CENSUS OF INDIA 1911

Census of India 1871-1951, 9 Sets In 384 Bindings (9788121258876) Rs. 700000

Census of India 1911, 23 Vols. In 41 Bindings (9788121271271) Rs. 69000

1. India - Report (9788121275071) Rs. 2475 (Vol. I, Pt. 1)
2. India - Tables (9788121275057) Rs. 2225 (Vol. I, Pt. 2)
3. Andaman and Nicobar Islands - Report & Tables (9788121275033) Rs. 900 (Vol. II, Pt. 1 & 2)
4. Assam - Report (9788121275019) Rs. 1000 (Vol. III, Pt. 1)
5. Assam - Tables (9788121274999) Rs. 1300 (Vol. III, Pt. 2)
6. Baluchistan - Report & Tables (9788121274975) Rs. 950 (Vol. IV, Pt. 1 & 2)
7. Bengal, Bihar And Orissa And Sikkim - Report (9788121274951) Rs. 3100 (Vol. V, Pt. 1)
8. Bengal - Tables (9788121274937) Rs. 2250 (Vol. V, Pt. 2)
9. Bihar And Orissa - Tables and Bengal And Sikkim - Chapter I of Administrative Volume (9788121274913) Rs. 1800 (Vol. V, Pt. 3 & 4)
10. City of Calcutta - Report and Tables and Administrative (9788121274876) Rs. 1300 (Vol. VI, Pt. 1 & 2 & 3)
11. Bombay - Report (9788121274814) Rs. 1950 (Vol. VII, Pt. 1)
12. Bombay - Imperial Tables and Administrative Report (9788121274791) Rs. 3300 (Vol. VII, Pt. 2 & 3)
13. Bombay (Town And Island) - Report And Tables (9788121274753) Rs. 1250 (Vol. VIII, Pt. 1 & 2)
14. Burma - Report (9788121274739) Rs. 2250 (Vol. IX, Pt. 1)
15. Burma - Tables (9788121274715) Rs. 1480 (Vol. IX, Pt. 2)
16. Central Provinces And Berar - Report (9788121274692) Rs. 1475 (Vol. X, Pt. 1)
17. Central Provinces And Berar - Tables (9788121274678) Rs. 1900 (Vol. X, Pt. 2)
18. Coorg - Report And Tables Madras - Report (9788121274630) Rs. 1740 (Vol. XI & Vol. XII, Pt. 1)
19. Madras - Imperial And Provincial Tables (9788121274616) Rs. 1500 (Vol. XII, Pt. 2)
20. Madras - Administrative Report and city of Madras (9788121274593) Rs. 630 (Vol. XII, Pt. 3 & 4)
21. North - West Frontier Province - Report & Tables (9788121274579) Rs. 2150 (Vol. XIII, Pt. 1 & 2)
22. Punjab - Report (9788121274555) Rs. 3000 (Vol. XIV, Pt. 1)
23. Punjab - Tables (9788121274531) Rs. 2200 (Vol. XIV, Pt. 2)
24. Punjab - Appendices To The - Imperial Tables (9788121274517) Rs. 950 (Vol. XIV, Pt. 3)
25. United Provinces of Agra And Oudh - Report (9788121274494) Rs. 2225 (Vol. XV, Pt. 1)
26. United Provinces of Agra And Oudh - Tables (9788121274470) Rs. 4000 (Vol. XV, Pt. 2)
27. United Provinces of Agra And Oudh - Provincial Tables And Appendices (9788121274456) Rs. 570 (Vol. XV, Pt. 3)
28. Baroda - Report (9788121274432) Rs. 2000 (Vol. XVI, Pt. 1)
29. Baroda State - The Imperial Tables (9788121274418) Rs. 850 (Vol. XVI, Pt. 2)
30. Central India Agency - Report And Tables (9788121274395) Rs. 1470 (Vol. XVII)
31. Cochin - Report And Imperial Tables (9788121274371) Rs. 1150 (Vol. XVIII, Pt. 1 & 2)
32. Hyderabad State - Report (9788121274357) Rs. 890 (Vol. XIX, Pt. 1)
33. Hyderabad State - Imperial And Provincial Tables (9788121274333) Rs. 1750 (Vol. XIX, Pt. 2)
34. Kashmir - Report (9788121274319) Rs. 950 (Vol. XX, Pt. 1)
35. Kashmir - Tables (9788121274296) Rs. 1170 (Vol. XX, Pt. 2)
36. Mysore - Report (9788121274272) Rs. 1200 (Vol. XXI, Pt. 1)
37. Mysore - Tables (9788121274258) Rs. 1500 (Vol. XXI, Pt. 2)
38. Rajputana And Ajmer-Merwara - Report (9788121274234) Rs. 1470 (Vol. XXII, Pt. 1)
39. Rajputana And Ajmer-Merwara - Tables (9788121274210) Rs. 1700 (Vol. XXII, Pt. 2)
40. Travancore - Report (9788121274197) Rs. 1870 (Vol. XXIII, Pt. 1)
41. Travancore - Imperial Tables (9788121274173) Rs. 870 (Vol. XXIII, Pt. 2)

Owing to the antiquity and rarity of this book, certain pages are regrettably absent, and readability is compromised due to the blurring of the original text. If you possess any insights regarding the availability of these missing sections, kindly inform us. Your assistance is crucial in ensuring the completion of this significant work for the benefit of future generations.

CENSUS OF INDIA, 1911

VOLUME - XIX

HYDERABAD STATE

PART II - IMPERIAL AND PROVINCIAL TABLES

M. ABDUL MAJEED

GYAN

Published by

Gyan Publishing House
5, Ansari Road
Daryaganj, New Delhi-110002
Phone: 011-47034999, 9811692060
E-mail: books@gyanbooks.com

Distribution Network
gyanbooks.com
India, USA, Canada, UK, Australia

ISBN: 978-81-212-7127-1 (Set) 23 Vols. In 41 Bindings

ISBN: 978-81-212-7433-3 (PB) Vol. XIX, Pt. II

First Published, 1913

2nd Impression 2024

Printed at: Gyan Press, Delhi.

CENSUS OF INDIA 1911

CENSUS OF INDIA, 1911.

VOLUME XIX.

HYDERABAD STATE.

PART II.

IMPERIAL AND PROVINCIAL TABLES.

SUPERINTENDENT,

M. ABDUL MAJEED, H. C. S.

Secunderabad:
CHEEKOTY VEERUNNAH & SONS, PRINTERS TO H. H. THE NIZAM'S GOVT.

1913.

Price—B. G. Rs. 3 or M. O. Rs. 3-8.

LIST OF ERRATA.

In Table I,	page 2,	column 2	against Osmanabad	*for*	2,743	*read*	3,517.
In Table I,	page 2,	column 2	against Bidar	*for*	5,857	*read*	5,083.
In Table II,	page 6,	column 3	against Aurangabad Division	*for*	2,455,105	*read*	2,445,105.
In Table VII,	page 39,	column 8	against Age 25 –30	*for*	10,065,522	*read*	1,065,522.
In Table VII,	page 39,	column 11	against Total	*for*	1,422,057	*read*	1,442,057.
In Table VII,	page 42,	column 47	against Musalman Total	*for*	446,264	*read*	646,264.
In Table VII,	page 47,	column 3	against Hindu age 5 –10	*for*	76,191	*read*	77,191.
In Table XIII,	page 136,	column 64	against Momin	*for*	20	*read*	205.
In Table XV,	page 215,	column 855	against Raichur	*for*	1,334	*read*	1,234.
In Table XV-D,	page 275,	column 8	against Group 44	*for*	Nil	*read*	29.
In Table XV-D,	page 280,	column 5	against Group 155	*for*	2,585	*read*	1,585.
In Table XVI,	page 311,	column 7	against Indian Christian	*for*	11,737	*read*	Nil.
In Table XVII,	page 318,	column 14	against State	*for*	3,586	*read*	3,587.
In Table XVII,	page 318,	column 14	against Hyderabad City	*for*	3,415	*read*	3,416.
In Table XVII,	page 318,	column 18	against State	*for*	4,545	*read*	4,544.
In Table XVII,	page 318,	column 18	against Hyderabad City	*for*	392	*read*	391.
In Provincial Table II,	page 345,	column 2	against Ekeli	*for*	11,997	*read*	11,179.

TABLE OF CONTENTS.

IMPERIAL TABLES I TO XVIII.

PROVINCIAL TABLES I & II.

TABLE I.

AREA, HOUSES AND POPULATION.

1. This table shows for each district the area, the number of towns and inhabited villages, the number of occupied houses and the total urban and rural population, male and female.

2. During the decade (1901—1911) a general re-adjustment of districts was effected on an extensive scale. The district of Lingsugur was abolished and its taluks transferred to Raichur and Gulbarga districts. The districts of Sirpur-Tandur, Elgandal and Indur have been designated as Adilabad, Karimnagar and Nizamabad respectively.

3. The difference between the areas here shown and those in the corresponding table of 1901 is due to inter-district changes referred to in 2 *supra*.

4. The Cantonment of Secunderabad including Bolarum, and the Residency Bazars have been treated as part of Hyderabad City; and the Cantonment of Aurangabad, as part of the town of Aurangabad.

Details of the area and population of these three localities under British administration are given below :—

Locality.	Area in sq. miles.	Occupied houses.	Persons.	Males.	Females.
Residency Bazars	·534	4,089	17,971	9,504	8,467
Secunderabad including Bolarum cantonment	17·17	24,586	113,490	60,755	52,735
Aurangabad Cantonment ...	3·53	2,786	11,953	6,699	5,254

5. The main statistics for Tahsils will be found in Provincial Tables I and II at the end of the volume.

TABLE I.

AREA, HOUSES AND POPULATION.

Serial No.	District.	Area in square miles.	Towns.	Villages.	Occupied Houses. Total.	Occupied Houses. In Towns.	Occupied Houses. In Villages.
	1	2	3	4	5	6	7
	Hyderabad State	***82,698***	***85***	***20,151***	***2,713,845***	***291,441***	***2,422,404***
1	Hyderabad City	50	1	...	111,509	111,509	...
2	Atraf-i-balda	2,561	2	868	104,527	2,488	102,039
	Warangal Division	***20,970***	***15***	***4,002***	***502,670***	***39,871***	***462,799***
3	Warangal	7,943	5	1,244	172,285	16,606	155,673
4	Karimnagar	5,733	7	1,135	209,963	18,189	191,774
5	Adilabad	7,294	3	1,623	120,422	5,076	115,346
	Medak Division	***17,739***	***13***	***4,058***	***594,654***	***23,932***	***570,722***
6	Medak	3,215	4	957	133,930	7,206	126,734
7	Nizamabad	3,273	5	761	122,612	9,120	113,492
8	Mahbubnagar	5,147	2	1,183	149,029	4,855	144,174
9	Nalgonda	6,104	2	1,197	189,083	2,751	186,332
	Aurangabad Division ..	***19,268***	***22***	***5,662***	***633,502***	***52,650***	***580,852***
10	Aurangabad	6,212	5	1,828	182,748	16,098	166,650
11	Bhir	4,132	4	1,019	134,038	9,027	125,011
12	Nander	3,797	6	1,302	146,065	10,963	135,102
13	Parbhani	5,127	7	1,513	170,651	15,962	154,689
	Gulbarga Division	***22,110***	***32***	***5,521***	***766,983***	***60,991***	***705,992***
14	Gulbarga	6,719	10	1,585	238,247	23,039	215,208
15	Osmanabad...	2,743	6	869	137,654	9,816	127,838
16	Raichur	6,791	9	1,658	208,765	17,243	191,522
17	Bidar	5,857	7	1,409	182,317	10,893	171,424

TABLE I

AREA, HOUSES AND POPULATION.

POPULATION.									
Persons.			Males			Females.			Serial No.
Total.	Urban.	Rural.	Total.	Urban.	Rural.	Total.	Urban.	Rural.	
8	9	10	11	12	13	14	15	16	
13,374,676	*1,295,305*	*12,079,371*	*6,797,118*	*660,940*	*6,136,178*	*6,577,558*	*634,365*	*5,943,193*	
500,623	500,623	...	258,454	258,454	...	242,169	242,169	...	1
520,159	8,279	511,880	265,184	4,062	261,122	254,975	4,217	250,758	2
2,657,477	*151,928*	*2,505,549*	*1,368,101*	*78,464*	*1,289,637*	*1,289,376*	*73,464*	*1,215,912*	
905,414	73,373	832,041	467,413	39,094	428,319	438,001	34,279	403,722	3
1,131,637	54,418	1,077,219	586,260	27,666	558,594	545,377	26,752	518,625	4
620,426	24,137	596,289	314,428	11,704	302,724	305,998	12,433	293,565	5
3,046,705	*111,049*	*2,935,656*	*1,548,882*	*55,912*	*1,492,970*	*1,497,823*	*55,137*	*1,442,686*	
687,137	33,280	653,857	348,410	16,765	331,645	338,727	16,515	322,212	6
568,009	41,795	526,214	283,621	20,919	262,702	284,388	20,876	263,512	7
747,178	21,100	726,078	379,712	10,676	369,036	367,466	10,424	357,042	8
1,044,381	14,874	1,029,507	537,139	7,552	529,587	507,242	7,322	499,920	9
2,976,541	*237,940*	*2,738,601*	*1,496,102*	*120,714*	*1,375,388*	*1,480,439*	*117,226*	*1,363,213*	
869,787	76,560	793,227	437,495	38,978	398,517	432,292	37,582	394,710	10
622,531	40,201	582,330	314,738	20,398	294,340	307,793	19,803	287,990	11
704,549	54,347	650,202	352,638	27,178	325,460	351,911	27,169	324,742	12
779,674	66,832	712,842	391,231	34,160	357,071	388,443	32,672	355,771	13
3,673,171	*285,486*	*3,387,685*	*1,860,395*	*143,334*	*1,717,061*	*1,812,776*	*142,152*	*1,670,624*	
1,150,983	105,555	1,045,428	582,447	53,329	529,118	568,536	52,226	516,310	14
635,977	42,790	593,187	324,969	21,697	303,272	311,008	21,093	289,915	15
996,684	82,232	914,452	503,541	41,059	462,482	493,143	41,173	451,970	16
889,527	54,909	834,618	449,438	27,249	422,189	440,089	27,660	412,429	17

TABLE II.

VARIATION IN POPULATION SINCE 1881.

This table compares the population as now ascertained with that of the three previous Censuses. The figures for the latter differ from those shown in the Reports of those Censuses owing to the reconstitution of districts during the decade 1901—1911. The effect of changes on the population of districts brought about by inter-district transfers has been calculated, and the figures have been adjusted accordingly.

II. During the decade, besides numerous other changes, the district of Lingsugar was abolished and its taluks transferred to Gulbarga and Raichur districts. The district of Adilabad was enlarged by the addition of taluks from its adjoining districts. The old districts of Elgandal, Sirpur-Tandur and Indur have been designated as Karimnagar, Adilabad and Nizamabad respectively.

TABLE II.

VARIATION IN POPULATION SINCE 1881.

Serial No.	District.	Persons.				Males.			
		1911.	1901.	1891.	1881.	1911.	1901.	1891.	1881.
	1	2	3	4	5	6	7	8	9
	Hyderabad State.	***13,374,676***	***11,141,142***	***11,537,040***	***9,845,594***	***6,797,118***	***5,673,629***	***5,873,129***	***5,002,137***
1	Hyderabad City ...	500,623	462.321	427,849	378,890	258,454	239,582	223,025	193,820
2	Atraf-i-balda ...	520,159	431.502	409.800	375.419	265,184	219,517	208,718	190,241
	Warangal Division.	***2,657,477***	***2,035,776***	***1,962,811***	***1,658,751***	***1,368,101***	***1,053,834***	***1,005,442***	***842,349***
3	Warangal ...	905,414	716.171	640,265	506.573	467,413	374,506	330,673	259,374
4	Karimnagar ...	1,131,637	835 324	872,671	745,274	586,260	435,803	449,159	379,241
5	Adilabad ...	620,426	484,281	449,875	406,904	314,428	243.525	225,610	203,734
	Medak Division.	***3,046,705***	***2,500,750***	***2,387,629***	***2,000,930***	***1,548,882***	***1,289,429***	***1,212,262***	***1,010,432***
6	Medak ...	687,137	531,359	534,438	467,809	348,410	272,639	271,821	236,371
7	Nizamabad ...	568,009	497,569	501.449	450.994	283,621	250,937	252,544	227,231
8	Mahbubnagar ...	747,178	601,749	575,120	467,153	379,712	304,342	291,067	234,913
9	Nalgonda ...	1,044,381	870,073	776,631	614,974	537,129	461,511	396,830	311,917
	Aurangabad Division.	***2,976,541***	***2,455,105***	***2,986,010***	***2,673,899***	***1,496,102***	***1,224,691***	***1,518,166***	***1,365,414***
10	Aurangabad ...	869,787	725,556	833,699	733,813	437,495	363,191	423,414	374,784
11	Bhir ...	622,531	492,258	642.722	558,745	314,738	248,151	328,530	286,170
12	Nander ...	704.549	580,245	704.189	695,207	352,638	289,186	355,560	352,531
13	Parbhani ...	779,674	647.046	805.400	685,834	391,231	324,163	410,662	351,929
	Gulbarga Division.	***3,673,171***	***3,265,688***	***3,362,941***	***2,758,005***	***1,860,395***	***1,646,576***	***1,705,516***	***1,399,881***
14	Gulbarga ...	1,150,983	1,054.145	941.273	752,212	582,447	533,787	477,353	380,015
15	Osmanabad ...	635 977	530,577	643.835	538,840	324,969	268,691	328,999	275,962
16	Raichur ...	996.681	933.015	897.223	696.769	503,541	468,254	453,010	351,965
17	Bidar ...	889.527	747,951	880.610	770,184	449,438	375 844	446,154	391,939

TABLE II.

VARIATION IN POPULATION SINCE 1881.

Females.				Variation { Increase (+). Decrease (—).			Net variation in period 1881—1911 Increase (+). Decrease (—).	Serial No.
1911.	1901.	1891.	1881.	1901 to 1911.	1891 to 1901.	1881 to 1891.		
10	11	12	13	14	15	16	17	
6,577,558	*5,467,513*	*5,663,911*	*4,843,457*	*+2,233,534*	*— 395,898*	*+ 1,691,446*	*+ 3,529,082*	
242,169	222,739	204,824	185,070	+ 38,302	+ 34,472	+ 48,959	+ 121,733	1
254,975	211,985	201,082	185,178	+ 88,657	+ 21,702	+ 34,381	+ 144,740	2
1,289,376	*981,942*	*957,369*	*816,402*	*+ 621,701*	*+ 72,965*	*+ 304,060*	*+ 998,726*	
438,001	341,665	309,592	247,199	+ 189,243	+ 75,906	+ 133,692	+ 398,841	3
545,377	399,521	423,512	366,033	+ 296,313	— 37,347	+ 127,397	+ 386,363	4
305,998	240,756	224,255	203,170	+ 136,145	+ 34,406	+ 42,971	+ 213,522	5
1,497,823	*1,211,321*	*1,175,367*	*990,498*	*+ 545,955*	*+ 113,121*	*+ 386,699*	*+ 1,045,775*	
338,727	258,720	262,617	231,438	+ 155,778	— 3,079	+ 66,629	+ 219,328	6
284,388	246,632	248,896	223,763	+ 70,440	— 3,871	+ 50,446	+ 117,015	7
367,466	297,407	284,053	232,240	+ 145,429	+ 26,629	+ 107,967	+ 280,025	8
507,242	408,562	379,801	303,057	+ 174,308	+ 93,442	+ 161,657	+ 429,407	9
1,480,439	*1,220,414*	*1,467,844*	*1,308,185*	*+ 531,436*	*— 540,905*	*+ 312,411*	*+ 302,942*	
432,292	362,365	410,285	359,029	+ 144,231	— 108,143	+ 99,886	+ 135,974	10
307,793	244,107	314,192	272,575	+ 130,273	— 150,464	+ 83,977	+ 63,786	11
351,911	291,059	348,629	342,676	+ 124,304	— 123,944	+ 8,982	+ 9,342	12
388,443	322,883	394,738	333,905	+ 132,628	— 158,354	+ 119,566	+ 93,840	13
1,812,776	*1,619,112*	*1,657,425*	*1,358,124*	*+ 407,483*	*— 97,253*	*+ 604,936*	*+ 915,166*	
568,536	520,358	463,920	372,197	+ 96,838	+ 112,872	+ 189,061	+ 398,771	14
311,008	261,886	314,836	262,878	+ 105,400	— 113,258	+ 104,995	+ 97,137	15
493,143	464,761	444,213	344,804	+ 63,639	+ 35,792	+ 200,454	+ 299,915	16
440,089	372,107	434,456	378,245	+ 141,576	— 132,659	+ 110,426	+ 119,343	17

TABLE III.

TOWNS AND VILLAGES CLASSIFIED BY POPULATION.

TABLE III.

TOWNS AND VILLAGES CLASSIFIED BY POPULATION.

Serial No.	District.	Total number of inhabited Towns and Villages.	Population.	Under 500		500—1,000		1,000—2,000		2,000—5,000	
				Number.	Population.	Number.	Population.	Number.	Population.	Number.	Population.
	1	2	3	4	5	6	7	8	9	10	11
	Hyderabad State ...	*20,236*	*13,374,676*	*11,684*	*2,945,668*	*5,220*	*3,687,144*	*2,511*	*3,409,391*	*730*	*1,998,624*
1	Hyderabad City... ...	1	500,623	...	...	...	...	...	...	...	...
2	Atraf-i-balda	870	520,159	515	125,620	205	146,473	123	165,904	25	70,002
	Warangal Division ...	*4,017*	*2,657,477*	*2,225*	*478,140*	*952*	*686,722*	*666*	*917,612*	*159*	*423,075*
3	Warangal	1,249	905,414	615	129,668	351	254,969	228	311,952	50	135,452
4	Karimnagar	1,142	1,131,637	358	110,141	356	260,896	322	443,759	99	262,423
5	Adilabad	1,626	620,426	1,252	238,331	245	170,857	116	161,901	10	25,200
	Medak Division ..	*4,111*	*3,046,705*	*1,949*	*519,839*	*1,223*	*874,148*	*711*	*965,667*	*213*	*565,417*
6	Medak...	961	687,137	490	126,745	294	210,178	139	194,466	41	107,153
7	Nizamabad	766	588,009	409	112,285	181	129,376	131	174,237	41	115,063
8	Mahbubnagar	1,185	747,178	636	160,659	344	240,919	167	236,443	36	98,057
9	Nalgonda	1,199	1,044,381	424	120,170	404	293,672	274	370,521	95	245,144
	Aurangabad Division.	*5,684*	*2,976,541*	*3,880*	*980,994*	*1,267*	*882,769*	*394*	*528,544*	*118*	*329,393*
10	Aurangabad	1,833	869,787	1,317	313,872	372	255,247	112	149,473	26	68,416
11	Bhir	1,023	622,531	620	170,387	278	195,323	84	107,815	36	103,734
12	Nander...	1,308	704,549	878	227,099	289	198,817	105	141,980	30	82,306
13	Parbhani	1,520	779,674	1,065	269,636	328	233,382	93	129,276	26	74,937
	Gulbarga Division ...	*5,553*	*3,673,171*	*3,115*	*841,075*	*1,573*	*1,097,035*	*617*	*831,664*	*215*	*610,737*
14	Gulbarga	1,595	1,150,963	853	235,572	464	324,483	185	253,738	83	230,363
15	Osmanabad	875	635,977	430	123,662	274	191,661	127	171,832	38	106,032
16	Raichur	1,667	996,684	1,042	276,552	421	293,890	143	190,296	51	153,812
17	Bidar	1,416	889,527	790	211,289	414	287,001	162	215,798	43	120,530

TABLE III.

TOWNS AND VILLAGES CLASSIFIED BY POPULATION.

5,000—10,000.		10,000—20,000.		20,000—50,000.		50,000—100,000.		100,000 and over.		Encampments, Boat and Railway Population unclassed.	Serial No.
Number.	Population.	Number.	Population.	Number.	Population.	Number.	Population.	Number.	Population.		
12	13	14	15	16	17	18	19	20	21	22	
68	*465,683*	*18*	*233,877*	*4*	*128,000*	...	...	*1*	*500,623*	*5,666*	
...	...	...	...	...	...	...	...	1	500,623	...	1
2	12,160	...	...	...	...	...	...	...	...	...	2
12	*88,699*	*2*	*27,602*	*1*	*35,627*	...	...	...	...	...	
3	21,832	1	15,914	1	35,627	...	...	...	...	...	3
6	42,730	1	11,688	...	...	...	...	...	...	...	4
3	24,137	...	...	...	...	...	...	...	...	...	5
13	*91,835*	*2*	*29,802*	...	...	...	...	...	...	...	
7	48,595	...	...	...	...	...	...	...	...	...	6
3	19,715	1	17,353	...	...	...	...	...	...	...	7
1	8,651	1	12,449	...	...	...	...	...	...	...	8
2	14,874	...	...	...	...	...	...	...	...	...	9
16	*106,860*	*8*	*107,413*	*1*	*34,902*	...	...	...	...	*5,666*	
3	18,614	2	29,263	1	34,902	...	...	...	...	...	10
3	18,189	2	27,083	...	...	...	...	...	...	...	11
5	36,722	1	17,625	...	...	...	...	...	...	...	12
5	33,335	3	33,442	...	...	...	...	...	...	5,666	13
25	*166,129*	*6*	*69,060*	*2*	*57,471*	...	...	...	...	...	
7	51,394	2	22,996	1	32,437	...	...	...	...	...	14
5	32,569	1	10,221	...	...	...	...	...	...	...	15
8	51,018	1	12,082	1	25,034	...	...	...	...	...	16
5	31,148	2	23,761	...	...	...	...	...	...	...	17

TABLE IV.

TOWNS CLASSIFIED BY POPULATION WITH VARIATION SINCE 1881.

1. Sagar and Hasanparti are now excluded as no longer coming under the category of a town.

2. Nine new towns (marked with an asterisk) are included in the Table, and figures for these for previous censuses are given from village list.

3. The figures for Yadgir for last decade are revised figures as those given for previous censuses are incorrect.

4. The town of Hanamkonda includes certain villages situated within its municipal limits which were not included before and the figures for previous censuses have been adjusted accordingly.

5. The population of troops numbering 4,698 stationed in Fort Golconda (Muhammadnagar) is included in the city population. Hence the number of inhabitants for that town appears to be far below the standard.

6. Hyderabad City and Aurangabad include cantonments. The units composing them are detailed below:—

1. Hyderabad	Persons.	Males.	Females.
City ...	365,064	186,162	178,902
Golconda Troops ...	4,098	2,033	2,065
Residency Bazars ...	17,971	9,504	8,467
Secunderabad including Bolarum ...	113,490	60,755	52,735
Total ...	500,623	258,454	242,169
2. Aurangabad	**Persons.**	**Males.**	**Females.**
Town ...	22,949	11,293	11,656
Cantonment ...	11,953	6,699	5,254
Total ...	34,902	17,992	16,910

7. As regards those towns for which figures for 1881 (column 7) or for 1881 and 1891 (columns 7 & 6) are not available, the variation shown in column 11 is for the period 1891—1911 or 1901—1911.

TABLE IV.

TOWNS CLASSIFIED BY POPULATION WITH VARIATION SINCE 1881.

Serial No.	Town.	District.	Municipality, Suburbs, Cantonment etc.	Population.			
				1911	1901	1891	1881
	1	2	3	4	5	6	7
1	Hyderabad City (Haidarabad)	......	Municipality and Cantt.	500,623	448,466	415,639	367,417
2	Hanamkonda	Warangal ...	Municipality ...	35,827	20,661	24,764	...
3	Aurangabad	Aurangabad... ...	Municipality and Cantt.	34,90[illegible]	36,837	3[illegible],887	30,219
4	Gulbarga	Gulbarga	Municipality ..	32,437	29,228	28,20[illegible]	22,824
5	Raichur	Raichur	do ...	25,034	22,167	23,174	15,387
6	Jalna	Aurangabad ...	do ...	18,993	20,270	19,128	16,199
7	Nander	Nander	do ..	17,625	14,184	13,1[illegible]5	14,091
8	Hingoli	Parbhani	do ...	17,507	17,256	11,966	14,8[illegible]4
9	Nizamabad	Nizamabad ...	do ..	17,353	12,571	11,482	10,264
10	Bhir	Bhir	do ...	16,010	17,671	18,994	17,398
11	Yellandlapad	Warangal	do ...	15,914	12,377	...	...
12	Bidar	Bidar	do ...	12,684	11,367	11,315	9,730
13	Narayanpet	Mahabubnagar ..	do ...	12,449	12,011	11,858	11,290
14	Gadwal	Raichur	......	12,082	10,195	14,672	12,207
15	Aland	Gulbarga	......	12,051	10,130	9,558	6,201
16	Jagtial	Karimnagar... ...	Municipality ...	11,688	11,181	9,538	7,302
17	Kalyani	Bidar	......	11,077	11,191	13,026	11,092
18	Mominabad (Amba) ...	Bhir	Municipality ...	11,073	12,628	13,923	12,052
19	Manwat	Parbhani	Municipality ..	11,00[illegible]	7,395	10,912	8,767
20	Yadgir	Gulbarga	do ...	10,945	9,365	...	...
21	Basmat	Parbhani	do ...	10,599	8,445	11,361	11,022
22	Kadirabad	Aurangabad... ..	do ...	10,270	11,159	11,402	9,876

TABLE IV.

TOWNS CLASSIFIED BY POPULATION WITH VARIATION SINCE 1881.

Variation, Increase (+) Decrease (—).			Variation in period 1881 to 1911. Increase (+) Decrease (—).	Males.			Females.			Serial No.
1901 to 1911.	1891 to 1901.	1881 to 1891.		1911.	1901.	1891.	1911.	1901.	1891.	
8	9	10	11	12	13	14	15	16	17	
+ 52,157	+ 33,427	+ 47,622	+ 133,206	258,454	232,295	216,324	242,169	216,171	198,715	1
+ 14,966	— 4,103	...	+ 10,863	18,324	10,861	12,802	17,303	9,800	11,962	2
— 1,935	+ 2,950	+ 3,668	+ 4,683	17,992	19,005	17,186	16,910	17,832	16,701	3
+ 3,200	+ 1,028	+ 5,366	+ 9,603	16,840	15,274	14,747	15,588	13,954	13,453	4
+ 2,869	— 1,009	+ 7,787	+ 9,647	12,681	9,982	11,836	12,353	12,183	11,338	5
— 1,277	+ 1,232	+ 2,920	+ 2,704	9,711	10,484	10,106	9,282	9,786	8,932	6
+ 3,441	+ 1,079	— 980	+ 3,534	9,281	7,249	6,488	8,344	6,935	6,617	7
+ 251	+ 5,290	— 2,838	+ 2,703	9,199	9,005	6,283	8,308	8,251	5,683	8
+ 4,482	+ 1,389	+ 1,218	+ 7,039	9,135	6,708	5,671	8,215	6,163	5,811	9
— 1,661	— 1,323	+ 1,596	— 1,388	8,074	9,036	9,533	7,936	8,635	9,461	10
+ 3,537	...	...	+ 3,537	9,891	7,508	...	6,023	4,869	...	11
+ 1,317	+ 52	+ 1,585	+ 2,954	6,316	5,713	5,643	6,368	5,654	5,672	12
+ 438	+ 123	+ 598	+ 1,159	6,206	5,992	5,880	6,243	6,019	6,008	13
+ 1,887	— 4,477	+ 2,465	— 125	5,965	5,117	7,917	6,117	5,078	6,755	14
+ 1,921	+ 592	+ 3,337	+ 5,850	6,158	5,125	4,887	5,893	5,005	4,651	15
+ 507	+ 1,643	+ 2,236	+ 4,386	6,032	5,995	4,899	5,656	5,186	4,639	16
— 114	— 1,835	+ 1,934	— 15	5,458	5,377	6,458	5,619	5,814	6,568	17
— 1,555	— 1,295	+ 1,871	— 979	5,581	6,594	7,135	5,492	6,034	6,788	18
+ 3,607	— 3,517	+ 2,145	+ 2,235	5,740	3,817	5,683	5,262	3,578	5,229	19
+ 1,580	...	...	+ 1,580	5,241	4,435	...	5,704	4,930	...	20
+ 2,154	— 2,916	+ 339	— 423	5,336	4,127	5,614	5,263	4,318	5,747	21
— 889	— 243	+ 1,526	+ 394	5,180	5,502	5,463	5,090	5,657	5,939	22

TABLE IV.

TOWNS CLASSIFIED BY POPULATION WITH VARIATION SINCE 1881.

Serial No.	Town.	District.	Municipality, Suburbs, Cantonment etc.	Population.			
				1911	1901	1891	1881
	1	2	3	4	5	6	7
23	Osmanabad	Osmanabad ...	Municipality ...	10,221	10,607	10,511	8,801
24	Kosgi	Gulbarga	......	9,683	8,228	8,418	7,946
25	Nirmal	Adilabad	Municipality ..	9,588	7,751	10,932	10,577
26	Siddipet	Medak	do ...	9,583	8,302	7,671	7,002
27	Chitapur	Gulbarga	......	9,355	* 8,150	* 8,818	...
28	Medak	Medak	Municipality ...	9,125	8,511	7,556	7,026
29	Khamam	Warangal	do ...	9,117	*8,713	* 9,062	...
30	Parbhani	Parbhani	do ...	9,081	9,958	10,102	7,996
31	Mahbubnagar	Mahbubnagar ...	do ...	8,651	7,605	6,222	4,680
32	Sadaseopet	Medak	do ...	8,625	6,672	7,350	8,775
33	Bhaisa	Nander	......	8,444	7,126	7,688	6,701
34	Karimnagar	Karimnagar ..	Municipality ...	8,347	5,752	6,348	5,436
35	Vemalwada	Karimnagar... ..	......	8,075	5,372	6,511	6,097
36	Shorapur	Gulbarga	Municipality ...	8,043	8,271	9,754	9,900
37	Thair (Ter)	Osmanabad	......	7,948	7,327	8,015	3,984
38	Deglur	Nander	......	7.800	6,917	6,578	6,808
39	Manthani	Karimnagar ...	......	7,759	6,680	6,046	5,794
40	Latur	Osmanabad	Municipality ...	7,574	10,479	9,063	8,648
41	Adilabad	Adilabad	do ...	7,560	6,303	6,084	5,522
42	Koppal	Raichur	......	7,555	8,903	6,991	5,083
43	Nalgonda	Nalgonda	Municipality ...	7,532	5,889	5,906	5,283
44	Armur	Nizamabad... ...	do ...	7,530	9,031	7,015	5,530
45	Parli	Bhir	......	7,478	7,289	7,659	7,090

TABLE IV.

TOWNS CLASSIFIED BY POPULATION WITH VARIATION SINCE 1881.

Variation. Increase (+) Decrease (—).			Variation in period 1881 to 1911. Increase (+) Decrease (—).	Males.			Females.			Serial No.
1901 to 1911.	1891 to 1901.	1881 to 1891.		1911.	1901.	1891.	1911.	1901.	1891.	
8	9	10	11	12	13	14	15	16	17	
— 386	+ 96	+ 1,710	+ 1,420	5,255	5,345	5,512	4,960	5,262	4,999	23
+ 1,455	— 190	+ 472	+ 1,737	4,850	4,078	4,105	4,833	4,150	4,313	24
+ 1,837	— 3,181	+ 355	— 989	4,580	3,745	5,188	5,008	4,006	5,744	25
+ 1,281	+ 631	+ 669	+ 2,581	4,964	4,298	3,899	4,619	4,004	3,772	26
+ 1,205	— 668	...	+ 537	4,676	*4,012	*4,454	4.679	*4,138	*4,354	27
+ 614	+ 955	+ 530	+ 2,099	4,380	4,421	3,575	4,745	4,090	3,981	28
+ 404	— 349	...	+ 55	4,539	*4,260	*4,408	4,578	*4,453	*4,654	29
— 877	— 144	+ 2,106	+ 1,085	4,817	5,129	5,233	4,264	4,829	4,869	30
+ 1,046	+ 1,383	+ 1,542	+ 3,971	4,470	3,950	3,272	4,181	3,655	2,950	31
+ 1,953	— 678	— 1,425	— 150	4,415	3,185	3,703	4,210	3,487	3,647	32
+ 1,318	— 562	+ 987	+ 1,743	4,103	3,385	3,785	4.341	3,741	3,903	33
+ 2,595	— 596	+ 912	+ 2,911	4,393	2,910	3,479	3,954	2,842	2,869	34
+ 2,703	— 1,139	+ 414	+ 1,978	4,060	2,954	3.279	4,015	2,418	3,232	35
— 228	— 1,483	— 146	— 1,857	3,899	4,601	4,635	4,144	4,270	5,119	36
+ 621	— 688	+ 4,031	+ 3,964	3,991	3,667	4,077	3,957	3,660	3,938	37
+ 883	+ 339	— 230	+ 992	3,772	3,378	3,282	4,028	3,539	3,296	38
+ 1,079	+ 634	+ 252	+ 1,965	3,814	3,375	2,897	3,945	3,305	3,149	39
— 2,905	+ 1,416	+ 415	— 1,074	3,843	5,548	4,730	3,731	4,931	4,333	40
+ 1,257	+ 219	+ 562	+ 2,038	3,689	2,976	2,862	3,871	3,327	3,222	41
— 1,345	+ 1,912	+ 1,908	+ 2,475	3,916	4,511	3,553	3,642	4,392	3,438	42
+ 1,643	— 17	+ 623	+ 2,249	3,736	2,981	2,960	3,796	2,908	2,946	43
— 1,501	+ 2,016	+ 1,485	+ 2,000	3,628	4,435	3,409	3,903	4,596	3,606	44
+ 189	— 370	+ 569	+ 388	3,838	3,892	3,966	3,640	3,397	3,693	45

TABLE IV.

TOWNS CLASSIFIED BY POPULATION WITH VARIATION SINCE 1881.

Serial No.	Town.	District.	Municipality, Suburbs, Cantonment etc.	Population.			
				1911	1901	1891	1881
	1	2	3	4	5	6	7
46	Bhongir	Nalgonda	Municipality ...	7,342	5,806	4,938	...
47	Peddapalli	Karimnagar... ...	......	7,260	• 2,783	• 5,995	...
48	Udgir	Bidar	Municipality ...	7,213	5,984	6,722	7,141
49	Urus-Karimabad	Warangal	......	7,173	• 5,784	• 4,964	...
50	Pathri	Parbhani	......	7,095	5,828	6,726	6,572
51	Kondalwadi	Nander	......	7,018	6,557	5,936	7,570
52	Bodhan	Nizamabad	Municipality ..	6,99[illegible]	6,438	5.841	5,898
53	Paithan	Aurangabad... ...	......	6,989	8,638	8,788	10,874
54	Chinnur	Adilabad	......	6,989	6,561	5,719	5,721
55	Mudgal	Raichur	Municipality ...	6,947	7,729	6,641	5,064
56	Mudhol	Nander	......	6,876	6,040	6,624	6,177
57	Deodrug	Raichur	Municipality ...	6,837	6,773	7,213	4,587
58	Homnabad	Atraf-i-balda ...	......	6,798	7,136	7,736	7,199
59	Manvi	Raichur	Municipality ...	6,679	6,253	5,669	...
60	Gangawati	Raichur	do ..	6,663	6,245	6,138	...
61	Mukher	Nander	......	6,584	6,148	6,019	5,795
62	Tandur	Gulbarga	......	6,504	5.930	4,278	...
63	Kohir	Bidar	Municipality ...	6,486	6.379	6,557	7,027
64	Bhalki	Bidar	......	6,268	5,788	5,383	5,163
65	Moram	Osmanabad	......	6,130	5,692	5,874	4,079
66	Koratla	Karimnagar	......	6,068	5,524	5,892	5,522
67	Kodangal	Gulbarga	Municipality ...	6,062	5.099	5,296	...
68	Gangakher	Parbhani	......	5,997	5,007	6,653	5,517

TABLE IV

TOWNS CLASSIFIED BY POPULATION WITH VARIATION SINCE 1881.

Variation. Increase (+) Decrease (—) 1901 to 1911	1891 to 1901	1881 to 1891	Variation in period 1881 to 1911. Increase (+) Decrease (—).	Males. 1911	Males. 1901	Males. 1891	Females. 1911	Females. 1901	Females. 1891	Serial No.
8	9	10	11	12	13	14	15	16	17	
+ 1,536	+ 868	...	+ 2,404	3,816	2,974	2,432	3,526	2,832	2,506	46
+ 4,477	— 3,212	...	+ 1,265	3,745	*1,532	*2,948	3,515	*1,251	*3,047	47
+ 1,229	— 738	— 419	+ 72	3,619	3,061	3,362	3,594	2,923	3,360	48
+ 1,389	+ 820	...	+ 2,209	3,586	*2,937	*2,461	3,587	*2,847	*2,503	49
+ 1,267	— 898	+ 154	+ 523	3,501	2,782	3,358	3,594	3,046	3,368	50
+ 461	+ 621	— 1,634	— 552	3,403	3,181	2,890	3,615	3,376	3,046	51
+ 578	+ 597	— 57	+ 1,098	3,355	3,187	2,791	3,661	3,251	3,050	52
— 1,649	— 159	— 2,086	— 3,885	3,376	4,162	4,318	3,613	4,476	4,470	53
+ 423	+ 842	— 2	+ 1,268	3,435	3,320	2,879	3,554	3,241	2,840	54
— 782	+ 1,088	+ 1,577	+ 1,883	3,455	3,825	3,258	3,492	3,904	3,383	55
+ 836	— 584	+ 447	+ 699	3,311	2,893	3,153	3,565	3,147	3,471	56
+ 64	— 440	+ 2,626	+ 2,250	3,334	3,343	3,524	3,503	3,430	3,689	57
— 338	— 600	+ 537	— 401	3,322	3,516	3,728	3,476	3,620	4,008	58
+ 426	+ 584	...	+ 1,010	3,359	3,097	2,803	3,320	3,156	2,866	59
+ 418	+ 107	...	+ 525	3,238	3,037	3,036	3,425	3,208	3,102	60
+ 436	+ 129	+ 224	+ 789	3,308	3,170	3,004	3,276	2,978	3,015	61
+ 574	+ 1,652	...	+ 2,226	3,344	3,146	2,129	3,160	2,784	2,149	62
+ 107	— 178	— 470	— 541	3,154	3,093	3,118	3,332	3,286	3,439	63
+ 480	+ 405	+ 220	+ 1,105	3,158	2,884	2,663	3,110	2,904	2,720	64
+ 458	— 182	+ 1,795	+ 2,071	3,126	2,867	3,028	3,024	2,825	2,846	65
+ 544	— 368	+ 370	+ 546	3,010	2,810	2,944	3,058	2,714	2,948	66
+ 963	— 197	...	+ 766	3,010	2,538	2,567	3,052	2,561	2,729	67
+ 990	— 1,646	+ 1,136	+ 48[illegible]	2,878	2,482	3,364	3,119	2,525	3,289	68

TABLE IV.

TOWNS CLASSIFIED BY POPULATION WITH VARIATION SINCE 1881.

Serial No.	Town.	District.	Municipality, Suburbs, Cantonment etc.	Population.			
				1911	1901	1891	1881
	1	2	3	4	5	6	7
69	Sangareddipet	Medak	Municipality ...	5,947	* 4,8[illegible]9	* 4,993	...
70	Ekeli	Bidar	......	5,889	* 4,920	* 5,133	...
71	Manjlegaon	Bhir	......	5,640	5,698	5,556	...
72	Shahabad	Gulbarga	......	5,607	5,105	3,452	...
73	Sindhnur	Raichur	......	5,578	5,242	4,763	...
74	Sonepet	Parbhani	......	5,551	5,759	8,090	6,407
75	Warangal Fort	Warangal	......	5,542	* 4,741	* 3,433	...
76	Tuljapur	Osmanabad	Municipality ...	5,451	6,612	6,862	5,938
77	Owsa	Osmanabad	do ...	5,446	6,026	6,091	5,640
78	Vaijapur	Aurangabad ...	......	5,406	5,451	5,411	5,300
79	Alikher	Bidar	......	5,292	5,740	4,345	...
80	Dharmapuri	Karimnagar ...	......	5,221	* 4,948	* 4,361	...
81	Lingampet	Nizamabad	......	5,189	5,102	4,719	...
82	Seram...	Gulbarga	Municipality ...	4,868	5,503	4,245	...
83	Kallur	Raichur	......	4,854	6,456	3,653	...
84	Balkonda	Nizamabad	......	4,727	5,118	4,565	...
85	Muhammadnagar (Fort Golconda).	Atraf-i-balda ...	......	1,481	* 4,179	* 1,840	...

TABLE IV.

TOWNS CLASSIFIED BY POPULATION WITH VARIATION SINCE 1881.

Variation. Increase (+) Decrease (—). 1901 to 1911	1891 to 1901	1881 to 1891	Variation in period 1881 to 1911. Increase (+) Decrease (—).	Males. 1911	Males. 1901	Males. 1891	Females. 1911	Females. 1901	Females. 1891	Serial No.
8	9	10	11	12	13	14	15	16	17	
+ 1,138	— 184	...	+ 954	3,006	* 2,364	* 2,524	2,941	* 2,445	* 2,469	69
+ 969	— 213	...	+ 756	2,914	* 2,516	* 2,527	2,975	* 2,404	* 2,606	70
— 58	+ 142	...	+ 84	2,905	2,816	2,778	2,735	2,852	2,778	71
+ 502	+ 1,653	...	+ 2,155	2,886	2,674	1,767	2,721	2,431	1,635	72
+ 336	+ 479	...	+ 815	2,733	2,623	2,392	2,845	2,619	2,371	73
— 208	— 2,331	+ 1,683	— 856	2,689	2,819	4,075	2,862	2,940	4,015	74
+ 801	+ 1,308	...	+ 2,109	2,754	* 2,653	* 1,682	2,788	* 2,088	* 1,751	75
— 1,161	— 250	+ 924	— 487	2,766	3,322	3,519	2,685	3,290	3,343	76
— 580	— 65	+ 451	— 194	2,716	2,952	3,056	2,730	3,074	3,035	77
— 45	+ 40	+ 111	+ 106	2,719	2,693	2,730	2,687	2,758	2,681	78
— 448	+ 1,395	...	+ 947	2,630	2,824	2,112	2,662	2,916	2,233	79
+ 273	+ 647	...	+ 920	2,612	* 2,615	* 2,033	2,609	* 2,333	* 2,268	80
+ 87	+ 383	...	+ 470	2,658	2,854	2,370	2,531	2,248	2,349	81
— 635	+ 1,258	...	+ 623	2,416	2,722	2,134	2,452	2,781	2,111	82
— 1,602	+ 2,803	...	+ 1,201	2,378	3,129	1,771	2,476	3,327	1,882	83
— 391	+ 553	...	+ 162	2,163	2,333	2,038	2,564	2,785	2,527	84
— 2,698	+ 2,339	...	— 359	740	* 2,194	* 914	741	* 1,985	* 926	85

TABLE V.

TOWNS ARRANGED TERRITORIALLY WITH POPULATION BY RELIGION.

TABLE V.

TOWNS ARRANGED TERRITORIALLY WITH POPULATION BY RELIGION.

Serial No.	District.	Town, Municipality, Suburbs, Cantonment.	Population			INDO-								
						Hindu.			Jain.			Sikh.		
			Persons.	Males.	Females.	Persons.	Males.	Females.	Persons.	Males.	Females.	Persons.	Males.	Females.
	1	2	3	4	5	6	7	8	9	10	11	12	13	14
	All Towns		*1,295,305*	*660,940*	*634,365*	*826,607*	*421.649*	*404,958*	*3.817*	*2,009*	*1,808*	*2,594*	*1,509*	*1,085*
1		Hyderabad City Municipality and Cantonment.	500,623	258,452	242,169	262,131	135,638	126,493	379	223	156	978	644	334
	Atraf-i-balda		*8,279*	*4,062*	*4,217*	*5,414*	*2,671*	*2,743*	*48*	*25*	*23*	...	...	...
2		Homnabad ...	6,798	3,322	3,476	4,545	2,258	2,287	48	25	23	...	...	...
3		Muhammadnagar (Fort Golconda).	1,481	740	741	869	413	456	...	...	...	...	...	...
	Warangal		*73,373*	*39,094*	*34,279*	*58,002*	*31,037*	*26,965*	*14*	*9*	*5*	*204*	*96*	*108*
4		Hanamkonda .. Municipality	35,627	18,324	17,303	27,653	14,163	13,490	4	2	2	197	92	105
5		Yellandlapad .. Municipality	15,914	9,891	6,023	13,449	8,389	5,060	...	...	...	5	3	2
6		Khamam . Municipality	9.117	4,539	4,578	6,594	3,285	3,309	..	...	...	2	1	1
7		Urus-Karimabad	7,173	3.586	3,587	5,933	2,980	2,953	10	7	3	...	...	...
8		Warangal Fort..	5,542	2,754	2 783	4.373	2,220	2,153	...	...	...	...	...	...
	Karimnagar		*54,418*	*27,666*	*26,752*	*46,408*	*23,382*	*23,026*	*58*	*31*	*27*	*130*	*68*	*62*
9		Jagtial ... Municipality	11,638	6,032	5,656	9.933	5,135	4,798	...	...	...	...	...	...
10		Karimnagar ... Municipality	8,347	4,393	3,954	5,750	2,981	2,769	58	31	27	130	68	62
11		Vemalwada ...	8,075	4,060	4,015	7.599	3,738	3,861	...	...	...	...	...	...
12		Manthani ...	7,759	3,814	3,945	7,368	3,589	3,779	...	...	...	...	...	...
13		Peddapalli ...	7,260	3,745	3,515	6,038	3,072	2,966	...	...	...	...	...	...
14		Koratla ...	6,038	3,010	3,058	4.763	2,400	2,363	...	...	...	...	...	...
15		Dharmapuri ..	5,221	2,612	2,609	4,957	2,470	2,487	...	...	...	...	..	..
	Adilabad		*24,137*	*11,704*	*12,433*	*19,372*	*9,300*	*10,072*	*2*	*2*	...	*17*	*10*	*7*
16		Nirmal ... Municipality	9.588	4,580	5,008	7,528	3,553	3,975	...	...	...	...	...	...
17		Adilabad ... Municipality	7,560	3,689	3,871	5,738	2,740	2,998	2	2	...	17	10	7
18		Chinnur ..	6.989	3,435	3,554	6,106	3,007	3,099	...	...	...	...	...	...
	Medak		*33,280*	*16,765*	*16,515*	*25,147*	*12,697*	*12,450*	*17*	*7*	*10*	*16*	*9*	*7*
19		Siddipet ... Municipality	9,583	4,964	4,619	8,007	4,171	3,836	...	...	...	...	...	...

TABLE V.

TOWNS ARRANGED TERRITORIALLY WITH POPULATION BY RELIGION.

ARYAN. Arya. Persons.	Males.	Females.	Brahmo. Persons.	Males.	Females.	Buddhist. Persons.	Males.	Females.	Musalman. Persons.	Males.	Females.	Christian. Persons.	Males.	Females.	Parsi. Persons.	Males.	Females.	Jew. Persons.	Males	Females.	Animist. Persons.	Males.	Females.	Serial No.
15	16	17	18	19	20	21	22	23	24	25	26	27	28	29	30	31	32	33	34	35	36	37	38	
109	***55***	***54***	***36***	***18***	***18***	***20***	***8***	***12***	***439,138***	***222,522***	***216,616***	***20,798***	***11,970***	***8,828***	***1,189***	***641***	***548***	***12***	***8***	***4***	***985***	***551***	***434***	
90	44	46	35	17	18	13	6	7	219.893	111,770	108,126	16.240	9,623	6,617	808	443	365	12	8	4	41	38	3	1
...	...	...	...	...	...	...	...	...	***2,783***	***1,348***	***1,435***	***34***	***18***	***16***	...	...	...	...	...	...	...	...	...	
...	...	...	...	...	...	...	...	...	2.193	1,030	1,163	12	9	3	...	...	...	...	...	...	...	...	...	2
...	...	...	...	...	...	...	...	...	590	318	272	22	9	13	...	...	...	...	...	...	...	...	...	3
6	***3***	***3***	***1***	***1***	...	...	...	...	***14,088***	***7,358***	***6,730***	***925***	***504***	***421***	***55***	***30***	***25***	...	...	...	***78***	***56***	***22***	
...	...	...	...	...	...	...	...	...	7.504	3,922	3,582	241	131	110	27	13	14	...	...	...	1	1	...	4
...	...	...	...	...	...	...	...	...	1.815	1,129	686	590	324	266	17	11	6	...	...	...	38	35	3	5
6	3	3	1	1	...	...	...	...	2.370	1,174	1,196	94	49	45	11	6	5	...	...	...	39	20	19	6
...	...	...	...	...	...	...	...	...	1,230	599	631	...	...	...	...	...	...	...	...	...	...	...	...	7
...	...	...	...	...	...	...	...	...	1,159	534	625	...	...	...	...	...	...	...	...	...	...	...	...	8
...	...	...	...	...	...	...	...	...	***7,628***	***4,091***	***3,537***	***187***	***90***	***97***	...	...	...	...	...	...	***7***	***4***	***3***	
...	...	...	...	...	...	...	...	...	1.735	887	848	19	9	10	...	...	...	...	...	...	1	1	...	9
...	...	...	...	...	...	...	...	...	2,251	1,237	1,014	153	76	82	...	...	...	...	...	...	...	...	...	10
...	...	...	...	...	...	...	...	...	473	322	151	...	...	...	...	...	...	...	...	...	...	...	...	11
...	...	...	...	...	...	...	...	...	385	222	163	...	...	...	...	...	...	...	...	...	6	[illegible]	[illegible]	12
...	...	...	...	...	...	...	...	...	1.212	668	544	10	5	[illegible]	...	...	...	...	...	...	...	...	...	13
...	...	...	...	...	...	...	...	...	1.305	610	695	...	...	...	...	...	...	...	...	...	...	...	...	14
...	...	...	...	...	...	...	...	...	234	142	122	...	...	...	...	...	...	...	...	...	...	...	...	15
...	...	...	...	...	...	...	...	...	***4,724***	***2,374***	***2,350***	***11***	***8***	***3***	...	...	...	...	...	...	***11***	***10***	***1***	
...	...	...	...	...	...	...	...	...	2,057	1,025	1,032	3	2	1	...	...	...	...	...	...	...	...	...	16
...	...	...	...	...	...	...	...	...	1.790	925	865	2	2	...	...	...	...	...	...	...	11	10	1	17
...	...	...	...	...	...	...	...	...	877	424	453	6	[illegible]	[illegible]	...	...	...	...	...	...	...	...	...	18
1	...	***1***	...	...	...	...	...	...	***7,599***	***3,799***	***3,800***	***451***	***222***	***229***	***2***	***1***	***1***	...	...	...	***47***	***29***	***18***	
...	...	...	...	...	...	...	...	...	1,505	755	750	71	[illegible]	[illegible]	...	...	...	...	...	...	...	...	...	19

TABLE V.

TOWNS ARRANGED TERRITORIALLY WITH POPULATION BY RELIGION.

Serial No.	District.	Town, Municipality, Suburbs, Cantonment.	Population.			Hindu.			Jain.			INDO- Sikh		
			Persons.	Males.	Females.	Persons.	Males.	Females.	Persons.	Males.	Females.	Persons.	Males.	Females
	1	2	3	4	5	6	7	8	9	10	11	12	13	14
20	**Medak**—*contd.*	Medak Municipality ..	**9,125**	4,390	4,745	**6,312**	3,085	3,257	...	...	...	**5**	5	...
21		Sadaseopet ... Municipality	**8,625**	4,415	4,210	**6,859**	3,492	3,367	**17**	7	10	...	...	...
22		Sangareddipet.. Municipality	**5,947**	3,006	2,941	**3,939**	1,949	1,990	...	...	...	**11**	4	7
	Nizamabad		***41,795***	***20,919***	***20,876***	***32,623***	***16,290***	***16,333***	***7***	***6***	***1***	***121***	***59***	***62***
23		Nizamabad .. Municipality	**17,353**	9,135	8,218	**12,411**	6,504	5,907	**7**	6	1	**114**	56	58
24		Armur ... Municipality	**7,530**	3,628	3,902	**6,517**	3,130	3,387	...	...	...	...	...	...
25		Bodhan ... Municipality	**6,996**	3,335	3,661	**5,250**	2,477	2,773	...	...	...	...	...	...
26		Lingampet ...	**5,189**	2,658	2,531	**4,760**	2,450	2,319	...	...	...	**7**	3	4
27		Balkonda ...	**4,727**	2,163	2,564	**3,676**	1,729	1,947	...	...	...	...	...	...
	Mahbubnagar.		***21,100***	***10,676***	***10,424***	***16,595***	***8,342***	***8,253***	...	...	...	***24***	***12***	***12***
28		Narayanpet ... Municipality	**12,449**	6,206	6,243	**11,015**	5,472	5,543	...	...	...	...	...	...
29		Mahbubnagar ... Municipality	**8,651**	4,470	4,181	**5,580**	2,870	2,710	...	...	...	**24**	12	12
	Nalgonda.		***14,874***	***7,552***	***7,322***	***9,778***	***4,974***	***4,804***	...	...	...	***28***	***16***	***12***
30		Nalgonda ... Municipality	**7,532**	3,736	3,796	**4,199**	2,056	2,143	...	...	...	**28**	16	12
31		Bhongir .. Municipality	**7,342**	3,816	3,526	**5,579**	2,918	2,661	...	...	...	...	...	...
	Aurangabad		***76,560***	***38,978***	***37,582***	***48,056***	***24,590***	***23,466***	***371***	***212***	***159***	***102***	***59***	***43***
32		Aurangabad .. Municipality and Cantonment	**34,902**	17,992	16,910	**19,247**	9,960	9,287	**79**	43	36	**98**	57	41
33		Jalna ... Municipality	**18,993**	9,711	9,282	**12,891**	6,593	6,298	**68**	46	22	**4**	2	2
34		Kadirabad ... Municipality	**10,270**	5,180	5,090	**6,957**	3,619	3,338	**91**	51	40	...	...	...
35		Paithan ...	**6,983**	3,376	3,613	**4,907**	2,376	2,531	**47**	24	23	...	...	...
36		Vaijapur ...	**5,406**	2,719	2,687	**4,054**	2,042	2,012	**83**	48	38	...	...	...
	Bhir.		***40,201***	***20,398***	***19,803***	***29,100***	***14,759***	***14,341***	***454***	***226***	***228***	***19***	***15***	***4***
37		Bhir ... Municipality	**16,010**	8,074	7,936	**10,886**	5,452	5,434	**50**	30	20	**16**	12	4
38		Mominabad .. (Amba) Municipality	**11,073**	5,581	5,492	**7,997**	4,045	3,952	**224**	106	118	**1**	1	...
39		Parli ..	**7,478**	3,838	3,640	**5,953**	3,059	2,894	**114**	57	57	**2**	2	...

TABLE V.

TOWNS ARRANGED TERRITORIALLY WITH POPULATION BY RELIGION.

ARYAN.									MUSALMAN.			CHRISTIAN.			PARSI.			JEW.			ANIMIST.			Serial No.
ARYA.			BRAHMO.			BUDDHIST.																		
Persons.	Males.	Females.	Persons.	Males.	Females.	Persons.	Males.	Females.	Persons.	Males.	Females.	Persons.	Males.	Females.	Persons.	Males.	Females.	Persons.	Males.	Females.	Persons.	Males.	Females.	
15	16	17	18	19	20	21	22	23	24	25	26	27	28	29	30	31	32	33	34	35	36	37	38	
...	...	...	...	...	...	...	...	...	2,355	1,080	1,275	377	182	195	...	...	...	...	...	...	46	28	18	20
1	1	...	...	..	...	...	..	...	1,749	913	833	1	1	...	...	...	...	...	...	...	1	1	...	21
...	...	...	...	...	...	...	...	...	1,993	1,051	942	2	1	1	2	1	1	...	...	...	...	...	...	22
...	...	...	...	...	...	...	...	...	*8,941*	*4,508*	*4,433*	*80*	*45*	*35*	*9*	*2*	*7*	...	...	...	*14*	*9*	*5*	
...	..	...	...	...	...	...	...	...	4,740	2,525	2,215	72	42	30	9	2	7	...	...	...	...	...	...	23
...	...	...	...	...	...	...	...	...	991	486	505	8	3	5	...	...	...	...	..	...	14	9	5	24
...	...	...	...	...	...	...	...	..	1,746	858	888	...	...	...	...	...	...	...	...	...	...	...	...	25
...	...	...	...	...	...	...	...	...	413	205	208	...	...	...	...	...	...	...	...	...	...	...	...	26
...	...	...	...	...	...	..	...	...	1,051	434	617	..	...	...	...	...	...	...	...	...	...	...	...	27
...	...	.	...	...	...	...	...	...	*4,287*	*2,242*	*2,045*	*183*	*74*	*109*	...	...	...	...	...	...	*11*	*6*	*5*	
...	...	...	...	...	...	...	...	...	1,433	733	700	1	1	...	...	...	...	...	...	...	...	...	...	28
...	...	...	...	...	...	...	...	...	2,854	1,509	1,345	182	73	109	...	...	...	...	...	...	11	6	5	29
...	...	...	...	...	...	...	...	...	*4,807*	*2,437*	*2,370*	*249*	*122*	*127*	*10*	*2*	*8*	...	...	...	*2*	*1*	*1*	
...	...	...	...	...	...	...	...	...	3,034	1,557	1,527	221	107	114	...	...	...	...	...	...	...	...	...	30
...	...	...	...	...	...	...	...	...	1,723	880	843	28	15	13	10	2	8	...	...	...	2	1	1	31
...	...	...	...	...	...	*7*	*2*	*5*	*26,402*	*13,300*	*13,102*	*1,295*	*645*	*650*	*191*	*100*	*91*	...	...	...	*136*	*70*	*66*	
...	...	...	...	...	...	7	2	5	14,517	7,454	7,063	837	414	423	115	61	54	...	...	...	2	1	1	32
...	...	...	...	...	...	...	...	...	5,547	2,828	2,719	403	204	199	59	28	31	...	...	...	21	10	11	33
...	...	...	...	...	...	...	...	...	3,155	1,474	1,681	50	25	25	17	11	6	...	...	...	...	...	...	34
...	...	...	...	...	...	...	...	...	2,035	976	1,059	...	...	...	...	...	...	...	...	...	...	...	...	35
...	...	..	...	...	...	...	...	...	1,148	568	580	5	2	3	...	...	...	...	...	...	113	59	54	36
...	...	...	...	...	...	...	...	..	*10,624*	*5,396*	*5,228*	*2*	*1*	*1*	*1*	*1*	...	...	...	...	*1*	...	*1*	
...	...	...	...	...	...	...	...	...	5,058	2,580	2,478	...	...	...	...	...	...	...	...	...	...	...	...	37
...	...	...	...	...	...	...	...	...	2,848	1,428	1,420	2	1	1	...	...	...	..	...	...	1	...	1	38
...	...	...	...	...	..	...	...	...	1,409	720	689	...	...	...	...	...	...	...	..	..	...		...	39

TABLE V.

TOWNS ARRANGED TERRITORIALLY WITH POPULATION BY RELIGION.

Serial No.	District.	Town, Municipality, Suburbs, Cantonment.	Population			Indo-								
						Hindu.			Jain.			Sikh.		
			Persons.	Males.	Females.	Persons.	Males.	Females.	Persons.	Males.	Females.	Persons.	Males.	Females.
	1	2	3	4	5	6	7	8	9	10	11	12	13	14
40	**Bhir**—(*contd.*)	Manjlegaon ..	**5,640**	2,905	2,735	**4,264**	2,203	2,061	**66**	33	33	...	...	...
	Nander.		***54,347***	***27,178***	***27,169***	***35,710***	***17,837***	***17,873***	***171***	***92***	***79***	***798***	***433***	***365***
41		Nander Municipality ...	**17,625**	9,281	8,344	**9,275**	4,892	4,383	**42**	23	19	**774**	419	355
42		Bhaisa ...	**8,444**	4,103	4,341	**5,434**	2,631	2,803	**3**	2	1	...	...	...
43		Deglur ..	**7,800**	3,772	4,028	**5,669**	2,780	2,889	**56**	34	22	**5**	3	2
44		Kondalwadi ...	**7,018**	3,403	3,615	**5,705**	2,742	2,963	**4**	2	2	...	...	...
45		Mudhol ...	**6,876**	3,311	3,565	**4,485**	2,186	2,299	...	...	...	**19**	11	8
46		Mukher ..	**6,584**	3,308	3,276	**5,142**	2,606	2,536	**66**	31	35	...	...	...
	Parbhani.		***66,832***	***34,160***	***32,672***	***47,886***	***24,651***	***23,235***	***621***	***300***	***321***	***67***	***37***	***30***
47		Hingoli Municipality ..	**17,507**	9,199	8,308	**13,014**	6,958	6,056	**152**	76	76	**13**	9	4
48		Manwat Municipality ...	**11,002**	5,740	5,262	**8,868**	4,677	4,191	**243**	112	131	**3**	2	1
49		Basmat Municipality ..	**10,599**	5,336	5,263	**7,233**	3,629	3,604	**34**	18	16	...	...	...
50		Parbhani Municipality ..	**9,031**	4,817	4,214	**5,725**	3,006	2,719	**24**	15	9	**27**	16	11
51		Pathri ..	**7,095**	3,501	3,594	**4,148**	2,039	2,109	**40**	20	20	...	...	...
52		Gungakher ..	**5,997**	2,878	3,119	**4,611**	2,241	2,370	**47**	20	27	...	...	...
53		Sonepet ...	**5,551**	2,689	2,862	**4,257**	2,101	2,156	**81**	39	42	**24**	10	14
	Gulbarga.		***1,05,555***	***53,329***	***52,226***	***66,167***	***33,455***	***33,712***	***769***	***410***	***359***	***16***	***12***	***4***
54		Gulbarga Municipality ..	**32,437**	16,849	15,588	**17,189**	9,002	8,187	**130**	77	53	**4**	3	1
55		Aland ...	**12,051**	6,158	5,893	**5,461**	2,861	2,600	**529**	276	253	...	...	...
56		Yadgir Municipality .	**10,945**	5,241	5,704	**6,493**	3,110	3,383	**54**	28	26	...	...	...
57		Kosgi ..	**9,633**	4,850	4,933	**8,037**	4,046	3,991	...	...	...	...	...	...
58		Chitapur ...	**9,355**	4,676	4,679	**6,280**	3,122	3,158	**5**	3	2	...	...	...
59		Shorapur Municipality ...	**8,043**	3,899	4,144	**5,904**	2,843	3,061	**17**	10	7	...	...	...
60		Tandur ...	**6,504**	3,344	3,160	**4,659**	2,383	2,276	**3**	3	...	...	...	...
61		Kodangal Municipality ..	**6,062**	3,010	3,052	**4,783**	2,363	2,420	...	...	...	...	...	...
62		Shahabad ...	**5,607**	2,886	2,721	**3,897**	2,014	1,883	**22**	13	9	**12**	9	3

TABLE V.

TOWNS ARRANGED TERRITORIALLY WITH POPULATION BY RELIGION.

ARYAN.																								
ARYA.			BRAHAMO.			BUDDHIST.			MUSALMAN.			CHRISTIAN.			PARSI.			JEW.			ANIMIST.			Serial No.
Persons.	Males.	Females.	Persons.	Males.	Females.	Persons	Males.	Females.	Persons.	Males.	Females.	Persons	Males.	Females.	Persons.	Males.	Females.	Persons.	Males.	Females.	Persons.	Males.	Females.	
15	16	17	18	19	20	21	22	23	24	25	26	27	28	29	30	31	32	33	34	35	36	37	38	
...	...	...	...	...	...	...	...	...	1,309	668	611	...	...	...	1	1	...	...	...	...	...	...	...	40
...	...	...	...	...	...	...	...	...	*17,619*	*8,790*	*8,829*	*20*	*12*	*8*	*29*	*14*	*15*	...	...	...	...	...	...	
...	...	...	...	...	...	...	...	...	7,492	3,925	3,567	15	10	5	27	12	15	...	...	...	...	...	...	41
...	...	...	...	...	...	...	...	...	3,007	1,470	1,537	...	...	...	...	...	...	...	...	...	...	...	...	42
...	...	...	...	...	...	...	...	...	2,070	955	1,115	...	...	...	...	...	...	...	...	...	...	...	...	43
...	...	...	...	...	...	...	...	...	1,309	659	650	...	...	...	...	...	...	...	...	...	...	...	...	44
...	...	...	...	...	...	...	...	...	2,372	1,114	1,258	...	...	...	...	...	...	...	...	...	...	...	...	45
...	...	...	...	...	...	...	...	...	1,369	667	702	5	2	3	2	2	...	...	...	...	...	...	...	46
12	*7*	*5*	...	...	...	...	...	...	*17,845*	*8,965*	*8,880*	*94*	*52*	*42*	*18*	*7*	*11*	...	...	...	*289*	*141*	*148*	
12	7	5	...	...	...	...	...	...	3,937	1,938	1,999	31	19	12	11	3	8	...	...	...	287	139	148	47
...	...	...	...	...	...	...	...	...	1,839	919	939	...	...	...	...	...	...	...	...	...	...	...	...	48
...	...	...	...	...	...	...	...	...	3,298	1,687	1,611	4	2	2	...	...	...	...	...	...	...	...	...	49
...	...	...	...	...	...	...	...	...	3,237	1,74[illegible]	1,494	59	31	28	7	4	3	...	...	...	2	2	...	50
...	...	...	...	...	...	...	...	...	2,937	1,41[illegible]	1,465	...	...	...	...	...	...	...	...	...	...	...	...	51
...	...	...	...	...	...	...	...	...	1,339	617	722	...	...	...	...	...	...	...	...	...	...	...	...	52
...	...	...	...	...	...	...	...	...	1,189	539	650	...	...	...	...	...	...	...	...	...	...	...	...	53
...	...	...	...	...	...	...	...	...	*38,037*	*19,145*	*18,892*	*246*	*134*	112	*40*	*20*	*20*	...	...	...	*289*	*153*	*136*	
...	...	...	...	...	...	...	...	...	14,998	7,703	7,295	97	52	45	19	12	7	...	...	...	...	...	...	54
...	...	...	...	...	...	...	...	...	5,859	2,917	2,912	...	...	...	...	...	...	...	...	...	199	104	95	55
...	...	...	...	...	...	...	...	...	4,384	2,093	2,291	9	6	3	2	1	1	...	...	...	...	...	...	56
...	...	...	...	...	...	...	...	...	1,639	800	839	8	4	4	...	...	...	...	...	...	...	...	...	57
...	...	...	...	...	...	...	...	...	3,070	1,551	1,519	...	...	...	...	...	...	...	...	...	...	...	...	58
...	...	...	...	...	...	...	...	...	2,121	1,045	1,076	...	...	...	1	1	...	...	...	...	...	...	...	59
...	...	...	...	...	...	...	...	...	1,813	946	867	29	12	17	...	...	...	...	...	...	...	...	...	60
...	...	...	...	...	...	...	...	...	1,234	621	613	...	...	...	...	...	...	...	...	...	42	23	19	61
...	...	...	...	...	...	...	...	...	1,518	766	752	92	52	40	18	6	12	...	...	...	48	26	22	62

TOWNS ARRANGED TERRITORIALLY WITH POPULATION BY RELIGION.

Serial No.	District.	Town, Municipality, Suburbs, Cantonment.	Population.			Indo-: Hindu.			Indo-: Jain.			Indo-: Sikh.		
			Persons.	Males.	Females.	Persons.	Males.	Females.	Persons.	Males.	Females.	Persons.	Males.	Females.
	1	2	3	4	5	6	7	8	9	10	11	12	13	14
63	**Gulbarga-(*contd.*)**	Seram Municipality ...	**4,868**	2,416	2,452	**3,455**	1,705	1,750	...	...	...	...	...	...
	Osmanabad.		***42,790***	***21,697***	***21,093***	***32,789***	***16,639***	***16,150***	***523***	***264***	***259***	***6***	***4***	***2***
64		Osmanabad Municipality ...	**10,221**	5,255	4,966	**7,059**	3,631	3,428	**355**	175	180	...	...	...
65		Thair (Ter) ..	**7,948**	3,991	3,957	**7,280**	3,659	3,621	**3**	...	3	...	...	...
66		Latur Municipality ...	**7,574**	3,843	3,731	**5,274**	2,683	2,591	**52**	29	23	**6**	4	2
67		Moram ...	**6,150**	3,126	3,024	**4.917**	2,502	2,415	**72**	37	35	...	...	...
68		Tuljapur Municipality ...	**5,451**	2,766	2,685	**4,888**	2,460	2,428	**41**	23	18	...	...	...
69		Owsa Municipality ..	**5,446**	2,716	2,730	**3,371**	1,704	1,667	...	...	...	...	...	...
	Raichur.		***82,232***	***41,059***	***41,173***	***59,434***	***29,241***	***30,193***	***235***	***135***	***100***	***16***	***11***	***5***
70		Raichur Municipality ..	**25,034**	12,681	12,353	**19.245**	9,578	9,667	**16**	9	7	...	...	...
71		Gadwal ..	**12,082**	5,965	6,117	**9.172**	4,459	4,713	...	...	...	...	...	...
72		Koppal ...	**7.558**	3,916	3,642	**4,755**	2,413	2,342	**105**	62	43	...	...	...
73		Mudgal Municipality ...	**6,947**	3,455	3,492	**4,114**	2,048	2,066	...	...	...	...	...	...
74		Deodrug Municipality ...	**6,837**	3,334	3,503	**5,003**	2,423	2,580	...	...	...	...	...	...
75		Manvi Municipality ...	**6.679**	3,359	3,320	**4.908**	2,430	2,478	**2**	2	...	...	...	...
76		Gangawati Municipality ...	**6,663**	3,238	3,425	**4.571**	2,182	2,389	...	...	...	**8**	5	3
77		Sindhnur ...	**5,578**	2,733	2,845	**3.790**	1,827	1,963	**112**	62	50	**8**	6	2
78		Kallur ...	**4,854**	2,378	2,476	**3,876**	1,881	1,995	...	...	...	...	...	...
	Bidar.		***54,909***	***27,249***	***27,660***	***31,995***	***16,146***	***15,849***	***157***	***67***	***90***	***52***	***24***	***28***
79		Bidar Municipality ...	**12,684**	6,316	6,368	**6,011**	3,089	2,922	**25**	11	14	**16**	8	8
80		Kalyani ...	**11,077**	5,458	5,619	**5.783**	2,863	2,920	**27**	9	18	...	...	...
81		Udgir Municipality ...	**7.213**	3,619	3,594	**4.492**	2,292	2,200	**76**	36	40	**29**	13	16
82		Kohir Municipality ...	**6,486**	3,154	3,332	**3,293**	1,694	1,599	...	...	...	**7**	3	4
83		Bhalki ...	**6,268**	3,158	3,110	**5,041**	2,561	2,480	**9**	3	6	...	...	...
84		Ekeli ...	**5,889**	2,914	2,975	**3,776**	1,885	1,891	**20**	8	12	...	...	...
85		Alikher ..	**5,292**	2,630	2,662	**3 599**	1,762	1,837	...	...	...	...	...	...

TABLE V.

TOWNS ARRANGED TERRITORIALLY WITH POPULATION BY RELIGION.

ARYAN.																								
ARYA.			BRAHAMO.			BUDHIST.			MUSALMAN.			CHRISTIAN.			PARSI.			JEW.			ANIMIST.			Serial No.
Persons.	Males.	Females.	Persons.	Males.	Females.	Persons.	Males.	Females.	Persons.	Males.	Females.	Persons	Males.	Females.	Persons.	Males.	Females.	Persons.	Males.	Females	Persons.	Males.	Females.	
15	16	17	18	19	20	21	22	23	24	25	26	27	28	29	30	31	32	33	34	35	36	37	38	
...	...	...	...	...	...	...	...	...	1,402	703	699	11	8	3	...	...	...	...	...	...	...	...	...	63
...	...	...	...	...	...	...	...	...	***9,438***	***4,766***	***4,672***	***22***	***12***	***10***	***12***	***12***	...	...	...	...	...	...	...	
...	...	...	...	...	...	...	...	...	2,782	1,430	1,352	15	9	6	10	10	...	...	...	...	...	...	...	64
...	...	...	...	...	...	...	...	...	665	332	333	...	...	...	...	...	...	...	...	...	...	...	...	65
...	...	...	...	...	...	...	...	...	2,234	1,123	1,111	7	3	4	1	1	...	...	...	...	...	...	...	66
...	...	...	...	...	...	...	...	...	1,161	587	574	...	...	...	...	...	...	...	...	...	...	...	...	67
...	...	...	...	...	...	...	...	...	521	282	239	...	...	...	1	1	...	...	...	...	...	...	...	68
...	...	...	...	...	...	...	...	...	2,075	1,012	1,063	...	...	...	...	...	...	...	...	...	...	...	...	69
...	...	...	...	...	...	...	...	...	***21,874***	***11,311***	***10,563***	***659***	***352***	***307***	***14***	***9***	***5***	...	...	...	...	...	...	
...	...	...	...	...	...	...	...	...	5,502	2,937	2,565	265	151	114	6	6	...	...	...	...	...	...	...	70
...	...	...	...	...	...	...	...	...	2,871	1,478	1,393	37	26	11	2	2	...	...	...	...	...	...	...	71
...	...	...	...	...	...	...	...	...	2,687	1,436	1,251	11	5	6	...	...	...	...	...	...	...	...	...	72
...	...	...	...	...	...	...	...	...	2,487	1,237	1,250	346	170	176	...	...	...	...	...	...	...	...	...	73
...	...	...	...	...	...	...	...	...	1,834	911	923	...	...	...	...	...	...	...	...	...	...	...	...	74
...	...	...	...	...	...	...	...	...	1,763	926	837	...	...	...	6	1	5	...	...	...	...	...	...	75
...	...	...	...	...	...	...	...	...	2,084	1,051	1,033	...	...	...	...	...	...	...	...	...	...	...	...	76
...	...	...	...	...	...	...	...	...	1,668	838	830	...	...	...	...	...	...	...	...	...	...	...	...	77
...	...	...	...	...	...	...	...	...	978	497	481	...	...	...	...	...	...	...	...	...	...	...	...	78
...	...	...	...	...	...	...	...	...	***22,546***	***10,922***	***11,624***	***100***	***56***	***44***	...	...	...	...	...	...	***59***	***34***	***25***	
...	...	...	...	...	...	...	...	...	6,536	3,155	3,381	94	52	42	...	...	...	...	...	...	2	1	1	79
...	...	...	...	...	...	...	...	...	5,266	2,585	2,681	1	1	...	...	...	...	...	...	...	...	...	...	80
...	...	...	...	...	...	...	...	...	2,616	1,278	1,338	...	...	...	...	...	...	...	...	...	...	...	...	81
...	...	...	...	...	...	...	...	...	3,181	1,454	1,727	5	3	2	...	...	...	...	...	...	...	...	...	82
...	...	...	...	...	...	...	...	...	1,218	594	624	...	...	...	...	...	...	...	...	...	...	...	...	83
...	...	...	...	...	...	...	...	...	2,036	988	1,048	...	...	...	...	...	...	...	...	...	57	33	24	84
...	...	...	...	...	...	...	...	...	1,693	868	825	...	...	...	...	...	...	...	...	...	...	...	...	85

TABLE VI.

RELIGION.

TABLE VI.

RELIGION.

Serial No.	District.	Population.			INDO[illegible]					
					Hindu.			Jain.		
		Persons.	Males.	Females.	Persons.	Males.	Females.	Persons.	Males.	Females.
	1	2	3	4	5	6	7	8	9	10
	Hyderabad State ...	***13,374,676***	***6,797,118***	***6,577,558***	***11,626,146***	***5,897,158***	***5,728,988***	***21,026***	***11,032***	***9,9[illegible]***
1	Hyderabad City ...	**500,623**	258,454	242,169	**262,131**	135,638	126,493	**379**	223	1[illegible]
2	Atraf-i-balda ...	**520,159**	265,184	254,975	**455,203**	231,505	223,698	**110**	58	[illegible]
	Warangal Division ...	***2,657,477***	***1,368,101***	***1,289,376***	***2,323,038***	***1,194,071***	***1,128,967***	***226***	***115***	***11[illegible]***
3	Warangal	**905,414**	467,413	438,001	**723,884**	372,793	351,091	**35**	21	1[illegible]
4	Karimnagar	**1,131,637**	586,260	545,377	**1,074,654**	556,441	518,213	**64**	35	[illegible]
5	Adilabad	**620,426**	314,428	305,998	**524,500**	264,837	259,663	**127**	59	[illegible]
	Medak Division ...	***3,046,705***	***1,548,882***	***1,497,823***	***2,753,155***	***1,397,884***	***1,355,271***	***142***	***72***	***7[illegible]***
6	Medak	**687,137**	348,410	338,727	**615,552**	312,690	302,862	**120**	57	[illegible]
7	Nizamabad	**568,009**	283,621	284,388	**523,159**	261,053	262,106	**18**	13	[illegible]
8	Mahbubnagar	**747,178**	379,712	367,466	**672,750**	341,109	331,641	...	...	...
9	Nalgonda	**1,044,381**	537,139	507,242	**941,694**	483,032	458,662	**4**	2	[illegible]
	Aurangabad Division .	***2,976,541***	***1,496,102***	***1,480,439***	***2,627,633***	***1,317,224***	***1,310,409***	***13,490***	***7,019***	***6,47[illegible]***
10	Aurangabad	**869,787**	437,495	432,292	**734,252**	367,581	366,671	**5,496**	2,880	**2,61[illegible]**
11	Bhir	**622,531**	314,738	307,793	**566,054**	285,573	280,481	**3,389**	1,820	**1,5[illegible]**
12	Nander	**704,549**	352,638	351,911	**627,652**	313,495	314,157	**940**	477	**46[illegible]**
13	Parbhani	**779,674**	391,231	388,443	**699,675**	350,575	349,100	**3,665**	1,842	**1,82[illegible]**
	Gulbarga Division ...	***3,673,171***	***1,860,395***	***1,812,776***	***3,204,986***	***1,620,836***	***1,584,150***	***6,679***	***3,545***	***3,13[illegible]***
14	Gulbarga	**1,150,983**	582,447	568,536	**970,405**	490,220	480,185	**1,613**	880	**7[illegible]**
15	Osmanabad	**635,977**	324,969	311,008	**572,433**	292,192	280,241	**3,429**	1,817	**1,6[illegible]**
16	Raichur	**996,684**	503,541	493,143	**900,417**	453,629	446,788	**707**	393	**3[illegible]**
17	Bidar	**889,527**	449,438	440,089	**761,731**	384,795	376,936	**930**	455	**4[illegible]**

TABLE VI.

RELIGION.

ARYAN.																
Sikh.			Arya.			Brahmo.			Buddhist.			Musalman.			Serial No.
Persons.	Males.	Females.	Persons.	Males.	Females.	Persons.	Males.	Females.	Persons.	Males.	Females.	Persons.	Males.	Females.	
11	12	13	14	15	16	17	18	19	20	21	22	23	24	25	
4,726	*2,643*	*2,083*	*173*	*90*	*83*	*36*	*18*	*18*	*20*	*8*	*12*	*1,380,990*	*706,821*	*674,169*	
978	644	334	90	44	46	35	17	18	13	6	7	219,896	111,770	108,126	1
61	36	25	...	...	...	...	...	...	...	...	...	59,342	30,602	28,740	2
650	*336*	*314*	*8*	*4*	*4*	*1*	*1*	...	...	...	...	*126,270*	*66,897*	*59,373*	
306	160	146	8	4	4	1	1	...	...	...	...	50,079	26,709	23,370	3
210	111	99	...	...	...	...	...	...	...	...	...	46,523	24,345	22,178	4
134	65	69	...	...	...	...	...	...	...	...	...	29,668	15,843	13,825	5
581	*312*	*269*	*62*	*34*	*28*	...	...	...	...	...	...	*220,428*	*111,379*	*109,049*	
151	83	68	1	1	...	...	...	...	...	...	...	65,084	32,269	32,815	6
271	137	134	61	33	28	...	...	...	...	...	...	41,951	21,036	20,915	7
64	38	26	...	...	...	...	...	...	...	...	...	59,521	30,353	29,168	8
95	54	41	...	...	...	...	...	...	...	...	...	53,872	27,721	26,151	9
2,088	*1,103*	*985*	*12*	*7*	*5*	...	...	...	*7*	*2*	*5*	*308,012*	*157,875*	*150,137*	
195	107	88	...	...	...	...	...	...	7	2	5	111,449	57,629	53,820	10
346	183	163	...	...	...	...	...	...	...	...	...	51,900	26,749	25,151	11
1,323	700	623	...	...	...	...	...	...	...	...	...	72,189	36,708	35,481	12
224	113	111	12	7	5	...	...	...	...	...	...	72,474	36,789	35,685	13
368	*212*	*156*	*1*	*1*	...	...	...	...	...	...	...	*447,042*	*228,298*	*218,744*	
61	41	20	1	1	...	...	...	...	...	...	...	169,326	86,152	83,174	14
87	47	40	...	...	...	...	...	...	...	...	...	59,443	30,602	28,846	15
62	35	27	...	...	...	...	...	...	...	...	...	93,478	48,102	45,076	16
158	89	69	...	...	...	...	...	...	...	...	...	124,790	63,142	61,648	17

TABLE VI.

RELIGION—(*Continued.*)

		Christian.			Parsi.			Jew.			Animistic.		
		Persons.	Males.	Females.	Persons.	Males.	Females.	Persons.	Males.	Females.	Persons.	Males.	Females.
		26	27	28	29	30	31	32	33	34	35	36	37
	Hyderabad State ..	***54,296***	***29,495***	***24,801***	***1,529***	***822***	***707***	***12***	***8***	***4***	***285,722***	***149,023***	***136,69[illegible]***
1	Hyderabad City ..	16,240	9,623	6,617	808	443	365	12	8	4	41	38	[illegible]
2	Atraf-i-balda ..	1,291	686	605	85	42	43	...	...	...	4,067	2,255	1,81[illegible]
	Warangal Division ..	***12,593***	***6,507***	***6,086***	***108***	***55***	***53***	...	...	...	***194,583***	***100,115***	***94,4[illegible]***
3	Warangal ..	11,979	6,202	5,777	101	50	51	...	...	...	119,021	61,473	57,54[illegible]
4	Karimnagar ..	586	286	300	2	1	1	...	...	...	9,598	5,041	4,557
5	Adilabad ...	28	19	9	5	4	1	...	...	...	65,964	33,601	32,36[illegible]
	Medak Division ...	***13,940***	***7,285***	***6,655***	***32***	***14***	***18***	...	...	...	***58,365***	***31,902***	***26,46[illegible]***
6	Medak ..	2,203	1,124	1,079	10	7	3	...	...	...	4,016	2,179	1,837
7	Nizamabad ..	720	375	345	9	2	7	...	...	...	1,820	972	84[illegible]
8	Mahbubnagar ...	451	221	230	...	...	...	...	...	...	14,392	7,991	6,401
9	Nalgonda ...	10,566	5,565	5,001	13	5	8	...	...	...	38,137	20,760	17,37[illegible]
	Aurangabad Division ...	***6,849***	***3,513***	***3,336***	***342***	***175***	***167***	...	...	...	***18,108***	***9,184***	***8,924***
10	Aurangabad ..	6,369	3,222	3,147	225	118	107	...	...	...	11,794	5,956	5,83[illegible]
11	Bhir ..	2	1	1	5	5	...	...	...	...	835	407	42[illegible]
12	Nander ...	69	40	29	40	24	16	...	...	...	2,336	1,194	1,14[illegible]
13	Parbhani ...	409	250	159	72	28	44	...	...	...	3,143	1,627	1,516
	Gulbarga Division ...	***3,383***	***1,881***	***1,502***	***154***	***93***	***61***	...	...	...	***10,558***	***5,529***	***5,029***
14	Gulbarga ...	1,044	633	411	91	51	40	...	...	...	8,442	4,469	3,97[illegible]
15	Osmanabad ..	252	130	122	22	18	4	...	...	...	306	163	14[illegible]
16	Raichur ...	1,711	920	791	41	24	17	...	...	...	268	136	13[illegible]
17	Bidar ...	376	198	178	...	...	...	...	...	...	1,542	759	7[illegible]

TABLE VII.

AGE, SEX AND CIVIL CONDITION.

This table shows the distribution of the population by age, sex and civil condition and is divided into three parts.

Part I shows the distribution, for the State as a whole, of the total population by each religion.

Part II shows the distribution, for districts, of the total population by main religions.

Part III gives similar details for the City of Hyderabad.

Part I.
Total Population.

TABLE VII.

AGE, SEX AND CIVIL CONDITION.

Religion and Age.	Population.			Unmarried.		
	Persons.	Males.	Females.	Persons.	Males.	Females.
1	2	3	4	5	6	7
All Religions.						
Total	*13,374,676*	*6,797,118*	*6,577,558*	*4,963,166*	*3,022,032*	*1,941,134*
0—1	371,040	179,458	191,582	369,351	178,918	190,433
1—2	254,336	120,746	133,590	251,849	120,085	131,764
2—3	470,646	226,711	243,935	463,148	224,800	238,348
3—4	413,504	197,604	215,900	403,029	194,879	208,150
4—5	414,133	206,101	208,032	397,201	202,028	195,173
Total 0—5	*1,923,659*	*930,620*	*993,039*	*1,884,578*	*920,710*	*963,868*
5—10	1,695,021	857,599	837,422	1,472,158	823,363	648,795
10—15	1,392,802	764,794	628,008	846,011	641,523	204,488
15—20	1,004,122	499,688	504,434	334,330	296,326	38,004
20—25	1,164,165	536,898	627,267	184,269	163,080	21,189
25—30	1,223,496	631,250	592,246	94,589	79,219	15,370
30—35	1,190,977	584,516	606,461	50,120	35,722	14,398
35—40	727,312	402,969	324,343	22,219	14,903	7,316
40—45	972,672	504,379	468,293	27,789	17,431	10,858
45—50	438,854	253,855	184,999	10,059	6,822	3,237
50—55	686,953	353,934	333,019	15,668	9,859	5,809
55—60	174,675	99,381	75,294	4,316	3,011	1,305
60—65	461,796	222,792	239,004	9,148	5,400	3,748
65—70	80,558	42,351	38,207	1,765	1,091	674
70 & over	237,614	112,092	125,522	6,147	3,572	2,575
Hindu.						
Total	*11,626,146*	*5,897,158*	*5,728,988*	*4,188,681*	*2,561,643*	*1,627,038*
0—1	324,100	156,497	167,603	322,494	155,986	166,508
1—2	225,778	107,072	118,706	223,344	106,425	116,919
2—3	412,897	198,821	214,076	405,556	196,981	208,575
3—4	362,487	173,378	189,109	352,278	170,779	181,599
4—5	359,006	178,881	180,125	342,821	175,102	167,719
Total 0—5	*1,684,268*	*814,649*	*869,619*	*1,646,593*	*805,273*	*841,320*
5—10	1,469,492	743,647	725,845	1,256,469	711,568	544,901
10—15	1,204,040	662,127	541,913	691,683	545,570	146,113
15—20	871,698	432,742	438,956	265,375	241,533	23,842
20—25	1,006,989	461,425	545,564	138,281	121,819	16,462
25—30	1,065,817	549,561	516,256	70,303	58,256	12,047
30—35	1,036,323	508,357	527,966	39,316	27,144	12,172
35—40	636,756	350,714	286,042	17,973	11,685	6,288
40—45	844,916	437,735	407,181	23,035	14,055	8,980
45—50	386,557	222,189	164,368	8,631	5,768	2,863
50—55	596,775	306,266	290,509	13,172	8,180	4,992
55—60	152,500	86,044	66,456	3,674	2,551	1,123
60—65	398,649	191,004	207,645	7,695	4,463	3,232
65—70	69,961	36,389	33,572	1,473	900	573
70 & over	201,405	94,309	107,096	5,008	2,878	2,130

TABLE VII.

Part I.

AGE, SEX AND CIVIL CONDITION.

Total Population.

Married.			Widowed.		
Persons.	Males.	Females.	Persons.	Males.	Females.
8	9	10	11	12	13
6,969,453	***3,495,695***	***3,473,758***	***1,422,057***	***279,391***	***1,162,666***
1,594	520	1,074	95	20	75
2,319	638	1,681	168	23	145
7.269	1,853	5,416	229	58	171
10.104	2,661	7,443	371	64	307
16.219	3,920	12,299	713	153	560
37,505	***9,592***	***27,913***	***1,576***	***318***	***1,258***
215,739	32,646	183,093	7.124	1,590	5,534
531,449	119,116	412,333	15.342	4,155	11,187
650,394	198,711	451,683	19.398	4.651	14.747
939.418	365,008	574,410	40,478	8.810	31,668
10,065,522	536,552	528,970	63,385	15,479	47,906
1,029.764	528,124	501,640	111,093	20,670	90,423
611.452	369,837	241,615	93,641	18,229	75,412
731,281	453,174	278,107	213,602	33,774	179,828
315,969	225,555	90,414	112,826	21.478	91,348
408,650	289,528	109,122	262,635	44,547	218,088
102,026	80,877	21,149	68,333	15,493	52,840
207.161	171,388	35,773	245,487	46,004	199,483
36.127	30,995	5,132	42,666	10,265	32,401
86,996	74,592	12,404	144.471	33,928	110,543
6,162,316	***3,088,085***	***3,074,231***	***1,275,149***	***247,430***	***1,027,719***
1.520	492	1,028	86	19	67
2,270	624	1,646	164	23	141
7.121	1,787	5,234	220	53	167
9.746	2,537	7,209	363	62	301
15,505	3,638	11,867	680	141	539
36,162	***9,078***	***27,084***	***1,513***	***298***	***1,215***
206,430	30,635	175,795	6,593	1,444	5,149
498,368	112,848	385,520	13,989	3,709	10,280
588,365	186,826	401,539	17.958	4,383	13,575
832,338	331,661	500,677	36,370	7,945	28,425
938,835	477,508	461,267	56,649	13,707	42,942
897,955	462,946	435,009	99,052	18,267	80,785
534,693	322,911	211,782	84,090	16,118	67,972
632,679	393,586	239,093	189,202	30,094	159,108
276,615	197,176	79,439	101.311	19,245	82,066
352,031	258,358	93,673	231.572	39,728	191,844
87,897	69,611	18,286	60.929	13,822	47,047
176,436	146.140	30,296	214,518	40,401	174,117
30,910	26,463	4,447	37,578	9,026	28,552
72,572	62,248	10,324	123,825	29,183	94,642

Part I.

Total Population.

TABLE VII.

AGE, SEX AND CIVIL CONDITION.

Religion and Age.		Population.			Unmarried.			Married.			Widowed.		
		Persons.	Males.	Females.	Persons.	Males.	Females	Persons.	Males.	Females.	Persons.	Males.	Females.
14		15	16	17	18	19	20	21	22	23	24	25	26
Jain.	Total	*21,026*	*11,032*	*9,994*	*7,720*	*4,943*	*2,777*	*10,346*	*5,165*	*5,181*	*2,960*	*924*	*2,036*
	0—1	581	259	322	574	256	318	4	3	1	3	...	3
	1—2	344	154	190	339	153	186	5	1	4	...	...	...
	2—3	597	294	303	576	280	296	19	14	5	2	...	2
	3—4	452	216	236	442	212	230	7	4	3	3	...	3
	4—5	560	253	307	525	233	292	33	19	14	2	1	1
	Total 0—5	*2,534*	*1,176*	*1,358*	*2,456*	*1,134*	*1,322*	*68*	*41*	*27*	*10*	*1*	*9*
	5—10	2,397	1,197	1,200	2,120	1,134	986	264	60	204	13	3	10
	10—15	2,200	1,239	961	1,408	1,066	342	768	162	606	24	11	13
	15—20	1,657	852	805	528	496	32	1,091	348	743	38	8	30
	20—25	1,854	899	955	389	369	20	1,370	515	855	95	15	80
	25—30	1,973	1,061	912	233	250	13	1,547	747	800	163	64	99
	30—35	1,869	984	885	183	164	19	1,452	743	709	234	77	157
	35—40	1,399	758	641	108	92	16	1,051	603	448	240	63	177
	40—45	1,479	816	663	106	101	5	939	623	366	384	92	292
	45—50	868	502	366	40	34	6	554	382	172	274	86	188
	50—55	1,092	605	487	43	34	9	537	398	139	512	173	339
	55—60	397	250	147	16	15	1	200	159	41	181	76	105
	60—65	771	417	354	34	31	3	238	246	42	419	140	309
	65—70	179	104	75	13	13	...	73	59	14	93	32	61
	70 & over	357	172	185	13	10	3	94	79	15	250	83	167
Sikh.	Total	*4,726*	*2,643*	*2,083*	*1,888*	*1,232*	*656*	*2,343*	*1,270*	*1,073*	*495*	*141*	*354*
	0—1	119	65	54	119	65	54	...	...	...	...	...	...
	1—2	85	41	44	85	41	44	...	...	...	...	...	...
	2—3	136	65	71	135	67	70	1	...	1	...	...	...
	3—4	138	57	81	137	56	81	1	1	...	...	...	...
	4—5	116	46	70	115	45	70	1	1	...	...	...	...
	Total 0—5	*594*	*274*	*320*	*591*	*272*	*319*	*3*	*2*	*1*	...	...	...
	5—10	542	291	251	502	279	223	38	12	26	2	...	2
	10—15	381	227	154	274	201	73	106	26	80	1	...	1
	15—20	307	180	127	145	134	11	154	45	109	8	1	7
	20—25	483	262	221	159	152	7	308	108	200	13	2	14
	25—30	416	225	191	64	58	6	328	155	173	24	12	12
	30—35	528	285	243	58	49	9	436	224	212	34	12	22
	35—40	299	194	105	19	18	1	240	160	80	40	16	24
	40—45	359	231	128	18	18	...	300	206	94	41	7	34
	45—50	144	86	58	14	13	1	96	65	31	34	8	26
	50—55	258	147	111	10	8	2	158	119	39	90	20	70
	55—60	73	42	31	5	4	1	42	34	8	26	4	22
	60—65	190	112	78	19	17	2	73	68	5	98	27	71
	65—70	40	21	19	3	3	...	16	14	2	21	4	17
	70 & over	112	66	46	7	6	1	45	32	13	60	28	32

TABLE VII.

AGE, SEX AND CIVIL CONDITION.

Part I.
Total Population.

Religion and Age.	Population.			Unmarried.			Married.			Widowed.		
	Persons.	Males.	Females.	Persons.	Males.	Females.	Persons.	Males.	Females.	Persons.	Males.	Females.
27	28	29	30	31	32	33	34	35	36	37	38	39
Arya Samaj.												
Total	*173*	*90*	*83*	*68*	*41*	*27*	*88*	*46*	*42*	*17*	*3*	*14*
0—1	2	2	...	2	2	...	...	...	...	...	...	...
1—2	1	...	1	1	...	1	...	...	...	...	...	...
2—3	1	...	1	1	...	1	...	...	...	...	...	...
3—4	8	3	5	7	2	5	1	1	...	...	...	...
4—5	9	2	7	9	2	7	...	..	...	...	...	...
Total 0—5	*21*	*7*	*14*	*20*	*6*	*14*	*1*	*1*	...	...	...	...
5—10	20	11	9	18	10	8	2	1	1	...	...	...
10—15	23	14	9	17	13	4	6	1	5	...	...	...
15—20	9	4	5	4	3	1	5	1	4	...	...	...
20—25	25	12	13	6	6	...	19	6	13	...	...	...
25—30	9	4	5	...	...	...	9	4	5	...	...	...
30—35	25	17	8	1	1	...	22	15	7	2	1	1
35—40	8	8	...	1	1	...	7	7	...	...	...	...
40—45	11	4	7	...	...	...	8	4	4	3	...	3
45—50	3	2	1	...	...	...	1	1	...	2	1	1
50—55	6	3	3	1	1	...	3	2	1	2	...	2
55—60	2	2	...	...	...	...	2	2	...	...	...	...
60—65	6	2	4	...	...	...	1	1	...	5	1	4
65—70	2	...	2	...	...	...	1	...	1	1	...	1
70 & over	3	...	3	...	...	...	1	...	1	2	...	2
Brahmo Samaj.												
Total.	*36*	*18*	*18*	*13*	*6*	*7*	*20*	*10*	*10*	*3*	*2*	*1*
0—1	4	3	1	4	3	1	...	...	...	...	...	...
1—2	...	...	...	...	...	...	...	...	...	...	...	...
2—3	1	...	1	1	...	1	..	...	...	...	...	...
3—4	1	...	1	1	...	1	...	...	...	...	...	...
4—5	...	...	...	...	...	...	...	...	...	...	...	...
Total 0—5	*6*	*3*	*3*	*6*	*3*	*3*	...	...	...	...	...	...
5—10	4	1	3	4	1	3	...	...	...	...	...	...
10—15	2	...	2	1	...	1	1	...	1	...	...	...
15—20	3	...	3	...	...	...	3	...	3	...	...	...
20—25	4	2	2	1	1	...	3	1	2	...	...	...
25—30	3	2	1	...	...	...	3	2	1	...	...	...
30—35	3	2	1	...	...	...	3	2	1	...	...	...
35—40	2	2	...	...	...	...	2	2	...	...	...	...
40—45	6	4	2	1	1	...	4	2	2	1	1	...
45—50	1	1	...	...	...	...	...	...	...	1	1	...
50—55	1	...	1	...	...	...	...	...	...	1	...	1
55—60	...	...	...	...	...	...	...	...	...	...	...	...
60—65	1	1	...	...	...	...	1	1	...	...	...	...
65—70	...	...	...	...	...	...	...	...	...	...	...	...
70 & over	...	...	...	...	...	...	...	...	...	...	...	...

Part I.

Total Population.

TABLE VII.

AGE, SEX AND CIVIL CONDITION.

Religion and Age.	Population.			Unmarried.			Married.			Widowed.		
	Persons.	Males.	Females.	Persons.	Males.	Females.	Persons.	Males.	Females.	Persons.	Males.	Females.
40	41	42	43	44	45	46	47	48	49	50	51	52
Buddhist.												
Total	*20*	*8*	*12*	*12*	*5*	*7*	*6*	*3*	*3*	*2*	...	*2*
0—1	3	2	1	3	2	1	...	...	...	...	...	...
1—2	1	1	...	1	1	...	...	...	...	...	...	...
2—3	...	...	...	...	...	...	...	...	...	...	...	...
3—4	...	...	...	...	...	...	...	...	...	...	...	...
4—5	...	...	...	...	...	...	...	...	...	...	...	...
Total 0—5	*4*	*3*	*1*	*4*	*3*	*1*	...	...	...	...	...	...
5—10	3	1	2	3	1	2	...	...	...	...	...	...
10—15	...	...	...	...	...	...	...	...	...	...	...	...
15—20	3	...	3	2	...	2	1	...	1	...	...	...
20—25	3	...	3	2	...	2	1	...	1	...	...	...
25—30	...	...	...	...	...	...	...	...	...	...	...	...
30—35	2	1	1	...	...	...	2	1	1	...	...	...
35—40	3	2	1	1	1	...	1	1	...	1	...	1
40—45	1	...	1	...	...	...	...	...	...	1	...	1
45—50	...	...	...	...	...	...	...	...	...	...	...	...
50—55	1	1	...	...	...	...	1	1	...	...	...	...
55—60	...	...	...	...	...	...	...	...	...	...	...	...
60—65	...	...	...	...	...	...	...	...	...	...	...	...
65—70	...	...	...	...	...	...	...	...	...	...	...	...
70 & over	..	...	...	...	...	...	...	...	...	...	...	...
Musalman.												
Total	*1,380,990*	*706,821*	*674,169*	*593,038*	*352,479*	*240,559*	*446,264*	*328,278*	*317,986*	*141,688*	*26,064*	*115,624*
0—1	**36,059**	17,648	18,411	**36,058**	17,647	18,411	**1**	1	...	...	...	...
1—2	**22.435**	10.778	11,657	**22,434**	10,778	11,656	**1**	...	1	...	...	...
2—3	**42,674**	20,629	22,045	**42.670**	20,625	22,045	**4**	4	...	...	...	...
3—4	**36,507**	17,372	19,135	**36.387**	17,324	19,063	**120**	48	72	...	...	...
4—5	**40,621**	20,226	20,395	**40.159**	20,019	20,140	**462**	207	255	...	...	...
Total 0—5	*178,296*	*86,653*	*91,643*	*177,708*	*86,393*	*91,315*	*588*	*260*	*328*	...	...	...
5—10	**170,504**	85,612	84,892	**164.331**	84,101	80,230	**5,757**	1,393	4,364	**416**	118	298
10—15	**148,779**	80,349	68,430	**120,606**	75,149	45,457	**27,083**	4,873	22,210	**1,090**	327	763
15—20	**107,023**	53,754	53,272	**55 530**	44,156	11,380	**50.331**	9,398	40,933	**1,159**	200	959
20—25	**121 630**	59,415	65,215	**35,399**	31,666	3,733	**85.814**	27,086	58,728	**3,417**	663	2,754
25—30	**125.685**	65,089	60,596	**18,635**	15,868	2,767	**101.325**	47,828	53,497	**5.725**	1,393	4,332
30—35	**121.511**	59,198	62,313	**7,624**	5,926	1,698	**103,753**	51,331	52,422	**10,134**	1,941	8,193
35—40	**73,303**	41,878	31,425	**3,344**	2.472	872	**61,741**	37,738	24,003	**8,218**	1,668	6,550
40—45	**103,692**	53,349	50,343	**3,793**	2,675	1,121	**79,004**	47,634	31,370	**20,892**	3,040	17,852
45—50	**43,253**	25,887	17,366	**1.149**	842	307	**32,196**	23,223	8,973	**9,908**	1,822	8,086
50—55	**74.118**	38,725	35,393	**2,111**	1,417	694	**45.526**	33,353	12,173	**26.481**	3,955	22,526
55—60	**18,730**	11,090	7,640	**522**	375	147	**11,838**	9,421	2,417	**6,370**	1,294	5,076
60—65	**52.606**	26,187	26,419	**1,152**	735	417	**25.207**	20,789	4,418	**25,247**	4,663	21,584
65—70	**9.056**	5,015	4,041	**215**	131	84	**4,399**	3,854	545	**4,442**	1,039	3,412
70 & over	**29,801**	14,629	15,181	**910**	573	337	**11,702**	10,097	1,605	**17,189**	3,950	13,239

TABLE VII.

AGE, SEX AND CIVIL CONDITION.

Part I.
Total Population.

Religion and Age.	Population.			Unmarried.			Married.			Widowed.		
	Persons.	Males.	Females.	Persons.	Males.	Females.	Persons.	Males.	Females.	Persons.	Males.	Females.
53	54	55	56	57	58	59	60	61	62	63	64	65
Christian.												
Total	*54,296*	*29,495*	*24,801*	*28,207*	*17,217*	*10,990*	*22,662*	*11,565*	*11,097*	*3,427*	*713*	*2,714*
0—1	**1,660**	823	837	**1,654**	819	835	**5**	3	2	**1**	1	...
1—2	**821**	378	443	**819**	376	443	**2**	2	...	...	...	...
2—3	**1,699**	801	898	**1,693**	799	894	**5**	1	4	**1**	1	...
3—4	**1,814**	870	944	**1,801**	867	934	**13**	3	10	...	...	...
4—5	**1,591**	775	816	**1,570**	767	803	**21**	8	13	...	...	...
Total 0—5	**7,585**	3,647	3,938	**7,537**	3,628	3,909	**46**	17	29	**2**	2	...
5—10	**7,059**	3,545	3,505	**6,869**	3,496	3,373	**172**	47	125	**9**	2	7
10—15	**5,947**	3,133	2,814	**5,208**	3,021	2,187	**728**	109	619	**11**	3	8
15—20	**4,456**	2,146	2,310	**2,608**	1,843	765	**1,812**	299	1,513	**36**	4	32
20—25	**6,729**	4,179	2,550	**3,298**	3,056	242	**3,342**	1,111	2,231	**89**	12	77
25—30	**5,547**	3,284	2,263	**1,643**	1,469	174	**3,733**	1,769	1,964	**171**	46	125
30—35	**4,573**	2,408	2,165	**458**	335	123	**3,854**	2,027	1,827	**261**	46	215
35—40	**2,753**	1,633	1,123	**178**	130	48	**2,363**	1,454	909	**215**	49	166
40—45	**3,237**	1,836	1,431	**167**	105	62	**2,618**	1,662	956	**482**	69	413
45—50	**1,406**	861	545	**68**	36	32	**1,057**	769	288	**281**	56	225
50—55	**2,138**	1,215	923	**60**	34	26	**1,469**	1,072	397	**609**	109	500
55—60	**549**	337	212	**39**	20	19	**341**	277	64	**169**	40	129
60—65	**1,255**	698	557	**31**	16	15	**691**	566	125	**533**	116	417
65—70	**241**	132	109	**12**	7	5	**106**	91	15	**123**	34	89
70 & over	**797**	411	356	**31**	21	10	**330**	295	35	**436**	125	311
Parsi.												
Total	*1,529*	*822*	*707*	*701*	*361*	*340*	*712*	*409*	*303*	*116*	*52*	*64*
0—1	**24**	10	14	**24**	10	14	...	...	...	...	...	...
1—2	**21**	13	8	**21**	13	8	...	...	...	...	...	...
2—3	**27**	7	20	**27**	7	20	...	...	...	...	...	...
3—4	**29**	11	18	**29**	11	18	...	...	...	...	...	...
4—5	**29**	16	13	**29**	16	13	...	...	...	...	...	...
Total 0—5	*130*	*57*	*73*	*130*	*57*	*73*	...	...	...	...	...	...
5—10	**128**	43	85	**128**	43	85	...	...	...	...	...	...
10—15	**155**	67	88	**146**	61	85	**7**	5	2	**2**	1	1
15—20	**116**	55	61	**100**	54	46	**16**	1	15	...	...	...
20—25	**173**	109	64	**89**	57	32	**83**	52	31	**1**	...	1
25—30	**141**	65	76	**50**	34	16	**90**	31	59	**1**	...	1
30—35	**153**	97	56	**37**	36	1	**115**	61	54	**1**	...	1
35—40	**108**	60	48	**5**	5	...	**97**	51	46	**6**	4	2
40—45	**105**	71	34	**9**	8	1	**81**	54	27	**15**	9	6
45—50	**85**	58	27	**2**	2	...	**75**	49	26	**8**	7	1
50—55	**76**	50	26	**1**	1	...	**61**	40	21	**14**	9	5
55—60	**47**	31	16	...	...	...	**38**	28	10	**9**	3	6
60—65	**42**	21	21	**2**	2	...	**23**	16	7	**17**	3	14
65—70	**18**	13	5	...	...	...	**11**	8	3	**7**	5	2
70 & over	**52**	25	27	**2**	1	1	**15**	13	2	**35**	11	24

Part I.

Total Population.

TABLE VII.

AGE, SEX AND CIVIL CONDITION.

Religion and Age.	Population. Persons.	Population. Males.	Population. Females.	Unmarried. Persons.	Unmarried. Males.	Unmarried. Females.	Married. Persons.	Married. Males.	Married. Females.	Widowed. Persons.	Widowed. Males.	Widowed. Females.
66	67	68	69	70	71	72	73	74	75	76	77	78
Jew.												
Total	*12*	*8*	*4*	*7*	*5*	*2*	*5*	*3*	*2*	...	...	...
0—1	...	...	...	...	...	...	...	...	...	...	...	...
1—2	...	...	...	...	...	...	...	...	...	...	...	...
2—3	...	...	...	...	...	...	...	...	...	...	...	...
3—4	...	...	...	...	...	...	...	...	...	...	...	...
4—5	1	...	1	1	...	1	...	...	...	...	...	...
Total 0—5	*1*	...	*1*	*1*	...	*1*	...	...	...	...	...	...
5—10	1	...	1	1	...	1	...	...	...	...	...	...
10—15	2	2	...	2	2	...	...	...	...	...	...	...
15—20	1	1	...	1	1	...	...	...	...	...	...	...
20—25	2	2	...	2	2	...	...	...	...	...	...	...
25—30	3	2	1	...	...	...	3	2	1	...	...	...
30—35	...	...	...	...	...	...	...	...	...	...	...	...
35—40	1	...	1	...	...	...	1	...	1	...	...	...
40—45	...	...	...	...	...	...	...	...	...	...	...	...
45—50	1	1	...	...	...	...	1	1	...	...	...	...
50—55	...	...	...	...	...	...	...	...	...	...	...	...
55—60	...	...	...	...	...	...	...	...	...	...	...	...
60—65	...	...	...	...	...	...	...	...	...	...	...	...
65—70	...	...	...	...	...	...	...	...	...	...	...	...
70 & over	...	...	...	...	...	...	...	...	...	...	...	...
Animist.												
Total ...	*285,722*	*149,023*	*136,699*	*142,831*	*84,100*	*58,731*	*124,691*	*60,861*	*63,830*	*18,200*	*4,062*	*14,138*
0—1	**8,488**	4,149	4,339	**8,419**	4,128	4,291	**64**	21	43	**5**	...	5
1—2	**4.850**	2,309	2,541	**4.805**	2,298	2,507	**41**	11	30	**4**	...	4
2—3	**12,614**	6,094	6,520	**12,489**	6,043	6,446	**119**	47	72	**6**	4	2
3—4	**12,068**	5,697	6,371	**11.847**	5,628	6,219	**216**	67	149	**5**	2	3
4—5	**12.200**	5,902	6,293	**11.972**	5,844	6,128	**197**	47	150	**31**	11	20
Total 0—5	*60,220*	*24,151*	*26,069*	*49,532*	*23,941*	*25,591*	*637*	*193*	*444*	*51*	*17*	*34*
5—10	**44.880**	23,251	21,629	**41,713**	22,730	18,983	**3.076**	498	2,578	**91**	23	68
10—15	**31,273**	17,636	13,637	**26,666**	16,440	10,226	**4,382**	1,092	3,290	**225**	104	121
15—20	**18,846**	9,954	8,892	**10.031**	8,106	1,925	**8,616**	1,793	6,823	**199**	55	144
20—25	**23,273**	10,593	12,680	**6,643**	5,952	691	**16,140**	4,468	11,672	**490**	173	317
25—30	**23,902**	11,957	11,945	**3,631**	3,284	347	**19,619**	8,416	11,203	**652**	257	395
30—35	**25,990**	13.167	12,823	**2,443**	2,067	376	**22.172**	10,774	11,398	**1,375**	326	1,049
35—40	**12,677**	7,720	4,957	**590**	499	91	**11.256**	6,910	4,346	**831**	311	520
40—45	**18.836**	10,333	8,503	**657**	468	189	**15,598**	9,403	6,195	**2,581**	463	2,119
45—50	**6,536**	4,268	2,263	**155**	127	28	**5,374**	3,869	1,485	**1,007**	252	755
50—55	**12,488**	6,922	5,566	**270**	184	86	**8,864**	6,185	2,679	**3,354**	553	2,801
55—60	**2,377**	1,585	792	**60**	46	14	**1,668**	1,345	323	**649**	194	455
60—65	**8,276**	4,350	3,926	**215**	136	79	**4,441**	3,561	880	**3,620**	653	2,967
65—70	**1.061**	677	384	**49**	37	12	**611**	506	105	**401**	134	267
70 & over	**5,067**	2,459	2,628	**176**	83	93	**2,237**	1,828	409	**2,674**	548	2,126

TABLE VII.

AGE, SEX AND CIVIL CONDITION.

Part II.
Districts.

District.	Religion	Religion and Age.	Population. Persons.	Population. Males.	Population. Females.	Unmarried. Persons.	Unmarried. Males.	Unmarried. Females.	Married. Persons.	Married. Males.	Married. Females.	Widowed. Persons.	Widowed. Males.	Widowed. Females.
		1	2	3	4	5	6	7	8	9	10	11	12	13
Atraf-i-balda.	All Religions	Total ...	*520,159*	*265,184*	*254,975*	*192,981*	*120,219*	*72,762*	*267,777*	*133,939*	*133,838*	*59,401*	*11,026*	*48,375*
		0—5	71,110	34,618	36,492	70,655	34,473	36,182	442	139	303	13	6	7
		5—10	63.529	31,767	31,762	56,465	30,966	25,499	6,892	789	6,103	172	12	160
		10—15	52,998	29,042	23,956	32,341	26,103	6,238	20,174	2,868	17,306	483	71	412
		15—20	40.570	20,004	20,566	14,860	13,332	1,528	24,977	6,536	18,441	733	136	597
		20—40	162,716	81,547	81,169	15,122	13,163	1,959	135,777	66,338	69,439	11,817	2,046	9,771
		40—60	92.604	49,663	42,941	2,663	1,634	1,029	63,343	43,436	19,907	26,598	4,593	22,005
		60 & over	36,632	18,543	18,089	875	548	327	16,172	13,833	2,339	19,585	4,162	15,423
	Hindu.	Total ...	*455,203*	*231,505*	*223,698*	*164,177*	*103,045*	*61,132*	*237,958*	*118,590*	*119,368*	*53,068*	*9,870*	*43,198*
		0—5	62,762	30,580	32,182	62,317	30,439	31,878	432	135	297	13	6	7
		5—10	55,545	27,795	27,750	48,706	27,057	21,649	6,673	726	5,947	166	12	154
		10—15	46.053	25,131	20,922	26,502	22,367	4,135	19,109	2,696	16,413	442	68	374
		15—20	35.346	17,475	17,871	11,737	11,092	645	22,928	6,250	16,678	681	133	548
		20—40	142,770	71,395	71,375	11,939	10,301	1,638	120,106	59,286	60,820	10,725	1,808	8,917
		40—60	81,101	43,238	37,863	2,266	1,343	923	54,947	37,719	17,228	23,888	4,176	19,712
		60 & over	31,626	15,891	15,735	710	446	264	13,763	11,778	1,985	17,153	3,667	13,486
	Musalman.	Total ...	*59,342*	*30,602*	*28,740*	*25,858*	*15,357*	*10,501*	*27,534*	*14,199*	*13,335*	*5,950*	*1,046*	*4,904*
		0—5	7,390	3,564	3,826	7,383	3,560	3,823	7	4	3	...	...	...
		5—10	7,162	3,522	3,640	6,955	3,462	3,493	201	60	141	6	...	6
		10—15	6,337	3,526	2,811	5,306	3,363	1,943	992	160	832	39	3	36
		15—20	4.810	2,311	2,499	2,874	2,055	819	1,886	253	1,633	50	3	47
		20—40	18,292	9,262	9,030	2,827	2,551	276	14,425	6,490	7,935	1,040	221	819
		40—60	10.693	5,946	4,747	363	268	95	7,781	5,308	2,473	2,549	370	2,179
		60 & over	4,658	2,471	2,187	150	98	52	2,242	1,924	318	2,266	447	1,817
	Christian.	Total ...	*1,291*	*686*	*605*	*712*	*420*	*292*	*488*	*248*	*240*	*91*	*18*	*73*
		0—5	170	90	80	170	90	80	...	...	...	...	...	...
		5—10	195	98	97	182	96	86	13	2	11	...	...	...
		10—15	172	102	70	155	98	57	17	4	13	...	...	...
		15—20	133	74	59	101	64	37	30	10	20	2	...	2
		20—40	394	204	190	88	65	23	285	135	150	21	4	17
		40—60	180	94	86	13	6	7	122	80	42	45	8	37
		60 & over	47	24	23	3	1	2	21	17	4	23	6	17
	Animist.	Total ...	*4,067*	*2,255*	*1,812*	*2,126*	*1,341*	*785*	*1,686*	*839*	*847*	*255*	*75*	*180*
		0—5	763	375	388	760	375	385	3	...	3	...	...	...
		5—10	604	342	262	600	341	259	4	1	3	...	...	...
		10—15	401	269	132	350	261	89	50	8	42	1	...	1
		15—20	258	135	123	131	112	19	127	23	104	...	...	...
		20—40	1,179	638	541	254	233	21	899	394	505	26	11	15
		40—60	585	355	230	19	16	3	465	307	158	101	32	69
		60 & over	277	141	136	12	3	9	138	106	32	127	32	95

Part II.

Districts.

TABLE VII.

AGE, SEX AND CIVIL CONDITION.

District.	Religion and Age.		Population.			Unmarried.			Married.			Widowed.		
			Persons.	Males.	Females.	Persons.	Males.	Females.	Persons.	Males.	Females.	Persons.	Males.	Females.
	1		2	3	4	5	6	7	8	9	10	11	12	13
Warangal.	All Religions.	Total ...	*905,414*	*467,413*	*438,001*	*395,283*	*236,436*	*158,847*	*426,693*	*216,685*	*210,008*	*83,438*	*14,292*	*69,146*
		0—5	**132,731**	64,286	68,445	**131,904**	64,052	67,852	**777**	217	560	**50**	17	33
		5—10	**127,169**	64,295	62,874	**121,833**	63,627	58,206	**5,105**	640	4,465	**231**	25	203
		10—15	**104,079**	57,379	46,700	**78,828**	54,496	24,332	**24,603**	2,835	21,768	**648**	48	600
		15—20	**69,955**	36,089	33,866	**31,164**	27,128	4,036	**37,537**	8,838	28,699	**1,254**	123	1,131
		20—40	**276,922**	140,468	136,454	**27,680**	24,627	3,053	**231,052**	113,011	118,041	**18,190**	2,830	15,360
		40—60	**142,628**	78,606	64,022	**2,869**	1,926	943	**103,625**	70,844	32,781	**36,134**	5,836	30,298
		60 & over	**51,930**	26,290	25,640	**1,005**	580	425	**23,994**	20,300	3,694	**26,931**	5,410	21,521
	Hindu.	Total ...	*723,884*	*372,793*	*351,091*	*303,352*	*183,165*	*120,187*	*349,556*	*177,582*	*171,984*	*70,966*	*12,046*	*58,920*
		0—5	**104,157**	50,555	53,602	**103,484**	50,389	53,095	**637**	160	477	**36**	6	30
		5—10	**99,421**	50,299	49,122	**94,481**	49,776	44,705	**4,739**	498	4,241	**201**	25	176
		10—15	**83,274**	45,877	37,397	**59,803**	43,267	16,536	**22,870**	2,565	20,305	**601**	45	556
		15—20	**56,904**	29,197	27,707	**23,536**	20,996	2,540	**32,227**	8,090	24,137	**1,141**	111	1,030
		20—40	**221,482**	112,103	109,379	**19,029**	16,818	2,211	**186,671**	92,971	93,700	**15,782**	2,314	13,468
		40—60	**116,017**	63,334	52,683	**2,245**	1,477	768	**83,119**	56,889	26,230	**30,653**	4,968	25,685
		60 & over	**42,629**	21,428	21,201	**774**	442	332	**19,303**	16,409	2,894	**22,552**	4,577	17,975
	Musalman.	Total ...	*50,079*	*26,709*	*23,370*	*23,565*	*14,175*	*9,390*	*22,285*	*11,876*	*10,409*	*4,229*	*658*	*3,571*
		0—5	**6,630**	3,202	3,428	**6,620**	3,197	3,423	**10**	5	5	...	...	...
		5—10	**6,764**	3,349	3,415	**6,664**	3,323	3,341	**84**	23	61	**16**	3	13
		10—15	**5,732**	3,143	2,589	**5,181**	3,078	2,103	**539**	65	474	**12**	...	12
		15—20	**3,824**	2,136	1,688	**2,242**	1,963	279	**1,533**	171	1,362	**49**	2	47
		20—40	**16,082**	8,657	7,425	**2,617**	2,426	191	**12,613**	6,088	6,525	**852**	143	709
		40—60	**8,148**	4,730	3,418	**187**	145	42	**6,098**	4,324	1,774	**1,863**	261	1,602
		60 & over	**2,899**	1,492	1,407	**54**	43	11	**1,408**	1,200	208	**1,437**	249	1,118
	Christian.	Total ...	*11,979*	*6,202*	*5,777*	*5,791*	*3,361*	*2,430*	*5,479*	*2,721*	*2,758*	*709*	*120*	*589*
		0—5	**1,828**	846	982	**1,822**	844	978	**6**	2	4	...	...	...
		5—10	**1,714**	856	858	**1,676**	848	828	**37**	8	29	**1**	...	1
		10—15	**1,373**	765	608	**1,217**	742	475	**150**	23	127	**6**	...	6
		15—20	**988**	486	502	**503**	411	92	**477**	75	402	**8**	...	8
		20—40	**3,762**	1,908	1,854	**532**	488	44	**3,105**	1,396	1,709	**125**	24	101
		40—60	**1,731**	1,000	731	**28**	19	9	**1,378**	933	445	**325**	48	277
		60 & over	**583**	341	242	**13**	9	4	**326**	284	42	**244**	48	196
	Animist.	Total ...	*119,021*	*61,473*	*57,548*	*62,384*	*35,625*	*26,759*	*49,158*	*24,398*	*24,760*	*7,479*	*1,450*	*6,029*
		0—5	**20,068**	9,666	10,402	**19,931**	9,605	10,326	**123**	50	73	**14**	11	3
		5—10	**19,220**	9,763	9,457	**18,963**	9,652	9,311	**244**	111	133	**13**	...	13
		10—15	**13,664**	7,57[illegible]	6,089	**12,597**	7,391	5,206	**1,038**	181	857	**29**	3	26
		15—20	**8,201**	4,251	3,950	**4,859**	3,741	1,118	**3,286**	500	2,786	**56**	10	46
		20—40	**35,450**	17,723	17,727	**5,473**	4,870	603	**28,558**	12,509	16,049	**1,419**	344	1,075
		40—60	**16,638**	9,485	7,153	**397**	280	117	**12,965**	8,653	4,312	**3,276**	552	2,724
		60 & over	**5,780**	3,010	2,770	**164**	86	78	**2,944**	2,394	550	**2,672**	530	2,142

TABLE VII.

AGE, SEX AND CIVIL CONDITION.

Part II

Districts.

District.	Religion.	Age.	Population. Persons.	Population. Males.	Population. Females.	Unmarried. Persons.	Unmarried. Males.	Unmarried. Females.	Married. Persons.	Married. Males.	Married. Females.	Widowed. Persons.	Widowed. Males.	Widowed. Females.
	1		2	3	4	5	6	7	8	9	10	11	12	13
Karimnagar.	All Religions.	Total ...	*1,131,637*	*586,260*	*545,377*	*452,663*	*277,532*	*175,131*	*579,656*	*292,481*	*287,175*	*99,318*	*16,247*	*83,071*
		0—5	176,652	86,489	90,163	174,661	85,927	88,734	1,913	545	1,368	78	17	61
		5—10	156,351	81,353	74,998	142,618	79,599	63,019	13,305	1,701	11,604	428	53	375
		10—15	127,865	72,987	54,878	80,833	65,689	15,144	46,236	7,233	39,003	796	65	731
		15—20	88,374	45,392	42,982	30,092	27,211	2,881	56,848	18,042	38,806	1,434	139	1,295
		20—40	347,290	175,581	171,709	20,576	17,025	3,551	305,229	155,601	149,628	21,485	2,955	18,530
		40—60	175,575	94,469	81,106	2,984	1,627	1,357	127,925	85,831	42,094	44,666	7,011	37,655
		60 & over	59,530	29,989	29,541	899	454	445	28,200	23,528	4,672	30,431	6,007	24,424
	Hindu.	Total ...	*1,074,654*	*556,441*	*518,213*	*425,299*	*261,269*	*164,030*	*554,363*	*279,527*	*274,836*	*94,992*	*15,645*	*79,347*
		0—5	168,462	82,464	85,998	166,496	81,917	84,579	1,888	530	1,358	78	17	61
		5—10	148,056	76,191	70,865	134,494	75,482	59,012	13,140	1,659	11,481	422	50	372
		10—15	121,320	69,293	52,027	75,005	62,094	12,911	45,536	7,135	38,401	779	64	715
		15—20	84.102	43,107	40,995	27,644	25,155	2,489	55,053	17,814	37,239	1,405	138	1,267
		20—40	329,778	166,462	163,316	17,971	14,671	3,300	291,091	148,935	142,156	20,716	2,856	17,860
		40—60	166,626	89,605	77,021	2,838	1,525	1,313	121,106	81,318	39,788	42,682	6,762	35,920
		60 & over.	56.310	28,319	27,991	851	425	426	26,549	22,136	4,413	28,910	5,758	23,152
	Musalman.	Total ...	*46,523*	*24,345*	*22,178*	*21,856*	*13,097*	*8,759*	*20,983*	*10,761*	*10,222*	*3,684*	*487*	*3,197*
		0—5	6,446	3,173	3,273	6,428	3,159	3,269	18	14	4	...	...	...
		5—10	6,650	3,321	3,329	6,519	3,288	3,231	126	31	95	5	2	3
		10—15	5.337	3,005	2,332	4,721	2,923	1,798	602	81	521	14	1	13
		15—20	3,577	1,941	1,636	2,019	1,745	274	1,536	195	1,341	22	1	21
		20—40	14,397	7,531	6,866	2,020	1,884	136	11,712	5,563	6,149	665	84	581
		40—60	7.401	3,968	3,433	111	75	36	5,598	3,695	1,903	1,692	193	1,494
		60 & over.	2.715	1,406	1,309	38	23	15	1,391	1,182	209	1,286	201	1,085
	Christian.	Total ...	*586*	*286*	*300*	*312*	*158*	*154*	*241*	*124*	*117*	*33*	*4*	*29*
		0—5	90	31	59	89	31	58	1	...	1	...	...	...
		5—10	89	45	44	86	44	42	3	1	2	...	...	...
		10—15	85	44	41	75	44	31	10	...	10	...	...	...
		15—20	63	22	41	39	22	17	22	...	22	2	...	2
		20—40	171	94	77	22	17	5	144	76	68	5	1	4
		40—60	76	44	32	1	...	1	55	42	13	20	2	18
		60 & over	12	6	6	...	...	...	6	5	1	6	1	5
	Animist.	Total ...	*9,598*	*5,041*	*4,557*	*5,104*	*2,949*	*2,155*	*3,906*	*1,986*	*1,920*	*588*	*106*	*482*
		0—5	1,620	803	817	1,614	802	812	6	1	5	...	...	...
		5—10	1,524	781	743	1,490	771	719	33	9	24	1	1	...
		10—15	1,101	632	469	1,019	615	404	79	17	62	3	...	3
		15—20	615	313	302	386	285	101	224	28	196	5	...	5
		20—40	2,853	1,456	1,397	551	443	108	2,207	999	1,208	95	14	81
		40—60	1,412	812	600	34	27	7	1,116	737	379	262	48	214
		60 & over	473	244	229	10	6	4	241	195	46	222	43	179

Part II.

Districts.

TABLE VII.

AGE, SEX AND CIVIL CONDITION.

District.	Religion and Age.	Population. Persons.	Population. Males.	Population. Females.	Unmarried. Persons.	Unmarried. Males.	Unmarried. Females.	Married. Persons.	Married. Males.	Married. Females	Widowed. Persons.	Widowed. Males.	Widowed. Females.
	1	2	3	4	5	6	7	8	9	10	11	12	13
Adilabad.	**All Religions.** Total ..	*620,426*	*314,428*	*305,998*	*233,569*	*138,728*	*94,841*	*329.535*	*165,182*	*164,353*	*57,322*	*10,518*	*46,804*
	0—5	102,516	49,511	53,005	98.693	48,473	50,220	3.624	1,003	2,621	199	35	164
	5—10	92,808	46,889	45,919	73.570	42,656	30,914	18.595	4,107	14,489	642	126	516
	10—15	63,570	35,477	28,093	34,185	25,365	8,820	28.450	9,823	18,627	935	289	646
	15—20	38,824	19,292	19,532	10,477	9,085	1,392	27.575	9,982	17,593	772	225	547
	20—40	198,469	99,554	98,915	13.846	11,414	2,432	172.291	85,207	87,084	12,322	2,933	9,389
	40—60	94,728	50,617	44,111	2.236	1,429	807	66.468	45,146	21,322	26,024	4,042	21,982
	60 & over	29,511	13,088	16,123	562	306	256	12,531	9,914	2,617	16,418	2,868	13,550
	Hindu. Total ...	*524,500*	*264,837*	*259,663*	*192,193*	*113,453*	*78,740*	*282,648*	*142,521*	*140,127*	*49,659*	*8,863*	*40,796*
	0—5	86,897	42,052	44,845	83,419	41,113	42,306	3.299	908	2,391	179	31	148
	5—10	78,161	39,363	38,798	61,586	35,459	26,127	15.992	3,785	12,207	583	119	464
	10—15	53,918	30,049	23,869	27,101	20,732	6,369	26.051	9,111	16,940	766	206	560
	15—20	32,810	16,162	16,648	8,000	6,962	1,038	24,149	9,008	15,141	661	192	469
	20—40	167,447	83,627	83,820	9,840	7,801	2,039	146,915	73,439	73,476	10,692	2,387	8,305
	40—60	80,379	42,603	37,776	1,828	1,156	672	55.750	38,001	17,749	22,801	3,446	19,355
	60 & over	24,888	10,981	13,907	419	230	189	10.492	8,269	2,223	13,977	2,482	11,495
	Musalman. Total ..	*29,668*	*15,843*	*13,825*	*13,275*	*8,150*	*5,125*	*13.400*	*7,259*	*6,141*	*2,993*	*434*	*2,559*
	0—5	4,212	2,081	2,131	4.195	2,075	2,120	17	6	11	...	...	...
	5—10	4,274	2,230	2,044	4,090	2,174	1,916	169	56	113	15	...	15
	10—15	2,843	1,677	1,166	2,318	1,570	748	506	105	401	19	2	17
	15—20	1,909	978	931	958	794	164	928	182	746	23	2	21
	20—40	10,219	5,570	4,649	1,520	1,400	120	8.025	4,053	3,972	674	117	557
	40—60	4,631	2,626	2,005	143	108	35	3.153	2,350	803	1,335	168	1,167
	60 & over	1,580	681	899	51	29	22	602	507	95	927	145	782
	Christian. Total ...	*28*	*19*	*9*	*12*	*9*	*3*	*12*	*8*	*4*	*4*	*2*	*2*
	0—5	3	1	2	3	1	2	...	...	...	...	...	...
	5—10	1	...	1	1	...	1	...	...	...	...	...	...
	10—15	...	...	...	...	...	...	...	...	...	...	...	...
	15—20	3	3	...	3	3	...	...	..	...	...	...	...
	20—40	16	11	5	5	5	...	8	5	3	3	1	2
	40—60	5	4	1	...	...	...	4	3	1	1	1	...
	60 & over.	...	...	...	...	...	...	..	...	...	...	...	...
	Animist. Total ...	*65,964*	*33,601*	*32,363*	*27,994*	*17,060*	*10,934*	*33,334*	*15,326*	*18,008*	*4,636*	*1,215*	*3,421*
	0—5	11.361	5,359	6,002	11,034	5,267	5,767	307	88	219	20	4	16
	5—10	10.338	5,281	5,057	7,868	5,008	2,860	2,426	266	2,160	44	7	37
	10—15	6,788	3,741	3,047	4,754	3,055	1,699	1,885	605	1,280	149	81	68
	15—20	4,080	2,134	1,946	1,509	1,319	190	2,483	784	1,699	88	31	57
	20—40	20,711	10,311	10,400	2,474	2,201	273	17,277	7,683	9,594	960	427	533
	40—60	9,662	5,358	4,304	263	163	100	7,527	4,770	2,757	1,872	425	1,447
	60 & over.	3.024	1,417	1,607	92	47	45	1,429	1,130	299	1,503	240	1,263

TABLE VII.

Part II.

AGE, SEX AND CIVIL CONDITION.

Districts.

District.	Religion and Age.	Population.			Unmarried.			Married.			Widowed.		
		Persons.	Males.	Females.	Persons.	Males.	Females.	Persons.	Males.	Females.	Persons.	Males.	Females.
	1	2	3	4	5	6	7	8	9	10	11	12	13
Medak.	**All Religions.** Total ...	*687,137*	*348,410*	*338,727*	*252,183*	*157,780*	*94,403*	*365,926*	*176,317*	*179,609*	*79,028*	*14,313*	*64,715*
	0–5	95,262	46,155	49,107	94,229	45,929	48,307	982	219	763	51	14	37
	5–10	84,975	43,108	41,367	76,687	42,258	34,429	8,037	811	7,226	251	39	212
	10–15	69,827	39,597	30,230	43,068	36,269	6,799	26,269	3,252	23,017	490	76	414
	15–20	53,316	26,136	27,180	17,803	16,592	1,211	34,660	9,461	25,199	853	83	770
	20–40	215,112	106,113	108,999	16,578	14,215	2,363	182,403	89,345	93,058	16,131	2,553	13,578
	40–60	119,617	62,533	57,084	2,838	1,904	934	82,043	54,740	27,303	34,736	5,889	28,847
	60 & over.	49,028	24,768	24,260	980	620	360	21,532	18,489	3,043	26,516	5,659	20,857
	Hindu. Total ...	*615,552*	*312,690*	*302,862*	*220,788*	*139,179*	*81,609*	*323,099*	*160,414*	*162,685*	*71,665*	*13,097*	*58,568*
	0–5	85,764	41,630	44,134	84,844	41,439	43,405	876	179	697	44	12	32
	5–10	75,488	38,361	37,127	67,495	37,603	29,892	7,791	745	7,049	199	13	186
	10–15	63,067	35,411	26,656	36,549	32,214	4,335	25,089	3,158	21,931	429	39	390
	15–20	48,204	23,747	24,457	15,286	14,515	771	32,109	9,155	22,954	809	77	732
	20–40	193,207	95,598	97,609	13,373	11,305	2,068	165,004	81,922	83,082	14,830	2,371	12,459
	40–60	107,433	56,167	51,266	2,433	1,599	834	73,452	49,110	24,342	31,548	5,458	26,090
	60 & over.	43,389	21,776	21,613	808	504	304	18,775	16,145	2,630	23,806	5,127	18,679
	Musalman. Total ..	*65,084*	*32,269*	*32,815*	*28,348*	*16,775*	*11,573*	*29,830*	*14,377*	*15,453*	*6,906*	*1,117*	*5,789*
	0–5	8,455	4,018	4,437	8,361	3,981	4,383	91	37	54	...	...	...
	5–10	8,593	4,268	4,331	8,338	4,186	4,152	210	56	154	51	26	25
	10–15	7,022	3,771	3,251	5,918	3,655	2,263	1,046	79	967	58	37	21
	15–20	4,684	2,163	2,521	2,304	1,898	406	2,342	250	2,092	38	5	33
	20–40	19,953	9,539	10,417	2,926	2,683	243	15,803	6,695	9,108	1,227	161	1,066
	40–60	11,176	5,780	5,396	355	270	85	7,817	5,105	2,712	3,004	405	2,599
	60 & over.	5,192	2,730	2,462	143	102	41	2,521	2,145	376	2,528	483	2,045
	Christian. Total ...	*2,203*	*1,124*	*1,079*	*992*	*570*	*422*	*1,065*	*534*	*531*	*146*	*20*	*126*
	0–5	313	142	171	303	140	166	7	2	5	...	...	...
	5–10	313	161	152	301	159	142	12	2	10	...	...	...
	10–15	292	173	119	238	168	70	54	5	49	...	...	...
	15–20	161	75	86	69	54	15	91	20	71	1	1	...
	20–40	685	325	360	57	35	22	605	286	319	23	4	19
	40–60	325	187	138	15	9	6	243	171	72	67	7	60
	60 & over	114	61	53	6	5	1	53	48	5	55	8	47
	Animist. Total ...	*4,016*	*2,179*	*1,837*	*1,955*	*1,190*	*765*	*1,804*	*922*	*882*	*257*	*67*	*190*
	0–5	708	361	347	698	358	340	8	1	7	2	2	...
	5–10	550	301	249	529	293	236	20	8	12	1	...	1
	10–15	413	217	196	342	213	129	68	4	64	3	...	3
	15–20	251	143	108	139	120	19	109	23	86	3	...	3
	20–40	1,166	605	561	193	173	20	927	411	516	41	16	25
	40–60	629	369	260	30	22	8	498	331	167	101	16	85
	60 & over	299	183	116	19	6	13	174	144	30	106	33	73

Part II.

Districts.

TABLE VII.

AGE, SEX AND CIVIL CONDITION.

District.	Religion and Age.	Population. Persons.	Population. Males.	Population. Females.	Unmarried. Persons.	Unmarried. Males.	Unmarried. Females.	Married. Persons.	Married. Males.	Married. Females.	Widowed. Persons.	Widowed. Males.	Widowed. Females.
	1	2	3	4	5	6	7	8	9	10	11	12	13
Nizamabad.	**All Religions.** Total ...	***568,009***	***283,621***	***284,388***	***184,229***	***114,468***	***69,761***	***314,498***	***156,521***	***157,977***	***69,282***	***12,632***	***56,650***
	0—5	**78,691**	38,349	40,342	**75,924**	37,721	38,203	**2,695**	622	2,073	**72**	6	66
	5—10	**70,787**	36,078	34,709	**55,337**	33,705	21,632	**14,989**	2,289	12,700	**461**	84	377
	10—15	**56,150**	30,947	25,203	**27,188**	22,916	4,272	**28,339**	7,861	20,478	**623**	170	453
	15—20	**41,571**	20,159	21,412	**10,122**	9,140	982	**30,635**	10,796	19,839	**814**	223	591
	20—40	**187,071**	91,827	95,244	**12,508**	9,205	3,303	**159,749**	79,937	79,812	**14,814**	2,685	12,129
	40—60	**98,511**	50,795	47,716	**2,404**	1,355	1,049	**64,504**	43,932	20,572	**31,603**	5,508	26,095
	60 & over	**35,228**	15,466	19,762	**746**	426	320	**13,587**	11,084	2,503	**20,895**	3,956	16,939
	Hindu. Total ...	***523,159***	***261,053***	***262,106***	***165,072***	***102,558***	***62,514***	***293,809***	***146,670***	***147,139***	***64,278***	***11,825***	***52,453***
	0—5	**72,965**	35,551	37,414	**70,305**	34,943	35,362	**2,588**	602	1,986	**72**	6	66
	5—10	**64,992**	33,139	31,853	**49,833**	30,829	19,004	**14,714**	2,228	12,486	**445**	82	363
	10—15	**51,585**	28,453	23,132	**23,588**	20,585	3,003	**27,413**	7,704	19,709	**584**	164	420
	15—20	**38,308**	18,622	19,686	**8,713**	7,910	803	**28,830**	10,495	18,335	**765**	217	548
	20—40	**172,434**	84,531	87,903	**9,828**	6,729	3,099	**148,748**	75,272	73,476	**13,858**	2,530	11,328
	40—60	**90,636**	46,642	43,994	**2,145**	1,185	960	**59,177**	40,307	18,870	**29,314**	5,150	24,164
	60 & over	**32,239**	14,115	18,124	**660**	377	283	**12,339**	10,062	2,277	**19,240**	3,676	15,564
	Musalman. Total ...	***41,951***	***21,036***	***20,915***	***18,001***	***11,150***	***6,851***	***19,254***	***9,148***	***10,106***	***4,696***	***738***	***3,958***
	0—5	**5,263**	2,584	2,679	**5,242**	2,571	2,671	**21**	13	8	...	...	...
	5—10	**5,430**	2,746	2,684	**5,203**	2,691	2,512	**213**	54	159	**14**	1	13
	10—15	**4,280**	2,330	1,950	**3,388**	2,182	1,206	**858**	144	714	**34**	4	30
	15—20	**3,074**	1,439	1,635	**1,325**	1,158	167	**1,706**	276	1,430	**43**	5	38
	20—40	**13,752**	6,820	6,932	**2,528**	2,350	178	**10,316**	4,327	5,989	**908**	143	765
	40—60	**7,367**	3,860	3,507	**236**	154	82	**4,979**	3,381	1,598	**2,152**	325	1,827
	60 & over	**2,785**	1,257	1,528	**79**	44	35	**1,161**	953	208	**1,545**	260	1,285
	Christian. Total ...	***720***	***375***	***345***	***284***	***163***	***121***	***357***	***186***	***171***	***79***	***26***	***53***
	0—5	**112**	53	59	**111**	52	59	**1**	1	...	...	...	...
	5—10	**84**	47	37	**78**	45	33	**5**	1	4	**1**	1	...
	10—15	**48**	24	24	**33**	23	10	**14**	...	14	**1**	1	...
	15—20	**58**	21	37	**19**	14	5	**35**	6	29	**4**	1	3
	20—40	**264**	141	123	**37**	26	11	**211**	109	102	**16**	6	10
	40—60	**118**	74	44	**4**	2	2	**80**	59	21	**34**	13	21
	60 & over	**33**	15	21	**2**	1	1	**11**	10	1	**23**	4	19
	Animist. Total ...	***1,820***	***972***	***848***	***743***	***512***	***231***	***891***	***423***	***468***	***186***	***37***	***149***
	0—5	**317**	145	172	**234**	141	93	**83**	4	79	...	...	...
	5—10	**242**	129	113	**189**	123	66	**53**	6	47	...	...	...
	10—15	**198**	115	83	**152**	104	48	**42**	10	32	**4**	1	3
	15—20	**111**	69	42	**57**	51	6	**53**	18	35	**1**	...	1
	20—40	**500**	272	228	**90**	78	12	**386**	189	197	**24**	5	19
	40—60	**313**	179	134	**17**	12	5	**214**	150	64	**82**	17	65
	60 & over	**139**	63	76	**4**	3	1	**60**	46	14	**75**	14	61

TABLE VII.

Part II.

AGE, SEX AND CIVIL CONDITION.

Districts.

District.	Religion and Age.	Population.			Unmarried.			Married.			Widowed.		
		Persons.	Males.	Females.	Persons.	Males.	Females.	Persons.	Males.	Females.	Persons.	Males.	Females.
	1	2	3	4	5	6	7	8	9	10	11	12	13
Mahbubnagar.	All Religions. Total ...	*747,178*	*379,712*	*367,466*	*285,879*	*175,257*	*110,622*	*378,834*	*190,199*	*188,635*	*82,465*	*14,256*	*68,209*
	0—5	105,947	50,597	55,350	104.907	50,360	54,547	998	233	765	42	4	38
	5—10	95,364	48,438	46,926	86,185	47,565	38,620	8,937	846	8,091	242	27	215
	10—15	78,366	43,126	35,240	49,511	38,407	11,104	28.254	4,651	23,603	601	68	533
	15—20	58,479	28,378	30,101	19,841	18,130	1,711	37,656	10,134	27,522	982	114	868
	20—40	234,351	118,372	115,979	20,795	17,895	2,900	196,688	97,716	98,972	16,868	2,761	14,107
	40—60	127,641	67,866	59.775	3,570	2,251	1,319	86.371	59,539	26,832	37.700	6,076	31,624
	60 & over	47,030	22,935	24,095	1,070	649	421	19,930	17,080	2,850	26,030	5,206	20,824
	Hindu. Total ...	*672,750*	*341,109*	*331,641*	*251,713*	*154,628*	*97,085*	*345,464*	*173,310*	*172,154*	*75,573*	*13,171*	*62,402*
	0—5	95,587	45,533	50,054	94,563	45,299	49,264	983	230	753	41	4	37
	5—10	85,210	43,275	41,935	76,323	42,468	33,855	8,670	783	7,887	217	24	193
	10—15	70,226	38,565	31,661	42,637	34,008	8,629	27.011	4,493	22,518	578	64	514
	15—20	53,046	25,591	27,455	16,922	15,724	1,198	35,185	9,757	25,428	939	110	829
	20—40	211,243	106,508	104,735	17,147	14,640	2,507	178,441	89,322	89,119	15,655	2,546	13,109
	40—60	115,553	61,282	54,274	3,170	1,930	1,240	77,626	53,661	23,965	34,760	5,691	29,069
	60 & over	41,882	20,355	21,527	951	559	392	17,548	15,064	2,434	23,383	4,732	18,651
	Musalman. Total ...	*59,521*	*30,353*	*29,168*	*26,202*	*15,646*	*10,556*	*27,303*	*13,819*	*13,484*	*6,016*	*888*	*5,128*
	0—5	7,716	3,768	3,948	7,708	3,765	3,941	10	3	7	...	...	...
	5—10	7,908	3,928	3,980	7,672	3,879	3,793	216	46	170	20	3	17
	10—15	6,502	3,593	2,909	5.418	3,456	1,962	1,063	134	928	22	3	19
	15—20	4,420	2,212	2,208	2,348	1,905	443	2,034	303	1,731	38	4	34
	20—40	18,654	9,433	9,221	2,699	2,374	325	14.865	6,888	7,977	1,090	171	919
	40—60	10,007	5,287	4,720	266	195	71	7,157	4,772	2,385	2,584	320	2,264
	60 & over	4,314	2,132	2,182	93	72	21	1,959	1,673	286	2,262	387	1,875
	Christian. Total ...	*451*	*221*	*230*	*257*	*123*	*134*	*170*	*95*	*75*	*24*	*3*	*21*
	0—5	86	38	48	86	38	48	...	...	...	...	...	...
	5—10	49	18	31	45	14	31	4	4	...	...	...	...
	10—15	42	12	30	41	12	29	1	...	1	...	...	...
	15—20	36	18	18	26	14	12	10	4	6	...	...	...
	20—40	123	51	72	17	5	12	102	46	56	4	...	4
	40—60	101	78	23	42	40	2	45	36	9	14	2	12
	60 & over.	14	6	8	...	...	...	8	5	3	6	1	5
	Animist. Total ...	*14,392*	*7,991*	*6,401*	*7,633*	*4,844*	*2,839*	*5,861*	*2,953*	*2,908*	*848*	*194*	*654*
	0—5	2,548	1,252	1,296	2,542	1,252	1,290	5	...	5	1	...	[illegible]
	5—10	2,191	1,214	977	2,140	1,202	938	46	12	34	5	...	5
	10—15	1,592	953	639	1,412	928	484	179	24	155	1	1	...
	15—20	974	555	419	543	485	58	423	70	356	5	...	5
	20—40	4,307	2,366	1,941	928	873	55	3.281	1,419	1,812	118	44	74
	40—60	1,964	1,211	753	92	86	6	1,531	1,062	469	341	63	278
	60 & over.	816	440	376	26	18	8	413	336	77	377	86	291

Part II.

Districts.

TABLE VII.

AGE, SEX AND CIVIL CONDITION.

District.	Religion and Age.	Population.			Unmarried.			Married.			Widowed.		
		Persons.	Males.	Females.	Persons.	Males.	Females.	Persons.	Males.	Females.	Persons.	Males.	Females.
	1	2	3	4	5	6	7	8	9	10	11	12	13
Nalgonda.	All Religions. Total ...	*1,044,381*	*537,139*	*507,242*	*451,211*	*274,197*	*177,014*	*499,252*	*248,266*	*250,986*	*93,918*	*14,676*	*79,242*
	0—5	162,649	78,293	84,356	161,771	78,024	83,747	843	263	580	35	6	29
	5—10	142,773	72,065	70,708	136,146	71,447	64,699	6,425	590	5,835	202	28	174
	10—15	122,321	67,907	54,414	87.068	64,930	22,138	34,527	2,949	31,578	726	28	698
	15—20	87,956	45,104	42,852	36,653	34,191	2,462	49,823	10,816	39,007	1,480	97	1,383
	20—40	310,265	157,166	153,099	25,809	23,262	2,547	284,014	131,456	132,558	20.442	2,448	17,994
	40—60	157,253	85,332	71,921	2,797	1,775	1,022	114,852	77,777	37,075	39,604	5,780	33,824
	60 & over.	61,164	31,272	29,892	967	568	399	28,768	24,415	4,353	31.429	6,289	25,140
	Hindu. Total ...	*941,694*	*483,032*	*458,662*	*398,000*	*242,339*	*155,661*	*456,940*	*227,137*	*229,803*	*86,754*	*13,556*	*73,198*
	0—5	145,987	70,083	75,904	145,145	69,831	75,314	808	246	562	34	6	28
	5—10	127,462	64,103	63,359	120.988	63,531	57,457	6,277	546	5,731	197	26	171
	10—15	110,166	61,192	48,974	75,958	58,340	17,618	33,497	2.829	30,668	711	23	688
	15—20	80,472	41,014	39,458	32,152	30,377	1,775	46,885	10,544	36,341	1,435	93	1,342
	20—40	280,396	141,742	138,654	20,506	18,316	2,190	240,715	121,172	119,543	19,175	2,254	16,921
	40—60	142,286	76,891	65,395	2,429	1,489	940	103,178	70,039	33,139	36,679	5,363	31,316
	60 & over.	54,925	28,007	26,918	822	455	367	25,580	21,761	3,819	38,523	5,791	22,732
	Musalman. Total ...	*53,872*	*27,721*	*26,151*	*26,346*	*15,805*	*10,541*	*22,775*	*11,251*	*11,524*	*4,751*	*665*	*4,086*
	0—5	7,452	3,686	3,766	7,435	3,677	3,758	17	9	8	...	...	...
	5—10	7,559	3,824	3,735	7,484	3,806	3,678	74	17	57	1	1	...
	10—15	6,395	3,360	3,035	5,813	3,310	2,503	576	49	527	6	1	5
	15—20	4,279	2,269	2,010	2,488	2,135	353	1,765	132	1,633	25	2	24
	20—40	16,105	8,212	7,893	2,854	2,666	188	12,324	5,434	6,890	927	112	815
	40—60	8,516	4,575	3,941	205	158	47	6,311	4,161	2,150	2,000	256	1,744
	60 & over.	3,566	1,795	1,771	67	53	14	1.708	1,449	259	1,791	293	1,498
	Christian. Total ...	*10,566*	*5,565*	*5,001*	*5,062*	*2,932*	*2,130*	*4,896*	*2,527*	*2,369*	*608*	*106*	*502*
	0—5	1,694	833	861	1,688	831	857	6	2	4	...	...	...
	5—10	1,465	755	710	1,442	746	696	23	9	14	...	...	...
	10—15	1,354	736	618	1,177	720	457	176	16	160	1	...	1
	15—20	829	416	413	448	371	77	372	45	327	9	...	9
	20—40	3,250	1,682	1,568	285	251	34	2,830	1,408	1,422	135	23	112
	40—60	1,460	850	610	15	9	6	1,198	806	392	247	35	212
	60 & over.	514	293	221	7	4	3	291	241	50	216	48	168
	Animist. Total ...	*38,137*	*20,760*	*17,377*	*21,756*	*13,094*	*8,662*	*14,585*	*7,320*	*7,265*	*1,796*	*346*	*1,450*
	0—5	7,505	3,683	3,822	7,492	3,677	3,815	12	6	6	1	...	1
	5—10	6,273	3,381	2,892	6.219	3,362	2,857	50	18	32	4	1	3
	10—15	4,398	2,615	1,783	4,112	2,556	1,556	278	55	223	8	4	4
	15—20	2,369	1,401	968	1,562	1,305	257	797	94	703	10	2	8
	20—40	10,466	5,503	4,963	2,153	2,020	133	8,109	3,424	4,685	204	59	145
	40—60	4.974	3,003	1,971	147	118	29	4,154	2,761	1,393	673	124	549
	60 & over.	2,152	1,174	978	71	56	15	1,185	962	223	893	156	740

TABLE VII.

Part II.

AGE, SEX AND CIVIL CONDITION.

Districts.

District.	Religion and Age.		Population.			Unmarried.			Married.			Widowed.		
			Persons.	Males.	Females.	Persons.	Males.	Females.	Persons.	Males.	Females.	Persons.	Males.	Females.
	1		2	3	4	5	6	7	8	9	10	11	12	13
Aurangabad.	All Religions.	Total ...	*869,787*	*437,495*	*432,292*	*315,865*	*189,315*	*126,550*	*463,517*	*230,631*	*232,886*	*90,405*	*17,549*	*72,856*
		0—5	**130,051**	61,791	68,260	**127,180**	60,845	66,335	**2,616**	890	1,726	**255**	56	199
		5—10	**110,351**	56,676	53,675	**93,904**	53,486	40,418	**15,792**	3,014	12,778	**655**	176	479
		10—15	**88,098**	46,802	41,296	**49,653**	38,032	11,621	**36,750**	8,449	28,301	**1,695**	321	1,374
		15—20	**65,316**	31,546	33,770	**19,041**	16,692	2,349	**45,071**	14,506	30,565	**1,204**	348	856
		20—40	**289,175**	143,253	145,922	**21,081**	16,930	4,131	**247,901**	121,608	126,293	**20,213**	4,715	15,498
		40—60	**141,283**	75,776	65,507	**3,858**	2,653	1,205	**96,395**	66,380	30,015	**41,030**	6,743	34,287
		60 & over	**45,513**	21,651	23,862	**1,168**	677	491	**18,992**	15,784	3,208	**25,353**	5,190	20,163
	Hindu.	Total ...	*734,252*	*367,581*	*366,671*	*256,132*	*154,879*	*101,253*	*400,313*	*197,795*	*202,518*	*77,807*	*14,907*	*62,900*
		0—5	**111,090**	52,714	58,376	**108,334**	51,822	56,512	**2,507**	839	1,668	**249**	53	196
		5—10	**93,415**	48,239	45,176	**77,861**	45,334	32,527	**14,977**	2,759	12,218	**577**	146	431
		10—15	**71,993**	38,590	33,403	**38,131**	30,675	7,456	**32,564**	7,696	24,868	**1,298**	219	1,079
		15—20	**54,663**	25,976	28,687	**13,577**	12,537	1,040	**40,039**	13,136	26,903	**1,047**	303	744
		20—40	**244,638**	120,152	124,486	**14,272**	11,922	2,350	**212,940**	104,173	108,767	**17,426**	4,057	13,369
		40—60	**120,016**	63,839	56,177	**3,030**	2,055	975	**81,474**	56,053	25,421	**35,512**	5,731	29,781
		60 & over	**38,437**	18,071	20,366	**927**	534	393	**15,812**	13,129	2,673	**21,698**	4,398	17,300
	Musalman.	Total ...	*111,449*	*57,629*	*53,820*	*49,470*	*28,487*	*20,983*	*51,466*	*27,066*	*24,400*	*10,513*	*2,076*	*8,437*
		0—5	**15,061**	7,200	7,861	**15,021**	7,185	7,836	**40**	15	25	...	...	...
		5—10	**13,737**	6,767	6,970	**13,070**	6,559	6,511	**612**	188	424	**55**	20	35
		10—15	**13,672**	6,903	6,769	**9,830**	6,193	3,637	**3,461**	619	2,842	**381**	91	290
		15—20	**8,756**	4,684	4,072	**4,722**	3,570	1,152	**3,911**	1,083	2,828	**123**	31	92
		20—40	**36,424**	19,106	17,318	**5,960**	4,389	1,571	**23,208**	14,219	13,089	**2,256**	498	1,758
		40—60	**17,808**	9,987	7,821	**670**	486	184	**12,523**	8,695	3,828	**4,615**	805	3,809
		60 & over	**5,991**	2,932	3,009	**197**	105	92	**2,711**	2,247	464	**3,083**	630	2,453
	Christian.	Total ...	*6,369*	*3,222*	*3,147*	*2,749*	*1,526*	*1,223*	*3,239*	*1,628*	*1,611*	*381*	*68*	*313*
		0—5	**1,043**	515	528	**1,022**	507	515	**19**	6	13	**2**	2	...
		5—10	**848**	415	433	**791**	402	389	**52**	13	39	**5**	...	5
		10—15	**685**	355	330	**501**	315	186	**182**	38	144	**2**	2	...
		15—20	**521**	241	28[illegible]	**223**	167	62	**293**	73	220	**2**	1	1
		20—40	**2,181**	1,089	1,092	**161**	112	49	**1,923**	957	969	**94**	20	74
		40—60	**873**	499	374	**36**	18	18	**632**	459	203	**175**	22	153
		60 & over	**215**	108	107	**9**	5	4	**105**	82	23	**101**	21	80
	Animist.	Total ..	*11,794*	*5,956*	*5,838*	*5,135*	*2,972*	*2,163*	*5,667*	*2,717*	*2,950*	*992*	*267*	*725*
		0—5	**2,050**	1,000	1,050	**2,028**	994	1,034	**19**	6	13	**3**	...	3
		5—10	**1,643**	891	752	**1,560**	860	700	**70**	21	49	**13**	10	3
		10—15	**1,113**	606	507	**757**	540	217	**344**	58	286	**12**	8	4
		15—20	**888**	394	494	**343**	268	75	**524**	115	409	**21**	11	10
		20—40	**3,98[illegible]**	1,884	2,101	**373**	254	119	**3,357**	1,554	1,803	**255**	76	179
		40—60	**1,56[illegible]**	86[illegible]	697	**57**	40	17	**1,110**	748	362	**393**	75	318
		60 & over	**555**	318	237	**17**	16	1	**243**	215	28	**235**	87	208

Part II.

Districts.

TABLE VII.

AGE, SEX AND CIVIL CONDITION.

District.	Religion and Age.		Population.			Unmarried.			Married.			Widowed.		
			Persons.	Males.	Females.	Persons.	Males.	Females.	Persons.	Males.	Females.	Persons.	Males.	Females.
	1		2	3	4	5	6	7	8	9	10	11	12	13
Bhir.	All Religions.	Total ...	*622,531*	*314,738*	*307,793*	*215,217*	*131,170*	*84,047*	*341,333*	*169,728*	*171,695*	*65,981*	*13,840*	*21,415*
		0— 5	**94,189**	45,152	49,037	**92,323**	44,774	47,549	**1,810**	361	1,449	**56**	17	39
		5—10	**75,517**	38,169	37,348	**62,598**	36,441	26,157	**12,601**	1,638	10,963	**318**	90	228
		10—15	**58,212**	31,977	26,235	**31,925**	25,014	6,911	**25,619**	6,735	18,384	**668**	228	440
		15—20	**42,934**	21,106	21,828	**11,478**	10,722	756	**30,672**	10,159	20,513	**784**	225	559
		20—40	**211,710**	104,908	106,802	**13,848**	12,015	1,833	**182.829**	89,368	93,461	**15,033**	3,525	11,508
		40—60	**108,126**	57,877	50,249	**2,437**	1,782	655	**74,608**	50,366	24,242	**31,081**	5,729	25,352
		60 & over	**31,843**	15,549	16,294	**608**	422	186	**13,194**	11,101	2,093	**18.041**	4,026	14,015
	Hindu.	Total	*566,054*	*285,573*	*280,481*	*191,873*	*116,839*	*74,734*	*314,222*	*156,086*	*158,136*	*60,259*	*12,648*	*47,611*
		0— 5	**85,935**	41,136	44,849	**84,149**	40,768	43,381	**1,780**	351	1,429	**56**	17	39
		5—10	**68,588**	34,612	33,976	**56,055**	32,958	23,097	**12,236**	1,574	10,662	**297**	80	217
		10—15	**52,586**	28,830	23,756	**27,685**	22,107	5,578	**24,252**	6,505	17,747	**649**	218	431
		15—20	**38,912**	19,064	19,848	**9,645**	9,116	529	**28,540**	9,732	18,808	**727**	216	511
		20—40	**193,006**	95,424	97,582	**11,440**	9,968	1,472	**167,726**	82,181	85,545	**13.840**	3,275	10,565
		40—60	**98,310**	52,517	45,793	**2,067**	1,538	529	**67,838**	45,764	22,074	**28,405**	5,215	23,190
		60 & over	**28,667**	13,990	14,677	**532**	384	148	**11,850**	9,979	1,871	**16,285**	3,627	12,658
	Musalman.	Total ...	*51,900*	*26,749*	*25,151*	*21,648*	*13,084*	*8,564*	*25,042*	*12,629*	*12,413*	*5,210*	*1,036*	*4,174*
		0— 5	**7,580**	3,723	3,857	**7,557**	3,715	3,842	**23**	8	15	...	...	...
		5—10	**6,345**	3,263	3,082	**5,999**	3,199	2,800	**326**	54	272	**20**	10	10
		10—15	**5,079**	2,839	2,240	**3,862**	2,640	1,222	**1,200**	190	1,010	**17**	9	8
		15—20	**3,658**	1,854	1,804	**1,695**	1,484	211	**1,910**	361	1,549	**53**	9	44
		20—40	**17,270**	8,743	8,527	**2,144**	1,815	329	**14,059**	6,709	7,350	**1,067**	219	848
		40—60	**9,012**	4,911	4,131	**329**	205	124	**6,269**	4,263	2,006	**2,444**	443	2,001
		60 & over	**2,926**	1,416	1,510	**62**	26	36	**1,255**	1,044	211	**1,609**	346	1,263
	Jain.	Total ...	*3,389*	*1,820*	*1,569*	*1,411*	*933*	*478*	*1,549*	*748*	*801*	*429*	*139*	*290*
		0— 5	**401**	191	210	**396**	190	206	**5**	1	4	...	...	...
		5—10	**399**	203	196	**369**	196	173	**29**	7	22	**1**	...	1
		10—15	**437**	254	183	**309**	226	83	**126**	27	99	**2**	1	1
		15—20	**280**	145	135	**101**	93	8	**175**	52	123	**4**	...	4
		20—40	**1,078**	559	519	**193**	187	6	**771**	341	430	**114**	31	83
		40—60	**610**	356	254	**33**	32	1	**377**	260	117	**200**	64	136
		60 & over	**184**	112	72	**10**	9	1	**66**	60	6	**108**	43	65
	Animist.	Total ...	*835*	*407*	*428*	*413*	*213*	*200*	*360*	*183*	*177*	*62*	*11*	*51*
		0— 5	**158**	67	91	**157**	67	90	**1**	...	1	...	...	...
		5—10	**132**	64	68	**123**	61	62	**9**	3	6	...	...	...
		10—15	**78**	41	37	**42**	28	14	**36**	13	23	...	...	...
		15—20	**57**	25	32	**22**	16	6	**35**	9	26	...	...	...
		20—40	**247**	124	123	**61**	35	26	**175**	89	86	**11**	...	11
		40—60	**119**	67	52	**6**	5	1	**89**	56	33	**24**	6	18
		60 & over	**44**	19	25	**2**	1	1	**15**	13	2	**27**	5	22

TABLE VII.

AGE, SEX AND CIVIL CONDITION.

Part II.

Districts.

District.	Religion and Age.	Population.			Unmarried.			Married.			Widowed.		
		Persons.	Males.	Females.	Persons.	Males.	Females.	Persons.	Males.	Females.	Persons.	Males.	Females.
	1	2	3	4	5	6	7	8	9	10	11	12	13
Nander.	All Religions. Total ...	*704,549*	*352,638*	*351,911*	*218,462*	*134,821*	*83,641*	*399,011*	*200,405*	*198,606*	*87,076*	*17,412*	*69,664*
	0—5	**101,873**	51,573	53,300	**102,023**	51,074	50,949	**2,805**	489	2,316	**45**	10	35
	5—10	**83,252**	41,750	40,502	**62,224**	38,595	23,629	**19,668**	3,040	16,628	**360**	115	245
	10—15	**62,408**	34,361	28,047	**27,551**	22,910	4,641	**33,792**	10,961	22,831	**1,065**	490	575
	15—20	**44,021**	20,852	23,169	**9,525**	8,567	958	**33,411**	11,828	21,583	**1,085**	457	628
	20—40	**244,444**	121,620	122,824	**13,664**	11,321	2,343	**212,011**	105,157	106,854	**18,769**	5,142	13,627
	40—60	**123,749**	65,366	61,383	**2,644**	1,838	806	**82,724**	56,832	25,892	**41,381**	6,696	34,685
	60 & over...	**39,802**	17,116	22,686	**831**	516	315	**14,600**	12,098	2,502	**24,371**	4,502	19,869
	Hindu. Total ...	*627,652*	*313,495*	*314,157*	*187,616*	*116,265*	*71,351*	*361,268*	*181,243*	*180,025*	*78,768*	*15,987*	*62,781*
	0—5	**93,587**	46,144	47,443	**90,753**	45,654	45,099	**2,789**	480	2,309	**45**	10	35
	5—10	**72,920**	36,832	36,088	**53,201**	33,758	19,443	**19,366**	2,966	16,400	**353**	108	245
	10—15	**55,275**	30,298	24,977	**22,319**	19,249	3,070	**31,920**	10,578	21,342	**1,036**	471	565
	15—20	**38,789**	18,398	20,391	**7,491**	6,772	719	**30,262**	11,183	19,079	**1,036**	443	593
	20—40	**218,682**	108,671	110,011	**10,817**	8,830	2,017	**190,734**	95,045	95,689	**17,101**	4,796	12,305
	40—60	**113,372**	58,212	55,160	**2,276**	1,563	713	**73,506**	50,498	23,008	**37,590**	6,151	31,439
	60 & over...	**35,027**	14,940	20,087	**729**	439	290	**12,691**	10,493	2,198	**21,607**	4,008	17,599
	Musalman. Total ...	*72,189*	*36,708*	*35,481*	*28,924*	*17,380*	*11,544*	*35,430*	*18,023*	*17,407*	*7,835*	*1,305*	*6,530*
	0—5	**10,512**	5,067	5,445	**10,505**	5,067	5,438	**7**	...	7	...	...	...
	5—10	**8,750**	4,612	4,138	**8,494**	4,546	3,948	**250**	60	190	**6**	6	...
	10—15	**6,726**	3,826	2,900	**4,965**	3,464	1,501	**1,736**	347	1,389	**25**	15	10
	15—20	**4,964**	2,334	2,630	**1,937**	1,712	225	**2,982**	610	2,372	**45**	12	33
	20—40	**24,203**	12,186	12,017	**2,617**	2,303	314	**19,999**	9,557	10,442	**1,587**	326	1,261
	40—60	**12,575**	6,684	5,891	**323**	230	93	**8,671**	5,950	2,721	**3,581**	504	3,077
	60 & over.	**4,459**	1,939	2,460	**83**	58	25	**1,785**	1,499	286	**2,591**	442	2,149
	Sikh. Total ...	*1,323*	*700*	*623*	*502*	*333*	*169*	*670*	*330*	*340*	*151*	*37*	*114*
	0—5	**169**	78	91	**169**	78	91	...	...	...	...	...	...
	5—10	**170**	96	74	**151**	91	60	**19**	5	14	...	...	...
	10—15	**118**	71	47	**71**	59	12	**47**	12	35	...	...	...
	15—20	**79**	41	38	**28**	26	2	**49**	14	35	**2**	1	1
	20—40	**412**	190	222	**49**	45	4	**341**	143	198	**22**	2	20
	40—60	**247**	144	103	**17**	17	...	**174**	117	57	**56**	10	46
	60 & over	**128**	80	48	**17**	17	...	**40**	39	1	**71**	24	47
	Animist. Total ...	*2,336*	*1,194*	*1,142*	*1,060*	*598*	*462*	*1,110*	*553*	*557*	*166*	*43*	*123*
	0—5	**499**	233	266	**490**	224	266	**9**	9	...	...	...	...
	5—10	**230**	151	139	**278**	142	136	**11**	8	3	**1**	1	...
	10—15	**197**	114	83	**139**	93	4[illegible]	**54**	17	37	**4**	4	...
	15—20	**122**	49	73	**50**	39	11	**71**	9	62	**1**	1	...
	20—40	**760**	379	381	**90**	87	3	**658**	286	372	**12**	6	6
	40—60	**349**	205	144	**12**	12	...	**246**	177	69	**91**	16	75
	60 & over	**119**	63	56	**1**	1	...	**61**	47	14	**57**	15	42

Part II.

Districts.

TABLE VII.

AGE, SEX AND CIVIL CONDITION.

District.	Religion and Age.		Population. Persons.	Population. Males.	Population. Females.	Unmarried. Persons.	Unmarried. Males.	Unmarried. Females.	Married. Persons.	Married. Males.	Married. Females.	Widowed. Persons.	Widowed. Males.	Widowed. Females.
	1		2	3	4	5	6	7	8	9	10	11	12	13
Parbhani.	All Religions.	Total ...	*779,674*	*391,231*	*388,443*	*250,037*	*150,639*	*99,398*	*442,786*	*222,374*	*220,412*	*86,851*	*18,218*	*68,633*
		0—5	120.891	57,736	63,155	116.380	53,758	59,622	4.383	957	3,429	125	21	104
		5—10	90,657	45,409	45,248	70,899	42,197	28,702	19,214	3,065	16,179	514	147	367
		10—15	69,181	38,007	31,174	31,734	25,464	6,270	36.352	12,065	24,287	1,095	478	617
		15—20	52,306	25,234	27,072	11,115	10,041	1,074	39,893	14,630	25,263	1,298	563	735
		20—40	267,715	132,622	135,093	15,915	13,292	2,623	232,592	113,831	118,761	19,208	5,499	13,709
		40—60	137,600	73,373	64,227	3,189	2,340	849	93,968	64,195	29,773	40.443	6,838	33,665
		60 & over.	41,324	18,850	22,474	805	517	258	16,351	13,631	2,720	24.168	4,672	19,496
	Hindu.	Total ..	699.675	*350,575*	*349,100*	*217,006*	*131,257*	*85,749*	*403,892*	*202,554*	*201,338*	*78,777*	*16,764*	*62,013*
		0—5	109.076	52,093	56,983	104,675	51,174	53,501	4,276	898	3,378	125	21	104
		5—10	81.055	40,599	40,456	61,787	37,501	24,286	18,774	2,960	15,814	491	138	356
		10—15	61,934	34,026	27,908	26,268	21,879	4,389	34,614	11,681	22,932	1,052	466	586
		15—20	46,656	22,455	24,201	8,634	7,917	717	36,798	13,991	22,807	1,224	547	677
		20—40	240,432	118,724	121,708	12,287	10,259	2,028	210.627	103,359	107,268	17.518	5,106	12,412
		40—60	123,979	66,080	57,899	2,690	2,048	642	84,524	57,749	26,775	36.765	6,283	30,482
		60 & over.	36,543	16,598	19,945	665	479	186	14,279	11,916	2,363	21,599	4,203	17,396
	Musalman.	Total ...	*72,474*	*36,789*	*35,685*	*30,129*	*17,696*	*12,433*	*35,019*	*17,865*	*17,154*	*7,326*	*1,228*	*6,098*
		0—5	10,628	5,099	5,529	10,554	5,064	5,490	74	35	39	...	...	...
		5—10	8,710	4,384	4,326	8.319	4,293	4,026	377	84	293	14	7	7
		10—15	6.575	3,627	2,948	5,058	3.298	1,760	1,487	321	1,166	30	8	22
		15—20	5,139	2,530	2.609	2,298	1,970	328	2,778	548	2,230	63	12	51
		20—40	24.675	12,540	12,135	3,316	2,753	563	19,825	9,454	10,371	1,534	333	1,201
		40—60	12,385	6,585	5,800	457	262	195	8.578	5,850	2,728	3,350	473	2,877
		60 & over.	4,362	2,024	2,338	127	56	71	1,900	1,573	327	2,335	395	1,940
	Jain.	Total ...	*3,665*	*1,842*	*1,823*	*1,091*	*663*	*428*	*2,049*	*1,008*	*1,041*	*525*	*171*	*354*
		0—5	450	200	250	438	194	242	14	6	8	...	...	...
		5—16	387	187	200	325	174	151	59	12	47	3	1	2
		10—15	315	166	149	137	117	20	171	46	125	7	3	4
		15—20	271	119	152	49	46	3	213	69	144	9	4	5
		20—40	1,295	653	642	108	102	6	1,076	511	565	111	40	71
		40—60	687	378	309	27	21	6	425	289	136	235	68	167
		60 & over.	260	139	121	9	9	...	91	75	16	160	55	105
	Animist.	Total ..	*3,143*	*1,627*	*1,516*	*1,495*	*846*	*649*	*1,478*	*742*	*736*	*170*	*39*	*131*
		0—5	649	313	336	627	295	332	22	18	4	...	...	...
		5—10	412	201	211	377	191	186	32	9	23	3	1	2
		10—15	296	163	133	227	148	79	65	15	50	4	...	4
		15—20	193	102	91	107	84	23	84	18	66	2	...	2
		20—40	1,000	49[illegible]	504	140	118	22	825	364	461	35	14	21
		40—60	460	2.7	183	14	8	6	377	258	119	69	11	58
		60 & over	133	75	58	3	2	1	73	60	13	57	18	44

TABLE VII.

Part II.

AGE, SEX AND CIVIL CONDITION.

Districts.

District.	Religion and Age.		Population.			Unmarried.			Married.			Widowed.		
			Persons.	Males.	Females.	Persons.	Males.	Females.	Persons.	Males.	Females.	Persons.	Males.	Females.
	1		2	3	4	5	6	7	8	9	10	11	12	13
Gulbarga.	All Religions.	Total ...	*1,150,983*	*582,447*	*568,536*	*403,727*	*245,242*	*158,485*	*611,329*	*307,877*	*303,452*	*135,927*	*29,328*	*106,599*
		0—5	151,245	74,951	79,294	149,631	73,727	75,904	4,449	1,202	3,247	165	22	143
		5—10	140,447	70,638	69,809	119,556	67,260	52,296	20,075	3,152	16,923	816	226	590
		10—15	120,523	65,774	54,749	69,900	53.066	16,834	48,960	12,074	36,886	1,663	634	1,029
		15—20	88,348	44,332	44,016	27,448	24,157	3,291	59,135	19,597	39,538	1,765	578	1,187
		20—40	366,524	180,364	186,160	29,420	22,838	6,582	309,366	151,866	157,500	27,738	5,660	22,078
		40—60	208,415	111,547	96,868	6,121	3,377	2,744	140,201	95,410	44,791	62,093	12,760	49,333
		60 & over.	72,481	34,841	37,640	1,651	817	834	29,143	24,576	4,567	41,687	9,448	32,239
	Hindu.	Total ...	*970,405*	*490,220*	*480,185*	*329,105*	*201,371*	*127,734*	*524,073*	*263,340*	*260,733*	*117,227*	*25,509*	*91,718*
		0—5	129,783	62,989	66,794	125,341	61,833	63,508	4,288	1,134	3,154	154	22	132
		5—10	118,219	59,408	58,811	98,365	56,271	42,094	19,078	2,916	16,162	776	221	555
		10—15	100,934	54,967	45,967	54,958	43,402	11,556	44,428	10,964	33,464	1,548	601	947
		15—20	74,524	37,237	37,287	20,800	18,864	1,936	52,090	17,819	34,271	1,634	554	1,080
		20—40	310,670	153,040	157,630	22,994	17,500	5,494	263,358	130,577	132,781	24,318	4,963	19,355
		40—60	176,232	94,102	82,130	5,218	2,810	2,408	117,308	80,069	37,239	53,706	11,223	42,483
		60 & over.	60,043	28,477	31,566	1,429	691	738	23,523	19,861	3,662	35,091	7,925	27,166
	Musalman.	Total ...	*169,326*	*86,152*	*83,174*	*69,620*	*40,886*	*28,734*	*81,971*	*41,738*	*40,233*	*17,735*	*3,528*	*14,207*
		0—5	22,572	11,070	11,502	22,447	11,012	11,435	125	58	67	...	...	...
		5—10	20,768	10,474	10,294	19,808	10,257	9,551	923	212	711	37	5	32
		10—15	18,510	10,176	8,334	14,156	9,122	5,034	4,248	1,025	3,223	106	29	77
		15—20	12,980	6,645	6,335	6,279	4,973	1,306	6,582	1,649	4,933	119	23	96
		20—40	52,298	25,398	26,900	5,888	4,886	1,002	43,167	19,873	23,294	3,243	639	2,604
		40—60	30,430	16,388	14,042	839	523	316	21,626	14,458	7,168	7,965	1,407	6,558
		60 & over.	11,768	6,001	5,767	203	113	90	5,300	4,463	837	6,265	1,425	4,840
	Christian.	Total ...	*1,044*	*633*	*411*	*418*	*272*	*146*	*553*	*337*	*216*	*73*	*24*	*49*
		0—5	128	68	60	128	68	60	...	...	...	...	...	...
		5—10	129	82	47	128	82	46	1	...	1	...	...	—
		10—15	82	59	23	61	53	8	21	6	15	...	...	...
		15—20	107	50	57	42	29	13	63	20	43	2	1	1
		20—40	385	237	149	50	36	14	324	195	129	11	6	5
		40—60	165	112	53	9	4	5	126	102	24	30	6	24
		60 & over.	48	25	23	...	...	...	18	14	4	30	11	19
	Animist.	Total ...	*8,442*	*4,469*	*3,973*	*3,993*	*2,320*	*1,673*	*3,867*	*1,989*	*1,878*	*582*	*160*	*422*
		0—5	1.583	725	858	1,543	718	825	30	7	23	10	...	10
		5—10	1,171	606	565	1,104	583	521	65	23	42	2	...	2
		10—15	843	487	356	619	414	205	218	71	147	6	2	4
		15—20	574	310	264	260	229	31	309	81	228	5	...	5
		20—40	2,532	1,328	1,204	408	338	70	2,022	954	1,068	102	36	66
		40—60	1,238	731	507	43	28	15	958	643	315	237	60	177
		60 & over.	501	282	219	16	10	6	265	210	55	220	62	158

Part II.

Districts.

TABLE VII.

AGE, SEX AND CIVIL CONDITION.

District.	Religion and Age.		Population. Persons.	Population. Males.	Population. Females.	Unmarried. Persons.	Unmarried. Males.	Unmarried. Females.	Married. Persons.	Married. Males.	Married. Females.	Widowed. Persons.	Widowed. Males.	Widowed. Females.
	1		2	3	4	5	6	7	8	9	10	11	12	13
Osmanabad.	All Religions.	Total ...	*635,977*	*324,969*	*311,008*	*225,733*	*139,869*	*85,864*	*340,627*	*169,455*	*171,172*	*69,617*	*15,645*	*53,972*
		0—5	**93,501**	45,110	48,391	**91,350**	44,620	46,730	**2,074**	468	1,606	**77**	22	55
		5—10	**74,074**	37,776	36,298	**63,814**	36,337	27,477	**9,936**	1,345	8,591	**324**	94	230
		10—15	**64,339**	35,496	28,843	**37,377**	29,178	8,199	**26,148**	6,089	20,059	**814**	229	585
		15—20	**46,334**	23,196	23,138	**13,801**	12,951	850	**31,524**	9,938	21,586	**1,009**	307	702
		20—40	**212,052**	105,668	106,384	**16,326**	14,553	1,773	**179,552**	87,301	92,251	**16,174**	3,814	12,360
		40—60	**111,956**	60,369	51,587	**2,375**	1,761	614	**77,154**	52,211	24,943	**32,427**	6,397	26,030
		60 & over.	**33,721**	17,354	16,367	**690**	469	221	**14,239**	12,103	2,136	**18,792**	4,782	14,010
	Hindu.	Total ...	*572,433*	*292,192*	*280,241*	*199,774*	*124,153*	*75,621*	*309,687*	*153,868*	*155,819*	*62,972*	*14,171*	*48,801*
		0—5	**84,522**	40,765	43,757	**82,400**	40,289	42,111	**2,046**	455	1,591	**76**	21	55
		5—10	**66,527**	33,935	32,592	**56,558**	32,535	24,023	**9,656**	1,308	8,348	**313**	92	221
		10—15	**57,698**	31,778	25,920	**32,509**	25,781	6,728	**24,420**	5,783	18,637	**769**	214	555
		15—20	**41,597**	20,769	20,828	**11,809**	11,178	631	**28,855**	9,307	19,548	**933**	284	649
		20—40	**191,512**	95,351	96,161	**13,923**	12,460	1,463	**162,854**	79,398	83,456	**14,735**	3,493	11,242
		40—60	**100,699**	54,192	46,507	**1,988**	1,503	485	**69,314**	46,908	22,406	**29,397**	5,781	23,616
		60 & over.	**29,878**	15,402	14,476	**587**	407	180	**12,542**	10,709	1,833	**16,749**	4,286	12,463
	Musalman.	Total ...	*59,448*	*30,602*	*28,846*	*24,363*	*14,698*	*9,665*	*28,977*	*14,592*	*14,385*	*6,108*	*1,312*	*4,796*
		0—5	**8,445**	4,082	4,363	**8,421**	4,073	4,318	**21**	9	15	...	...	...
		5—10	**7,030**	3,571	3,459	**6,785**	3,542	3,243	**237**	29	208	**8**	...	8
		10—15	**6,199**	3,465	2,734	**4,571**	3,175	1,396	**1,583**	277	1,311	**40**	13	27
		15—20	**4,453**	2,284	2,169	**1,897**	1,684	213	**2,488**	579	1,907	**70**	21	49
		20—40	**19,221**	9,629	9,592	**2,246**	1,946	300	**15,679**	7,401	8,278	**1,296**	282	1,014
		40—60	**10,495**	5,745	4,750	**346**	221	125	**7,364**	4,984	2,380	**2,785**	540	2,245
		60 & over.	**3,605**	1,826	1,779	**97**	57	40	**1,599**	1,313	286	**1,909**	456	1,453
	Christian.	Total ...	*252*	*130*	*122*	*101*	*54*	*47*	*140*	*74*	*66*	*11*	*2*	*9*
		0—5	**41**	20	21	**40**	19	21	**1**	1	...	...	...	...
		5—10	**35**	18	17	**31**	17	14	**4**	1	3	...	...	...
		10—15	**17**	12	5	**14**	10	4	**3**	2	1	...	...	...
		15—20	**15**	1	14	**4**	...	4	**11**	1	10	...	...	...
		20—40	**89**	44	45	**11**	8	3	**75**	36	39	**3**	...	3
		40—60	**43**	23	20	**1**	...	1	**35**	22	13	**7**	1	6
		60 & over.	**12**	12	...	...	...	...	**11**	11	...	**1**	1	...
	Jain.	Total ...	*3,429*	*1,817*	*1,612*	*1,299*	*847*	*452*	*1,627*	*817*	*810*	*503*	*153*	*350*
		0—5	**408**	203	205	**404**	200	204	**3**	3	...	**1**	...	1
		5—10	**420**	213	207	**385**	207	178	**32**	4	28	**3**	2	1
		10—15	**381**	216	165	**248**	190	58	**128**	24	104	**5**	2	3
		15—20	**247**	131	116	**83**	81	2	**158**	48	110	**6**	2	4
		20—40	**1,121**	587	534	**135**	129	6	**850**	421	429	**136**	37	99
		40—60	**646**	363	283	**38**	35	3	**380**	255	125	**228**	73	155
		60 & over.	**206**	104	102	**6**	5	1	**76**	62	14	**124**	37	87

TABLE VII.

AGE, SEX AND CIVIL CONDITION.

Part II.
Districts.

District.	Religion and Age.	Population. Persons.	Population. Males.	Population. Females.	Unmarried. Persons.	Unmarried. Males.	Unmarried. Females.	Married. Persons.	Married. Males.	Married. Females.	Widowed. Persons.	Widowed. Males.	Widowed. Females.
	1	2	3	4	5	6	7	8	9	10	11	12	13
Raichur.	All Religions. Total ...	*996.681*	*503,541*	*493.143*	*397,105*	*234,143*	*162,962*	*486,076*	*245,117*	*240,959*	*113,503*	*24,281*	*89,222*
	0—5	124,195	60,407	64,088	120,837	59,156	61,681	3,477	1,209	2,268	181	42	139
	5—10	130,737	64,830	65,907	116.623	61,811	54,812	13.267	2,843	10,424	847	176	671
	10—15	116.599	61,364	55,226	78,016	51,300	26,716	36.953	9,601	27,352	1,621	463	1,158
	15—20	80.333	40,764	39,599	31,980	26,313	5,667	46.295	13,960	32,336	2,087	491	1,596
	20—40	312,334	156,563	155,771	39,489	29,742	9,747	248,007	121,898	126,109	24,838	4,923	19,915
	40—60	178,008	93,447	84,561	7,931	4,619	3,345	115,973	77,723	38,250	54,071	11,105	42,966
	60 & over	54,157	26,166	27,991	2,195	1,202	994	22,103	17,883	4,220	29,858	7,081	22,777
	Hindu. Total ...	*909,417*	*453,629*	*446,788*	*356,822*	*209,827*	*146,995*	*440,288*	*221,911*	*218,377*	*103,307*	*21,891*	*81,416*
	0—5	112,787	54,643	58,144	109,140	53,398	55,742	3,466	1,203	2,263	181	42	139
	5—10	118,789	58,541	60,248	105.556	55,762	49,794	12.464	2,617	9,847	769	152	607
	10—15	105,338	55,392	49,946	69,399	45,933	23,466	34,464	9,078	25,386	1,475	381	1,094
	15—20	72,880	36,897	35,983	28.334	23,466	4,868	42,582	12,966	29,616	1,964	465	1,499
	20—40	281,993	140,784	141,209	35,249	26,202	9,047	224.025	110,212	113,813	22.719	4,370	18,349
	40—60	160,406	84,332	76,074	7,205	4,041	3,164	103,819	70,103	33,716	49,332	10,188	39,194
	60 & over	48,224	23,040	25,184	1,939	1,025	914	19,468	15,732	3,736	28,817	6,283	20,534
	Musalman. Total ...	*93,478*	*48,402*	*45,076*	*39,052*	*23,596*	*15,456*	*44,473*	*22,482*	*21,991*	*9,953*	*2,324*	*7,629*
	0—5	11.333	5,592	5,741	11.333	5,592	5,741	...	...	...	...	...	...
	5—10	11,577	6,076	5,501	10.714	5,841	4,873	783	221	565	77	14	63
	10—15	10,954	5,827	5,127	8.386	5,237	3,149	2,424	508	1,916	144	82	62
	15—20	7,273	3,773	3,500	3,551	2.780	771	3,601	967	2,634	121	26	95
	20—40	29,407	15,255	14,152	4,086	3,417	669	23.264	11,297	11,967	2,057	541	1,516
	40—60	17,132	8,829	8,303	731	556	175	11,824	7,387	4,437	4,577	886	3,691
	60 & over	5,802	3,050	2,752	251	173	78	2,574	2,102	472	2.977	775	2,202
	Christian. Total ...	*1,711*	*920*	*791*	*778*	*428*	*350*	*821*	*460*	*361*	*112*	*32*	*80*
	0—5	231	105	126	229	103	126	2	2	...	...	...	...
	5—10	211	136	105	229	132	97	12	4	8	...	...	...
	10—15	183	88	100	151	77	74	37	11	26	...	...	...
	15—20	127	52	75	61	39	22	65	13	53	...	...	...
	20—40	559	316	243	90	66	24	449	246	202	21	4	17
	40—60	239	175	114	17	11	6	213	149	64	59	15	44
	60 & over	73	48	28	1	...	1	43	35	8	32	13	19
	Jain. Total ...	*707*	*393*	*314*	*293*	*211*	*82*	*314*	*163*	*151*	*100*	*19*	*81*
	0—5	83	48	35	75	45	30	8	3	5	...	...	...
	5—10	83	49	37	81	48	33	5	1	4	...	...	...
	10—15	80	48	32	59	45	14	19	3	16	2	...	2
	15—20	43	23	20	29	19	1	22	4	18	1	...	1
	20—40	259	137	122	48	44	4	177	88	89	34	5	29
	40—60	123	74	49	8	8	...	76	57	19	39	9	30
	60 & over	33	14	19	2	2	...	7	7	...	24	5	19

Part II.

Districts.

TABLE VII.

AGE, SEX AND CIVIL CONDITION.

District.	Religion and Age.	Population.			Unmarried.			Married.			Widowed.		
		Persons.	Males.	Females.	Persons.	Males.	Females.	Persons.	Males.	Females.	Persons.	Males.	Females.
	1	2	3	4	5	6	7	8	9	10	11	12	13
Bidar.	All Religions. Total ...	*889,527*	*449,438*	*440,089*	*292,139*	*182,007*	*110,132*	*491,477*	*245,138*	*246,339*	*105,911*	*22,293*	*83,618*
	0—5	125,635	61,122	64,513	122,173	60,435	61,738	3,348	666	2,682	114	21	93
	5—10	103,516	51,865	51,651	82,591	49,183	33,408	20.341	2,521	17,820	584	161	423
	10—15	88,184	47,846	40,338	45,661	36,900	8,761	41,289	10,454	30,835	1.234	492	742
	15—20	61,285	30,687	30,598	17,259	15,654	1,605	42,852	14,575	28,277	1,174	458	716
	20—40	293,919	147,251	146,668	19,258	16,348	2,910	253,852	125,496	128,356	20,809	5,407	15,402
	40—60	160,390	84,468	75,922	3,955	2,738	1,217	107,291	72,706	34,585	49,144	9,024	40,120
	60 & over.	56,598	26,199	30,399	1,242	749	493	22,504	18,720	3,784	32,852	6,730	26,122
	Hindu. Total ...	*761,731*	*384,795*	*376,936*	*238,482*	*150,168*	*88,314*	*4,30,445*	*214,671*	*215,774*	*92,804*	*19,956*	*72,848*
	0—5	107,340	52,348	54,992	103,992	51,707	52,285	3,236	620	2,616	112	21	91
	5—10	87,300	43,779	43,521	67,369	41,312	26,057	19,423	2,329	17,094	508	138	370
	10—15	75,037	40,632	34,405	35,770	30,261	5,509	38,130	9,918	28,212	1,137	453	684
	15—20	52,160	26,043	26,117	12,966	12,042	924	38,136	13,568	24,568	1,058	433	625
	20—40	253,273	126,903	126,370	14,190	12,003	2,187	220,651	109,951	110,700	18,432	4,949	13,483
	40—60	138,815	73,049	65,766	3,212	2,258	954	92,213	62,653	29,560	43,390	8,138	35,252
	60 & over.	47,806	22,041	25,765	983	585	398	18,656	15,632	3,024	28,167	5,824	22,343
	Musalman. Total ...	*124,790*	*63,142*	*61,648*	*52,437*	*31,144*	*21,293*	*59,574*	*29,752*	*29,822*	*12,779*	*2,246*	*10,533*
	0—5	17,848	8,577	9,271	17,746	8,534	9,212	102	43	59	...	...	...
	5—10	15,841	7,913	7,928	14,884	7,708	7,176	887	185	702	70	20	50
	10—15	12,875	7,044	5,831	9,710	6,503	3,207	3,082	514	2,568	83	27	56
	15—20	8,920	4,552	4,368	4,219	3,548	671	4,588	979	3,609	113	25	88
	20—40	39,627	19,857	19,770	4.918	4,241	677	32.399	15,169	17,230	2,310	447	1,863
	40—60	21,085	11,148	9,937	714	455	259	14,751	9,843	4,908	5,620	850	4,770
	60 & over.	8,594	4,051	4,543	246	155	91	3,765	3,019	746	4,583	877	3,706
	Jain. Total ...	*930*	*455*	*475*	*313*	*197*	*116*	*463*	*219*	*244*	*154*	*39*	*115*
	0—5	115	43	72	113	43	70	...	...	...	2	...	2
	5—10	90	41	49	73	40	33	16	1	15	1	...	1
	10—15	90	56	34	56	47	9	31	7	24	3	2	1
	15—20	60	28	32	18	18	...	40	10	30	2	...	2
	20—40	320	160	160	31	29	2	259	124	135	30	7	23
	40—60	175	84	91	13	13	...	90	52	38	72	19	53
	60 & over.	80	43	37	9	7	2	27	25	2	44	11	33
	Animist. Total ...	*1,542*	*759*	*783*	*710*	*379*	*331*	*696*	*343*	*353*	*136*	*37*	*99*
	0—5	269	121	148	261	119	142	8	2	6	...	...	...
	5—10	210	94	116	197	89	108	10	3	7	3	2	1
	10—15	131	78	53	99	68	31	31	10	21	1	...	1
	15—20	105	50	55	48	41	7	56	9	47	1	...	1
	20—40	497	238	259	93	55	38	367	171	196	37	12	25
	40—60	242	135	107	10	7	3	185	119	66	47	9	38
	60 & over.	88	43	45	2	...	2	39	29	10	47	14	33

TABLE VII.

AGE, SEX AND CIVIL CONDITION.

Hyderabad City.

Part III. Cities.

Age.	Population.			Unmarried.			Married.			Widowed.		
	Persons.	Males.	Females.	Persons.	Males.	Females.	Persons.	Males.	Females.	Persons.	Males.	Females.
1	2	3	4	5	6	7	8	9	10	11	12	13
All Religions.	***500,623***	***258,454***	***242,169***	***196,886***	***120,212***	***76,674***	***241,124***	***125,377***	***115,747***	***62,613***	***12,865***	***49,748***
0—5	**50,219**	24,481	25,738	**49,935**	24,369	25,566	**266**	109	157	**18**	3	15
5—10	**53,711**	26,492	27,219	**51,105**	26,229	24,876	**2,529**	255	2,274	**77**	8	69
10—15	**50,101**	26,715	23,386	**41,172**	25,484	15,688	**8,734**	1,216	7,518	**195**	15	180
15—20	**44,170**	21,417	22,753	**21,671**	16,420	5,251	**21,829**	4,913	16,916	**670**	84	586
20—40	**175,869**	92,745	83,124	**29,301**	25,079	4,222	**132,842**	64,384	68,458	**13,726**	3,282	10,444
40—60	**92,079**	49,447	42,632	**2,938**	2,118	820	**60,481**	42,065	18,416	**28,660**	5,264	23,396
60 & over	**34,474**	17,157	17,317	**764**	513	251	**14,443**	12,435	2,008	**19,267**	4,209	15,058
Hindu.	***262,131***	***135,638***	***126,493***	***91,577***	***57,248***	***34,329***	***134,281***	***70,866***	***63,415***	***36,273***	***7,524***	***28,749***
0—5	**27,517**	13,369	14,148	**27,236**	13,258	13,978	**263**	108	155	**18**	3	15
5—10	**28,344**	14,176	14,168	**25,811**	13,932	11,879	**2,457**	236	2,221	**76**	8	68
10—15	**24,636**	13,643	10,993	**17,501**	12,676	4,825	**7,000**	954	6,046	**135**	13	122
15—20	**22,325**	10,988	11,337	**8,129**	6,910	1,219	**13,697**	4,011	9,686	**499**	67	432
20—40	**92,922**	49,042	43,880	**11,038**	9,179	1,859	**73,245**	37,901	35,344	**8,639**	1,962	6,677
40—60	**48,885**	26,149	22,736	**1,472**	1,034	438	**30,871**	21,890	8,981	**16,542**	3,225	13,317
60 & over	**17,502**	8,271	9,231	**390**	259	131	**6,742**	5,766	982	**10,364**	2,246	8,118
Musalman.	***219,896***	***111,770***	***108,126***	***93,944***	***55,353***	***38,591***	***100,948***	***51,441***	***49,507***	***25,004***	***4,976***	***20,028***
0—5	**20,753**	10,167	10,586	**20,751**	10,166	10,585	**2**	1	1	...	...	...
5—10	**23,400**	11,364	12,036	**23,333**	11,347	11,986	**66**	17	49	**1**	...	1
10—15	**23,741**	12,237	11,504	**22,005**	11,980	10,025	**1,676**	255	1,421	**60**	2	58
15—20	**20,306**	9,649	10,657	**12,380**	8,782	3,598	**7,763**	850	6,913	**163**	17	146
20—40	**74,547**	37,842	36,705	**13,836**	11,848	1,988	**55,950**	24,766	31,184	**4,761**	1,228	3,533
40—60	**40,902**	22,002	18,900	**1,303**	998	305	**28,064**	19,105	8,959	**11,535**	1,899	9,636
60 & over	**16,247**	8,509	7,738	**336**	232	104	**7,427**	6,447	980	**8,484**	1,830	6,654
Christian.	***16,240***	***9,623***	***6,617***	***10,395***	***6,990***	***3,405***	***4,750***	***2,368***	***2,382***	***1,095***	***265***	***830***
0—5	**1,746**	854	892	**1,745**	854	891	**1**	...	1	...	...	...
5—10	**1,783**	870	913	**1,779**	869	910	**4**	1	3	...	...	...
10—15	**1,543**	729	814	**1,501**	729	772	**42**	...	42	...	...	...

TABLE VII.

Part III.
Cities.

AGE, SEX AND CIVIL CONDITION.

Hyderabad City.

Age.	Population. Persons.	Population. Males.	Population. Females.	Unmarried Persons.	Unmarried Males.	Unmarried Females.	Married. Persons.	Married. Males.	Married. Females.	Widowed. Persons.	Widowed. Males.	Widowed. Females.
1	2	3	4	5	6	7	8	9	10	11	12	13
Christian (concld.)												
15—20	**1,339**	657	682	**1,035**	632	403	**298**	25	273	**6**	...	6
20—40	**7,362**	5,175	2,187	**4,157**	3,817	340	**2,945**	1,303	1,642	**260**	55	205
40—60	**1,876**	1,030	846	**147**	72	75	**1,242**	854	388	**487**	104	383
60 & over	**591**	308	283	**31**	17	14	**218**	185	33	**342**	106	236
Sikh.	***978***	***644***	***334***	***376***	***287***	***89***	***485***	***309***	***176***	***117***	***48***	***69***
0—5	**92**	42	50	**92**	42	50	...	...	...	...	...	...
5—10	**66**	39	27	**65**	39	26	**1**	...	1	...	...	...
10—15	**53**	37	16	**41**	31	10	**12**	6	6	...	...	...
15—20	**79**	58	21	**44**	44	...	**33**	14	19		...	2
20—40	**498**	354	144	**121**	120	1	**329**	206	123	**48**	28	20
40—60	**150**	90	60	**10**	9	1	**97**	72	25	**43**	9	34
60 & over	**40**	24	16	**3**	2	1	**13**	11	2	**24**	1	13
Parsi.	***808***	***443***	***365***	***377***	***201***	***176***	***364***	***213***	***151***	***67***	***29***	***38***
0—5	**59**	28	31	**59**	28	31	...	...	...	...	...	
5—10	**50**	12	38	**50**	12	38	...	...	...	...	...	
10—15	**86**	41	45	**85**	40	45	**1**	1	...	...	...	
15—20	**61**	31	30	**59**	31	28	**2**	...	2	...	...	
20—40	**301**	180	121	**115**	83	32	**181**	95	86	**5**	2	
40—60	**181**	118	63	**5**	4	1	**151**	97	54	**25**	17	
60 & over	**70**	33	37	**4**	3	1	**29**	20	9	**37**	10	
Others.	***570***	***336***	***234***	***217***	***133***	***84***	***296***	***180***	***116***	***57***	***23***	
0—5	**52**	21	31	**52**	21	31	...	...	...	...	...	
5—10	**68**	31	37	**67**	30	37	**1**	1	...	...	...	
10—15	**42**	28	14	**39**	28	11	**3**	...	3	...	...	
15—20	**60**	34	26	**24**	21	3	**36**	13	23	...	...	
20—40	**239**	152	87	**34**	32	2	**192**	113	79	**13**	7	
40—60	**85**	58	27	**1**	1	...	**56**	47	9	**28**	10	
60 & over.	**24**	12	12	...	...	...	**8**	6	2	**16**	6	

TABLE VIII.

EDUCATION BY RELIGION AND AGE.

1. This table, like Table VII, is divided into three parts. Part I shows the extent of literacy in the State as a whole among the total population and for each religion returned; Part II gives details for districts for the total district population and for each main religion; and Part III gives similar details for the City of Hyderabad.

2. The table shows the number of persons literate in their own vernaculars. The number of persons literate in English has also been shown separately.

3. Of the 9,801 (males 7,151, females 2,650) Christans literate in English, 7,641 (males 5,729, females 1,912) are Europeans and Anglo-Indians and 2,160 (males 1,422, females 738) are natives of India.

4. Of the 5,763 (males 3,633, females 2,130) literate Indian Christians 3,892 (males 2,427, females 1,465) are Protestants, 1,870 (males 1,206, females 664) are Roman Catholics and the remaining one (female 1) is Syrian.

Part I.

Total Population.

TABLE VIII.

EDUCATION BY RELIGION AND AGE.

Religion and Age.	POPULATION.											
	TOTAL.			LITERATE.			ILLITERATE.			LITERATE IN ENGLISH		
	Persons.	Males.	Females.	Persons.	Males.	Females	Persons.	Males.	Females.	Persons.	Males.	Females.
1	2	3	4	5	6	7	8	9	10	11	12	13
All Religions. Total ...	*13,374,676*	*6,797,118*	*6,577,558*	*368,166*	*344,089*	*24,077*	*13,006,510*	*6,453,029*	*6,553,481*	*26,526*	*22,965*	*3,561*
0—10	3,618,680	1,788,219	1,830,461	9,493	7,621	1,872	3,609,187	1,780,598	1,828,589	773	490	283
10—15	1,392,802	764,794	628,008	34,190	30,670	3,520	1,358,612	734,124	624,488	2,290	1,829	461
15—20	1,004,122	499,638	504,434	38,249	34,574	3,675	965,873	465,114	500,759	3,347	2,820	527
20 & over.	7,359,072	3,744,417	3,614,655	286,234	271,224	15,010	7,072,838	3,473,193	3,599,645	20,116	17,826	2,290
Hindu. Total ...	*11,626,146*	*5,897,158*	*5,728,988*	*266,968*	*256,095*	*10,873*	*11,359,178*	*5,641,063*	*5,718,115*	*8,838*	*8,483*	*355*
0—10	3,153,760	1,558,296	1,595,464	6,209	5,288	921	3,147,551	1,553,008	1,594,543	170	143	27
10—15	1,204,040	662,127	541,913	24,619	23,054	1,565	1,179,421	639,073	540,348	825	766	59
15—20	871,698	432,742	438,956	27,234	25,654	1,580	844,464	407,088	437,376	1,190	1,120	70
20 & over.	6,396,648	3,243,993	3,152,655	208,906	202,099	6,807	6,187,742	3,041,894	3,145,848	6,653	6,454	199
Jain. Total ...	*21,026*	*11,032*	*9,994*	*4,280*	*4,139*	*141*	*16,746*	*6,893*	*9,853*	*63*	*52*	*11*
0—10	4,931	2,373	2,558	110	93	17	4,821	2,280	2,541	2	1	1
10—15	2,200	1,239	961	392	376	16	1,808	863	945	8	7	1
15—20	1,657	852	805	409	396	13	1,248	456	792	12	11	1
20 & over.	12,238	6,568	5,670	3,369	3,274	95	8,869	3,294	5,575	41	33	8
Sikh. Total ...	*4,726*	*2,643*	*2,083*	*818*	*741*	*77*	*3,908*	*1,902*	*2,006*	*44*	*28*	*16*
0—10	1,136	565	571	21	15	6	1,115	550	565	...	...	...
10—15	381	227	154	53	48	5	328	179	149	5	2	3
15—20	307	180	127	68	57	11	239	123	116	5	2	3
20 & over.	2,902	1,671	1,231	676	621	55	2,226	1,050	1,176	34	24	10
Arya Samaj. Total ...	*173*	*90*	*83*	*46*	*37*	*9*	*127*	*53*	*74*	*21*	*18*	*3*
0—10	41	18	23	2	1	1	39	17	22	...	...	...
10—15	23	14	9	7	5	2	16	9	7	5	4	1
15—20	9	4	5	2	1	1	7	3	4	...	...	...
20 & over	100	54	46	35	30	5	65	24	41	16	14	2
Brahmo Samaj. Total ...	*36*	*18*	*18*	*15*	*11*	*4*	*21*	*7*	*14*	*5*	*5*	...
0—10	10	4	6	...	...	...	10	4	6	...	...	...
10—15	2	...	2	1	...	1	1	...	1	...	...	...
15—20	3	...	3	2	...	2	1	...	1	...	...	...
20 & over.	21	14	7	12	11	1	9	3	6	5	5	...

TABLE VIII.

Part I.

EDUCATION BY RELIGION AND AGE.

Total Population.

Religion and Age.	POPULATION.											
	TOTAL.			LITERATE.			ILLITERATE.			LITERATE IN ENGLISH.		
	Persons.	Males.	Females.	Persons.	Males.	Females.	Persons.	Males.	Females.	Persons.	Males.	Females.
1	2	3	4	5	6	7	8	9	10	11	12	13
Buddhist. Total ...	*20*	*8*	*12*	*12*	*5*	*7*	*8*	*3*	*5*	*2*	*2*	...
0—10	7	4	3	1	1	...	6	3	3	...	...	...
10—15	...	...	...	...	...	...	...	...	...	...	...	...
15—20	3	...	3	3	...	3	...	...	...	...	...	...
20 & over	10	4	6	8	4	4	2	...	2	2	2	...
Musalman. Total ...	*1,380,990*	*706,821*	*674,169*	*81,260*	*72,783*	*8,477*	*1,299,730*	*634,038*	*665,692*	*7,020*	*6,692*	*328*
0—10	348,800	172,265	176,535	2,259	1,703	556	346,541	170,562	175,979	150	110	40
10—15	148,779	80,349	68,430	7,518	6,263	1,255	141,261	74,086	67,175	727	665	62
15—20	107,026	53,754	53,272	9,042	7,657	1,385	97,984	46,097	51,887	1,230	1,172	58
20 & over	776,385	400,453	375,932	62,441	57,160	5,281	713,944	343,293	370,661	4,913	4,745	168
Christian. Total ...	*54,296*	*29,495*	*24,801*	*13,404*	*9,362*	*4,042*	*40,892*	*20,133*	*20,759*	*9,801*	*7,151*	*2,650*
0—10	14,635	7,192	7,443	806	471	335	13,829	6,721	7,108	422	221	201
10—15	5,947	3,133	2,814	1,435	827	608	4,512	2,306	2,206	650	347	303
15—20	4,456	2,146	2,310	1,361	731	630	3,095	1,415	1,680	841	474	367
20 & over	29,258	17,024	12,234	9,802	7,333	2,469	19,456	9,691	9,765	7,888	6,109	1,779
Parsi. Total ...	*1,529*	*822*	*707*	*1,106*	*692*	*414*	*423*	*130*	*293*	*726*	*528*	*198*
0—10	258	100	158	70	39	31	188	61	127	29	15	14
10—15	155	67	88	108	50	58	47	17	30	68	36	32
15—20	116	55	61	95	49	46	21	6	15	68	40	28
20 & over	1,000	600	400	833	554	279	167	46	121	561	437	124
Jew. Total ...	*12*	*8*	*4*	*10*	*8*	*2*	*2*	...	*2*	*6*	*6*	...
0—10	2	...	2	1	...	1	1	...	1	...	...	...
10—15	2	2	...	2	2	...	...	...	...	2	2	...
15—20	1	1	...	1	1	...	...	...	...	1	1	...
20 & over	7	5	2	6	5	1	1	...	1	3	3	...
Animist. Total ...	*285,722*	*149,023*	*136,699*	*247*	*216*	*31*	*285,475*	*148,807*	*136,668*	...	...	...
0—10	95,100	47,402	47,698	14	10	4	95,086	47,392	47,694	...	...	...
10—15	31,273	17,636	13,637	55	45	10	31,218	17,591	13,627	...	...	...
15—20	18,846	9,954	8,892	32	28	4	18,814	9,926	8,888	...	...	...
20 & over	140,503	74,031	66,472	146	133	13	140,357	73,898	66,459	...	...	...

Part II.

Districts.

TABLE VIII.

EDUCATION BY RELIGION AND AGE.

District.	Religion	Age.	POPULATION.											
			TOTAL.			LITERATE.			ILLITERATE.			LITERATE IN ENGLISH.		
			Persons.	Males.	Females.	Persons.	Males.	Females.	Persons.	Males.	Females.	Persons.	Males.	Females.
		1	2	3	4	5	6	7	8	9	10	11	12	13
Atraf-i-balda.	All Religions.	Total ...	*520,159*	*265,184*	*254,975*	*14,824*	*13,616*	*908*	*505,635*	*251,568*	*254,067*	*696*	*563*	*133*
		0—10	134,639	66,385	68,254	427	351	76	134,212	66,034	68,178	54	49	5
		10—15	52,998	29,042	23,956	1,309	1,185	124	51,689	27,857	23,832	95	86	9
		15—20	40,570	20,004	20,566	1,340	1,193	147	39,230	18,811	20,419	110	86	24
		20 & over.	291,952	149,753	142,199	11,448	10,887	561	280,504	138,866	141,638	437	342	95
	Hindu.	Total ..	*455,203*	*231,505*	*223,698*	*11,097*	*10,590*	*507*	*444,106*	*220,915*	*223,191*	*187*	*182*	*5*
		0—10	118,307	58,375	59,932	302	251	51	118,005	58,124	59,881	10	10	...
		10—15	46,053	25,131	20,922	961	890	71	45,092	24,241	20,851	33	33	...
		15—20	35,346	17,475	17,871	985	911	74	34,361	16,564	17,797	32	30	2
		20 & over	255,497	130,524	124,973	8,849	8,538	311	246,648	121,986	124,662	112	109	3
	Musalman.	Total ...	*59,342*	*30,602*	*28,740*	*2,842*	*2,623*	*219*	*56,500*	*27,979*	*28,521*	*173*	*164*	*9*
		0—10	14,552	7,086	7,466	62	43	19	14,490	7,043	7,447	9	8	1[illegible]
		10—15	6,337	3,526	2,811	278	233	45	6,061	3,293	2,768	35	33	2[illegible]
		15—20	4,810	2,311	2,499	273	238	38	4,534	2,073	2,461	39	38	...
		20 & over.	33,643	17,679	15,964	2,228	2,109	119	31,415	15,570	15,845	91	85	6
	Christian.	Total ...	*1,291*	*686*	*605*	*487*	*331*	*156*	*804*	*355*	*449*	*287*	*186*	*101*
		0—10	365	188	177	54	51	3	311	137	174	27	25	2
		10—15	172	102	70	58	54	4	114	48	66	17	15	2
		15—20	133	74	59	69	40	29	64	34	30	31	15	16
		20 & over.	621	322	299	306	186	120	315	136	179	212	131	8[illegible]
	Animist.	Total ...	*4,067*	*2,255*	*1,812*	*14*	*13*	*1*	*4,053*	*2,242*	*1,811*	...	...	...
		0—10	1,367	717	650	...	...	...	1,367	717	650	...	...	...
		10—15	401	269	132	1	1	...	400	268	132	...	...	...
		15—20	258	135	123	1	1	...	257	134	123	...	...	...
		20 & over.	2,041	1,134	907	12	11	1	2,029	1,123	906	...	...	...
Warangal.	All Religions.	Total ..	*905,414*	*467,413*	*438,001*	*22,243*	*21,045*	*1,198*	*883,171*	*446,368*	*436,803*	*1,065*	*898*	*167*
		0—10	259,900	128,581	131,319	536	453	83	259,364	128,128	131,236	19	14	5
		10—15	104,079	57,379	46,700	2,302	2,125	177	101,777	55,254	46,523	53	33	20
		15—20	69,955	36,089	33,866	2,424	2,264	160	67,531	33,825	33,706	127	101	26
		20 & over	471,480	245,364	226,116	16,981	16,203	778	454,499	229,161	225,338	866	750	116
	Hindu.	Total ...	*723,884*	*372,793*	*351,091*	*17,592*	*17,017*	*575*	*706,292*	*355,776*	*350,516*	*406*	*393*	*13*
		0—10	203,578	100,854	102,724	398	352	46	203,180	100,502	102,678	3	3	...
		10—15	83,274	45,877	37,397	1,840	1,754	86	81,434	44,123	37,311	18	16	2
		15—20	56,904	29,197	27,707	1,938	1,852	86	54,966	27,345	27,621	54	49	5
		20 & over	380,128	196,865	183,263	13,416	13,059	357	366,712	183,806	182,906	331	325	6
	Musalman.	Total ...	*50,079*	*26,709*	*23,370*	*3,524*	*3,225*	*299*	*46,555*	*23,484*	*23,071*	*189*	*183*	*6*
		0—10	13,394	6,551	6,843	90	67	23	13,304	6,484	6,820	5	5	...
		10—15	5,732	3,143	2,589	323	277	46	5,409	2,866	2,543	9	8	1
		15—20	3,824	2,136	1,688	346	320	26	3,478	1,816	1,662	18	17	1
		20 & over.	27,129	14,879	12,250	2,765	2,561	204	24,364	12,318	12,046	157	153	4
	Christian.	Total ...	*11,979*	*6,202*	*5,777*	*890*	*601*	*289*	*11,089*	*5,601*	*5,488*	*433*	*296*	*137*
		0—10	3,542	1,702	1,840	41	29	12	3,501	1,673	1,828	11	6	5
		10—15	1,373	765	608	106	66	40	1,257	699	568	26	9	17
		15—20	988	486	502	111	68	43	877	418	459	53	35	1[illegible]
		20 & over	6,076	3,249	2,827	632	438	194	5,444	2,811	2,633	343	246	97
	Animist.	Total ...	*119,021*	*61,473*	*57,548*	*77*	*67*	*10*	*118,944*	*61,406*	*57,538*	...	...	...
		0—10	39,288	19,429	19,859	3	2	1	39,285	19,427	19,858	...	...	...
		10—15	13,664	7,575	6,089	22	19	3	13,642	7,556	6,086	...	...	...
		15—20	8,201	4,251	3,950	11	11	...	8,190	4,240	3,950	...	...	...
		20 & over.	57,868	30,218	27,650	41	35	6	57,827	30,183	27,644	...	...	...

TABLE VIII.

Part II.

EDUCATION BY RELIGION AND AGE.

Districts.

District.	Religion	Age.	POPULATION.											
			Total.			Literate.			Illiterate.			Literate in English.		
			Persons.	Males.	Females.	Persons.	Males.	Females.	Persons.	Males.	Females.	Persons.	Males.	Females.
		1	2	3	4	5	6	7	8	9	10	11	12	13
Karimnagar.	All Religions.	Total ...	***1,131,637***	***586,260***	***545,377***	***22,436***	***21,548***	***888***	***1,109,201***	***564,712***	***544,489***	***130***	***110***	***20***
		0—10	**333.003**	167,842	165,161	**466**	411	55	**332.537**	167,431	165,106	**5**	4	1
		10—15	**127,865**	72,987	54,878	**2,194**	2,082	112	**125.671**	70,905	54,766	**4**	4	...
		15—20	**88.374**	45,392	42,982	**2.319**	2,188	131	**85.055**	43,204	42,851	**9**	5	4
		20 & over.	**582,395**	300,039	282,356	**17.457**	16,867	590	**564 938**	283,172	281,766	**112**	97	15
	Hindu.	Total ...	***1,074,654***	***556,441***	***518 213***	***19,505***	***18,788***	***717***	***1,035,149***	***537,653***	***517,496***	***60***	***53***	***7***
		0—10	**316.518**	159,655	156,863	**416**	373	43	**316.102**	159,282	156,820	**2**	2	...
		10—15	**121.320**	69,293	52,027	**1,930**	1,844	86	**119.390**	67,449	51,941	**4**	4	...
		15—20	**84.102**	43,107	40,995	**1.931**	1,887	94	**82.121**	41,220	40,901	**4**	2	2
		20 & over.	**552,714**	284,386	268,328	**15.178**	14,684	494	**537,536**	269,702	267,834	**50**	45	5
	Musalman.	Total ...	***46,523***	***24,345***	***22.178***	***2,741***	***2,631***	***110***	***43,782***	***21,714***	***22,068***	***32***	***31***	***1***
		0—10	**13.095**	6,491	6,602	**43**	35	8	**13.053**	6,459	6,594	...	...	...
		10—15	**5.337**	3,005	2,332	**234**	222	12	**5.103**	2,783	2,320	...	...	...
		15—20	**3,577**	1,941	1,636	**291**	281	13	**3 283**	1 660	1,623	**1**	1	...
		20 & over.	**24.513**	12,905	11,608	**2,170**	2,093	77	**22,343**	10,812	11,531	**31**	30	1
	Christian.	Total ...	***586***	***286***	***300***	***144***	***85***	***59***	***442***	***201***	***241***	***38***	***26***	***12***
		0—10	**179**	76	103	**7**	3	4	**172**	73	99	**3**	2	1
		10—15	**85**	44	41	**27**	13	14	**58**	31	27	...	...	...
		15—20	**63**	22	41	**41**	17	24	**22**	5	17	**4**	2	2
		20 & over.	**259**	144	115	**69**	52	17	**190**	92	98	**31**	22	9
	Animist.	Total ...	***9,598***	***5,041***	***4,557***	***3***	***3***	...	***9,595***	***5,038***	***4,557***	...	...	...
		0—10	**3,144**	1,584	1,560	...	...	...	**3,144**	1,584	1,560	...	...	...
		10—15	**1,101**	632	469	**1**	1	...	**1.100**	631	469	...	...	..
		15—20	**615**	313	302	...	...	...	**615**	313	302	...	...	..
		20 & over.	**4,738**	2,512	2,226	**2**	2	...	**4,736**	2,510	2,226	...	...	...
Adilabad.	All Religions.	Total ...	***620,426***	***314,428***	***305,998***	***7,887***	***7,599***	***288***	***612,539***	***306,829***	***305,710***	***143***	***110***	***33***
		0—10	**195,324**	96,400	98,924	**163**	129	34	**195,161**	96,271	98,890	**4**	2	2
		10—15	**63,570**	35,477	28,093	**729**	695	34	**62.841**	34,782	28,059	**5**	5	...
		15—20	**38,824**	19,292	19,532	**675**	644	31	**38,149**	18,648	19,501	**8**	4	4
		20 & over.	**322,708**	163,259	159,449	**6,320**	6.131	189	**316,388**	157,128	159,260	**126**	99	27
	Hindu.	Total ...	***524,500***	***264,837***	***259,663***	***6,466***	***6,238***	***228***	***518,034***	***258,599***	***259,435***	***93***	***63***	***30***
		0—10	**165.058**	81,415	83,643	**126**	99	27	**164.932**	81,316	83,616	**4**	2	2
		10—15	**53.918**	30,049	23,869	**624**	599	25	**53,294**	29,450	23,844	**5**	5	...
		15—20	**32,810**	16,162	16,648	**564**	542	22	**32,246**	15,620	16,626	**6**	2	4
		20 & over.	**272,714**	137,211	135,503	**5,152**	4.998	154	**267,562**	132,213	135,349	**78**	54	24
	Musalman.	Total ...	***29,668***	***15,843***	***13,825***	***1,328***	***1,282***	***46***	***28,340***	***14,561***	***13,779***	***37***	***35***	***2***
		0—10	**8,486**	4,311	4,175	**30**	25	5	**8.456**	4,286	4,170	...	...	...
		10—15	**2,843**	1,677	1,166	**95**	89	6	**2.748**	1,588	1,160	...	...	...
		15—20	**1,909**	978	931	**98**	90	8	**1.811**	888	923	...	...	...
		20 & over	**16,430**	8,877	7,553	**1,105**	1,078	27	**15,325**	7,799	7,526	**37**	35	2
	Christian.	Total ...	***28***	***19***	***9***	***20***	***18***	***2***	***8***	***1***	***7***	***11***	***10***	***1***
		0—10	**4**	1	3	**1**	1	..	**3**	...	3	...	..	...
		10—15	...	...	...	...	...	...	...	...	...	...	...	...
		15—20	**3**	3	...	**3**	3	...	...	...	...	**2**	2	...
		20 & over.	**21**	15	6	**16**	14	2	**5**	1	4	**9**	8	1
	Animist.	Total ..	***65,964***	***33,601***	***32,363***	***49***	***40***	***9***	***65,915***	***33,561***	***32,354***	...	...	...
		0—10	**21.699**	10,640	11.059	**5**	3	2	**21.694**	10,637	11.057	...	...	...
		10—15	**6,788**	3.741	3,047	**6**	4	2	**6,782**	3,737	3,045	...	...	...
		15—20	**4,080**	2.134	1,946	**7**	6	1	**4.073**	2,128	1,945	...	...	...
		20 & over	**33,397**	17,086	16,311	**31**	27	4	**33,366**	17,059	16,307	...	...	...

Part II.

Districts.

TABLE VIII.

EDUCATION BY RELIGION AND AGE.

District.	Religion	Age.	POPULATION.											
			Total.			Literate.			Illiterate.			Literate in English.		
			Persons.	Males.	Females.	Persons.	Males.	Females.	Persons.	Males.	Females.	Persons.	Males.	Females.
		1	2	3	4	5	6	7	8	9	10	11	12	13
Medak.	All Religions.	Total ...	*687,137*	*348,410*	*338,727*	*21,568*	*20,432*	*1,136*	*665,569*	*327,978*	*337,591*	*413*	*372*	*41*
		0—10	180,237	89,263	90,974	623	509	114	179,614	88.754	90,860	5	5	...
		10—15	69.827	39,597	30,230	2,260	2,086	174	67,567	37,511	30,056	37	36	1
		15—20	53,316	26,136	27,180	2,357	2,194	163	50.959	23,942	27,017	83	74	9
		20 & over.	383,757	193,414	190,343	16,328	15,643	685	367,429	177,771	189,658	288	257	31
	Hindu.	Total ...	*615,552*	*312,690*	*302,862*	*17,086*	*16,462*	*624*	*598,466*	*296,228*	*302,238*	*133*	*128*	*5*
		0—10	161.252	79,991	81,261	408	348	60	160.844	79,643	81,201	2	2	...
		10—15	62,067	35,411	26,656	1.707	1,636	71	60,360	33,775	26,585	2	2	...
		15—20	48,204	23,747	24.457	1.808	1,718	90	46,396	22,029	24.367	11	9	2
		20 & over.	344,029	173,541	170,488	13,133	12,760	403	330,866	160,781	170,085	118	115	3
	Musalman.	Total ..	*65,084*	*32,269*	*32,815*	*3,906*	*3,619*	*287*	*61,178*	*28,650*	*32,528*	*184*	*183*	*1*
		0—10	17,054	8,286	8,768	127	108	19	16,927	8,178	8,749	...	...	...
		10—15	7,022	3,771	3,251	397	357	40	6.625	3,414	3,211	31	31	...
		15—20	4.684	2,163	2,521	496	453	43	4,188	1,710	2,478	63	62	1
		20 & over.	36,324	18,049	18,275	2,886	2,701	185	33,438	15,348	18,090	90	90	...
	Christian.	Total ...	*2,203*	*1,124*	*1,079*	*488*	*275*	*213*	*1,715*	*849*	*866*	*85*	*51*	*34*
		0—10	626	303	323	84	49	35	542	254	288	3	3	...
		10—15	292	173	119	145	82	63	147	91	56	1	...	1
		15—20	161	75	86	49	19	30	112	56	56	8	2	6
		20 & over.	1,124	573	551	210	125	85	914	448	466	73	46	27
	Animist.	Total ...	*4,016*	*2,179*	*1,837*	*14*	*14*	...	*4,002*	*2,165*	*1,837*	...	...	...
		0—10	1,258	662	596	3	3	...	1,255	659	596	...	...	...
		10—15	413	217	196	1	1	...	412	216	196	...	...	...
		15—20	251	143	108	...	...	...	251	143	108	...	...	...
		20 & over	2,094	1,157	937	10	10	...	2,084	1,147	937	...	...	...
Nizamabad.	All Religions.	Total ..	*568,009*	*283,621*	*284,388*	*11,265*	*10,871*	*394*	*556,744*	*272,750*	*283,994*	*224*	*195*	*29*
		0—10	149,478	74,427	75,051	215	188	27	149,283	74.239	75,024	6	4	2
		10—15	56.150	30,947	25,203	841	799	42	55,309	30,148	25,161	14	12	2
		15—20	41.571	20,159	21,412	1,055	1,002	53	40,516	19,157	21,359	22	16	6
		20 & over	320,810	158,088	162,722	9,154	8,882	272	311,656	149,206	162,450	182	163	19
	Hindu.	Total ..	*523,159*	*261,053*	*262,106*	*9,598*	*9,300*	*298*	*513,561*	*251,753*	*261,808*	*108*	*106*	*2*
		0—10	137,957	68,690	69,267	173	150	23	137,784	68,540	69,244	2	2	...
		10—15	51,585	28,453	23,132	718	681	37	50,867	27,772	23,095	2	2	...
		15—20	38.308	18,622	19,686	882	851	31	37,426	17,771	19,655	9	9	...
		20 & over	295,309	145,288	150,021	7,825	7,618	207	287,484	137,670	149,814	95	93	2
	Musalman.	Total ...	*41,951*	*21,036*	*20,915*	*1,502*	*1,449*	*53*	*40,449*	*19,587*	*20,862*	*56*	*53*	*3*
		0—10	10,693	5,330	5.363	34	33	1	10,659	5,297	5,362	...	...	...
		10—15	4,280	2,330	1,950	110	106	4	4,170	2,224	1,946	9	8	1
		15—20	3,074	1,439	1,635	148	138	10	2,926	1,301	1,625	5	4	1
		20 & over	23,904	11,937	11,967	1,210	1,172	38	22,694	10,765	11,929	42	41	1
	Christian.	Total ...	*720*	*375*	*345*	*88*	*55*	*33*	*632*	*320*	*312*	*52*	*34*	*18*
		0—10	196	100	96	5	4	1	191	96	95	3	2	1
		10—15	48	24	24	3	3	...	45	21	24	2	2	...
		15—20	58	21	37	10	3	7	48	18	30	2	1	1
		20 & over	418	230	188	70	45	25	348	185	163	45	29	16
	Animist.	Total ...	*1,820*	*972*	*848*	*18*	*15*	*3*	*1,802*	*957*	*845*	...	...	...
		0—10	559	274	285	2	1	1	557	273	284	...	...	...
		10—15	198	115	83	2	2	...	196	113	83	...	...	...
		15—20	111	69	42	4	4	...	107	65	42	...	...	...
		20 & over.	952	514	438	10	8	2	942	506	436	...	...	...

TABLE VIII.

EDUCATION BY RELIGION AND AGE.

Part II.
Districts.

District.	Religion and Age.	POPULATION. Total. Persons.	Total. Males.	Total. Females.	Literate. Persons.	Literate. Males.	Literate. Females.	Illiterate. Persons.	Illiterate. Males.	Illiterate. Females.	Literate in English. Persons.	Literate in English. Males.	Literate in English. Females.
	1	2	3	4	5	6	7	8	9	10	11	12	13
Mahbubnagar.	All Religions. Total ...	*747,178*	*379,712*	*367,466*	*18,575*	*17,666*	*909*	*728,603*	*362,046*	*366,557*	*195*	*150*	*45*
	0–10	201,311	99,035	102,276	392	307	91	200,913	98,728	102,185	16	6	10
	10–15	78,366	43,126	35,240	1,652	1,540	112	76,714	41,586	35,128	22	6	16
	15–20	58,479	28,378	30,101	1,767	1,645	122	56,712	26,733	29,979	12	6	6
	20 & over.	409,022	209,173	199,849	14,758	14,174	584	394,264	194,999	199,265	145	132	13
	Hindu. Total ...	*672,750*	*341,109*	*331,641*	*15.506*	*14,791*	*715*	*657,244*	*326,318*	*330,926*	*78*	*78*	...
	0–10	180,797	88,808	91,989	302	241	61	180,495	88,567	91,928	1	1	...
	10–15	70,226	38,565	31,661	1,334	1,252	82	68,892	37,313	31,579	2	2	...
	15–20	53,046	25,591	27,455	1,561	1,461	100	51,485	24,130	27,355	...	...	...
	20 & over.	368,681	188,145	180,536	12,309	11,837	472	356,372	176,308	180,064	75	75	...
	Musalman. Total ...	*59,521*	*30,353*	*29,168*	*2,846*	*2,738*	*108*	*56,675*	*27,615*	*29,060*	*28*	*28*	...
	0–10	15,624	7,696	7,928	72	58	14	15,552	7,638	7,914	...	...	...
	10–15	6.502	3,593	2,909	276	266	10	6,226	3,327	2,899	1	1	...
	15–20	4,420	2,212	2,208	179	168	11	4,241	2,044	2,197	...	...	...
	20 & over.	32,975	16,852	16,123	2,319	2,246	73	30,656	14,606	16,050	27	27	...
	Christian. Total ...	*451*	*221*	*230*	*184*	*98*	*86*	*267*	*123*	*144*	*89*	*44*	*45*
	0–10	135	56	79	24	8	16	111	48	63	15	5	10
	10–15	42	12	30	29	9	20	13	3	10	19	3	16
	15–20	36	18	18	26	15	11	10	3	7	12	6	6
	20 & over.	238	135	103	105	66	39	133	69	64	43	30	13
	Animist. Total ...	*14,392*	*7,991*	*6,401*	*33*	*33*	...	*14,359*	*7,958*	*6,401*	...	...	...
	0–10	4,739	2,466	2,273	...	...	...	4,739	2,466	2,273	...	...	...
	10–15	1,592	953	639	13	13	...	1,579	940	639	...	...	...
	15–20	974	555	419	1	1	...	973	554	419	...	...	...
	20 & over.	7,087	4,017	3,070	19	19	...	7,068	3,998	3,070	...	...	...
Nalgonda.	All Religions. Total ...	*1,044,381*	*537,139*	*507,242*	*22,306*	*21,133*	*1,173*	*1,022,075*	*516,006*	*506,069*	*221*	*201*	*20*
	0–10	305,422	150,358	155,064	515	398	117	304.907	149,960	154,947	5	2	3
	10–15	122,321	67,907	54,414	2.388	2,182	206	119,933	65,725	54,208	10	10	...
	15–20	87,956	45,104	42.852	2.566	2,392	174	85.390	42,712	42.678	18	13	5
	20 & over.	528,682	273,770	254,912	16,837	16,161	676	511,845	257,609	254,236	188	176	12
	Hindu. Total ...	*941,694*	*483,032*	*458,662*	*18,062*	*17,398*	*664*	*923,632*	*465,634*	*457,998*	*83*	*79*	*4*
	0–10	273,449	134,186	139,263	347	291	56	273,102	133,895	139,207	1	1	...
	10–15	110,166	61,192	48,974	1.895	1,817	78	108,271	59,375	48,896	7	7	...
	15–20	80,472	41,014	39,458	2,106	1,996	110	78,366	39,018	39,348	4	3	1
	20 & over.	477,607	246,640	230,967	13,714	13,294	420	463,893	233,346	230,547	71	68	3
	Musalman. Total ...	*53,872*	*27,721*	*26,151*	*3,683*	*3,369*	*314*	*50,189*	*24,352*	*25,837*	*71*	*71*	...
	0–10	15,011	7.510	7,501	117	85	32	14,894	7,425	7.469	...	...	...
	10–15	6,395	3,360	3,035	366	291	75	6,029	3,069	2,960	2	2	...
	15–20	4.279	2,269	2,010	379	347	32	3,900	1,922	1,978	6	6	...
	20 & over.	28,187	14,582	13,605	2,821	2,646	175	25,366	11,936	13,430	63	63	...
	Christian. Total ...	*10,566*	*5,565*	*5,001*	*521*	*336*	*185*	*10,045*	*5,229*	*4,816*	*63*	*49*	*14*
	0–10	3,159	1,588	1,571	50	22	28	3,109	1,566	1,543	3	1	2
	10–15	1,354	736	618	124	73	51	1,230	663	567	1	1	...
	15–20	829	416	413	79	47	32	750	369	381	8	4	4
	20 & over.	5,224	2,825	2,399	268	194	74	4,956	2,631	2,325	51	43	8
	Animist. Total ...	*38,137*	*20,760*	*17,377*	*3*	*3*	...	*38,134*	*20,757*	*17,377*	...	...	...
	0–10	13,778	7,064	6,714	...	...	...	13.778	7,064	6,714	...	...	...
	10–15	4,398	2,615	1,783	...	...	...	4,398	2,615	1,783	...	...	...
	15–20	2,369	1,401	968	...	...	...	2,369	1,401	968	...	...	...
	20 & over.	17,592	9,680	7,912	3	5	...	17,589	9,677	7,912	...	...	...

Part II.

Districts.

TABLE VIII.

EDUCATION BY RELIGION AND AGE.

District.	Religion and Age.	POPULATION. Total. Persons.	Total. Males.	Total. Females.	Literate. Persons.	Literate. Males.	Literate. Females.	Illiterate. Persons.	Illiterate. Males.	Illiterate. Females.	Literate in English. Persons.	Literate in English. Males.	Literate in English. Females.
	1	2	3	4	5	6	7	8	9	10	11	12	13
Aurangabad.	All Religions. Total ...	*869,787*	*437,495*	*432,292*	*21,577*	*19,809*	*1,768*	*848,210*	*417,686*	*430,524*	*1,033*	*926*	*107*
	0—10	240,402	118,467	121,935	683	487	196	239,719	117,980	121,739	13	8	5
	10—15	88,098	46,802	41,296	2,135	1,767	368	85,963	45,035	40,928	69	61	8
	15—20	65,316	31,546	33,770	2,338	2,021	317	62,978	29,525	33,453	135	127	8
	20 & over.	475,971	240,680	235,291	16,421	15,534	887	459,550	225,146	234,404	816	730	86
	Hindu. Total ...	*734,252*	*367,581*	*366,671*	*15,378*	*14,609*	*769*	*718,874*	*352,972*	*365,902*	*420*	*402*	*18*
	0—10	204,505	100,953	103,552	412	302	110	204,093	100,651	103,442	3	2	1
	10—15	71,993	38,590	33,403	1,439	1,250	189	70,554	37,340	33,214	22	19	3
	15—20	54,663	25,976	28,687	1,590	1,472	118	53,073	24,504	28,569	64	63	1
	20 & over.	403,091	202,062	201,029	11,937	11,585	352	391,154	190,477	200,677	331	318	13
	Musalman. Total ...	*111,449*	*57,629*	*53,820*	*4,004*	*3,405*	*599*	*107,445*	*54,224*	*53,221*	*274*	*264*	*10*
	0—10	28,798	13,967	14,831	181	125	56	28,617	13,842	14,775	5	4	1
	10—15	13,672	6,903	6,769	422	324	98	13,250	6,579	6,671	30	27	3
	15—20	8,756	4,684	4,072	501	376	125	8,255	4,308	3,947	48	47	1
	20 & over.	60,223	32,075	28,148	2,900	2,580	320	57,323	29,495	27,828	191	186	5
	Christian. Total ...	*6,369*	*3,222*	*3,147*	*813*	*525*	*288*	*5,556*	*2,697*	*2,859*	*244*	*185*	*59*
	0—10	1,891	930	961	45	26	19	1,846	904	942	5	2	3
	10—15	685	355	330	168	101	67	517	254	263	13	13	...
	15—20	524	241	283	105	52	53	419	189	230	16	12	4
	20 & over.	3,269	1,696	1,573	495	346	149	2,774	1,350	1,424	210	158	52
	Animist. Total ...	*11,794*	*5,956*	*5,838*	*36*	*28*	*8*	*11,758*	*5,928*	*5,830*	...	...	...
	0—10	3,693	1,891	1,802	1	1	...	3,692	1,890	1,802	...	...	...
	10—15	1,113	606	507	9	4	5	1,104	602	502	...	...	...
	15—20	888	394	494	8	5	3	880	389	491	...	...	...
	20 & over	6,100	3,065	3,035	18	18	...	6,082	3,047	3,035	...	...	...
Bhir.	All Religions. Total ...	*622,531*	*314,738*	*307,793*	*15,829*	*15,456*	*373*	*606,702*	*299,282*	*307,420*	*479*	*478*	*1*
	0—10	169,706	83,321	86,385	362	347	15	169,344	82,974	86,370	1	1	...
	10—15	58,212	31,977	26,235	1,508	1,473	35	56,704	30,504	26,200	9	9	...
	15—20	42,934	21,106	21,828	1,489	1,453	36	41,445	19,653	21,792	32	32	...
	20 & over	351,679	178,834	173,345	12,470	12,183	287	339,209	166,151	173,058	437	436	1
	Hindu. Total ...	*566,054*	*285,573*	*280,481*	*13,397*	*13,099*	*298*	*552,657*	*272,474*	*280,183*	*146*	*146*	...
	0—10	154,573	75,748	78,825	300	291	9	154,273	75,457	78,816	...	...	...
	10—15	52,586	28,830	23,756	1,261	1,242	19	51,325	27,588	23,737	8	8	...
	15—20	38,912	19,064	19,848	1,275	1,244	31	37,637	17,820	19,817	27	27	...
	20 & over	319,983	161,931	158,052	10,561	10,322	239	309,422	151,609	157,813	111	111	...
	Musalman. Total ...	*51,900*	*26,749*	*25,151*	*1,644*	*1,577*	*67*	*50,256*	*25,172*	*25,084*	*328*	*328*	...
	0—10	13,925	6,986	6,939	50	44	6	13,875	6,942	6,933	1	1	...
	10—15	5,079	2,839	2,240	157	142	15	4,922	2,697	2,225	1	1	...
	15—20	3,658	1,854	1,804	136	131	5	3,522	1,723	1,799	5	5	...
	20 & over	29,238	15,070	14,168	1,301	1,260	41	27,937	13,810	14,127	321	321	...
	Jain. Total ...	*3,389*	*1,820*	*1,569*	*775*	*768*	*7*	*2,614*	*1,052*	*1,562*	*2*	*2*	...
	0—10	800	394	406	12	12	...	788	382	406	...	...	...
	10—15	437	254	183	90	89	1	347	165	182	...	...	...
	15—20	280	145	135	78	78	...	202	67	135	...	...	...
	20 & over.	1,872	1,027	845	595	589	6	1,277	438	839	2	2	...
	Animist. Total ...	*835*	*407*	*428*	...	...	...	*835*	*407*	*428*	...	...	...
	0—10	290	131	159	...	...	...	290	131	159	...	...	...
	10—15	78	41	37	...	...	...	78	41	37	...	...	...
	15—20	57	25	32	...	...	...	57	25	32	...	...	...
	20 & over.	410	210	200	...	...	...	410	210	200	...	...	...

TABLE VIII.

Part II.

Districts.

EDUCATION BY RELIGION AND AGE.

District.	Religion and Age.		POPULATION. Total. Persons.	Total. Males.	Total. Females.	Literate. Persons.	Literate. Males.	Literate. Females.	Illiterate. Persons.	Illiterate. Males.	Illiterate. Females.	Literate in English. Persons.	Literate in English. Males.	Literate in English. Females.
	1		2	3	4	5	6	7	8	9	10	11	12	13
Nander.	All Religions.	Total ...	*704,549*	*352,638*	*351,911*	*14,753*	*14,352*	*401*	*689,796*	*338,286*	*351,510*	*283*	*272*	*11*
		0—10	187,125	93,323	93,802	363	334	29	186,762	92,989	93,773	3	2	1
		10—15	62,403	34,361	28,047	1,202	1,173	29	61,206	33,188	28,018	12	12	...
		15—20	44,021	20,852	23,169	1,368	1,297	71	42,653	19,555	23,098	24	21	3
		20 & over	410,995	204,102	206,893	11,820	11,548	272	399,175	192,554	206,621	244	237	7
	Hindu.	Total ...	*627,652*	*313,495*	*314,157*	*11,645*	*11,378*	*267*	*616,007*	*302,117*	*313,890*	*149*	*148*	*1*
		0—10	166,507	82,976	83,531	276	262	14	166,231	82,714	83,517	1	1	...
		10—15	55,275	30,298	24,977	964	944	20	54,311	29,354	24,957	6	6	...
		15—20	38,789	18,398	20,391	1,062	1,019	43	37,727	17,379	20,348	19	18	1
		20 & over	367,081	181,823	185,258	9,343	9,153	190	357,738	172,670	185,068	123	123	...
	Musalman.	Total ...	*72,189*	*36,708*	*35,481*	*2,716*	*2,608*	*108*	*69,473*	*34,100*	*35,373*	*79*	*77*	*2*
		0—10	19,262	9,679	9,583	69	55	14	19,193	9624	9,569	1	...	1
		10—15	6,726	3,826	2,900	210	203	7	6,516	3,623	2,893	...	...	...
		15—20	4,964	2,334	2,630	272	247	25	4,692	2,087	2,605	2	2	...
		20 & over	41,237	20,869	20,368	2,165	2,103	62	39,072	18,766	20,306	76	75	1
	Sikh.	Total ...	*1,323*	*700*	*623*	*154*	*149*	*5*	*1,169*	*551*	*618*	*5*	*5*	...
		0—10	339	174	165	11	11	...	328	163	165	...	...	...
		10—15	118	71	47	11	10	1	107	61	46	2	2	...
		15—20	79	41	38	13	13	...	66	28	38	...	...	...
		20 & over	787	414	373	119	115	4	668	299	369	3	3	...
	Animist.	Total ...	*2,336*	*1,194*	*1,142*	...	...	...	*2,336*	*1,194*	*1,142*	...	...	...
		0—10	789	384	405	...	...	...	789	384	405	...	...	...
		10—15	197	114	83	...	...	...	197	114	83	...	...	...
		15—20	122	49	73	...	...	...	122	49	73	...	...	...
		20 & over	1,228	647	581	...	...	...	1,228	647	581	...	...	...
Parbhani.	All Religions.	Total ...	*779,674*	*391,231*	*388,443*	*19,113*	*18,393*	*720*	*760,561*	*372,838*	*387,723*	*747*	*670*	*77*
		0—10	211,548	103,145	108,403	455	388	67	211,093	102,757	108,336	25	15	10
		10—15	69,181	38,007	31,174	1,617	1,538	79	67,531	36,469	31,095	43	34	9
		15—20	52,303	25,234	27,072	1,625	1,561	64	50,681	23,673	27,008	67	59	8
		20 & over	446,639	224,845	221,794	15,416	14,906	510	431,223	209,939	221,284	612	562	50
	Hindu.	Total ...	*699,675*	*350,575*	*349,100*	*15,671*	*15,160*	*511*	*684,004*	*335,415*	*348,589*	*414*	*406*	*8*
		0—10	190,131	92,692	97,439	353	312	41	189,778	92,380	97,398	2	2	...
		10—15	61,934	34,026	27,908	1,328	1,275	53	60,606	32,751	27,855	25	24	1
		15—20	46,656	22,455	24,201	1,338	1,292	46	45,318	21,163	24,155	42	40	2
		20 & over	400,954	201,402	199,552	12,652	12,281	371	388,302	189,121	199,181	345	340	5
	Musalman.	Total ...	*72,474*	*36,789*	*35,685*	*2,608*	*2,489*	*119*	*69,866*	*34,300*	*35,566*	*113*	*108*	*5*
		0—10	19,338	9,483	9,855	67	55	12	19,271	9,428	9,843	2	2	...
		10—15	6,575	3,627	2,948	222	205	17	6,353	3,422	2,931	4	3	1
		15—20	5,139	2,530	2,609	219	208	11	4,920	2,322	2,598	7	7	...
		20 & over	41,422	21,149	20,273	2,100	2,021	79	39,322	19,128	20,194	100	96	4
	Jain.	Total ...	*3,665*	*1,842*	*1,823*	*532*	*519*	*13*	*3,133*	*1,323*	*1,810*	*5*	*2*	*3*
		0—10	837	387	450	13	10	3	824	377	447	1	1	...
		10—15	315	166	149	50	49	1	265	117	148	1	1	...
		15—20	271	119	152	41	41	...	230	78	152	...	...	...
		20 & over	2,242	1,170	1,072	428	419	9	1,814	751	1,063	3	...	3
	Animist.	Total ...	*3,143*	*1,627*	*1,516*	...	...	...	*3,143*	*1,627*	*1,516*	...	...	...
		0—10	1,061	514	547	...	...	...	1,061	514	547	...	...	...
		10—15	296	163	133	...	...	...	296	163	133	...	...	...
		15—20	193	102	91	...	...	...	193	102	91	...	...	...
		20 & over	1,593	848	745	...	...	...	1,593	848	745	...	...	...

Part II.

Districts.

TABLE VIII.

EDUCATION BY RELIGION AND AGE.

District.	Religion and Age.	POPULATION. Total. Persons.	Total. Males.	Total. Females.	Literate. Persons.	Literate. Males.	Literate. Females.	Illiterate. Persons.	Illiterate. Males.	Illiterate. Females.	Literate in English. Persons.	Literate in English. Males.	Literate in English. Females.
	1	2	3	4	5	6	7	8	9	10	11	12	13
Gulbarga.	All Religions. Total ...	*1,150,983*	*582,447*	*568,536*	*28,230*	*27,372*	*858*	*1,122,753*	*555,075*	*567,678*	*917*	*830*	*87*
	0—10	294,692	145,589	149,103	717	659	58	293,975	144,930	149,045	20	17	3
	10—15	120,523	65,774	54,749	2,832	2,724	108	117,691	63,050	54,641	86	78	8
	15—20	88,348	44,332	44,016	2,938	2,795	143	85,410	41,537	43,873	133	121	12
	20 & over.	647,420	326,752	320,668	21,743	21,194	549	625,677	305,558	320,119	678	614	64
	Hindu. Total ...	*970,405*	*490,220*	*480,185*	*22,707*	*22,232*	*475*	*947,698*	*467,988*	*479,710*	*482*	*468*	*14*
	0—10	248,002	122,397	125,605	551	521	30	247,451	121,876	125,575	6	6	...
	10—15	100,934	54,967	45,967	2,210	2,154	56	98,724	52,813	45,911	46	44	2
	15—20	74,524	37,237	37,287	2,328	2,249	79	72,196	34,988	37,208	76	71	5
	20 & over.	546,945	275,619	271,326	17,618	17,308	310	529,327	258,311	271,016	354	347	7
	Musalman. Total ...	*169,326*	*86,152*	*83,174*	*4,849*	*4,565*	*284*	*164,477*	*81,587*	*82,890*	*248*	*231*	*17*
	0—10	43,340	21,544	21,796	133	115	18	43,207	21,429	21,778	8	6	2
	10—15	18,510	10,176	8,334	579	529	50	17,931	9,647	8,284	32	28	4
	15—20	12,980	6,645	6,335	537	486	51	12,443	6,159	6,284	43	41	2
	20 & over.	94,496	47,787	46,709	3,600	3,435	165	90,896	44,352	46,544	165	156	9
	Christian. Total ...	*1,044*	*633*	*411*	*205*	*146*	*59*	*839*	*487*	*352*	*132*	*87*	*45*
	0—10	257	150	107	13	10	3	244	140	104	6	5	1
	10—15	82	59	23	11	10	1	71	49	22	4	3	1
	15—20	107	50	57	20	12	8	87	38	49	9	4	5
	20 & over.	598	374	224	161	114	47	437	260	177	113	75	38
	Animist. Total ...	*8,442*	*4,469*	*3,973*	...	...	...	*8,442*	*4,469*	*3,973*	...	...	...
	0—10	2,754	1,331	1,423	...	...	...	2,754	1,331	1,423	...	...	...
	10—15	843	487	356	...	...	...	843	487	356	...	...	...
	15—20	574	310	264	...	...	...	574	310	264	...	...	...
	20 & over	4,271	2,341	1,930	...	...	...	4,271	2,341	1,930	...	...	...
Osmanabad.	All Religions. Total ...	*635,977*	*324,969*	*311,008*	*16,683*	*16,092*	*591*	*619,294*	*308,877*	*310,417*	*200*	*194*	*6*
	0—10	167,575	82,886	84,689	433	393	40	167,142	82,493	84,649	2	2	...
	10—15	64,339	35,496	28,843	1,471	1,397	74	62,868	34,099	28,769	16	15	1
	15—20	46,334	23,196	23,138	1,606	1,531	75	44,728	21,665	23,963	15	14	1
	20 & over.	357,729	183,391	174,338	13,173	12,771	402	344,556	170,620	173,936	167	163	4
	Hindu. Total ...	*572,433*	*292,192*	*280,241*	*14,219*	*13,755*	*464*	*558,214*	*278,437*	*279,777*	*135*	*135*	...
	0—10	151,049	74,700	76,349	372	339	33	150,677	74,361	76,316	1	1	...
	10—15	57,698	31,778	25,920	1,244	1,187	57	56,454	30,591	25,863	8	8	...
	15—20	41,597	20,769	20,828	1,374	1,316	58	40,223	19,453	20,770	12	12	...
	20 & over.	322,089	164,945	157,144	11,229	10,913	316	310,860	154,032	156,828	114	114	...
	Musalman. Total ...	*59,448*	*30,602*	*28,846*	*1,686*	*1,599*	*87*	*57,762*	*29,003*	*28,759*	*34*	*34*	...
	0—10	15,475	7,653	7,822	42	39	3	15,433	7,614	7,819	1	1	...
	10—15	6,199	3,465	2,734	147	135	12	6,052	3,330	2,722	4	4	...
	15—20	4,453	2,284	2,169	165	150	15	4,288	2,134	2,154	...	...	...
	20 & over.	33,321	17,200	16,121	1,332	1,275	57	31,989	15,925	16,064	29	29	...
	Christian. Total ...	*252*	*130*	*122*	*21*	*18*	*3*	*231*	*112*	*119*	*12*	*9*	[illegible]
	0—10	76	38	38	...	...	...	76	38	38	...	...	...
	10—15	17	12	5	1	1	...	16	11	5	1	1	...
	15—20	15	1	14	1	...	1	14	1	13	1	...	1
	20 & over.	144	79	65	19	17	2	125	62	63	10	8	2
	Jain. Total ...	*3,429*	*1,817*	*1,612*	*721*	*687*	*34*	*2,708*	*1,130*	*1,578*	*6*	*6*	...
	0—10	828	416	412	19	15	4	809	401	408	...	...	...
	10—15	381	216	165	78	74	4	303	142	161	2	2	...
	15—20	247	131	116	65	64	1	182	67	115	2	2	...
	20 & over.	1,973	1,054	919	559	534	25	1,414	520	894	2	2	...

TABLE VIII.

Part II. District.

EDUCATION BY RELIGION AND AGE.

District.	Religion and Age.	Population. Total. Persons.	Total. Males.	Total. Females.	Literate. Persons.	Literate. Males.	Literate. Females.	Illiterate. Persons.	Illiterate. Males.	Illiterate. Females.	Literate in English. Persons.	Literate in English. Males.	Literate in English. Females.
	1	2	3	4	5	6	7	8	9	10	11	12	13
Raichur.	All Religions. Total ...	*996,684*	*503,541*	*493,143*	*20,225*	*18,945*	*1,280*	*976,459*	*484,896*	*491,863*	*612*	*503*	*109*
	0—10	255,232	125,237	129,995	576	459	117	254,656	124,778	129,878	26	20	6
	10—15	116,590	61,364	55,226	1,632	1,436	196	114,958	59,928	55,030	49	39	10
	15—20	80,333	40,764	39,599	2,216	2,002	214	78,147	38,762	39,385	70	50	20
	20 & over.	544,499	276,176	268,323	15,801	15,048	753	528,698	261,128	267,570	467	394	73
	Hindu. Total ...	*900,417*	*453,629*	*446,788*	*15,840*	*14,952*	*888*	*884,577*	*438,677*	*445,900*	*320*	*297*	*23*
	0—10	231,576	113,184	118,392	419	326	93	231,157	112,858	118,299	9	6	3
	10—15	105,338	55,392	49,946	1,374	1,228	146	103,964	54,164	49,800	23	22	1
	15—20	72,880	36,897	35,983	1,703	1,547	156	71,177	35,350	35,827	42	36	6
	20 & over.	490,623	248,156	242,467	12,344	11,851	493	478,279	236,305	241,974	246	233	13
	Musalman. Total ..	*93,478*	*48,402*	*45,076*	*3,901*	*3,643*	*258*	*89,577*	*44,759*	*44,818*	*77*	*73*	*4*
	0—10	22,910	11,668	11,242	121	104	17	22,789	11,564	11,225	1	1	...
	10—15	10,954	5,827	5,127	212	180	32	10,742	5,647	5,095	5	5	...
	15—20	7,273	3,773	3,500	470	440	30	6,803	3,333	3,470	8	8	...
	20 & over	52,341	27,134	25,207	3,098	2,919	179	49,243	24,215	25,028	63	59	4
	Christian. Total ...	*1,711*	*920*	*791*	*296*	*183*	*113*	*1,415*	*737*	*678*	*201*	*126*	*75*
	0—10	472	241	231	22	17	5	450	224	226	16	13	3
	10—15	188	88	100	28	13	15	160	75	85	20	12	8
	15—20	127	52	75	30	7	23	97	45	52	18	6	12
	20 & over.	924	539	385	216	146	70	708	393	315	147	95	52
	Jain. Total ...	*707*	*393*	*314*	*147*	*142*	*5*	*560*	*251*	*309*	...	...	...
	0—10	169	97	72	8	7	1	161	90	71	...	...	...
	10—15	80	48	32	15	14	1	65	34	31	...	...	...
	15—20	43	23	20	8	6	2	35	17	18	...	...	...
	20 & over.	415	225	190	116	115	1	299	110	189	...	...	...
Bidar	All Religions. Total ...	*889,527*	*449,438*	*440,089*	*18,572*	*17,930*	*642*	*870,955*	*431,508*	*439,447*	*173*	*161*	*12*
	0—10	229,151	112,987	116,164	354	304	50	228,797	112,683	116,114	2	2	...
	10—15	88,184	47,846	40,338	1,573	1,494	79	86,611	46,352	40,259	13	13	...
	15—20	61,235	30,687	30,598	1,867	1,786	81	59,418	28,901	30,517	34	30	4
	20 & over.	510,907	257,918	252,989	14,778	14,346	432	496,129	243,572	252,557	124	116	8
	Hindu. Total ...	*761,731*	*384,795*	*376,936*	*15,171*	*14,735*	*436*	*746,560*	*370,060*	*376,500*	*80*	*76*	*4*
	0—10	191,640	96,127	95,513	261	224	37	191,379	95,903	95,476	2	2	...
	10—15	75,037	40,632	34,405	1,268	1,216	52	73,769	39,416	34,353	7	7	...
	15—20	52,160	26,043	26,117	1,549	1,496	53	50,611	24,547	26,064	9	8	1
	20 & over.	439,894	221,993	217,901	12,093	11,799	294	427,801	210,194	217,607	62	59	3
	Musalman. Total ...	*124,790*	*63,142*	*61,648*	*3,205*	*3,016*	*189*	*121,585*	*60,126*	*61,459*	*74*	*72*	*2*
	0—10	33,689	16,490	17,199	82	69	13	33,607	16,421	17,186	...	...	...
	10—15	12,875	7,044	5,831	288	262	26	12,587	6,782	5,805	6	6	...
	15—20	8,920	4,552	4,368	303	279	24	8,617	4,273	4,344	22	22	...
	20 & over	69,306	35,056	34,250	2,532	2,406	126	66,774	32,650	34,124	46	44	2
	Jain. Total ...	*930*	*455*	*475*	*140*	*135*	*5*	*790*	*320*	*470*	...	..	...
	0—10	205	84	121	3	3	...	202	81	121	...	...	...
	10—15	90	56	34	11	11	...	79	45	34	...	...	...
	15—20	60	28	32	9	9	...	51	19	32	...	...	...
	20 & over.	575	287	288	117	112	5	458	175	283	...	...	...
	Animist. Total ...	*1,542*	*759*	*783*	...	...	...	*1,542*	*759*	*783*	...	...	...
	0—10	479	215	264	...	...	...	479	215	264	...	...	...
	10—15	131	78	53	...	...	...	131	78	53	...	...	...
	15—20	105	50	55	...	...	...	105	50	55	...	...	...
	20 & over.	827	416	411	...	...	...	827	416	411	...	...	...

Part III.

Cities.

TABLE VIII.

EDUCATION BY RELIGION AND AGE.

Hyderabad City.

Religion and Age.	POPULATION.											
	Total.			Literate.			Illiterate.			Literate in English.		
	Persons.	Males.	Females.	Persons.	Males.	Females.	Persons.	Males.	Females.	Persons.	Males.	Females.
1	2	3	4	5	6	7	8	9	10	11	12	13
All Religions. Total ...	***500,623***	***258,454***	***242,169***	***72,380***	***61,830***	***10,550***	***428,243***	***196,624***	***231,619***	***18,997***	***16,334***	***2,663***
0–10	**103,930**	50,973	52,957	**2,207**	1,504	703	**101,723**	49,469	52,254	**567**	337	230
10–15	**50,101**	26,715	23,386	**6,545**	4,974	1,571	**43,558**	21,741	21,815	**1,753**	1,376	377
15–20	**44,170**	21,417	22,753	**8,299**	6,606	1,693	**35,871**	14,811	21,060	**2,448**	2,061	387
20 & over.	**302,422**	159,349	143,073	**55,329**	48,746	6,583	**247,093**	110,603	136,490	**14,229**	12,560	1,669
Hindu. Total ...	***262,131***	***135,638***	***126,493***	***28,028***	***25,591***	***2,437***	***234,103***	***110,047***	***124,056***	***5,544***	***5,323***	***221***
0–10	**55,861**	27,545	28,316	**793**	606	187	**55,068**	26,939	28,129	**121**	100	21
10–15	**24,636**	13,643	10,993	**2,522**	2,085	437	**22,114**	11,558	10,556	**607**	557	50
15–20	**22,325**	10,988	11,337	**3,190**	2,801	389	**19,135**	8,187	10,948	**779**	741	38
20 & over.	**159,309**	83,462	75,847	**21,523**	20,099	1,424	**137,786**	63,363	74,423	**4,037**	3,925	112
Musalman. Total ...	***219,896***	***111,770***	***108,126***	***34,275***	***28,945***	***5,330***	***185,621***	***82,825***	***102,796***	***5,023***	***4,757***	***266***
0–10	**44,153**	21,531	22,622	**939**	643	296	**43,214**	20,888	22,326	**117**	82	35
10–15	**23,741**	12,237	11,504	**3,204**	2,442	762	**20,537**	9,795	10,742	**558**	508	50
15–20	**20,306**	9,649	10,657	**4,223**	3,305	918	**16,083**	6,344	9,739	**964**	912	52
20 & over.	**131,696**	68,353	63,343	**25,909**	22,555	3,354	**105,787**	45,798	59,989	**3,384**	3,255	129
Christian. Total ...	***16,240***	***9,623***	***6,617***	***8,936***	***6,465***	***2,471***	***7,304***	***3,158***	***4,146***	***7,909***	***5,876***	***2,033***
0–10	**3,529**	1,724	1,805	**430**	232	198	**3,099**	1,492	1,607	**310**	147	163
10–15	**1,543**	729	814	**715**	389	326	**828**	340	488	**534**	282	252
15–20	**1,339**	657	682	**785**	429	356	**554**	228	326	**654**	373	281
20 & over.	**9,829**	6,513	3,316	**7,006**	5,415	1,591	**2,823**	1,098	1,725	**6,411**	5,074	1,337
Parsi. Total ...	***808***	***443***	***365***	***663***	***399***	***264***	***145***	***44***	***101***	***454***	***322***	***132***
0–10	**109**	40	69	**40**	21	19	**69**	19	50	**18**	8	10
10–15	**86**	41	45	**70**	31	39	**16**	10	6	**46**	23	23
15–20	**61**	31	30	**52**	29	23	**9**	2	7	**41**	26	15
20 & over	**552**	331	221	**501**	318	183	**51**	13	38	**349**	265	84
Sikh. Total ...	***978***	***644***	***334***	***237***	***226***	***11***	***741***	***418***	***323***	***11***	***11***	...
0–10	**158**	81	77	**2**	1	1	**156**	80	76	...	...	...
10–15	**53**	37	16	**8**	8	...	**45**	29	16	...	...	...
15–20	**79**	58	21	**17**	17	...	**62**	41	21	**1**	1	...
20 & over.	**688**	468	220	**210**	200	10	**478**	268	210	**10**	10	...

TABLE IX.

EDUCATION BY SELECTED CASTES, TRIBES OR RACES.

This table repeats the information given in Table viii in respect of education, with this difference that, whereas in that Table the population is distributed by age and religion, it is here arranged according to caste and tribe. Moreover, in Table viii the whole population is dealt with, but this table refers only to more important castes and tribes selected for the purpose, the minor castes and tribes having been left out of account altogether.

TABLE IX.

EDUCATION BY SELECTED CASTES, TRIBES OR RACES.

Caste, Tribe or Race and Locality.	POPULATION.									LITERATE IN ENGLISH.		
	TOTAL.			LITERATE.			ILLITERATE.					
	Persons.	Males.	Females.	Persons.	Males.	Females.	Persons.	Males.	Females.	Persons.	Males.	Females.
1	2	3	4	5	6	7	8	9	10	11	12	13
HINDU.												
Bhoi.												
State ...	*177,004*	*89,369*	*87,635*	*479*	*454*	*25*	*176,525*	*88,915*	*87,610*	*8*	*8*	..
Telingana ...	124,509	62,894	61,705	353	332	21	124,156	62,472	61,684	6	6	...
City ..	7,565	4,041	3,524	149	145	4	7,416	3,526	3,890	4	4	...
Districts ..	116,944	58,763	58,181	204	187	17	116,740	58,576	58,164	2	2	...
Marathwara ...	52,495	26,565	25,930	126	122	4	52,369	26,443	25,926	2	2	...
Brahman.												
State ..	*261,241*	*133,192*	*128,049*	*68,325*	*65,069*	*3,256*	*192,916*	*68,123*	*124,793*	*3,026*	*2,947*	*79*
Telingana ..	98,014	50,412	47,602	26,127	24,602	1,525	71,887	25,810	46,077	1,921	1,876	[illegible]
City ..	25,819	13,950	11,869	6,151	5,849	302	19,668	8,101	11,567	1,560	1,529	[illegible]
Districts ..	72,195	36,462	35,733	19,976	18,753	1,223	52,219	17,709	34,510	361	347	[illegible]
Marathwara ..	163,227	82,780	80,447	42,198	40,467	1,731	121,029	42,313	78,716	1,105	1,071	34
Chakala.												
State ..	*175,626*	*89,791*	*85,835*	*280*	*276*	*4*	*175,346*	*89,515*	*85,831*	*7*	*7*	...
Telingana ..	173,424	88,655	84,769	233	232	1	173,191	88,423	84,768	7	7	..
City ...	4,379	2,216	2,163	48	47	1	4,331	2,149	2,162	7	7	...
Districts ..	169,045	86,439	82,606	185	185	...	168,860	86,274	82,606	...	...	...
Chambhar.												
State ..	*70,618*	*35,993*	*34,625*	*64*	*61*	*3*	*70,554*	*35,932*	*34,622*	*1*	*1*	...
Marathwara ...	59,437	30,078	29,359	56	54	2	59,381	30,024	29,357	1	1	...
Dewang or Koshti.												
State ..	*71,400*	*36,257*	*35,143*	*1,799*	*1,756*	*43*	*69,601*	*34,501*	*35,100*	*2*	*2*	...
Telingana ...	21,796	11,276	10,520	194	183	11	21,602	11,093	10,509	...	...	...
Marathwara ...	49,604	24,981	24,623	1,605	1,573	32	47,999	23,408	24,591	2	2	...
Dhangar.												
State ...	*488,609*	*245,387*	*243,222*	*1,472*	*1,437*	*35*	*487,137*	*243,950*	*243,187*	*16*	*14*	*2*
Telingana ...	41,641	21,268	20,373	288	280	8	41,353	20,988	20,365	3	1	2
City ..	8,349	4,155	4,194	104	101	3	8,245	4,054	4,191	1	1	..
Districts ..	33,292	17,113	16,179	184	179	5	33,108	16,934	16,174	2	...	2
Marathwara ...	446,968	224,119	222,849	1,184	1,157	27	445,784	222,962	222,822	13	13	...
Dhobi.												
State ..	*66,598*	*33,600*	*32,998*	*200*	*197*	*3*	*66,398*	*33,403*	*32,995*	*1*	*1*	...
Marathwara ..	54,231	27,444	26,787	188	187	1	54,043	27,257	26,786	...	...	...
Golla.												
State ..	*460,760*	*234,629*	*226,131*	*2,124*	*2,037*	*87*	*458,636*	*232,592*	*226,044*	*222*	*207*	*15*
Telingana ..	420,971	214,643	206,328	1,796	1,721	75	419,175	212,922	206,253	211	196	[illegible]
City ...	3,647	1,866	1,781	[illegible]	444	48	3,155	1,422	1,733	193	179	14
Districts ..	417,324	212,777	204,547	1,304	1,277	27	416,020	211,500	204,520	18	17	1
Marathwara ..	39,789	19,986	19,803	328	316	12	39,461	19,670	19,791	11	11	...

TABLE IX.

EDUCATION BY SELECTED CASTES, TRIBES OR RACES.

Caste, Tribe or Race and Locality.	POPULATION.									LITERATE IN ENGLISH.		
	Total.			Literate.			Illiterate.					
	Persons.	Males.	Females.	Persons.	Males.	Females.	Persons.	Males.	Females.	Persons.	Males.	Females.
1	2	3	4	5	6	7	8	9	10	11	12	13
HINDU—(contd).												
Goundla												
State ...	*306,071*	*156,381*	*149,690*	*2,521*	*2,453*	*68*	*303,550*	*153,928*	*149,622*	*9*	*9*	...
Telingana ..	302,677	154,630	148,047	2,521	2,453	68	300,156	152,177	147,979	9	9	...
Hatkar.												
State ...	*67,934*	*34,727*	*33,207*	*806*	*786*	*20*	*67,128*	*33,941*	*33,187*	*45*	*45*	...
Marathwara ...	61,116	31,179	29,937	695	681	14	60,421	30,498	29,923	45	45	...
Kalal.												
State ...	*75,339*	*38,366*	*36,973*	*1,272*	*1,238*	*34*	*74,067*	*37,128*	*36,939*	*43*	*43*	...
Telingana ...	38,640	19,788	18,852	543	537	6	38,097	19,251	18,846	5	5	...
City ..	3,956	2,130	1,826	172	172	...	3,784	1,958	1,826	3	3	...
Districts ..	34,684	17,658	17,026	371	365	6	34,313	17,293	17,020	2	2	...
Marathwara ...	36,699	18,578	18,121	729	701	28	35,970	17,877	18,093	38	38	...
Kapu.												
State ...	*648,254*	*330,902*	*317,352*	*16,273*	*15,882*	*391*	*631,981*	*315,020*	*316,961*	*322*	*318*	*4*
Telingana ...	611,446	312,438	299,008	15,553	15,190	363	595,893	297,248	298,645	318	314	4
City ..	13,269	6,617	6,652	1,121	1,060	61	12,148	5,557	6,591	180	177	3
Districts ...	598,177	305,821	292,356	14,432	14,130	302	583,745	291,691	292,054	138	137	1
Marathwara ...	36,808	18,464	18,344	720	692	28	36,088	17,772	18,316	4	4	...
Koli.												
State ...	*266,840*	*134,432*	*132,408*	*1,424*	*1,397*	*27*	*265,416*	*133,035*	*132,381*	*11*	*11*	...
Telingana ...	18,590	9,737	8,853	205	201	4	18,385	9,536	8,849	8	8	...
Marathwara ...	248,250	124,695	123,555	1,219	1,196	23	247,031	123,499	123,532	3	3	...
Komati.												
State ..	*223,380*	*114,121*	*109,259*	*39,303*	*37,944*	*1,359*	*184,077*	*76,177*	*107,900*	*292*	*279*	*13*
Telingana ...	182,739	93,663	89,076	32,547	31,416	1,131	150,192	62,247	87,945	239	226	13
City ..	5,526	3,000	2,526	2,148	1,709	439	3,378	1,291	2,087	102	93	9
Districts ..	177,213	90,663	86,550	30,399	29,707	692	146,814	60,956	85,858	137	133	4
Marathwara ...	40,641	20,458	20,183	6,756	6,528	228	33,885	13,930	19,955	53	53	...
Kummara, Kumbhar.												
State ...	*151,986*	*77,980*	*74,006*	*604*	*574*	*30*	*151,382*	*77,406*	*73,976*	*45*	*45*	...
Telingana ...	84,962	43,660	41,302	270	254	16	84,692	43,406	41,286	41	41	...
City ..	1,847	900	947	94	80	14	1,753	820	933	41	41	...
Districts .	83,115	42,760	40,355	176	174	2	82,939	42,586	40,353	...	..	...
Marathwara ...	67,024	34,320	32,704	334	320	14	66,690	34,000	32,690	4	4	...
Kurma.												
State ...	*144,688*	*75,144*	*69,544*	*1,034*	*1,018*	*16*	*143,654*	*74,126*	*69,528*	*95*	*95*	...
Telingana ...	141,793	73,675	68,118	1,033	1,017	16	140,760	72,658	68,102	95	95	...
City ..	1,836	934	902	342	330	12	1,494	604	890	93	93	...
Districts ...	139,957	72,741	67,216	691	687	4	139,266	72,054	67,212	2	2	...

TABLE IX.

EDUCATION BY SELECTED CASTES, TRIBES OR RACES.

Caste, Tribe or Race and Locality.	POPULATION.									LITERATE IN ENGLISH.		
	TOTAL.			LITERATE.			ILLITERATE.					
	Persons.	Males.	Females.	Persons.	Males.	Females.	Persons.	Males.	Females.	Persons.	Males.	Females.
1	2	3	4	5	6	7	8	9	10	11	12	13
					HINDU—(*contd*).							
Lingayat.												
State ...	*757,611*	*381,201*	*376,410*	*32,102*	*31,331*	*771*	*725,509*	*349,870*	*375,639*	*189*	*185*	*4*
Telingana ...	80,914	41,034	39,880	6,274	5,989	285	74,640	35,045	39,595	94	93	1
City ...	1,964	1,010	954	330	277	53	1,634	733	901	65	65	...
Districts ...	78,950	40,024	38,926	5,944	5,712	232	78,006	34,312	38,694	29	28	1
Marathwara ...	676,697	340,167	336,530	25,828	25,342	486	650,869	314,825	336,044	95	92	3
Lohar.												
State ...	*47,844*	*24,828*	*23,016*	*724*	*711*	*13*	*47,120*	*24,117*	*23,003*	*1*	*1*	...
Telingana ...	23,498	12,376	11,122	474	469	5	23,024	11,907	11,117	...	...	...
Marathwara ...	24,346	12,452	11,894	250	242	8	24,096	12,210	11,886	1	1	...
Madiga, Mang.												
State ...	*1,145,352*	*581,519*	*563,833*	*801*	*738*	*63*	*1,144,551*	*580,781*	*563,770*	*48*	*45*	*3*
Telingana ...	754,219	385,407	368,812	486	441	45	753,733	384,966	368,767	39	36	3
City ...	6,975	3,468	3,507	125	123	2	6,850	3,345	3,505	20	18	2
Districts ...	747,244	381,939	365,305	361	318	43	746,883	381,621	365,262	19	18	1
Marathwara ...	391,133	196,112	195,021	315	297	18	390,818	195,815	195,003	9	9	...
Mahar, Mala.												
State ...	*1,137,589*	*574,385*	*563,204*	*3,984*	*3,693*	*291*	*1,133,605*	*570,692*	*562,913*	*1,204*	*1,160*	*44*
Telingana ..	505,850	256,455	249,395	3,090	2,854	236	502,760	253,601	249,159	1,081	1,041	40
City ...	57,755	28,933	28,822	2,470	2,283	187	55,285	26,650	28,635	1,045	1,011	34
Districts ...	448,095	227,522	220,573	620	571	49	447,475	226,951	220,524	36	30	6
Marathwara ...	631,739	317,930	313,809	894	839	55	630,845	317,091	313,754	123	119	4
Mali.												
State ..	*107,097*	*54,230*	*52,867*	*498*	*478*	*20*	*106,599*	*53,752*	*52,847*	...	...	...
Marathwara ...	101,946	51,556	50,390	464	451	13	101,482	51,105	50,377	...	...	...
Mangala.												
State ...	*76,514*	*39,754*	*36,760*	*563*	*551*	*12*	*75,951*	*39,203*	*36,748*	*25*	*24*	
Telingana ...	71,042	36,954	34,088	493	484	9	70,549	36,470	34,079	24	24	...
City ...	5,937	3,447	2,492	182	175	7	5,755	3,270	2,485	23	23	
Districts ..	65,105	33,509	31,596	311	309	2	64,794	33,200	31,594	1	1	
Maratha.												
State ..	*1,538,874*	*772,878*	*765,996*	*18,119*	*17,448*	*671*	*1,520,755*	*755,430*	*765,325*	*410*	*388*	*22*
Telingana ...	143,028	72,601	70,427	3,576	3,417	159	139,452	69,184	70,268	228	211	17
City ...	6,296	3,200	3,096	1,249	1,183	66	5,047	2,017	3,030	181	176	
Districts ...	136,732	69,401	67,331	2,327	2,234	93	134,405	67,167	67,238	47	35	12
Marathwara ...	1,395,846	700,277	695,569	14,543	14,031	512	1,381,303	686,246	695,057	182	177	5

TABLE IX.

EDUCATION BY SELECTED CASTES, TRIBES OR RACES.

Caste, Tribe or Race and Locality.	POPULATION.									LITERATE IN ENGLISH.		
	TOTAL.			LITERATE.			ILLITERATE.					
	Persons.	Males.	Females.	Persons.	Males.	Females.	Persons.	Males.	Females.	Persons.	Males.	Females.
1	2	3	4	5	6	7	8	9	10	11	12	13
HINDU—(*contd.*)												
Munnur.												
State ...	228,354	115,120	113,234	3,621	3,516	105	224,733	111,604	113,129	120	117	3
Telingana ...	183,605	94,152	92,453	3,331	3,234	97	183,274	90,918	92,356	119	116	3
City ...	12,814	6,262	6,552	1,041	1,019	25	11,800	5,243	6,557	102	99	3
Districts ...	173,761	87,890	85,871	2,287	2,215	72	171,474	85,675	85,799	17	17	...
Marathwara ...	41,749	20,968	20,781	290	282	8	41,459	20,686	20,773	1	1	...
Mutrasi.												
State ...	260,770	134,473	126,297	3,008	2,938	70	257,762	131,535	126,227	71	71	...
Telingana ...	256,561	132,293	124,268	2,956	2,889	67	253,605	129,404	124,201	71	71	...
City ...	10,196	5,105	5,091	893	876	17	9,303	4,229	5,074	57	57	...
Districts ...	246,365	127,188	119,177	2,063	2,013	50	244,302	125,175	119,127	14	14	...
Nahvi, (Warik).												
State ...	58,974	30,019	28,955	271	262	9	58,703	29,757	28,946	4	4	...
Marathwara ...	53,036	27,001	26,035	261	252	9	52,775	26,749	26,026	4	4	...
Panchal.												
State ...	117,710	59,990	57,720	4,606	4,528	78	113,104	55,462	57,642	18	17	1
Telingana ...	87,919	44,972	42,947	3,867	3,804	63	84,052	41,168	42,884	9	9	...
City ...	2,844	1,487	1,357	276	260	16	2,568	1,227	1,341	8	8	...
Districts ...	85,075	43,485	41,590	3,591	3,544	47	81,484	39,941	41,543	1	1	...
Marathwara ...	29,791	15,018	14,773	739	724	15	29,052	14,294	14,758	9	8	1
Rajput.												
State ...	61,637	31,296	30,341	4,494	4,087	407	57,143	27,209	29,934	351	324	27
Telingana ...	21,584	11,101	10,483	2,520	2,244	276	19,064	8,857	10,207	287	264	23
City ...	7,012	3,606	3,406	1,364	1,149	215	5,648	2,457	3,191	253	233	20
Districts ...	14,572	7,495	7,077	1,156	1,095	61	13,416	6,400	7,016	34	31	3
Marathwara ...	40,053	20,195	19,858	1,974	1,843	131	38,079	18,352	19,727	64	60	4
Sale.												
State ...	343,130	175,968	167,162	4,562	4,479	83	338,568	171,489	167,079	33	30	3
Telingana ...	295,999	151,897	144,102	3,867	3,805	62	292,132	148,092	144,040	31	28	3
City ...	5,283	2,778	2,505	490	470	20	4,793	2,308	2,485	24	23	1
Districts ...	290,716	149,119	141,597	3,377	3,335	42	287,339	145,784	141,555	7	5	2
Marathwara ...	47,131	24,071	23,060	695	674	21	46,436	23,397	23,039	2	2	...
Satani.												
State ...	27,883	14,589	13,294	3,210	3,079	131	24,673	11,510	13,163	54	53	1
Telingana ...	24,607	12,867	11,740	3,092	2,963	129	21,515	9,904	11,611	52	51	1
Sunar.												
State ...	88,037	45,278	42,759	5,795	5,667	128	82,242	39,611	42,631	32	31	1
Telingana ...	46,937	24,439	22,498	3,651	3,590	61	43,286	20,849	22,437	13	13	...
City ...	3,348	1,659	1,689	331	326	5	3,017	1,333	1,684	11	11	...
Districts ...	43,589	22,780	20,809	3,320	3,264	56	40,269	19,516	20,753	2	2	...
Marathwara ...	41,100	20,839	20,261	2,144	2,077	67	38,956	18,762	20,194	19	18	1

TABLE IX

EDUCATION BY SELECTED CASTES, TRIBES OR RACES.

Caste, Tribe or Race and Locality.	POPULATION.									LITERATE IN ENGLISH.		
	Total.			Literate.			Illiterate.					
	Persons.	Males.	Females.	Persons.	Males.	Females.	Persons.	Males.	Females.	Persons.	Males.	Females.
1	2	3	4	5	6	7	8	9	10	11	12	13
HINDU—(*concluded.*)												
Sutar.												
State ...	*69,205*	*35,118*	*34,087*	*1,110*	*1,075*	*35*	*68,095*	*34,043*	*34,052*	*10*	*10*	...
Telingana ...	23,038	11,694	11,344	451	438	13	22,587	11,256	11,331	...	...	...
Marathwara ...	46,167	23,424	22,743	659	637	22	45,508	22,787	22,721	10	10	...
Telaga.												
State ...	*458,622*	*233,206*	*225,416*	*5,989*	*5,555*	*434*	*452,633*	*227,651*	*224,982*	*641*	*598*	[illegible]
Telingana ...	413,061	209,666	203,395	5,497	5,095	402	407,564	204,571	202,993	564	524	[illegible]
City ...	12,363	6,213	6,150	1,482	1,193	289	10,881	5,020	5,861	460	424	[illegible]
Districts ...	400,698	203,453	197,245	4,015	3,902	113	396,683	199,551	197,132	104	100	[illegible]
Marathwara ...	45,561	23,540	22,021	492	460	32	45,069	23,080	21,989	77	74	3
Teli.												
State ...	*56,944*	*28,620*	*28,324*	*1,248*	*1,227*	*21*	*55,696*	*27,393*	*28,303*	*5*	*5*	...
Marathwara ...	49,360	24,822	24,538	1,125	1,104	21	48,235	23,718	24,517	3	3	...
Uppara.												
State ...	*57,000*	*29,098*	*27,902*	*497*	*477*	*20*	*56,503*	*28,621*	*27,882*	*1*	*1*	...
Telingana ...	21,161	11,166	9,995	223	221	2	20,938	10,945	9,993	1	1	...
Marathwara ...	35,839	17,932	17,907	274	256	18	35,565	17,676	17,889	...	...	...
Velama.												
State ...	*83,787*	*42,705*	*41,082*	*2,641*	*2,581*	*60*	*81,146*	*40,124*	*41,022*	*8*	*8*	...
Telingana ...	48,877	24,972	23,905	2,443	2,386	57	46,434	22,586	23,848	8	8	...
Marathwara ...	34,910	17,733	17,177	198	195	3	34,712	17,538	17,174	...	...	...
Waddar.												
State ...	*131,799*	*67,696*	*64,103*	*278*	*260*	*18*	*131,521*	*67,436*	*64,085*	...	...	...
Telingana ...	75,526	38,748	36,778	63	58	5	75,463	38,690	36,773	...	...	...
Marathwara ...	56,273	28,948	27,325	215	202	13	56,058	28,746	27,312	...	...	...
Wanjari.												
State ...	*174,039*	*87,843*	*86,196*	*1,344*	*1,305*	*39*	*172,695*	*86,538*	*86,157*	*2*	*2*	...
Telingana ...	34,384	17,607	16,777	325	302	23	34,059	17,305	16,754	2	2	...
Marathwara ...	139,655	70,236	69,419	1,019	1,003	16	*138,636*	69,233	69,403	...	...	...
MUSALMAN.												
Mughal												
State ...	*33,411*	*17,685*	*15,726*	*3,657*	*3,188*	*469*	*29,754*	*14,497*	*15,257*	*370*	*344*	[illegible]
Marathwara ...	20,785	11,125	9,660	1,022	913	109	19,763	10,212	9,551	46	45	

TABLE IX.

EDUCATION BY SELECTED CASTES, TRIBES OR RACES.

Caste, Tribe or Race and Locality.	POPULATION.									LITERATE IN ENGLISH.		
	TOTAL.			LITERATE.			ILLITERATE.					
	Persons.	Males.	Females.	Persons.	Males.	Females.	Persons.	Males.	Females.	Persons.	Males.	Females.
1	2	3	4	5	6	7	8	9	10	11	12	13
MUSALMAN—(*concluded.*)												
Pathan												
State ...	*135,148*	*71,167*	*63,981*	*10,372*	*9,397*	*975*	*124,776*	*61,770*	*63,006*	*926*	*900*	*26*
Telingana ..	**51,244**	27,528	23,716	**6,427**	5,821	606	**41,317**	21,707	23,110	**688**	671	17
City ...	24,960	13,362	11,598	4,143	3,671	469	20,817	9,688	11,129	586	573	13
Districts ...	26,284	14,166	12,118	2,284	2,147	137	20,500	12,019	11,981	102	98	4
Marathwara ...	**83,904**	43,639	40,265	**3,945**	3,576	369	**79,959**	40,063	39,896	**238**	229	9
Shaik.												
State ...	*985,019*	*499,495*	*485,524*	*48,451*	*43,961*	*4,490*	*936,568*	*455,534*	*481,034*	*3,640*	*3,472*	*168*
Telingana ...	**450,982**	229,280	221,702	**33,764**	30,138	3,626	**417,218**	199,142	218,076	**2,946**	2,795	151
City ...	150,618	76,219	74,399	18,760	15,953	2,807	131,858	60,266	71,592	2,488	2,349	139
Districts ...	300,364	153,061	147,303	15,004	14,185	819	285,360	138,876	146,481	458	446	12
Marathwara ...	**534,037**	270,215	263,822	**14,687**	13,823	864	**519,350**	256,392	262,958	**694**	677	17
Sayyed.												
State ...	*189,874*	*99,142*	*90,432*	*18,319*	*15,837*	*2,482*	*171,255*	*83,305*	*87,950*	*2,047*	*1,941*	*106*
Telingana ...	**82,137**	42,280	39,857	**13,479**	11,352	2,127	**68,658**	30,928	37,730	**1,806**	1,711	95
City ...	34,940	17,377	17,563	9,287	7,562	1,725	25,653	9,815	15,838	1,644	1,555	89
Districts ...	47,197	24,903	22,294	4,192	3,790	402	43,005	21,113	21,892	162	156	6
Marathwara ...	**107,437**	56,862	50,575	**4,840**	4,485	355	**102,597**	52,377	50,220	**241**	230	11
CHRISTIAN.												
Indian Christian.												
State ...	*45,908*	*23,638*	*22,273*	*5,763*	*3,633*	*2,130*	*40,145*	*20,002*	*20,143*	*2,160*	*1,422*	*738*
Telingana ...	**36,293**	18,600	17,693	**4,445**	2,746	1,699	**31,848**	15,854	15,994	**1,816**	1,216	600
City ...	9,220	4,549	4,678	2,092	1,277	815	7,128	3,225	3,863	1,227	850	377
Districts ...	27,073	14,056	12,016	2,353	1,469	884	24,720	12,589	12,131	589	366	223
ANIMIST.												
Gond.												
State ...	*124,341*	*62,583*	*61,758*	*59*	*49*	*10*	*124,282*	*62,534*	*61,748*	...	...	...
Telingana ...	**123,503**	62,155	61,348	**59**	49	10	**123,444**	62,106	61,338	...	...	...
Lambada.												
State ...	*142,044*	*76,703*	*65,341*	*185*	*164*	*21*	*141,859*	*76,539*	*65,320*	...	...	...
Telingana ...	**125,849**	68,304	57,545	**149**	136	13	**125,700**	68,168	57,532	...	...	...
Marathwara ...	**16,195**	8,399	7,796	**36**	28	8	**16,159**	8,371	7,788	...	...	...

TABLE X.

LANGUAGE.

1. The following statement shows how individual dialects returned in the schedules are grouped under languages to which, according to the new Scheme of Classification, they belong :—

Serial No.	Language.	Dialects.
1	2	3
1	Eastern Hindi	Pardesi.
2	Gondi	Koya.
3	Gujarati	Bohari, Jain, Kathiyawadi, Khatri, Kagari, Parsi, Patkari, Rangari, Sorathi, and Thakori.
4	Marathi	Are, Dhangari, Goanese, Kathodi, Konkani, and Panchali.
5	Rajasthani	Bikaneri, Marwari and Rangri.
6	Sindhi	Kachchi.
7	Western Hindi	Braj-Bhasha, Bondili, Hindostani, Hindi, Lodhi, and Urdu.
8	Western Panjabi	Multani and Peshawari.

2. The number of persons returned as speaking each of the dialects mentioned in column 3 will be found in the Appendix at the end of the table.

TABLE X.

LANGUAGE.

Serial No.	DISTRICT.	POPULATION.			GROUP A.—		
					BHILI.		
		Persons.	Males.	Females.	Persons.	Males.	Females.
	1	2	3	4	5	6	7
	Hyderabad State ...	***13,374,676***	***6,797,118***	***6,577,558***	***7,01 2***	***3,463***	***3,549***
1	Hyderabad City	**500,623**	258,454	242,169	**8**	8	...
2	Atraf-i-balda...	**520,159**	265,184	254,975	...	...	...
	Warangal Division ...	***2,657,477***	***1,368,101***	***1,289,376***	***35***	***10***	***25***
3	Warangal...	**905,414**	467,413	438,001	...	...	...
4	Karimnagar	**1,131,637**	586,260	545,377	...	...	...
5	Adilabad	**620,426**	314,428	305,998	**35**	10	25
	Medak Division ...	***3,046,705***	***1,548,882***	***1,497,823***	...	...	...
6	Medak	**687,137**	348,410	338,727	...	...	...
7	Nizamabad	**568,009**	283,621	284,388	...	..	...
8	Mahbabnagar	**747,178**	379,712	367,466	...	...	...
9	Nalgonda...	**1,044,381**	537,139	507,242	...	...	...
	Aurangabad Division. ...	***2,976,541***	***1,496,102***	***1,480,439***	***6,812***	***3,407***	***3,405***
10	Aurangabad...	**869,787**	437,495	432,292	**6,357**	3,204	3,153
11	Bhir	**622,531**	314,738	307,793	**382**	161	221
12	Nander	**704,549**	352,638	351,911	...	...	...
13	Parbhani	**779,674**	391,231	388,443	**73**	42	31
	Gulbarga Division ...	***3,673,171***	***1,860,395***	***1,812,776***	***157***	***38***	***119***
14	Gulbarga	**1,150,983**	582,447	568,536	...	...	...
15	Osmanabad	**635,977**	324,969	311,008	...	...	...
16	Raichur	**996,684**	503,541	493,143	...	...	...
17	Bidar	**889,527**	449,438	440,089	**157**	38	119

TABLE X.

LANGUAGE.

VERNACULARS OF INDIA.—(1) VERNACULARS OF THE STATE.									Serial No.
CANARESE.			GONDI.			KAIKADI.			
Persons.	Males.	Females.	Persons.	Males.	Females..	Persons.	Males.	Females.	
8	9	10	11	12	13	14	15	16	
1,680,005	*843,815*	*836,190*	*73,939*	*38,890*	*35,049*	*2,763*	*1,380*	*1,383*	
2,296	1,427	869	**2**	...	2	**11**	1	10	1
9,988	5,767	4,221	...	...	...	...	...	...	2
1,619	*901*	*718*	*73,583*	*38,717*	*34,866*	*681*	*357*	*324*	
39	21	18	**15,874**	8,420	7,454	...	...	...	3
10	6	4	**388**	202	186	...	...	...	4
1,570	874	696	**57,321**	30,095	27,226	**681**	357	324	5
22,970	*11,706*	*11,264*	*130*	*74*	*56*	...	...	...	
1,340	600	740	**130**	74	56	...	...	...	6
9,261	4,635	4,626	...	...	...	...	...	...	7
12,337	6,449	5,888	...	...	...	...	...	...	8
32	22	10	...	...	...	...	...	...	9
40,950	*20,856*	*20,094*	*224*	*99*	*125*	*1,128*	*553*	*575*	
733	404	329	...	...	...	**143**	74	69	10
1,219	718	501	...	...	...	**405**	199	206	11
38,121	19,054	19,067	**224**	99	125	**323**	165	158	12
877	680	197	...	...	...	**257**	115	142	13
1,602,182	*803,158*	*799,024*	...	...	...	*943*	*469*	*474*	
680,617	340,291	340,326	...	...	...	...	...	...	14
22,478	11,459	11,019	...	...	...	**217**	101	116	15
625,706	313,315	312,391	...	...	...	...	...	...	16
273,381	138,093	135,288	...	...	...	**726**	368	358	17

TABLE X.

LANGUAGE.

Serial No.	DISTRICT.	GROUP A.—VERNACULARS OF INDIA.					
		KOLHATI.			LAMBADI.		
		Persons.	Males.	Females.	Persons.	Males.	Females.
	1	17	18	19	20	21	22
	Hyderabad State ...	***262***	***129***	***133***	***237,899***	***124,852***	***113,047***
1	Hyderabad City ...	...	...	...	78	69	9
2	Atraf-i-balda	...	...	...	10.621	5,713	4,908
	Warangal Division ...	***68***	***47***	***21***	***77,887***	***39,932***	***37,955***
3	Warangal	...	...	...	56,007	29,537	26,470
4	Karimnagar	...	...	...	7,949	4,174	3,775
5	Adilabad	68	47	21	13,931	6,221	7,710
	Medak Division ...	...	...	...	***75,573***	***39,776***	***35,797***
6	Medak	...	...	...	4,200	2,212	1,988
7	Nizamabad	...	...	...	10.791	5,140	5,651
8	Mahabubnagar	...	...	...	17,316	8,983	8,333
9	Nalgonda	...	...	...	43,266	23,441	19,825
	Aurangabad Division ...	***194***	***82***	***112***	***33,620***	***17,827***	***15,793***
10	Aurangabad	68	42	26	12,009	6,375	5,634
11	Bhir	98	32	66	4,322	2,276	2,046
12	Nander	28	8	20	9,476	5,004	4,472
13	Parbhani	...	...	...	7,813	4,172	3,641
	Gulbarga Division ...	...	...	...	***40,120***	***21,535***	***18,585***
14	Gulbarga	...	...	...	26.717	14,421	12,296
15	Osmanabad	...	...	...	1,515	798	717
16	Raichur	...	...	...	4,941	2,641	2,300
17	Bidar	...	...	...	6,947	3,675	3,272

TABLE X.

LANGUAGE.

(1) VERNACULARS OF THE STATE.

Marathi.			Pardhi.			Telugu.			Serial No.
Persons.	Males.	Females.	Persons.	Males.	Females.	Persons.	Males.	Females.	
23	24	25	26	27	28	29	30	31	
3,498,758	*1,763,997*	*1,734,761*	*834*	*416*	*418*	*6,367,578*	*3,249,365*	*3,118,213*	
15,699	7,948	7,751	32	17	15	185,318	93,240	92,078	1
33,430	16,741	16,689	3	...	3	401,403	203,229	198,174	2
151,435	*77,604*	*73,831*	...	...	...	*2,235,174*	*1,148,558*	*1,086,616*	
6,870	3,514	3,326	...	...	...	780,668	401,409	379,259	3
9,775	5,204	4,571	...	...	...	1,073,957	556,158	517,799	4
134,790	68,856	65,934	...	...	...	380,549	190,991	189,558	5
17,202	*9,037*	*8,165*	*90*	*51*	*39*	*2,738,136*	*1,395,391*	*1,342,745*	
2,683	1,427	1,256	2	2	...	624,569	317,070	307,499	6
8,354	4,439	3,915	17	6	11	497,117	247,723	249,394	7
4,228	2,154	2,074	64	39	25	662,080	338,949	323,131	8
1,937	1,017	920	7	4	3	954,370	491,649	462,721	9
2,367,161	*1,186,310*	*1,180,851*	*342*	*155*	*187*	*147,361*	*73,674*	*73,687*	
691,261	344,311	346,950	39	15	24	3,843	1,808	2,035	10
559,641	285,953	273,688	68	30	38	1,781	892	889	11
442,903	220,916	221,987	...	..	...	132,443	65,719	66,724	12
673,356	335,130	338,226	235	110	125	9,291	5,255	4,039	13
913,831	*466,357*	*447,474*	*367*	*193*	*174*	*669,186*	*335,273*	*324,913*	
37,749	19,906	17,843	...	...	...	229,669	117,388	112,281	14
542,481	276,690	265,791	367	193	174	3,858	1,996	1,862	15
3,311	1,884	1,427	...	...	...	282,451	143,666	138,785	16
330,290	167,877	162,413	...	...	...	144,208	72,223	71,935	17

TABLE X.

LANGUAGE.

Serial No.	DISTRICT.	GROUP A—VERNACULARS OF INDIA.					
		WADARI.			WESTERN HINDI (URDU.)		
		Persons.	Males.	Females.	Persons.	Males.	Females.
	1	32	33	34	35	36	37
	Hyderabad State ..	***1,048***	***602***	***446***	***1,341,622***	***677,492***	***664,130***
1	Hyderabad City	1	1	...	244,709	124,343	120,366
2	Atraf-i-balda	401	240	161	60,624	31,346	29,278
	Warangal Division ..	***45***	***39***	***6***	***108,181***	***57,147***	***51,034***
3	Warangal	7	6	1	41,544	22,092	19,452
4	Karimnagar	...	...	...	38,283	19,820	18,463
5	Adilabad	38	33	5	28,354	15,235	13,119
	Medak Division	***65***	***27***	***38***	***186,388***	***89,421***	***96,967***
6	Medak	...	...	...	52,660	26,035	26,625
7	Nizamabad	15	1	14	41,169	20,938	20,231
8	Mahabubnagar	50	2[illegible]	24	49,726	22,426	27,300
9	Nalgonda	...	...	...	42,833	20,022	22,811
	Aurangabad Division ...	***408***	***225***	***183***	***305,815***	***152,608***	***153,207***
10	Aurangabad	119	73	46	114,591	59,056	55,535
11	Bhir	156	76	80	44,399	18,999	25,400
12	Nander	65	35	30	74,584	37,789	36,795
13	Parbhani	68	41	27	72,241	36,764	35,477
	Gulbarga Division	***128***	***70***	***58***	***435,905***	***222,627***	***213,278***
14	Gulbarga	14	14	...	168,759	86,260	82,499
15	Osmanabad	70	36	34	59,879	30,869	29,010
16	Raichur	40	19	21	77,715	40,618	37,097
17	Bidar	4	1	3	129,552	64,880	64,672

TABLE X.

LANGUAGE.

(I) VERNACULARS OF THE STATE.			TOTAL GROUP A.			Serial No.
YERUKALA.			(I) VERNACULARS OF THE STATE.			
Persons.	Males.	Females.	Persons.	Males.	Females.	
38	39	40	41	42	43	
7,398	*3,888*	*3,510*	*13,219,118*	*6,708,289*	*6,510,829*	
347	168	179	448,501	227,222	221,279	1
1,106	759	347	517,576	263,795	253,781	2
2,706	*1,385*	*1,321*	*2,651,414*	*1,364,697*	*1,286,717*	
2,084	1,057	1,027	903,093	466,086	437,007	3
622	328	294	1,130,984	585,892	545,092	4
...	...	...	617,337	312,719	304,618	5
2,542	*1,236*	*1,306*	*3,043,096*	*1,546,719*	*1,496,377*	
349	191	158	685,933	347,611	338,322	6
191	95	96	566,915	282,977	283,938	7
833	404	429	746,634	379,430	367,204	8
1,169	546	623	1,043,614	536,701	506,913	9
4	*2*	*2*	*2,904,019*	*1,455,798*	*1,448,221*	
...	...	...	829,163	415,362	413,801	10
...	...	...	612,471	309,336	303,135	11
4	2	2	698,171	348,791	349,380	12
...	...	...	764,214	382,309	381,905	13
693	*338*	*355*	*3,654,512*	*1,850,058*	*1,804,454*	
500	228	272	1,144,025	578,508	565,517	14
...	...	...	630,865	322,142	308,723	15
193	110	83	994,357	502,253	492,101	16
...	...	...	885,235	447,155	438,110	17

TABLE X.

LANGUAGE.

Serial No.	DISTRICT.	GROUP A.—VERNACULARS OF INDIA.					
		BENGALI.			BIHARI.		
		Persons.	Males.	Females.	Persons.	Males.	Females.
	1	44	45	46	47	48	49
	Hyderabad State ...	***194***	***171***	***23***	***142***	***83***	***59***
1	Hyderabad City	149	138	11	72	41	31
2	Atraf-i-balda	...	...	...	...	...	...
	Warangal Division ...	...	...	...	***11***	***7***	***4***
3	Warangal	...	...	...	...	...	...
4	Karimnagar	...	...	...	...	...	...
5	Adilabad	...	...	...	11	7	4
	Medak Division	***43***	***31***	***12***	...	...	...
6	Medak	1	1	...	...	...	...
7	Nizamabad	37	27	10	...	...	...
8	Mahabubnagar	...	...	...	...	...	...
9	Nalgonda	5	3	2	...	...	...
	Aurangabad Division. ...	***1***	***1***	...	***59***	***35***	***24***
10	Aurangabad	...	...	...	10	5	5
11	Bhir	...	...	...	...	...	...
12	Nander	...	...	...	13	5	8
13	Parbhani	1	1	...	36	25	11
	Gulbarga Division ...	***1***	***1***	...	...	...	...
14	Gulbarga	...	...	...	...	...	...
15	Osmanabad	1	1	...	...	...	...
16	Raichur	...	...	...	...	...	...
17	Bidar	...	...	...	...	...	...

TABLE X.

LANGUAGE.

(II)—VERNACULARS FOREIGN TO THE STATE.									
Eastern Hindi.			Ghisadi.			Gujarati.			Serial No.
Persons.	Males.	Females.	Persons.	Males.	Females.	Persons.	Males.	Females.	
50	51	52	53	54	55	56	57	58	
6,609	***3,507***	***3,102***	***371***	***181***	***190***	***14,984***	***8,670***	***6,314***	
3	3	...	...	...	...	**3,056**	1,730	1,326	1
...	...	...	...	...	...	**373**	221	152	2
72	***69***	***3***	...	...	...	***671***	***310***	***361***	
...	...	...	...	...	...	**479**	227	252	3
...	...	...	...	...	...	**18**	9	9	4
72	69	3	...	...	...	**174**	74	100	5
...	...	...	...	...	...	***706***	***466***	***240***	
...	...	...	...	...	...	**501**	353	148	6
...	...	...	...	...	...	**77**	54	23	7
...	...	...	...	...	...	**61**	20	41	8
...	...	...	...	...	...	**67**	39	28	9
6,534	***3,435***	***3,099***	***367***	***177***	***190***	***6,513***	***3,943***	***2,570***	
5,907	3,181	2,726	**19**	7	12	**4,169**	2,545	1,624	10
213	56	157	**52**	24	28	**285**	165	120	11
52	23	29	**215**	103	112	**555**	394	161	12
362	175	187	**81**	43	38	**1,504**	839	665	13
...	...	...	***4***	***4***	...	***3,665***	***2,000***	***1,665***	
...	...	...	...	...	...	**1,831**	1,013	818	14
...	...	...	**4**	4	...	**682**	360	322	15
...	...	...	...	...	...	**260**	147	113	16
...	...	...	...	...	...	**892**	480	412	17

TABLE X.

LANGUAGE.

Serial No.	DISTRICT.	GROUP A.—VERNACULARS OF INDIA.								
		MALAYALAM.			ORIYA.			PANJABI.		
		Persons	Males.	Females	Persons	Males.	Females.	Persons	Males.	Females.
	1	59	60	61	62	63	64	65	66	67
	Hyderabad State ...	***243***	***215***	***28***	***265***	***137***	***128***	***3,414***	***2,143***	***1,271***
1	Hyderabad City	125	107	18	260	136	124	887	693	194
2	Atraf-i-balda	...	...	...	...	...	...	40	20	20
	Warangal Division ...	...	...	...	...	...	...	***648***	***402***	***246***
3	Warangal	...	...	...	...	...	...	160	90	70
4	Karimnagar	...	...	...	...	...	...	146	78	68
5	Adilabad	...	...	...	...	...	...	342	234	108
	Medak Division	***1***	...	***1***	...	...	...	***138***	***68***	***70***
6	Medak	...	...	...	...	...	...	37	16	21
7	Nizamabad	...	...	...	...	...	...	60	27	33
8	Mahabubnagar	...	...	...	...	...	...	15	9	6
9	Nalgonda	1	...	1	...	...	...	26	16	10
	Aurangabad Division ..	***8***	***6***	***2***	***1***	***1***	...	***1,369***	***760***	***609***
10	Aurangabad	3	3	...	...	...	...	268	141	127
11	Bhir	...	...	...	...	...	...	120	79	41
12	Nander	...	...	...	...	...	...	896	496	400
13	Parbhani	5	3	2	1	1	...	85	44	41
	Gulbarga Division ...	***109***	***102***	***7***	***4***	...	***4***	***332***	***200***	***132***
14	Gulbarga	10	10	...	...	...	...	241	131	110
15	Osmanabad	...	...	...	...	...	...	26	22	4
16	Raichur	96	89	7	...	...	...	22	19	3
17	Bidar	3	3	...	4	...	4	42	28	15

TABLE X.

LANGUAGE.

(II)—Vernaculars foreign to the State.									Serial No.
Pashto.			Rajasthani.			Sindhi.			
Persons.	Males.	Females.	Persons.	Males.	Females.	Persons.	Males.	Females.	
68	69	70	71	72	73	74	75	76	
786	***618***	***168***	***50,208***	***27,665***	***22,543***	***307***	***268***	***39***	
370	314	56	9,583	5,162	4,421	93	71	22	1
...	...	...	180	45	135	...	...	...	2
4	***4***	...	***579***	***273***	***306***	***62***	***60***	***2***	
4	4	...	165	87	78	3	1	2	3
...	...	...	190	92	98	...	...	...	4
...	...	...	224	94	130	59	59	...	5
13	***10***	***3***	***644***	***354***	***290***	***10***	***10***	...	
11	8	3	114	56	58	...	...	...	6
...	...	...	337	188	149	...	...	...	7
...	...	...	137	76	61	...	...	...	8
2	2	...	56	34	22	10	10	...	9
319	***238***	***81***	***31,260***	***17,451***	***13,809***	***138***	***125***	***13***	
42	24	18	11,716	6,349	5,367	51	42	9	10
88	53	35	7,725	4,126	3,599	...	...	...	11
65	62	3	2,477	1,429	1,048	83	79	4	12
124	99	25	9,342	5,547	3,795	4	4	...	13
80	***52***	***28***	***7,962***	***4,380***	***3,582***	***4***	***2***	***2***	
19	19	...	2,006	1,112	894	1	1	...	14
4	4	...	3,310	1,837	1,473	...	...	...	15
...	...	...	343	152	191	...	...	...	16
57	29	28	2,303	1,279	1,024	3	1	2	17

TABLE X.

LANGUAGE.

Serial No.	DISTRICT.	GROUP A.—VERNACULARS OF INDIA.					
		TAMIL.			WESTERN HINDI.		
		Persons.	Males.	Females.	Persons.	Males.	Females.
	1	77	78	79	80	81	82
	Hyderabad State ..	***25,027***	***13,228***	***11,799***	***37,814***	***21,538***	***16.276***
1	Hyderabad City ...	**18,885**	9,680	9,205	**8,281**	5,563	2,718
2	Atraf-i-balda ...	**1,081**	593	488	**675**	391	284
	Warangal Division ..	***1,072***	***651***	***421***	***2,186***	***1,137***	***1 049***
3	Warangal ...	**797**	482	315	**304**	192	112
4	Karimnagar ...	**247**	146	101	**7**	5	2
5	Adilabad ...	**28**	23	5	**1,875**	940	935
	Medak Division	***1,015***	***584***	***431***	***345***	***192***	***153***
6	Medak ..	**281**	161	120	**45**	33	12
7	Nizamabad ...	**226**	135	91	**84**	51	33
8	Mahabubnagar ...	**153**	89	64	**20**	9	11
9	Nalgonda ..	**355**	199	156	**195**	99	97
	Aurangabad Division ...	***1,317***	***766***	***551***	***22,676***	***12,295***	***10,381***
10	Aurangabad ...	**609**	336	273	**17,117**	9,121	7,996
11	Bhir ...	**248**	124	124	**1,104**	657	447
12	Nander ..	**96**	66	30	**1,702**	1,044	658
13	Parbhani ...	**364**	240	124	**2,753**	1,473	1,280
	Gulbarga Division ...	***1,657***	***954***	***703***	***3.651***	***1,960***	***1,691***
14	Gulbarga ...	**767**	454	313	**1.589**	921	668
15	Osmanabad ..	**64**	37	27	**875**	463	412
16	Raichur ...	**790**	441	349	**369**	194	175
17	Bidar ..	**36**	22	14	**818**	382	436

TABLE X.

LANGUAGE:

(II)—Vernaculars foreign to the State.						Total Group A.			
Western Panjabi.			Others.			(II)—Vernaculars foreign to the State.			Serial No.
Persons	Males.	Females.	Persons.	Males.	Females.	Persons.	Males.	Females.	
83	84	85	86	87	88	89	90	91	
15	***13***	***2***	***213***	***126***	***87***	***140,592***	***78,563***	***62,029***	
...	...	...	62	34	28	41,826	23,672	18,154	1
...	...	...	...	...	...	2,349	1,270	1,079	2
...	...	...	...	...	...	***5,305***	***2,913***	***2,392***	
...	...	...	...	...	...	1,912	1,083	829	3
...	...	...	...	...	...	608	330	278	4
...	...	...	...	...	...	2,785	1,500	1,285	5
11	***11***	...	***70***	***46***	***24***	***2,996***	***1,772***	***1,224***	
11	11	...	1	1	...	1,002	640	362	6
...	...	...	69	45	24	890	527	363	7
...	...	...	...	...	...	386	203	183	8
...	...	...	...	...	...	718	402	316	9
4	***2***	***2***	***81***	***46***	***35***	***70,647***	***39,281***	***31,366***	
...	...	...	...	...	...	39,911	21,754	18,157	10
...	...	...	...	...	...	9,835	5,284	4,551	11
...	...	...	...	...	...	6,154	3,701	2,453	12
4	2	2	81	46	35	14,747	8,542	6,205	13
...	...	...	...	...	...	***17,469***	***9,655***	***7,814***	
...	...	...	...	...	...	6,464	3,681	2,803	14
...	...	...	...	...	...	4,966	2,728	2,238	15
...	...	...	...	...	...	1,880	1,042	838	16
...	...	...	...	...	...	4,159	2,224	1,935	17

TABLE X.

LANGUAGE.

Serial No.	DISTRICT.	GROUP B.—VERNACULARS OF ASIATIC					
		ARABIC.			PERSIAN.		
		Persons.	Males.	Females.	Persons.	Males.	Females.
.	1	92	93	94	95	96	97
	Hyderabad State ..	***5,683***	***3,881***	***1,802***	***256***	***129***	***127***
1	Hyderabad City ...	2.852	2,224	628	98	59	[illegible]
2	Atraf-i-balda ...	36	35	1	...	...	...
	Warangal Division ..	***383***	***275***	***108***	***1***	...	***1***
3	Warangal ..	69	56	13	...	...	...
4	Karimnagar ..	21	19	2	1	...	1
5	Adilabad ...	293	200	93	...	...	..
	Medak Division ...	***336***	***205***	***131***	***49***	***24***	***25***
6	Medak ...	68	54	14	...	...	...
7	Nizamabad ...	123	75	48	49	24	25
8	Mahbubnagar ..	124	56	68	...	...	...
9	Nalgonda ...	21	20	1	...	...	...
	Aurangabad Division ...	***1,393***	***761***	***632***	***37***	***17***	***20***
10	Aurangabad ...	451	242	209	10	4	6
11	Bhir ...	221	115	106	...	...	...
12	Nander ...	167	115	52	27	13	14
13	Parbhani ...	554	289	265	...	...	...
	Gulbarga Division ...	***683***	***381***	***302***	***73***	***29***	***44***
14	Gulbarga ...	286	180	106	73	29	44
15	Osmanabad ...	129	88	41	...	...	...
16	Raichur ...	170	56	114	...	...	...
17	Bidar ...	98	57	41	...	...	...

TABLE X.

LANGUAGE.

COUNTRIES BEYOND INDIA.			TOTAL GROUP B.			
OTHERS.			VERNACULARS OF ASIATIC COUNTRIES BEYOND INDIA.			Serial No.
Persons.	Males.	Females.	Persons.	Males.	Females.	
98	99	100	101	102	103	
38	*18*	*20*	*5,977*	*4,028*	*1,949*	
25	16	9	2,973	2,299	674	1
...	...	...	36	35	1	2
...	...	...	*384*	*275*	*109*	
...	...	...	69	56	13	3
...	...	...	22	19	3	4
...	...	...	293	200	93	5
...	...	...	*385*	*229*	*156*	
...	...	...	68	54	14	6
...	...	...	172	99	73	7
...	...	...	124	56	68	8
...	...	...	21	20	1	9
1	*1*	...	*1,431*	*779*	*652*	
...	...	...	461	246	215	10
...	...	...	221	115	106	11
1	1	...	195	129	66	12
...	...	...	554	289	265	13
12	*1*	*11*	*768*	*411*	*357*	
12	1	11	371	210	161	14
...	...	...	129	88	41	15
...	...	...	170	56	114	16
...	...	...	98	57	41	17

TABLE X.

LANGUAGE.

Serial No.	DISTRICT.	GROUP C.—EUROPEAN					
		ENGLISH.			GERMAN.		
		Persons.	Males.	Females.	Persons.	Males.	Females.
	1	104	105	106	107	108	109
	Hyderabad State ...	***8,843***	***6,174***	***2,669***	***18***	***6***	***12***
1	Hyderabad City ...	7,219	5,212	2,007	6	3	3
2	Atraf-i-balda ..	195	84	111	...	...	...
	Warangal Division ...	***371***	***216***	***155***	...	...	...
3	Warangal ...	337	188	149	...	...	...
4	Karimnagar ...	23	19	4	...	...	...
5	Adilabad ..	11	9	2	...	...	...
	Medak Division ..	***216***	***159***	***57***	***12***	***3***	***9***
6	Medak ..	134	105	29	...	...	...
7	Nizamabad ...	32	18	14	...	...	...
8	Mahabubnagar ..	27	22	5	7	1	6
9	Nalgonda ..	23	14	9	5	2	3
	Aurangabad Division ..	***429***	***238***	***191***	...	...	...
10	Aurangabad ..	237	127	110	...	...	...
11	Bhir ...	4	3	1	...	...	...
12	Nander ..	29	17	12	...	...	...
13	Parbhani ...	159	91	68	...	...	...
	Gulbarga Division ..	***413***	***265***	***148***	...	...	...
14	Gulbarga ...	121	66	55	...	...	...
15	Osmanabad ..	17	11	6	...	...	...
16	Raichur ...	270	186	84	...	...	...
17	Bidar ...	5	2	3	...	...	...

TABLE X.

LANGUAGE:

LANGUAGES.						TOTAL GROUP C.			Serial No.
PORTUGUESE.			OTHERS.			EUROPEAN LANGUAGES.			
Persons.	Males.	Females.	Persons.	Males.	Females.	Persons.	Males.	Females.	
110	111	112	113	114	115	116	117	118	
70	*44*	*26*	*58*	*14*	*44*	*8,989*	*6,238*	*2,751*	
56	36	20	42	10	32	7,323	5,261	2,062	1
...	...	...	3	...	3	198	84	114	2
...	...	...	*3*	...	*3*	*374*	*216*	*158*	3
...	...	...	3	...	3	340	188	152	
...	...	...	...	...	...	23	19	4	4
...	...	...	...	...	...	11	9	2	5
...	...	...	...	...	...	*228*	*162*	*66*	
...	...	...	...	...	...	134	105	29	6
...	...	...	...	...	...	32	18	14	7
...	...	...	...	...	...	34	23	11	8
...	...	...	...	...	...	28	16	12	9
5	*2*	*3*	*10*	*4*	*6*	*444*	*244*	*200*	
5	2	3	10	4	6	252	133	119	10
...	...	...	...	...	...	4	3	1	11
...	...	...	...	...	...	29	17	12	12
...	...	...	...	...	...	159	91	68	13
9	*6*	*3*	...	...	...	*422*	*271*	*151*	
2	2	...	...	...	...	123	68	55	14
...	...	...	...	...	...	17	11	6	15
7	4	3	...	...	...	277	190	87	16
...	...	...	...	...	...	5	2	3	17

TABLE X.

LANGUAGE.

Details of languages included under "Others."			
Language.	Persons.	Males.	Females.
1	119	120	121
"OTHER LANGUAGES."	*309*	*158*	*151*
Vernaculars of India foreign to the State ..	*213*	*126*	*87*
Agari	2	2	...
Beldari	80	45	35
Burmese	1	...	1
Kashmiri	4	1	3
Katari	42	22	20
Kayasthi	76	49	27
Koli	3	3	...
Sanskrit	5	4	1
Vernaculars of Asiatic countries beyond India ...	*38*	*18*	*20*
Japanese	8	1	7
Somali	2	2	...
Turkey	28	15	13
European languages	*58*	*14*	*44*
Dutch	1	...	1
French	18	5	13
Irish	1	...	1
Italian	36	8	28
Russian	3	1	2

Appendix to Table X.

LANGUAGE.

APPENDIX TO TABLE X.

LANGUAGE.

Serial No.	Language.	Dialect.	POPULATION.			DISTRIBUTION					
						HYDERABAD CITY.			ATHAF-I-BALDA.		
			Persons.	Males.	Females.	Persons.	Males.	Females.	Persons.	Males.	Females.
	1		2	3	4	5	6	7	8	9	10
1	Eastern Hindi ..	Pardesi ...	**6,609**	3,507	3,102	**3**	3	...	...	...	...
2	Gondi ...	Koya ..	**8,043**	4,039	4,004	**2**	...	2	...	...	...
3	Gujarati	Bohari ..	**17**	17	...	**17**	17	...	...	...	...
		Jain ..	**85**	42	43	...	...	...	...	...	...
		Kathiyawadi ...	**9**	7	2	...	...	...	...	...	...
		Khatri ...	**396**	202	194	**16**	4	12	..	...	...
		Nagari ..	**233**	191	42	**195**	173	22	...	...	...
		Parsi ...	**75**	39	36	**4**	3	1	**19**	9	10
		Patkari ...	**142**	54	88	...	...	...	...	...	...
		Rangari ...	**48**	27	21	...	...	...	...	...	...
		Sorathi ..	**239**	101	138	...	...	...	...	...	...
		Thakori ..	**79**	10	69	...	...	...	...	...	...
4	Marathi	Are ...	**2,378**	1,225	1,153	...	...	...	**241**	177	64
		Dhangari ..	**11**	5	6	...	...	...	...	...	...
		Goanese ...	**86**	64	22	**48**	37	11	...	...	...
		Kathodi ...	**42**	22	20	**42**	22	20	...	...	...
		Konkani ..	**29**	17	12	**28**	16	12	...	...	...
		Panchali ...	**12**	5	7	...	...	...	..	...	...
5	Rajasthani	Bikaneri ...	**13**	6	7	...	...	...	...	...	...
		Marwari ...	**49,547**	27,309	22,238	**9,581**	5,162	4,419	**180**	4[illegible]	13[illegible]
		Rangri ...	**255**	140	115	...	...	...	...	...	...
6	Sindhi	Kachchi ...	**307**	268	39	**93**	71	22	...	...	...
7	Western Hindi	Braj-Basha ...	**237**	129	108	**3**	3	...	...	...	...
		Bondili ...	**103**	46	57	...	...	...	...	...	...
		Hindostani ...	**24,280**	13,038	11,242	**162**	141	21	**673**	390	2[illegible]
		Hindi ...	**12,261**	7,837	4,424	**8,116**	5,419	2,697	**2**	1	1
		Lodhi ...	**49**	11	38	..	...	...	...	...	...
		Urdu ...	**1,341,622**	677,492	664,130	**244,709**	124,343	120,366	**60,624**	31,346	29,27[illegible]
8	Western Panjabi	Multani ..	**4**	2	2	...	...	...	...	...	...
		Peshawari ..	**11**	11	...	...	...	...	...	...	...

APPENDIX TO TABLE X.

LANGUAGE.

BY DISTRICT.															Serial No.
Warangal.			Karimnagar.			Adilabad.			Medak.			Nizamabad.			
Persons.	Males.	Females.	Persons.	Males.	Females.	Persons.	Males.	Females.	Persons.	Males.	Females.	Persons.	Males.	Females.	
11	12	13	14	15	16	17	18	19	20	21	22	23	24	25	
...	...	...	...	...	...	**72**	69	3	...	...	...	...	...	...	1
7,873	3,942	3,931	**38**	23	15	...	...	...	**130**	74	56	...	...	...	2
...	...	...	...	...	...	...	...	...	...	...	...	...	...	...	
...	...	...	...	...	...	...	...	...	...	...	...	...	...	...	
...	...	...	...	...	...	...	...	...	...	...	...	...	...	...	
...	...	...	...	...	...	**27**	9	18	...	...	...	**12**	10	2	
12	7	5	...	...	...	**1**	...	1	...	...	...	**4**	1	3	3
10	6	4	...	...	...	...	...	...	...	...	...	...	...	...	
29	14	15	**17**	8	9	...	...	...	**60**	28	32	...	...	...	
...	...	...	...	...	...	...	...	...	**48**	27	21	...	...	...	
239	101	138	...	...	...	...	...	...	...	...	...	...	...	...	
...	...	...	...	...	...	...	...	...	...	...	...	...	...	...	
58	32	26	**1,627**	818	809	...	...	...	**8**	5	3	**254**	98	156	
...	...	...	...	...	...	...	...	...	...	...	...	...	...	...	
...	...	...	...	...	...	...	...	...	...	...	...	...	...	...	4
...	...	...	...	...	...	...	...	...	...	...	...	...	...	...	
...	...	...	...	...	...	...	...	...	...	...	...	...	...	...	
...	...	...	...	...	...	...	...	...	...	...	...	...	...	...	
...	...	...	...	...	...	...	...	...	...	...	...	...	...	...	
147	79	68	**190**	92	98	**224**	94	130	**102**	50	52	**337**	188	149	5
...	...	...	...	...	...	...	...	...	...	...	...	...	...	...	
3	1	2	...	...	...	**59**	59	...	...	...	...	...	...	...	6
...	...	...	...	...	...	**1**	...	1	...	...	...	...	...	...	
...	...	...	**2**	...	2	...	...	...	...	...	...	...	...	...	
285	181	104	**5**	5	...	**1,846**	929	917	**43**	31	12	**70**	48	22	7
19	11	8	...	...	...	**28**	11	17	**2**	2	...	**14**	3	11	
...	...	...	...	...	...	...	...	...	...	...	...	...	...	...	
41,544	22,092	19,452	**38,283**	19,820	18,463	**28,354**	15,235	13,119	**52,660**	26,035	26,625	**41,169**	20,938	20,231	
...	...	...	...	...	...	...	...	...	...	...	...	...	...	...	8
...	...	...	...	...	...	...	...	...	**11**	11	...	...	...	...	

APPENDIX TO TABLE X.

LANGUAGE.

Serial No.	Language.	Dialect.	DISTRIBUTION: Mahbubnagar. Persons.	Mahbubnagar. Males.	Mahbubnagar. Females.	Nalgonda. Persons.	Nalgonda. Males.	Nalgonda. Females.	Aurangabad. Persons.	Aurangabad. Males.	Aurangabad. Females.	Bhir. Persons.	Bhir. Males.	Bhir. Females.
	1		26	27	28	29	30	31	32	33	34	35	36	37
1	Eastern Hindi	Pardesi	...	...	...	...	...	...	5,907	3,181	2,726	213	56	157
2	Gondi.	Koya	...	...	...	...	...	...	...	...	...	...	...	...
3	Gujarati	Bohari	...	...	...	...	...	...	...	...	...	...	...	...
		Jain	...	...	...	...	...	...	7	2	5	...	...	...
		Kathiyawadi	...	...	...	...	...	...	...	...	...	...	...	...
		Khatri	14	9	5	...	...	...	9	4	5	...	...	...
		Nagari	...	...	...	...	...	...	...	...	...	...	...	...
		Parsi	...	...	...	1	1	...	...	...	...	4	4	...
		Patkari	27	...	27	9	4	5	...	...	...	...	...	...
		Rangari	...	...	...	...	...	...	...	...	...	...	...	...
		Sorathi	...	...	...	...	...	...	...	...	...	...	...	...
		Thakori	...	...	...	...	...	...	79	10	69	...	...	...
4	Marathi	Are	129	69	60	61	26	35	...	...	...	...	...	...
		Dhangari	...	...	...	...	...	...	11	5	6	...	...	...
		Goanese	...	...	...	...	...	...	35	2	11	...	...	...
		Kathodi	...	...	...	...	...	...	...	...	...	...	...	...
		Konkani	...	...	...	...	...	...	...	...	...	...	...	...
		Panchali	...	...	...	...	...	...	...	...	...	...	...	...
5	Rajasthani	Bikaneri	...	...	...	...	...	...	13	6	7	...	...	...
		Marwari	137	76	61	56	34	22	11,192	6,063	5,129	7,716	4,118	3,598
		Rangri	...	...	...	...	...	...	242	130	112	9	8	1
6	Sindhi	Kachchi	...	...	...	10	10	...	51	42	9	...	...	...
7	Western Hindi	Braj-Basha	...	...	...	...	...	...	190	95	95	13	10	3
		Bondili	...	...	...	6	...	6	...	...	...	95	46	49
		Hindostani	15	6	9	190	99	91	15,662	8,273	7,389	851	530	321
		Hindi	5	3	2	...	...	...	332	268	64	145	71	74
		Lodhi	...	...	...	...	...	...	49	11	38	...	...	...
		Urdu	49,726	22,426	27,300	42,833	20,022	22,811	114,591	59,056	55,535	44,399	18,999	25,400
8	Western Panjabi	Multani	...	...	...	...	...	...	...	...	...	...	...	...
		Peshawari	...	...	...	...	...	...	...	...	...	...	...	...

APPENDIX TO TABLE X.

LANGUAGE —(*concluded.*)

BY DISTRICT.																		
NANDER.			PARBHANI.			GULBARGA.			OSMANABAD.			RAICHUR.			BIDAR.			Serial No.
Persons.	Males.	Females.	Persons.	Males.	Females.	Persons.	Males.	Females.	Persons.	Males.	Females.	Persons.	Males.	Females.	Persons.	Males.	Females.	
38	39	40	41	42	43	44	45	46	47	48	49	50	51	52	53	54	55	
52	23	29	362	175	187	...	...	...	...	...	...	...	...	...	...	...	...	1
...	...	...	...	...	...	...	...	...	...	...	...	...	...	...	...	...	...	2
...	...	...	...	...	..	...	...	...	...	...	...	...	...	...	...	...	...	
5	3	2	10	6	4	...	...	...	1	1	...	...	...	...	62	30	32	
...	...	...	9	7	2	...	...	...	...	...	...	...	...	...	...	...	...	
19	9	10	...	...	...	295	153	142	4	4	...	...	..	...	...	...	...	
...	...	...	21	10	11	...	...	...	...	...	...	...	...	...	...	...	...	3
9	4	5	6	1	5	21	10	11	1	1	...	...	...	...	...	...	...	
...	...	...	...	...	...	...	...	...	...	...	...	...	...	...	...	...	...	
...	...	...	...	...	...	...	...	...	...	...	...	...	...	...	...	...	...	
...	...	...	...	...	...	...	...	...	...	...	...	...	...	...	...	...	...	
..	...	...	...	...	...	...	...	...	...	...	...	...	...	...	...	...	...	
...	...	...	...	...	...	...	...	...	...	...	...	...	...	...	...	...	...	
...	...	...	...	...	...	...	...	...	...	...	...	...	...	...	...	...	...	
1	1	...	...	...	...	...	...	...	...	...	...	1	1	...	...	...	...	4
...	...	...	...	...	...	...	...	...	...	...	...	...	...	...	...	...	...	
...	...	...	...	...	...	...	...	...	...	...	...	1	1	...	...	...	...	
...	...	...	12	5	7	...	...	...	...	...	...	...	...	...	...	...	...	
...	...	...	...	...	...	...	...	...	...	...	...	...	...	...	...	...	...	
2,440	1,414	1,026	9,321	5,536	3,785	1,976	1,090	886	3,310	1,837	1,473	343	152	191	2,295	1,279	1,016	5
2	...	2	2	2	...	...	...	...	...	...	...	...	...	...	...	...	...	
83	79	4	4	4	...	1	1	...	...	...	...	...	...	...	3	1	2	6
4	1	3	5	4	1	...	...	...	...	...	...	6	2	4	15	14	1	
...	...	...	..	...	...	...	...	...	...	...	...	...	...	...	...	...	...	
1,113	668	445	1,710	882	828	...	...	...	717	390	327	302	152	150	636	313	323	7
585	372	213	1,038	587	451	1,589	921	668	158	73	85	61	40	21	167	55	112	
...	...	...	...	...	...	...	...	...	...	...	...	...	...	...	...	...	...	
74,584	37,789	36,795	72,241	36,764	35,477	168,759	86,260	82,499	59,879	30,869	29,010	77,715	40,618	37,097	129,552	64,880	64,672	
...	...	...	4	2	2	...	...	...	...	...	...	...	...	...	...	...	...	8
...	...	...	...	...	...	...	...	...	...	...	...	..	...	...	...	...	...	

TABLE XI.

BIRTH-PLACE.

This table deals with the birth-places of the population enumerated in the State. It is divided into eight parts according to the following scheme of classification.

Serial No.	Part.	Birth-place.
1.	A—I	Born in India——Born within the State.
2.	A—II	Born in India——Born in Provinces and States in India beyond the Hyderabad State.
3.	B	Born in other Asiatic countries.
4.	C	Born in Europe.
5.	D	Born in Africa.
6.	E	Born in America.
7.	F	Born in Australasia.
8.	G	Born at Sea.

TABLE XI.
BIRTH-PLACE.

Serial No.	District, State, Province, or country where born.	DISTRICT OF STATE					
		POPULATION OF THE STATE.			HYDERABAD CITY.		
		Persons.	Males.	Females.	Persons.	Males.	Females.
	1	2	3	4	5	6	7
	Total Population ...	***13,374,676***	***6,797,118***	***6,577,558***	***500,623***	***258,454***	***242,169***
	A—BORN IN INDIA ...	***13,367,080***	***6,790,681***	***6,576,399***	***494,788***	***253,378***	***241,410***
	I.—Born within the State ...	***13,113,963***	***6,665,244***	***6,448,719***	***449,623***	***226,017***	***223,606***
1	Hyderabad City ...	**415,827**	206,435	208,592	**387,451**	190,292	197,159
2	Atraf-i-balda ...	**503,818**	256,733	247,085	**16,563**	8,632	7,931
	Warangal Division ...	***2,585,769***	***1,330,000***	***1,255,769***	***4,997***	***2,984***	***2,013***
3	Warangal	**864,259**	445,260	418,999	**1,778**	949	829
4	Karimnagar	**1,161,873**	602,940	558,933	**2,236**	1,437	799
5	Adilabad	**559,637**	281,800	277,837	**983**	598	385
	Medak Division ...	***3,070,753***	***1,565,106***	***1,505,647***	***22,532***	***13,561***	***8,971***
6	Medak	**685,082**	349,711	335,371	**10,595**	6,158	4,437
7	Nizamabad	**583,158**	293,389	289,769	**4,610**	3,006	1,604
8	Mahbubnagar	**759,242**	385,762	373,480	**4.662**	2,913	1,749
9	Nalgonda	**1,043,271**	536,244	507,027	**2,665**	1,484	1,181
	Aurangabad Division ...	***2,903,138***	***1,462,906***	***1,440,232***	***8,036***	***4,661***	***3,375***
10	Aurangabad	**839,894**	423,313	416,581	**4.017**	2,363	1,654
11	Bhir	**619,006**	315,589	303,417	**1,370**	767	603
12	Nander	**700,491**	352,689	347,802	**1,127**	663	464
13	Parbhani	**743,747**	371,315	372,432	**1,522**	868	654
	Gulbarga Division ...	***3,635,458***	***1,844,064***	***1,791,394***	***10,044***	***5,887***	***4,157***
14	Gulbarga	**1,132,087**	571,845	560,242	**4,047**	2,363	1,684
15	Osmanabad	**609,312**	315,632	293,680	**328**	129	199
16	Raichur	**990,191**	500,578	489,613	**1.729**	1,039	690
17	Bidar	**903,868**	456,009	447,859	**3,940**	2,356	1,584
	II.—Born in Provinces and States beyond the State..	***253,117***	***125,437***	***127,680***	***45,165***	***27,358***	***17,807***
	Provinces	***229,385***	***109,537***	***119,848***	***34,069***	***20,285***	***13,784***
	(a) Provinces adjacent to the State ...	***207,419***	***94,358***	***113,061***	***21,864***	***11,727***	***10,137***
18	Bombay (including Aden)...	**118,653**	50,702	67,951	**3,634**	2,122	1,512
19	Central Provinces and Berar	**20,945**	8,956	11,989	**3,112**	1,440	1,672
20	Madras (including Laccadives) ...	**67,821**	34,700	33,121	**15,118**	8,165	6,953
	(b) Other Provinces in India..	***21,966***	***15,179***	***6,787***	***12,205***	***8,558***	***3,647***
21	Ajmer-Merwara ...	**6,698**	4,188	2,510	**1,096**	670	426
22	Baluchistan (Districts and Administered Territories).	**110**	100	10	**14**	11	3
23	Bengal	**734**	547	187	**388**	241	147
24	Burma	**185**	72	113	**138**	60	78
25	Coorg	**1**	...	1	...	...	...
26	Eastern Bengal and Assam	**5**	4	1	**2**	1	1
27	North West Frontier Province (Districts and Administered Territories) ...	**364**	317	47	**271**	241	30
28	Punjab	**4,470**	3,324	1,146	**3,567**	2,756	811
29	United Provinces of Agra and Oudh	**9,399**	6,627	2,772	**6,729**	4,578	2,151
	States and Agencies ..	***19,769***	***13,150***	***6,619***	***9,561***	***6,026***	***3,535***
30	Baluchistan (Agency Tracts)	**71**	71	...	...	...	...
31	Baroda	**204**	106	98	**61**	36	25
32	Bombay States... ..	**177**	170	7	...	...	...
33	Central India Agency ...	**565**	264	301	**235**	137	98
34	Central Provinces States ...	**2**	1	1	...	...	...
35	Cochin ...	**10**	5	5	**6**	1	5
36	Kashmir ...	**83**	64	19	**28**	16	12
37	Mysore ..	**3,880**	2,547	1,333	**2,347**	1,343	1,004
38	Punjab States ..	**399**	233	166	**368**	220	148
39	Rajputana Agency ..	**14,271**	9,612	4,659	**6,417**	4,200	2,217
40	Travancore ...	**6**	2	4	**4**	2	2
41	United Provinces States ...	**101**	75	26	**95**	69	26
42	**French and Portuguese Settlements**	***288***	***184***	***104***	***219***	***141***	***78***
43	**India,** *Unspecified* ...	***3,675***	***2,566***	***1,109***	***1,316***	***906***	***410***

TABLE XI.

BIRTH-PLACE.

WHERE ENUMERATED.												
ATRAF-I-BALDA.			WARANGAL.			KARIMNAGAR.			ADILABAD.			Serial No.
Persons.	Males.	Females.	Persons.	Males.	Females.	Persons.	Males.	Females.	Persons.	Males.	Females.	
8	9	10	11	12	13	14	15	16	17	18	19	
520,159	*265,184*	*254,975*	*905,414*	*467,413*	*438,001*	*1,131,637*	*586,260*	*545,377*	*620,426*	*314,428*	*305,998*	
520,003	*265,074*	*254,929*	*905,285*	*467,313*	*437,972*	*1,131,606*	*586,237*	*545,369*	*620,312*	*314,333*	*305,979*	
517,604	*263,391*	*254,213*	*876,502*	*452,951*	*423,551*	*1,130,848*	*585,716*	*545,132*	*601,301*	*305,801*	*295,500*	
5,257	2,938	2,319	3,123	1,918	1,205	897	535	362	1,101	726	375	1
464,255	237,581	226,674	392	219	173	67	44	23	21	13	8	2
3,243	*1,633*	*1,610*	*855,313*	*441,331*	*413,982*	*1,125,005*	*582,779*	*542,226*	*567,971*	*287,480*	*280,491*	
1,595	833	762	844,599	435,472	409,1[illegible]	2,682	1,309	1,373	601	103	498	3
1,622	780	842	10,660	5,836	4,824	1,121,592	581,169	540,423	12,226	7,863	4,363	4
26	20	6	54	23	31	731	301	430	555,144	279,514	275,630	5
32,021	*15,769*	*16,252*	*16,676*	*8,818*	*7,858*	*4,399*	*2,078*	*2,321*	*8,105*	*4,362*	*3,743*	
9,194	4,708	4,486	433	324	109	2,360	1,077	1,283	1,034	456	578	6
1,274	734	540	450	314	136	1,490	688	802	6,439	3,594	2,845	7
9,942	4,443	5,499	126	78	48	25	20	5	604	291	313	8
11,611	5,884	5,727	15,667	8,102	7,565	524	293	231	28	21	7	9
3,865	*1,510*	*2,355*	*315*	*212*	*103*	*364*	*205*	*159*	*18,698*	*10,789*	*7,819*	
287	94	193	172	125	47	46	21	25	1,451	1,075	376	10
424	39	385	25	21	4	8	6	2	1,704	684	1,020	11
2,976	1,295	1,681	98	56	42	258	167	91	12,012	6,720	5,292	12
178	82	96	20	10	10	52	11	41	3,441	2,310	1,131	13
8,963	*3,960*	*5,003*	*683*	*453*	*230*	*116*	*75*	*41*	*5,495*	*2,431*	*3,064*	
2,631	1,200	1,431	303	194	109	37	27	10	1,555	579	976	14
774	112	662	7	4	3	2	...	2	445	157	288	15
489	207	282	158	104	54	16	10	6	345	251	94	16
5,069	2,441	2,628	215	151	64	61	38	23	3,150	1,444	1,706	17
2,399	*1,683*	*716*	*28,783*	*14,362*	*14,421*	*758*	*521*	*237*	*19,011*	*8,532*	*10,479*	
1,368	*857*	*511*	*28,359*	*14,090*	*14,269*	*589*	*409*	*180*	*18,334*	*8,079*	*10,255*	
1,257	*782*	*475*	*27,343*	*13,265*	*14,078*	*536*	*370*	*166*	*18,265*	*8,039*	*10,226*	
248	110	138	330	229	101	33	23	10	9,594	4,426	5,168	18
240	237	3	222	164	58	85	23	62	8,085	3,223	4,862	19
769	435	334	26,791	12,872	13,919	418	324	94	586	390	196	20
111	*75*	*36*	*1,016*	*825*	*191*	*53*	*39*	*14*	*69*	*40*	*29*	
13	6	7	45	35	10	10	6	4	44	34	10	21
...	...	...	...	...	...	...	...	...	...	...	...	22
12	6	6	26	17	9	7	2	5	...	...	...	23
3	...	3	6	3	3	...	...	...	...	...	...	24
...	...	...	...	...	...	...	...	...	...	...	...	25
...	...	...	1	1	...	...	...	...	...	...	...	26
1	1	...	7	7	...	...	...	...	...	...	...	27
11	11	...	56	29	27	13	12	1	25	6	19	28
71	51	20	875	733	142	22	19	4	...	..	...	29
684	*619*	*65*	*274*	*174*	*100*	*143*	*88*	*55*	*437*	*232*	*205*	
...	...	...	...	...	...	...	...	...	...	...	...	30
18	...	18	1	1	...	...	...	...	1	...	1	31
...	...	...	1	1	...	...	...	...	...	...	...	32
...	...	...	36	28	8	...	...	...	140	4	136	33
...	...	...	...	...	...	...	...	...	...	...	...	34
...	...	...	2	2	...	...	...	...	...	...	...	35
7	6	1	8	8	...	...	...	...	...	...	...	36
637	601	36	103	61	42	36	22	14	17	15	2	37
...	...	...	...	...	...	...	...	...	...	...	..	38
22	12	10	123	73	50	107	66	41	279	213	66	39
...	...	...	...	...	...	...	...	...	...	...	...	40
...	...	...	...	...		...	...	...	...	...	...	41
7	*1*	*6*	*5*	*3*	*2*	...	...	...	...	...	...	42
340	*206*	*134*	*145*	*95*	*50*	*26*	*24*	*2*	*240*	*221*	*19*	43

TABLE XI.

BIRTH-PLACE.

Serial No.	District, State, Province, or country where born.	DISTRICT OF STATE					
		MEDAK.			NIZAMABAD.		
		Persons.	Males.	Females.	Persons.	Males.	Females.
	1	20	21	22	23	24	25
	Total Population ...	687,137	348,410	338,727	568,009	283,621	284,388
	A—BORN IN INDIA ...	686,985	348,293	338,692	567,914	283,540	284,374
	I.—Born within the State ...	684,884	347,071	337,813	566,959	282,901	284,058
1	Hyderabad City ...	3,049	1,657	1,392	1,438	858	[illegible]
2	Atraf-i-balda	11,444	4,972	6,472	346	154	192
	Warangal Division ...	6,312	2,705	3,607	5,137	1,855	3,282
3	Warangal	834	446	388	157	71	86
4	Karimnagar	5,466	2,248	3,218	4,754	1,671	3,083
5	Adilabad	12	11	1	226	113	113
	Medak Division	661,028	336,227	324,801	554,463	277,885	276,578
6	Medak	651,324	332,604	318,720	3,804	1,383	2,421
7	Nizamabad	3,016	1,168	1,848	550,519	276,413	274,106
8	Mahbubnagar	2,312	1,026	1,286	45	31	14
9	Nalgonda	4,376	1,429	2,947	95	58	37
	Aurangabad Division ...	568	239	329	4,247	1,596	2,651
10	Aurangabad	230	119	111	136	85	51
11	Bhir	20	13	7	53	24	29
12	Nander	304	102	202	4,002	1,457	2,545
13	Parbhani	14	5	9	56	30	26
	Gulbarga Division ...	2,483	1,271	1,212	1,330	553	777
14	Gulbarga	353	217	136	195	106	89
15	Osmanabad	6	2	4	5	2	3
16	Raichur	159	116	43	58	34	24
17	Bidar	1,965	936	1,029	1,072	411	661
	II.—Born in Provinces and States beyond the State..	2,101	1,222	879	955	639	316
	Provinces	1,763	993	770	731	472	259
	(a) Provinces adjacent to the State	1,672	934	738	532	323	209
18	Bombay (including Aden)...	591	315	276	168	98	70
19	Central Provinces and Berar	31	19	12	28	22	6
20	Madras (including Laccadives)	1,050	600	450	336	203	133
	(b) Other Provinces in India...	91	59	32	199	149	50
21	Ajmere-Merwara ...	4	4	...	152	118	34
22	Baluchistan (Districts and Administered Territories).	...	...	...	...	...	...
23	Bengal	4	3	1	3	3	...
24	Burma	6	1	5	2	...	2
25	Coorg	...	...	...	...	...	...
26	Eastern Bengal and Assam	...	...	...	...	...	...
27	North West Frontier Province (Districts and Administered Territories) ...	...	...	...	2	2	...
28	Punjab	35	27	8	14	7	[illegible]
29	United Provinces of Agra and Oudh	42	24	18	26	19	[illegible]
	States and Agencies ...	244	176	68	154	112	[illegible]
30	Baluchistan (Agency Tracts)	71	71	...	...	...	...
31	Baroda	2	2	...	17	10	[illegible]
32	Bombay States... ...	...	...	...	...	...	...
33	Central India agency ...	4	1	3	2	1	[illegible]
34	Central Provinces States ...	...	...	...	...	...	...
35	Cochin ...	...	...	...	...	...	...
36	Kashmir ...	23	21	2	...	...	...
37	Mysore ...	70	48	22	26	17	[illegible]
38	Punjab States ...	...	...	...	...	...	...
39	Rajputana Agency ...	74	33	41	109	84	[illegible]
40	Travancore ...	...	...	...		...	...
41	United Provinces States ...	...	...	...	...	...	...
42	**French and Portuguese Settlements**	...	...	...	...	...	...
43	**India,** *Unspecified* ...	94	53	41	70	55	[illegible]

TABLE XI.

BIRTH-PLACE.

WHERE ENUMERATED.												
MAHBUBNAGAR.			NALGONDA.			AURANGABAD.			BHIR.			Serial No.
Persons.	Males.	Females.	Persons.	Males.	Females.	Persons.	Males.	Females.	Persons.	Males.	Females.	
26	27	28	29	30	31	32	33	34	35	36	37	
747,178	*379,712*	*367,466*	*1,044,381*	*537,139*	*507,242*	*869,787*	*437,495*	*432,292*	*622,531*	*314,738*	*307,793*	
747,112	*379,662*	*367,450*	*1,044,317*	*537,087*	*507,230*	*869,541*	*437,311*	*432,230*	*622,440*	*314,672*	*307,768*	
746,605	*378,769*	*366,836*	*1,030,206*	*529,845*	*500,361*	*834,200*	*419,969*	*414,231*	*605,265*	*308,885*	*296,380*	
532	310	222	1,638	978	660	1,931	917	1,014	367	214	153	1
2,270	959	1,311	5,945	2,999	2,946	25	3	22	7	6	1	2
150	*79*	*71*	*13,097*	*6,446*	*6,651*	*158*	*113*	*45*	*31*	*16*	*15*	
74	40	34	11,222	5,552	5,670	49	30	19	7	5	2	3
66	35	31	1,863	887	976	56	44	12	6	5	1	4
10	4	6	12	7	5	53	39	14	18	6	12	5
739,109	*375,926*	*363,183*	*1,009,116*	*519,165*	*489,951*	*565*	*330*	*235*	*146*	*83*	*63*	
450	218	232	2,988	1,266	1,722	57	20	37	8	3	5	6
38	18	20	181	112	69	447	263	184	134	77	57	7
735,350	374,226	361,124	1,187	442	745	61	47	14	4	3	1	8
3,271	1,464	1,807	1,004,760	517,345	487,415	...	...	...	...	...	...	9
79	*50*	*29*	*121*	*74*	*47*	*830,557*	*418,176*	*412,381*	*596,617*	*306,063*	*290,554*	
30	26	4	45	29	16	822,008	414,236	407,772	3,227	1,112	2,115	10
2	2	...	3	1	2	5,418	2,634	2,784	589,708	303,596	286,112	11
45	22	23	65	42	23	416	149	267	443	229	214	12
2	...	2	8	2	6	2,715	1,157	1,558	3,239	1,126	2,113	13
3,465	*1,445*	*2,020*	*289*	*183*	*106*	*964*	*430*	*534*	*8,097*	*2,503*	*5,594*	
2,293	956	1,337	92	57	35	224	98	126	153	84	69	14
6	4	2	13	8	5	271	116	155	6,560	1,938	4,622	15
1,124	459	665	59	37	22	138	93	45	9	6	3	16
42	26	16	125	81	44	331	123	208	1,375	475	900	17
1,507	*893*	*614*	*14,111*	*7,242*	*6,869*	*35,341*	*17,342*	*17,999*	*17,175*	*5,787*	*11,388*	
1,307	*775*	*532*	*13,930*	*7,127*	*6,803*	*32,071*	*15,031*	*17,040*	*16,444*	*5,281*	*11,163*	
1,273	*764*	*509*	*13,848*	*7,068*	*6,780*	*29,650*	*13,519*	*16,131*	*15,624*	*4,740*	*10,884*	
362	192	170	156	96	60	25,491	12,006	13,485	15,441	4,630	10,811	18
14	14	...	20	15	5	3,038	939	2,099	171	102	69	19
897	558	339	13,672	6,957	6,715	1,121	574	547	12	8	4	20
34	*11*	*23*	*82*	*59*	*23*	*2,421*	*1,512*	*909*	*820*	*541*	*279*	
4	2	2	22	14	8	1,209	623	586	680	441	239	21
2	2	...	...	...	...	47	40	7	10	10	...	22
2	1	1	14	13	1	183	174	9	4	3	1	23
10	...	10	4	2	2	4	1	3	...	...	...	24
...	...	...	1	...	1	...	...	...	...	...	...	25
...	...	...	...	...	...	...	...	...	...	...	...	26
...	...	...	8	6	2	17	6	11	21	21	...	27
7	3	4	6	5	1	263	118	145	35	30	5	28
9	3	6	27	19	8	698	550	148	70	36	34	29
128	*76*	*52*	*81*	*42*	*39*	*2,805*	*1,938*	*817*	*649*	*435*	*214*	
...	...	...	...	...	...	...	...	...	...	...	...	30
1	1	...	...	...	...	39	34	5	3	1	2	31
...	...	...	...	...	...	...	...	...	8	8	...	32
1	1	...	2	...	2	37	23	14	15	12	3	33
...	...	...	...	...	...	...	...	...	...	...	...	34
...	...	...	1	1	...	...	...	...	...	...	...	35
4	4	...	...	...	...	8	3	5	...	...	...	36
42	28	14	36	12	24	100	93	7	2	1	1	37
...	...	...	...	...	...	...	...	...	...	...	...	38
80	42	38	42	29	13	2,621	1,835	786	621	413	208	39
...	...	...	...	...	...	...	...	...	...	...	...	40
...	...	...	...	...	...	...	...	...	...	...	...	41
...	...	...	...	...	...	*36*	*26*	*10*	...	...	...	42
72	*42*	*30*	*100*	*73*	*27*	*429*	*297*	*132*	*82*	*71*	*11*	43

TABLE XI.

BIRTH-PLACE.

Serial No.	District, State, Province, or country where born.	DISTRICT OF STATE. Nander. Persons.	Nander. Males.	Nander. Females.	Parbhani. Persons.	Parbhani. Males.	Parbhani. Females.
	1	38	39	40	41	42	43
	Total Population	*704,549*	*352,638*	*351,911*	*779,674*	*391,231*	*388,4*[illegible]
	A—BORN IN INDIA	*704,422*	*352,529*	*351,893*	*779,507*	*391,094*	*388,41*[illegible]
	I.—Born within the State	*695,638*	*347,515*	*348,123*	*761,292*	*381,576*	*379,71*[illegible]
1	Hyderabad City	1,587	961	626	2,397	1,528	86[illegible]
2	Atraf-i-balda	573	165	408	388	183	20[illegible]
	Warangal Division	*2,686*	*1,539*	*1,147*	*943*	*696*	*24*[illegible]
3	Warangal	105	55	50	317	22[illegible]	9[illegible]
4	Karimnagar	747	522	225	432	337	9[illegible]
5	Adilabad	1,834	962	872	194	134	[illegible]
	Medak Division	*11,164*	*5,238*	*5,926*	*2,620*	*1,702*	*91*[illegible]
6	Medak	505	293	212	496	274	22[illegible]
7	Nizamabad	10,514	4,858	5,656	2,007	1,357	65[illegible]
8	Mahbubnagar	69	35	34	62	51	1[illegible]
9	Nalgonda	76	52	24	55	20	3[illegible]
	Aurangabad Division	*670,408*	*335,340*	*335,068*	*750,631*	*375,331*	*375,30*[illegible]
10	Aurangabad	833	468	365	6,667	3,181	3,48[illegible]
11	Bhir	703	393	310	10,677	4,674	6,00[illegible]
12	Nander	662,342	331,632	330,710	9,103	5,194	3,909
13	Parbhani	6,530	2,847	3,683	724,184	362,282	361,902
	Gulbarga Division	*9,220*	*4,272*	*4,948*	*4,313*	*2,135*	*2,17*[illegible]
14	Gulbarga	448	267	181	504	258	246
15	Osmanabad	414	247	167	742	410	332
16	Raichur	52	38	14	243	131	112
17	Bidar	8,306	3,720	4,586	2,824	1,336	1,488
	II.—Born in Provinces and States beyond the State	*8,784*	*5,014*	*3,770*	*18,215*	*9,518*	*8,697*
	Provinces	*7,867*	*4,375*	*3,492*	*15,964*	*7,970*	*7,994*
	(a) **Provinces adjacent to the State**	*6,686*	*3,551*	*3,135*	*13,686*	*6,454*	*7,232*
18	Bombay (including Aden)	2,739	1,496	1,243	11.173	5,438	5,735
19	Central Provinces and Berar	3,656	1,883	1,773	2,040	739	1,301
20	Madras (including Laccadives)	291	172	119	473	277	196
	(b) **Other Provinces in India.**	*1,181*	*824*	*357*	*2,278*	*1,516*	*762*
21	Ajmere-Merwara	658	448	210	1,768	1,113	65[illegible]
22	Baluchistan (Districts and Administered Territories).	4	4	...	23	23	...
23	Bengal	37	37	...	20	20	...
24	Burma	1	1	...	6	1	5
25	Coorg	...	...	...	...	...	...
26	Eastern Bengal and Assam.	2	2	...	...	...	...
27	North West Frontier Province (Districts and Administered Territories)	7	6	1	1	1	...
28	Punjab	233	163	70	99	90	[illegible]
29	United Provinces of Agra and Oudh	239	163	76	361	26[illegible]	9[illegible]
	States and Agencies	*719*	*491*	*228*	*1,926*	*1,358*	*56*[illegible]
30	Baluchistan (Agency Tracts.)	...	...	...	...	...	...
31	Baroda	1	1	...	36	8	2[illegible]
32	Bombay States	...	...	...	...	...	...
33	Central India Agency	7	5	2	67	44	2[illegible]
34	Central Provinces States	...	...	...	1	1	...
35	Cochin	...	...	...	...	...	...
36	Kashmir	...	...	...	1	1	...
37	Mysore	23	18	5	57	39	1[illegible]
38	Punjab States	...	...	...	13	...	1[illegible]
39	Rajputana Agency	688	467	221	1,746	1,260	4[illegible]
40	Travancore	...	...	...	...	...	...
41	United Provinces States	...	...	...	5	5	...
42	**French and Portuguese Settlements**	*2*	*2*	...	*1*	*1*	...
43	**India,** *Unspecified*	*196*	*146*	*50*	*324*	*189*	*13*[illegible]

TABLE XI.

BIRTH-PLACE.

WHERE ENUMERATED.												
GULBARGA.			OSMANABAD.			RAICHUR.			BIDAR.			Serial No.
Persons.	Males.	Females.	Persons.	Males.	Females.	Persons.	Males.	Females.	Persons.	Males.	Females	
44	45	46	47	48	49	50	51	52	53	54	55	
1,150,983	*582,447*	*568,536*	*635,977*	*324,969*	*311,008*	*996,684*	*503,541*	*493,143*	*889,527*	*449,438*	*440,089*	
1,150,872	*582,362*	*568,510*	*635,897*	*324,915*	*310,982*	*996,595*	*503,476*	*493,119*	*889,484*	*449,408*	*440,076*	
1,130,881	*572,379*	*558,502*	*609,922*	*315,877*	*294,045*	*986,181*	*498,284*	*487,897*	*887,052*	*448,297*	*438,755*	
2,032	1,300	732	537	328	209	885	499	386	807	475	332	1
832	490	342	3	2	1	42	19	23	645	292	353	2
279	*211*	*68*	*27*	*14*	*13*	*47*	*32*	*15*	*373*	*87*	*286*	
151	114	37	20	10	10	31	24	7	37	22	15	3
95	68	27	3	1	2	5	2	3	44	35	9	4
33	29	4	4	3	1	11	6	5	292	30	262	5
3,961	*1,884*	*2,077*	*51*	*33*	*18*	*1,327*	*590*	*737*	*3,470*	*1,455*	*2,015*	
207	128	79	8	5	3	14	12	2	1,605	782	823	6
126	94	32	36	23	13	65	25	40	1,812	645	1,167	7
3,538	1,607	1,931	1	1	...	1,225	534	691	29	14	15	8
90	55	35	6	4	2	23	19	4	24	14	10	9
611	*385*	*226*	*8,774*	*2,731*	*6,043*	*115*	*98*	*17*	*9,222*	*5,446*	*3,776*	
191	130	61	238	107	131	66	53	13	250	89	161	10
158	76	82	8,051	2,385	5,666	6	6	...	676	268	408	11
191	139	52	267	143	124	37	34	3	6,805	4,645	2,160	12
71	40	31	218	96	122	6	5	1	1,491	444	1,047	13
1,122,166	*568,109*	*555,057*	*600,530*	*312,769*	*287,761*	*983,765*	*497,046*	*486,719*	*872,535*	*440,542*	*431,993*	
1,113,902	562,924	550,978	1,110	427	683	1,249	620	629	3,091	1,468	1,623	14
1,429	788	641	595,527	310,963	284,564	18	10	8	2,765	742	2,023	15
3,011	1,567	1,434	61	38	23	982,465	496,391	486,074	85	57	28	16
4,934	2,830	2,104	3,832	1,341	2,491	33	25	8	866,594	438,275	428,319	17
19,991	*9,983*	*10,008*	*25,975*	*9,038*	*16,937*	*10,414*	*5,192*	*5,222*	*2,432*	*1,111*	*1,321*	
19,226	*9,515*	*9,711*	*25,442*	*8,673*	*16,769*	*9,845*	*4,786*	*5,059*	*2,076*	*815*	*1,257*	
18,895	*9,269*	*9,626*	*24,953*	*8,353*	*16,600*	*9,683*	*4,671*	*5,012*	*1,652*	*529*	*1,123*	
18,257	8,872	9,385	24,792	8,247	16,545	4,089	1,942	2,147	1,555	460	1,095	18
44	27	17	109	70	39	22	14	8	28	25	3	19
594	370	224	52	36	16	5,572	2,715	2,857	69	44	25	20
331	*246*	*85*	*489*	*320*	*169*	*162*	*115*	*47*	*424*	*290*	*134*	
183	143	40	395	248	147	98	79	19	314	204	110	21
8	8	...	...	...	...	...	...	...	2	2	...	22
5	5	...	5	4	1	19	15	4	5	3	2	23
1	1	...	...	...	...	4	2	2	...	...	...	24
...	...	...	...	...	...	...	...	...	...	...	...	25
...	...	...	...	...	...	...	...	...	...	...	...	26
2	2	...	14	11	3	...	...	...	13	13	...	27
29	12	17	23	16	7	21	14	7	33	25	8	28
100	75	25	52	41	11	20	5	15	57	43	14	29
681	*405*	*276*	*507*	*345*	*162*	*474*	*332*	*142*	*302*	*251*	*51*	
...	...	...	...	...	...	...	...	...	...	...	...	30
18	6	12	3	3	...	3	3	...	...	...	...	31
...	...	...	7	...	7	...	...	...	161	161	...	32
...	...	...	9	6	3	...	...	...	10	2	8	33
...	...	...	...	...		1	...	1	...	...	...	34
1	1	...	...	...	...	...	...		...	...	...	35
3	2	1	...	...	...	...	...	...	1	1	...	36
125	60	65	4	2	2	243	183	60	12	4	8	37
10	10	...	8	3	5	...	...	...	...	...	...	38
524	326	198	476	331	145	225	146	79	117	82	35	39
...	...	...	...	...	...	2	...	2	...	...	...	40
...	...	...	...	...	...	...	...	...	1	1	...	41
16	*8*	*8*	...	...	...	*1*	*1*	...	*1*	*1*	...	42
68	*55*	*13*	*26*	*20*	*6*	*94*	*73*	*21*	*53*	*40*	*13*	43

TABLE XI.

BIRTH-PLACE.

Serial No.	District, State, Province, or country where born.	DISTRICT OF STATE.					
		Population of the State.			Hyderabad City.		
		Persons.	Males.	Females.	Persons.	Males.	Females.
	1	56	57	58	59	60	61
	B. Born in other Asiatic Countries.	***3,507***	***2,882***	***625***	***1,998***	***1,682***	***316***
44	Afghanistan ..	468	367	101	180	163	17
45	Arabia ..	2,864	2,394	470	1,684	1,425	259
46	Bhotan ...	12	12	...	12	12	...
47	Ceylon ..	20	9	11	13	5	8
48	Hongkong ..	1	1	...	1	1	...
49	Japan ..	3	...	3	3	...	3
50	Nepal ...	19	12	7	9	7	2
51	Persia ..	90	59	31	67	42	25
52	Straits Settlements and Malaya.	29	27	2	29	27	2
53	Turkey in Asia ...	1	1	...	...	...	...
	C. Born in Europe ...	***3,936***	***3,444***	***492***	***3,701***	***3,293***	***408***
54	United Kingdom— ..	3,790	3,359	431	3,581	3,225	356
	England and Wales ..	3,615	3,238	377	3,437	3,120	317
	Scotland	72	53	19	49	39	10
	Ireland	103	68	35	95	66	29
55	Austria Hungary ...	5	1	4	5	1	4
56	Belgium	1	1	...	1	1	...
57	France	12	6	6	11	6	5
58	Germany	3	2	1	3	2	1
59	Gibraltar	1	...	1	1	...	1
60	Italy	66	42	24	61	40	21
61	Malta	1	...	1	...	...	...
62	Rumania	1	1	...	1	1	...
63	Russia	11	6	5	6	4	2
64	Spain	3	2	1	3	2	1
65	Switzerland	1	1	...	1	1	...
66	Turkey in Europe ..	13	13	...	9	9	...
67	Europe, *Unspecified* ..	28	10	18	18	1	17
	D. Born in Africa ...	***98***	***87***	***11***	***97***	***86***	***11***
68	Egypt	8	8	...	8	8	...
69	Mauritius	1	...	1	1	...	1
70	Africa, *Unspecified* ...	89	79	10	88	78	10
	E. Born in America ..	***40***	***13***	***27***	***27***	***8***	***19***
71	Canada	1	...	1	1	...	1
72	Jamaica	3	...	3	3	...	3
73	Newfoundland ..	1	1	...	1	1	...
74	United States	1	...	1	...	...	...
75	America, *Unspecified* ...	34	12	22	22	7	15
	F. Born in Australasia ..	***11***	***9***	***2***	***9***	***8***	***1***
76	Australia	4	3	1	2	2	...
77	Java	4	4	...	4	4	...
78	New Zealand	2	1	1	2	1	1
79	Tasmania	1	1	...	1	1	...
	G. Born at sea ...	***4***	***2***	***2***	***3***	***2***	***1***
80	At Sea...	4	2	2	3	2	1

TABLE XI.

BIRTH-PLACE.

WHERE ENUMERATED.												
ATRAF-I-BALDA.			WARANGAL.			KARIMNAGAR.			ADILABAD.			Serial No.
Persons.	Males.	Females.	Persons.	Males.	Females.	Persons.	Males.	Females.	Persons.	Males.	Females	
62	63	64	65	66	67	68	69	70	71	72	73	
111	*79*	*32*	*74*	*62*	*12*	*20*	*18*	*2*	*114*	*95*	*19*	
16	6	10	6	6	...	...	...	...	3	2	1	44
93	73	20	67	56	11	20	18	2	109	91	18	45
...	...	...	...	...	...	...	...	...	...	...	...	46
2	...	2	1	...	1	...	...	...	...	...	...	47
...	...	...	...	...	...	...	...	...	...	...	...	48
...	...	...	...	...	...	...	...	...	...	...	...	49
...	...	...	...	...	...	...	...	...	1	1	...	50
...	...	...	...	...	...	...	...	...	...	...	...	51
...	...	...	...	...	...	...	...	...	...	...	...	52
...	...	...	...	...	...	...	...	...	1	1	...	53
44	*31*	*13*	*48*	*36*	*12*	*11*	*5*	*6*	...	...	...	
44	31	13	38	27	11	11	5	6	...	...	...	54
40	29	11	34	24	10	6	2	4	...	...	...	
4	2	2	3	3	...	3	2	1	...	...	...	
...	...	...	1	...	1	2	1	1	...	...	...	
...	...	...	...	...	...	...	...	...	...	...	...	55
...	...	...	...	...	...	...	...	...	...	...	...	56
...	...	...	...	...	...	...	...	...	...	...	...	57
...	...	...	...	...	...	...	...	...	...	...	...	58
...	...	...	...	...	...	...	...	...	...	...	...	59
...	...	...	...	...	...	...	...	...	...	...	...	60
...	...	...	...	...	...	...	...	...	...	...	...	61
...	...	...	...	...	...	...	...	...	...	...	...	62
...	...	...	...	...	...	...	...	...	...	...	...	63
...	...	...	...	...	...	...	...	...	...	...	...	64
...	...	...	...	...	...	...	...	...	...	...	...	65
...	...	...	...	...	...	...	...	...	...	...	...	66
...	...	...	10	9	1	...	...	...	...	...	...	67
...	...	...	...	...	...	...	...	...	...	...	...	
...	...	...	...	...	...	...	...	...	...	...	...	68
...	...	...	...	...	...	...	...	...	...	...	...	69
...	...	...	...	...	...	...	...	...	...	...	...	70
...	...	...	*7*	*2*	*5*	...	...	...	...	...	...	
...	...	...	...	...	...	...	...	...	...	...	...	71
...	...	...	...	...	...	...	...	...	...	...	...	72
...	...	...	...	...	...	...	...	...	...	...	...	73
...	...	...	...	...	...	...	...	...	...	...	...	74
...	...	...	7	2	5	...	...	...	...	...	...	75
1	...	*1*	...	...	...	...	...	...	...	...		
1	...	1	...	...	...	...	...	...	...	...	...	76
...	...	...	...	...	...	...	...	...	...	...	...	77
...	...	...	...	...	...	...	...	...	...	...	...	78
...	...	...	...	...	...	...	...	...	...	...	...	79
...	...	...	...	...	...	...	...	...	...	...	...	
...	...	...	...	...	...	...	...	...	...	...	...	80

TABLE XI.

BIRTH-PLACE.

Serial No.	District, State, Province, or country where born.	DISTRICT OF STATE.					
		MEDAK.			NIZAMABAD.		
		Persons.	Males.	Females	Persons.	Males.	Females.
	1	74	75	76	77	78	79
	B. Born in other Asiatic Countries.	*133*	*111*	*22*	*89*	*80*	*9*
44	Afghanistan ...	40	22	18	6	6	...
45	Arabia ...	92	88	4	83	74	9
46	Bhotan ...	...	...	...	...	...	...
47	Ceylon ...	1	1	...	...	...	...
48	Hongkong ...	...	...	...	...	...	...
49	Japan ..	...	...	...	...	...	...
50	Nepal ..	...	...	...	...	...	...
51	Persia ...	...	...	...	...	...	...
52	Straits Settlements and Malaya	...	...	...	...	...	...
53	Turkey in Asia ...	...	...	...	...	...	...
	C. Born in Europe ..	*19*	*6*	*13*	*5*	...	*5*
54	United Kingdom— ..	19	6	13	5	...	5
	England and Wales ..	17	6	11	5	..	5
	Scotland ..	1	...	1	...	...	...
	Ireland ..	1	...	1	..	...	...
55	Austria Hungary ..	...	...	...	...	...	...
56	Belgium ...	...	...	...	...	...	...
57	France	...	...	...	...	...	...
58	Germany	...	...	...	...	...	...
59	Gibraltar	...	...	...	...	...	...
60	Italy	...	...	...	...	...	...
61	Malta	...	...	...	...	...	...
62	Rumania	...	...	...	...	...	...
63	Russia	...	...	...	...	...	...
64	Spain	...	...	...	...	...	...
65	Switzerland	...	...	...	...	...	...
66	Turkey in Europe ..	...	...	..	...	...	...
67	Europe, *Unspecified* ..	...	...	...	...	...	...
	D. Born in Africa	...	...	...	*1*	*1*	...
68	Egypt	...	...	...	...	...	...
69	Mauritius ..	...	...	...	...	...	...
70	Africa, *Unspecified* ..	...	...	...	1	1	...
	E. Born in America ..	...	...	...	...	...	...
71	Canada	...	...	...	...	...	...
72	Jamaica	...	...	...	...	...	...
73	Newfoundland ..	...	...	...	...	...	...
74	United States	...	...	...	...	...	..
75	America, *Unspecified* ..	...	...	...	...	...	...
	F. Born in Australasia ..	...	...	...	...	...	...
76	Australia	...	...	...	...	...	...
77	Java	...	...	...	...	...	...
78	New Zealand	...	...	...	...	...	...
79	Tasmania	...	...	...	...	...	...
	G. Born at Sea ...	...	...	...	...	...	...
80	At Sea	...	...	...	...	...	...

TABLE XI.

BIRTH-PLACE.

WHERE ENUMERATED.												
MAHBUBNAGAR.			NALGONDA.			AURANGABAD.			BHIR.			Serial No.
Persons.	Males.	Females.	Persons.	Males.	Females.	Persons.	Males.	Females.	Persons.	Males.	Females.	
80	81	82	83	84	85	86	87	88	89	90	91	
55	*42*	*13*	*56*	*48*	*8*	*205*	*158*	*47*	*91*	*66*	*25*	
2	2	...	...	...	...	68	34	34	33	31	2	44
50	39	11	56	48	8	136	123	13	57	34	23	45
...	...	...	...	...	...	...	...	...	...	...	...	46
...	...	...	...	...	...	...	...	...	...	...	...	47
...	...	...	...	...	...	...	...	...	...	...	...	48
...	...	...	...	...	...	...	...	...	...	...	...	49
3	1	2	...	...	...	1	1	...	1	1	...	50
...	...	...	...	...	...	...	...	...	...	...	...	51
...	...	...	...	...	...	...	...	...	...	...	...	52
...	...	...	...	...	...	...	...	...	...	...	...	53
7	*6*	*1*	*8*	*4*	*4*	*39*	*24*	*15*	...	...	...	54
7	6	1	3	2	1	38	24	14	...	...	...	
7	6	1	3	2	1	31	21	10	...	...	...	
...	...	...	...	...	...	1	2	4	...	...	...	
...	...	...	...	...	...	1	1	...	...	...	...	
...	...	...	...	...	...	...	...	...	...	...	...	55
...	...	...	...	...	...	...	...	...	...	...	...	56
...	...	...	...	...	...	1	...	1	...	...	...	57
...	...	...	...	...	...	...	...	...	...	...	...	58
...	...	...	...	...	...	...	...	...	...	...	...	59
...	...	...	...	...	...	...	...	...	...	...	...	60
...	...	...	...	...	...	...	...	...	...	...	...	61
...	...	...	...	...	...	...	...	...	...	...	...	62
...	...	...	5	2	3	...	...	...	...	...	...	63
...	...	...	...	...	...	...	...	...	...	...	...	64
...	...	...	...	...	...	...	...	...	...	...	...	65
...	...	...	...	...	...	...	...	...	...	...	...	66
...	...	...	...	...	...	...	...	...	...	...	...	67
...	...	...	...	...	...	...	...	...	...	...	...	
...	...	...	...	...	...	...	...	...	...	...	...	68
...	...	...	...	...	...	...	...	...	...	...	...	69
...	...	...	...	...	...	...	...	...	...	...	...	70
4	*2*	*2*	...	...	...	*1*	*1*	...	...	...	...	
...	...	...	...	...	...	...	...	...	...	...	...	71
...	...	...	...	...	...	...	...	...	...	...	...	72
...	...	...	...	...	...	...	...	...	...	...	...	73
...	...	...	...	...	...	...	...	...	...	...	...	74
4	2	2	...	...	...	1	1	...	...	...	...	75
...	...	...	...	...	...	*1*	*1*	...	...	...	...	
...	...	...	...	...	...	1	1	...	...	...	...	76
...	...	...	...	...	...	...	...	...	...	...	...	77
...	...	...	...	...	...	...	...	...	...	...	...	78
...	...	...	...	...	...	...	...	...	...	...	...	79
...	...	...	...	...	...	...	...	...	...	...	...	
...	...	...	...	...	...	...	...	...	...	...	...	80

TABLE XI.

BIRTH-PLACE.

Serial No.	District, State, Province, or country where born.	DISTRICT OF STATE.					
		NANDER.			PARBHANI.		
		Persons.	Males.	Females.	Persons.	Males.	Females.
	1	92	93	94	95	96	97
	B. Born in other Asiatic Countries	*124*	*106*	*18*	*145*	*124*	*25*
44	Afghanistan	50	42	8	34	33	1
45	Arabia	73	63	10	114	90	24
46	Bhotan	...	...	...	...	...	...
47	Ceylon	...	...	...	...	...	...
48	Hongkong	...	...	...	...	...	...
49	Japan	...	...	...	...	...	...
50	Nepal	1	1	...	...	...	...
51	Persia ...	...	...	...	1	1	..
52	Straits Settlements and Malaya	...	...	...	...	...	...
53	Turkey in Asia ...	...	...	...	...	...	...
	C. Born in Europe ...	*3*	*3*	...	*18*	*13*	*5*
54	United Kingdom— ...	...	...	...	16	12	4
	England and Wales ..	...	...	..	15	11	4
	Scotland ...	...	...	..	1	1	...
	Ireland ...	...	...	...	...	...	...
55	Austria Hungary ...	...	...	...	...	...	...
56	Belgium	...	...	...	...	...	...
57	France	...	...	...	...	...	...
58	Germany	...	...	...	...	...	...
59	Gibraltar	..	...	...	...	...	...
60	Italy	...	...	..	2	1	1
61	Malta	...	...	...	...	...	...
62	Rumania	...	...	...	...	...	...
63	Russia	...	...	...	...	...	...
64	Spain	...	...	...	...	...	...
65	Switzerland	...	...	...	...	...	...
66	Turkey in Europe ..	3	3	...	...	...	...
67	Europe, *Unspecified* ..	...	...	...	...	...	...
	D. Born in Africa ..	...	...	...	...	...	...
68	Egypt	...	...	...	...	...	...
69	Mauritius	...	...	...	...	..	...
70	Africa, *Unspecified* ..	...	...	...	...	...	...
	E. Born in America ...	...	...	...	...	...	...
71	Canada	...	...	...	...	...	...
72	Jamaica	...	...	...	...	...	...
73	Newfoundland ...	...	...	...	...	...	...
74	United States	...	...	...	...	...	...
75	America, *Unspecified* ...	...	...	...	...	...	...
	F. Born in Australasia ...	...	...	...	...	...	...
76	Australia	...	...	...	...	...	...
77	Java ...	...	...	...	...	...	...
78	New Zealand	...	...	...	...	...	...
79	Tasmania	...	...	...	...	...	...
	G. Born at Sea ...	...	...	...	...	...	...
80	At Sea	...	...	...	...	...	...

TABLE XI.

BIRTH-PLACE.

WHERE ENUMERATED.												
GULBARGA.			OSMANABAD.			RAICHUR.			BIDAR.			Serial No.
Persons.	Males.	Females.	Persons.	Males.	Females.	Persons.	Males.	Females.	Persons.	Males.	Females.	
98	99	100	101	102	103	104	105	106	107	108	109	
98	*75*	*23*	*80*	*54*	*26*	*68*	*52*	*16*	*42*	*30*	*12*	
9	7	2	12	5	7	2	2	...	7	6	1	44
67	52	15	68	49	19	63	47	16	32	24	8	45
...	...	...	...	...	...	...	...	...	...	...	...	46
...	...	...	...	...	...	3	3	...	...	...	...	47
...	...	...	...	...	...	...	...	...	...	...	...	48
...	...	...	...	...	...	...	...	...	...	...	...	49
...	...	...	...	...	...	...	...	...	3	...	3	50
22	16	6	...	...	...	...	...	...	...	...	...	51
...	...	...	...	...	...	...	...	...	...	...	...	52
...	...	...	...	...	...	...	...	...	...	...	...	53
13	*10*	*3*	...	...	...	*20*	*13*	*7*	...	...	...	
12	10	2	...	...	...	16	11	5	...	...	...	54
[illegible]	[illegible]	[illegible]	...	...	...	11	10	1	...	...	...	
[illegible]	[illegible]	...	...	...	...	[illegible]	[illegible]	1	...	...	...	
...	...	...	...	...	...	[illegible]	...	[illegible]	...	...	...	
...	...	...	...	...	...	...	...	...	...	...	...	55
...	...	...	...	...	...	...	...	...	...	...	...	56
...	...	...	...	...	...	...	...	...	...	...	...	57
...	...	...	...	...	...	...	...	...	...	...	...	58
...	...	...	...	...	...	...	...	...	...	...	...	59
...	...	...	...	...	...	3	1	2	...	...	...	60
1	...	1	...	...	...	...	...	...	...	...	...	61
...	...	...	...	...	...	...	...	...	...	...	...	62
...	...	...	...	...	...	...	...	...	...	...	...	63
...	...	...	...	...	...	...	...	...	...	...	...	64
...	...	...	...	...	...	...	...	...	...	...	...	65
...	...	...	...	...	...	1	1	...	...	...	...	66
...	...	...	...	...	...	...	...	...	...	...	...	67
...	...	...	...	...	...	...	...	...	...	...	...	
...	...	...	...	...	...	...	...	...	...	...	...	68
...	...	...	...	...	...	...	...	...	...	...	...	69
...	...	...	...	...	...	...	...	...	...	...	...	70
...	...	...	...	...	...	...	...	...	*1*	...	*1*	
...	...	...	...	...	...	...	...	...	...	...	...	71
...	...	...	...	...	...	...	...	...	...	...	...	72
...	...	...	...	...	...	...	...	...	...	...	...	73
...	...	...	...	...	...	...	...	...	1	...	1	74
...	...	...	...	...	...	...	...	...	...	...	...	75
...	...	...	...	...	...	...	...	...	...	...	...	
...	...	...	...	...	...	...	...	...	...	...	...	76
...	...	...	...	...	...	...	...	...	...	...	...	77
...	...	...	...	...	...	...	...	...	...	...	...	78
...	...	...	...	...	...	...	...	...	...	...	...	79
...	...	...	...	...	...	1	...	1	...	...	...	
...	...	...	...	...	...	1	...	1	...	...	...	80

TABLE XII.

INFIRMITIES.

Part I.—Distribution by Age.

Part II.—Distribution by Districts.

1. The infirmities recorded at the census were insanity, deaf-mutism, blindness and leprosy.

2. The table is divided into two parts——Part I shows the distribution of the persons afflicted according to age, and Part II their distribution according to locality. In 1901 Part II of the table was not prepared for districts.

3. Some unfortunate persons were returned as suffering from more than one infirmity. In the table they have been shown under each. This explains why the total "Population afflicted" in columns 2, 3 and 4 does not quite agree with the total of the figures for each separate infirmity. The following is a list of these double entries :—

INFIRMITIES.	Persons.	Males.	Females.
Total ...	*171*	*93*	*78*
Insane and Blind	18	9	9
Insane and Lepers	2	1	1
Insane and Deaf-mutes	101	53	48
Deaf-mutes and Blind	28	14	14
Deaf-mutes and Lepers	11	8	3
Blind and Lepers.	11	8	3

TABLE XII.

INFIRMITIES.

Part I.
Distribution by Age.

AGE.	Population Afflicted.			Insane.			Deaf-mutes.			Blind.			Lepers.		
	Persons.	Males.	Females.	Persons.	Males.	Females.	Persons.	Males.	Females.	Persons.	Males.	Females.	Persons.	Males.	Females.
1	2	3	4	5	6	7	8	9	10	11	12	13	14	15	16
Total ...	***26,831***	***15,025***	***11,806***	***2,560***	***1,547***	***1,013***	***4,421***	***2,522***	***1,899***	***16,263***	***8,287***	***7,976***	***3,758***	***2,762***	[illegible]
0—1 ...	**124**	72	52	...	...	...	**1**	...	1	**123**	72	51	...	...	...
1—2 ..	**123**	71	52	**2**	1	1	**3**	3	...	**117**	66	51	**1**	1	...
2—3 ...	**231**	136	95	**8**	3	5	**22**	12	10	**200**	121	79	**2**	1	1
3—4 ..	**260**	139	121	**16**	3	13	**70**	41	29	**175**	96	79	**2**	...	[illegible]
4—5 ..	**356**	199	157	**33**	25	8	**116**	57	59	**208**	117	91	**2**	1	
Total 0—5 ..	***1,094***	***617***	***477***	***59***	***32***	***27***	***212***	***113***	***99***	***823***	***472***	***351***	***7***	***3***	[illegible]
5—10 ..	**2,000**	1,146	854	**199**	122	77	**644**	358	286	**1,149**	664	485	**30**	18	[illegible]
10—15 ...	**2,254**	1,321	933	**306**	179	127	**671**	375	296	**1,203**	722	480	**100**	56	[illegible]
15—20 ..	**1,807**	1,025	782	**267**	134	133	**467**	251	216	**959**	561	398	**137**	68	[illegible]
20—25 ..	**2,282**	1,312	970	**275**	162	113	**541**	329	212	**1,244**	674	570	**237**	152	[illegible]
25—30 ..	**2,284**	1,386	898	**293**	193	100	**468**	282	186	**1,206**	676	530	**334**	246	[illegible]
30—35 ..	**2,576**	1,441	1,135	**291**	179	112	**402**	256	146	**1,424**	688	736	**471**	327	1
35—40 ..	**1,563**	936	627	**167**	113	54	**224**	129	95	**823**	423	400	**353**	272	[illegible]
40—45 ..	**2,493**	1,429	1,064	**237**	150	87	**338**	188	150	**1,299**	626	673	**632**	473	1
45—50 .	**1,218**	753	465	**117**	81	36	**119**	63	56	**681**	373	308	**304**	229	
50—55 ..	**2,237**	1,229	1,008	**168**	95	73	**159**	88	71	**1,384**	646	738	**532**	402	[illegible]
55—60 ..	**617**	383	234	**44**	32	12	**32**	19	13	**400**	218	182	**146**	115	
60—65 ..	**2,099**	1,014	1,085	**83**	46	37	**91**	46	45	**1,634**	700	934	**302**	228	
65—70 ..	**412**	204	208	**18**	11	7	**14**	8	6	**328**	144	184	**54**	48	[illegible]
70 & over .	**1,895**	829	1,066	**36**	18	18	**39**	17	22	**1,707**	700	1,007	**119**	96	

TABLE XII.

INFIRMITIES.

Part II.

Distribution by Districts.

	DISTRICT.	POPULATION AFFLICTED.			INSANE.			DEAF-MUTES.			BLIND.			LEPERS.		
		Persons.	Males.	Females.	Persons.	Males.	Females.	Persons.	Males.	Females.	Persons.	Males.	Females.	Persons.	Males.	Females.
	1	2	3	4	5	6	7	8	9	10	11	12	13	14	15	16
	State ...	***26,831***	***15,025***	***11,806***	***2,560***	***1,547***	***1,013***	***4,421***	***2,522***	***1,899***	***16,263***	***8,287***	***7,976***	***3,758***	***2,762***	***996***
	Hyderabad City ...	**628**	414	214	**285**	213	72	**82**	46	36	**215**	124	91	**49**	33	16
2	Atraf-i-balda	**1,141**	621	520	**122**	68	54	**185**	94	91	**693**	350	343	**148**	112	36
	Warangal Division ...	***4,503***	***2,558***	***1,945***	***712***	***401***	***311***	***962***	***569***	***393***	***2,266***	***1,187***	***1,079***	***625***	***431***	***194***
3	Warangal	**1,601**	887	714	**235**	116	119	**461**	256	205	**718**	384	334	**216**	141	75
4	Karimnagar	**1,898**	1,154	744	**332**	199	133	**319**	204	115	**964**	534	430	**305**	230	75
5	Adilabad	**1,004**	517	487	**145**	86	59	**182**	109	73	**584**	269	315	**104**	60	44
	Medak Division ...	***7,444***	***4,187***	***3,257***	***859***	***477***	***382***	***1,286***	***758***	***528***	***4,177***	***2,106***	***2,071***	***1,176***	***872***	***304***
6	Medak	**1,881**	1,087	794	**262**	151	111	**255**	156	99	**983**	471	512	**387**	311	76
7	Nizamabad	**1,235**	716	519	**138**	76	62	**164**	88	76	**590**	307	283	**345**	246	99
8	Mahbubnagar	**2,136**	1,142	994	**178**	88	90	**415**	240	175	**1,371**	688	683	**186**	132	54
9	Nalgonda	**2,192**	1,242	950	**281**	162	119	**452**	274	178	**1,233**	640	593	**258**	183	75
	Aurangabad Division	***6,233***	***3,311***	***2,922***	***227***	***150***	***77***	***757***	***411***	***346***	***4,607***	***2,283***	***2,324***	***664***	***483***	***181***
0	Aurangabad	**1,463**	733	730	**49**	30	19	**135**	64	71	**1,120**	541	579	**160**	99	61
1	Bhir..	**1,412**	805	607	**56**	37	19	**151**	88	63	**960**	496	464	**252**	188	64
2	Parbhani	**1,823**	966	857	**54**	40	14	**206**	118	88	**1,479**	737	742	**95**	80	15
3	Nander	**1,535**	807	728	**68**	43	25	**265**	141	124	**1,048**	509	539	**157**	116	41
	Gulbarga Division ..	***6,882***	***3,934***	***2,948***	***355***	***238***	***117***	***1,149***	***644***	***505***	***4,305***	***2,237***	***2,068***	***1,096***	***831***	***265***
	Gulbarga	**2,093**	1,146	947	**142**	88	54	**402**	208	194	**1,247**	620	627	**314**	238	76
	Raichur	**1,077**	639	438	**66**	47	19	**247**	144	103	**593**	344	249	**172**	105	67
	Osmanabad	**1,490**	915	575	**39**	29	10	**184**	103	81	**882**	468	414	**388**	316	72
	Bidar	**2,222**	1,234	938	**108**	74	34	**316**	189	127	**1,583**	805	778	**222**	172	50

TABLE XII-A.

INFIRMITIES BY SELECTED CASTES, TRIBES OR RACES.

1. In 1901 this table, being optional, was not prepared for the selected castes, tribes or races in the State. It has now been prepared for the first time and confined to 38 castes representing 92 per cent. of the Hindu population, to 4 communities of the Musalmans representing 97 per cent. of the Musalman population, to 2 communuities of the christians representing 90 per cent. of the christian population, to 4 tribes of the animists representing 97 per cent. of the animist population, and lastly to the Jains representing 76 per cent. of the population under " Other religions."

2. Persons suffering from more than one infirmity (see title page of Table XII) have been counted separately for each infirmity.

TABLE XII-A.

INFIRMITIES BY SELECTED CASTES, TRIBES OR RACES.

Serial No.	CASTE, TRIBE OR RACE.	Population dealt with.			Insane.		
		Persons.	Males.	Females.	Persons.	Males.	Females.
	1	2	3	4	5	6	7
	All religions	***13,374,676***	***6,797,118***	***6,577,558***	***2,560***	***1,547***	***1,013***
	Hindu	***11,626,146***	***5,897,158***	***5,728,988***	***2,180***	***1,292***	***888***
1	Bhoi	177.004	89,369	87,635	34	21	13
2	Brahman	231.241	133,192	128,049	89	67	22
3	Chakala	175,626	89,791	85,835	58	28	30
4	Chambhar	70,618	35,993	34,625	6	4	2
5	Dewang or Koshti	71,400	36,257	35,143	8	6	2
6	Dhangar	483,609	245,387	243,222	41	23	18
7	Dhobi	66,598	33,600	32,998	7	5	2
8	Golla	460,760	234,629	226,131	109	62	47
9	Goundla	303,071	156,381	149,690	88	53	35
10	Hatkar	67,934	34,727	33,207	4	1	3
11	Kalal	75.339	38,366	36,973	27	13	14
12	Kapu	648.254	330,902	317,352	201	124	77
13	Koli	266.840	134,432	132,408	28	21	7
14	Komati	223.380	114,121	109,259	92	65	27
15	Kummara, Kumbhar	151,986	77,980	74,006	45	26	19
16	Kurma	144,688	75,144	69,544	29	14	15
17	Lingayet	757,611	381,201	376,410	91	58	33
18	Lohar	47,844	24,828	23,016	5	5	...
19	Madiga, Mang	1,145,352	581,519	563,833	243	136	107
20	Mahar, Mala	1,137,589	574,385	563,204	193	95	98
21	Mali	107,097	54,230	52,867	4	4	...
22	Mangala	73.514	39,754	36,760	22	8	14
23	Maratha	1,538,874	772,878	765,996	86	54	32
24	Munnur	223,354	115,120	113,234	45	28	17
25	Mutrasi	230,770	134 473	126,297	65	41	24
26	Nahvi (Warik)	58.974	30,019	28,955	6	4	2
27	Panchal	117,710	59,990	57,720	13	7	6
28	Rajput	61.337	31,296	30,341	9	6	3
29	Sale	343.130	175,968	167,162	74	39	35
30	Satani	27,833	14,589	13,294	10	7	3
31	Sunar	88,037	45,278	42,759	46	33	13
32	Sutar	69.205	35,118	34,087	7	4	3
33	Telaga	458.622	233,206	225,416	112	54	58
34	Teli	56.944	28,620	28,324	2	2	...
35	Uppara	57,000	29,098	27,902	5	2	3
36	Velama	83,787	42,705	41,082	18	11	7
37	Waddar	131,799	67,696	64,103	39	20	19
38	Wanjari	174,039	87,843	86,196	21	15	6
39	Others	941,026	477,073	463,953	198	126	72
	Musalman	***1,380,990***	***706,821***	***674,169***	***332***	***228***	***104***
40	Mughal	33,411	17,685	15,726	3	2	1
41	Pathan	135.148	71,167	63,981	34	24	10
42	Shaikh	935,019	499,495	485.524	239	170	69
43	Sayyed	189.574	99,142	90,432	49	26	23
44	Others	37,838	19,332	18,506	7	6	1
	Christian	***54.296***	***29,495***	***24,801***	***7***	***4***	***3***
45	Anglo-Indian	3.004	1,548	1.456	...	...	...
46	Indian Christian	45,908	23.635	22,273	7	4	3
	Animist	***285,722***	***149,023***	***136,699***	***41***	***23***	***18***
47	Bhil	9.921	5,036	4.885	...	...	...
48	Erkala	2.013	969	1,044	11	2	9
49	Gond	124,341	62,583	61,758	11	4	7
50	Lambada	142,044	76,703	65,341	19	17	2
	Other religions	***27,522***	***14,621***	***12,901***	...	...	...
51	Jain	21,026	11,032	9,994	...	...	...

TABLE XII-A.

INFIRMITIES BY SELECTED CASTES, TRIBES OR RACES.

Deaf-Mutes.			Blind.			Lepers.			
Persons.	Males.	Females.	Persons.	Males.	Females.	Persons.	Males.	Females.	Serial No.
8	9	10	11	12	13	14	15	16	
4,421	2,822	1,899	16,263	8,287	7,976	3,758	2,762	996	
3,931	2,213	1,718	14,826	7,521	7,305	3,378	2,482	896	
85	44	41	235	114	121	99	65	34	1
94	49	45	361	203	158	48	34	14	2
89	52	37	268	137	131	81	52	29	3
9	4	5	68	42	26	19	13	6	4
15	12	3	44	23	21	9	4	5	5
100	55	45	634	313	321	99	76	23	6
8	4	4	38	13	25	3	...	3	7
168	102	66	709	341	368	107	75	32	8
125	57	68	389	222	167	81	66	15	9
37	23	14	113	62	51	12	10	2	10
22	8	14	78	36	42	22	13	9	11
242	137	105	672	383	289	139	105	34	12
103	54	49	337	156	181	76	62	14	13
129	77	52	522	301	221	101	80	21	14
95	49	46	289	135	154	76	42	34	15
60	41	19	243	112	131	29	24	5	16
221	124	97	610	318	292	107	78	29	17
15	11	4	35	23	12	10	8	2	18
336	211	155	1,231	631	600	462	331	131	19
311	156	155	1,406	695	711	416	315	101	20
15	11	4	83	80	33	23	17	6	21
37	23	14	117	59	58	26	15	11	22
334	184	150	2,279	1,055	1,224	357	265	92	23
75	38	37	296	147	149	95	75	90	24
105	57	48	304	135	169	125	100	25	25
16	2	14	111	67	44	9	5	4	26
22	14	8	67	41	26	15	11	4	27
19	12	7	43	12	31	13	6	7	28
114	69	45	327	181	146	97	75	22	29
29	17	12	69	32	37	15	8	7	30
64	40	24	158	97	61	40	29	11	31
33	17	16	108	61	47	12	9	3	32
192	123	69	588	301	287	170	114	56	33
13	7	6	78	39	39	21	17	4	34
15	6	9	42	28	14	7	6	1	35
58	37	21	116	72	44	23	17	6	36
68	32	36	122	66	56	21	13	8	37
46	21	25	236	110	126	65	52	13	38
382	233	149	1,400	708	692	248	195	53	39
382	236	146	1,165	619	546	311	237	74	
8	4	4	17	14	3	5	4	1	40
29	16	13	107	53	54	21	16	5	41
291	183	108	835	469	416	240	180	60	42
47	27	20	135	69	66	36	29	7	43
7	6	1	21	14	7	9	8	1	44
14	9	5	59	29	30	11	8	3	
...	...	...	1	...	1	1	...	1	45
14	9	5	58	29	29	10	8	2	46
94	64	30	207	114	93	56	33	23	
7	6	1	5	4	1	3	1	2	47
25	18	7	23	15	8	6	3	3	48
32	18	14	93	41	52	20	12	8	49
30	22	8	86	54	32	27	17	10	50
...	...	...	6	4	2	2	2	...	
...	...	...	6	4	2	2	2	...	51

TABLE XIII.

CASTE, TRIBE, RACE, OR NATIONALITY.

1. This table deals in alphabetical order with the main castes, tribes, or races returned in the State, and the total number of males and females belonging to each.

2. Details are given for 57 Hindu castes, 6 Musalman communities, 4 Christian communities and races and 5 Animistic tribes.

TABLE XIII.

CASTE, TRIBE, RACE, OR NATIONALITY.

Serial No.	Caste, Tribe, Race, or Nationality.	Hyderabad State.		Hyderabad City.		Atraf-i-Balda.		Warangal.	
		Males.	Females.	Males.	Females.	Males.	Females.	Males.	Females.
	1	2	3	4	5	6	7	8	9
	HINDU.								
1	Bedar ...	103,803	104,293	1,873	1,854	135	138	141	107
2	Bhoi ...	89,369	87,635	4,041	3,524	1,460	1,443	5,054	4,812
3	Bogam ...	3,097	7,284	169	220	330	390	456	707
4	Brahman ...	133,192	128,049	13,950	11,869	2,612	2,523	6,625	6,239
5	Burud ...	12,538	11,960	242	244	255	279	476	471
6	Chakala ...	89,791	85,835	2,216	2,163	6,980	6,955	14,138	13,105
7	Chambhar ...	35,993	34,625	2,140	1,678	59	47	34	34
8	Darzi or Simpi ...	24.828	23.119	2,214	2,102	692	664	2,473	2,094
9	Dasri ...	6.320	5,922	67	46	561	479	603	403
10	Dewang or Koshti ..	36,257	35,143	4	2	103	48	171	147
11	Dhangar ...	245,387	243.222	4,155	4,194	1,580	1,074	...	...
12	Dhobi ...	33,600	32,996	...	...	...	...	..	...
13	Dhor ..	6,830	6.411	115	142	21	14	...	...
14	Gandla ...	6,888	6.127	202	208	282	233	437	406
15	Golla ...	234,629	226,131	1,866	1,781	14,689	14,601	35,652	33,394
16	Gossain ...	15.976	13,895	310	182	242	183	342	333
17	Gouli ...	9,862	9,469	1,433	1,412	101	87	124	115
18	Goundla ...	156.381	149,690	298	298	17,039	16,981	23,220	21,580
19	Gurav ...	9,267	8,255	...	...	...	...	...	...
20	Hatkar ...	34,727	33,207	20	36	1,523	1,459	...	...
21	Idiga ...	12.582	12,329	...	...	...	...	65	52
22	Kalal ...	38,366	36,973	2,130	1,826	666	539	2.248	2,235
23	Kapu ...	330,902	317,352	6,617	6,652	29,292	28,334	47,946	46,572
24	Kasar ...	7,689	6,833	74	43	350	377	40	36
25	Koli ...	134,432	132,408	513	391	149	115	136	90
26	Komati ...	114,121	109,259	3,000	2,526	7,052	6,587	13,645	13,120
27	Kumbhar ..	37,446	35,058	792	778	601	321	61	59
28	Kummara ..	40,534	38,948	168	169	3.141	3,009	5,451	5,482
29	Kurma ...	75.144	69,544	934	902	9,565	9,352	4,400	4,130
30	Kurmi ..	11,819	11,259	2,295	2,074	5	...	6	3
31	Lingayet ...	381,201	376,410	1,010	954	9,400	9,347	2,344	1,921
32	Lohar ..	24,828	23.016	170	205	1,078	937	289	299
33	Madiga ...	410.474	393,919	2,461	2,398	37,082	36,182	52,262	48,777
34	Mahar ...	346.974	342,569	...	...	...	...	...	...
35	Mala ..	237,411	230,635	28,933	28,822	18,563	18,529	27,483	25,969
36	Mali ...	54,230	52,867	62	40	16	17	71	52
37	Mang ...	171.045	169.914	1,007	1,109	38	25	47	13
38	Mangala ...	39,754	36,760	3.445	2,492	3,719	3,570	4,254	4,205
39	Maratha ...	772.378	765.996	3,200	3,096	4,223	4,064	4,814	4,640
40	Mochi ...	3,999	3,024	712	654	132	52	492	22[illegible]

TABLE XIII.

CASTE, TRIBE, RACE, OR NATIONALITY.

Karimnagar.		Adilabad.		Medak.		Nizamabad.		Mahbubnagar.		Serial No.
Males.	Females.	Males.	Females.	Males.	Females.	Males.	Females.	Males.	Females.	
10	11	12	13	14	15	16	17	18	19	
196	188	999	845	124	108	35	25	849	803	1
11,318	11,456	8,130	8,056	2,892	2,817	11,740	11,670	15,383	15,203	2
215	825	63	132	100	781	87	433	275	848	3
6,887	6,844	3,451	3,428	3,210	3,199	3,784	3,730	4,239	4,288	4
1,942	1,307	1,380	1,226	853	888	3,029	3,022	911	905	5
19,700	18,106	...	...	9,679	9,607	7,640	7,693	10,003	9,265	6
28	19	3,147	3,039	35	40	346	265	5	6	7
3,922	3,573	1,898	1,841	1,090	1,093	1,955	1,953	476	425	8
1,040	1,031	128	118	399	316	452	420	682	660	9
149	143	9,860	9,352	31	20	90	40	...	...	10
285	269	11,006	10,928	245	108	1,549	1,475	1,173	1,109	11
55	50	6,101	6,161	...	...	...	...	...	...	12
141	122	101	174	77	75	...	...	5	6	13
1,900	1,493	629	678	642	625	945	906	444	432	14
42,472	39,245	4,875	4,872	17,498	17,201	12,699	12,663	31,793	31,751	15
452	361	317	254	74	67	76	98	38	28	16
28	14	968	817	57	13	68	73	...	...	17
32,749	29,664	5,026	4,363	15,091	15,004	7,228	7,273	11,216	11,210	18
...	...	816	809	768	570	...	...	65	92	19
88	75	905	769	177	123	500	479	335	829	20
164	150	10	6	2,200	2,112	591	572	4,248	4,151	21
4,466	4,436	3,876	3,583	2,374	2,339	437	429	2,007	2,000	22
61,277	55,099	13,046	12,891	29,399	27,751	25,142	25,120	37,245	36,279	23
863	727	771	466	165	151	80	93	127	125	24
145	119	7,817	7,355	22	12	559	529	303	162	25
16,393	14,676	4,807	4,334	12,051	12,071	7,848	7,822	10,395	9,809	26
...	...	2,232	2,222	68	33	391	377	603	365	27
8,347	7,412	183	178	5,226	5,177	3,114	3,073	3,604	3,418	28
13,189	11,723	56	48	12,366	12,282	4,300	4,200	15,409	14,200	29
...	...	101	109	223	115	21	17	458	359	30
2,859	2,873	2,610	2,608	7,017	6,932	3,743	3,736	8,301	8,340	31
2,395	2,104	2,527	2,083	946	731	1,749	1,770	1,675	1,643	32
70,487	65,502	2,593	2,304	41,020	39,940	28,985	28,900	59,763	58,158	33
...	...	31,093	30,708	306	210	61	52	...	...	34
43,875	41,979	...	...	31,018	29,420	26,587	26,553	18,396	17,789	35
211	206	1,890	1,855	233	134	...	...	...	...	36
...	...	10,014	9,126	521	433	43	29	...	...	37
6,603	5,839	...	...	4,990	4,781	3,595	3,516	4,287	4,159	38
8,710	8,014	42,990	42,861	1,781	1,693	3,154	3,148	905	888	39
46	26	97	97	165	152	36	36	69	79	40

TABLE XIII.

CASTE, TRIBE, RACE, OR NATIONALITY.

Serial No.	Caste, Tribe, Race or Nationality.	Nalgonda.		Aurangabad.		Bhir.		Nander.	
		Males.	Females.	Males.	Females.	Males.	Females.	Males.	Females.
	1	20	21	22	23	24	25	26	27
	HINDU.—(*contd.*)								
1	Bedar ...	27	8	221	147	109	76	697	[illegible]
2	Bhoi ...	2,786	2,724	1,080	1,059	1,045	1,061	5,164	[illegible]
3	Bogam ...	828	1,168	2	5	126	265	30	[illegible]
4	Brahman ...	5,654	5,442	15,003	14,936	11,179	10,714	7,020	[illegible]
5	Burud ...	549	434	206	209	55	44	612	[illegible]
6	Chakala ...	18,299	17,875	...	...	...	...	...	...
7	Chambhar ...	121	138	6,337	6,300	4,266	3,964	1,721	[illegible]
8	Darzi or Simpi ...	2,615	2,339	1,222	1,191	519	399	1,471	[illegible]
9	Dasri ...	688	591	2	2	3	2	131	[illegible]
10	Dewang or Koshti ...	868	768	1,455	1,407	2,301	2,241	3,405	[illegible]
11	Dhangar ...	1,275	1,216	20,380	20,336	17,309	17,284	13,997	[illegible]
12	Dhobi ...	...	...	2,407	2,410	1,757	1,446	5,769	[illegible]
13	Dhor ...	46	45	975	959	825	722	377	[illegible]
14	Gandla ...	324	307	...	...	...	...	348	[illegible]
15	Golla ...	53,099	50,820	11	9	...	...	7,009	[illegible]
16	Gossain ...	138	124	2,000	1,753	2,003	1,951	1,740	[illegible]
17	Gouli ...	...	...	1,096	1,031	597	592	1,600	[illegible]
18	Goundla ...	42,763	41,674	93	81	...	...	...	...
19	Gurav ...	...	...	523	470	848	639	783	[illegible]
20	Hatkar ...	...	...	1,158	1,187	2,090	1,922	5,597	[illegible]
21	Idiga ...	...	...	...	...	...	...	...	...
22	Kalal ...	1,584	1,465	1,256	1,205	243	196	1,574	[illegible]
23	Kapu ...	62,474	60,310	25	13	15	2	1,602	[illegible]
24	Kasar ...	217	173	1,341	1,350	1,009	857	329	[illegible]
25	Koli ...	93	80	5,545	5,480	1,550	1,502	15,859	[illegible]
26	Komati ...	18,472	18,131	560	520	442	470	6,290	[illegible]
27	Kumbhar ...	556	380	4,454	4,439	2,194	2,077	3,024	[illegible]
28	Kummara ...	9,182	8,849	1,989	1,989	...	...	...	...
29	Kurma ...	13,456	11,281	168	133	...	...	...	...
30	Kurmi ...	...	...	7,796	7,747	127	108	180	
31	Lingayat ...	3,750	3,169	3,317	3,219	5,026	4,877	25,874	[illegible]
32	Lohar ...	1,547	1,440	2,211	2,200	1,522	1,371	1,052	[illegible]
33	Madiga ...	79,054	75,897	99	92	...	...	49	
34	Mahar ...	...	...	45,000	44,730	28,874	28,784	38,169	[illegible]
35	Mala ...	30,140	29,364	...	...	...	...	53	
36	Mali ...	191	173	15,254	15,226	8,710	8,693	1.664	[illegible]
37	Mang ...	30	18	13,191	13,179	14,170	13,784	23,013	[illegible]
38	Mangala ...	6,061	5,526	245	243	...	...	5	
39	Maratha ...	2,824	2,023	158,453	158,490	122,095	122,088	77,459	[illegible]
40	Mochi ...	119	104	570	466	159	49	64	

TABLE XIII.

CASTE, TRIBE, RACE, OR NATIONALITY.

Parbhani.		Gulbarga.		Osmanabad.		Raichur.		Bidar.		Serial No.
Males.	Females.	Males.	Females.	Males.	Females.	Males.	Females.	Males.	Females.	
28	29	30	31	32	33	34	35	36	37	
320	348	25,432	25,217	1,113	1,074	70,314	71,538	1,218	1,142	1
1,526	1,508	906	717	347	303	16,003	15,725	494	422	2
...	...	240	270	3	11	172	859	1	4	3
11,009	10,984	10,337	9,938	8,581	8,231	11,483	11,316	8,174	7,314	4
239	204	639	633	176	145	549	453	425	423	5
...	...	...	...	...	...	1,136	1,066	...	...	6
3,377	3,360	3,072	2,904	5,529	5,457	3,276	3,196	2,500	2,478	7
434	428	695	616	381	365	2,213	2,015	560	554	8
18	23	1,294	1,267	1	2	200	119	51	34	9
2,206	2,212	7,778	7,727	1,268	1,190	3,072	3,001	3,496	3,410	10
17,474	17,477	50,451	50,370	20,543	20,312	53,023	52,018	31,136	31,105	11
1,469	1,491	5,437	5,363	1,840	1,851	5,295	5,006	3,470	2,465	12
911	927	891	823	1,197	1,039	150	117	998	901	13
...	...	355	235	3	...	281	202	96	68	14
34	34	2,057	1,973	12	7	10,088	10,096	765	754	15
3,448	3,428	681	537	1,861	1,629	35	11	2,219	1,238	16
804	782	1,219	1,169	403	333	807	835	557	544	17
41	34	75	46	95	80	1,272	1,282	175	140	18
981	957	911	737	2,135	1,983	150	115	1,239	1,121	19
14,037	14,022	1,268	1,206	329	301	1,907	1,873	4,793	3,899	20
...	...	98	80	...	...	5,206	5,200	...	...	21
500	472	8,220	8,170	334	321	4,441	4,387	2,010	1,970	22
90	87	5,730	5,779	42	16	6,505	6,172	4,455	4,363	23
[illegible]	893	269	208	421	365	593	531	138	119	24
[illegible]	2,622	62,897	62,736	4,565	4,281	8,947	8,971	22,694	22,127	25
2,027	2,099	2,506	2,497	283	245	4,506	4,372	3,844	3,747	26
4,827	4,818	4,771	4,646	2,098	1,893	8,309	7,238	2,465	2,423	27
1	2	...	...	5	3	183	187	...	...	28
...	...	11	7	...	...	1,266	1,234	24	22	29
155	131	11	9	28	19	103	96	310	345	30
8,865	8,825	106,051	105,444	24,932	23,246	79,081	78,219	87,021	86,838	31
1,062	1,056	1,656	1,545	1,203	1,048	2,763	2,722	983	927	32
...	...	802	413	...	...	34,064	33,564	1,753	1,775	33
55,453	55,445	50,098	48,016	37,219	36,510	16,233	15,249	44,463	44,357	34
172	156	151	55	...	...	2,040	1,945	...	...	35
12,849	12,859	3,403	3,378	7,290	6,864	782	119	1,604	1,650	36
13,474	13,144	35,455	35,392	16,569	16,541	6,989	6,604	36,495	36,436	37
...	...	329	320	...	...	1,848	1,898	272	209	38
136,523	137,597	20,040	19,917	123,672	118,578	3,959	3,654	58,076	57,791	39
130	120	317	273	...	...	843	624	48	28	40

TABLE XIII.

CASTE, TRIBE, RACE, OR NATIONALITY.

Serial No.	Caste, Tribe, Race, or Nationality.	Hyderabad State.		Hyderabad City.		Atraf-i-Balda.		Warangal.	
		Males.	Females.	Males.	Females.	Males.	Females.	Males.	Females.
	1	38	39	40	41	42	43	44	45
	HINDU.—(*concld.*)								
41	Munnur ...	115,120	113,234	6,262	6,582	4,222	4,078	1,026	[illegible]
42	Mutrasi ...	131,473	126,297	5,105	5,091	12,158	11,200	20,524	18,800
43	Nahvi (Warik) ...	30,019	28,955	20	18	...	...	...	...
44	Panchal ...	59,990	57,720	1,487	1,357	2,536	2,514	11,112	10,060
45	Rajput ...	31,293	30,341	3,606	3,406	1,516	1,489	1,162	1,151
46	Rangari ...	11,521	10,987	408	342	458	416	111	[illegible]
47	Sale ...	175,958	167,162	2,778	2,505	8,374	8,044	20,570	18,882
48	Satani ...	14,589	13,294	441	420	[illegible]	462	1,782	1,514
49	Sunar ...	45,278	42,759	1,659	1,689	2,147	2,077	782	639
50	Sutar ...	35,118	34,087	1	6	874	818	101	104
51	Telaga ...	233.206	225,416	6,213	6,150	14,020	13,544	29,563	28,933
52	Teli ...	28,620	28,324	401	333	168	189	206	167
53	Uppara ...	29.098	27,902	473	389	677	575	1,289	1,131
54	Velama ...	42,705	41,082	7	20	625	573	4,144	3,686
55	Waddar ...	67,898	64.103	307	335	2,338	2,216	8,350	7,781
56	Wakligar ..	19.381	19 116	3	2	...	...	...	...
57	Wanjari ...	87.843	86.196	83	91	1,157	1,094	1,317	1,27[illegible]
58	Others ...	210,673	203,970	13,696	10,671	6,02[illegible]	5,454	14,454	14,016
	MUSALMAN.								
59	Ladaf ...	15,574	15,147	203	161	28[illegible]	110	3,725	[illegible]
60	Momin ...	2,755	2,439	114	100	201	109	776	[illegible]
61	Mughal ...	17.683	15,726	3,724	3.579	[illegible]	828	355	[illegible]
62	Pathan ...	71.167	63,981	13,362	11,598	3,747	2,119	1,586	[illegible]
63	Sayyed ...	99,142	90,432	17,377	17,563	5,059	4,072	3,113	2,78[illegible]
64	Shaik ...	499,495	485,524	76,219	74.399	20,720	22,002	17,154	14,8[illegible]
65	Others ...	1,003	920	771	786	...	...	...	...
	CHRISTIAN.								
66	Anglo-Indian ...	1,548	1,456	1,030	1,073	129	95	94	[illegible]
67	Armenian ...	1	1	1	1	...	...	...	...
68	European ..	4,311	1,071	4,050	865	67	51	51	[illegible]
69	Indian Christian ...	23.635	22,273	4,542	4,678	490	459	6,057	5,6[illegible]
	ANIMIST.								
70	Andh ..	1,364	1.281	...	...	...	...	...	...
71	Bhil ...	5,036	4,885	...	...	...	...	...	...
72	Erkala ...	969	1.044	1	...	...	...	12	[illegible]
73	Gond ...	62,583	61,758	...	...	...	...	32,372	32,7[illegible]
74	Lambada ...	76,703	65,341	26	2	2,255	1,812	28,924	24,[illegible]
75	Others ...	2,368	2,410	11	1	...	...	165	[illegible]

TABLE XIII.

CASTE, TRIBE, RACE, OR NATIONALITY.

Karimnagar.		Adilabad.		Medak.		Nizamabad.		Mahbubnagar.		Serial No.
Males.	Females.	Males.	Females.	Males.	Females.	Males.	Females.	Males.	Females.	
46	47	48	49	50	51	52	53	54	55	
23,242	21,656	18,540	18,405	8,040	7,920	23,008	23,466	5,539	5,577	41
14,802	13,694	88	85	34,500	33,841	9,194	9,183	11,141	9,402	42
...	...	2,998	2,902	...	...	...	...	...	...	43
12,002	12,016	814	803	6,181	6,158	677	670	471	421	44
766	776	599	568	1,357	1,094	761	717	768	737	45
325	325	564	403	480	419	343	313	433	411	46
51,246	48,010	2,700	2,597	19,490	19,342	17,182	17,100	8,038	8,037	47
2,901	2,557	2,039	2,000	1,231	1,202	1,114	1,092	985	806	48
5,780	4,677	2,470	2,370	1,796	1,637	3,661	3,607	2,825	2,898	49
7	4	2,705	2,698	1,711	1,436	1,833	1,885	3,296	3,299	50
50,361	47,503	3,232	2,680	21,634	20,825	23,002	23,090	38,231	38,125	51
415	414	2,229	2,274	67	47	202	220	72	114	52
1,259	1,038	585	431	810	688	221	214	5,138	4,904	53
11,693	11,889	1,475	1,341	294	217	1,720	1,742	1,969	1,899	54
3,020	2,922	1,963	1,906	2,206	2,125	2,236	2,153	5,811	5,794	55
...	...	...	...	36	13	...	...	...	...	56
4,298	4,210	5,566	5,322	1,331	1,132	2,253	2,621	51	26	57
10,727	10,512	27,859	32,242	6,393	5,642	10,987	11,753	10,654	9,907	58
2,940	2,708	724	617	759	902	492	516	524	550	59
4	3	12	68	10	18	6	16	12	9	60
417	400	320	289	325	359	358	327	241	241	61
1,296	1,250	1,971	2,133	1,868	1,859	1,098	990	1,361	1,391	62
2,567	2,013	2,179	1,767	4,091	3,866	2,017	2,180	3,103	2,941	63
17,121	15,804	10,637	8,951	25,152	25,809	17,054	16,837	25,112	24,036	64
...	...	...	...	64	2	11	39	...	...	65
7	1	8	1	14	8	14	3	...	3	66
...	...	...	...	...	...	...	...	...	...	67
5	6	1	...	7	14	1	7	8	5	68
274	293	10	8	1,103	1,057	360	335	213	222	69
...	...	1,347	1,258	...	...	...	...	...	...	70
...	...	1,077	1,018	...	...	...	...	...	...	71
...	...	237	391	24	16	...	...	16	9	72
1,814	1,689	27,965	26,847	1	...	1	...	1	1	73
3,227	2,868	2,806	2,573	2,154	1,821	971	848	7,213	5,650	74
...	...	169	236	...	...	...	...	761	741	75

TABLE XIII.

CASTE, TRIBE, RACE, OR NATIONALITY.

Serial No.	Caste, Tribe, Race, or Nationality.	Nalgonda.		Aurangabad.		Bhir.		Nander.	
		Males.	Females.	Males.	Females.	Males.	Females.	Males.	Females.
	1	56	57	58	59	60	61	62	63
	HINDU.—(*concld.*)								
41	Munnur ...	4,273	3,793	79	68	10	1	14,535	14,7[illegible]
42	Mutrasi ...	24,481	22,882	...	...	6	4	765	74[illegible]
43	Nahvi (Warik) ...	...	...	4,308	4,299	3,284	2,949	3,53[illegible]	3,44[illegible]
44	Panchal ...	9,692	8,948	251	190	153	117	1,238	1,21[illegible]
45	Rajput ...	566	545	3,749	3,717	1,093	968	1,739	1,74[illegible]
46	Rangari ...	190	189	971	904	640	591	1,811	1,8[illegible]
47	Sale ...	21,519	19,585	1,445	1,360	724	752	5,056	[illegible]
48	Satani ...	1,888	1,587	5	2	5	9	230	2[illegible]
49	Sunar ...	3,319	2,904	4,314	4,285	2,989	2,753	2,316	2,[illegible]
50	Sutar ...	1,166	1,094	3,609	3,651	3,084	2,763	3,149	3,0[illegible]
51	Telaga ...	23,410	22,555	1,754	1,727	116	135	210	19[illegible]
52	Teli ...	28	28	6,207	6,233	2,448	2,490	2,300	2,[illegible]
53	Uppara ...	714	625	310	302	248	157	3,232	3,62[illegible]
54	Velama ...	3,045	2,698	87	63	902	654	1,095	1,12[illegible]
55	Waddar ...	12,622	11,646	739	648	690	636	1,849	1,83[illegible]
56	Wakligar ...	...	...	...	...	...	...	37	3[illegible]
57	Wanjari ...	1,551	1,008	9,905	9,890	29,391	29,364	4,242	4,19[illegible]
58	Others ..	14,728	14,519	14,203	15,119	8,622	7,978	12,430	12,06[illegible]
	MUSALMAN.								
59	Ladaf ...	3,369	3,200	7	3	55	65	527	5[illegible]
60	Momin ...	2	2	...	...	65	99	203	1[illegible]
61	Mughal ..	226	207	2,636	2,789	706	520	707	6[illegible]
62	Pathan ..	1,239	1,068	10,281	8,594	4,003	3,4[illegible]2	4,559	4,[illegible]
63	Sayyed ...	2,774	2,669	8,331	8,172	3,316	2,328	7,537	5,94[illegible]
64	Shaik ...	20,111	19,005	36,374	34,262	18,604	13,687	23,034	23,7[illegible]
65	Others ...	...	...	...	...	...	...	141	[illegible]
	CHRISTIAN.								
66	Anglo-Indian ..	7	6	29	30	1	1	15	
67	Armenian ...	...	...	...	...	...	...	...	...
68	European ...	7	1	44	31	...	...	...	...
69	Indian Christian ...	5,551	4,994	3,149	3,086	...	...	25	[illegible]
	ANIMIST.								
70	Andh ...	...	...	7	8	10	...	...	..
71	Bhil ...	...	...	3,576	3,519	216	208	...	—
72	Erkala ...	5	12	14	10	22	16	14	...
73	Gond ...	1	...	75	109	...	...	14	[illegible]
74	Lambada ...	20,728	17,337	2,284	2,197	159	204	1,166	1,[illegible]
75	Others ...	26	28	...	...	...	...	...	...

TABLE XIII.

CASTE, TRIBE, RACE, OR NATIONALITY.

Parbhani.		Gulbarga.		Osmanabad.		Raichur.		Bidar.		Serial No.
Males.	Females.	Males.	Females.	Males.	Females.	Males.	Females.	Males.	Females.	
64	65	66	67	68	69	70	71	72	73	
118	137	2,38?	2,216	10	...	1,953	1,757	1,875	1,834	41
75	69	298	295	15	13	502	471	519	435	42
3,756	3,751	3,786	3,700	2,841	2,754	2,233	2,192	3,263	2,946	43
148	140	4,557	4,553	994	905	4,204	4,199	3,473	3,453	44
1,263	1,249	5,411	5,393	1,760	1,651	3,292	3,270	1,888	1,870	45
1,508	1,494	2,163	2,134	295	285	177	166	649	621	46
1,320	1,277	5,043	5,020	476	401	7,796	7,533	2,211	1,689	47
...	...	263	139	...	...	1,143	1,079	76	70	48
3,129	3,076	1,538	1,514	1,789	1,743	3,012	3,056	1,752	1,576	49
3,307	3,255	2,010	1,928	2,411	2,395	3,774	3,767	2,080	1,924	50
477	470	10,702	9,916	160	149	8,000	7,769	2,121	1,659	51
4,904	4,967	1,787	1,436	2,600	2,587	3,262	3,231	1,314	1,200	52
494	492	4,515	4,465	1,481	1,397	5,847	5,676	1,805	1,796	53
375	382	211	175	1,609	1,500	164	194	13,350	13,088	54
1,698	1,641	7,290	7,282	1,649	1,149	13,098	12,244	1,935	1,891	55
2	5	291	228	...	...	16,731	16,636	2,281	2,201	56
12,334	12,254	2,737	2,351	3,371	3,177	206	206	8,050	7,982	57
17,680	15,590	18,667	16,806	6,452	5,900	8,106	9,195	7,082	6,601	58
113	177	1,234	1,334	57	52	...	...	564	608	59
20	206	1,077	1,062	25	53	...	...	43	78	60
493	463	1,907	1,878	479	379	3,342	2,256	855	739	61
6,385	6,190	5,989	5,561	3,755	3,437	4,023	3,571	4,644	5,156	62
3,712	3,119	13,357	10,795	3,561	2,464	8,957	8,492	8,091	9,259	63
25,881	25,530	62,572	62,544	22,725	22,461	32,080	30,757	48,945	45,808	64
...	...	16	...	...	...	...	...	...	...	65
49	43	43	28	11	4	96	68	1	2	66
...	...	...	...	...	...	...	...	...	...	67
21	6	22	19	...	...	26	18	1	1	68
180	110	568	364	119	118	798	705	196	175	69
...	...	...	...	...	...	...	...	...	...	70
156	135	...	...	5	5	6	...	...	...	71
38	59	551	481	18	16	...	...	17	17	72
339	283	...	...	...	...	...	...	...	...	73
1,094	1,039	2,859	2,401	84	81	132	130	621	620	74
...	...	1,059	1,091	56	41	...	...	121	146	75

TABLE XIV.

CIVIL CONDITION BY AGE FOR SELECTED CASTES.

This table like table IX deals, not with the whole population, but with certain selected castes, races and tribes in the two natural divisions, Telingana (City and Districts) and Marathwara, where they are specially numerous.

TABLE XIV.

CIVIL CONDITION BY AGE FOR SELECTED CASTES.

Serial No.	Caste, Tribe or Race.	Locality.	Sex.	Population dealt with.	Unmarried. Total.	0—5	5—12	12—15	15—20	20—40	40 and over.
	1	2	3	4	5	6	7	8	9	10	11
	HINDU.										
1	Bhoi ...	Hyderabad State ...	Male ...	***89,369***	***39,394***	***15,758***	***12,210***	***5,280***	***3,211***	***2,384***	***551***
			Female ...	***87,635***	***23,394***	***16,437***	***5,782***	***910***	***146***	***108***	***11***
		Telingana ...	Male ...	62,804	28,949	10,090	9,916	4,006	2,598	2,009	330
			Female ...	61,705	16,472	11,666	4,412	247	85	58	4
		City ...	Male ...	4,041	1,308	458	380	151	127	137	55
			Female ...	3,524	1,217	628	402	164	18	5	...
		Districts ...	Male ...	58,763	27,641	9,632	9,536	3,855	2,471	1,872	275
			Female ..	58,181	15,255	11,038	4,010	83	67	53	4
		Marathwara ...	Male ...	26,565	10,445	5,668	2,294	1,274	613	375	221
			Female ...	25,930	6,922	4,771	1,370	663	61	50	7
2	Brahman ...	Hyderabad State ...	Male ..	***133,192***	***54,574***	***20,438***	***15,541***	***7,975***	***5,410***	***4,441***	***769***
			Female ...	***128,049***	***31,541***	***19,383***	***10,740***	***727***	***319***	***263***	***109***
		Telingana ...	Male ...	50,412	21,112	7,936	5,473	3,042	1,879	2,323	459
			Female ...	47,602	11,464	7,062	3,311	632	251	175	33
		City ...	Male ...	13,950	5,725	3,029	1,567	819	210	67	33
			Female ...	11,869	2,767	2,510	58	75	99	20	5
		Districts ...	Male ...	36,462	15,387	4,907	3,906	2,223	1,669	2,256	426
			Female ...	35,733	8,697	4,552	3,253	557	152	155	28
		Marathwara ...	Male ...	82,780	33,462	12,502	10,068	4,933	3,531	2,118	310
			Female ...	80,447	20,077	12,321	7,429	95	68	88	76
3	Chakala ...	Hyderabad State ...	Male ...	***89,791***	***41,392***	***13,297***	***14,513***	***6,466***	***3,974***	***2,516***	***626***
			Female ...	***85,835***	***29,667***	***15,095***	***10,941***	***2,435***	***546***	***423***	***227***
		Telingana ...	Male ...	88,655	40,908	13,011	14,379	6,438	3,960	2,501	619
			Female ...	84,769	29,269	14,907	10,886	2,361	495	405	215
		City ...	Male ...	2,216	856	270	263	75	80	95	73
			Female ...	2,163	757	342	251	97	52	9	6
		Districts ...	Male ...	86,439	40,052	12,741	14,116	6,363	3,880	2,406	546
			Female ...	82,606	28,512	14,565	10,635	2,264	443	396	209
4	Chambhar...	Hyderabad State ...	Male ...	***35,993***	***13,581***	***4,773***	***4,574***	***1,951***	***1,079***	***887***	***317***
			Female ...	***34,625***	***10,731***	***5,496***	***3,382***	***1,051***	***306***	***356***	***140***
		Marathwara ...	Male ...	30,078	11,354	4,007	3,891	1,610	930	628	288
			Female ...	29,359	9,018	4,708	2,777	881	253	282	117
5	Dewang or Koshti.	Hyderabad State ...	Male ...	***36,257***	***14,636***	***5,556***	***4,938***	***1,771***	***1,078***	***1,010***	***283***
			Female ...	***35,143***	***10,217***	***5,132***	***2,985***	***1,335***	***348***	***277***	***140***
		Telingana ...	Male ...	11,276	4,563	1,896	1,749	436	252	179	51
			Female ...	10,520	3,199	1,756	1,051	246	55	65	26
		Marathwara ...	Male ...	24,981	10,073	3,660	3,189	1,335	826	831	232
			Female ...	24,623	7,018	3,376	1,934	1,089	293	212	114
6	Dhangar ...	Hyderabad State ...	Male ...	***245,387***	***93,661***	***37,673***	***30,583***	***16,837***	***4,464***	***3,565***	***539***
			Female ...	***243,222***	***69,706***	***47,689***	***20,297***	***1,411***	***153***	***124***	***32***
		Telingana ...	Male ..	21,268	9,926	4,058	3,000	1,659	615	483	111
			Female ...	20,373	5,171	3,092	1,476	384	126	81	12
		City ...	Male ...	4,155	1,547	447	548	238	181	112	21
			Female ...	4,194	992	456	456	12	32	27	9
		Districts ...	Male ...	17,113	8,379	3,611	2,452	1,421	434	371	90
			Female ...	16,179	4,179	2,636	1,020	372	94	54	2
		Marathwara ...	Male ...	224,119	83,735	33,615	27,583	15,178	3,849	3,082	428
			Female ...	222,849	64,535	44,597	18,821	1,027	27	43	20

TABLE XIV.

CIVIL CONDITION BY AGE FOR SELECTED CASTES.

Married.							Widowed.							Serial No.
Total.	0—5	5—12	12—15	15—20	20—40	40 and over.	Total.	0—5	5—12	12—15	15—20	20—40	40 and over.	
12	13	14	15	16	17	18	19	20	21	22	23	24	25	
45,197	***389***	***4,851***	***4,960***	***4,434***	***16,919***	***13,644***	***4,778***	***19***	***54***	***116***	***370***	***1,228***	***2,991***	1
53,214	***224***	***4,601***	***7,712***	***10,128***	***17,831***	***12,718***	***11,027***	***30***	***150***	***140***	***343***	***2,487***	***7,877***	
30,474	101	492	818	3,432	14,343	11,288	3,381	6	21	56	249	667	2,382	
36,465	173	2,914	5,703	6,832	14,455	6,388	8,768	28	135	62	146	1,975	6,422	
2,470	16	21	66	116	1,200	1,051	263	5	13	20	25	44	155	
1,806	41	64	93	342	1,075	191	501	...	...	6	12	112	371	
28,004	85	471	752	3,316	13,143	10,237	3,118	1	8	36	223	623	2,227	
34,659	132	2,850	5,610	6,490	13,380	6,197	8,267	28	135	56	134	1,863	6,051	
14,723	288	4,359	4,142	1,002	2,576	2,356	1,397	13	33	60	121	561	609	
16,749	51	1,687	2,009	3,296	3,376	6,330	2,259	2	15	78	197	512	1,455	
72,247	***220***	***1,455***	***3,131***	***13,552***	***29,183***	***24,736***	***6,371***	***22***	***54***	***80***	***130***	***674***	***5,411***	2
71,182	***616***	***6,028***	***9,159***	***13,219***	***24,352***	***17,808***	***25,326***	***32***	***195***	***551***	***1,248***	***6,619***	***16,651***	
26,166	78	572	1,249	3,918	11,507	8,842	3,134	1	14	26	110	576	2,407	
25,814	115	1,356	3,201	5,454	10,292	5,396	10,324	11	71	197	345	2,543	7,157	
7,728	25	373	712	2,598	2,935	1,085	497	...	5	21	68	93	310	
8,027	57	168	1,349	2,789	2,825	839	1,075	...	4	98	76	321	576	
18,438	53	199	537	1,320	8,572	7,757	2,637	1	9	5	42	483	2,097	
17,787	58	1,188	1,852	2,665	7,467	4,557	9,249	11	67	99	269	2,222	6,581	
46,081	142	883	1,882	9,634	17,646	15,894	3,237	21	40	54	20	98	3,004	
45,368	501	4,672	5,958	7,765	14,060	12,412	15,002	21	124	381	903	4,076	9,494	
46,207	***175***	***476***	***2,166***	***3,488***	***21,594***	***18,308***	***2,192***	***14***	***33***	***73***	***175***	***603***	***1,294***	3
46,256	***165***	***3,158***	***3,633***	***8,068***	***21,914***	***9,318***	***9,912***	***7***	***46***	***170***	***365***	***2,642***	***6,682***	
45,681	173	457	2,155	3,395	21,406	18,095	2,066	8	18	60	130	567	1,283	
45,773	164	3,151	3,614	8,010	21,728	9,106	9,727	7	45	162	344	2,588	6,581	
1,134	34	60	104	142	258	536	226	6	14	11	12	35	148	
1,138	52	15	78	221	574	198	268	...	...	7	3	96	162	
44,547	139	397	2,051	3,253	21,148	17,559	1,840	2	4	49	118	532	1,135	
44,635	112	3,136	3,536	7,789	21,154	8,908	9,459	7	45	155	341	2,492	6,419	
19,613	***186***	***677***	***1,206***	***2,250***	***8,318***	***6,976***	***2,799***	***17***	***50***	***88***	***188***	***729***	***1,727***	4
18,851	***283***	***1,580***	***1,724***	***3,059***	***7,877***	***4,328***	***5,043***	***11***	***77***	***189***	***160***	***1,114***	***3,492***	
17,344	145	592	925	2,970	6,791	5,921	1,380	14	50	78	168	441	629	
16,086	239	1,361	1,424	2,684	6,531	3,847	4,255	5	69	180	144	927	2,930	
19,145	***180***	***771***	***1,600***	***2,616***	***7,647***	***6,331***	***2,476***	***19***	***61***	***113***	***142***	***745***	***1,396***	5
19,890	***243***	***2,317***	***2,401***	***3,106***	***7,373***	***4,450***	***5,036***	***3***	***56***	***104***	***230***	***1,298***	***3,345***	
6,172	26	342	633	656	2,802	1,713	541	2	11	15	24	155	334	
5,734	62	828	565	858	2,596	825	1,587	2	29	7	17	331	1,201	
12,973	154	429	967	1,960	4,845	4,618	1,935	17	50	98	118	590	1,062	
14,156	181	1,489	1,836	2,248	4,777	3,625	3,449	1	27	97	213	967	2,144	
141,525	***959***	***3,789***	***9,224***	***16,156***	***61,428***	***49,969***	***10,201***	***10***	***32***	***47***	***59***	***2,722***	***7,331***	6
144,234	***1,155***	***11,309***	***22,580***	***24,101***	***58,026***	***27,063***	***29,282***	***74***	***261***	***553***	***2,188***	***8,236***	***17,970***	
10,589	44	364	1,140	1,880	4,465	2,696	753	2	15	16	33	257	430	
12,429	76	477	2,100	2,790	5,107	1,879	2,773	7	32	54	97	813	1,770	
2,409	1	21	49	326	1,180	826	199	...	...	...	12	56	131	
2,140	6	142	150	329	1,198	315	1,062	...	4	2	18	229	809	
8,180	43	343	1,091	1,554	3,279	1,870	551	2	15	16	21	201	299	
10,289	70	335	1,950	2,461	3,909	1,564	1,711	7	28	52	79	584	961	
130,936	915	3,425	8,084	14,276	56,963	47,273	9,448	8	17	31	26	2,465	6,901	
131,805	1,079	10,832	20,480	21,311	52,919	25,184	26,509	67	229	499	2,091	7,423	16,200	

TABLE XIV.

CIVIL CONDITION BY AGE FOR SELECTED CASTES.

Serial No.	Caste, Tribe or Race.	Locality.	Sex.	Population dealt with.	Unmarried.						
					Total.	0—5	5—12	12—15	15—20	20—40	40 and over.
	1	2	3	26	27	28	29	30	31	32	33
	HINDU.— *(contd.)*										
7	Dhobi ...	Hyderabad State ...	Male ...	33,600	12,844	4,708	4,266	1,655	1,113	762	340
			Female ...	32,998	11,109	5,619	3,238	1,325	626	190	111
		Marathwara ...	Male ...	27,444	10,152	3,535	3,233	1,334	1,019	709	322
			Female ...	26,787	8,742	4,308	2,428	1,184	586	147	89
8	Golla ...	Hyderabad State ...	Male ...	234,629	104,756	34,064	36,244	16,350	11,527	5,427	1,144
			Female ...	226,131	63,262	39,646	22,573	684	214	100	45
		Telingana ...	Male ...	214,643	97,148	31,016	33,824	15,290	10,803	5,218	997
			Female ...	206,328	58,627	35,777	22,186	541	104	13	6
		City ...	Male ...	1,866	722	290	196	27	95	112	2
			Female ...	1,781	478	299	153	7	14	5	...
		Districts ...	Male ...	212,777	96,426	30,726	33,628	15,263	10,708	5,106	995
			Female ...	204,547	58,149	35,478	22,033	534	90	8	6
		Marathwara ...	Male ...	19,986	7,608	3,048	2,420	1,060	724	209	147
			Female ...	19,803	4,635	3,869	387	143	110	87	39
9	Goundla ...	Hyderabad State ...	Male ...	156,381	73,420	22,358	26,461	11,260	8,369	3,847	1,125
			Female ...	149,690	38,895	25,209	13,342	109	86	52	97
		Telingana ...	Male ...	154,630	72,862	22,147	26,312	11,149	8,313	3,832	1,109
			Female ...	148,047	38,332	24,942	13,224	24	25	30	87
10	Hatkar ...	Hyderabad State ...	Male ...	34,727	13,384	6,121	4,198	1,712	673	498	182
			Female ...	33,207	11,093	6,326	3,205	1,222	179	111	50
		Marathwara ...	Male ...	31,179	12,087	5,548	3,870	1,521	587	418	143
			Female ...	29,937	10,157	5,724	3,015	1,128	144	100	46
11	Kalal ...	Hyderabad State ...	Male ...	38,366	15,011	5,224	4,462	2,420	1,541	1,042	322
			Female ...	36,973	11,304	5,092	3,753	1,462	594	275	128
		Telingana ...	Male ...	19,788	8,683	3,123	2,736	1,285	824	553	163
			Female ...	18,852	5,625	2,435	1,893	695	366	176	60
		City ...	Male ...	2,130	832	265	177	118	114	94	64
			Female ...	1,826	395	163	168	23	22	18	1
		Districts ...	Male ...	17,658	7,851	2,857	2,559	1,167	710	459	99
			Female ...	17,026	5,230	2,272	1,725	672	344	158	59
		Marathwara ...	Male ...	18,578	6,328	2,102	1,726	1,135	717	489	159
			Female ...	18,121	5,679	2,657	1,860	767	228	99	68
12	Kapu	Hyderabad State ...	Male ...	330,902	145,184	54,433	40,264	24,759	17,338	7,801	589
			Female ...	317,352	85,657	44,202	34,035	5,735	1,332	202	151
		Telingana ...	Male ...	312,438	139,428	52,471	38,407	23,691	16,900	7,475	484
			Female ...	299,008	80,949	41,866	32,608	5,153	1,157	59	106
		City ...	Male ...	6,617	2,826	875	612	603	275	378	83
			Female ...	6,652	1,725	823	603	116	146	24	13
		Districts ...	Male ...	305,821	136,602	51,596	37,795	23,088	16,625	7,097	401
			Female ...	292,356	79,224	41,043	32,005	5,037	1,011	35	93
		Marathwara ...	Male ...	18,464	5,756	1,962	1,857	1,068	438	326	105
			Female ...	18,344	4,708	2,336	1,427	582	175	143	45

TABLE XIV.

CIVIL CONDITION BY AGE FOR SELECTED CASTES.

Married.							Widowed.							
Total.	0—5	5—12	12—15	15—20	20—40	40 and over.	Total.	0—5	5—12	12—15	15—20	20—40	40 and over.	Serial No.
34	35	36	37	38	39	40	41	42	43	44	45	46	47	
19,421	***263***	***701***	***1,225***	***3,499***	***7,863***	***6,173***	***1,335***	***2***	***21***	***84***	***89***	***178***	***961***	7
17,291	***182***	***1,331***	***1,602***	***3,068***	***7,690***	***3,418***	***4,598***	***6***	***77***	***108***	***252***	***1,355***	***2,800***	
16,283	248	596	1,016	2,589	6,033	5,801	1,009	2	19	84	81	75	748	
14,111	131	1,229	1,291	2,243	5,080	3,237	3,934	1	62	103	237	1,161	2,370	
124,425	***382***	***2,284***	***8,649***	***9,501***	***57,890***	***45,749***	***5,443***	***24***	***148***	***251***	***445***	***1,110***	***3,470***	8
129,259	***478***	***8,464***	***22,144***	***24,100***	***49,888***	***24,185***	***33,610***	***15***	***203***	***568***	***979***	***8,337***	***23,508***	
113,546	271	1,672	7,525	7,972	53,915	42,191	3,949	4	74	185	350	740	2,596	
117,521	424	7,856	20,731	22,087	44,507	21,916	30,180	11	155	372	762	7,453	21,428	
1,074	5	4	1	28	502	534	70	...	...	...	1	12	57	
864	1	1	46	73	499	244	439	...	...	...	1	117	321	
112,472	266	1,668	7,524	7,944	53,413	41,657	3,879	4	74	185	349	728	2,539	
116,657	423	7,855	20,685	22,014	44,008	21,672	29,741	11	153	373	761	7,336	21,107	
10,879	81	612	1,124	1,529	3,975	3,558	1,499	20	74	66	95	370	874	
11,733	54	608	1,413	2,013	5,381	2,269	3,430	4	50	195	217	884	2,080	
79,483	***135***	***1,318***	***4,037***	***5,623***	***36,897***	***31,473***	***3,478***	***24***	***53***	***63***	***350***	***382***	***2,606***	9
91,406	***303***	***5,038***	***16,241***	***19,858***	***31,986***	***17,980***	***19,389***	***18***	***103***	***277***	***688***	***4,724***	***13,579***	
78,653	118	1,290	4,003	5,522	36,644	31,076	3,115	10	23	54	286	259	2,483	
90,635	296	5,017	16,164	19,768	31,717	17,673	19,080	16	100	262	641	4,613	13,445	
18,796	***99***	***500***	***916***	***4,294***	***8,836***	***4,151***	***2,547***	***10***	***39***	***92***	***191***	***546***	***1,669***	10
17,769	***169***	***997***	***2,274***	***3,476***	***7,246***	***3,616***	***4,345***	***8***	***68***	***108***	***215***	***1,169***	***2,777***	
16,868	71	425	842	3,705	7,815	3,950	2,284	7	30	81	162	439	1,565	
15,992	135	862	2,198	3,269	6,232	3,296	3,788	8	58	95	208	1,029	2,390	
20,720	***141***	***726***	***1,168***	***2,397***	***9,923***	***6,368***	***2,635***	***23***	***68***	***87***	***183***	***595***	***1,679***	11
20,267	***265***	***1,744***	***1,719***	***3,265***	***9,378***	***3,896***	***5,402***	***13***	***48***	***91***	***239***	***1,338***	***3,673***	
9,994	67	223	461	1,050	4,745	3,436	1,112	3	11	17	33	281	767	
10,083	128	879	847	1,454	4,346	2,430	3,144	6	24	44	114	709	2,247	
1,186	5	15	31	94	537	501	112	...	...	...	19	28	65	
1,040	29	67	139	154	412	230	391	...	...	8	30	80	273	
8,807	62	213	430	956	4,211	2,935	1,000	3	11	17	14	253	702	
9,043	89	812	708	1,301	3,933	2,200	2,753	6	24	36	81	629	1,974	
10,727	74	498	704	1,347	5,175	2,929	1,523	20	57	70	150	314	912	
10,184	137	865	872	1,811	5,033	1,166	2,258	7	24	47	125	629	1,126	
178,204	***393***	***4,085***	***12,206***	***14,559***	***85,873***	***61,088***	***7,514***	***29***	***86***	***113***	***43***	***2,271***	***4,972***	12
179,211	***620***	***18,287***	***23,200***	***26,852***	***72,660***	***37,892***	***52,484***	***34***	***363***	***471***	***1,331***	***12,678***	***37,607***	
166,350	374	3,784	11,156	12,149	81,753	57,134	6,660	14	57	26	8	2,177	4,378	
169,647	503	17,201	22,288	25,210	68,891	35,554	48,412	33	335	373	1,012	11,487	35,172	
3,539	38	32	66	247	1,900	1,256	252	1	...	1	...	78	172	
3,139	91	104	195	595	1,629	525	1,788	4	1	1	51	425	1,306	
162,811	336	3,752	11,099	11,902	79,853	55,878	6,408	13	57	25	8	2,099	4,206	
165,508	412	17,097	22,093	24,615	67,262	35,029	46,624	29	334	372	961	11,062	33,866	
11,854	19	301	1,050	2,410	4,120	3,954	854	15	29	87	35	91	594	
9,564	117	1,086	912	1,342	3,769	2,338	4,072	1	28	98	319	1,191	2,435	

TABLE XIV.

CIVIL CONDITION BY AGE FOR SELECTED CASTES.

Serial No.	Caste, Tribe or Race.	Locality.	Sex.	Population dealt with.	Unmarried.						
					Total.	0—5	5—12	12—15	15—20	20—40	40 and over.
	1	2	3	48	49	50	51	52	53	54	55
	HINDU.—(contd.)										
13	Koli ..	Hyderabad State ...	Male ...	***134,432***	***51,389***	***21,558***	***16,799***	***7,486***	***4,119***	***1,146***	***281***
			Female ...	***132,408***	***33,711***	***22,317***	***9,838***	***1,235***	***121***	***117***	***86***
		Telingana ...	Male ...	9,737	3,849	1,772	1,299	305	205	227	41
			Female ..	8,853	2,459	1,364	808	158	46	56	27
		Marathwara ...	Male ...	124,695	47,540	19,786	15,500	7,181	3,914	919	24[illegible]
			Female ...	123,555	31,252	20,953	9,027	1,077	75	61	59
14	Komati ...	Hyderabad State ...	Male ...	***114,121***	***49,348***	***18,255***	***13,260***	***8,612***	***6,673***	***1,901***	***647***
			Female ...	***109,259***	***32,096***	***15,169***	***11,532***	***4,032***	***739***	***378***	***246***
		Telingana ...	Male ...	93,663	41,767	15,260	11,166	7,218	5,952	1,660	511
			Female ...	89,076	25,759	12,215	9,406	3,348	339	27[illegible]	179
		City ...	Male ...	3,000	1,269	487	310	174	147	10[illegible]	4[illegible]
			Female ...	2,526	996	626	150	78	65	57	2[illegible]
		Districts ...	Male ...	90,663	40,498	14,773	10,856	7,044	5,805	1,551	469
			Female ...	86,550	24,763	11,589	9,256	3,270	274	21[illegible]	159
		Marathwara ...	Male ..	20,458	7,581	2,995	2,094	1,394	721	241	136
			Female ..	20,183	6,337	2,954	2,126	684	400	106	67
15	Kummara or Kumbhar.	Hyderabad State ...	Male ..	***77,980***	***32,010***	***12,827***	***9,456***	***4,448***	***3,225***	***1,608***	***449***
			Female ...	***74,006***	***26,062***	***14,171***	***7,880***	***2,435***	***846***	***473***	***257***
		Telingana ...	Male ...	43,660	19,326	7,349	5,791	2,873	2,178	893	242
			Female ...	41,302	14,451	8,121	4,317	1,144	472	249	149
		City ...	Male ...	900	343	114	102	52	42	2[illegible]	10
			Female ...	947	307	138	151	9	...	5	4
		Districts ...	Male ...	42,760	18,983	7,235	5,689	2,821	2,136	870	232
			Female ...	40,355	14,144	7,983	4,166	1,135	472	244	144
		Marathwara ...	Male ...	34,320	12,684	5,478	3,665	1,575	1,047	712	207
			Female ...	32,704	11,611	6,050	3,563	1,291	374	224	109
16	Kurma ...	Hyderabad State ...	Male ...	***75,144***	***32,759***	***12,815***	***9,684***	***4,744***	***2,892***	***2,113***	***511***
			Female ...	***69,544***	***21,188***	***10,196***	***7,402***	***2,179***	***805***	***547***	***329***
		Telingana ...	Male ...	73,675	32,324	12,627	9,574	4,636	2,873	2,107	507
			Female ...	68,118	20,668	10,004	7,321	2,106	436	501	300
		City ...	Male ...	934	318	110	90	35	35	42	[illegible]
			Female ...	902	128	60	29	28	1	10	...
		Districts ...	Male ...	72,741	32,006	12,517	9,484	4,601	2,838	2,065	501
			Female ...	67,216	20,540	9,944	7,292	2,078	435	491	30[illegible]
17	Lingayet ...	Hyderabad State ...	Male ...	***381,201***	***144,700***	***63,784***	***43,485***	***22,184***	***11,250***	***2,141***	***1,856***
			Female ...	***376,410***	***107,106***	***62,787***	***28,424***	***9,409***	***3,882***	***1,562***	***1,042***
		Telingana ...	Male ...	41,034	18,051	6,883	4,741	3,220	2,182	681	34[illegible]
			Female ...	39,880	11,052	5,268	3,667	1,142	400	349	226
		City ...	Male ...	1,010	374	108	124	41	31	45	2[illegible]
			Female ...	954	355	138	149	39	22	...	7
		Districts ...	Male ...	40,024	17,677	6,775	4,617	3,179	2,151	636	319
			Female ...	38,926	10,697	5,130	3,518	1,103	378	349	219
		Marathwara ...	Male ...	340,167	126,649	56,901	38,744	18,964	9,068	1,460	1,512
			Female ...	336,530	96,054	57,519	24,757	8,267	3,482	1,213	816

TABLE XIV.

CIVIL CONDITION BY AGE FOR SELECTED CASTES.

Married.							Widowed.							Serial No.
Total.	0—5	5—12	12—15	15—20	20—40	40 and over.	Total.	0—5	5—12	12—15	15—20	20—40	40 and over.	
56	57	58	59	60	61	62	63	64	65	66	67	68	69	
79,520	***135***	***2,533***	***7,927***	***8,260***	***36,277***	***25,388***	***3,523***	***33***	***60***	***91***	***79***	***887***	***2,403***	13
77,402	***641***	***6,401***	***11,368***	***13,562***	***33,232***	***12,198***	***21,295***	***26***	***265***	***624***	***900***	***5,134***	***14,346***	
5,219	24	177	121	291	3,011	1,595	669	4	11	5	28	230	391	
4,728	71	692	301	553	2,227	884	1,666	6	22	19	53	398	1,168	
74,301	111	2,356	7,806	7,969	32,266	23,793	2,854	29	49	86	51	627	2,012	
72,674	570	5,709	11,067	13,009	31,005	11,314	19,629	20	243	605	847	4,736	13,178	
67,126	***119***	***1,403***	***3,349***	***6,057***	***25,717***	***23,481***	***4,647***	***13***	***68***	***176***	***349***	***1,120***	***2,921***	14
57,170	***261***	***5,193***	***6,268***	***9,426***	***22,445***	***13,577***	***19,993***	***13***	***136***	***363***	***781***	***5,541***	***13,159***	
48,037	80	1,165	2,901	4,094	21,654	18,143	3,859	1	39	135	287	1,106	2,291	
46,354	167	4,487	5,329	7,985	18,302	10,084	16,963	9	111	324	672	4,668	11,179	
1,570	...	12	25	118	1,014	401	161	...	...	...	...	35	126	
1,399	3	65	155	270	786	120	131	...	3	3	12	51	62	
46,467	80	1,153	2,876	3,976	20,640	17,742	3,698	1	39	135	287	1,071	2,165	
44,955	164	4,422	5,174	7,715	17,516	9,964	16,832	9	108	321	660	4,617	11,117	
12,089	39	238	448	1,963	4,063	5,338	788	12	29	41	62	14	630	
10,816	94	706	939	1,441	4,143	3,493	3,030	4	25	39	109	873	1,980	
43,235	***213***	***1,272***	***3,820***	***4,747***	***17,684***	***15,499***	***2,735***	***14***	***71***	***112***	***175***	***716***	***1,647***	15
38,316	***353***	***2,886***	***3,860***	***5,839***	***14,089***	***11,289***	***9,628***	***8***	***86***	***140***	***465***	***2,211***	***6,718***	
23,316	67	595	1,895	2,136	10,424	8,199	1,018	2	16	19	17	23	941	
21,385	107	1,637	2,414	3,776	7,621	5,830	5,466	5	22	26	185	1,165	4,063	
498	11	27	39	43	223	155	59	...	...	9	5	12	33	
469	3	22	20	85	230	109	171	...	...	...	4	38	129	
22,818	56	568	1,856	2,093	10,201	8,044	959	2	16	10	12	11	908	
20,916	104	1,615	2,394	3,691	7,391	5,721	5,295	5	22	26	181	1,127	3,934	
19,919	146	677	1,925	2,611	7,260	7,300	1,717	12	55	93	158	693	706	
16,931	246	1,249	1,446	2,063	6,468	5,459	4,162	3	64	114	280	1,046	2,655	
40,736	***89***	***634***	***2,328***	***3,824***	***18,955***	***14,906***	***1,649***	***2***	***9***	***41***	***26***	***186***	***1,415***	16
38,087	***173***	***3,881***	***3,663***	***5,677***	***16,165***	***8,528***	***10,299***	***3***	***41***	***126***	***226***	***2,147***	***7,786***	
40,022	83	616	2,302	3,635	18,780	14,606	1,329	1	4	29	3	66	1,226	
37,427	164	3,857	3,614	5,498	15,971	8,323	10,023	3	38	115	192	2,048	7,627	
425	5	2	...	18	186	214	191	...	1	4	2	45	139	
507	4	4	...	36	294	169	267	...	...	...	...	47	220	
39,597	78	614	2,302	3,617	18,594	14,392	1,138	1	3	25	1	21	1,087	
36,920	160	3,853	3,614	5,462	15,677	8,154	9,756	3	38	115	192	2,001	7,407	
215,872	***896***	***7,079***	***22,294***	***22,686***	***81,001***	***81,916***	***20,629***	***101***	***555***	***609***	***553***	***6,426***	***12,385***	17
207,027	***1,465***	***18,012***	***20,592***	***26,775***	***83,949***	***56,234***	***62,277***	***123***	***698***	***2,962***	***3,581***	***13,256***	***41,687***	
21,361	65	354	773	2,428	9,308	8,433	1,622	1	19	18	64	626	894	
20,639	105	1,855	2,015	2,968	9,174	4,522	8,189	9	65	180	337	1,900	5,698	
548	...	...	13	20	281	234	88	...	...	3	...	9	76	
506	6	8	13	80	218	181	93	...	...	2	4	16	71	
20,813	65	354	760	2,408	9,027	8,199	1,534	1	19	15	64	617	818	
20,133	99	1,847	2,002	2,888	8,956	4,341	8,096	9	65	178	333	1,884	5,627	
194,511	831	6,725	21,521	20,258	71,693	73,483	19,007	100	536	591	489	5,800	11,491	
186,388	1,360	16,157	18,577	23,807	74,775	51,712	54,088	114	633	2,782	3,244	11,356	35,959	

TABLE XIV.

CIVIL CONDITION BY AGE FOR SELECTED CASTES.

Serial No.	Caste, Tribe or Race.	Locality.	Sex.	Population dealt with.	Unmarried.						
					Total	0—5	5—12	12—15	15—20	20—40	40 and over.
	1	2	3	70	71	72	73	74	75	76	77
	HINDU.— *(contd.)*										
18	Lohar ...	Hyderabad State ...	Male ...	***24,828***	***10,435***	***3,947***	***3,153***	***1,474***	***885***	***747***	***229***
			Female ..	***23,016***	***7,456***	***3,807***	***2,472***	***619***	***216***	***257***	***85***
		Telingana ...	Male ...	12,376	5,374	1,726	1,839	784	562	368	[illegible]
			Female ..	11,122	3,718	1,885	1,389	267	75	76	[illegible]
		Marathwara ...	Male ...	12,452	5,061	2,221	1,314	690	323	379	[illegible]
			Female ..	11,891	3,738	1,922	1,083	352	141	181	[illegible]
19	Madiga, Mang	Hyderabad State ...	Male ...	***581,519***	***265,032***	***109,553***	***79,957***	***33,389***	***25,787***	***14,999***	***1,347***
			Female ...	***563,833***	***187,125***	***110,715***	***64,321***	***7,724***	***2,205***	***1,797***	***363***
		Telingana ...	Male ...	385,407	184,998	68,768	56,469	25,687	20,893	12,267	964
			Female ...	368,812	129,101	77,326	48,424	2,931	120	185	[illegible]
		City ...	Male ...	3,468	1,440	564	422	243	139	48	[illegible]
			Female ...	3,507	944	385	257	120	21	87	[illegible]
		Districts ...	Male ...	381,939	183,558	68,204	56,047	25,394	20,754	12,219	[illegible]
			Female ...	365,305	128,157	76,941	48,167	2,811	99	98	41
		Marathwara ...	Male ...	196,112	80,034	40,785	23,488	7,752	4,894	2,732	385
			Female ...	195,021	58,024	33,389	15,897	4,793	2,085	1,612	[illegible]
20	Mahar, Mala.	Hyderabad State ...	Male ...	***574,385***	***250,358***	***98,381***	***76,726***	***38,934***	***24,886***	***8,550***	***2,881***
			Female ...	***563,204***	***182,634***	***95,455***	***59,605***	***18,811***	***4,912***	***3,293***	***558***
		Telingana ...	Male ...	256,455	117,689	39,610	35,281	22,115	16,385	3,232	1,066
			Female ...	249,395	78,387	38,614	27,355	9,642	1,767	742	267
		City ...	Male ..	28,933	12,400	1,468	3,535	1,850	2,062	2,684	801
			Female ...	28,822	7,592	3,227	3,039	977	319	20	[illegible]
		Districts ...	Male ...	227,522	105,289	38,142	31,746	20,265	14,323	548	[illegible]
			Female ...	220,573	70,795	35,387	24,316	8,665	1,448	722	[illegible]
		Marathwara ...	Male ...	317,930	132,669	58,771	41,445	16,819	8,501	5,318	[illegible]
			Female ...	313,809	104,247	56,841	32,250	9,169	3,145	2,551	291
21	Mali ...	Hyderabad State ...	Male ...	***54,233***	***22,098***	***9,202***	***7,734***	***2,662***	***1,231***	***957***	***312***
			Female ...	***52,867***	***16,846***	***9,107***	***5,706***	***1,063***	***496***	***274***	***200***
		Marathwara ...	Male ...	51,556	21,111	8,692	7,462	2,569	1,165	919	[illegible]
			Female ...	50,390	15,856	8,513	5,425	992	467	264	[illegible]
22	Mangala ...	Hyderabad State ...	Male ...	***39,754***	***16,847***	***6,518***	***4,765***	***2,317***	***1,783***	***1,124***	***346***
			Female ..	***36,760***	***12,357***	***5,885***	***4,124***	***1,533***	***372***	***290***	***153***
		Telingana ...	Male ..	36,954	15,905	6,938	4,559	2,213	1,695	1,078	321
			Female ...	34,088	11,336	5,425	3,847	1,375	306	253	[illegible]
		City ...	Male ...	3,445	1,396	572	380	188	142	95	[illegible]
			Female ...	2,492	725	362	238	35	40	47	[illegible]
		Districts ...	Male ...	33,509	14,509	5,466	4,179	2,025	1,554	983	[illegible]
			Female ...	31,596	10,611	5,063	3,609	1,340	260	206	[illegible]
23	Maratha ...	Hyderabad State ...	Male ..	***772,878***	***314,044***	***112,328***	***92,449***	***48,825***	***29,111***	***24,780***	***6,560***
			Female ...	***765,996***	***222,127***	***109,169***	***78,017***	***25,346***	***4,651***	***4,538***	***406***
		Telingana ...	Male ...	72,601	28,183	10,435	8,471	3,751	2,495	2,565	[illegible]
			Female ..	70,427	21,359	12,321	6,283	1,973	303	321	[illegible]
		City ...	Male ...	3,200	1,076	261	248	170	168	188	[illegible]
			Female ...	3,096	780	352	324	35	32	24	[illegible]
		Districts ...	Male ...	69,401	27,107	10,174	8,223	3,581	2,327	2,377	[illegible]
			Female ...	67,331	20,579	11,969	5,959	1,938	271	297	[illegible]
		Marathwara ...	Male ...	700,277	285,861	101,893	83,969	45,074	26,616	22,215	[illegible]
			Female ..	695,569	200,768	96,848	71,734	23,373	4,348	4,217	[illegible]

TABLE XIV.

CIVIL CONDITION BY AGE FOR SELECTED CASTES.

Married.							Widowed.							Serial No.
Total.	0—5	5—12	12—15	15—20	20—40	40 and over.	Total.	0—5	5—12	12—15	15—20	20—40	40 and over.	
78	79	80	81	82	83	84	85	86	87	88	89	90	91	
12,850	**58**	**363**	**780**	**1,536**	**5,291**	**4,822**	**1,543**	**14**	**40**	**21**	**123**	**409**	**936**	18
12,351	**132**	**919**	**1,287**	**1,952**	**4,684**	**3,377**	**3,209**	**14**	**35**	**122**	**157**	**734**	**2,147**	
6,424	15	159	369	741	2,860	2,280	578	2	6	4	50	124	392	
5,833	35	404	591	824	2,253	1,756	1,541	2	9	20	37	398	1,075	
6,426	43	204	411	795	2,431	2,542	965	12	34	17	73	285	544	
6,488	97	515	695	1,128	2,431	1,621	1,668	12	26	102	120	336	1,072	
297,094	**735**	**3,597**	**13,085**	**22,948**	**142,372**	**114,357**	**19,393**	**193**	**342**	**512**	**1,405**	**8,087**	**11,854**	19
303,269	**1,834**	**22,134**	**32,604**	**43,893**	**119,115**	**83,985**	**73,439**	**94**	**448**	**1,412**	**2,492**	**18,009**	**50,984**	
190,523	324	1,773	4,246	13,712	96,778	73,690	9,886	6	33	92	336	2,561	6,858	
196,567	674	16,039	24,630	27,714	72,535	54,975	43,144	70	228	386	621	10,509	31,330	
1,910	4	3	32	51	1,270	550	118	...	2	3	1	40	72	
1,969	6	40	43	165	1,357	349	603	...	...	1	42	162	398	
188,613	320	1,770	4,214	13,661	95,508	73,140	9,768	6	31	89	335	2,521	6,786	
194,607	662	15,999	24,587	27,549	71,178	54,026	42,541	70	228	385	579	10,347	30,932	
106,571	411	1,824	8,849	9,236	45,594	40,667	9,507	187	309	420	1,069	2,526	4,996	
106,702	860	6,095	7,974	16,179	46,580	29,014	30,295	24	220	1,026	1,871	7,506	19,634	
301,115	**1,356**	**7,746**	**12,168**	**27,206**	**139,640**	**112,999**	**22,912**	**74**	**314**	**523**	**1,178**	**6,629**	**14,194**	20
305,520	**2,670**	**22,967**	**27,306**	**49,999**	**140,030**	**62,848**	**75,080**	**106**	**981**	**2,095**	**3,376**	**17,243**	**51,249**	
130,617	405	2,214	4,354	11,079	61,742	50,823	8,149	48	62	101	349	1,997	5,592	
136,373	647	10,546	11,677	19,925	67,485	26,093	34,635	36	187	210	667	8,318	25,217	
16,146	81	612	1,102	2,359	7,118	4,874	387	40	40	53	62	37	155	
16,243	97	1,921	839	2,461	6,690	4,235	4,987	6	56	50	107	1,317	3,451	
114,471	324	1,602	3,252	8,720	54,624	45,949	7,762	8	22	48	287	1,960	5,437	
120,130	559	8,625	10,838	17,464	61,795	21,858	29,648	30	131	160	560	7,001	21,766	
170,198	951	5,532	7,814	16,127	77,898	62,176	14,763	26	252	422	829	4,632	8,602	
169,147	2,923	12,421	15,629	30,074	72,545	36,455	40,415	70	794	1,885	2,709	8,925	26,032	
28,688	**198**	**709**	**2,633**	**3,672**	**11,873**	**9,606**	**3,444**	**1**	**19**	**113**	**207**	**849**	**2,255**	21
28,795	**321**	**2,426**	**3,143**	**4,452**	**11,138**	**7,318**	**7,226**	**22**	**105**	**220**	**343**	**1,662**	**4,873**	
27,216	192	650	2,537	3,408	11,121	9,308	3,229	1	19	105	164	788	2,152	
27,689	302	2,315	3,076	4,311	10,684	7,001	6,845	22	102	213	321	1,568	4,619	
21,228	**71**	**258**	**1,579**	**1,592**	**8,647**	**9,081**	**1,679**	**6**	**16**	**19**	**227**	**751**	**660**	22
18,809	**58**	**1,320**	**1,887**	**2,935**	**7,192**	**5,417**	**5,594**	**7**	**39**	**76**	**269**	**1,272**	**3,930**	
19,909	53	235	1,495	1,478	8,061	8,587	1,149	3	7	9	197	573	351	
17,528	55	1,299	1,782	2,744	6,868	4,780	5,224	7	35	51	214	1,175	3,742	
1,923	26	26	84	150	1,029	608	126	...	1	...	4	28	93	
1,273	...	51	78	190	732	222	494	1	1	6	5	104	377	
17,936	27	209	1,411	1,328	7,032	7,979	1,014	3	6	9	193	545	258	
16,255	55	1,248	1,704	2,554	6,136	4,558	4,730	6	34	45	209	1,071	3,365	
420,874	**1,897**	**13,036**	**22,105**	**42,675**	**190,210**	**150,951**	**37,960**	**73**	**495**	**899**	**3,255**	**12,286**	**20,952**	23
418,428	**2,503**	**32,675**	**44,290**	**54,222**	**180,204**	**101,534**	**128,441**	**163**	**2,733**	**4,239**	**8,074**	**29,271**	**83,961**	
41,796	334	2,059	1,657	3,278	20,529	13,939	2,622	23	50	62	185	634	1,668	
38,529	611	4,173	2,287	3,704	17,214	10,540	10,539	25	95	112	116	2,946	8,144	
1,910	33	10	17	119	1,204	527	214	...	...	...	2	52	160	
1,519	3	8	122	331	696	287	797	...	2	...	9	142	614	
39,890	301	2,049	1,610	3,159	19,325	13,412	2,408	23	50	62	183	582	1,508	
37,010	608	4,093	2,165	3,373	17,518	9,253	9,742	25	94	112	107	1,904	7,500	
379,078	1,563	10,977	20,448	39,397	169,681	137,012	35,338	50	445	837	3,070	11,652	19,281	
[illegible]	1,892	28,502	42,003	50,318	162,990	90,994	117,902	138	2,637	4,127	7,958	27,225	75,817	

TABLE XIV.

CIVIL CONDITION BY AGE FOR SELECTED CASTES.

Serial No.	Caste, Tribe or Race.	Locality.	Sex.	Population dealt with.	Unmarried. Total.	0—5	5—12	12—15	15—20	20—40	40 and over.
	1	2	3	92	93	94	95	96	97	98	99
	HINDU.— *(contd.)*										
24	Munnur ...	Hyderabad State ...	Male ...	***115,120***	***47,862***	***19,840***	***13,322***	***6,410***	***5,581***	***2,163***	***54***
			Female ..	***113,234***	***26,327***	***18,783***	***5,652***	***1,082***	***277***	***323***	***21***
		Telingana ...	Male ..	94,152	40,762	17,195	10,826	5,467	5,091	1,772	41
			Female ...	92,453	21,005	15,426	4,378	789	129	169	11
		City ...	Male ...	6,262	2,441	853	664	449	306	113	5
			Female ...	6,582	1,683	720	655	57	61	86	4
		Districts ...	Male ..	87,890	38,321	16,342	10,162	5,018	4,785	1,659	35
			Female ..	85,871	19,322	14,646	3,723	732	68	83	7
		Marathwara ...	Male ..	20,968	7,100	2,645	2,496	943	490	391	13
			Female ..	20,781	5,322	3,357	1,274	293	148	154	9
25	Mutrasi ...	Hyderabad State ...	Male ...	***134,473***	***61,086***	***22,502***	***18,652***	***9,217***	***6,221***	***4,011***	***48***
			Female ...	***126,297***	***37,222***	***22,461***	***11,415***	***2,515***	***644***	***115***	***7***
		Telingana ...	Male ..	132,293	60,380	22,123	18,473	9,142	6,173	3,994	47
			Female ...	124,268	36,632	22,174	11,268	2,427	619	82	6
		City ...	Male ..	5,105	2,270	928	539	373	187	237	
			Female ...	5,091	1,879	893	583	243	119	28	1
		Districts ...	Male ..	127,188	58,110	21,195	17,934	8,769	5,986	3,757	46
			Female ...	119,177	34,753	21,281	10,685	2,184	500	54	4
26	Nahvi (Warik.)	Hyderabad State ...	Male ..	***30,019***	***11,890***	***4,530***	***3,651***	***1,660***	***1,095***	***782***	***20***
			Female ..	***28,955***	***8,636***	***_4,617***	***2,481***	***828***	***338***	***269***	***10***
		Marathwara ...	Male ..	27,001	10,508	3,943	3,247	1,411	1,002	719	18
			Female ..	26,035	7,293	3,804	2,096	726	317	251	9
27	Panchal ..	Hyderabad State ...	Male ..	***59,990***	***25,600***	***10,058***	***6,931***	***3,788***	***2,991***	***1,449***	***38***
			Female ..	***57,720***	***18,926***	***9,920***	***6,154***	***1,521***	***815***	***400***	***11***
		Telingana ...	Male ..	44,972	20,456	7,920	5,536	2,983	2,549	1,175	29
			Female ..	42,947	14,289	7,268	4,934	1,120	608	309	4
		City ...	Male ...	1,487	688	263	96	147	97	44	4
			Female ..	1,357	465	160	211	40	30	22	
		Districts ...	Male ...	43,485	19,768	7,657	5,440	2,836	2,452	1,131	25
			Female ..	41,590	13,824	7,108	4,724	1,080	578	287	4
		Marathwara ...	Male ..	15,018	5,144	2,138	1,395	805	412	274	9
			Female ..	14,772	4,637	2,652	1,219	401	207	91	6
28	Rajput ...	Hyderabad State ...	Male ..	***31,296***	***12,772***	***4,619***	***3,619***	***1,944***	***1,447***	***826***	***31***
			Female ...	***30,341***	***10,636***	***5,304***	***3,319***	***1,135***	***433***	***287***	***18***
		Marathwara ...	Male ...	20,195	7,778	3,028	2,383	1,056	763	367	1?
			Female ..	19,858	6,755	3,504	1,967	633	215	216	1?
29	Sale ...	Hyderabad State ..	Male ..	***175,968***	***79,876***	***32,979***	***25,157***	***12,511***	***7,035***	***1,691***	[illegible]
			Female ...	***167,162***	***55,206***	***29,382***	***20,870***	***3,238***	***811***	***580***	[illegible]
		Telingana ...	Male ..	151,897	70,939	29,054	22,467	11,339	6,308	1,391	[illegible]
			Female ...	144,102	47,861	25,241	18,593	2,636	662	467	[illegible]
		City ...	Male ...	2,778	1,225	510	357	136	178	35	[illegible]
			Female ..	2,505	587	290	255	26	8	6	[illegible]
		Districts ...	Male ...	149,119	69,714	28,544	22,110	11,203	6,130	1,356	[illegible]
			Female ...	141,597	47,274	24,951	18,338	2,610	654	461	[illegible]
		Marathwara ...	Male ...	24,071	8,937	3,925	2,696	1,172	727	300	[illegible]
			Female .	23,060	7,345	4,141	2,277	602	149	113	[illegible]

TABLE XIV.

CIVIL CONDITION BY AGE FOR SELECTED CASTES.

Married.							Widowed.							Serial No.
Total.	0—5	5—12	12—15	15—20	20—40	40 and over.	Total.	0—5	5—12	12—15	15—20	20—40	40 and over.	
100	101	102	103	104	105	106	107	108	109	110	111	112	113	
60,357	***458***	***2,267***	***2,580***	***9,136***	***27,189***	***18,727***	***6,901***	***30***	***87***	***284***	***426***	***1,406***	***4,668***	24
68,731	***385***	***8,850***	***11,169***	***7,959***	***28,711***	***11,657***	***18,176***	***31***	***166***	***208***	***662***	***4,118***	***12,991***	
47,906	424	1,642	2,004	7,564	21,367	14,905	5,484	15	26	207	338	1,012	3,886	
57,447	306	7,270	10,116	6,519	23,208	10,028	14,001	20	103	103	401	3,126	10,248	
3,393	32	45	81	380	1,429	1,426	428	10	15	67	20	86	230	
3,096	3	131	187	388	1,942	444	1,803	...	5	...	17	293	1,488	
44,513	392	1,597	1,923	7,184	19,938	13,479	5,056	5	11	140	318	926	3,656	
54,351	303	7,139	9,929	6,131	21,265	9,584	12,198	20	98	103	384	2,833	8,760	
12,451	34	625	576	1,572	5,822	3,822	1,417	15	61	77	88	394	782	
11,284	79	1,580	1,053	1,440	5,503	1,629	4,175	11	63	105	261	992	2,743	
66,954	***107***	***482***	***878***	***5,305***	***32,556***	***27,626***	***6,433***	***6***	***18***	***64***	***227***	***1,460***	***4,658***	25
72,084	***388***	***3,775***	***9,643***	***14,848***	***28,616***	***14,814***	***16,991***	***62***	***162***	***135***	***547***	***3,773***	***12,312***	
65,830	98	469	835	5,122	32,053	27,253	6,083	6	11	60	210	1,333	4,463	
71,062	354	3,699	9,486	14,499	28,357	14,667	16,574	56	146	111	506	3,661	12,094	
2,336	21	43	69	118	1,358	727	499	3	3	5	12	157	319	
2,278	1	35	97	414	1,435	296	934	...	...	...	6	199	729	
63,494	77	426	766	5,004	30,695	26,526	5,584	3	8	55	198	1,176	4,144	
68,784	353	3,664	9,389	14,085	26,922	14,371	15,640	56	146	111	500	3,462	11,365	
16,028	***102***	***501***	***1,072***	***2,073***	***6,920***	***5,360***	***2,101***	***8***	***37***	***58***	***178***	***617***	***1,203***	26
15,769	***210***	***1,579***	***1,886***	***2,597***	***6,377***	***3,120***	***4,550***	***13***	***65***	***81***	***274***	***1,142***	***2,975***	
14,719	76	433	964	1,648	6,525	5,073	1,774	8	36	56	175	508	991	
14,605	186	1,487	1,774	2,288	5,916	2,924	4,137	12	62	75	269	974	2,745	
30,863	***112***	***477***	***914***	***2,248***	***14,820***	***12,292***	***3,527***	***14***	***45***	***82***	***134***	***851***	***2,401***	27
29,576	***214***	***2,269***	***2,478***	***4,148***	***13,170***	***7,297***	***9,218***	***15***	***79***	***151***	***303***	***2,075***	***6,595***	
22,715	80	243	648	1,692	10,811	9,241	1,801	4	16	26	34	293	1,428	
21,884	112	1,615	1,763	3,196	9,370	5,828	6,774	6	42	76	164	1,501	4,985	
724	20	17	32	80	336	239	75	1	4	1	6	18	45	
789	30	45	22	223	227	242	103	...	1	3	2	17	80	
21,991	60	226	616	1,612	10,475	9,002	1,726	3	12	25	28	275	1,383	
21,095	82	1,570	1,741	2,973	9,143	5,586	6,671	6	41	73	162	1,484	4,905	
8,148	32	234	266	556	4,009	3,051	1,726	10	29	56	100	558	973	
7,692	102	654	715	952	3,800	1,469	2,444	9	37	75	139	574	1,610	
15,232	***58***	***336***	***534***	***1,568***	***6,325***	***6,411***	***3,292***	***2***	***13***	***98***	***260***	***961***	***1,958***	28
14,420	***176***	***1,100***	***1,173***	***2,232***	***5,809***	***3,930***	***5,285***	***17***	***68***	***89***	***206***	***1,211***	***3,694***	
10,119	47	295	379	1,124	3,890	4,384	2,358	2	13	78	243	704	1,258	
9,895	155	733	914	1,598	3,866	2,629	3,208	15	59	82	133	791	2,128	
89,143	***224***	***1,717***	***2,307***	***8,772***	***41,490***	***34,633***	***6,949***	***7***	***35***	***234***	***461***	***1,527***	***4,685***	29
91,173	***341***	***7,509***	***7,700***	***14,844***	***38,212***	***22,567***	***20,783***	***20***	***142***	***290***	***650***	***4,608***	***15,073***	
75,639	184	1,463	1,803	6,488	37,451	28,250	5,319	1	18	182	325	1,029	3,764	
78,521	259	6,584	6,377	12,476	33,106	19,719	17,720	17	101	172	411	3,952	13,067	
1,422	...	8	13	73	712	616	131	..	1	...	2	27	101	
1,370	8	79	104	302	686	191	548	..	...	...	14	252	282	
74,217	184	1,455	1,790	6,415	36,739	27,634	5,188	1	17	182	323	1,002	3,663	
77,151	251	6,505	6,273	12,174	32,420	19,528	17,172	17	101	172	397	3,700	12,785	
13,504	40	254	504	2,284	4,039	6,383	1,630	6	17	52	136	498	921	
12,652	82	925	1,323	2,368	5,106	2,848	3,063	3	41	118	239	656	2,006	

TABLE XIV.

CIVIL CONDITION BY AGE FOR SELECTED CASTES.

Serial No.	Caste, Tribe or Race.	Locality.	Sex.	Population dealt with.	Unmarried.						
					Total.	0—5	5—12	12—15	15—20	20—40	40 and over.
	1	2	3	114	115	116	117	118	119	120	121
	HINDU.— *(contd.)*										
30	Satani ...	Hyderabad State ...	Male ..	***14,589***	***6,225***	***2,791***	***1,655***	***846***	***521***	***323***	***89***
			Female ..	***13,294***	***4,542***	***2,397***	***1,491***	***399***	***137***	***95***	***23***
		Telingana ...	Male ...	12,867	5,644	2,488	1,506	760	500	310	[illegible]
			Female ...	11,740	3,929	2,032	1,372	335	88	82	[illegible]
31	Sunar ...	Hyderabad State ...	Male ...	***45,278***	***18,741***	***7,255***	***5,063***	***2,696***	***1,920***	***1,428***	***379***
			Female ...	***42,759***	***13,352***	***6,961***	***4,292***	***1,169***	***435***	***312***	***183***
		Telingana ...	Male ...	24,439	11,038	4,176	2,929	1,679	1,221	813	[illegible]
			Female ...	22,498	6,950	3,386	2,454	644	239	167	[illegible]
		City ...	Male ...	1,659	680	260	188	103	86	31	[illegible]
			Female ...	1,689	511	362	111	26	2	9	1
		Districts ...	Male ...	22,780	10,358	3,916	2,741	1,576	1,135	782	[illegible]
			Female ...	20,809	6,439	3,024	2,343	618	237	158	[illegible]
		Marathwara ...	Male ...	20,839	7,703	3,079	2,134	1,017	699	615	[illegible]
			Female ...	20,261	6,402	3,575	1,838	525	196	145	[illegible]
32	Sutar ...	Hyderabad State ...	Male ...	***35,118***	***13,413***	***4,908***	***3,866***	***1,719***	***1,377***	***1,202***	***344***
			Female ...	***34,087***	***10,704***	***5,678***	***3,352***	***983***	***332***	***224***	***135***
		Telingana ...	Male ...	11,694	4,669	1,660	1,209	653	589	454	164
			Female ...	11,344	3,412	1,791	920	418	122	105	56
		Marathwara ...	Male ...	23,424	8,744	3,245	2,657	1,066	788	748	[illegible]
			Female ...	22,743	7,292	3,887	2,432	565	210	119	79
33	Telaga ...	Hyderabad State ...	Male ..	***233,206***	***107,435***	***37,806***	***34,034***	***16,028***	***11,848***	***7,424***	***595***
			Female ..	***225,416***	***75,798***	***38,016***	***25,587***	***7,762***	***2,202***	***1,385***	***876***
		Telingana ...	Male ...	209,666	97,695	34,039	30,869	14,822	10,770	6,786	409
			Female ...	203,395	68,403	34,715	23,358	6,837	1,632	1,039	792
		City ...	Male ...	6,213	2,228	435	645	437	310	330	71
			Female ...	6,150	1,698	728	666	111	87	61	45
		Districts ...	Male ...	203,453	95,467	33,604	30,224	14,385	10,460	6,456	338
			Female ...	197,245	66,705	33,987	22,692	6,726	1,545	1,008	747
		Marathwara ...	Male ...	23,540	9,740	3,767	3,165	1,206	778	638	186
			Female ...	22,021	7,395	3,301	2,229	925	570	286	84
34	Teli ..	Hyderabad State ...	Male ...	***28,620***	***10,887***	***4,592***	***2,884***	***1,471***	***970***	***703***	***261***
			Female ...	***28,324***	***10,026***	***5,467***	***2,774***	***957***	***363***	***300***	***165***
		Marathwara ...	Male ...	24,822	9,558	4,041	2,557	1,243	834	633	[illegible]
			Female ...	24,538	8,747	4,661	2,576	821	302	235	152
35	Uppara ...	Hyderabad State ...	Male ...	***29,098***	***11,193***	***4,280***	***3,653***	***1,548***	***916***	***613***	***183***
			Female ..	***27,932***	***8,561***	***4,098***	***2,543***	***819***	***600***	***389***	***112***
		Telingana ...	Male ...	11,163	4,878	1,714	1,533	750	443	338	100
			Female ...	9,995	2,694	1,284	1,035	211	62	72	30
		Marathwara ...	Male ...	17,932	6,315	2,565	2,120	798	473	275	83
			Female ...	17,907	5,867	2,514	1,508	608	538	317	82

TABLE XIV.

CIVIL CONDITION BY AGE FOR SELECTED CASTES.

Married.							Widowed.							Serial No.
Total.	0—5	5—12	12—15	15—20	20—40	40 and over.	Total.	0—5	5—12	12—15	15—20	20—40	40 and over.	
122	123	124	125	126	127	128	129	130	131	132	133	134	135	
7,354	24	93	318	818	3,291	2,810	1,010	3	7	10	64	240	686	30
6,654	31	424	509	909	2,423	2,358	2,098	6	23	33	76	543	1,417	
6,414	21	89	242	645	3,039	2,408	779	...	...	1	16	172	590	
5,927	25	413	479	800	2,072	2,138	1,884	6	16	24	57	473	1,308	
23,136	93	449	899	2,201	9,871	9,623	3,401	7	15	98	283	906	2,092	31
22,265	169	1,735	2,180	3,233	8,870	6,078	7,142	15	87	140	243	1,725	4,932	
11,783	31	143	375	1,040	5,462	4,732	1,618	...	3	45	190	393	987	
11,459	29	741	961	1,514	4,876	3,335	4,089	2	22	38	108	972	2,947	
895	...	2	12	40	444	397	84	...	...	...	...	22	62	
914	...	6[illegible]	43	101	567	138	264	...	1	...	8	97	158	
10,888	31	141	363	1,000	5,018	4,335	1,534	...	3	45	190	371	925	
10,545	29	679	921	1,410	4,309	3,197	3,825	2	21	38	100	875	2,789	
11,353	62	306	524	1,161	4,409	4,891	1,783	7	12	53	93	513	1,105	
10,806	140	994	1,216	1,719	3,994	2,743	3,053	13	65	102	135	753	1,985	
18,995	71	426	1,095	2,353	7,793	7,257	2,710	5	21	56	186	697	1,745	32
18,398	194	1,677	1,490	2,496	6,707	5,834	4,985	12	49	109	247	1,181	3,387	
6,378	19	125	351	1,056	2,607	2,220	647	3	1	9	55	163	416	
6,241	21	563	468	797	1,981	2,411	1,691	1	5	19	31	357	1,278	
12,617	52	301	744	1,297	5,186	5,037	2,063	2	20	47	131	534	1,329	
12,157	173	1,114	1,022	1,699	4,726	3,423	3,294	11	44	90	216	824	2,109	
114,162	356	1,162	2,988	8,101	55,904	45,651	11,609	7	49	78	745	2,896	7,834	33
113,390	406	8,341	9,823	18,185	50,788	25,847	36,228	30	181	318	1,004	8,121	26,574	
102,123	273	762	2,342	6,948	52,092	39,706	9,848	6	28	58	454	2,451	6,851	
102,639	296	7,428	8,405	15,926	47,281	23,303	32,353	28	140	260	853	7,093	23,979	
3,527	18	86	98	276	1,911	1,188	458	...	13	23	68	128	226	
2,978	5	142	110	314	1,602	805	1,474	11	2	19	7	320	1,115	
98,596	255	726	2,244	6,672	50,181	38,518	9,390	6	15	35	386	2,323	6,625	
99,661	291	7,286	8,295	15,612	45,679	22,498	30,879	17	138	241	846	6,773	22,864	
12,039	83	400	646	1,159	3,812	5,94[illegible]	1,761	1	21	20	291	415	983	
10,751	110	913	1,418	2,259	3,507	2,544	3,87[illegible]	2	41	58	151	1,028	2,595	
15,162	66	473	824	1,778	6,165	5,856	2,571	8	29	71	172	653	1,638	34
14,053	213	1,351	1,419	2,418	5,282	3,370	4,245	5	62	99	280	942	2,857	
12,987	61	366	6[illegible]2	1,475	5,273	5,130	2,277	8	27	58	151	572	1,461	
12,103	194	1,178	1,305	2,126	4,543	2,757	3,688	5	49	80	201	826	2,467	
15,095	37	230	652	1,714	6,947	6,415	2,810	24	52	111	212	639	1,772	35
14,777	159	1,292	1,441	2,188	6,096	3,601	4,564	4	40	110	236	1,125	3,049	
5,767	12	42	165	46[illegible]	2,822	2,260	521	...	...	9	68	120	824	
5,555	25	494	527	87[illegible]	2,446	1,190	1,746	2	9	17	74	415	1,229	
9,328	25	187	487	1,249	3,225	4,155	2,289	24	52	102	144	519	1,448	
9,222	134	798	914	1,315	3,650	2,411	2,818	2	31	93	162	710	1,820	

TABLE XIV.

CIVIL CONDITION BY AGE FOR SELECTED CASTES.

Serial No.	Caste, Tribe or Race.	Locality.	Sex.	Population dealt with.	Unmarried.						
					Total.	0—5	5—12	12—15	15—20	20—40	40 and over.
	1	2	3	136	137	138	139	140	141	142	143
	HINDU.— (*concld.*)										
36	Velama ..	Hyderabad State ...	Male ...	***42,705***	***18,648***	***6,421***	***5,287***	***2,647***	***2,132***	***1,864***	***297***
			Female ...	***41,082***	***12,894***	***6,703***	***4,282***	***1,291***	***315***	***227***	***76***
		Telingana ...	Male ...	24,972	12,289	4,207	3,254	1,732	1,478	1,388	[illegible]
			Female ..	23,905	8,700	4,269	3,166	917	223	99	[illegible]
		Marathwara ...	Male ...	17,733	6,359	2,214	2,033	915	654	476	[illegible]
			Female ...	17,177	4,194	2,434	1,116	374	92	128	[illegible]
37	Waddar ..	Hyderabad State ...	Male ...	***67,696***	***29,586***	***11,910***	***9,414***	***3,595***	***2,555***	***1,722***	***390***
			Female ...	***64,103***	***23,088***	***10,911***	***7,463***	***2,961***	***956***	***502***	***295***
		Telingana ...	Male ...	38,748	18,790	7,361	5,432	2,403	1,858	1,415	[illegible]
			Female ...	36,778	13,180	6,242	4,512	1,757	387	199	[illegible]
		Marathwara ...	Male ...	28,948	10,796	4,549	3,982	1,192	697	307	[illegible]
			Female ...	27,325	9,908	4,669	2,951	1,204	569	303	[illegible]
38	Wanjari ...	Hyderabad State ...	Male ...	***87,843***	***36,599***	***15,056***	***11,171***	***4,762***	***3,608***	***1,712***	***290***
			Female ...	***86,196***	***28,346***	***14,259***	***10,038***	***2,003***	***1,299***	***507***	***240***
		Telingana ...	Male ...	17,607	7,569	2,979	1,742	1,206	1,000	512	[illegible]
			Female ...	16,777	6,019	3,168	1,884	456	269	207	[illegible]
		Marathwara ...	Male ...	70,236	29,030	12,077	9,429	3,556	2,608	1,200	[illegible]
			Female ...	69,419	22,327	11,091	8,154	1,547	1,030	300	[illegible]
	MUSALMAN.										
39	Mughal ...	Hyderabad State ...	Male ...	***17,685***	***9,113***	***3,086***	***2,566***	***1,518***	***1,039***	***727***	***177***
			Female ..	***15,726***	***7,070***	***2,829***	***2,017***	***1,137***	***526***	***463***	***98***
		Marathwara ...	Male ...	11,125	5,971	2,264	1,733	1,047	606	258	[illegible]
			Female ...	9,660	4,369	1,947	1,165	684	252	234	[illegible]
40	Pathan ...	Hyderabad State ...	Male ...	***71,167***	***33,573***	***9,391***	***9,868***	***4,645***	***4,595***	***4,278***	***796***
			Female ...	***63,981***	***23,832***	***9,529***	***8,460***	***3,087***	***1,418***	***974***	***364***
		Telingana ...	Male ..	27,528	14,160	3,257	4,149	1,880	2,143	2,283	[illegible]
			Female ...	23,716	9,331	3,459	3,645	1,239	575	301	112
		City ...	Male ...	13,362	6,706	1,467	1,909	966	1,089	1,135	[illegible]
			Female ...	11,598	4,712	1,634	1,828	738	343	149	[illegible]
		Districts ...	Male ...	14,166	7,454	1,790	2,240	914	1,054	1,148	[illegible]
			Female ...	12,118	4,619	1,825	1,817	501	232	152	[illegible]
		Marathwara ...	Male ...	43,639	19,413	6,134	5,719	2,765	2,452	1,995	[illegible]
			Female ...	40,265	14,501	6,070	4,815	1,848	843	675	[illegible]
41	Sayyed ..	Hyderabad State ...	Male ...	***99,142***	***47,149***	***12,754***	***13,672***	***6,706***	***5,996***	***6,924***	***1,097***
			Female ...	***90,432***	***32,113***	***12,098***	***12,628***	***4,368***	***1,586***	***1,062***	***371***
		Telingana ...	Male ...	42,280	21,959	4,697	6,170	3,064	3,372	4,095	[illegible]
			Female ...	39,857	15,523	5,345	6,033	2,478	1,045	489	[illegible]
		City ...	Male ..	17,377	9,034	1,625	2,528	1,297	1,570	1,840	[illegible]
			Female ..	17,563	6,880	2,235	2,760	1,030	578	215	[illegible]
		Districts ...	Male ...	24,903	12,925	3,072	3,642	1,767	1,802	2,255	[illegible]
			Female ..	22,294	8,643	3,110	3,273	1,448	467	274	[illegible]
		Marathwara ...	Male ..	56,862	25,190	8,057	7,502	3,642	2,621	2,829	[illegible]
			Female ..	50,575	16,590	6,753	6,595	1,890	541	573	[illegible]

TABLE XIV.

CIVIL CONDITION BY AGE FOR SELECTED CASTES.

Married.							Widowed.							Serial No.
Total.	0—5	5—12	12—15	15—20	20—40	40 and over.	Total.	0—5	5—12	12—15	15—20	20—40	40 and over.	
144	145	146	147	148	149	150	151	152	153	154	155	156	157	
21,808	***93***	***405***	***1,049***	***1,662***	***9,808***	***8,791***	***2,249***	***9***	***35***	***40***	***116***	***570***	***1,479***	36
20,996	***243***	***1,379***	***2,004***	***2,788***	***9,249***	***5,333***	***7,192***	***16***	***59***	***65***	***155***	***1,658***	***5,239***	
11,594	40	143	308	519	5,343	5,241	1,089	...	3	1	19	209	857	
10,983	82	391	783	1,466	4,514	3,617	4,322	3	36	47	93	992	3,151	
10,214	53	262	741	1,143	4,165	3,550	1,160	9	32	29	97	361	622	
10,113	161	988	1,221	1,322	4,735	1,086	2,870	13	23	18	62	666	2,098	
35,282	***187***	***827***	***1,150***	***5,094***	***18,338***	***9,686***	***2,828***	***11***	***70***	***123***	***259***	***730***	***1,635***	37
33,704	***240***	***1,674***	***3,260***	***6,652***	***14,495***	***7,383***	***7,311***	***9***	***81***	***141***	***325***	***1,682***	***5,103***	
18,855	76	269	575	3,346	9,479	5,110	1,103	2	8	10	24	246	819	
18,718	65	939	1,709	3,462	7,871	4,732	4,880	1	11	76	150	1,071	3,571	
16,427	111	558	575	1,748	8,859	4,576	1,725	9	62	113	235	490	815	
14,996	175	735	1,551	3,250	6,624	2,651	2,431	8	40	65	175	611	1,552	
46,805	***384***	***2,101***	***2,186***	***4,823***	***22,507***	***14,804***	***4,439***	***10***	***70***	***130***	***178***	***1,165***	***2,886***	38
45,661	***1,029***	***4,010***	***4,933***	***6,188***	***19,602***	***9,899***	***12,189***	***23***	***168***	***490***	***917***	***2,734***	***7,857***	
9,446	27	161	411	1,814	4,816	2,187	592	2	4	4	39	128	415	
8,755	79	715	877	1,334	3,222	2,528	2,003	14	22	35	60	461	1,391	
37,359	357	1,946	1,775	3,609	17,661	12,017	3,847	8	66	126	139	1,037	2,471	
36,906	950	3,295	4,056	4,854	16,380	7,371	10,186	9	146	455	857	2,253	6,466	
7,387	...	***173***	***320***	***644***	***2,991***	***3,259***	***1,185***	...	***19***	***102***	***99***	***313***	***652***	39
7,015	...	***150***	***559***	***972***	***3,070***	***2,264***	***1,641***	...	***10***	***89***	***89***	***353***	***1,109***	
4,999	...	115	174	950	1,864	1,879	165	...	15	29	7	16	99	
4,407	...	127	446	605	1,755	1,474	884	...	8	61	66	211	535	
64,404	...	***236***	***517***	***1,910***	***18,007***	***13,734***	***3,190***	...	***4***	***22***	***70***	***787***	***2,307***	40
31,499	...	***604***	***1,781***	***4,540***	***17,047***	***7,527***	***8,650***	...	***29***	***75***	***184***	***1,992***	***6,370***	
12,137	...	38	103	465	5,389	6,142	1,231	...	...	...	34	303	894	
10,702	...	155	465	1,539	5,867	2,676	3,683	...	7	10	63	817	2,781	
6,020	...	9	40	250	2,576	3,145	636	...	...	...	7	169	469	
5,031	...	20	152	713	2,882	1,272	1,847	...	2	2	19	351	1,470	
6,117	...	29	63	215	2,813	2,997	595	...	...	...	27	131	434	
5,663	...	135	313	826	2,985	1,404	1,836	...	5	8	44	463	1,316	
22,267	...	198	414	1,415	12,618	7,592	1,959	...	4	22	36	481	1,414	
20,797	...	449	1,316	3,001	11,180	4,851	4,967	...	22	65	121	1,175	3,584	
47,117	...	***357***	***676***	***2,266***	***22,473***	***21,345***	***4,876***	...	***15***	***44***	***140***	***1,205***	***3,472***	41
43,569	...	***843***	***3,314***	***5,728***	***23,446***	***10,238***	***14,750***	...	***31***	***198***	***295***	***3,222***	***11,004***	
18,602	...	120	143	396	8,846	9,097	1,719	...	...	1	14	421	1,283	
17,829	...	283	973	2,506	9,573	4,491	6,505	...	8	76	152	1,440	4,829	
7,609	...	31	50	125	3,626	3,777	734	...	...	...	2	176	556	
7,531	...	34	499	1,065	4,196	1,737	3,152	...	2	60	56	606	2,428	
10,997	...	89	93	271	5,220	5,326	985	...	...	1	12	245	727	
10,298	...	249	474	1,441	5,377	2,757	3,353	...	6	16	96	834	2,411	
28,515	...	237	532	1,879	13,627	12,248	3,157	...	15	43	126	784	2,189	
25,740	...	560	2,341	3,222	13,873	5,744	8,245	...	23	122	143	1,782	6,175	

TABLE XIV.

CIVIL CONDITION BY AGE FOR SELECTED CASTES.

Serial No.	Caste, Tribe or Race.	Locality.	Sex.	Population dealt with.	Unmarried. Total.	0–5	5–12	12–15	15–20	20–40	40 and over.
	1	2	3	158	159	160	161	162	163	164	165
	MUSALMAN.—(concld.)										
42	Shaik ...	Hyderabad State ...	Male ..	***499,495***	***250,462***	***73,115***	***62,124***	***46,647***	***34,732***	***30,788***	***3,056***
			Female ...	***485,524***	***171,834***	***69,938***	***59,126***	***25,504***	***9,172***	***6,935***	***1,159***
		Telingana ...	Male ..	229,280	120,506	35,478	23,704	26,301	15,740	15,083	1,197
			Female ...	221,702	78,551	30,399	27,927	12,049	4,701	2,661	814
		City ...	Male ...	76,219	40,820	11,241	10,435	6,859	5,932	5,589	761
			Female ..	74,399	25,866	11,215	6,797	3,830	2,221	1,476	327
		Districts ...	Male ..	153,061	79,686	24,234	13,269	19,445	12,808	9,494	436
			Female ...	147,303	52,685	19,184	21,130	8,219	2,480	1,185	487
		Marathwara ...	Male ...	270,215	129,956	37,637	38,420	20,343	15,992	15,705	1,859
			Female ...	263,822	93,283	39,539	31,199	13,455	4,471	4,274	345
	CHRISTIAN.										
43	Indian Christian.	Hyderabad State ...	Male ..	***23,635***	***12,454***	***3,730***	***3,940***	***1,629***	***1,309***	***1,663***	***183***
			Female ...	***22,273***	***9,170***	***3,946***	***3,309***	***1,265***	***355***	***209***	***86***
		Telingana ...	Male ...	18,600	10,281	2,862	3,256	1,311	1,124	1,566	162
			Female ..	17,693	7,386	3,074	2,750	1,051	289	162	60
		City ...	Male ..	4,542	2,864	812	814	147	229	823	39
			Female ...	4,678	1,894	893	528	304	89	15	5
		Districts ...	Male ..	14,058	7,417	2,050	2,442	1,164	895	743	123
			Female ...	13,015	5,492	2,181	2,162	747	200	147	55
	ANIMIST.										
44	Gond ...	Hyderabad State ...	Male ..	***62,583***	***32,764***	***18,821***	***10,967***	***2,147***	***550***	***254***	***25***
			Female ...	***61,758***	***24,501***	***15,105***	***7,638***	***1,402***	***288***	***55***	***13***
		Telingana ...	Male ...	62,155	32,613	18,756	10,913	2,128	541	251	24
			Female ...	61,348	24,346	15,017	7,593	1,384	284	5[illegible]	1[illegible]
45	Lambada ...	Hyderabad State ...	Male ...	***76,703***	***42,874***	***18,622***	***12,360***	***3,960***	***3,445***	***4,419***	***68***
			Female ...	***65,341***	***30,681***	***15,750***	***11,319***	***2,338***	***794***	***431***	***49***
		Telingana ...	Male ...	68,304	39,049	17,045	11,237	3,299	3,177	4,245	46
			Female ...	57,545	27,522	14,088	10,368	2,018	678	344	27
		Marathwara ...	Male ...	8,399	3,825	1,577	1,123	661	268	174	22
			Female ...	7,796	3,159	1,662	951	320	116	8[illegible]	22

TABLE XIV.

CIVIL CONDITION BY AGE FOR SELECTED CASTES.

Married.							Widowed.							Serial No.
Total.	0—5	5—12	12—15	15—20	20—40	40 and over.	Total.	0—5	5—12	12—15	15—20	20—40	40 and over.	
166	167	168	169	170	171	172	173	174	175	176	177	178	179	
229,470	...	901	2,345	8,297	114,941	102,986	19,563	...	74	238	805	4,388	14,358	42
235,719	...	4,049	11,847	30,985	132,920	55,918	77,971	...	231	857	1,768	15,292	59,823	
100,065	...	357	698	2,320	49,636	47,054	8,709	...	11	62	270	2,022	6,844	
103,941	...	1,654	4,788	14,468	61,285	21,746	39,210	...	76	246	770	7,585	30,533	
31,143	...	64	119	582	15,268	15,000	4,256	...	...	1	208	1,102	2,945	
34,535	...	151	798	4,798	22,589	6,284	13,998	...	6	27	76	2,576	11,313	
68,922	...	293	579	1,788	34,268	31,994	4,453	...	11	61	62	920	3,399	
69,406	...	1,503	3,995	9,670	38,746	15,492	15,212	...	70	219	694	5,009	19,220	
129,405	...	544	1,647	5,977	65,305	55,932	10,854	...	63	176	285	2,366	8,014	
131,778	...	2,395	7,059	16,517	71,635	34,172	38,761	...	155	611	998	7,707	29,290	
10,088	...	6	97	404	5,454	4,127	1,653	...	...	5	33	301	754	43
10,459	...	10	410	1,464	6,015	2,566	2,644	...	...	25	129	629	1,861	
7,691	...	...	57	247	4,058	3,349	628	...	...	2	22	151	453	
8,198	...	8	298	1,040	4,739	2,112	2,109	...	...	20	112	494	1,488	
1,550	...	...	...	12	887	651	128	...	...	...	...	34	94	
2,118	...	...	46	118	1,237	717	671	...	...	6	78	169	418	
6,141	...	...	57	231	3,151	2,698	500	...	...	2	22	117	359	
6,085	...	8	253	927	3,562	1,391	1,438	...	...	14	34	325	1,065	
28,643	52	646	1,777	2,077	14,148	9,942	1,176	...	6	7	11	418	734	44
30,769	18	1,387	2,858	3,324	17,881	5,261	6,488	...	42	64	396	997	4,989	
28,406	53	641	1,754	2,032	14,059	9,867	1,196	...	6	7	7	401	715	
30,571	18	1,388	2,879	3,208	17,807	5,214	6,431	...	42	64	386	983	4,936	
28,606	69	417	482	906	13,339	13,393	5,223	106	143	1,123	1,142	628	2,081	45
27,261	191	891	1,072	2,813	15,944	6,750	7,259	2	16	75	1,100	1,061	5,042	
24,537	52	209	399	127	11,425	11,901	4,718	106	125	1,100	1,115	462	1,810	
23,528	171	475	846	2,374	13,870	5,802	6,465	2	13	67	1,051	843	4,509	
4,069	17	108	159	379	1,914	1,492	105	...	18	22	27	166	271	
3,823	20	110	126	439	2,074	948	814	...	8	11	49	218	533	

TABLE XV.

OCCUPATION OR MEANS OF LIVELIHOOD.

PART A.—GENERAL TABLE.

1. For the purpose of this table, a classified scheme of occupations based on that drawn up by M. Bertillon has been framed by the Census Commissioner. All occupations are divided into 4 main classes, and sub-divided into 12 sub-classes, 55 orders and 169 groups.

2. The table comprises 5 parts, A. B. C. D. and E. Part A. deals with the whole population of the State by city and districts. Part B. shows the subsidiary occupations of the actual workers among the agriculturists only. Part C. contains information as to the strength returned for certain mixed occupations. Part D. purposes to show distribution by religion of the total population for the State and for the City. Part E. embodies the results of the Industrial Census and its scope is explained in the title page prefixed to it.

TABLE XV.

OCCUPATION OR MEANS OF LIVELIHOOD.

PART A.—GENERAL TABLE.

Serial Number.	District.	Class A.—Production. Sub-Class I.—Exploitation. Total Order 1 (a): Total workers and dependants.	Actual workers. Total. Males.	Actual workers. Total. Females.	Actual workers. Partially agriculturist. Males.	Actual workers. Partially agriculturist. Females.	Dependants.	Order 1.—Pasture and agriculture. 1.—Income from rent of agricultural land. Total workers and dependants.	Actual workers. Total. Males.	Actual workers. Total. Females.	Dependants.
	1	2	3	4	5	6	7	8	9	10	11
	Hyderabad State ...	*7,619,505*	*2,408,868*	*1,737,615*	*24,715*	*20,662*	*3,473,022*	*731,803*	*234,108*	*113,407*	*384,288*
1	Hyderabad City ...	33,425	13,445	1,206	...	...	18,774	5,327	1,351	263	3,713
2	Atraf-i-balda ...	250,194	77,680	66,387	135	108	106,127	15,317	6,495	2,150	6,672
	Warangal Division ...	*1,427,930*	*450,848*	*374,875*	*1,884*	*982*	*602,207*	*94,452*	*30,381*	*17,796*	*46,275*
3	Warangal ..	485,183	152,554	134,957	602	117	197,672	45,982	16,129	8,920	20,933
4	Karimnagar ...	526,858	165,275	150,304	979	774	211,279	24,368	8,432	3,914	12,022
5	Adilabad ...	415,889	133,019	89,614	303	91	193,256	24,102	5,820	4,962	12,320
	Medak Division ...	*1,498,578*	*483,798*	*458,706*	*11,318*	*12,887*	*556,074*	*174,424*	*65,061*	*40,684*	*68,679*
6	Medak ...	287,826	99,404	75,414	5,394	7,342	113,008	71,590	25,898	16,895	29,597
7	Nizamabad ...	297,094	83,340	87,350	536	88	126,404	18,258	6,756	3,302	8,200
8	Mahbubnagar ..	309,160	128,377	128,139	1,123	1,666	142,318	35,803	16,002	6,428	13,373
9	Nalgonda ...	514,498	172,681	167,478	4,267	3,791	174,341	48,773	17,20.	11,059	17,509
	Aurangabad Division	*2,043,662*	*667,573*	*431,215*	*5,870*	*2,355*	*943,874*	*180,623*	*64,975*	*19,450*	*96,158*
10	Aurangabad ..	618,088	198,601	112,908	2,346	1,003	306,579	91,584	26,741	11,637	53,206
11	Bhir ..	460,637	160,745	104,607	1,049	171	195,285	24,747	8,234	1,152	15,361
12	Nander ..	500,374	164,257	113,229	1,097	471	222,888	40,423	21,259	3,565	15,569
13	Parbhani ...	463,563	143,970	100,471	1,378	710	219,122	23,869	8,711	3,096	12,062
	Gulbarga Division ...	*2,366,716*	*715,524*	*405,226*	*5,508*	*4,330*	*1,245,966*	*261,660*	*65,845*	*33,064*	*162,781*
14	Gulbarga ...	674,862	214,261	110,734	2,644	1,891	349,867	92,850	28,649	12,233	51,968
15	Osmanabad ..	491,247	159,164	99,351	935	271	232,732	14,427	3,224	2,255	9,949
16	Raichur ...	605,084	165,522	89,835	946	1,739	349,729	97,999	20,108	11,483	66,413
17	Bidar ...	595,523	176,57[illegible]	105,308	1,013	429	313,638	56,384	13,869	7,093	[illegible]

TABLE XV.

OCCUPATION OR MEANS OF LIVELIHOOD.

PART A.—GENERAL TABLE.

of raw materials.

of the surface of the earth.

(a) Ordinary cultivation.

2.—Ordinary cultivators.				3.—Agents, managers of landed estates (not planters), clerks, rent collectors, etc.				4.—Farm servants and field labourers.						Serial Number.
Total workers and dependants.	Actual workers. Total. Males.	Actual workers. Total. Females.	Dependants.	Total workers and dependants.	Actual workers. Total. Males.	Actual workers. Total. Females.	Dependants.	Total workers and dependants.	Actual workers. Total. Males.	Actual workers. Total. Females.	Actual workers. Partially agriculturist. Males.	Actual workers. Partially agriculturist. Females.	Dependants.	
12	13	14	15	16	17	18	19	20	21	22	23	24	25	
4,064,950	***1,367,676***	***727,383***	***1,969,891***	***34,840***	***16,353***	...	***18,187***	***2,788,212***	***790,731***	***896,825***	***24,715***	***20,662***	***1,100,656***	
3,771	1,480	393	1,898	22,200	10,099	...	12,101	2,127	515	550	...	...	1,062	1
120,512	44,779	22,587	53,146	5	2	...	3	114,360	26,404	41,650	135	108	46,306	2
758,623	***262,299***	***137,428***	***358,896***	...	...	...	...	***574,855***	***158,168***	***219,651***	***1,884***	***982***	***197,036***	
262,218	93,067	47,161	121,990	...	...	...	...	176,983	43,358	78,876	602	117	54,749	3
281,417	98,130	51,039	132,248	...	...	...	...	221,073	58,713	95,351	979	774	67,009	4
214,988	71,102	39,228	104,658	...	...	...	...	176,793	56,097	45,421	303	91	75,278	5
736,107	***259,282***	***178,309***	***298,546***	***156***	***82***	...	***74***	***587,891***	***159,403***	***239,713***	***11,318***	***12,887***	***188,775***	
109,634	41,623	23,932	44,079	...	...	..	...	106,603	32,683	34,587	5,394	7,342	39,832	6
163,008	44,323	38,898	79,787	...	...	...	...	115,828	32,261	45,150	536	84	38,417	7
183,776	71,595	41,803	70,378	...	...	...	...	179,581	40,776	80,238	1,123	1,666	58,567	8
279,689	101,711	73,676	104,302	156	82	...	74	185,880	53,683	79,738	4,265	3,791	52,459	9
1,187,889	***391,310***	***216,934***	***549,645***	***4,782***	***2,095***	...	***2,687***	***699,368***	***209,193***	***194,831***	***5,870***	***2,355***	***295,344***	
332,025	108,673	58,009	165,343	4,676	2,038	...	2,638	189,803	61,149	43,262	2,346	1,003	85,392	10
263,214	97,722	52,012	113,480	...	...	...	...	172,676	54,789	51,443	1,019	171	66,444	11
296,584	94,856	58,054	143,674	95	49	...	46	163,272	43,063	51,610	1,097	471	63,599	12
266,066	90,059	48,859	127,148	11	8	...	3	173,617	45,192	48,516	1,378	710	79,909	13
,288,048	***408,556***	***171,732***	***707,760***	***7,397***	***4,075***	...	***3,322***	***809,611***	***237,048***	***200,430***	***5,508***	***4,330***	***372,133***	
331,073	104,423	51,518	175,132	387	109	...	278	250,552	81,080	46,983	2,614	1,891	122,489	14
273,166	93,155	34,201	145,810	132	90	...	42	203,522	62,695	62,895	905	271	77,972	15
374,071	113,239	43,908	216,924	6,506	3,685	...	2,821	126,508	28,495	34,442	946	1,739	63,571	16
309,788	97,729	42,105	169,894	372	191	...	181	229,029	61,778	56,110	1,013	429	108,141	17

TABLE XV.

OCCUPATION OR MEANS OF LIVELIHOOD.

PART A.—GENERAL TABLE.

Class A.—Production

Sub Class I.—Exploitation

Serial Number.	District.	Total Order 1 (b). Total workers and dependants.	Total Order 1 (b). Actual workers. Total. Males.	Total Order 1 (b). Actual workers. Total. Females.	Total Order 1 (b). Actual workers. Partially agriculturist. Males.	Total Order 1 (b). Actual workers. Partially agriculturist. Females.	Total Order 1 (b). Dependants.	Order 1 (b).—Growers of special products. 5 Tea, coffee, cinchona and indigo plantations. Total workers and dependants.	5 Tea, coffee, cinchona and indigo plantations. Actual workers. Total. Males.	5 Tea, coffee, cinchona and indigo plantations. Actual workers. Total. Females.	5 Tea, coffee, cinchona and indigo plantations. Actual workers. Partially agriculturist. Males.	5 Tea, coffee, cinchona and indigo plantations. Actual workers. Partially agriculturist. Females.	5 Tea, coffee, cinchona and indigo plantations. Dependants.
	1	26	27	28	29	30	31	32	33	34	35	36	37
	Hyderabad State ...	***22,804***	***8,137***	***5,349***	***522***	***286***	***9,318***	...	...	...	...	...	...
1	Hyderabad City ...	3,988	1,249	1,085	...	...	1,654	...	...	...	...	...	...
2	Atraf-i-balda ..	7	...	...	...	...	7	...	...	...	...	...	...
	Warangal Division .	***1,754***	***670***	***397***	***4***	...	***687***	...	...	...	...	...	...
3	Warangal ..	42	15	...	...	...	27	...	...	...	...	...	...
4	Karimnagar ...	151	33	38	...	...	80	...	...	...	...	...	...
5	Adilabad ...	1,561	622	359	4	...	580	...	...	...	...	...	...
	Medak Division ...	***3,143***	***1,589***	***570***	***365***	***190***	***984***	...	...	...	...	...	...
6	Medak	2,456	1,315	446	323	179	695	...	...	...	...	...	...
7	Nizamabad ...	...	...	...	...	...	...	...	...	...	...	...	...
8	Mahbubnagar ...	641	269	113	42	...	259	...	...	...	...	...	...
9	Nalgonda... ...	46	5	11	...	11	30	...	...	...	...	...	...
	Aurangabad Division	***7,174***	***2,501***	***2,078***	***112***	***80***	***2,595***	...	...	...	...	...	...
10	Aurangabad ...	3,205	1,135	889	93	70	1,181	...	...	...	...	...	...
11	Bhir	2,317	783	790	17	9	744	...	...	...	...	...	...
12	Nander	104	21	32	...	...	51	...	...	...	...	...	...
13	Parbhani ...	1,548	562	367	2	1	619	...	...	...	...	...	...
	Gulbarga Division ...	***6,738***	***2,128***	***1,219***	***41***	***16***	***3,391***	...	...	...	...	...	...
14	Gulbarga ..	5,029	1,580	818	35	10	2,631	...	...	...	...	...	...
15	Osmanabad ...	259	75	19	3	...	165	...	...	...	...	...	...
16	Raichur	12	7	3	1	...	2	...	...	...	...	...	...
17	Bidar	1,487	466	379	2	6	592	...	...	...	...	...	...

TABLE XV.

OCCUPATION OR MEANS OF LIVELIHOOD.

PART A.—GENERAL TABLE.

of raw materials —(*contd*).

of the surface of the earth.—(*contd*).

and market gardening. 6—Fruit, flower, vegetable, betel, vine, arecanut, etc., growers. Total workers and dependants.	Actual workers. Total. Males.	Females.	Partially agriculturist. Males.	Females.	Dependants.	Total Order 1 (c). Total workers and dependants.	Actual workers. Total. Males.	Females.	Partially agriculturist. Males.	Females.	Dependants.	Order 1 (c)—Forestry. 7—Forest officers, rangers, guards, etc. Total workers and dependants.	Actual workers. Total. Males.	Females.	Partially agriculturist. Males.	Females	Dependants.	Serial Number.
38	39	40	41	42	43	44	45	46	47	48	49	50	51	52	53	54	55	
22,804	*8,137*	*5,349*	*522*	*286*	*9,318*	*41,774*	*12,248*	*7,285*	*1,415*	*1,121*	*22,241*	*869*	*351*	..	*3*	...	*518*	
3,938	1,249	1,085	...	...	1,654	3,420	1,224	299	...	...	1,897	352	185	...	...	...	168	1
7	...	...	...	...	7	2,421	1,172	43	48	1	1,206	266	52	...	...	...	214	2
1,784	*670*	*397*	*4*	...	*687*	*18,770*	*4,996*	*3,531*	*765*	*588*	*10,243*	*213*	*95*	...	...	...	*118*	
42	15	...	...	...	27	9,942	2,277	2,206	122	12	5,399	213	95	...	...	...	118	3
151	33	38	...	...	80	8,642	2,619	1,250	643	576	4,773	...	...	...	...	...	...	4
1,561	622	350	4	.	589	186	100	15	...	..	71	...	...	...	...	...	...	5
3,143	*1,589*	*570*	*365*	*190*	*984*	*12,088*	*3,829*	*2,530*	*586*	*529*	*6,029*	*2*	*2*	..	...	...	...	
2,456	1,315	446	323	179	695	4,899	1,402	921	252	284	2,576	2	2	..	...	...	...	6
...	...	...	...	...	...	2,468	998	440	195	12	1,040	...	...	...	...	...	...	7
641	269	113	42	...	259	3,196	708	844	74	10	1,642	...	...	...	...	...	...	8
46	5	11	...	11	30	1,525	431	323	65	123	771	...	...	...	...	...	...	9
7,174	*2,501*	*2,078*	*112*	*80*	*2,595*	*1,146*	*463*	*271*	*7*	*1*	*412*	*31*	*15*	...	*3*	...	*16*	
3,205	1,135	829	93	70	1,181	123	59	10	5	...	54	25	9	...	3	...	16	10
2,317	783	790	17	9	714	667	234	212	...	...	220	...	...	...	...	...	...	11
104	21	32	...	...	51	356	170	48	2	1	138	6	6	...	...	...	...	12
1,548	562	367	2	1	619	...	...	...	...	...	...	...	...	..	...	...	...	13
6,738	*2,128*	*1,219*	*41*	*16*	*3,391*	*3,929*	*864*	*611*	*9*	*2*	*2,454*	*4*	*2*	...	.	..	*2*	
5,029	1,580	816	35	10	2,681	1,959	623	461	9	...	875	...	...	...	...	..		14
259	75	19	8	...	165	4	8	...	...	...	1	...	...	...	..	...	...	15
13	7	3	1	...	3	1,683	114	137	...	2	1,432	...	...	...	...	...	...	16
1,437	466	379	2	6	592	283	124	13	...	...	146	4	2	...	...	...	2	17

TABLE XV.

OCCUPATION OR MEANS OF LIVELIHOOD.

PART A.—GENERAL TABLE.

Serial Number.	District.	Class A.—Production. Sub-Class I—Exploitation. Order 1 (c)—Forestry.—(concld). 8—Wood-cutters, fire-wood, lac, catechu, rubber, etc., collectors and charcoal burners. Total workers and dependants.	Actual workers. Total. Males.	Actual workers. Total. Females.	Actual workers. Partially agriculturist. Males.	Actual workers. Partially agriculturist. Females.	Dependants.	Total Order 1 (d). Total workers and dependants.	Actual workers. Total. Males.	Actual workers. Total. Females.	Actual workers. Partially agriculturist. Males.	Actual workers. Partially agriculturist. Females.	Dependants.
	1	56	57	58	59	60	61	62	63	64	65	66	67
	Hyderabad State ..	***49,905***	***11,897***	***7,285***	***1,412***	***1,121***	***21,723***	***597,728***	***240,754***	***105,916***	***16,882***	***5,413***	***251,05***
1	Hyderabad City ...	3,067	1,039	299	...	...	1,729	6,721	1,805	958	...	...	3,95
2	Atraf-i-balda ...	2,155	1,120	43	48	1	992	26,915	11,490	5,425	236	211	10,00
	Warangal Division ...	***18,557***	***4,901***	***3,531***	***765***	***588***	***10,125***	***122,104***	***58,441***	***17,480***	***2,834***	***1,176***	***46,18***
3	Warangal ...	9,729	2,182	2,266	122	12	5,281	47,995	20,906	8,956	893	86	18,13
4	Karimnagar ...	8,642	2,619	1,250	643	576	4,773	55,861	29,647	5,798	1,785	979	20,41
5	Adilabad ...	180	100	15	...	...	71	18,248	7,888	2,726	156	111	7,62
	Medak Division ...	***12,086***	***3,527***	***2,530***	***586***	***529***	***6,029***	***162,527***	***70,862***	***31,993***	***5,787***	***2,014***	***59,67***
6	Medak ...	4,897	1,400	921	252	384	2,576	31,365	11,918	6,075	1,708	897	13,37
7	Nizamabad ..	2,468	988	440	105	12	1,040	28,771	14,853	5,092	1,176	179	8,2
8	Mahbubnagar ..	3,196	708	846	74	10	1,642	31,311	14,363	4,917	618	99	12,0
9	Nalgonda ..	1,525	431	823	65	129	771	71,077	29,728	15,309	2,278	839	26,0
	Aurangabad Division.	***1,115***	***448***	***271***	***4***	***1***	***396***	***106,015***	***41,396***	***20,810***	***1,325***	***447***	***43,8***
10	Aurangabad ..	98	50	10	2	...	38	30,335	8,681	6,514	725	226	15,1
11	Bhir ..	667	234	213	...	...	220	16,573	9,266	1,933	169	58	5,2
12	Nander ...	350	164	48	2	1	138	20,845	9,108	5,313	182	73	6,8
13	Parbhani ...	...	...	...	...	...	...	38,262	14,341	7,050	249	90	16,8
	Gulbarga Division ...	***3,925***	***862***	***611***	***9***	***2***	***2,452***	***173,446***	***56,760***	***29,250***	***6,707***	***1,565***	***87,4***
14	Gulbarga ...	1,959	625	461	9	...	875	52,403	18,113	8,971	1,515	256	25,3
15	Osmanabad ...	4	3	...	...	...	1	18,212	7,612	4,086	64	46	6,3
16	Raichur ...	1,683	114	137	...	2	1,432	67,601	17,838	8,996	4,434	901	40,7
17	Bidar ...	279	122	13	...	...	144	35,230	13,197	7,197	694	302	14

TABLE XV.

OCCUPATION OR MEANS OF LIVELIHOOD.

PART A.—GENERAL TABLE.

of raw materials.—(*contd*).

of the surface of the earth.—(*contd*).

Order 1 (*d*)—Raising of farm stock.

9 – Cattle and buffalo breeders and keepers.						10 — Sheep, goat and pig breeders.						11 — Breeders of other animals (horses, mules, camels, asses, etc).						Serial Number.
Total workers and dependants.	Actual workers.				Dependants.	Total workers and dependants.	Actual workers.				Dependants.	Total workers and dependants.	Actual workers.				Dependants.	
	Total.		Partially agriculturist.				Total.		Partially agriculturist.				Total.		Partially agriculturist.			
	Males.	Females.	Males.	Females.			Males.	Females.	Males.	Females.			Males.	Females.	Males.	Females.		
68	69	70	71	72	73	74	75	76	77	78	79	80	81	82	83	84	85	
42,418	***13,153***	***10,446***	***545***	***445***	***18,819***	***109,739***	***38,398***	***19,916***	***5,055***	***785***	***51,425***	***413***	***224***	***2***	...	...	***187***	
4,034	1,141	628	...	...	2,265	95	43	15	...	...	37	214	112	...	...	...	102	1
1,558	509	641	9	6	708	94	70	...	1	...	24	56	36	...	...	...	20	2
9,246	***3,501***	***2,902***	***112***	***129***	***2,843***	***3,496***	***1,390***	***574***	***94***	***48***	***1,532***	***76***	***43***	***2***	...	...	***31***	
4,360	1,654	1,379	51	38	1,327	21	21	...	...	...	...	5	3	1	...	...	1	3
2,988	1,157	1,053	59	43	676	64	23	20	...	...	21	8	6	1	...	...	1	4
2,000	690	470	2	48	840	3,411	1,346	554	94	48	1,511	63	34	...	...	...	29	5
9,109	***4,115***	***1,794***	***324***	***116***	***3,200***	***3,707***	***1,783***	***334***	***328***	***14***	***1,590***	***55***	***24***	...	...	...	***31***	
1,949	615	306	112	...	1,028	338	74	80	32	14	184	...	...	...	...	...	...	6
5,810	3,282	718	191	21	1,310	384	126	87	4	...	171	...	...	...	..	...	...	7
236	92	79	2	...	65	1,002	302	20	...	...	680	52	22	...	...	...	30	8
1,114	126	691	19	95	297	1,983	1,281	147	280	...	555	3	2	...	...	...	1	9
7,270	***1,444***	***1,962***	***45***	***68***	***3,864***	***31,317***	***7,960***	***7,611***	***909***	***156***	***15,746***	***12***	***9***	...	...	...	***3***	
3,548	262	1,034	4	10	2,252	9,051	3,359	1,753	586	32	3,939	...	...	...	...	...	...	10
1,084	510	211	20	11	363	3,497	1,244	748	137	45	1,505	...	...	...	...	...	...	11
1,278	439	295	9	26	494	2,375	959	311	128	46	1,105	...	...	...	...	...	...	12
1,360	183	422	12	21	755	16,394	2,308	4,799	61	33	9,197	12	9	...	...	...	3	13
10,901	***2,443***	***2,519***	***55***	***126***	***5,939***	***71,030***	***27,152***	***11,382***	***3,726***	***567***	***32,496***	...	...	...	...	...	...	
4,729	1,411	1,033	11	53	2,285	23,627	8,358	3,687	1,316	195	11,582	...	..	...	...	...	...	14
114	55	6	1	...	53	3,099	1,917	531	55	29	1,551	...	...	...	...	...	...	15
5,111	761	1,310	20	72	3,043	28,049	11,005	4,835	1,903	207	12,209	...	...	..	...	...	...	16
947	216	170	23	1	561	15,355	5,872	2,329	452	136	7,154	...	...	...	...	...	...	17

TABLE XV.

OCCUPATION OR MEANS OF LIVELIHOOD.

PART A—GENERAL TABLE.

Serial Number.	District.	Class A—Production											
		Sub-Class I.—Exploitation											
		Order 1 (d)—Raising of farm stock.—(concld).						Order 1 (e)—Raising of small animals					
		12—Herdsmen, shepherds, goatherds, etc.						13—Birds, bees, silkworms, etc.					
		Total workers and dependants.	Actual workers. Total.		Actual workers. Partially agriculturist.		Dependants.	Total workers and dependants.	Actual workers. Total.		Actual workers. Partially agriculturist.		Dependants.
			Males.	Females.	Males.	Females.			Males.	Females.	Males.	Females.	
1		86	87	88	89	90	91	92	93	94	95	96	97
	Hyderabad State ...	***445,158***	***188,979***	***75,552***	***11,282***	***4,183***	***180,627***	***18***	***11***	...	***6***	...	[illegible]
1	Hyderabad City ...	2,378	509	315	...	...	1,554	...	...	...	...	...	...
2	Atraf-i-balda ...	24,907	10,875	4,784	226	205	9,248	...	...	...	...	...	...
	Warangal Division ...	***109,286***	***53,507***	***14,002***	***2,628***	***999***	***41,777***	...	...	...	...	...	...
3	Warangal ..	43,6.9	1?,228	7,576	842	48	16,805	...	...	...	...	...	...
4	Karimnagar ..	52,903	28,461	4,724	1,726	986	10,718	...	...	...	...	...	...
5	Adilabad ...	12,774	5,818	1,702	60	15	5,254	...	...	...	...	...	...
	Medak Division ...	***149,656***	***64,949***	***29,861***	***5,131***	***1,884***	***54,851***	***11***	***5***	...	...	...	[illegible]
6	Medak ...	29,081	11,229	5,689	1,564	883	12,163	11	5	...	...	...	[illegible]
7	Nizamabad ...	22,577	11,445	4,887	981	158	6,245	...	...	...	...	...	...
8	Mahbubnagar ...	30,021	13,947	4,818	616	99	11,256	...	...	...	...	...	...
9	Nalgonda ...	67,977	28,819	14,471	1,970	744	25,187	...	...	...	...	...	...
	Aurangabad Division.	***67,416***	***31,983***	***11,237***	***371***	***223***	***24,196***	...	...	...	...	...	...
10	Aurangabad ...	17,736	5,060	3,727	133	184	8,349		...	...	...	...	
11	Bhir ...	11,992	7,512	974	12	2	3,506	...	...	...	...	...	
12	Nander ...	17,192	7.660	4,707	50	1	4,825	...	...	...	...	...	
13	Parbhani ...	20,496	11,751	1,829	176	86	6,916	...	...	...	...	...	
	Gulbarga Division ...	***91,515***	***27,165***	***15,349***	***2,926***	***872***	***49,001***	***7***	***6***	...	***6***	...	
14	Gulbarga ...	24,047	8,314	4,251	188	8	11,452	...	...	...	...	...	
15	Osmanabad ...	14,099	5,640	3,549	8	17	4,910	...	...	...	...	...	
16	Raichur ...	34,441	6,072	2,851	2,511	622	25,518	7	6	...	6	...	
17	Bidar ...	18,928	7,109	4,696	219	225	7,121	...	...	...	...	...	

TABLE XV.

OCCUPATION OR MEANS OF LIVELIHOOD.

PART A.—GENERAL TABLE.

of raw materials.—(*contd*).

of the surface of the earth.—(*contd*).

Total Order 2.						Order 2.—Fishing and hunting. 14.—Fishing.						
Total workers and dependants.	Actual workers. Total. Males.	Actual workers. Total. Females.	Actual workers. Partially agriculturist. Males.	Actual workers. Partially agriculturist. Females.	Dependants.	Total workers and dependants.	Actual workers. Total. Males.	Actual workers. Total. Females.	Actual workers. Partially agriculturist. Males.	Actual workers. Partially agriculturist. Females.	Dependants.	Serial Number.
98	99	100	101	102	103	104	105	106	107	108	109	
107,889	***51,427***	***6,286***	***8,276***	***1,026***	***50,176***	***78,269***	***37,954***	***5,520***	***7,589***	***990***	***34,795***	
1,325	600	...	...	...	725	818	395	...	...	...	423	1
5,790	2,985	265	162	2	2,540	1,773	820	255	84	1	698	2
28,898	***13,357***	***1,739***	***1,231***	***114***	***13,802***	***23,728***	***10,788***	***1,643***	***1,196***	***114***	***11,295***	
8,943	4,145	735	215	2	4,063	4,549	1,952	668	185	2	1,929	3
12,769	6,492	50	780	69	6,227	12,510	6,343	43	776	69	6,124	4
7,186	2,720	954	236	43	3,512	6,669	2,493	934	235	43	3,242	5
34,546	***15,843***	***2,490***	***2,041***	***552***	***16,211***	***21,348***	***10,209***	***1,930***	***1,596***	***518***	***9,209***	
8,903	3,873	680	848	71	4,350	4,143	2,033	638	551	71	1,472	6
10,674	5,501	296	650	437	4,877	10,633	5,470	294	650	437	4,869	7
5,153	2,235	228	181	2	2,690	2,755	1,226	129	115	...	1,400	8
9,816	4,226	1,286	362	42	4,294	3,817	1,480	869	277	10	1,468	9
8,478	***3,266***	***858***	***767***	***80***	***4,354***	***7,098***	***3,041***	***818***	***752***	***79***	***3,239***	
3,348	1,172	481	433	11	1,695	2,872	1,046	446	429	10	1,380	10
1,132	201	43	3	2	888	323	150	39	3	2	134	11
2,376	1,062	128	271	14	1,186	2,344	1,044	128	262	14	1,172	12
1,622	831	206	60	53	585	1,559	801	205	58	53	553	13
28,852	***15,374***	***934***	***4,075***	***278***	***12,544***	***23,504***	***12,701***	***872***	***3,961***	***278***	***9,931***	
3,831	1,680	373	117	1	1,778	2,436	940	311	52	1	1,185	14
393	144	8	5	...	241	234	96	8	5	...	150	15
22,343	12,814	198	3,849	161	9,331	18,633	11,110	198	3,849	164	7,525	16
2,285	736	355	104	113	1,194	1,981	555	355	55	113	1,071	17

TABLE XV.

OCCUPATION OR MEANS OF LIVELIHOOD.

PART A.—GENERAL TABLE.

Serial Number.	Districts.	Class A.—Production. Sub-Class I.—Exploitation of the surface of the earth—(concld). Order 2.—Fishing and hunting—(concld). 15—Hunting. Total workers and dependants.	Actual workers. Total. Males.	Actual workers. Total. Females.	Actual workers. Partially agriculturist. Males.	Actual workers. Partially agriculturist. Females.	Dependants.	Sub-Class II.—Extraction. Total Order 3. Total workers and dependants.	Actual workers. Total. Males.	Actual workers. Total. Females.	Actual workers. Partially agriculturist. Males.	Actual workers. Partially agriculturist. Females.	Dependants.
	1	110	111	112	113	114	115	116	117	118	119	120	121
	Hyderabad State ...	***29,620***	***13,473***	***766***	***687***	***36***	***15,381***	***15,325***	***8,224***	***2,328***	...	...	***4,773***
1	Hyderabad City ..	507	205	...	...	...	302	323	276	...	...	...	47
2	Atraf-i-balda ...	4,017	2,165	10	78	1	1,842	...	...	...	...	...	...
	Warangal Division ...	***5,170***	***2,569***	***94***	***35***	...	***2,507***	***11,550***	***6,302***	***1,996***	...	...	***3,252***
3	Warangal ...	4,394	2,193	67	30	...	2,131	11,550	6,302	1,996	...	...	3,252
4	Karimnagar ...	259	149	7	4	...	103	...	...	...	...	...	...
5	Adilabad ...	517	227	20	1	...	270	...	...	...	...	...	...
	Medak Division ...	***13,198***	***5,636***	***560***	***445***	***34***	***7,002***	...	...	...	...	...	...
6	Medak ...	4,760	1,846	42	294	...	2,878	...	...	...	...	...	...
7	Nizamabad ...	41	31	2	...	...	8	...	...	...	...	...	...
8	Mahbubnagar ...	2,398	1,009	99	66	2	1,290	...	...	...	...	...	...
9	Nalgonda ...	5,993	2,756	417	85	32	2,826	...	...	...	...	...	...
	Aurangabad Division.	***1,380***	***225***	***40***	***15***	***1***	***1,115***	***556***	***106***	...	...	...	***450***
10	Aurangabad ...	476	126	35	4	1	315	...	...	...	...	...	...
11	Bhir ...	809	51	4	...	...	754	...	...	...	...	...	...
12	Nander ..	32	18	...	9	...	14	39	17	...	...	...	22
13	Parbhani ...	63	30	1	2	...	32	517	89	...	...	...	428
	Gulbarga Division ...	***5,348***	***2,673***	***62***	***114***	...	***2,613***	***2,896***	***1,540***	***332***	...	...	***1,024***
14	Gulbarga ...	1,395	740	62	65	...	593	29	21	...	...	...	8
15	Osmanabad ...	139	48	...	...	...	91	...	...	...	...	...	...
16	Raichur ..	3,510	1,704	...	...	...	1,806	2,867	1,519	332	...	...	1,016
17	Bidar ..	304	181	...	49	...	123	...	...	...	...	...	...

TABLE XV.

OCCUPATION OR MEANS OF LIVELIHOOD.

PART A.—GENERAL TABLE.

of raw materials.—(*contd*).

of minerals.

Order 3—Mines.												Order 4—Quarries of hard rocks.						
5—Coal mines and petroleum wells.						17—Mines and metallic minerals (gold, iron, manganese, etc.).						18—Other minerals (jade, diamonds, limestone, etc.).						
Total orkers and ·pend-ınts.	Actual workers. Total. Males.	Actual workers. Total. Females.	Actual workers. Partially agricul-turist. Males.	Actual workers. Partially agricul-turist. Females.	Dependants.	Total work-ers and depend-ants.	Actual workers. Total. Males.	Actual workers. Total. Females.	Actual workers. Partially agricul-turist. Males.	Actual workers. Partially agricul-turist. Females.	Dependants.	Total workers and depend-ants.	Actual workers. Total. Males.	Actual workers. Total. Females.	Actual workers. Partially agricul-turist. Males.	Actual workers. Partially agricul-turist. Females.	Dependants.	Serial Number.
122	123	124	125	126	127	128	129	130	131	132	133	134	135	36	137	138	139	
11,872	***6,377***	***1,996***	...	...	***3,399***	***3,453***	***1,647***	***332***	...	...	***1,474***	***3,149***	***1,510***	***452***	***129***	***8***	***1,187***	
322	275	...	...	..	47	1	1	...	...	...	...	189	92	21	...	...	76	1
...	...	...	...	...	...	...	...	...	...	...	...	...	...	...	...	...	...	2
11,550	***6,302***	***1,996***	...	...	***3,252***	...	...	...	...	...	...	...	...	...	...	...	...	
11,550	6,302	1,996	...	...	3,252	...	...	...	...	...	...	...	...	...	...	...	...	3
...	...	...	...	...	...	...	...	...	...	...	...	...	...	...	...	...	...	4
...	...	...	...	...	...	...	...	...	...	...	...	...	...	...	...	...	...	5
...	...	...	...	...	...	...	...	...	...	...	...	***12***	***3***	...	...	...	***9***	
...	...	...	...	...	...	...	...	...	...	...	...	12	3	...	...	...	9	6
...	...	...	...	...	...	...	...	...	...	...	...	...	...	...	...	...	...	7
...	...	...	...	...	...	...	...	...	...	...	...	...	...	...	...	...	...	8
...	...	...	...	...	...	...	...	...	...	...	...	...	...	...	...	...	...	9
...	...	...	...	...	...	***556***	***106***	...	...	...	***450***	***2,520***	***1,077***	***428***	***56***	***8***	***1,015***	
...	...	...	...	...	...	...	...	...	...	...	...	986	458	198	1	...	335	10
..	...	...	...	...	...	...	...	...	...	...	...	903	345	189	...	...	369	11
..	...	...	...	...	...	39	17	...	...	...	22	530	215	41	6	8	274	12
..	...	...	...	...	...	517	89	...	...	...	428	101	64	...	49	...	37	13
..	...	...	...	...	...	***2,896***	***1,540***	***332***	...	...	***1,024***	***428***	***338***	***3***	***73***	...	***87***	
..	...	...	...	...	...	29	21	...	...	...	8	343	288	3	53	...	52	14
..	...	...	...	...	...	...	...	...	...	...	...	...	...	...	...	...	...	15
..	...	...	...	...	...	2,867	1,519	332	...	...	1,016	...	...	...	...	...	...	16
..	...	...	...	...	...	...	...	...	...	...	...	85	50	...	20	...	35	17

TABLE XV.

OCCUPATION OR MEANS OF LIVELIHOOD.

PART A.—GENERAL TABLE.

Serial Number.	District.	Class A.—Production of raw materials—(concld). Sub-class II.—Extraction of minerals.—(concld). Total Order 5. Total workers and dependants.	Total Order 5. Actual workers. Total. Males.	Total Order 5. Actual workers. Total. Females.	Total Order 5. Actual workers. Partially agriculturist. Males.	Total Order 5. Actual workers. Partially agriculturist. Females.	Total Order 5. Dependants.	Order 5—Saltpetre, etc. 19—Rock, sea and marsh salt. Total workers and dependants.	19. Actual workers. Total. Males.	19. Actual workers. Total. Females.	19. Actual workers. Partially agriculturist. Males.	19. Actual workers. Partially agriculturist. Females.	19. Dependants.	20—Extraction of saltpetre, alum and other substances soluble in water. Total workers and dependants.	20. Actual workers. Total. Males.	20. Actual workers. Total. Females.	20. Actual workers. Partially agriculturist. Males.	20. Actual workers. Partially agriculturist. Females.	20. Dependants.
	1	140	141	142	143	144	145	146	147	148	149	150	151	152	153	154	155	156	15[7]
	Hyderabad State ...	...	...	...		...	...	...	...	...	...	...	...	...	...	...	...	...	...
1	Hyderabad City ...	...	...	...	...	...	...	...	...	...	...	...	...	...	...	...	...	...	...
2	Atraf-i-balda ...	...	...	...	...	...	...	...	...	...	...	...	...	...	...	...	...	...	...
	Warangal Division ...	...	...	...	...	...	...	...	...	...	...	...	...	...	...	...	...	...	...
3	Warangal	...	...	...	...	...	...	...	...	...	...	...	...	...	...	...	...	...	...
4	Karimnagar	...	...	...	...	...	...	...	...	...	...	...	...	...	...	...	...	...	...
5	Adilabad	...	...	...	...	...	...	...	...	...	...	...	...	...	...	...	...	...	...
	Medak Division ...	...	...	...	...	...	...	...	...	...	...	...	...	...	...	...	...	...	...
6	Medak	...	...	...	...	...	...	...	...	...	...	...	...	...	...	...	...	...	...
7	Nizamabad	...	...	...	...	...	...	...	...	...	...	...	...	...	...	...	...	...	...
8	Mahbubnagar ...	...	...	...	...	...	...	...	...	...	...	...	...	...	..	...	...	...	...
9	Nalgonda	...	...	...	...	...	...	...	...	...	...	...	...	...	...	...	...	...	...
	Aurangabad Division	...	...	..	...	...	...	...	...	...	...	...	...	...	...	...	...	...	...
10	Aurangabad	...	...	...	...	...	...	...	...	...	...	...	...	...	...	...	...	...	...
11	Bhir	...	...	...	...	...	...	...	...	...	...	...	...	...	...	...	...	...	...
12	Nander	...	...	...	...	...	...	...	...	...	...	...	...	...	...	...	...	...	...
13	Parbhani	...	...	...	...	...	...	...	...	...	...	...	...	...	...	...	...	...	...
	Gulbarga Division ...	...	...	...	...	...	...	...	...	...	...	...	...	...	...	...	...	...	...
14	Gulbarga	...	...	...	...	...	...	...	...	...	...	...	...	...	...	...	...	...	...
15	Osmanabad	...	...	...	...	...	...	...	...	...	...	...	...	...	...	...	...	...	...
16	Raichur	...	...	...	...	...	...	...	...	...	...	...	...	...	...	...	...	...	...
17	Bidar	...	...	...	...	...	...	...	...	...	...	...	...	...	...	...	...	...	...

TABLE XV.

OCCUPATION OR MEANS OF LIVELIHOOD.

PART A.—GENERAL TABLE.

Class B.—Preparation and supply of material substances.												
Sub-Class III—Industry.												
Total Order 6.						Order 6.—Textiles. 21.—Cotton ginning, cleaning and pressing.						Serial Number.
Total workers and dependants.	Actual workers. Total. Males.	Actual workers. Total. Females.	Actual workers. Partially agriculturist. Males.	Actual workers. Partially agriculturist. Females.	Dependants.	Total workers and dependants.	Actual workers. Total. Males.	Actual workers. Total. Females.	Actual workers. Partially agriculturist. Males.	Actual workers. Partially agriculturist. Females.	Dependants.	
158	159	160	161	162	163	164	165	166	167	168	169	
517,750	***174,159***	***106,746***	***12,562***	***5,496***	***236,845***	***69,943***	***16,737***	***20,636***	***1,272***	***818***	***32,570***	
7,033	2,541	553	...	...	3,939	1,455	635	102	...	...	718	1
22,691	7,673	4,394	419	122	10,624	1,533	507	595	11	2	931	2
157,697	***52,632***	***34,849***	***2,688***	***1,874***	***70,216***	***26,370***	***6,721***	***9,044***	***470***	***374***	***10,605***	
36,795	13,199	7,378	504	313	16,218	7,089	2,330	1,374	53	28	3,385	3
101,570	32,662	24,142	1,888	1,431	44,766	17,588	3,807	7,188	362	317	6,593	4
19,332	6,771	3,329	296	130	9,232	1,693	534	482	55	29	677	5
150,371	***52,183***	***32,976***	***3,336***	***1,856***	***65,212***	***32,229***	***6,090***	***9,278***	***365***	***274***	***16,861***	
33,034	9,082	8,032	841	666	15,870	9,043	1,021	2,370	55	26	5,652	6
30,175	13,421	5,621	908	469	11,133	7,243	1,947	1,882	68	98	3,414	7
36,899	13,002	6,548	785	280	17,349	12,502	2,609	3,615	171	139	6,278	8
50,263	16,678	12,725	802	441	20,860	3,441	513	1,411	71	11	1,517	9
70,072	***23,882***	***13,305***	***2,256***	***503***	***32,885***	***4,384***	***1,640***	***825***	***180***	***63***	***1,919***	
15,957	4,107	1,805	790	30	10,045	372	159	54	...	...	159	10
15,558	7,063	3,649	252	31	4,846	404	203	12	73	...	189	11
21,014	7,261	4,298	1,019	330	9,455	1,301	461	396	80	60	444	12
17,543	5,451	3,553	195	112	8,539	2,307	817	363	27	3	1,127	13
109,886	***35,248***	***20,669***	***3,863***	***1,141***	***53,969***	***3,672***	***1,144***	***992***	***246***	***105***	***1,536***	
41,155	14,609	6,701	1,503	298	19,755	2,182	705	760	6	80	717	14
13,735	3,923	1,913	88	44	7,699	215	38	23	1	...	154	15
23,786	7,051	5,429	1,582	182	11,306	1,090	361	165	237	25	564	16
31,210	9,575	6,626	690	617	15,009	185	40	44	2	...	101	17

TABLE XV.

OCCUPATION OR MEANS OF LIVELIHOOD.

PART A.—GENERAL TABLE.

Class B.—Preparation and supply

Sub-Class III.—

Order 6.—

Serial Number.	District.	22.—Cotton spinning, sizing, and weaving. Total workers and dependants.	Actual workers. Total. Males.	Females.	Partially agriculturist. Males.	Females.	Dependants.	23.—Jute spinning, pressing and weaving. Total workers and dependants.	Actual workers. Total. Males.	Females.	Partially agriculturist. Males.	Females.	Dependants.
	1	170	171	172	173	174	175	176	177	178	179	180	181
	Hyderabad State ...	***202,748***	***107,226***	***60,586***	***6,408***	***2,915***	***134,922***	***1,098***	***757***	***10***	***5***	...	***331***
1	Hyderabad City ...	3,225	1,173	281	...	...	1,764	...	...	...	...	...	...
2	Atraf-i-balda ...	14,121	4,779	2,817	187	77	6,525	...	...	...	...	...	...
	Warangal Division ...	***96,005***	***33,637***	***17,906***	***1,610***	***911***	***44,462***	***56***	***33***	...	***3***	...	***2.***
3	Warangal ...	25,776	9,030	5,271	408	244	11,475	56	33	...	3	...	2:
4	Karimnagar ...	56,674	20,522	10,016	1,034	580	26,136	...	...	...	...	...	...
5	Adilabad ...	13,555	4,085	2,619	168	87	6,851	...	...	...	...	...	...
	Medak Division ...	***84,870***	***33,945***	***17,235***	***1,944***	***1,033***	***33,390***	***191***	***61***	...	...	...	***13***
6	Medak ...	18,212	6,237	4,482	635	475	7,493	191	61	...	...	...	13
7	Nizamabad ...	16,969	9,008	2,489	540	141	5,472	...	...	...	...	...	...
8	Mahbubnagar ...	9,450	4,504	1,175	201	12	3,771	...	...	...	...	...	...
9	Nalgonda ...	39,939	14,196	9,089	568	405	16,654	...	...	...	...	...	...
	Aurangabad Division ...	***46,284***	***16,162***	***9,869***	***1,220***	***209***	***20,583***	***798***	***628***	***2***	...	...	***16***
10	Aurangabad ...	8,087	2,117	1,049	649	18	4,921	...	...	...	...	...	..
11	Bhir ...	11,101	5,413	2,769	134	1	2,919	7	3	2	...	...	5
12	Nander ...	15,214	5,296	2,954	371	116	6,964	1	1	...	...	...	..
13	Parbhani ...	11,882	3,336	2,797	66	74	5,749	787	624	...	...	...	16
	Gulbarga Division ...	***58,542***	***17,825***	***12,778***	***1,447***	***685***	***28,239***	***56***	***35***	***8***	***2***	...	***1***
14	Gulbarga ...	16,745	6,404	2,627	781	106	7,714	...	...	...	...	...	...
15	Osmanabad ...	3,968	1,327	459	24	10	2,182	...	...	...	...	...	...
16	Raichur ...	18,021	4,052	5,035	415	157	8,934	...	...	...	...	...	..
17	Bidar ...	19,808	5,742	4,657	227	412	9,409	56	35	8	2	...	1

TABLE XV.

OCCUPATION OR MEANS OF LIVELIHOOD.

PART A.—GENERAL TABLE.

of material substances.—(*contd*).

Industry.—(*contd*).

Textiles.—(*contd*).

24.—Rope, twine and string.						25.—Other fibres (cocoanut, aloes, flax, hemp, straw, etc.).						26.—Wool carders and spinners, weavers of woollen blankets, carpets, etc.						Serial Number.
Total workers and dependants.	Actual workers.				Dependants.	Total workers and dependants.	Actual workers.				Dependants.	Total workers and dependants.	Actual workers.				Dependants.	
	Total.		Partially agriculturist.				Total.		Partially agriculturist.				Total.		Partially agriculturist.			
	Males.	Females.	Males.	Females.			Males.	Females.	Males.	Females.			Males.	Females.	Males.	Females.		
182	183	184	185	186	187	188	189	190	191	192	193	194	195	196	197	198	199	
28,954	***9,468***	***6,575***	***566***	***246***	***12,911***	***10***	***6***	...	...	...	***4***	***89,095***	***31,486***	***14,518***	***3,029***	***1,267***	***43,094***	
52	36	...	...	...	16	...	...	...	...	...	...	53	27	...	...	...	26	1
1,132	601	29	7	...	502	...	...	...	...	...	...	5,012	1,544	989	213	43	2,479	2
17,331	***5,028***	***4,734***	***280***	***228***	***7,569***	...	...	...	...	...	...	***18,840***	***6,578***	***2,716***	***303***	***343***	***6,246***	
660	238	271	6	1	151	...	...	...	...	...	...	2,719	1,349	394	32	36	976	3
16,671	4,790	4,463	274	227	7,418	...	...	...	...	...	...	9,661	3,363	2,192	217	297	4,101	4
...	...	...	...	...	...	...	...	...	...	...	...	3,160	1,861	130	54	10	1,169	5
9,028	***3,291***	***1,518***	***187***	***18***	***4,309***	...	...	...	...	...	...	***20,289***	***7,273***	***4,002***	***789***	***526***	***9,014***	
340	152	...	11	...	188	...	...	...	...	...	...	3,855	1,046	855	128	165	1,954	6
2,007	688	452	46	2	867	...	...	...	...	...	...	2,450	1,221	423	253	227	806	7
6,572	2,329	1,025	130	12	3,219	...	...	...	...	...	...	7,747	3,314	616	275	115	3,817	8
109	33	41	...	4	35	...	...	...	...	...	...	6,237	1,692	2,108	133	18	2,437	9
191	***75***	***15***	***9***		***101***	...	...	...	...	...	...	***11,452***	***3,564***	***2,039***	***434***	***213***	***5,849***	
106	31	9	7	...	66	...	...	...	...	...	...	3,294	1,007	273	78	5	2,015	10
...	...	...	...	...	...	...	...	...	...	...	...	3,169	1,139	731	20	28	1,29	11
35	15	6	...	...	14	...	...	...	...	...	...	3,165	887	785	241	145	1,493	12
50	29	...	2	...	21	...	...	...	...	...	...	1,224	531	251	95	35	1,042	13
1,220	***527***	***279***	***83***	...	***414***	***10***	***6***	...	...	...	***4***	***36,749***	***12,500***	***4,769***	***1,290***	***143***	***19,480***	
226	176	3	81	...	47	10	6	...	...	...	4	18,295	6,201	2,718	645	109	9,376	14
643	266	101	2	...	276	...	...	...	...	...	...	8,251	2,149	1,160	50	12	4,912	15
...	...	...	...	...	...	...	...	...	...	...	...	2,967	1,624	67	393	...	1,276	16
351	8:	175	...	...	91	...	...	...	...	...	...	7,236	2,526	824	193	22	3,886	17

TABLE XV.

OCCUPATION OR MEANS OF LIVELIHOOD.

PART A.—GENERAL TABLE.

Serial Number.	District.	Class B.—Preparation and supply / Sub-Class III.— / Order 6.— 27.—Silk spinners and weavers. Total workers and dependants.	Actual workers. Total. Males.	Actual workers. Total. Females.	Actual workers. Partially agriculturist. Males.	Actual workers. Partially agriculturist. Females.	Dependants.	28.—Hair, camel and horse hair, bristles work, brush-makers, etc. Total workers and dependants.	Actual workers. Total. Males.	Actual workers. Total. Females.	Actual workers. Partially agriculturist. Males.	Actual workers. Partially agriculturist. Females.	Dependants.	29.—Persons occupied with feathers. Total workers and dependants.	Actual workers. Total. Males.	Actual workers. Total. Females.	Actual workers. Partially agriculturist. Males.	Actual workers. Partially agriculturist. Females.	Dependants.
	1	200	201	202	203	204	205	206	207	208	209	210	211	212	213	214	215	216	21
	Hyderabad State ...	***1,901***	***652***	***374***	***10***	...	***875***	***77***	***47***	...	***1***	...	***30***	***204***	***122***	...	...	...	***8.***
1	Hyderabad City ...	352	8[illegible]	87	...	...	179	2	2	...	...	...	...	38	23	...	...	...	1
2	Atraf-i-balda ...	...	...	...	...	...	...	...	...	...	...	...	...	...	...	...	...	...	...
	Warangal Division	***6***	***3***	***2***	...	...	***1***	***47***	***21***	...	...	...	***26***	...	...	...	...	...	...
3	Warangal ..	...	...	...	...	...	...	47	21	...	...	...	26	...	...	...	...	...	...
4	Karimnagar ..	6	3	2	...	...	1	...	...	...	...	...	...	...	...	...	...	...	...
5	Adilabad ..	...	...	...	...	...	...	...	...	...	...	...	...	...	...	...	...	...	...
	Medak Division ..	***703***	***283***	***128***	***10***	...	***295***	...	...	...	...	...	...	...	...	...	...	...	...
6	Medak ..	259	92	44	10	...	123	...	...	...	...	...	...	...	...	...	...	...	...
7	Nizamabad ...	119	63	19	...	...	37	...	...	...	...	...	...	...	...	...	..	...	...
8	Mahbubnagar ..	120	45	36	...	...	39	...	...	...	...	...	...	...	...	...	...	...	..
9	Nalgonda ..	205	83	26	...	...	96	...	...	...	...	...	...	...	...	...	...	...	...
	Aurangabad Division	***747***	***253***	***151***	...	...	***343***	***28***	***24***	...	***1***	...	***4***	***109***	***69***	...	...	...	***41***
10	Aurangabad ...	698	231	145	...	...	322	...	...	...	...	...	...	...	...	...	...	...	..
11	Bhir ...	...	...	...	...	...	...	...	...	...	...	...	...	100	65	...	...	...	3
12	Nander ...	1	...	1	...	...	...	...	...	...	...	...	...	9	4	...	...	...	5
13	Parbhani ...	48	22	5	...	...	21	28	24	...	1	...	4	...	...	...	..	...	..
	Gulbarga Division ...	***93***	***27***	***9***	...	...	***57***	...	...	...	...	..	...	***57***	***30***	...	...	...	***27***
14	Gulbarga ...	...	...	...	...	...	...	...	...	...	...	...	...	...	...	...	...	...	...
15	Osmanabad ...	86	25	9	...	...	52	...	...	...	...	...	...	...	...	...	...	...	...
16	Raichur ...	...	...	...	...	...	...	...	...	...	...	...	..	57	30	...	...	...	2[illegible]
17	Bidar ...	7	2	...	...	...	5	...	...	...	...	...	...	...	...	...	...	...	...

TABLE XV.

OCCUPATION OR MEANS OF LIVELIHOOD.

PART A—GENERAL TABLE.

of material substances.—(*contd*).

Industry.—(*contd*).

Textiles.—(*concld*).

30.—Dyeing, bleaching, printing, preparation and sponging of textiles.						31.—Other (lace, crape, embroideries, fringes, etc.) and insufficiently described textile industries.						Total Order 7.						Serial Number.
Total workers and dependants.	Actual workers.				Dependants.	Total workers and dependants.	Actual workers.				Dependants.	Total workers and dependants.	Actual workers.				Dependants.	
	Total.		Partially agriculturist.				Total.		Partially agriculturist.				Total.		Partially agriculturist.			
	Males.	Females.	Males.	Females.			Males.	Females.	Males.	Females.			Males.	Females.	Males.	Females.		
218	219	220	221	222	223	224	225	226	227	228	229	230	231	232	233	234	235	
22,310	***7,134***	***4,015***	***1,269***	***250***	***11,161***	***1,413***	***524***	***35***	***2***	...	***854***	***15,930***	***6,634***	***1,921***	***318***	***56***	***7,375***	
665	195	48	...	...	422	1,193	359	35	...	...	799	396	147	29	...	...	220	1
593	242	164	1	...	187	...	...	...	...	...	...	...	...	...	...	...	...	2
2,230	***804***	***447***	***22***	***18***	***1,279***	***112***	***107***	...	...	...	***5***	***813***	***311***	***128***	***21***	...	***374***	
438	141	68	2	4	229	10	7	...	...	...	3	...	...	...	...	...	...	3
868	72	281	1	10	515	102	100	...	...	...	2	633	223	121	21	...	289	4
924	291	98	19	4	535	...	...	...	...	...	...	180	88	7	...	...	85	5
3,260	***1,277***	***818***	***39***	***6***	***1,165***	***101***	***53***	...	***2***	...	***48***	***7,756***	***4,021***	***907***	***65***	***5***	***2,828***	
1,112	459	331	...	...	322	22	14	...	2	...	8	1,595	597	353	40	2	645	6
1,387	494	356	1	1	537	...	...	...	...	...	...	...	...	...	...	...	...	7
508	202	81	8	2	225	...	...	...	...	...	...	6,160	3,423	554	25	3	2,183	8
253	122	50	30	3	81	79	39	...	...	...	40	1	1	...	...	...	...	9
6,075	***1,462***	***704***	***412***	***18***	***3,909***	***7***	***5***	...	...	...	***2***	***2,669***	***630***	***229***	***19***	***1***	***1,810***	
3,400	562	276	56	7	2,562	...	...	...	...	...	...	1,677	219	74	7	...	1,365	10
777	240	135	25	2	402	...	...	...	...	...	...	379	237	14	10	...	128	11
1,281	592	156	327	9	533	7	5	...	...	...	2	394	139	73	2	1	182	12
617	63	137	4	...	412	...	...	...	...	...	...	219	36	68	...	...	115	13
9,487	***3,454***	***1,834***	***795***	***208***	***4,199***	...	...	...	...	...	...	***4,296***	***1,525***	***628***	***213***	***50***	***2,143***	
3,697	1,207	593	40	3	1,897	...	...	...	...	...	...	961	443	87	1	...	431	14
572	118	161	2	22	293	...	...	...	...	...	...	653	107	67	14	3	389	15
1,651	984	162	537	...	505	...	...	...	...	...	...	279	46	73	...	...	160	16
3,567	1,145	918	216	183	1,594	...	...	...	...	...	...	2,403	839	401	198	47	1,163	17

TABLE XV.

OCCUPATION OR MEANS OF LIVELIHOOD.

PART A.—GENERAL TABLE.

Serial Number.	District.	Class B.—Preparation and supply											
		Sub-Class III.—											
		Order 7.—Hides, skins and hard											
		32.—Tanners, curriers, leather dressers, and dyers, etc.						33.—Makers of leather articles, such as trunks, water bags, etc.					
		Total workers and dependants.	Actual workers. Total. Males.	Actual workers. Total. Females.	Actual workers. Partially agriculturist. Males.	Actual workers. Partially agriculturist. Females.	Dependants.	Total workers and dependants.	Actual workers. Total. Males.	Actual workers. Total. Females.	Actual workers. Partially agriculturist. Males.	Actual workers. Partially agriculturist. Females.	Dependants.
	1	236	237	238	239	240	241	242	243	244	245	246	247
	Hyderabad State ...	***7,061***	***2,067***	***1,064***	***222***	***51***	***3,930***	***7,946***	***4,144***	***784***	***86***	***5***	***3,018***
1	Hyderabad City ...	161	41	28	...	...	92	37	23	1	...	...	13
2	Atraf-i-balda ...	...	...	...	...	...	...	...	...	...	...	...	...
	Warangal Division ...	***8***	***2***	...	...	...	***6***	***805***	***309***	***128***	***21***	...	***368***
3	Warangal ...	...	...	...	...	...	...	...	...	...	...	...	...
4	Karimnagar ...	...	...	...	...	...	...	633	223	121	21	...	289
5	Adilabad ...	8	2	...	...	...	6	172	86	7	...	...	79
	Medak Division ...	***1,440***	***487***	***342***	...	...	***611***	***6,316***	***3,534***	***565***	***65***	***5***	***2,217***
6	Medak ...	1,440	487	342	...	...	611	155	110	11	40	2	34
7	Nizamabad ...	...	...	...	...	...	...	...	...	...	...	...	...
8	Mahbubnagar ...	...	...	...	...	...	...	6,16[illegible]	3,423	554	25	3	2,183
9	Nalgonda ...	...	...	...	...	...	...	1	1	...	...	...	...
	Aurangabad Division ...	***2,356***	***437***	***222***	***9***	***1***	***1,707***	***119***	***42***	***7***	...	...	***70***
10	Aurangabad ...	1,677	218	74	7	...	1,385	...	...	...	...	...	...
11	Bhir ...	87	50	7	...	...	30	110	33	7	...	...	7[illegible]
12	Nander ...	373	123	73	2	1	177	9	9	...	...	...	...
13	Parbhani ...	219	36	68	...	...	115	...	...	...	...	...	...
	Gulbarga Division ...	***3,096***	***1,110***	***472***	***213***	***50***	***1,514***	***669***	***236***	***83***	...	...	***350***
14	Gulbarga ...	278	212	4	1	...	62	431	98	82	...	...	2[illegible]
15	Osmanabad ...	651	196	67	14	3	388	2	1	...	...	...	1
16	Raichur ...	...	...	...	...	...	...	...	...	...	...	...	...
17	Bidar ...	2,167	702	401	198	47	1,064	236	137	...	...	...	99

TABLE XV.

OCCUPATION OR MEANS OF LIVELIHOOD.

PART A.—GENERAL TABLE.

of material substances.—(*contd*).

Industry —(*contd*).

materials from the animal kingdom.—(*concld*).

34.—Furriers.						35-Bone, ivory, horn, shell, etc, workers.						Total Order 8.						
Total workers and dependants.	Actual workers. Total. Males.	Actual workers. Total. Females.	Actual workers. Partially agriculturist. Males.	Actual workers. Partially agriculturist. Females.	Dependants.	Total workers and dependants.	Actual workers. Total. Males.	Actual workers. Total. Females.	Actual workers. Partially agriculturist. Males.	Actual workers. Partially agriculturist. Females.	Dependants.	Total workers and dependants.	Actual workers. Total. Males.	Actual workers. Total. Females.	Actual workers. Partially agriculturist. Males.	Actual workers. Partially agriculturist. Females.	Dependants.	Serial Number.
248	249	250	251	252	253	254	555	256	257	258	259	260	261	262	263	264	265	
462	*223*	...	...	...	*239*	*461*	*200*	*73*	*10*	...	*188*	*146,747*	*55,611*	*19,837*	*5,370*	*1,415*	*71,299*	
193	83	...	...	...	115	...	...	...	...	...	...	4,008	1,544	219	...	...	2,245	1
...	...	...	...	...	...	...	...	...	...	...	...	4,448	1,751	939	48	25	1,758	2
...	...	...	...	...	...	...	...	...	...	...	...	*34,828*	*13,880*	*5,440*	*1,516*	*455*	*15,508*	
...	...	...	...	...	...	...	...	...	...	..	...	14,511	6,620	2,089	836	56	5,802	3
...	...	...	...	...	...	...	...	...	...	...	...	14,036	4,737	2,660	583	342	6,639	4
...	...	...	...	...	...	...	...	...	...	...	...	6,281	2,523	691	97	57	3,067	5
...	...	...	...	...	...	...	...	...	...	...	...	*32,696*	*12,195*	*6,037*	*1,146*	*468*	*14,464*	
...	...	...	...	...	...	...	...	...	...	...	..	8,072	3,137	1,646	392	170	3,289	6
...	...	...	...	...	...	...	...	...	...	...	...	5,345	2,179	1,165	240	96	2,001	7
...	...	...	...	...	...	...	...	...	...	...	...	7,330	2,648	1,391	142	90	3,291	8
...	..	...	...	...	...	...	...	...	...	...	...	11,949	4,231	1,835	372	112	5,883	9
12	*7*	...	...	...	*5*	*182*	*154*	...	*10*	..	*28*	*27,943*	*10,680*	*2,768*	*1,088*	*129*	*14,525*	
...	...	...	...	...	...	...	...	...	...	...	...	8,769	4,111	666	522	28	3,992	10
...	...	...	...	...	...	182	154	...	10	...	28	4,450	1,584	502	82	22	2,364	11
12	7	...	...	...	5	...	...	...	...	...	.	7,389	2,436	811	144	9	4,142	12
...	...	..	...	...	...	...	...	...	...	...	...	7,335	2,519	789	310	70	4,027	13
252	*133*	...	...	...	*119*	*279*	*46*	*73*	...	...	*169*	*42,824*	*15,591*	*4,434*	*1,602*	*338*	*22,799*	
252	133	...	...	...	119	...	...	..	...	...	...	14,711	6,257	1,369	457	63	7,085	14
...	..	...	...	...	...	...	...	...	...	...	...	7,112	2,539	588	169	15	3,985	15
...	...	...	...	...	...	279	46	73	...	...	160	12,014	3,243	1,796	723	163	6,975	16
...	...	...	...	...	...	...	...	...	...	...	...	8,987	3,552	661	253	97	4,774	17

TABLE XV.

OCCUPATION OR MEANS OF LIVELIHOOD.

PART A.—GENERAL TABLE.

Class B.—Preparation and supply

Sub-Class III.—

Order 8.—Wood.—(*concld*).

Serial Number.	District.	36.—Sawyers, carpenters, turners and joiners, etc.						37.—Basket makers and other industries of woody material including leaves.					
		Total workers and dependants.	Actual workers.				Dependants.	Total workers and dependants.	Actual workers.				Dependants.
			Total.		Partially agriculturist.				Total		Partially agriculturist.		
			Males.	Females.	Males.	Females.			Males.	Females.	Males.	Females.	
	1	266	267	268	269	270	271	272	273	274	275	276	277
	Hyderabad State ...	**87,903**	**36,290**	**3,955**	**3,629**	**479**	**47,658**	**58,844**	**19,321**	**15,882**	**1,741**	**936**	**23,641**
1	Hyderabad City ...	3,405	1,436	99	...	...	1,870	603	108	120	...	...	375
2	Atraf-i-balda ...	1,422	642	178	42	3	602	3,026	1,109	761	6	22	1,156
	Warangal Division ...	**17,698**	**6,788**	**1,210**	**780**	**77**	**9,700**	**17,130**	**7,092**	**4,230**	**736**	**378**	**5,808**
3	Warangal	5,720	2,109	403	421	13	3,208	8,791	4,511	1,686	415	43	2,594
4	Karimnagar	6,877	2,391	532	262	17	3,954	7,159	2,316	2,128	321	325	2,683
5	Adilabad	5,101	2,288	275	97	47	2,538	1,180	235	416	...	10	529
	Medak Division ...	**15,155**	**6,349**	**892**	**564**	**137**	**7,914**	**17,841**	**5,846**	**5,145**	**582**	**331**	**6,559**
6	Medak	2,880	1,186	256	110	68	1,438	5,192	1,951	1,390	282	102	1,851
7	Nizamabad	1,683	793	35	80	4	855	3,662	1,386	1,130	160	92	1,146
8	Mahbubnagar ...	3,541	1,639	177	74	48	1,725	3,789	1,009	1,214	68	42	1,566
9	Nalgonda	7,051	2,731	424	300	17	3,896	4,898	1,500	1,411	72	95	1,987
	Aurangabad Division..	**22,367**	**9,310**	**978**	**1,020**	**59**	**12,079**	**5,576**	**1,340**	**1,790**	**38**	**70**	**2,446**
10	Aurangabad	7,368	3,569	256	516	19	3,543	1,401	542	410	6	9	449
11	Bhir	3,206	1,211	140	63	10	1,855	1,244	373	362	19	12	509
12	Nander	6,024	2,228	345	140	6	3,451	1,365	208	466	4	3	691
13	Parbhani	5,769	2,302	237	301	24	3,230	1,566	217	552	9	46	797
	Gulbarga Division ...	**27,856**	**11,765**	**598**	**1,223**	**203**	**15,493**	**14,968**	**3,826**	**3,836**	**379**	**135**	**7,306**
14	Gulbarga	9,844	4,631	173	304	40	5,040	4,867	1,626	1,216	153	23	2,025
15	Osmanabad	5,738	2,114	266	143	8	3,358	1,374	425	322	26	7	627
16	Raichur	5,102	2,036	21	547	73	3,045	6,912	1,207	1,775	176	90	3,930
17	Bidar	7,172	2,984	138	229	82	4,050	1,815	568	523	24	15	724

TABLE XV.

OCCUPATION OR MEANS OF LIVELIHOOD.

PART A.—GENERAL TABLE.

of material substances.—(*contd*).

Industry.—(*contd*).

Total Order 9. Total workers and dependants.	Total Order 9. Actual workers. Total. Males.	Total Order 9. Actual workers. Total. Females.	Total Order 9. Actual workers. Partially agriculturist. Males.	Total Order 9. Actual workers. Partially agriculturist. Females.	Total Order 9. Dependants.	Order 9.—Metals. 38.—Forging and rolling of iron and other metals. Total workers and dependants.	38. Actual workers. Total. Males.	38. Actual workers. Total. Females.	38. Actual workers. Partially agriculturist. Males.	38. Actual workers. Partially agriculturist. Females.	38. Dependants.	39.—Plough and agricultural implement makers. Total workers and dependants.	39. Actual workers. Total. Males.	39. Actual workers. Total. Females.	39. Actual workers. Partially agriculturist. Males.	39. Actual workers. Partially agriculturist. Females.	39. Dependants.	Serial Number.
278	279	280	281	282	283	284	285	286	287	288	289	290	291	292	293	294	295	
88,772	***30,665***	***10,956***	***3,338***	***1,223***	***47,151***	***409***	***246***	...	***42***	...	***163***	***9***	***3***	...	...	...	...	
2,312	1,061	40	...	...	1,211	...	...	...	...	...	...	9	3	...	...	...	...	1
3,775	1,605	514	50	51	1,656	...	...	...	..	...	...	...	...	...	...	...	...	2
20,991	***6,916***	***2,958***	***931***	***413***	***11,117***	...	...	...	...	...	...	...	...	...	...	...	...	
6,158	2,508	536	347	10	3,114	...	...	...	...	...	...	...	..	...	...	...	...	3
11,025	3,278	1,956	489	397	5,781	...	...	...	..	...	..	...	...	...	...	...	...	4
3,808	1,130	456	95	6	2,222	...	...	...	...	...	...	...	...	...	...	...	...	5
28,687	***9,543***	***5,086***	***970***	***898***	***14,058***	...		...	...	...	...	...	...	...	...	...	...	
6,442	2,131	1,190	389	516	3,121	...	...	...	...	...	...	...	...	...	...	...	...	6
9,736	3,062	2,056	255	117	4,618	...	...	...	...	...	...	...	...	...	...	...	...	7
2,817	858	447	80	13	1,512	...	...	...	..	...	...	...	...	...	...	...	...	8
9,692	3,492	1,393	246	152	4,807	...	...	...	...	...	...	...	...	...	...	...	...	9
13,375	***5,119***	***1,014***	***695***	***52***	***7,242***	...	...	...	...	...	...	...	...	...	...	...	...	
4,087	1,695	234	381	17	2,158	...	...	...	...	...	...	...	...	...	...	...	...	10
2,273	928	187	49	7	1,158	...	..	...	...	...	...	...	...	...	...	..	...	11
3,034	1,261	222	148	15	1,551	...	...	...	...	...	...	...	...	...	...	...	...	12
3,981	1,235	371	117	13	2,375	...	...	...	...	...	...	...	...	...	...	...	...	13
19,632	***6,421***	***1,344***	***692***	***109***	***11,867***	***409***	***246***	...	***42***	...	***163***	...	...	...	...	...	...	
5,760	2,196	624	136	16	2,940	...	...	..	...	...	...	...	...	...	...	...	...	14
2,308	817	161	54	25	1,330	...	...	...	...	...	...	...	...	...	...	...	...	15
7,161	1,906	116	330	3	5,139	409	246	...	42	...	163	...	...	...	...	...	...	16
4,403	1,502	443	172	65	2,458	...	...	...	...	...	...	...	...	...	...	...	...	17

TABLE XV.

OCCUPATION OR MEANS OF LIVELIHOOD.

PART A.—GENERAL TABLE.

Class B.—Preparation and supply

Sub-Class III.—

Order 9.—

Serial Number.	District.	40.—Makers of arms, guns, etc. — Total workers and dependants.	Actual workers — Total — Males.	Actual workers — Total — Females.	Actual workers — Partially agriculturist — Males.	Actual workers — Partially agriculturist — Females.	Dependants.	41.—Other workers in iron and makers of implements and tools principally or exclusively of iron. — Total Workers and Dependants.	Actual workers — Total — Males.	Actual workers — Total — Females.	Actual workers — Partially agriculturist — Males.	Actual workers — Partially agriculturist — Females.	Dependants.
	1	296	297	298	299	300	301	302	303	304	305	306	307
	Hyderabad State ...	***257***	***126***	***19***	***6***	...	***112***	***73,586***	***24,296***	***9,652***	***2,679***	***1,017***	***39,638***
1	Hyderabad City ...	46	25	...	...	...	21	1,161	497	38	...	...	626
2	Atraf-i balda ..	13	11	...	1	...	2	2,362	826	436	46	27	1,1[illegible]
	Warangal Division ...	***130***	***57***	***16***	...	...	***57***	***16,835***	***5,533***	***2,654***	***822***	***404***	***8,668***
3	Warangal ...	30	10	1	...	...	19	4,894	2,062	411	317	9	2,421
4	Karimnagar ...	90	40	15	...	...	35	8,28[illegible]	2,391	1,788	418	389	4,104
5	Adilabad ..	1[illegible]	7	...	...	...	3	3,67	1,080	455	87	6	2,14[illegible]
	Medak Division ..	***34***	***22***	***3***	***5***	...	***9***	***23,282***	***7,338***	***4,351***	***770***	***427***	***11,593***
6	Medak ..	...	...	...	...	...	...	3,946	1,292	860	263	158	1,794
7	Nizamabad ..	33	21	3	5	...	9	8,238	2,475	1,784	241	106	3,979
8	Mahbubnagar ..	...	...	...	...	...	...	2,595	762	405	77	11	1,42[illegible]
9	Nalgonda ..	1	1	...	...	...	...	8,503	2,809	1,302	189	1[illegible]2	4,[illegible]
	Aurangabad Division .	***18***	***6***	...	...	...	***12***	***12,022***	***4,626***	***873***	***584***	***50***	***6,525***
10	Aurangabad ...	...	...	...	...	...	...	3,653	1,522	215	342	17	1,9[illegible]
11	Bhir ...	19	6	...	...	...	12	2,130	889	151	44	7	1,0[illegible]
12	Nander ...	...	...	...	...	...	...	2,560	935	219	84	15	1,[illegible]
13	Parbhani ...	...	...	...	...	...	...	3,679	1,220	283	114	11	2,17[illegible]
	Gulbarga Division ...	***16***	***5***	...	...	...	***11***	***17,904***	***8,476***	***1,300***	***457***	***109***	***11,125***
14	Gulbarga ...	...	...	...	...	...	...	5,709	2,166	624	134	16	2,9[illegible]
15	Osmanabad ...	...	...	...	...	...	...	2,062	748	146	51	25	1,1[illegible]
16	Raichur ..	...	...	...	...	...	...	5,970	1,236	88	165	3	4,64[illegible]
17	Bidar ...	16	5	...	...	...	11	4,163	1,326	442	107	65	2,395

TABLE XV.

OCCUPATION OR MEANS OF LIVELIHOOD.

PART A.—GENERAL TABLE.

of material substances.—(*contd*).

Industry.—(*contd.*)

Metals.—(*concld*).

42.—Workers in brass, copper and bell metal.						43.—Workers in other metals (tin, zinc, lead, quicksilver, etc.).						44.—Workers in mints, die-sinkers, etc.						
Total workers and dependants.	Actual workers. Total. Males.	Actual workers. Total. Females.	Actual workers. Partially agriculturist. Males.	Actual workers. Partially agriculturist. Females.	Dependants.	Total workers and dependants.	Actual workers. Total. Males.	Actual workers. Total. Females.	Actual workers. Partially agriculturist. Males.	Actual workers. Partially agriculturist. Females.	Dependants.	Total workers and dependants.	Actual workers. Total. Males.	Actual workers. Total. Females.	Actual workers. Partially agriculturist. Males.	Actual workers. Partially agriculturist. Females.	Dependants.	Serial Number.
308	309	310	311	312	313	314	315	316	317	318	319	320	321	322	323	324	325	
12,925	***5,284***	***1,253***	***516***	***206***	***6,388***	***1,096***	***521***	***23***	***83***	...	***547***	***490***	***189***	***4***	***12***	...	***297***	
194	102	...	...	...	92	496	270	2	...	...	224	406	164	...	...	...	242	1
1,400	768	78	3	24	554	...	...	...	...	...	...	...	...	...	...	...	...	2
3,972	***1,299***	***288***	***101***	***9***	***2,385***	***34***	***27***	...	***8***	...	***7***	...	...	...	...	...	...	
1,234	436	124	30	1	674	...	...	...	...	...	...	...	...	...	...	...	..	3
2,652	847	163	71	8	1,642	...	...	...	...	...	...	...	...	..	...	...	...	4
86	16	1	...	...	69	34	27	...	8	...	7	...	...	...	...	...	...	5
5,303	***2,133***	***739***	***155***	***171***	***2,440***	***68***	***50***	***2***	***40***	...	***16***	...	...	...	...	...	...	
2,428	789	323	86	158	1,311	68	50	2	40	...	16	...	...	...	...	...	...	6
1,465	566	269	9	11	630	...	...	...	...	...	...	...	...	...	..	...	...	7
222	96	42	8	2	84	...	...	...	...	...	...	...	...	...	...	...	...	8
1,188	682	91	57	...	415	...	...	..	...	...	...	...	...	...	...	...	...	9
1,005	***364***	***123***	***76***	***2***	***518***	***330***	***123***	***18***	***35***	...	***189***	...	...	...	...	...	..	
178	79	3	4	...	96	256	94	16	35	...	146	...	...	...	...	...	...	10
114	29	34	5	...	51	11	4	2	...	...	5	...	...	...	..	...	...	11
418	241	3	64	...	174	56	25	...	...	...	31	...	...	...	..	...	..	12
295	15	83	3	2	197	7	...	...	...	...	7	...	...	...	...	...	..	13
1,051	***618***	***34***	***181***	...	***399***	***168***	***51***	***6***	...	...	***111***	***84***	***25***	***4***	***12***	...	***55***	
11	11	...	2	...	...	40	19	...	...	...	21	...	...	...	..	...	...	14
129	46	9	3	...	74	117	23	6	...	...	88	...	...	...	...	...	...	15
698	399	24	111	...	275	...	...	...	...	...	...	84	25	4	12	...	55	16
218	162	1	65	...	50	11	9	...	...	...	2	...	..	...	...	..	...	17

TABLE XV.

OCCUPATION OR MEANS OF LIVELIHOOD

PART A.—GENERAL TABLE.

Serial Number.	District.	Class B.—Preparation and supply — Sub-class III.— Total Order 10. — Total workers and dependants.	Actual workers. Total. Males.	Actual workers. Total. Females.	Actual workers. Partially agriculturist. Males.	Actual workers. Partially agriculturist. Females.	Dependants.	Order 10.— 45.—Makers of glass and crystal ware. — Total workers and dependants.	Actual workers. Total. Males.	Actual workers. Total. Females.	Actual workers. Partially agriculturist. Males.	Actual workers. Partially agriculturist. Females.	Dependants.
	1	326	327	328	329	330	331	332	333	334	335	336	337
	Hyderabad State ...	***103,514***	***37,591***	***18,566***	***4,953***	***1,481***	***47,357***	...	...	...	...	...	...
1	Hyderabad City ...	2,238	443	558	...	...	1,237	...	...	...	...	...	...
2	Atraf-i-balda ...	5,244	1,748	1,328	128	220	2,168	...	...	...	...	...	...
	Warangal Division ...	***23,737***	***8,513***	***4,639***	***1,281***	***247***	***10,585***	...	...	...	...	...	...
3	Warangal ...	6,137	2,276	1,297	448	23	2,564	...	...	...	...	...	...
4	Karimnagar ...	12,062	4,452	2,073	752	157	5,537	...	...	...	...	...	...
5	Adilabad ...	5,538	1,785	1,269	81	67	2,484	...	...	...	...	...	...
	Medak Division ...	***26,174***	***9,891***	***4,644***	***1,476***	***341***	***11,639***	...	...	...	...	...	...
6	Medak ...	6,835	2,360	1,161	276	148	3,314	...	...	...	...	...	...
7	Nizamabad ...	3,364	1,555	326	171	...	1,483	...	...	...	...	...	...
8	Mahbubnagar ...	4,202	1,732	595	244	32	1,875	...	...	...	...	...	...
9	Nalgonda ...	11,773	4,244	2,562	785	161	4,967	...	...	...	...	...	...
	Aurangabad Division	***24,839***	***10,123***	***3,564***	***1,272***	***115***	***11,152***	...	...	...	...	...	...
10	Aurangabad ...	7,271	3,498	588	854	50	3,185	...	...	...	...	...	...
11	Bhir ...	3,277	1,284	502	102	26	1,491	...	...	...	...	...	...
12	Nander ...	4,847	2,006	703	63	13	2,138	...	...	...	...	...	...
13	Parbhani ...	9,444	3,335	1,771	253	26	4,338	...	...	...	...	...	...
	Gulbarga Division ...	***21,282***	***6,873***	***3,833***	***796***	***558***	***10,576***	...	...	...	...	...	...
14	Gulbarga ...	9,015	2,416	1,721	352	230	4,878	...	...	...	...	...	...
15	Osmanabad ...	2,527	1,005	481	53	19	1,041	...	...	...	...	...	...
16	Raichur ...	5,816	2,065	826	192	122	2,925	...	...	...	...	...	...
17	Bider ...	3,924	1,387	805	199	187	1,732	...	...	...	...	...	...

TABLE XV.

OCCUPATION OR MEANS OF LIVELIHOOD.

PART A.—GENERAL TABLE.

of material substances.—(*contd*).

Industry.—(*contd*).

Ceramics.

46.—Makers of porcelain and crockery.						47.—Potters and earthen pipe and bowl makers.						48.—Brick and tile makers.						Serial Number.
Total workers and dependants.	Actual workers. Total.		Actual workers. Partially agriculturist.		Dependants.	Total workers and dependants.	Actual workers. Total.		Actual workers. Partially agriculturist.		Dependants.	Total workers and dependants.	Actual workers. Total.		Actual workers. Partially agriculturist.		Dependants.	
	Males.	Females.	Males.	Females.			Males.	Females.	Males.	Females.			Males.	Females.	Males.	Females.		
338	339	340	341	342	343	344	345	346	347	348	349	350	351	352	353	354	355	
...	...	...	...	...	...	**102,373**	**37,046**	**18,460**	**4,946**	**1,481**	**46,867**	**1,141**	**548**	**106**	**7**	...	**490**	
...	...	...	...	...	...	1,973	307	515	...	...	1,151	265	136	43	...	...	86	1
...	...	...	...	...	...	5,244	1,748	1,328	128	220	2,168	...	...	...	...	...	...	2
...	...	...	...	...	..	**23,135**	**8,200**	**4,619**	**1,274**	**247**	**10,316**	**602**	**313**	**20**	**7**	...	**269**	
...	...	...	...	..	...	6,137	2,276	1,297	448	23	2,564	...	...	...	...	...	...	3
...	...	...	...	...	...	11,856	4,324	2,073	745	157	5,459	206	128	...	7	...	78	4
...	...	...	...	...	...	5,142	1,600	1,249	81	67	2,293	396	185	20	...	...	191	5
...	...	...	...	...	...	**26,174**	**9,891**	**4,644**	**1,476**	**341**	**11,639**	...	...	...	...	...	...	
...	...	...	...	...	...	6,835	2,360	1,161	276	148	3,314	...	...	...	...	...	...	6
...	...	...	...	...	...	3,364	1,555	326	171	...	1,483	...	...	...	...	...	...	7
...	...	...	...	...	...	4,202	1,732	595	244	32	1,875	...	...	...	...	...	...	8
...	...	...	...	...	...	11,773	4,244	2,562	785	161	4,967	...	...	...	...	...	...	9
...	...	...	..	...	...	**24,865**	**10,027**	**3,521**	**1,272**	**115**	**11,017**	**274**	**96**	**43**	...	...	**135**	
...	...	...	...	...	...	6,987	3,402	545	854	50	3,050	274	96	43	...	...	135	10
...	...	...	...	...	...	3,277	1,284	502	102	26	1,491	...	...	...	...	...	...	11
...	...	...	...	...	...	4,847	2,006	703	63	13	2,138	...	...	...	...	...	...	12
...	...	...	...	...	...	9,444	3,335	1,771	253	26	4,338	...	...	...	...	...	...	13
...	...	...	...	...	...	**21,282**	**6,873**	**3,833**	**796**	**558**	**10,576**	...	...	...	...	...	...	
...	...	...	...	...	...	9,015	2,416	1,721	352	230	4,875	...	...	...	...	...	...	14
...	...	...	...	...	...	2,527	1,005	481	53	19	1,041	...	...	...	...	...	...	15
...	...	...	...	...	...	5,816	2,065	826	192	122	2,925	...	...	...	...	...	...	16
...	...	...	...	...	...	3,924	1,387	805	199	187	1,732	...	...	...	...	...	...	17

TABLE XV.

OCCUPATION OR MEANS OF LIVELIHOOD.

PART A.—GENERAL TABLE.

Class B.—Preparation and supply

Sub Class III.—

Serial Number.	District.	Order 10—Ceramics.—(concld) 49.—Others (mosaic, talc, mica, alabaster, etc., workers). Total workers and dependants.	Actual workers. Total. Males.	Actual workers. Total. Females.	Actual workers. Partially agriculturist. Males.	Actual workers. Partially agriculturist. Females.	Dependants.	Total Order 11. Total workers and dependants.	Actual workers. Total. Males.	Actual workers. Total. Females.	Actual workers. Partially agriculturist. Males.	Actual workers. Partially agriculturist. Females.	Dependants.
	1	356	357	358	359	360	361	362	363	364	365	366	[illegible]
	Hyderabad State ...	...	...	...	...	...	...	***19,211***	***7,568***	***2,704***	***1,275***	***445***	***8,93[illegible]***
1	Hyderabad City ...	...	...	...	...	...	...	448	218	13	...	...	21[illegible]
2	Atraf-i-balda ..	...	...	...	...	...	...	32	21	...	6	...	11
	Warangal Division ...	...	...	...	...	...	...	***3,659***	***1,618***	***693***	***316***	***66***	***1,351***
3	Warangal ..	...	...	...	...	...	...	883	365	199	7	3	31[illegible]
4	Karimnagar ...	...	...	...	...	...	...	2,597	1,137	494	285	68	96[illegible]
5	Adilabad ...	...	...	...	...	...	...	179	113	...	24	...	6[illegible]
	Medak Division ...	...	...	...	...	...	...	***1,090***	***537***	***76***	***40***	***8***	***477***
6	Medak	...	...	...	...	...	...	637	280	51	17	4	30[illegible]
7	Nizamabad ...	...	...	...	...	...	...	195	131	...	14	...	64
8	Mahbubnagar ...	...	...	...	...	...	...	179	114	9	9	4	56
9	Nalgonda... ...	...	...	...	...	...	...	79	12	16	...	...	5[illegible]
	Aurangabad Division.	...	...	...	...	...	...	***6,957***	***2,295***	***839***	***150***	***64***	***3,823***
10	Aurangabad ...	...	...	...	...	...	...	1,905	773	188	44	21	949
11	Bhir	...	..	...	...	...	...	1,436	304	218	30	2	9[illegible]
12	Nander	...	...	...	...	...	...	1,319	319	261	23	14	73[illegible]
13	Parbhani ...	...	...	...	...	...	...	2,295	899	177	53	27	1,219
	Gulbarga Division ...	...	...	...	...	...	...	***7,025***	***2,882***	***1,083***	***763***	***307***	***3,060***
14	Gulbarga ..	...	...	...	...	...	...	926	505	29	63	2	39[illegible]
15	Osmanabad ...	...	...	...	...	...	...	1,090	426	144	39	2	52[illegible]
16	Raichur	...	...	...	...	...	...	3,842	1,543	634	574	187	1,665
17	Bidar	...	...	...	...	...	...	1,167	408	276	87	116	48[illegible]

TABLE XV.

OCCUPATION OR MEANS OF LIVELIHOOD.

PART A.—GENERAL TABLE.

of material substances.—(contd).

Industry.—(contd)

Order 11.—Chemical products properly so called, and analogous.

50.—Manufacture of matches and explosive materials.						51.—Manufacture of ærated and mineral waters.						52.—Manufacturers of dyes, paint and ink.						Serial Number.
Total workers and dependants.	Actual workers. Total. Males.	Actual workers. Total. Females.	Actual workers. Partially agriculturist. Males.	Actual workers. Partially agriculturist. Females.	Dependants.	Total workers and dependants.	Actual workers. Total. Males.	Actual workers. Total. Females.	Actual workers. Partially agricultur ist. Males.	Actual workers. Partially agricultur ist. Females.	Dependants.	Total workers and dependants.	Actual workers. Total. Males.	Actual workers. Total. Females.	Actual workers. Partially agriculturist. Males.	Actual workers. Partially agriculturist. Females.	Dependants.	
368	369	370	371	372	373	374	375	376	377	378	379	380	381	382	383	384	385	
39	***20***	***4***	...	...	***15***	...	...	...	...	...	...	***15***	***23***	...	...	...	***27***	
39	20	4	...	...	15	...	...	...	...	...	...	15	23	...	...	...	27	1
...	...	...	...	...	...	...	...	...	...	...	...	...	...	...	...	...	...	2
...	...	...	...	...	...	...	...	...	...	...	...	...	...	...	...	...	...	
...	...	...	...	...	...	...	...	...	...	...	...	...	...	...	...	...	...	3
...	...	...	...	...	...	...	...	...	...	...	...	...	...	...	...	...	...	4
...	...	...	...	...	...	...	...	...	...	...	...	...	...	...	...	...	...	5
...	...	...	...	...	...	...	...	...	...	...	...	...	...	...	...	...	...	
...	...	...	...	...	...	...	...	...	...	...	...	...	...	...	...	...	...	6
...	...	...	...	...	...	...	...	...	...	...	...	...	...	...	...	...	...	7
...	...	...	...	...	...	...	...	...	...	...	...	...	...	...	...	...	...	8
...	...	...	...	...	...	...	...	...	...	...	...	...	...	...	...	...	...	9
...	...	...	...	...	...	...	...	...	...	...	...	...	...	...	...	...	...	
...	...	...	...	...	...	...	...	...	...	...	...	...	...	...	...	...	...	10
...	...	...	...	...	...	...	...	...	...	...	...	...	...	...	...	...	...	11
...	...	...	...	...	...	...	...	...	...	...	...	...	...	...	...	...	...	12
...	...	...	...	...	...	...	...	...	...	...	...	...	...	...	...	...	...	13
...	...	...	...	...	...	...	...	...	...	...	...	...	...	...	...	...	...	
...	...	...	...	...	...	...	...	...	...	...	...	...	...	...	...	...	...	14
...	...	...	...	...	...	...	...	...	...	...	...	...	...	...	...	...	...	15
...	...	...	...	...	...	...	...	...	...	...	...	...	...	...	...	...	...	16
...	...	...	...	...	...	...	...	...	...	...	...	...	...	...	...	...	...	17

TABLE XV.

OCCUPATION OR MEANS OF LIVELIHOOD.

PART A.—GENERAL TABLE.

Serial Number.	District.	Class B.—Preparation and supply — Sub-Class III.— — Order 11.—Chemical products. 53.—Manufacture and refining of vegetable and mineral oils. Total workers and dependants.	Actual workers. Total. Males.	Actual workers. Total. Females.	Actual workers. Partially agriculturist. Males.	Actual workers. Partially agriculturist. Females.	Dependants.	54.—Manufacture of paper, cardboard and papier-mache. Total workers and dependants.	Actual workers. Total. Males.	Actual workers. Total. Females.	Actual workers. Partially agriculturist. Males.	Actual workers. Partially agriculturist. Females.	Dependants.
	1	386	387	388	389	390	391	392	393	394	395	396	397
	Hyderabad State ...	***18,091***	***7,110***	***2,534***	***1,165***	***410***	***8,447***	***535***	***238***	...	...	...	***297***
1	Hyderabad City ...	345	170	6	...	...	169	...	...	...	...	...	...
2	Atraf-i-balda ...	32	21	...	6	...	11	...	...	...	...	...	...
	Warangal Division ..	***3,465***	***1,329***	***693***	***316***	***66***	***1,243***	***163***	***69***	...	...	...	***94***
3	Warangal ..	873	360	199	7	3	314	10	5	...	...	...	5
4	Karimnagar ..	2,444	1,073	494	285	63	877	153	64	...	...	...	89
5	Adilabad ..	148	96	...	24	...	52	...	...	...	...	...	...
	Medak Division ...	***1,064***	***522***	***76***	***40***	***8***	***466***	***8***	***5***	...	...	...	***3***
6	Medak ...	637	280	51	17	4	306	...	...	...	...	...	...
7	Nizamabad ..	169	116	...	14	..	53	8	5	...	...	...	3
8	Mahbubnagar ..	179	114	9	9	4	56	...	...	...	...	...	...
9	Nalgonda ..	79	12	16	...	...	51	...	...	...	...	...	...
	Aurangabad Division	***6,621***	***2,146***	***839***	***150***	***64***	***3,636***	***336***	***149***	...	...	...	***187***
10	Aurangabad ..	1,569	624	183	44	21	762	336	149	...	...	...	187
11	Bhir ..	1,438	304	218	30	2	916	...	...	...	...	...	...
12	Nander ..	1,319	319	261	23	14	739	...	...	...	...	...	...
13	Parbhani ...	2,295	899	177	53	27	1,219	...	...	...	...	...	...
	Gulbarga Division ...	***6,564***	***2,722***	***920***	***653***	***272***	***2,922***	***28***	***15***	...	...	...	***13***
14	Gulbarga ...	926	505	29	63	2	392	...	...	...	...	...	...
15	Osmanabad ...	1,090	426	144	39	2	520	...	...	...	...	...	...
16	Raichur ...	3,381	1,383	471	464	152	1,527	28	15	...	...	...	13
17	Bidar ...	1,167	406	276	87	116	483	...	...	...	...	...	...

TABLE XV.

OCCUPATION OR MEANS OF LIVELIHOOD.

PART A.—GENERAL TABLE.

of material substances.—(*contd*).

Industry.—(*contd*).

properly so-called and analogous.—(*concld*). 55.—Others (soap, candles, lac, catechu, perfumes and miscellaneous drugs.). Total workers and dependants.	Actual workers. Total. Males.	Total. Females.	Partially agriculturist. Males.	Partially agriculturist. Females.	Dependants.	Total Order 12. Total workers and dependants.	Actual workers. Total. Males.	Total. Females.	Partially agriculturist. Males.	Partially agriculturist. Females.	Dependants.	Order 12. 56.—Rice pounders and huskers and flour grinders. Total workers and Dependants.	Actual workers. Total. Males.	Total. Females.	Partially agriculturist. Males.	Partially agriculturist. Females.	Dependants.	Serial Number.
398	399	400	401	402	403	404	405	406	407	408	409	410	411	412	413	414	415	
496	**177**	**166**	**110**	**35**	**153**	**119,245**	**49,288**	**13,892**	**5,540**	**724**	**56,068**	**7,308**	**28**	**3,664**	**2**	**17**	**3,616**	
14	5	3	...	...	6	12,837	4,179	1,765	10	...	6,893	147	...	70	...	...	77	1
...	...	...	...	...	...	9,792	4,088	1,359	69	49	4,345	...	...	...	...	...	...	2
31	**17**	...	...	...	**14**	**39,728**	**18,041**	**3,075**	**2,519**	**72**	**18,612**	**64**	...	**45**	.	**3**	**19**	
...	...	...	...	...	...	11,902	4,974	1,197	905	...	5,731	...	...	...	...	...	...	3
...	...	...	...	...	...	27,108	12,777	1,725	1,599	69	12,606	...	...	...	...	...	...	4
31	17	...	...	...	14	718	290	153	15	3	275	64	...	45	...	3	19	5
18	**10**	...	...	...	**8**	**38,783**	**19,565**	**2,293**	**2,491**	**95**	**16,925**	**110**	**1**	**82**	...	...	**27**	
...	...	...	...	...	...	6,914	2,993	504	755	25	3,417	...	...	...	...	...	...	6
18	10	...	...	...	8	4,834	2,374	442	438	31	2,018	38	...	37	..	...	1	7
...	...	...	...	...	...	6,632	3,447	620	266	34	2,565	46	...	20	...	...	26	8
...	...	...	...	...	...	20,403	10,751	727	1,032	5	8,925	26	1	25	...	...	...	9
...	...	...	...	...	...	**4,687**	**1,113**	**815**	**119**	**295**	**2,759**	**149**	...	**66**	...	...	**83**	
...	...	...	...	...	...	1,417	385	77	19	3	955	...	...	...	...	...	...	10
...	...	...	...	...	...	411	101	63	8	...	247	...	...	...	...	...	...	11
...	...	...	...	...	...	1,024	226	160	6	1	638	149	...	66	...	...	83	12
...	...	...	...	...	...	1,835	401	515	86	291	919	...	...	...	...	...	...	13
433	**145**	**163**	**110**	**35**	**125**	**13,418**	**2,202**	**4,585**	**332**	**213**	**6,831**	**6,838**	**27**	**3,401**	**2**	**14**	**3,410**	
...	...	...	...	...	...	7,801	738	3,389	76	81	3,674	5,739	27	2,892	2	8	2,820	14
...	...	...	...	...	...	698	234	77	6	4	387	...	...	...	...	...	...	15
433	145	163	110	35	125	1,162	326	190	7	2	646	...	...	...	...	...	...	16
...	...	...	...	...	...	3,757	1,004	929	243	126	1,824	1,099	...	509	...	6	890	17

TABLE XV.

OCCUPATION OR MEANS OF LIVELIHOOD.

PART A.—GENERAL TABLE.

Serial Number.	District.	Class B.—Preparation and supply / Sub-Class III.— / Order 12.—Food / 57.—Bakers and biscuit makers. Total workers and dependants.	Actual workers. Total. Males.	Actual workers. Total. Females.	Actual workers. Partially agriculturist. Males.	Actual workers. Partially agriculturist. Females.	Dependants.	58.—Grain parchers, etc. Total workers and dependants.	Actual workers. Total. Males.	Actual workers. Total. Females.	Actual workers. Partially agriculturist. Males.	Actual workers. Partially agriculturist. Females.	Dependants.
	1	416	417	418	419	420	421	422	423	424	425	426	427
	Hyderabad State ...	***2,869***	***1,085***	***296***	...	...	***1,488***	***2,082***	***642***	***758***	***110***	***245***	***642***
1	Hyderabad City ..	2,789	1,057	280	...	...	1,452	1,132	300	310	...	...	522
2	Atraf-i-balda ..	10	...	6	...	...	4	91	26	32	...	...	[illegible]
	Warangal Division ...	...	...	...	...	...	...	...	...	...	...	...	...
3	Warangal ..	...	...	...	...	...	...	...	...	...	...	...	...
4	Karimnagar ..	...	...	...	...	...	...	...	...	...	...	...	...
5	Adilabad ...	...	...	...	...	...	...	...	...	...	...	...	...
	Medak Division ...	...	...	...	...	...	...	...	...	...	...	...	...
6	Medak ...	...	...	...	...	...	...	...	...	...	...	...	...
7	Nizamabad ...	...	...	...	...	...	...	...	...	...	...	...	...
8	Mahbubnagar ..	...	...	...	...	...	...	...	...	...	...	...	...
9	Nalgonda ...	...	...	...	...	...	...	...	...	...	...	...	...
	Aurangabad Division.	***70***	***28***	***10***	...	...	***32***	***639***	***164***	***445***	***55***	***245***	***30***
10	Aurangabad ...	64	28	10	...	...	26	...	...	...	...	...	...
11	Bhir ...	...	...	...	...	...	..	...	...	...	...	...	..
12	Nander ...	...	...	...	...	..	...	31	7	8	...	...	[illegible]
13	Parbhani ...	6	...	...	...	...	6	608	157	437	55	245	14
	Gulbarga Division ..	...	...	...	...	...	...	***220***	***152***	***11***	***55***	...	***57***
14	Gulbarga ...	...	...	...	...	...	...	...	...	...	...	...	...
15	Osmanabad ...	...	...	...	...	...	...	7	...	3	...	...	4
16	Raichur ...	...	...	...	...	...	...	86	35	8	...	...	43
17	Bidar ...	...	...	...	...	...	...	127	117	...	55	...	[illegible]

TABLE XV.

OCCUPATION OR MEANS OF LIVELIHOOD.

PART A.—GENERAL TABLE.

of material substances.—(*contd.*)

Industry.—(*contd*).

Industries.—(*contd*).

59.—Butchers.						60.—Fish curers.						61.—Butter, cheese and ghee makers.						Serial Number.
Total workers and dependants.	Actual workers.				Dependants.	Total workers and dependants.	Actual workers.				Dependants.	Total workers and dependants.	Actual workers.				Dependants.	
	Total.		Partially agriculturist.				Total.		Partially agriculturist.				Total.		Partially agriculturist.			
	Males.	Females.	Males.	Females.			Males.	Females.	Males.	Females.			Males.	Females.	Males.	Females.		
428	429	430	431	432	433	434	435	436	437	438	439	440	441	442	443	444	445	
21,192	***7,258***	***2,803***	***608***	***315***	***11,131***	***13***	***8***	***5***	...	...	...	...	...	...	...	...	...	
4,349	1,641	263	10	...	2,445	...	...	...	...	...	...		...	...	..	...	...	1
2,263	912	393	19	1	958	...	...	..	...	...	...	...	...	...	...	...	...	2
1,329	***492***	***216***	***41***	***5***	***621***	...	...	...	...	...	...	...	...	...	...	...	...	
414	151	48	25	...	212	...	...	...	..	...	...	...	...	...	...	...	...	3
285	62	61	5	5	162	...	...	...	...	...	..	...	...	...	...	...	...	4
630	276	107	11	...	247	...	..	...	...	...	...	...	...	...	...	...	...	5
3,723	***1,368***	***550***	***205***	***60***	***1,895***	...	..	...	...	...	...	...	...	...	...	...	...	
1,183	512	150	148	24	521	...	...	...	...	...	...	...	...	...	..	...	..	6
703	113	158	2	4	432	...	...	...	...	...	...	...	...	...	...	...	...	7
1,414	580	203	50	31	631	...	...	...	...	...	...	...	...	...	...	...	...	8
423	163	39	5	1	221	...	...	...	...	...	...	...	...	...	...	...	...	9
3,379	***796***	***253***	***60***	***50***	***2,330***	...	...	...	...	...	...	...	...	..	...	...	...	
1,305	337	62	19	3	906	...	..	...	...	...	...	...	...	...	...	...	...	10
382	88	58	8	...	236	...	...	...	...	...	...	..	...	...	...	...	...	11
748	185	73	4	1	490	...	...	...	...	...	...	...	...	...	..	...	...	12
944	186	60	29	46	698	...	...	...	...	...	...	...	...	...	...	...	...	13
6,149	***2,049***	***1,128***	***273***	***199***	***2,972***	***13***	***8***	***5***	...	...	...	...	...	...	...	...	...	
2,000	687	477	74	73	836	...	...	...	...	...	...	...	...	...	...	...	...	14
567	203	54	4	4	310	...	...	...	...	...	...	...	...	...	...	...	...	15
1,063	283	177	7	2	603	13	8	5	...	...	...	...	...	...	...	...	...	16
2,519	876	420	188	120	1,223	...	...	...	...	...	...	...	...	...	...	...	...	17

TABLE XV.

OCCUPATION OR MEANS OF LIVELIHOOD.

PART A.—GENERAL TABLE.

Class B.—Preparation and supply

Sub Class III.—

Order 12—Food

Serial Number.	District.	62.—Makers of sugar, molasses and gur. Total workers and dependants.	62. Actual workers. Total. Males.	62. Actual workers. Total. Females.	62. Actual workers. Partially agriculturist. Males.	62. Actual workers. Partially agriculturist. Females.	62. Dependants.	63.—Sweetmeat makers, preparers of jam and condiments, etc. Total workers and dependants.	63. Actual workers. Total. Males.	63. Actual workers. Total. Females.	63. Actual workers. Partially agriculturist. Males.	63. Actual workers. Partially agriculturist. Females.	63. Dependants.
	1	446	447	448	449	450	451	452	453	454	455	456	457
	Hyderabad State ...	***249***	***134***	...	...	...	***115***	***1,652***	***506***	***385***	***10***	...	***761***
1	Hyderabad City ...	...	...	...	...	...	...	1,048	325	328	...	...	395
2	Atraf-i-balda ...	...	...	...	...	...	...	...	...	...	...	...	...
	Warangal Division ...	...	...	...	...	...	...	***24***	***14***	***1***	***4***	...	***9***
3	Warangal	...	...	...	...	...	...	...	...	...	...	...	...
4	Karimnagar	...	...	...	...	...	...	...	...	...	...	...	...
5	Adilabad	...	..	...	...	...	...	24	14	1	4	...	9
	Medak Division ...	***249***	***134***	...	...	...	***115***	...	...	...	...	...	...
6	Medak	249	134	...	...	...	115	...	...	...	...	...	...
7	Nizamabad	...	...	...	...	...	...	...	...	...	...	...	...
8	Mahbubnagar ...	...	...	...	...	...	...	...	...	...	...	...	...
9	Nalgonda	...	...	...	...	...	..	...	...	...	...	...	...
	Aurangabad Division..	...	...	...	...	...	...	***427***	***116***	***36***	***4***	...	***275***
10	Aurangabad	...	...	...	...	...	...	48	20	5	...	...	23
11	Bhir	...	...	...	...	...	...	6	4	...	...	...	2
12	Nander	...	...	...	...	...	...	96	34	13	2	...	49
13	Parbhani	...	...	...	...	...	...	277	58	18	2	...	201
	Gulbarga Division ...	...	...	...	...	...	...	***153***	***51***	***20***	***4***	...	***82***
14	Gulbarga	...	...	...	...	...	...	17	9	...	2	...	8
15	Osmanabad	...	...	...	...	...	...	124	31	20	2	...	73
16	Raichur	...	...	...	...	...	...	...	...	...	...	...	...
17	Bidar	...	...	...	...	...	...	12	11	...	...	...	1

TABLE XV.

OCCUPATION OR MEANS OF LIVELIHOOD.

PART A.—GENERAL TABLE.

of material substances.—(*contd*).

Industry.—(*contd*).

Industries.—(*concld*).

64.—Brewers and distillers.						65.—Toddy drawers.						66.—Manufacturers of tobacco, opium and ganja.						
Total workers and dependants.	Actual workers. Total. Males.	Actual workers. Total. Females.	Partially agriculturist. Males.	Partially agriculturist. Females.	Dependants.	Total workers and dependants.	Actual workers. Total. Males.	Actual workers. Total. Females.	Partially agriculturist. Males.	Partially agriculturist. Females.	Dependants.	Total workers and dependants.	Actual workers. Total. Males.	Actual workers. Total. Females.	Partially agriculturist. Males.	Partially agriculturist. Females.	Dependants.	Serial Number.
458	459	460	461	462	463	464	465	466	467	468	469	470	471	472	473	474	475	
443	***204***	***31***	...	...	***208***	***79,852***	***38,858***	***5,233***	***4,809***	***146***	***35,761***	***3,585***	***565***	***677***	1	1	***2,343***	
403	187	26	...	...	190	384	250	...	...	...	134	2,585	419	488	...	...	1,678	1
...	...	...	...	...	...	7,416	3,144	925	50	48	3,347	12	6	3	...	...	3	2
...	...	...	...	...	...	***38,201***	***17,489***	***2,809***	***2,473***	***64***	***17,903***	***110***	***46***	***4***	***1***	...	***60***	
...	...	...	...	...	...	11,407	4,787	1,145	879	...	5,475	81	33	4	1	...	44	3
...	...	...	...	...	...	26,794	12,702	1,664	1,594	64	12,428	29	13	...	...	...	16	4
...	...	...	...	...	...	...	...	...	...	...	...	...	...	...	...	...	...	5
17	***8***	...	...	...	***9***	***33,851***	***17,975***	***1,499***	***2,286***	***34***	***14,377***	***833***	***79***	***162***	...	***1***	***592***	
...	...	..	...	...	...	4,740	2,332	194	607	...	2,214	742	15	160	...	1	567	6
...	...	...	..	...	...	4,015	2,204	245	436	27	1,566	78	57	2	...	...	19	7
17	8	...	...	...	9	5,145	2,853	397	216	3	1,895	10	6	...	...	...	4	8
...	...	...	...	...	...	19,951	10,586	663	1,027	4	8,702	3	1	...	...	...	2	9
23	***9***	***5***	...	...	***9***	...	...	..	...	...	...	...	...	...	...	...	...	
...	...	...	...	...	...	...	...	...	...	...	...	...	...	...	...	...	...	10
23	9	5	...	...	9	...	...	...	...	...	...	...	...	...	...	..	...	11
...	...	...	...	...	...	...	...	...	...	...	...	...	...	...	...	...	...	12
...	...	...	...	...	...	...	...	...	...	...	...	...	...	...	...	...	...	13
...	...	...	...	...	...	...	...	...	...	...	...	***45***	***15***	***20***	...	...	***10***	
...	...	...	...	...	...	...	...	...	...	...	...	45	15	20	...	...	10	14
...	...	...	...	...	...	...	...	...	...	...	...	...	...	...	...	...	...	15
...	...	...	...	...	...	...	...	...	...	...	...	...	...	...	...	...	...	16
...	...	...	...	...	...	...	...	...	...	...	...	...	...	...	...	...	...	17

TABLE XV.

OCCUPATION OR MEANS OF LIVELIHOOD.

PART A—GENERAL TABLE.

Serial Number.	District.	Class B.—Preparation and supply											
		Sub-Class III.—											
		Total Order 13.						Order 13.— 67.—Hat, cap and turban makers.					
		Total workers and dependants.	Actual workers. Total. Males.	Actual workers. Total. Females.	Actual workers. Partially agriculturist. Males.	Actual workers. Partially agriculturist. Females.	Dependants.	Total workers and dependants.	Actual workers. Total. Males.	Actual workers. Total. Females.	Actual workers. Partially agriculturist. Males.	Actual workers. Partially agriculturist. Females.	Dependants.
	1	476	477	478	479	480	481	482	483	484	485	486	487
	Hyderabad State ...	***642,448***	***234,466***	***115,228***	***24,489***	***7,910***	***292,784***	***391***	***202***	...	***7***	...	***18***
1	Hyderabad City ...	19,537	7,748	2,680	...	...	9,109	132	42	...	...	...	9
2	Atraf-i-balda ...	45,087	17,844	7,677	1,162	315	19,566	...	...	...	...	...	...
	Warangal Division ...	***168,998***	***61,589***	***30,070***	***6,188***	***1,551***	***77,348***	...	...	...	...	...	...
3	Warangal ...	60,352	22,172	11,191	2,740	283	26,989	...	...	...	...	...	...
4	Karimnagar ...	83,310	30,693	14,077	3,083	1,633	38,540	...	...	...	...	...	...
5	Adilabad ...	25,336	8,715	4,802	365	235	11,819	...	...	...	...	...	...
	Medak Division ...	***229,929***	***86,818***	***47,102***	***9,033***	***4,126***	***96,009***	...	...	...	...	...	...
6	Medak ...	59,835	19,941	13,217	2,264	1,603	26,677	...	...	...	...	...	...
7	Nizamabad ...	41,876	16,349	9,822	1,996	789	15,705	...	...	...	...	...	...
8	Mahbubnagar ...	51,329	17,574	16,924	1,783	979	22,831	...	...	...	...	...	...
9	Nalgonda ...	76,889	32,951	13,139	2,991	755	30,796	...	...	...	...	...	...
	Aurangabad Division	***71,059***	***23,643***	***11,572***	***2,776***	***372***	***35,844***	***92***	***30***	...	***6***	...	***6***
10	Aurangabad ...	25,747	8,056	3,562	1,326	85	14,170	25	19	...	...	...	
11	Bhir ...	14,770	4,789	3,236	363	82	6,745	5	2	...	...	...	
12	Nander ...	14,534	5,201	2,286	542	84	7,047	...	..	...	...	...	...
13	Parbhani ...	16,008	5,647	2,488	545	121	7,873	62	9	...	6	...	5
	Gulbarga Division ...	***107,838***	***36,833***	***16,127***	***5,300***	***1,846***	***54,878***	***167***	***130***	...	***1***	...	***3***
14	Gulbarga ...	34,539	10,791	6,617	1,094	673	17,131	100	97	...	1	...	
15	Osmanabad ...	18,648	6,265	1,614	413	72	10,749	...	...	...	...	...	...
16	Raichur ...	31,340	12,495	3,919	2,735	413	14,926	...	...	...	...	...	...
17	Bidar ...	23,311	7,262	3,977	1,058	388	12,072	67	33	...	...	...	[illegible]

TABLE XV.

OCCUPATION OR MEANS OF LIVELIHOOD.

PART A.—GENERAL TABLE.

of material substances.—(*contd*).

Industry.—(*contd*).

Industries of dress and the toilet.—(*contd*).

68.—Tailors, milliners, dress makers and darners, embroiderers on linen.						69.—Shoe, boot and sandal makers.						Serial Number.
Total workers and dependants.	Actual workers. Total.		Actual workers. Partially agriculturist.		Dependants.	Total workers and dependants.	Actual workers. Total.		Actual workers. Partially agriculturist.		Dependants.	
	Males.	Females.	Males.	Females.			Males.	Females.	Males.	Females.		
488	489	490	491	492	493	494	495	496	497	498	499	
70,859	*20,022*	*16,848*	*2,366*	*1,054*	*33,989*	*269,048*	*101,423*	*41,983*	*8,487*	*2,400*	*125,642*	
5,402	1,984	600	...	...	2,818	4,271	1,800	506	...	...	1,965	1
2,445	919	611	22	46	915	27,504	10,830	4,030	749	98	12,644	2
18,934	*5,949*	*4,440*	*474*	*173*	*8,545*	*67,406*	*27,089*	*7,418*	*1,884*	*180*	*32,899*	
5,821	1,884	1,353	98	21	2,584	25,893	9,715	3,522	940	17	12,656	3
8,382	2,532	2,155	267	102	3,695	34,617	14,594	2,808	857	158	17,215	4
4,731	1,532	932	109	50	2,267	6,896	2,780	1,088	87	5	3,028	5
17,487	*4,050*	*5,420*	*254*	*478*	*8,017*	*116,439*	*43,558*	*21,629*	*4,149*	*1,730*	*51,252*	
5,567	1,002	1,714	117	358	2,851	33,008	12,254	6,496	1,170	590	14,258	6
3,536	992	1,131	67	21	1,413	18,895	6,681	4,583	767	287	7,631	7
2,513	478	773	17	49	1,262	30,966	10,514	5,878	1,045	630	14,574	8
5,871	1,578	1,802	53	50	2,491	33,570	14,109	4,672	1,167	223	14,789	9
12,852	*3,288*	*2,890*	*797*	*80*	*6,674*	*20,063*	*6,620*	*3,478*	*435*	*91*	*9,965*	
6,704	1,615	1,425	626	12	3,664	6,083	1,786	755	130	17	3,542	10
1,951	446	514	80	46	991	6,016	2,023	1,418	84	9	2,575	11
2,852	809	617	87	17	1,426	2,860	976	486	99	20	1,398	12
1,345	418	334	4	5	593	5,104	1,835	819	122	45	2,450	13
13,739	*3,832*	*2,887*	*819*	*277*	*7,020*	*33,365*	*11,526*	*4,922*	*1,270*	*301*	*16,917*	
5,155	1,012	1,555	29	110	2,588	7,939	2,724	1,310	210	17	3,905	14
788	165	94	1	3	529	7,272	2,054	603	88	16	4,615	15
5,307	1,813	766	665	65	2,728	11,855	4,634	1,778	775	210	5,443	16
2,489	842	472	124	19	1,175	6,299	2,114	1,231	197	58	2,954	17

TABLE XV.

OCCUPATION OR MEANS OF LIVELIHOOD.

PART A.—GENERAL TABLE.

Class B.—Preparation and supply

Sub-class III.—

Order 13.—Industries

Serial Number.	District.	70.—Other industries pertaining to dress, gloves, socks, gaiters, belts, buttons, umbrellas, canes, etc. Total workers and dependants.	Actual workers. Total. Males.	Total. Females.	Partially agriculturist. Males.	Partially agriculturist. Females.	Dependants.	71.—Washing, cleaning and dyeing. Total workers and dependants.	Actual workers. Total. Males.	Total. Females.	Partially agriculturist. Males.	Partially agriculturist. Females.	Dependants.
	1	500	501	502	503	504	505	506	507	508	509	510	511
	Hyderabad State ...	***1,124***	***373***	***302***	***15***	...	***449***	***214,921***	***75,606***	***51,071***	***9,018***	***3,934***	***88,244***
1	Hyderabad City ...	...	...	...	...	...	...	6,067	1,909	1,574	...	...	2,584
2	Atraf-i-balda ...	...	...	...	...	...	...	10,417	3,944	2,829	249	146	3,644
	Warangal Division ...	***29***	***17***	***5***	***1***	...	***7***	***61,818***	***19,759***	***16,723***	***2,723***	***1,111***	***25,336***
3	Warangal ...	5	5	...	1	...	...	20,898	6,917	6,162	1,267	235	7,819
4	Karimnagar ...	24	12	5	...	...	7	31,488	10,105	8,289	1,353	735	13,094
5	Adilabad ...	...	...	...	...	...	...	9,432	2,737	2,272	103	141	4,423
	Medak Division ...	***1,091***	***354***	***297***	***14***	...	***440***	***74,959***	***30,063***	***18,341***	***3,380***	***1,660***	***26,555***
6	Medak ...	371	...	191	...	...	180	16,088	4,806	4,209	665	534	7,073
7	Nizamabad ...	94	36	4	...	...	54	15,751	7,273	3,767	887	468	4,711
8	Mahbubnagar ...	...	...	...	...	...	...	13,552	4,686	3,988	501	277	4,875
9	Nalgonda ...	626	318	102	14	...	206	29,568	13,298	6,377	1,327	381	9,833
	Aurangabad Division.	***4***	***2***	...	...	...	***2***	***21,884***	***7,048***	***4,475***	***583***	***158***	***10,361***
10	Aurangabad ...	4	2	...	...	...	2	8,155	2,842	1,125	189	41	4,153
11	Bhir ...	...	...	...	...	...	...	3,686	979	1,200	95	17	1,567
12	Nander ...	...	...	...	...	...	...	4,832	1,835	1,047	206	37	1,935
13	Parbhani ...	...	...	...	...	...	...	5,211	1,392	1,103	93	63	2,716
	Gulbarga Division ...	...	...	...	...	...	...	***39,776***	***12,883***	***7,129***	***2,083***	***859***	***19,764***
14	Gulbarga ...	...	...	...	...	...	...	14,831	3,864	3,414	405	539	7,5[illegible]
15	Osmanabad ...	...	...	...	...	...	...	5,816	2,356	769	196	38	2,691
16	Raichur ...	...	...	...	...	...	...	9,932	4,361	949	1,148	107	4,022
17	Bidar ..	...	...	...	...	...	...	9,197	2,302	1,997	334	175	4,898

TABLE XV.

OCCUPATION OR MEANS OF LIVELIHOOD.

PART A.—GENERAL TABLE.

of material substances.—(*contd.*)

Industry.—(*contd.*)

of dress and the toilet.—(*concld.*)

72.—Barbers, hair dressers and wig makers.						73.—Other industries connected with the toilet (tattooers, shampooers, bath houses, etc.)						Total Order 14.						Serial Number.
Total workers and dependants.	Actual workers. Total. Males.	Actual workers. Total. Females.	Actual workers. Partially agriculturist. Males.	Actual workers. Partially agriculturist. Females.	Dependants.	Total workers and dependants.	Actual workers. Total. Males.	Actual workers. Total. Females.	Actual workers. Partially agriculturist. Males.	Actual workers. Partially agriculturist. Females.	Dependants.	Total workers and dependants.	Actual workers. Total. Males.	Actual workers. Total. Females.	Actual workers. Partially agriculturist. Males.	Actual workers. Partially agriculturist. Females.	Dependants.	
512	513	514	515	516	517	518	519	520	521	522	523	524	525	526	527	528	529	
85,880	***36,672***	***5,013***	***4,552***	***522***	***44,198***	***225***	***168***	***11***	***14***	...	***46***	***255***	***126***	...	...	...	***129***	
3,665	2,013	...	...	...	1,652	...	...	...	...	...	...	215	103	...	...	...	112	1
4,721	2,151	207	142	25	2,363	...	...	...	...	...	...	...	...	...	...	...	...	2
20,810	***8,766***	***1,483***	***1,106***	***87***	***10,561***	***1***	...	***1***	...	...	...	***2***	...	...	...	...	***2***	
7,735	3,650	154	434	10	3,931	...	...	...	...	...	...	2	...	...	...	...	2	3
8,798	3,450	819	606	38	4,529	1	...	1	...	...	...	...	...	...	...	...	...	4
4,277	1,666	510	66	39	2,101	...	...	...	...	...	...	...	...	...	...	...	...	5
19,919	***8,793***	***1,408***	***1,236***	***288***	***9,721***	***34***	...	***10***	...	...	***24***	***38***	***23***	...	...	...	***15***	
4,501	1,879	607	312	121	2,315	...	...	...	...	...	...	...	...	...	...	...	...	6
3,600	1,367	337	274	13	1,896	...	...	...	...	...	...	...	...	...	...	...	...	7
4,264	1,896	275	220	23	2,093	34	...	10	...	...	24	...	...	...	...	...	...	8
7,254	3,651	186	430	101	3,417	...	...	...	...	...	...	38	23	...	...	...	15	9
16,164	***6,685***	***729***	***955***	***43***	***8,780***	...	...	...	...	...	...	...	...	...	...	...	...	
4,776	1,742	257	381	15	2,777	...	...	...	...	...	...	...	...	...	...	...	...	10
3,112	1,339	104	164	10	1,669	...	...	...	...	...	...	...	...	...	...	...	...	11
3,990	1,581	136	150	10	2,273	...	...	...	...	...	...	...	...	...	...	...	...	12
4,286	1,993	232	320	8	2,061	...	...	...	...	...	...	...	...	...	...	...	...	13
20,601	***8,294***	***1,189***	***1,113***	***109***	***11,118***	***190***	***168***	...	***14***	...	***22***	...	...	...	...	...	...	
6,324	2,926	338	435	7	3,060	190	168	...	14	...	22	...	...	...	...	...	...	14
4,772	1,710	148	128	15	2,914	...	...	...	...	...	...	...	...	...	...	...	...	15
4,246	1,687	426	147	31	2,133	...	...	...	...	...	...	...	...	...	...	...	...	16
5,259	1,971	277	403	56	3,011	...	...	...	...	...	...	...	...	...	...	...	...	17

TABLE XV.

OCCUPATION OR MEANS OF LIVELIHOOD.

PART A.—GENERAL TABLE.

Serial Number.	District.	Class B.—Preparation and supply											
		Sub Class III.—											
		Order 14.—Furniture industries.											
		74.—Cabinet makers, carriage painters, etc.						75.—Upholsterers, tent makers, etc.					
		Total workers and dependants.	Actual workers. Total.		Actual workers. Partially agriculturist.		Dependants.	Total workers and dependants.	Actual workers. Total.		Actual workers. Partially agriculturist.		Dependants.
			Males.	Females.	Males.	Females.			Males.	Females.	Males.	Females.	
	1	530	531	532	533	534	535	536	537	538	539	540	541
	Hyderabad State	*255*	*126*	...	...	...	*129*	...	...	...	...	...	...
1	Hyderabad City	215	103	...	...	...	112	...	...	...	...	...	...
2	Atraf-i-balda	...	...	...	...	...	...	...	...	...	...	...	...
	Warangal Division	*2*	...	...	...	...	*2*	...	...	...	...	...	...
3	Warangal	2	...	...	...	...	2	...	...	...	...	...	...
4	Karimnagar	...	...	...	...	...	...	...	...	...	...	...	...
5	Adilabad	...	...	...	...	...	...	...	...	...	...	...	...
	Medak Division	*38*	*23*	...	...	...	*15*	...	...	...	...	...	...
6	Medak	...	...	...	...	...	...	...	...	...	...	...	...
7	Nizamabad	...	...	...	...	...	...	...	...	...	...	...	...
8	Mahbubnagar	...	...	...	...	...	...	...	...	...	...	...	...
9	Nalgonda	38	23	...	...	...	15	...	...	...	...	...	...
	Aurangabad Division	...	...	...	...	...	...	...	...	...	...	...	...
10	Aurangabad	...	...	...	...	...	...	...	...	...	...	...	...
11	Bhir	...	...	...	...	...	...	...	...	...	...	...	...
12	Nander	...	...	...	...	...	...	...	...	...	...	...	...
13	Parbhani	...	...	...	...	...	...	...	...	...	...	...	...
	Gulbarga Division	...	...	...	...	...	...	...	...	...	...	...	...
14	Gulbarga	...	...	...	...	...	...	...	...	...	...	...	...
15	Osmanabad	...	...	...	...	...	...	...	...	...	...	...	...
16	Raichur	...	...	...	...	...	...	...	...	...	...	...	...
17	Bidar	...	...	...	...	...	...	...	...	...	...	...	...

TABLE XV.

OCCUPATION OR MEANS OF LIVELIHOOD.

PART A—GENERAL TABLE.

of material substances.—(*contd.*)

Industry.—(*contd.*)

Total Order 15.						Order 15.—Building industries.													
						76.—Lime burners, cement workers.						77.—Excavators, plinth builders and well sinkers.							Serial Number.
Total workers and dependants.	Actual workers.				Dependants.	Total workers and dependants.	Actual workers.				Dependants.	Total workers and dependants.	Actual workers.				Dependants.		
	Total.		Partially agriculturist.				Total.		Partially agriculturist.				Total.		Partially agriculturist.				
	Males.	Females.	Males.	Females.			Males.	Females.	Males.	Females.			Males.	Females.	Males.	Females.			
542	543	544	545	546	547	548	549	550	551	552	553	554	555	556	557	558	559		
111,194	*41,344*	*16,678*	*2,659*	*958*	*53,172*	*643*	*263*	*88*	*1*	...	*292*	*2,149*	*948*	*181*	*64*	*1*	*1,020*		
5,487	2,894	155	...	...	2,438	265	93	46	...	...	121	...	...	...	...	...	...	1	
3,408	1,330	435	48	36	1,643	61	21	12	...	...	28	253	94	32	...	...	127	2	
15,846	*4,898*	*3,214*	*228*	*166*	*7,734*	*28*	*23*	...	*1*	...	*5*	*481*	*197*	*50*	*2*	...	*234*		
6,781	2,015	1,660	73	21	3,109	...	...	...	...	...	...	73	23	19	...	...	31	3	
3,774	1,320	528	129	109	1,926	28	23	...	1	...	5	408	174	31	2	...	203	4	
5,288	1,563	1,026	26	36	2,699	...	...	...	...	...	...	...	...	.	...	...	...	5	
19,025	*7,986*	*3,233*	*658*	*94*	*7,806*	*54*	*34*	...	...	...	*20*	*1,415*	*657*	*99*	*62*	*1*	*659*		
4,761	1,474	1,256	196	9	2,031	...	...	...	...	...	...	181	117	...	...	...	64	6	
1,255	539	111	43	...	605	...	...	...	...	...	...	...	..	...	...	...	...	7	
4,150	1,839	581	172	15	1,730	54	34	...	...	...	20	524	196	41	24	1	287	8	
8,859	4,134	1,285	247	70	3,440	...	...	...	...	...	...	710	344	58	38	...	308	9	
17,327	*6,493*	*2,781*	*456*	*175*	*8,053*	*142*	*24*	*30*	...	...	*88*	...	...	...	...	...	...		
4,242	1,231	840	41	18	2,171	...	...	...	...	...	...	...	...	...	...	...	...	10	
2,219	952	414	143	35	853	28	12	7	...	...	9	...	...	...	...	...	...	11	
4,079	1,591	682	84	101	1,806	...	...	...	...	...	...	...	...	...	...	...	...	12	
6,787	2,719	845	183	21	3,223	114	12	23	...	...	79	...	...	...	...	...	...	13	
50,101	*17,743*	*6,860*	*1,269*	*487*	*25,498*	*93*	*63*	...	...	...	*30*	...	...	...	...	...	...		
17,942	7,973	2,128	566	81	7,841	...	...	...	...	...	...	...	...	...	...	...	...	14	
2,982	1,110	216	30	2	1,656	...	...	...	...	...	...	...	...	...	...	...	...	15	
18,289	5,455	2,710	475	265	10,124	93	63	...	...	...	30	...	...	...	...	...	...	16	
10,888	3,205	1,806	198	139	5,877	...	...	...	...	...	...	...	...	...	...	...	...	17	

TABLE XV.

OCCUPATION OR MEANS OF LIVELIHOOD.

PART A.—GENERAL TABLE.

Class B.—Preparation and supply

Sub-Class III.—

Order 15.—Building industries.—(concld).

Serial Number.	District.	78.—Stone and marble workers, masons and bricklayers. Total workers and dependants.	Actual workers. Total. Males.	Actual workers. Total. Females.	Actual workers. Partially agriculturist. Males.	Actual workers. Partially agriculturist. Females.	Dependants.	79.—Others (thatchers, building contractors, house painters, tilers, plumbers, locksmiths, etc.) Total workers and dependants.	Actual workers. Total. Males.	Actual workers. Total. Females.	Actual workers. Partially agriculturist. Males.	Actual workers. Partially agriculturist. Females.	Dependants.
	1	560	561	562	563	564	565	566	567	568	569	570	571
	Hyderabad State ..	***101,530***	***37,021***	***15,798***	***2,293***	***913***	***48,711***	***6,872***	***3,112***	***611***	***301***	***44***	***3,149***
1	Hyderabad City ...	5,142	2,763	99	...	...	2,280	80	33	10	...	...	37
2	Atraf-i-balda ...	2,961	1,150	373	48	26	1,438	133	65	18	...	10	50
	Warangal Division ...	***13,228***	***3,442***	***3,044***	***99***	***156***	***6,742***	***2,109***	***1,236***	***120***	***126***	***10***	***753***
3	Warangal ...	5,753	1,487	1,521	60	11	2,745	958	505	120	13	10	333
4	Karimnagar ...	2,712	602	497	13	109	1,613	626	521	...	113	...	105
5	Adilabad ...	4,763	1,353	1,026	26	36	2,384	525	210	...	...	...	315
	Medak Division ...	***17,362***	***7,244***	***3,134***	***596***	***93***	***6,984***	***194***	***51***	...	...	...	***143***
6	Medak ...	4,418	1,338	1,256	196	9	1,821	162	19	...	...	...	143
7	Nizamabad ...	1,223	507	111	43	...	605	32	32	...	...	...	...
8	Mahbubnagar ...	3,572	1,609	540	148	14	1,423	...	...	...	...	...	...
9	Nalgonda ...	8,149	3,790	1,227	209	70	3,132	...	...	...	...	...	...
	Aurangabad Division..	***15,206***	***5,732***	***2,390***	***454***	***175***	***7,084***	***1,979***	***737***	***361***	***2***	...	***881***
10.	Aurangabad ..	3,040	864	543	41	18	1,633	1,202	367	297	...	...	538
11	Bhir ..	1,495	602	365	146	35	528	696	338	42	2	...	316
12	Nander ..	4,064	1,578	682	84	101	1,804	15	13	...	...	...	2
13	Parbhani ...	6,607	2,688	800	183	21	3,119	66	19	22	...	...	25
	Gulbarga Division ...	***47,631***	***16,690***	***6,758***	***1,096***	***463***	***24,183***	***2,377***	***990***	***102***	***173***	***24***	***1,285***
14	Gulbarga ...	17,926	7,957	2,128	566	81	7,841	16	16	...	...	...	...
15	Osmanabad ...	2,982	1,110	216	30	2	1,656	...	...	...	...	...	...
16	Raichur ...	15,835	4,418	2,608	302	241	8,809	2,361	974	102	173	24	1,285
17	Bidar ...	10,888	3,205	1,806	198	139	5,877	...	...	...	...	...	...

TABLE XV.

OCCUPATION OR MEANS OF LIVELIHOOD.

PART A.—GENERAL TABLE.

of material substances.—(*contd*).

Industry.—(*contd*).

Total Order 16.						Order 16.—Construction of means of transport. 80—Cart, carriage, palki, etc., makers and wheel wrights.						Order 16.—Construction of means of transport. 81—Saddlers, harness makers, whip and lash makers.						Serial Number.
Total workers and dependants.	Actual workers. Total. Males.	Actual workers. Total. Females.	Actual workers. Partially agriculturist. Males.	Actual workers. Partially agriculturist. Females.	Dependants.	Total workers and dependants.	Actual workers. Total. Males.	Actual workers. Total. Females.	Actual workers. Partially agriculturist. Males.	Actual workers. Partially agriculturist. Females.	Dependants.	Total workers and dependants.	Actual workers. Total. Males.	Actual workers. Total. Females.	Actual workers. Partially agriculturist. Males.	Actual workers. Partially agriculturist. Females.	Dependants.	
572	573	574	575	576	577	578	579	580	581	582	583	584	585	586	587	588	589	
2,910	***1,832***	***28***	***139***	...	***1,050***	***2,518***	***1,681***	***24***	***38***	...	***813***	***392***	***151***	***4***	***101***	...	***237***	
2,135	1,411	12	...	...	712	2,113	1,404	12	...	...	697	22	7	...	...	...	15	1
376	253	12	14	...	111	376	253	12	14	...	111	...	...	...	...	...	...	2
29	***24***	...	***24***	...	***5***	***29***	***24***	...	***24***	...	***5***	...	...	...	...	...	...	
...	...	...	...	...	...	...	...	...	...	...	...	...	...	...	...	...	...	3
29	24	...	24	...	5	29	24	...	24	...	5	...	...	...	...	...	...	4
...	...	...	...	...	...	...	...	...	...	...	...	...	...	...	...	...	...	5
...	...	...	...	...	...	...	...	...	...	...	...	...	...	...	...	...	...	
...	...	...	...	...	...	...	...	...	...	...	...	...	...	...	...	...	...	6
...	...	...	...	...	...	...	...	...	...	...	...	...	...	...	...	...	...	7
...	...	...	...	...	...	...	...	...	...	...	...	...	...	...	...	...	...	8
...	...	...	...	...	...	...	...	...	...	...	...	...	...	...	...	...	...	9
32	***13***	***1***	...	...	***18***	...	...	...	...	...	...	***32***	***13***	***1***	...	...	***18***	
...	...	...	...	...	...	...	...	...	...	...	...	...	...	...	...	...	...	10
...	...	...	...	...	...	...	...	...	...	...	...	...	...	...	...	...	...	11
32	13	1	...	...	18	...	...	...	...	...	...	32	13	1	...	...	18	12
...	...	...	...	...	...	...	...	...	...	...	...	...	...	...	...	...	...	13
338	***131***	***3***	***101***	...	***204***	...	...	...	...	...	...	***338***	***131***	***3***	***101***	...	***204***	
...	...	...	...	...	...	...	...	...	...	...	...	...	...	...	...	...	...	14
9	4	2	...	...	3	...	...	...	...	...	...	9	4	2	...	...	3	15
...	...	...	...	...	...	...	...	...	...	...	...	...	...	...	...	...	...	16
329	127	1	101	...	201	...	...	...	...	...	...	329	127	1	101	...	201	17

TABLE XV.

OCCUPATION OR MEANS OF LIVELIHOOD.

PART A.—GENERAL TABLE.

Serial Number.	District.	Class B.—Preparation and supply											
		Sub-Class III.—											
		Order 16.—Construction of means of transport.—(concld).						Order 17.—Production and transmission of physical forces (heat, light, electricity, motive power, etc.)					
		82—Ship and boat builders.						83—Gas works, electric light and ice factories.					
		Total workers and dependants.	Actual workers.					Total Workers and Dependants.	Actual workers.				
			Total.		Partially agriculturist.		Dependants.		Total.		Partially agriculturist.		Dependants.
			Males.	Females.	Males.	Females.			Males.	Females.	Males.	Females.	
	1	590	591	592	593	594	595	596	597	598	599	600	601
	Hyderabad State	...	...	...	...	...	...	***78***	***42***	...	...	...	***36***
1	Hyderabad City	...	...	...	...	...	...	78	42	...	...	...	36
2	Atraf-i-balda	...	...	...	...	...	...	...	...	...	...	...	...
	Warangal Division	...	...	...	...	...	...	...	...	...	...	...	...
3	Warangal	...	...	...	...	...	...	...	...	...	...	...	...
4	Karimnagar	...	...	...	...	...	...	...	...	...	...	...	...
5	Adilabad	...	...	...	...	...	...	...	...	...	...	...	...
	Medak Division	...	...	...	...	...	...	...	...	...	...	...	...
6	Medak	...	...	...	...	...	...	...	...	...	...	...	...
7	Nizamabad	...	...	...	...	...	...	...	...	...	...	...	...
8	Mahbubnagar	...	...	...	...	...	...	...	...	...	...	...	...
9	Nalgonda	...	...	...	...	...	...	...	...	...	...	...	...
	Aurangabad Division	...	...	...	...	...	...	...	...	...	...	...	...
10	Aurangabad	...	...	...	...	...	...	...	...	...	...	...	...
11	Bhir	...	...	...	...	...	...	...	...	...	...	...	...
12	Nandor	...	...	...	...	...	...	...	...	...	...	...	...
13	Parbhani	...	...	...	...	...	...	...	...	...	...	...	...
	Gulbarga Divison	...	...	...	...	...	...	...	...	...	...	...	...
14	Gulbarga	...	...	...	...	...	...	...	...	...	...	...	...
15	Osmanabad	...	...	...	...	...	...	...	...	...	...	...	...
16	Raichur	...	...	...	...	...	...	...	...	...	...	...	...
17	Bidar	...	...	...	...	...	...	...	...	...	...	...	...

TABLE XV.

OCCUPATION OR MEANS OF LIVELIHOOD.

PART A.—GENERAL TABLE.

of material substances.—(*contd*).

Industry.—(*contd*).

Total Order 18.						Order 18.—Industries of luxury and those pertaining to literature and the arts and sciences.														
						84—Printers, lithographers, engravers, etc.						85—Newspaper and magazine managers and editors, others journalists, etc.							
Total workers and dependants.	Actual workers. Total. Males.	Actual workers. Total. Females.	Actual workers. Partially agriculturist. Males.	Actual workers. Partially agriculturist. Females.	Dependants.	Total workers and dependants.	Actual workers. Total. Males.	Actual workers. Total. Females.	Actual workers. Partially agriculturist. Males.	Actual workers. Partially agriculturist. Females.	Dependants.	Total workers and dependants.	Actual workers. Total. Males.	Actual workers. Total. Females.	Actual workers. Partially agriculturist. Males.	Actual workers. Partially agriculturist. Females.	Dependants	Serial Number.
602	603	604	605	606	607	608	609	610	611	612	613	614	615	616	617	618	619	
97,951	***34,780***	***9,831***	***3,392***	***1,038***	***53,340***	***697***	***346***	...	...	...	***351***	***47***	***24***	...	...	...	***23***	
6,074	2,300	583	...	...	3,191	485	248	...	...	...	237	47	24	...	...	...	23	1
4,161	1,419	546	75	45	2,196	2	1	...	...	...	1	...	...	...	...	...	...	2
23,770	***7,991***	***1,678***	***816***	***635***	***14,101***	***82***	***35***	...	...	...	***47***	...	...	...	...	...	...	
6,439	2,175	434	185	16	3,830	82	35	...	...	...	47	...	...	...	...	...	...	3
14,662	4,833	1,169	565	602	8,660	...	...	...	...	...	...	...	...	...	...	...	..	4
2,609	983	75	66	17	1,611	...	...	...	...	...	...	...	...	...	...	...	...	5
25,452	***8,942***	***3,703***	***1,215***	***182***	***12,807***	...	...	...	..	...	...	...	...	...	...	...	...	
6,995	2,409	1,530	656	51	3,056	...	...	...	...	...	...	...	...	...	...	...	...	6
3,957	1,421	381	150	17	2,155	...	...	...	...	...	...	...	...	...	...	...	...	7
5,313	1,620	758	164	65	2,935	...	...	...	...	...	...	...	...	...	...	...	..	8
9,187	3,495	1,031	215	46	4,661	...	...	...	...	...	...	...	...	...	...	...	...	9
20,694	***8,218***	***1,666***	***773***	***54***	***10,810***	***109***	***52***	...	...	...	***57***	...	...	...	...	...	...	
5,421	1,863	730	165	19	2,828	106	49	...	...	...	57	...	...	...	...	...	...	10
3,175	1,204	201	158	8	1,767	...	...	...	...	...	...	...	...	...	...	...	...	11
3,537	1,462	155	120	14	1,920	3	3	...	...	...	...	...	...	...	...	...	...	12
8,561	3,689	577	330	13	4,295	...	...	...	...	...	...	...	...	...	...	...	...	13
17,800	***5,910***	***1,655***	***513***	***122***	***10,235***	***19***	***10***	...	...	...	***9***	...	...	...	...	...	...	
6,280	1,925	961	168	10	3,394	19	10	...	...	...	9	...	...	...	...	...	...	14
3,232	1,015	108	81	9	2,109	...	...	...	...	...	...	...	...	...	...	...	...	15
3,528	1,410	152	104	2	1,936	...	...	...	...	...	...	...	...	...	..	...	...	16
4,760	1,560	434	160	101	2,766	...	...	...	...	..	...	...	...	...	...	...	...	17

TABLE XV.

OCCUPATION OR MEANS OF LIVELIHOOD

PART A.—GENERAL TABLE.

Serial Number.	District.	Class B.—Preparation and supply											
		Sub-Class III.—											
		Order 18.—Industries of luxury and those											
		86—Book binders and stitchers, envelope makers, etc.						87.—Makers of musical instruments.					
		Total workers and dependants.	Actual workers. Total. Males.	Actual workers. Total. Females.	Actual workers. Partially agriculturist. Males.	Actual workers. Partially agriculturist. Females.	Dependants.	Total workers and dependants.	Actual workers. Total. Males.	Actual workers. Total. Females.	Actual workers. Partially agriculturist. Males.	Actual workers. Partially agriculturist. Females.	Dependants.
	1	620	621	622	623	624	625	626	627	628	629	630	631
	Hyderabad State ...	***129***	***77***	...	...	...	***52***	***358***	***148***	***30***	...	...	***18***
1	Hyderabad City ...	83	41	...	...	...	42	65	36	...	...	...	2
2	Atraf-i-balda ...	...	...	...	...	...	...	...	...	...	...	...	...
	Warangal Division ..	...	...	...	...	...	...	***293***	***112***	***30***	...	...	***15***
3	Warangal ...	...	...	...	...	...	...	...	...	...	...	...	...
4	Karimnagar ...	...	...	...	...	...	...	293	112	30	...	...	1[illegible]
5	Adilabad ...	...	...	...	...	...	...	...	...	...	...	...	...
	Medak Division ...	...	...	...	...	...	...	...	...	...	...	...	...
6	Medak ...	...	...	...	...	...	...	...	...	...	...	...	...
7	Nizamabad ..	...	...	...	...	...	...	...	...	...	...	...	...
8	Mahbubnagar ...	...	...	...	...	...	...	...	...	...	...	...	...
9	Nalgonda ...	...	...	...	...	...	...	...	...	...	...	...	...
	Aurangabad Division.	***46***	***36***	...	...	...	***10***	...	...	...	...	...	...
10	Aurangabad ...	...	...	...	...	...	...	...	...	...	...	...	...
11	Bhir ..	...	...	...	...	...	...	...	...	...	...	...	...
12	Nander ...	46	36	...	...	...	10	...	...	...	...	...	...
13	Parbhani ...	...	...	...	...	...	...	...	...	...	...	...	...
	Gulbarga Division ...	...	...	...		...	...	...	...	...	...	...	...
14	Gulbarga ...	...	...	...	...	...	...	...	...	...	...	...	...
15	Osmanabad ..	...	...	...	...	...	...	...	...	...	...	...	...
16	Raichur ...	...	...	...	...	...	...	...	...	...	...	...	...
17	Bidar ...	...	...	...	...	...	...	...	...	...	...	...	...

TABLE XV.

OCCUPATION OR MEANS OF LIVELIHOOD.

PART A.—GENERAL TABLE.

of material substances.—(*contd*).

Industry.—(*contd*).

pertaining to literature and the arts and sciences.—(*contd*).

88—Makers of watches and clocks and optical, photographic and surgical instruments.						89—Workers in precious stones and metals, enamellers, imitation jewellery makers, gilders, etc.						90—Makers of bangles, rosaries, bead and other necklaces, spangles, lingams and sacred threads.						Serial Number.
Total workers and dependants.	Actual workers. Total. Males.	Actual workers. Total. Females.	Actual workers. Partially agriculturist. Males.	Actual workers. Partially agriculturist. Females.	Dependants.	Total workers and dependants.	Actual workers. Total. Males.	Actual workers. Total. Females.	Actual workers. Partially agriculturist. Males.	Actual workers. Partially agriculturist. Females.	Dependants.	Total workers and dependants.	Actual workers. Total. Males.	Actual workers. Total. Females.	Actual workers. Partially agriculturist. Males.	Actual workers. Partially agriculturist. Females.	Dependants.	
632	633	634	635	636	637	638	639	640	641	642	643	644	645	646	647	648	649	
204	***89***	...	...	...	***115***	***93,489***	***33,079***	***9,452***	***3,366***	***1,035***	***50,958***	***2,871***	***968***	***314***	***26***	***3***	***1,589***	
153	59	...	...	...	94	3,971	1,470	514	...	...	1,987	1,242	416	69	...	...	757	1
5	3	...	...	...	2	4,154	1,415	546	75	45	2,193	...	...	...	...	...	...	2
...	...	...	...	...	...	***23,071***	***7,696***	***1,612***	***799***	***635***	***13,763***	***298***	***139***	***30***	***17***	...	***129***	
...	...	...	...	...	...	6,317	2,110	434	184	16	3,773	33	26	...	1	...	7	3
...	...	...	...	...	...	14,094	4,603	1,108	549	602	8,383	[illegible]	113	30	16	...	122	4
...	...	...	...	...	...	2,660	983	70	66	17	1,607	...	...	...	...	...	...	5
1	***1***	...	...	...	...	***24,716***	***8,775***	***3,558***	***1,212***	***179***	***12,383***	***649***	***136***	***121***	***3***	***3***	***392***	
...	...	...	...	...	...	6,615	2,315	1,512	656	54	2,786	382	94	18	...	...	270	6
...	...	...	...	...	...	3,891	1,406	357	150	17	2,128	8	...	1	...	...	7	7
...	...	...	...	...	...	5,113	1,607	656	161	62	2,850	197	11	102	3	3	81	8
1	1	...	...	..	...	9,099	3,447	1,033	245	46	4,619	62	31	...	..	...	31	9
...	...	...	...	...	...	***20,142***	***7,996***	***1,572***	***767***	***54***	***10,574***	***395***	***134***	***94***	***6***	...	***167***	
...	...	...	...	...	...	5,315	1,814	730	165	19	2,771	...	...	...	..	...	...	10
...	...	...	...	...	...	3,142	1,183	204	155	8	1,755	33	21	...	[illegible]	...	12	11
...	...	...	...	...	...	3,401	1,387	136	126	14	1,878	87	36	19	...	...	32	12
...	...	...	...	...	...	8,284	3,612	502	327	13	4,170	275	77	73	[illegible]	...	123	13
45	***26***	...	...	...	***19***	***17,435***	***5,727***	***1,650***	***813***	***122***	***10,058***	***287***	***143***	...	...	...	***144***	
...	...	...	...	...	...	6,247	1,911	956	168	10	3,380	...	...	...	...	...	...	14
...	...	...	...	...	...	3,232	1,015	108	81	9	2,109	..	...	...	...	...	...	15
...	...	...	...	...	...	3,241	1,267	152	104	2	1,822	287	143	...	...	...	144	16
45	26	...	...	...	19	4,715	1,534	434	160	101	2,747	...	...	...	...	...	...	17

TABLE XV.

OCCUPATION OR MEANS OF LIVELIHOOD.

PART A.—GENERAL TABLE.

Class B.—Preparation and supply

Sub-Class III.—

Order 18.—Industries of luxury and those pertaining to literature and the arts and sciences.—(concld.

Serial Number.	District.	91—Toy, kite, cage, fishing tackle, etc. makers, taxidermists, etc. — Total workers and dependants.	Actual workers. Total. Males.	Actual workers. Total. Females.	Actual workers. Partially agriculturist. Males.	Actual workers. Partially agriculturist. Females.	Dependants.	92—Others, including managers, persons other than performers employed in theatres and other places of public entertainment, employees of public societies, race-course service, huntsmen, etc. — Total workers and dependants.	Actual workers. Total. Males.	Actual workers. Total. Females.	Actual workers. Partially agriculturist. Males.	Actual workers. Partially agriculturist. Females.	Dependants.
	1	650	651	652	653	654	655	656	657	658	659	660	661
	Hyderabad State ...	***125***	***34***	***35***	...	...	***56***	***31***	***15***	...	...	...	***16***
1	Hyderabad City ...	22	4	...	...	...	18	6	2	...	...	...	4
2	Atraf-i-balda ...	...	...	...	...	...	...	...	...	...	...	...	...
	Warangal Division ...	***19***	***5***	***6***	...	...	***8***	***7***	***4***		...	...	***3***
3	Warangal	...	...	...	...	...	...	7	4	...	...	...	3
4	Karimnagar	10	5	1	...	...	4	...	...	...	...	...	...
5	Adilabad	9	...	5	...	...	4	...	...	...	...	...	...
	Medak Division ...	***70***	***21***	***24***	...	...	***25***	***16***	***9***	...	...	...	***7***
6	Medak	...	...	...	...	...	...	...	...	...	...	...	...
7	Nizamabad	58	15	23	...	...	20	...	...	...	...	...	...
8	Mahbubnagar ...	3	2	...	...	...	1	...	...	...	...	...	...
9	Nalgonda	9	4	1	...	...	4	16	9	...	...	...	7
	Aurangabad Division	...	...	...	...	...	...	***2***	...	...	...	...	***2***
10	Aurangabad	...	...	...	...	...	...	...	...	..	...	...	...
11	Bhir	...	...	...	...	...	...	...	...	...	...	...	...
12	Nander	...	...	...	...	...	...	...	...	...	...	...	...
13	Parbhani	...	...	...	...	...	...	2	...	...	...	...	2
	Gulbarga Division ...	***14***	***4***	***5***	...	...	***5***	...	...	...	...	...	...
14	Gulbarga	14	4	5	...	...	5	...	...	...	...	...	...
15	Osmanabad	...	...	...	...	...	...	...	...	...	...	...	...
16	Raichur	...	...	...	...	...	...	...	...	...	...	...	...
17	Bidar	...	...	...	...	...	...	...	...	...	...	...	...

TABLE XV.

OCCUPATION OR MEANS OF LIVELIHOOD.

PART A.—GENERAL TABLE.

of material substances.—(*contd*).

Industry.—(*concld*). Order 19.—Industries concerned with refuse matter. 93.—Sweepers, scavengers, dust and sweeping contractors. Total workers and dependants.	Actual workers. Total. Males.	Actual workers. Total. Females.	Actual workers. Partially agriculturist. Males.	Actual workers. Partially agriculturist. Females	Dependants.	Sub-Class IV—Transport. Total Order 20. Total workers and dependants.	Actual workers. Total. Males.	Actual workers. Total. Females.	Actual workers. Partially agriculturist. Males.	Actual workers. Partially agriculturist. Females.	Dependants.	Order 20.—Transport by water. 94.—Harbour works, dockyards and pilots. Total workers and dependants.	Actual workers. Total. Males.	Actual workers. Total. Females.	Actual workers. Partially agriculturist. Males.	Actual workers. Partially agriculturist. Females.	Dependants.	Serial Number.
662	663	664	665	666	667	668	669	670	671	672	673	674	675	676	677	678	679	
6,728	***1,976***	***1,699***	***206***	***108***	***3,053***	***2,667***	***1,344***	***164***	***186***	***74***	***1,159***	...	...	...	...	...	...	
2,817	790	652	...	...	1,375	5	3	...	...	...	2	...	...	...	...	...	...	1
54	16	1	...	...	37	...	...	...	...	...	...	...	...	...	...	...	...	2
99	***35***	***6***	...	...	***58***	***977***	***376***	***105***	***64***	***51***	***496***	...	...	...	...	...	...	
63	31	...	...	...	32	157	42	35	4	1	79	...	...	...	...	...	...	3
...	...	...	...	...	...	820	333	70	60	59	417	...	...	...	...	...	...	4
36	4	6	...	...	26	...	...	...	...	...	...	...	...	...	...	...	...	5
1,478	***50***	***689***	***4***	***108***	***739***	***1,348***	***811***	***44***	***97***	***23***	***493***	...	...	...	...	...	...	
411	5	266	...	102	110	555	234	27	14	23	294	...	...	...	...	...	...	6
19	11	...	...	...	8	288	161	13	38	...	114	...	...	...	...	...	...	7
993	19	411	4	6	563	463	392	3	40	...	63	...	...	...	...	...	...	8
55	15	12	...	...	28	42	24	1	5	...	17	...	...	...	...	...	...	9
1,222	***697***	***62***	***178***	...	***463***	***332***	***149***	***15***	***25***	...	***168***	...	...	...	...	...	...	
326	74	21	3	...	231	140	58	15	...	...	67	...	...	...	...	...	...	10
183	98	36	...	...	49	120	74	...	25	...	46	...	...	...	...	...	...	11
45	24	...	...	...	21	19	10	...	...	...	9	...	...	...	...	...	...	12
668	501	5	175	...	162	53	7	...	...	...	46	...	...	...	...	...	...	13
1,058	***388***	***289***	***24***	...	***381***	***5***	***5***	...	...	...	...	...	...	...	...	...	...	
673	368	87	23	...	218	...	...	...	...	...	...	...	...	...	...	...	...	14
68	13	12	...	...	43	...	...	...	...	...	...	...	...	...	...	...	...	15
...	...	...	...	...	...	5	5	...	...	...	...	...	...	...	...	...	...	16
317	7	190	1	...	120	...	...	...	...	...	...	...	...	...	...	...	...	17

TABLE XV.

OCCUPATION OR MEANS OF LIVELIHOOD.

PART A.—GENERAL TABLE.

Serial Number.	District.	Class B.—Preparation and supply / Sub-Class IV.— / Order 20—Transport.											
		95.—Ship owners and their employees, ship brokers, ships officers, engineers, mariners and firemen.						96.—Persons employed on the maintenance of streams, rivers and canals (including construct[illegible]					
		Total workers and dependants.	Actual workers. Total. Males.	Actual workers. Total. Females.	Actual workers. Partially agriculturist. Males.	Actual workers. Partially agriculturist. Females.	Dependants.	Total workers and dependants.	Actual workers. Total. Males.	Actual workers. Total. Females.	Actual workers. Partially agriculturist. Males.	Actual workers. Partially agriculturist. Females.	Dependants.
	1	680	681	682	683	684	685	686	687	688	689	690	691
	Hyderabad State ...	...	...	...	...	...	...	***2,336***	***1,214***	***129***	***173***	***73***	***99***
1	Hyderabad City ...	...	...	...	...	...	...	...	...	...	...	...	...
2	Atraf-i-balda ...	...	...	...	...	...	...	...	...	...	...	...	...
	Warangal Division ...	...	...	...	...	...	...	***712***	***293***	***70***	***60***	***50***	***34***
3	Warangal ..	...	...	...	...	...	...	...	...	...	...	...	...
4	Karimnagar ...	...	...	...	...	...	...	712	293	70	60	50	34
5	Adilabad ...	...	...	...	...	...	...	...	...	...	...	...	...
	Medak Division ...	...	...	...	...	..	..	***1,329***	***794***	***44***	***88***	***23***	***49***
6	Medak	...	...	...	...	...	...	536	217	27	5	23	29
7	Nizamabad ..	...	...	...	...	...	...	288	161	13	38	...	11
8	Mahbubnagar ..	...	...	...	...	...	...	463	392	3	40	...	6
9	Nalgonda... ..	...	...	...	...	...	...	42	24	1	5	...	1
	Aurangabad Division	...	...	...	...	...	...	***295***	***127***	***15***	***25***	...	***15***
10	Aurangabad ..	...	...	...	...	...	...	122	46	15	...	...	6
11	Bhir	...	...	...	...	...	...	120	74	...	25	...	4
12	Nander	...	...	...	...	...	...	...	...	...	...	...	...
13	Parbhani ..	...	...	...	...	...	...	53	7	...	...	...	4
	Gulbarga Division ..	...	...	...	...	...	...	...	...	...	...	...	...
14	Gulbarga ..	...	...	...	...	...	...	...	...	...	...	...	...
15	Osmanabad ..	...	...	...	...	...	..	...	...	...	...	...	...
16	Raichur	...	...	...	...	...	...	...	...	...	...	...	...
17	Bidar	...	...	...	...	...	...	...	...	...	...	...	...

TABLE XV.

OCCUPATION OR MEANS OF LIVELIHOOD.

PART A.—GENERAL TABLE.

of material substances.—(*contd*).

Transport—(*contd*).

by water—(*concld.*) 97.—Boat owners, boatmen and towmen.						Total Order 21.						Order 21—Transport by road. 98.—Persons employed on the construction and maintenance of roads and bridges.						Serial Number.
Total workers and dependants.	Actual workers. Total. Males.	Actual workers. Total. Females.	Partially agriculturist. Males.	Partially agriculturist. Females.	Dependants.	Total workers and dependants.	Actual workers. Total. Males.	Actual workers. Total. Females.	Partially agriculturist. Males.	Partially agriculturist. Females.	Dependants.	Total workers and dependants.	Actual workers. Total. Males.	Actual workers. Total. Females.	Partially agriculturist. Males.	Partially agriculturist. Females.	Dependants.	
692	693	694	695	696	697	698	699	700	701	702	703	704	705	706	707	708	709	
331	**130**	**35**	**13**	**1**	**166**	**111,476**	**41,919**	**18,004**	**3,215**	**773**	**51,553**	**51,879**	**15,891**	**13,203**	**758**	**437**	**22,785**	
5	3	...	...	...	2	12,252	6,798	153	39	...	5,301	194	76	13	...	...	105	1
...	...	...	...	...	...	4,685	2,130	837	65	3	1,718	1,173	487	300	45	3	386	2
265	**83**	**35**	**4**	**1**	**147**	**21,386**	**8,131**	**4,023**	**502**	**206**	**9,232**	**11,941**	**4,082**	**3,297**	**237**	**181**	**4,562**	
157	43	35	4	1	79	11,016	4,049	2,404	294	64	4,563	5,817	1,789	1,960	177	62	2,068	3
108	40	...	...	...	68	6,680	2,883	1,126	207	90	2,671	3,777	1,610	853	60	67	1,314	4
...	...	...	...	...	...	3,690	1,199	493	1	52	1,998	2,347	683	481	...	52	1,180	5
19	**17**	...	**9**	...	**2**	**26,290**	**9,695**	**5,144**	**1,205**	**206**	**11,451**	**13,205**	**3,785**	**4,147**	**249**	**156**	**5,273**	
19	17	...	9	...	2	4,177	1,886	851	293	41	1,440	2,124	528	831	36	38	765	6
...	...	...	...	...	...	4,427	1,678	419	317	58	2,330	544	298	60	17	11	186	7
...	...	...	...	...	...	10,432	4,265	1,488	473	91	4,679	4,957	1,808	1,214	175	91	1,935	8
...	...	..	...	...	...	7,254	1,866	2,386	122	16	3,002	5,580	1,151	2,042	21	16	2,387	9
37	**22**	...	...	...	**15**	**23,193**	**7,972**	**3,796**	**248**	**71**	**11,425**	**13,930**	**4,372**	**2,986**	**146**	**64**	**6,572**	
18	12	...	...	...	6	2,481	613	370	23	4	1,498	835	245	203	3	...	387	10
...	...	...	...	...	...	2,640	1,195	663	56	1	782	1,123	425	509	25	...	189	11
19	10	...	...	...	9	6,229	2,036	1,045	72	56	3,148	4,388	1,147	900	27	54	2,341	12
...	...	...	...	...	...	11,843	4,128	1,718	97	10	5,997	7,584	2,555	1,374	91	10	3,655	13
5	**5**	...	...	...	...	**23,670**	**7,193**	**4,051**	**1,156**	**287**	**12,426**	**11,436**	**3,089**	**2,460**	**81**	**33**	**5,887**	
...	...	...	...	...	...	11,248	3,240	1,764	534	44	6,244	6,734	1,705	1,468	10	3	3,561	14
...	...	...	...	...	...	3,573	1,283	504	134	1	1,786	2,213	670	413	9	...	1,130	15
5	5	...	...	...	...	3,991	1,027	1,036	131	141	1,928	2,489	714	579	62	30	1,196	16
...	...	...	...	...	...	4,858	1,643	747	357	101	2,468	...	...	...	...	...	...	17

TABLE XV.

OCCUPATION OR MEANS OF LIVELIHOOD.

PART A.—GENERAL TABLE.

Class B.—Preparation and supply

Sub-Class IV.—

Order 21.—Transport

Serial Number.	District.	99.—Cart owners and drivers, coachmen, stable boys, tramway, mail Carriage, etc., managers and employes (excluding private servants.)						100—Palki, etc., bearers and owners.					
		Total workers and dependants.	Actual workers.				Dependants.	Total workers and dependants.	Actual workers.				Dependants.
			Total.		Partially agriculturist.				Total.		Partially agriculturist.		
			Males.	Females.	Males.	Females.			Males.	Females.	Males.	Females.	
	1	710	711	712	713	714	715	716	717	718	719	720	721
	Hyderabad State ...	***47,907***	***21,226***	***3,666***	***1,487***	***270***	***23,015***	***1,674***	***987***	***47***	***13***	***3***	***640***
1	Hyderabad City ...	9,439	5,467	16	19	...	3,962	357	165	...	...	...	192
2	Atraf-i-balda ...	3,047	1,323	533	19	...	1,191	376	279	...	1	...	97
	Warangal Division ...	***8,095***	***3,507***	***638***	***223***	***21***	***3,950***	***358***	***135***	***31***	...	***3***	***192***
3	Warangal ...	4,791	2,023	410	77	1	2,358	79	50	...	...	...	29
4	Karimnagar ...	2,179	1,075	224	145	20	880	272	80	31	...	3	161
5	Adilabad ...	1,125	409	4	1	...	712	7	5	...	...	...	2
	Medak Division ...	***12,141***	***5,331***	***981***	***823***	***50***	***5,829***	***561***	***390***	***16***	***12***	...	***155***
6	Medak ...	1,772	1,185	12	245	3	575	281	173	8	12	...	106
7	Nizamabad ...	3,731	1,248	359	300	47	2,124	138	129	...	...	...	9
8	Mahbubnagar ...	5,133	2,268	266	180	...	2,599	142	88	8	...	...	40
9	Nalgonda ...	1,505	630	344	98	...	531	...	...	...	...	...	...
	Aurangabad Division.	***7,015***	***2,647***	***563***	***88***	***4***	***3,805***	***9***	***5***	...	...	...	
10	Aurangabad ...	1,224	201	92	19	2	931	9	5	...	...	...	
11	Bhir ...	1,257	625	126	26	...	506	...	...	...	...	...	...
12	Nander ...	1,702	795	145	38	2	762	...	...	...	...	...	...
13	Parbhani ...	2,832	1,020	200	5	...	1,606	...	...	...	...	...	...
	Gulbarga Division ...	***8,170***	***2,951***	***941***	***315***	***195***	***4,278***	***13***	***13***	...	...	...	...
14	Gulbarga ...	2,881	990	223	52	13	1,668	13	13	...	...	...	...
15	Osmanabad ...	993	476	84	2	1	433	...	...	...	...	...	...
16	Raichur ...	1,254	313	338	69	111	603	...	...	...	...	...	...
17	Bidar	3,042	1,172	296	192	70	1,574	...	...	...	...	...	...

TABLE XV.

OCCUPATION OR MEANS OF LIVELIHOOD.

PART A.—GENERAL TABLE.

of material substances.—(*contd*).

Transport.—(*contd*).

by road —(*concld*).

101.—Pack elephant, camel, mule, ass and bullock, owners and drivers.						102.—Porters and messengers.						Total Order 22.						
Total workers and dependants.	Actual workers. Total. Males.	Actual workers. Total. Females.	Actual workers. Partially agriculturist. Males.	Actual workers. Partially agriculturist. Females.	Dependants.	Total workers and dependants.	Actual workers. Total. Males.	Actual workers. Total. Females.	Actual workers. Partially agriculturist. Males.	Actual workers. Partially agriculturist. Females.	Dependants.	Total workers and dependants.	Actual workers. Total. Males.	Actual workers. Total. Females.	Actual workers. Partially agriculturist. Males.	Actual workers. Partially agriculturist. Females.	Dependants.	Serial Number.
722	723	724	725	726	727	728	729	730	731	732	733	734	735	736	737	738	739	
1,335	***449***	***257***	***13***	...	***629***	***8,681***	***3,366***	***831***	***944***	***63***	***4,484***	***18,609***	***7,861***	***698***	***5***	***3***	***10,050***	
205	86	10	...	...	109	2,057	1,004	120	20	...	933	5,308	3,271	4	...	...	2,033	1
63	29	...	...	...	34	26	12	4	...	...	10	1,624	477	27	...	...	1,120	2
...	...	...	...	...	...	***992***	***407***	***57***	***42***	***1***	***528***	***3,237***	***1,204***	***112***	***1***	***3***	***1,921***	
...	...	...	...	...	...	329	187	34	40	1	108	3,231	1,204	109	1	3	1,918	3
...	...	...	...	...	...	452	118	18	2	...	316	6	...	3	...	..	3	4
...	...	...	...	...	...	211	102	5	...	...	104	...	...	...	...	...	...	5
...	...	...	...	...	...	***383***	***189***	...	***121***	...	***194***	***1,559***	***554***	***25***	...	...	***980***	
...	...	...	...	...	...	...	...	...	...	...	...	551	136	...	...	...	415	6
...	...	...	...	...	...	14	3	...	...	...	11	567	235	20	...	...	312	7
...	...	...	...	...	...	200	101	...	118	...	99	75	42	...	...	..	33	8
...	...	...	...	...	...	169	85	...	3	...	81	366	141	5	...	...	220	9
14	***8***	...	...	...	***6***	***2,225***	***940***	***247***	***14***	***3***	***1,038***	***6,160***	***1,907***	***509***	***4***	...	***3,744***	
...	...	...	...	...	...	413	162	75	1	2	176	1,288	708	69	4	...	511	10
...	...	...	...	...	...	260	145	28	5	1	87	...	...	...	...	...	...	11
10	8	...	...	...	2	129	86	...	7	...	43	132	35	32	...	...	65	12
4	...	...	...	...	4	1,423	547	144	1	..	732	4,740	1,164	408	...	...	3,168	13
1,053	***326***	***247***	***13***	...	***480***	***2,998***	***814***	***403***	***747***	***59***	***1,781***	***721***	***448***	***21***	...	...	***252***	
...	...	...	...	...	...	1,620	532	73	472	28	1,015	274	152	10	...	...	112	14
...	...	...	...	...	...	367	137	7	123	...	223	156	105	11	...	...	40	15
...	...	...	...	...	...	248	...	119	...	...	129	291	191	...	...	...	100	16
1,053	326	247	13	...	480	763	145	204	152	31	414	...	...	...	...	...	...	17

TABLE XV.

OCCUPATION OR MEANS OF LIVELIHOOD.

PART A.—GENERAL TABLE.

Class B.—Preparation and supply

Sub-class IV.—

Order 22.—Transport by rail.—(concld.)

Serial Number.	District.	103.—Railway employes of all kinds other than construction coolies.						104.—Labourers employed on railway construction.					
		Total workers and dependants.	Actual workers.				Dependants.	Total workers and dependants.	Actual workers.				Dependants.
			Total.		Partially agriculturist.				Total.		Partially agriculturist.		
			Males.	Females.	Males.	Females.			Males.	Females.	Males.	Females.	
	1	740	741	742	743	744	745	746	747	748	749	750	751
	Hyderabad State ...	***13,794***	***6,328***	***210***	***5***	***3***	***7,256***	***4,815***	***1,533***	***488***	...	...	***2,794***
1	Hyderabad City ...	4,616	2,848	3	...	...	1,765	692	423	1	...	...	268
2	Atraf-i-balda ...	1,268	351	...	...	...	917	356	126	27	...	...	203
	Warangal Division ...	***2,761***	***1,034***	***99***	***1***	***3***	***1,628***	***476***	***170***	***13***	...	...	***293***
3	Warangal ...	2,755	1,034	96	1	3	1,625	476	170	13	...	...	293
4	Karimnagar ...	6	...	3	...	...	3	...	...	...	...	...	...
5	Adilabad ...	..	...	...	...	...	...	...	...	...	...	...	...
	Medak Division ...	***1,193***	***403***	***2***	...	...	***788***	***366***	***151***	***23***	...	...	***192***
6	Medak ...	405	66	...	...	...	339	146	70	...	...	...	76
7	Nizamabad ...	505	221	1	...	...	283	62	14	19	...	...	29
8	Mahbubnagar ...	65	32	...	...	...	23	10	10	...	...	..	...
9	Nalgonda ...	218	84	1	...	..	133	148	57	4	...	...	87
	Aurangabad Division .	***3,303***	***1,289***	***93***	***4***	...	***1,921***	***2,857***	***618***	***416***	...	...	***1,823***
10	Aurangabad ...	726	422	...	4	...	304	562	286	69	...	...	207
11	Bhir ...	...	...	...	...	...	...	...	...	...	...	...	...
12	Nander ...	12	4	1	...	...	7	120	31	31	...	...	58
13	Parbhani ...	2,565	863	92	...	...	1,610	2,175	301	316	...	...	1,558
	Gulbarga Division ...	***653***	***403***	***13***	...	...	***237***	***68***	***45***	***8***	...	...	***15***
14	Gulbarga ...	274	152	10	...	...	112	...	...	...	...	...	...
15	Osmanabad ...	125	91	3	...	...	31	31	14	8	...	...	9
16	Raichur ...	254	160	...	...	...	94	37	31	...	...	...	6
17	Bidar ..	...	...	...	...	...	...	...	...	...	...	...	...

TABLE XV.

OCCUPATION OR MEANS OF LIVELIHOOD.

PART A—GENERAL TABLE.

of material substances.—(*contd.*)

Transport.—(*concld*). Order 23.—Post office, telegraph and telephone services. 105.—Post offices, telegraph and telephone services. Total workers and dependants.	Actual workers. Total. Males.	Actual workers. Total. Females.	Actual workers. Partially agriculturist. Males.	Actual workers. Partially agriculturist. Females.	Dependants.	Sub-Class V.—Trade. Order 24.—Banks, establishments of credit, exchange and insurance. 106.—Bank, managers, money-lenders, exchange and insurance agents, money changers and brokers and their employes. Total workers and dependants.	Actual workers. Total. Males.	Actual workers. Total. Females.	Actual workers. Partially agriculturist. Males.	Actual workers. Partially agriculturist. Females.	Dependants.	Order 25.—Brokerage commission and export. 107.—Brokers, commission agents, commercial travellers, warehouse owners and employes. Total workers and dependants.	Actual workers. Total. Males.	Actual workers. Total. Females.	Actual workers. Partially agriculturist. Males.	Actual workers. Partially agriculturist. Females.	Dependants.	Serial Number.
752	753	754	755	756	757	758	759	760	761	762	763	764	765	766	767	768	769	
1,199	437	...	17	...	762	22,223	7,313	2,382	712	120	12,528	3,588	794	532	15	25	2,262	
897	301	...	...	...	596	2,216	857	37	1	...	1,352	2,788	474	444	3	...	1,870	1
61	9	...	...	...	52	607	287	73	2[illegible]	5	247	...	...	...	...	...	...	2
11	7	...	...	...	4	3,391	1,210	462	76	15	1,719	226	99	35	...	...	92	
11	7	...	...	...	4	1,232	390	190	8	1	652	21	6	...	...	...	15	3
...	...	...	...	...	...	593	99	150	6	...	344	1	1	...	...	...	...	4
...	...	...	...	...	...	1,566	721	122	62	14	723	204	92	35	...	...	77	5
78	42	...	13	...	36	1,977	631	437	14	6	909	15	13	...	...	...	2	
...	...	...	...	...	...	119	53	36	...	4	30	14	12	...	...	...	2	6
7	5	...	13	...	2	613	92	140	6	2	381	...	...	...	...	..	...	7
60	35	...	...	...	25	970	350	259	7	...	361	...	...	...	...	...	...	8
11	2	...	...	...	9	275	136	2	1	...	137	1	1	...	...	...	...	9
93	53	...	4	...	40	7,561	2,585	509	496	38	4,467	149	29	...	2	...	120	
9	4	...	4	...	5	1,878	448	114	165	16	1,316	30	6	...	...	...	24	10
4[illegible]	29	...	...	...	18	1,113	380	167	89	3	566	...	...	...	...	...	...	11
1	1	...	...	...	...	1,295	527	68	85	10	700	46	12	...	1	...	34	12
36	19	..	...	...	17	3,275	1,230	160	157	9	1,885	73	11	...	1	...	62	13
59	25	...	...	...	34	6,441	1,743	864	103	56	3,834	410	179	53	10	25	178	
22	6	...	...	...	16	2,854	846	308	58	24	1,700	274	112	50	7	25	112	14
32	17	...	...	...	15	448	180	28	5	3	240	8	3	...	...	...	5	15
5	2	...	...	...	3	925	95	334	7	...	496	...	...	...	...	...	...	16
...	...	...	...	...	...	2,214	622	194	33	29	1,398	128	64	3	3	...	61	17

TABLE XV.

OCCUPATION OR MEANS OF LIVELIHOOD.

PART A.—GENERAL TABLE.

Class B.—Preparation and supply

Sub-Class V.—

Serial Number.	District.	Order 26.—Trade in textiles. 108.—Trade in piece-goods, wool, cotton, silk, hair and other textiles. Total workers and dependants.	Actual workers. Total. Males.	Actual workers. Total. Females.	Actual workers. Partially agriculturist. Males.	Actual workers. Partially agriculturist. Females.	Dependants.	27.—Trade in skins, leather and furs. 109.—Trade in skins, leather, furs, feathers, horn, etc. Total Workers and Dependants.	Actual workers. Total. Males.	Actual workers. Total. Females.	Actual workers. Partially agriculturist. Males.	Actual workers. Partially agriculturist. Females.	Dependants.
	1	770	771	772	773	774	775	776	777	778	779	[illegible]	[illegible]
	Hyderabad State ...	***81,139***	***32,680***	***9,108***	***3,359***	***469***	***39,351***	***15,218***	***6,165***	***2,163***	***1,201***	***465***	***6,890***
1	Hyderabad City ...	3,100	1,283	70	...	...	1,747	584	293	20	...	...	271
2	Atraf-i-balda ...	5,701	1,944	1,451	81	10	2,306	494	123	41	3	...	330
	Warangal Division ...	***25,333***	***11,500***	***2,817***	***703***	***114***	***11,016***	***2,818***	***1,082***	***555***	***126***	...	***1,181***
3	Warangal ...	8,622	4,561	651	174	19	3,410	780	420	18	76	...	342
4	Karimnagar ...	14,026	5,934	1,488	471	95	6,604	2,036	669	537	110	...	839
5	Adilabad ...	2,685	1,005	678	55	...	1,002	2	2	...	...	...	...
	Medak Division ...	***11,845***	***5,370***	***1,726***	***665***	***51***	***4,749***	***8,927***	***3,411***	***1,322***	***952***	***365***	***4,194***
6	Medak ...	4,280	2,348	342	443	10	1,590	5,570	2,598	592	893	255	2,380
7	Nizamabad ..	2,242	734	430	64	4	1,078	1,463	446	239	5	...	778
8	Mahbubnagar ...	2,574	1,171	588	94	22	815	1,191	136	403	15	100	652
9	Nalgonda ...	2,749	1,117	366	64	15	1,266	703	231	88	39	10	384
	Aurangabad Division.	***17,612***	***7,353***	***1,004***	***974***	***53***	***9,255***	***938***	***570***	***28***	***15***	...	***340***
10	Aurangabad ...	3,171	1,411	158	545	20	1,602	...	...	...	...	...	...
11	Bhir ...	1,576	817	97	44	1	662	523	389	...	12	...	134
12	Nander ...	4,239	1,840	164	132	2	2,235	256	122	19	3	...	115
13	Parbhani ...	8,626	3,285	585	253	30	4,756	159	59	9	...	...	91
	Gulbarga Division ...	***17,548***	***5,230***	***2,040***	***936***	***241***	***10,278***	***1,457***	***686***	***197***	***105***	***100***	***574***
14	Gulbarga ...	6,479	1,945	660	106	65	3,874	493	307	26	77	...	160
15	Osmanabad ...	1,513	578	187	36	...	748	133	35	3	...	...	95
16	Raichur ...	6,147	1,453	791	603	119	3,903	...	...	...	...	...	...
17	Bidar ...	3,409	1,254	402	191	57	1,753	831	344	168	28	100	319

TABLE XV.

OCCUPATION OR MEANS OF LIVELIHOOD.

PART A.—GENERAL TABLE.

of material substances.—(*contd*).

Trade.—(*contd*).

Order 28.—Trade in wood. 110.—Trade in wood (not fire-wood) cork, bark, etc. Total workers and dependants.	Actual workers. Total. Males.	Actual workers. Total. Females.	Partially agriculturist. Males.	Partially agriculturist. Females.	Dependants.	Order 29.—Trade in metals. 111.—Trade in metals, machinery, knife, tool etc., sellers. Total workers and dependants.	Actual workers. Total. Males.	Actual workers. Total. Females.	Partially agriculturist. Males.	Partially agriculturist. Females.	Dependants.	Order 30.—Trade in pottery. 112.—Trade in pottery. Total workers and dependants.	Actual workers. Total. Males.	Actual workers. Total. Females.	Partially agriculturist. Males.	Partially agriculturist. Females.	Dependants.	Serial Number.
782	783	784	785	786	787	788	789	790	791	792	793	794	795	796	797	798	799	
8,511	*2,593*	*2,005*	*127*	*334*	*3,913*	*959*	*326*	*93*	...	*8*	*540*	*11,228*	*2,503*	*3,211*	*296*	*385*	*5,514*	
696	261	225	...	...	210	620	148	49	...	...	423	695	36	330	...	...	329	1
12	8	...	...	...	4	88	67	...	...	...	21	449	175	67	27	9	207	2
1,221	*404*	*239*	*17*	*9*	*578*	*19*	*12*	*1*	...	...	*6*	*3,923*	*943*	*1,252*	*181*	*127*	*1,728*	
...	...	...	...	...	...	19	12	1	...	...	6	1,779	419	552	113	69	808	3
890	223	177	7	9	400	...	...	...	...	...	...	2,144	524	700	68	58	920	4
421	181	62	10	...	178	...	...	...	...	...	...	...	...	...	...	...	...	5
3,418	*889*	*1,051*	*25*	*127*	*1,478*	*137*	*68*	*32*	...	*8*	*37*	*4,970*	*942*	*1,339*	*82*	*233*	*2,689*	
15	...	8	...	...	7	...	...	...	...	..	...	1,711	335	481	36	104	895	6
72	50	...	...	...	22	...	...	...	...	...	...	1,172	304	206	...	9	662	7
2,326	529	741	...	92	1,056	7	3	...	...	..	4	1,225	301	363	46	69	561	8
1,005	310	302	25	35	393	130	65	32	...	8	33	862	2	289	...	51	571	9
1,528	*476*	*129*	*39*	*19*	*923*	*44*	*15*	...	...	...	*29*	*410*	*77*	*162*	*4*	*14*	*171*	
482	116	49	3	...	317	...	...	..	...	...	...	116	49	19	4	3	48	10
30	8	5	...	...	17	...	...	...	...	...	...	...	...	...	...	...	...	11
795	230	63	36	19	502	19	9	...	..	...	10	294	28	143	...	11	123	12
221	122	12	...	..	87	25	6	...	...	...	19	...	...	...	...	...	...	13
1,636	*555*	*361*	*46*	*179*	*720*	*51*	*16*	*11*	...	...	*24*	*781*	*330*	*61*	*2*	*2*	*390*	
847	295	174	10	108	378	51	16	11	...	...	24	...	...	...	...	...	...	14
118	30	33	...	...	55	...	...	...	...	...	...	...	...	...	...	...	...	15
...	..	...	...	...	...	...	...	...	...	...	...	54	...	31	...	2	23	16
671	230	154	36	71	287	...	...	...	...	...	...	727	330	30	2	...	367	17

TABLE XV.

OCCUPATION OR MEANS OF LIVELIHOOD.

PART A.—GENERAL TABLE.

Serial Number.	District.	Class B.—Preparation and supply											
		Sub-Class V.—											
		Order 31.—Trade in Chemical products. 113—Trade in chemical products (drugs, dyes, paints, petroleum, explosives, etc.)						Total Order 32.					
		Total workers and dependants.	Actual workers. Total. Males.	Actual workers. Total. Females.	Actual workers. Partially agriculturist. Males.	Actual workers. Partially agriculturist. Females.	Dependants.	Total workers and dependants.	Actual workers. Total. Males.	Actual workers. Total. Females.	Actual workers. Partially agriculturist. Males.	Actual workers. Partially agriculturist. Females.	Dependants.
	1	800	801	802	803	804	805	806	807	808	809	810	811
	Hyderabad State ...	*2,454*	*713*	*394*	*44*	*8*	*1,347*	*241,975*	*69,324*	*65,721*	*9,448*	*3,404*	*106,930*
1	Hyderabad City ...	1,577	393	206	...	...	978	6,789	2,166	982	5	...	3,641
2	Atraf-i-balda ..	34	25	...	..	...	9	18,076	6,219	5,231	189	102	6,626
	Warangal Division ...	*73*	*24*	*15*	*11*	...	*34*	*63,138*	*15,265*	*19,757*	*2,228*	*1,157*	*28,116*
3	Warangal	53	14	10	11	...	29	24,385	6,633	5,933	1,259	318	11,819
4	Karimnagar	20	10	5	...	...	5	33,943	7,433	12,964	891	775	13,546
5	Adilabad	...	...	...	...	...	...	4,810	1,199	860	78	64	2,751
	Medak Division ...	*718*	*250*	*167*	*33*	*8*	*301*	*98,922*	*29,370*	*29,139*	*5,184*	*1,659*	*40,413*
6	Medak	115	31	48	13	8	36	21,886	7,382	4,611	2,207	549	9,895
7	Nizamabad	58	43	...	...	...	15	11,937	4,064	3,364	237	128	4,509
8	Mahbubnagar ...	545	176	119	20	...	250	15,938	4,328	4,393	482	109	7,217
9	Nalgonda	...	...	...	...	...	...	49,159	13,596	16,771	2,228	873	18,792
	Aurangabad Division	*43*	*16*	*6*	...	...	*21*	*9,834*	*2,350*	*1,735*	*233*	*16*	*5,749*
10	Aurangabad	26	9	6	...	...	11	4,941	841	986	52	10	3,114
11	Bhir	...	...	...	...	...	...	319	68	121	6	...	130
12	Nander	17	7	...	...	...	10	1,946	608	242	122	3	1,096
13	Parbhani	...	...	...	...	...	...	2,628	833	386	53	3	1,409
	Gulbarga Division ...	*9*	*5*	...	...	...	*4*	*45,216*	*13,954*	*8,877*	*1,639*	*470*	*22,385*
14	Gulbarga	...	...	...	...	...	...	20,638	5,580	3,620	744	116	11,438
15	Osmanabad	...	...	...	...	...	...	1,178	611	66	1	...	501
16	Raichur	9	5	...	...	...	4	16,042	5,496	4,003	683	305	6,543
17	Bidar	...	...	...	...	...	...	7,358	2,267	1,188	211	49	3,903

TABLE XV.

OCCUPATION OR MEANS OF LIVELIHOOD.

PART A.—GENERAL TABLE.

of material substances—(*contd.*)

Trade—(*contd.*)

Order 32—Hotels, cafes, restaurants, etc..

114.—Vendors of wine, liquors, aerated waters, etc.						115.—Owners and managers of hotels, cookshops, sarais, etc., and their employes.						Serial Number.
Total workers and dependants.	Actual workers.				Dependants.	Total workers and dependants.	Actual workers.				Dependants.	
	Total.		Partially agriculturist.				Total.		Partially agriculturist.			
	Males.	Females.	Males.	Females.			Males.	Females.	Males.	Females.		
812	813	814	815	816	817	818	819	820	821	822	823	
241,714	***69,248***	***65,656***	***9,437***	***3,404***	***106,810***	***261***	***76***	***65***	***11***	...	***120***	
6,610	2,142	917	3	...	3,551	179	24	65	2	...	90	1
18,076	6,219	5,231	189	102	6,626	...	...	...	...	...	...	2
63,138	***16,265***	***19,757***	***2,228***	***1,157***	***28,116***	...	...	...	...	...	...	
24,385	6,633	5,933	1,259	318	11,819	...	...	...	...	...	...	3
33,943	7,433	12,964	891	775	13,546	...	...	...	...	...	...	4
4,810	1,199	860	78	64	2,751	...	...	...	...	...	...	5
98,922	***29,370***	***29,139***	***5,154***	***1,659***	***40,413***	...	...	...	...	...	...	
21.888	7,382	4,611	2,207	549	9,895	...	...	...	...	...	...	6
11,937	4,064	3,364	237	128	4,509	...	...	...	...	...	...	7
15.938	4,328	4,393	482	109	7,217	...	...	...	...	...	...	8
49,159	13,596	16,771	2,228	873	18,792	...	...	...	...	...	...	9
9,816	***2,335***	***1,735***	***228***	***16***	***5,746***	***18***	***15***	...	***5***	...	***3***	
4,935	836	986	47	10	3,114	5	5	...	5	...	...	10
319	68	121	6	...	130	...	...	...	...	...	...	11
1,946	608	242	122	3	1,096	...	...	...	...	...	...	12
2,615	823	386	53	3	1,406	13	10	...	...	...	3	13
45,152	***13,917***	***8,877***	***1,635***	***470***	***22,358***	***64***	***37***	...	***4***	...	***27***	
20,574	5,543	3,620	740	116	11,411	64	37	...	4	...	27	14
1,178	611	66	1	...	501	...	...	...	...	...	...	15
16,042	5,496	4,003	693	305	6,543	...	...	...	...	...	...	16
7,358	2,267	1,188	211	49	3,903	...	...	...	...	...	...	17

TABLE XV.

OCCUPATION OR MEANS OF LIVELIHOOD.

PART A—GENERAL TABLE.

Serial Number.	District.	Class B.—Preparation and supply / Sub-Class V.— / Total Order 33.						Order 33.—Other trade in / 116.—Fish dealers.					
		Total workers and dependants.	Actual workers. Total.		Actual workers. Partially agriculturist.		Dependants.	Total workers and dependants.	Actual workers. Total.		Actual workers. Partially agriculturist.		Dependants.
			Males.	Females.	Males.	Females.			Males.	Females.	Males.	Females.	
	1	824	825	826	827	828	829	830	831	832	833	834	835
	Hyderabad State ...	***391,941***	***115,556***	***85,851***	***10,806***	***6,620***	***190,834***	***24,960***	***5,318***	***7,722***	***362***	***712***	***11,920***
1	Hyderabad City ...	30,529	6,486	6,394	14	...	17,649	1,232	82	318	...	...	[illegible]
2	Atraf-i-balda ...	15,901	6,282	3,359	195	77	6,260	276	273	...	6	...	[illegible]
	Warangal Division ...	***108,340***	***33,360***	***26,463***	***2,520***	***2,171***	***48,517***	***6,750***	***797***	***3,232***	***71***	***331***	***2,721***
3	Warangal ...	27,392	8,902	6,123	578	288	12,367	...	...	...	...	...	...
4	Karimnagar ..	64,712	17,440	17,622	1,778	1,841	29,650	6,572	722	3,195	71	330	[illegible]
5	Adilabad ...	16,236	7,018	2,718	164	42	6,500	178	75	37	...	1	[illegible]
	Medak Division ...	***104,911***	***30,495***	***25,762***	***3,736***	***2,477***	***48,654***	***10,419***	***2,421***	***2,629***	***103***	***276***	***5,369***
6	Medak ...	35,997	10,268	8,687	2,202	1,770	17,042	1,365	79	271	7	102	1,015
7	Nizamabad ...	17,596	5,917	3,812	349	167	7,867	1,069	528	...	1	...	541
8	Mahbubnagar ...	33,159	9,253	8,498	590	464	15,408	7,213	1,814	1,896	95	161	[illegible]
9	Nalgonda ...	18,159	5,057	4,765	595	76	8,837	772	...	462	...	13	[illegible]
	Aurangabad Division.	***59,642***	***19,125***	***9,190***	***1,959***	***597***	***31,327***	***3,120***	***985***	***458***	***136***	***33***	***1,677***
10	Aurangabad ...	12,410	3,334	2,482	587	100	6,594	546	101	45	...	...	[illegible]
11	Bhir ...	9,091	3,497	1,564	438	47	4,030	601	304	73	126	1	[illegible]
12	Nander ...	12,977	4,904	1,770	352	223	6,303	592	144	113	...	32	[illegible]
13	Parbhani ...	25,164	7,390	3,374	582	227	14,400	1,381	436	227	10	...	[illegible]
	Gulbarga Division ...	***72,618***	***19,808***	***14,383***	***2,382***	***1,298***	***38,427***	***3,163***	***760***	***1,085***	***46***	***72***	***1,318***
14	Gulbarga ...	26,766	6,020	6,999	[illegible]	442	13,747	329	144	43	31	...	[illegible]
15	Osmanabad ...	5,764	2,059	662	109	15	3,043	82	39	1	...	...	42
16	Raichur ...	20,585	6,055	3,001	1,171	139	11,529	2,401	534	892	...	...	[illegible]
17	Bidar ...	19,503	5,674	3,721	646	702	10,108	348	43	149	15	72	[illegible]

TABLE XV.

OCCUPATION OR MEANS OF LIVELIHOOD.

PART A.—GENERAL TABLE.

of material substances.—(*contd.*)

Trade.—(*contd.*)

food stuffs.

117.—Grocers and sellers of vegetable oil, salt and other condiments.						118.—Sellers of milk, butter, ghee, poultry, eggs, etc.						Serial Number.
Total workers and dependants.	Actual workers.				Dependants.	Total workers and dependants.	Actual workers.				Dependants.	
	Total.		Partially agriculturist.				Total.		Partially agriculturist.			
	Males.	Females.	Males.	Females.			Males.	Females.	Males.	Females.		
836	837	838	839	840	841	842	843	844	845	846	847	
112,156	***32,155***	***21,919***	***3,220***	***1,618***	***58,082***	***17,040***	***2,193***	***6,209***	***308***	***441***	***8,638***	
3,224	600	819	...	...	1,805	1,664	191	365	10	...	1,108	1
2,824	893	604	42	15	1,327	560	109	204	...	...	247	2
22,921	***5,594***	***5,784***	***507***	***462***	***11,543***	***5,294***	***469***	***3,046***	***1***	***118***	***1,779***	
2,504	694	529	29	9	1,371	1,678	238	749	...	33	691	3
14,224	3,653	3,590	392	422	6,987	3,616	231	2,297	1	85	1,088	4
6,103	1,247	1,683	86	31	3,191	...	...	...	...	...	...	5
16,764	***4,758***	***4,155***	***648***	***465***	***7,851***	***9,486***	***1,413***	***2,580***	***297***	***323***	***5,493***	
8,262	2,421	2,200	400	380	3,641	5,155	1,006	888	276	286	3,261	6
4,163	754	1,217	121	69	2,192	832	403	124	21	...	305	7
2,375	781	446	54	14	1,148	3,202	3	1,391	...	33	1,808	8
1,964	802	292	73	2	870	297	1	177	...	4	119	9
32,338	***11,349***	***4,896***	***1,200***	***199***	***16,093***	***36***	***11***	***14***	...	...	***11***	
6,735	1,894	1,857	460	83	2,984	...	...	...	...	...	...	10
6,658	2,775	1,035	295	32	2,848	...	...	...	...	...	...	11
5,436	2,201	620	117	50	2,615	36	11	14	...	...	11	12
13,509	4,479	1,384	328	34	7,646	...	...	...	...	...	...	13
34,085	***8,961***	***5,661***	***823***	***477***	***19,463***	...	...	...	...	...	...	
12,994	3,409	2,959	244	71	6,626	...	...	...	...	...	...	14
4,000	1,287	427	84	14	2,286	...	...	...	...	...	...	15
8,062	1,728	580	242	63	5,734	...	...	...	...	...	...	16
9,029	2,537	1,695	253	329	4,797	...	...	...	...	...	...	17

TABLE XV.

OCCUPATION OR MEANS OF LIVELIHOOD.

PART A.—GENERAL TABLE.

Class B.—Preparation and supply

Sub-Class V.—

Order 33.—Other trade in

Serial Number.	District.	119.—Sellers of sweetmeats, sugar, gur, and molasses. Total workers and dependants.	Actual workers. Total. Males.	Females.	Partially agriculturist. Males.	Females.	Dependants.	120.—Cardamom, betel-leaf, vegetables, fruit and areca nut sellers. Total workers and dependants.	Actual workers. Total. Males.	Females.	Partially agriculturist. Males.	Females.	Dependants.
	1	848	849	850	851	852	853	854	855	856	857	858	859
	Hyderabad State ...	***4,656***	***990***	***1,188***	***46***	***8***	***2,478***	***97,564***	***27,214***	***28,019***	***2,725***	***2,269***	***42,331***
1	Hyderabad City ...	991	160	133	...	...	698	11,726	2,137	2,964	4	...	[illegible]
2	Atraf-i-balda ...	55	10	11	...	...	34	3,288	1,110	1,084	10	28	[illegible]
	Warangal Division ...	***1,244***	***235***	***317***	***6***	***6***	***692***	***38,564***	***12,387***	***10,304***	***824***	***708***	***15,873***
3	Warangal ..	507	119	120	5	...	268	9,539	2,219	3,234	211	221	[illegible]
4	Karimnagar ...	470	82	137	1	6	251	22,054	5,898	6,533	572	485	[illegible]
5	Adilabad ...	267	34	60	...	...	173	6,971	4,240	487	41	2	[illegible]
	Medak Division ...	***1,343***	***314***	***571***	***34***	...	***458***	***22,740***	***6,873***	***7,327***	***1,133***	***751***	***8,549***
6	Medak	1,123	203	555	33	...	365	7,796	2,931	1,841	837	550	[illegible]
7	Nizamabad ...	38	4	4	...	...	30	3,503	1,175	1,323	49	46	[illegible]
8	Mahbubnagar ...	16	12	...	...	...	4	7,036	2,475	1,945	88	130	[illegible]
9	Nalgonda... ...	166	95	12	1	...	59	4,405	292	2,218	159	25	[illegible]
	Aurangabad Division	***237***	***88***	***36***	...	***2***	***113***	***6,168***	***1,339***	***1,746***	***159***	***158***	***3,085***
10	Aurangabad ...	...	...	...	...	...	...	1,049	125	214	16	4	[illegible]
11	Bhir	92	22	11	...	2	59	903	198	209	9	4	[illegible]
12	Nander	103	57	16	...	...	30	674	187	199	8	6	[illegible]
13	Parbhani ...	42	9	9	...	...	24	3,542	829	1,124	126	144	[illegible]
	Gulbarga Division ...	***786***	***183***	***120***	***6***	...	***483***	***15,078***	***3,368***	***4,594***	***595***	***624***	***7,116***
14	Gulbarga ..	...	...	...	...	...	...	7,388	844	2,967	110	299	[illegible]
15	Osmanabad ...	77	51	...	...	...	26	1,050	473	175	8	1	[illegible]
16	Raichur	422	117	42	6	...	263	3,102	1,334	327	379	25	[illegible]
17	Bidar	287	15	78	...	...	194	3,538	817	1,125	98	299	[illegible]

TABLE XV.

OCCUPATION OR MEANS OF LIVELIHOOD.

PART A.—GENERAL TABLE.

of material substances.—(*contd*).

Trade.—(*contd*).

food stuffs.—(*contd.*)

121.—Grain and pulse dealers.						122.—Tobacco, opium, ganja, ect., sellers.						
Total workers and dependants.	Actual workers.				Dependants.	Total workers and dependants.	Actual workers.				Dependants.	Serial Number.
	Total.		Partially agriculturist.				Total.		Partially agriculturist.			
	Males.	Females.	Males.	Females.			Males.	Females.	Males.	Females.		
860	861	862	863	864	865	866	867	868	869	870	871	
106,171	*37,380*	*14,815*	*3,179*	*1,364*	*53,976*	*4,615*	*1,354*	*690*	*4*	*11*	*2,571*	
7,162	2,404	825	...	...	3,933	2,703	707	416	...	...	1,580	1
5,827	2,535	719	107	18	2,573	112	67	7	...	...	38	2
24,758	*10,043*	*2,979*	*755*	*502*	*11,736*	*330*	*96*	*57*	*2*	*9*	*177*	
8,134	3,245	1,018	142	13	3,871	29	18	3	...	...	8	3
14,348	5,600	1,544	581	482	7,204	280	78	52	2	9	150	4
2,270	1,198	417	32	7	661	21	...	2	...	...	19	5
35,136	*12,088*	*6,068*	*1,299*	*528*	*16,980*	*625*	*150*	*40*	...	*2*	*435*	
11,672	3,483	2,672	649	442	5,517	322	133	6	...	...	183	6
7,332	2,965	957	157	46	3,410	253	6	23	...	...	224	7
5,891	1,907	899	136	8	3,085	26	1	11	...	2	14	8
10,241	3,733	1,540	357	32	4,968	24	10	...	...	...	14	9
15,845	*4,699*	*1,681*	*432*	*199*	*9,465*	*249*	*127*	*15*	*2*	...	*107*	
3,474	987	262	84	7	2,225	201	95	15	2	...	91	10
591	181	124	8	8	286	...	...	...	...	...	...	11
5,745	2,138	758	223	135	2,849	...	...	...	...	...	...	12
6,035	1,393	537	117	49	4,105	48	32	...	...	...	16	13
17,443	*5,611*	*2,543*	*586*	*117*	*9,289*	*596*	*207*	*155*	...	...	*234*	
5,927	1,565	1,030	71	72	3,332	86	44	...	...	...	42	14
457	172	34	16	...	251	26	14	1	...	...	11	15
5,424	1,782	1,094	220	43	2,548	72	13	15	...	...	44	16
5,635	2,092	385	279	2	3,158	412	136	139	...	...	137	17

TABLE XV.

OCCUPATION OR MEANS OF LIVELIHOOD.

PART A.—GENERAL TABLE.

Serial Number.	District.	Class B.—Preparation and supply											
		Sub-Class V.—											
		Order 33.—Other trade in food stuffs—(concld).											
		123.— Dealers in sheep, goats and pigs.						124.—Dealers in hay, grass and fodder.					
		Total workers and dependants.	Actual workers. Total. Males.	Actual workers. Total. Females.	Actual workers. Partially agriculturist. Males.	Actual workers. Partially agriculturist. Females.	Dependants.	Total workers and dependants.	Actual workers. Total. Males.	Actual workers. Total. Females.	Actual workers. Partially agriculturist. Males.	Actual workers. Partially agriculturist. Females.	Dependants.
	1	872	873	874	875	876	877	878	879	880	881	882	883
	Hyderabad State ...	***19,400***	***7,664***	***3,189***	***637***	***117***	***8,547***	***5,379***	***1,288***	***1,800***	***325***	***80***	***2,291***
1	Hyderabad City ...	26	9	...	...	...	17	1,801	196	554	...	...	1,051
2	Atraf-i-balda ...	2,895	1,239	728	30	16	828	64	46	2	...	...	16
	Warangal Division ...	***8,053***	***3,679***	***481***	***354***	***34***	***3,893***	***426***	***60***	***263***	...	***1***	***103***
3	Warangal ...	4,710	2,308	278	191	12	2,124	201	31	142	...	...	28
4	Karimnagar ...	3,012	1,172	190	158	22	1,650	136	4	84	...	...	48
5	Adilabad ..	331	199	13	5	...	119	89	25	37	...	1	27
	Medak Division ...	***7,779***	***2,457***	***1,890***	***222***	***67***	***3,432***	***619***	***21***	***502***	...	***65***	***96***
6	Medak ...	82	...	50	...	10	32	220	12	204	...	...	4
7	Nizamabad ..	384	76	155	...	1	153	22	6	9	...	5	7
8	Mahbubnagar ...	7,084	2,257	1,672	217	56	3,155	316	3	238	...	60	75
9	Nalgonda ...	229	124	13	5	...	92	61	...	51	...	...	10
	Aurangabad Division	***583***	***241***	***90***	***29***	...	***252***	***1,066***	***286***	***254***	***1***	***6***	***526***
10	Aurangabad ...	371	132	72	25	...	167	34	...	17	...	6	17
11	Bhir ...	...	...	...	...	...	...	246	17	112	...	...	117
12	Nander ...	181	90	18	4	...	73	210	76	32	...	...	102
13	Parbhani ...	31	19	...	...	...	12	576	193	93	1	...	290
	Gulbarga Division ...	***64***	***39***	...	***2***	...	***25***	***1,403***	***679***	***225***	***324***	***8***	***499***
14	Gulbarga ...	...	...	...	...	...	...	42	14	...	...	...	28
15	Osmanabad ...	7	5	...	1	...	2	65	18	24	...	...	23
16	Raichur ...	...	...	...	...	...	...	1,099	647	51	324	8	401
17	Bidar ...	57	34	...	1	...	23	197	...	150	...	...	47

TABLE XV.

OCCUPATION OR MEANS OF LIVELIHOOD.

PART A.—GENERAL TABLE.

of material substances—(*contd.*)

Trade.—(*contd.*)

Order 34.—Trade in clothing and toilet articles. 125.—Trade in ready-made clothing and other articles of dress and the toilet (hats, umbrellas, socks, ready-made shoes, perfumes, etc.						Total Order 35.						Serial Number.
Total workers and dependants.	Actual workers.				Dependants.	Total workers and dependants.	Actual workers.				Dependants.	
	Total.		Partially agriculturist.				Total.		Partially agriculturist.			
	Males.	Females.	Males.	Females.			Males.	Females.	Males.	Females.		
884	885	886	887	888	889	890	891	892	893	894	895	
16,682	***4,688***	***3,395***	***603***	***227***	***8,839***	***7,670***	***2,960***	***1,099***	***129***	***113***	***3,611***	
1,476	376	175	...	...	925	665	247	106	...	...	312	1
1,406	641	87	20	1	678	507	299	54	13	1	154	2
2,284	***574***	***582***	***45***	***12***	***1,128***	***1,292***	***353***	***316***	***25***	***2***	***623***	
877	176	285	13	...	416	228	98	40	...	...	90	3
1,281	326	297	19	12	658	736	115	254	11	...	367	4
126	72	...	13	...	54	328	140	22	14	2	166	5
6,066	***1,471***	***1,301***	***326***	***157***	***3,294***	***3,567***	***1,420***	***484***	***46***	***95***	***1,663***	
3,557	906	280	315	155	2,371	1,117	450	183	37	29	484	6
928	432	221	6	2	275	219	54	64	...	4	101	7
1,424	75	793	...	...	556	2,099	885	178	9	56	1,036	8
157	58	7	5	...	92	132	31	59	...	6	42	9
2,053	***754***	***349***	***31***	***54***	***950***	***967***	***385***	***37***	***29***	...	***545***	
186	49	89	6	...	48	473	263	...	12	...	210	10
718	204	156	10	13	353	5	3	...	...	...	2	11
329	166	8	...	...	155	356	79	17	17	...	260	12
820	335	96	15	41	389	133	40	20	...	...	73	13
3,337	***872***	***901***	***181***	***3***	***1,864***	***672***	***256***	***102***	***16***	***15***	***314***	
1,349	327	537	92	1	485	197	101	3	16	...	93	14
490	138	40	10	2	312	163	44	54	...	15	65	15
347	20	128	...	...	199	42	20	...	...	...	22	16
1,151	387	196	79	...	568	270	91	45	...	...	134	17

TABLE XV.

OCCUPATION OR MEANS OF LIVELIHOOD.

PART A.—GENERAL TABLE.

Class B.—Preparation and supply

Sub-Class V.—

Order 35.—Trade in furniture.

Serial Number.	District.	126.—Trade in furniture, carpets, curtains and bedding. Total workers and dependants.	Actual workers. Total. Males.	Actual workers. Total. Females.	Partially agriculturist. Males.	Partially agriculturist. Females.	Dependants.	127.—Hardware, cooking utensils, porcelain, crockery, glassware, bottles, articles for gardening, the cellar, etc. Total workers and dependants.	Actual workers. Total. Males.	Actual workers. Total. Females.	Partially agriculturist. Males.	Partially agriculturist. Females.	Dependants.
	1	896	897	898	899	900	901	902	903	904	905	906	907
	Hyderabad State ...	***6,117***	***2,206***	***1,027***	***107***	***113***	***2,884***	***1,553***	***784***	***72***	***22***	...	***727***
1	Hyderabad City ...	571	220	73	...	...	278	94	27	33	...	...	34
2	Atraf-i-balda ...	507	299	54	13	1	154	...	...	...	...	...	...
	Warangal Division ...	***979***	***203***	***301***	***25***	***2***	***475***	***313***	***150***	***15***	...	...	***148***
3	Warangal ...	211	88	40	...	...	83	17	10	...	...	...	7
4	Karimnagar ...	629	78	242	11	...	309	107	37	12	...	...	58
5	Adilabad ...	139	37	19	14	2	83	189	103	3	...	...	83
	Medak Division ...	***3,210***	***1,148***	***484***	***45***	***95***	***1,578***	***357***	***272***	...	***1***	...	***84***
6	Medak ...	773	183	183	36	29	407	344	267	...	1	...	77
7	Nizamabad ...	219	54	64	...	4	101	...	...	...	...	...	...
8	Mahbubnagar ...	2,097	881	178	9	56	1,035	2	1	...	...	...	1
9	Nalgonda ...	121	27	59	...	6	35	11	4	...	...	...	7
	Aurangabad Division ...	***377***	***136***	***36***	***8***	...	***205***	***590***	***249***	***1***	***21***	...	***348***
10	Aurangabad ...	128	83	...	...	...	45	345	180	...	12	...	165
11	Bhir ...	5	3	...	...	...	2	...	...	...	...	...	...
12	Nander ...	164	22	16	8	...	126	192	57	1	9	...	134
13	Parbhani ...	80	28	20	...	...	32	53	12	...	...	...	41
	Gulbarga Division ...	***473***	***200***	***79***	***16***	***15***	***194***	***199***	***56***	***23***	...	...	***120***
14	Gulbarga ...	156	81	...	16	...	75	41	20	3	...	...	1
15	Osmanabad ...	163	44	54	...	15	65	...	...	...	...	...	...
16	Raichur ...	41	19	...	...	...	22	1	1	...	...	...	...
17	Bidar ...	113	56	25	...	...	32	157	35	20	...	...	[illegible]

TABLE XV.

OCCUPATION OR MEANS OF LIVELIHOOD.

PART A.—GENERAL TABLE.

of material substances.—(*contd*).

Trade—(*contd*).

Order 36.—Trade in building materials. 128.—Trade in building materials (stones, bricks, plaster, cement, sand, tiles, thatch, etc.						Order 37.—Trade in means of transport. 129.—Dealers and hirers of elephants, camels, horses, cattle, asses, mules, etc., sellers (not makers) of carriages, saddlery, etc.						Order 38.—Trade in fuel. 130.—Dealers in fire-wood, charcoal, coal, cowdung, etc.						Serial Number.
Total workers and dependants.	Actual workers. Total. Males.	Actual workers. Total. Females.	Actual workers. Partially agriculturist. Males.	Actual workers. Partially agriculturist. Females.	Dependants.	Total workers and dependants.	Actual workers. Total. Males.	Actual workers. Total. Females.	Actual workers. Partially agriculturist. Males.	Actual workers. Partially agriculturist. Females.	Dependants.	Total workers and dependants.	Actual workers. Total. Males.	Actual workers. Total. Females.	Actual workers. Partially agriculturist. Males.	Actual workers. Partially agriculturist. Females.	Dependants.	
908	909	910	911	912	913	914	915	916	917	918	919	920	921	922	923	924	925	
1,2[illegible]	***495***	***85***	...	...	***680***	***15,597***	***5,838***	***1,814***	***496***	***154***	***7,948***	***25,880***	***7,063***	***6,379***	***639***	***879***	***12,438***	
319	111	47	...	...	161	417	97	21	...	...	299	2,535	543	619	...	...	1,373	1
...	...	...	...	...	...	375	257	5	...	...	113	644	248	183	13	3	[illegible]13	2
62	***3***	***16***	...	...	***43***	***1,462***	***372***	***196***	***22***	..	***894***	***1,595***	***651***	***272***	***7***	***4***	***[illegible]72***	
...	...	...	...	...	...	833	191	146	...	...	496	655	301	50	5	...	304	3
62	3	16	...	...	43	568	161	50	22	...	357	505	167	138	2	4	200	4
...	...	...	...	...	...	61	20	...	...	...	41	435	163	84	...	...	168	5
233	***106***	***2***	...	...	***125***	***9,246***	***3,426***	***1,163***	***375***	***150***	***4,657***	***8,460***	***2,367***	***2,027***	***141***	***469***	***4,066***	
190	84	...	...	...	106	3,712	1,228	695	181	146	1,789	4,364	1,162	1,273	76	437	1,929	6
...	...	...	...	...	...	868	153	168	7	2	547	1,788	508	371	61	26	909	7
24	13	2	..	...	9	2,042	924	35	2	...	1,083	1,971	572	332	3	4	1,067	8
19	9	...	...	...	10	2,624	1,121	265	185	2	1,238	337	125	51	1	2	161	9
92	***48***	***20***	...	...	***24***	***1,590***	***800***	***130***	***29***	***4***	***660***	***4,691***	***1,199***	***1,257***	***15***	***23***	***2,235***	
...	...	...	...	...	...	86	55	...	...	...	31	623	149	174	1	1	300	10
...	...	...	...	...	...	401	175	21	5	...	205	791	50	316	2	...	425	11
92	48	20	...	...	24	657	415	22	15	4	220	1,004	162	360	12	22	482	12
...	...	...	...	...	..	446	155	87	..	...	204	2,273	838	407	...	..	1,028	13
554	***227***	...	...	...	***327***	***2,507***	***886***	***299***	***79***	...	***1,322***	***7,955***	***2,055***	***2,021***	***463***	***380***	***3,879***	
550	225	...	...	..	325	2,062	712	283	59	...	1,067	4,921	530	1,637	22	295	2,754	14
...	...	...	...	...	...	31	22	...	10	...	9	478	196	56	4	4	226	15
...	...	...	...	...	...	75	23	...	8	...	52	1,889	1,164	194	437	81	531	16
4	2	...	...	...	2	339	129	16	2	...	194	667	165	134	...	...	363	17

TABLE XV.

OCCUPATION OR MEANS OF LIVELIHOOD.

PART A.—GENERAL TABLE.

Serial Number.	District.	Total Order 39. Total workers and dependants.	Actual workers. Total. Males.	Actual workers. Total. Females.	Actual workers. Partially agriculturist. Males.	Actual workers. Partially agriculturist. Females.	Dependants.	Class B.—Preparation and supply / Sub-Class V.— / Order 39.—Trade in articles of luxury and those / 131.—Dealers in precious stones, jewellery (real and imitation) clocks, optical instruments, etc. Total workers and dependants.	Actual workers. Total. Males.	Actual workers. Total. Females.	Actual workers. Partially agriculturist. Males.	Actual workers. Partially agriculturist. Females.	Dependants.
	1	926	927	928	929	930	931	932	933	934	935	936	937
	Hyderabad State ...	***46,316***	***12,453***	***12,069***	***961***	***760***	***21,794***	***7,265***	***2,008***	***2,061***	***211***	***49***	***3,196***
1	Hyderabad City ...	3,595	1,222	485	...	...	1,688	1,012	212	234	...	...	56
2	Atraf-i-balda ...	2,416	838	613	9	30	959	66	25	7	1	...	34
	Warangal Division ...	***9,206***	***2,377***	***2,475***	***92***	***113***	***4,354***	***619***	***246***	***31***	***16***	...	***342***
3	Warangal	4,737	1,138	1,508	44	110	2,091	382	99	30	2	...	253
4	Karimnagar	2,425	792	543	42	2	1,090	237	147	1	14	...	89
5	Adilabad	2,044	447	424	6	1	1,173	...	...	...	...	...	...
	Medak Division ...	***16,166***	***3,757***	***5,400***	***358***	***356***	***7,009***	***4,820***	***1,221***	***1,696***	***178***	***49***	***1,903***
6	Medak	3,819	723	1,722	55	62	1,374	2,067	595	740	48	43	73
7	Nizamabad	6,386	1,471	1,919	142	258	2,993	114	42	19	...	...	53
8	Mahbubnagar ...	4,022	1,186	1,054	145	16	1,782	2,590	576	937	130	6	1,077
9	Nalgonda	1,939	377	705	16	20	857	49	8	...	...	...	41
	Aurangabad Division.	***6,997***	***2,402***	***1,197***	***300***	***38***	***3,488***	***469***	***281***	...	***15***	...	***186***
10	Aurangabad	2,298	991	188	232	26	1,119	171	153	...	10	...	18
11	Bhir	1,229	255	400	26	4	574	21	15	...	...	...	6
12	Nander	1,128	320	172	36	1	636	35	17	...	...	...	18
13	Parbhani	2,342	836	347	6	7	1,159	242	96	...	5	...	14
	Gulbarga Division ..	***7,942***	***1,857***	***1,989***	***202***	***223***	***4,096***	***279***	***23***	***93***	***1***	...	***165***
14	Gulbarga	2,249	399	818	62	101	1,032	3	3	...	...	...	...
15	Osmanabad	1,154	385	150	26	4	619	9	5	1	...	...	[illegible]
16	Raichur	1,635	266	377	25	47	1,042	224	...	92	...	...	13
17	Bidar	2,854	807	644	89	71	1,403	43	15	...	1	...	2

TABLE XV.

OCCUPATION OR MEANS OF LIVELIHOOD.

PART A—GENERAL TABLE.

of material substances.—(*contd.*)

Trade.—(*contd.*)

pertaining to letters and the arts, sciences.												Order 40.—Trade in refuse matter.						
132.—Dealers in common bangles, bead necklaces, fans, small articles, toys, hunting and fishing tackle, flowers, etc.						133.—Publishers, booksellers, stationers, dealers in music pictures, musical instruments and curiosities.						134.—Dealers in rags, stable refuse, etc.						
Total workers and dependants.	Actual workers.				Dependants.	Total workers and dependants.	Actual workers.				Dependants.	Total workers and dependants.	Actual workers.				Dependants.	Serial Number.
	Total.		Partially agriculturist.				Total.		Partially agriculturist.				Total.		Partially agriculturist.			
	Males.	Females.	Males.	Females.			Males.	Females.	Males.	Females.			Males.	Females.	Males.	Females.		
938	939	940	941	942	943	944	945	946	947	948	949	950	951	952	953	954	955	
38,144	***10,151***	***9,960***	***718***	***711***	***18,033***	***907***	***294***	***48***	***32***	...	***565***	...	...	...	...	...	...	
2,215	881	251	...	...	1,083	368	129	...	...	...	239	...	...	...	...	...	...	1
2,339	813	604	8	30	922	5	...	2	...	...	3	...	...	...	...	...	...	2
8,289	***2,055***	***2,428***	***76***	***113***	***3,806***	***298***	***76***	***16***	...	...	***206***	...	...	...	...	...	...	
4,276	1,004	1,470	42	110	1,802	79	35	8	...	...	36	...	...	...	...	...	...	3
1,969	604	534	28	2	831	219	41	8	...	...	170	...	...	...	...	...	...	4
2,044	447	424	6	1	1,173	...	...	...	...	...	...	...	...	...	...	...	...	5
11,275	***2,518***	***3,694***	***178***	***307***	***5,063***	***71***	***18***	***10***	***2***	...	***43***	...	...	...	...	...	...	
1,742	121	982	7	19	639	10	7	...	..	...	3	...	...	...	...	..	...	6
6,265	1,427	1,900	142	258	2,938	7	2	...	...	...	5	...	...	...	...	...	...	7
1,427	608	117	15	10	702	5	2	...	...	...	3	...	...	...	...	...	...	8
1,841	362	695	14	20	784	49	7	10	2	...	32	...	...	...	...	...	...	9
6,827	***2,121***	***1,106***	***285***	***38***	***3,300***	***1***	...	***1***	...	...	...	...	...	...	...	...	...	
2,127	835	188	222	26	1,101	...	...	...	...	...	...	...	...	...	...	...	...	10
1,208	240	400	26	4	563	...	...	...	...	...	...	...	...	...	...	...	...	11
1,092	303	171	36	1	618	1	...	1	...	...	...	...	...	...	...	...	...	12
2,100	740	347	1	7	1,013	...	...	...	...	...	...	...	...	...	...	...	...	13
7,499	***1,763***	***1,877***	***171***	***223***	***3,859***	***164***	***71***	***19***	***30***	...	***74***	...	...	..	...	...	...	
2,246	396	818	62	101	1,032	...	...	...	...	...	...	...	...	...	...	...	...	14
1,145	380	149	26	4	616	...	...	...	...	...	...	...	...	...	...	...	...	15
1,461	266	285	25	47	910	...	...	...	...	...	...	...	...	...	...	...	...	16
2,617	721	625	58	71	1,301	164	71	19	30	...	74	...	...	...	...	...	...	17

TABLE XV.

OCCUPATION OR MEANS OF LIVELIHOOD.

PART A.—GENERAL TABLE.

Serial Number.	District.	Class B.—Preparation and supply — Sub-Class V.— Total Order 41. Total workers and dependants.	Total Order 41. Actual workers. Total. Males.	Total Order 41. Actual workers. Total. Females.	Total Order 41. Actual workers. Partially agriculturist. Males.	Total Order 41. Actual workers. Partially agriculturist. Females.	Total Order 41. Dependants.	Order 41.—Trade of — 135.—Shopkeepers otherwise unspecified. Total workers and dependants.	135. Actual workers. Total. Males.	135. Actual workers. Total. Females.	135. Actual workers. Partially agriculturist. Males.	135. Actual workers. Partially agriculturist. Females.	135. Dependants.
	1	956	957	958	959	960	961	962	963	964	965	966	967
	Hyderabad State ...	***241,787***	***85,825***	***34,645***	***6,783***	***1,224***	***121,317***	***239,765***	***85,082***	***34,311***	***6,775***	***1,197***	***120,372***
1	Hyderabad City ...	12,365	3,705	1,829	20	...	6,831	12,304	3,676	1,829	20	...	6,799
2	Atraf-i-balda ...	11,793	3,994	2,116	274	82	5,683	11,786	3,991	2,116	274	82	5,679
	Warangal Division ...	***33,587***	***11,319***	***5,411***	***1,055***	***115***	***16,857***	***33,468***	***11,270***	***5,398***	***1,055***	***115***	***16,800***
3	Warangal ...	15,581	5,343	2,140	329	19	8,098	15,557	5,333	2,134	329	19	8,090
4	Karimnagar ...	8,636	2,966	1,042	420	70	4,628	8,541	2,927	1,035	420	70	4,579
5	Adilabad ...	9,370	3,010	2,229	306	26	4,131	9,370	3,010	2,229	306	26	4,131
	Medak Division ...	***68,420***	***26,697***	***10,506***	***2,370***	***523***	***31,217***	***67,349***	***26,385***	***10,228***	***2,370***	***498***	***30,736***
6	Medak ...	11,719	3,696	1,399	789	155	6,624	11,386	3,658	1,272	789	146	6,456
7	Nizamabad ...	13,959	5,232	1,653	675	62	7,074	13,439	4,988	1,577	675	61	6,874
8	Mahbubnagar ...	15,272	7,332	2,238	389	93	5,702	15,130	7,330	2,173	380	78	5,627
9	Nalgonda ...	27,470	10,437	5,216	526	213	11,817	27,394	10,409	5,206	526	213	11,779
	Aurangabad Division.	***45,716***	***13,675***	***5,837***	***802***	***182***	***26,204***	***45,439***	***13,544***	***5,820***	***802***	***182***	***26,075***
10	Aurangabad ...	13,937	2,679	2,008	201	120	9,250	13,905	2,658	2,008	201	120	9,239
11	Bhir ...	6,257	1,647	598	178	12	4,012	6,024	1,549	581	178	12	3,894
12	Nander ...	8,937	2,547	1,194	77	36	5,196	8,925	2,535	1,194	77	36	5,196
13	Parbhani ...	16,585	6,802	2,037	346	14	7,746	16,585	6,802	2,037	346	14	7,746
	Gulbarga Division ...	***69,906***	***26,435***	***8,946***	***2,262***	***322***	***34,525***	***69,419***	***26,216***	***8,920***	***2,254***	***320***	***34,283***
14	Gulbarga ...	27,770	9,125	4,981	957	175	13,664	27,537	8,992	4,979	949	175	13,566
15	Osmanabad ...	11,569	4,124	760	163	36	6,685	11,345	4,047	743	163	36	6,555
16	Raichur ...	16,549	8,666	1,478	499	53	6,405	16,549	8,666	1,478	499	53	6,405
17	Bidar ...	14,018	4,520	1,727	643	58	7,771	13,988	4,511	1,720	643	56	7,757

TABLE XV.

OCCUPATION OR MEANS OF LIVELIHOOD.

PART A.—GENERAL TABLE.

of material substances.—(*concld*).

Trade.—(*concld*).

other sorts.

136.—Itinerant traders, pedlars, hawkers, etc.						137.—Conjurors, acrobats, fortune tellers, reciters, exhibitors of curiosities and wild animals.						138.—Other trades (including farmers of pounds, tolls and markets).						Serial Number.
Total workers and dependants.	Actual workers.				Dependants.	Total workers and dependants.	Actual workers.				Dependants.	Total workers and dependants.	Actual workers.				Dependants.	
	Total.		Partially agriculturist.				Total.		Partially agriculturist.				Total.		Partially agriculturist.			
	Males.	Females.	Males.	Females.			Males.	Females.	Males.	Females.			Males.	Females.	Males.	Females.		
968	969	970	971	972	973	974	975	976	977	978	979	980	981	982	983	984	985	
30	...	***29***	...	...	***1***	***1,992***	***743***	***305***	***8***	***27***	***944***	...	...	...	...	...	...	
...	...	...	...	...	...	61	29	...	...	...	32	...	...	...	...	...	...	1
...	...	...	...	...	...	7	3	...	...	...	4	...	...	...	...	...	...	2
...	...	...	...	...	...	***119***	***49***	***13***	...	...	***57***	...	...	...	...	...	...	
...	...	...	...	...	...	24	10	6	...	...	8	...	...	...	...	...	...	3
...	...	...	...	...	...	95	39	7	...	...	49	...	...	...	...	...	...	4
...	...	...	...	...	...	...	...	...	...	...	...	...	...	...	...	...	...	5
30	...	***29***	...	...	***1***	***1,041***	***312***	***249***	...	***25***	***480***	...	...	...	...	...	...	
30	...	29	...	...	1	303	38	98	...	9	167	...	...	...	...	...	...	6
...	...	...	...	...	...	520	244	76	...	1	200	...	...	...	...	...	...	7
...	...	...	...	...	...	142	2	65	...	15	75	...	...	...	...	...	...	8
...	...	...	...	...	...	76	28	10	...	...	38	...	...	...	...	...	...	9
...	...	...	...	...	...	***277***	***131***	***17***	...	...	***129***	...	...	...	...	...	...	
...	...	...	...	...	...	32	21	...	...	...	11	...	...	...	...	...	...	10
...	...	...	...	...	...	233	98	17	...	...	118	...	...	...	...	...	...	11
...	...	...	...	...	...	12	12	...	...	...	...	...	...	...	...	...	...	12
...	...	...	...	...	...	...	...	...	...	...	...	...	...	...	...	...	...	13
...	...	...	...	...	...	***487***	***219***	***26***	***8***	***2***	***242***	...	...	...	...	...	...	
...	...	...	...	...	...	233	133	2	8	...	98	...	...	...	...	...	...	14
...	...	...	...	...	...	224	77	17	...	...	130	...	...	...	...	...	...	15
...	...	...	...	...	...	...	...	...	...	...	...	...	...	...	...	...	...	16
...	...	...	...	...	...	30	9	7	...	2	14	...	...	...	...	...	...	17

TABLE XV.

OCCUPATION OR MEANS OF LIVELIHOOD.

PART A.—GENERAL TABLE.

Serial Number.	District.	Class C.—Public administration											
		Sub-Class VI.—											
		Total Order 42.						Order 42.— 139.—Army (Imperial.)					
		Total workers and dependants.	Actual workers. Total.		Actual workers. Partially agriculturist.		Dependants.	Total workers and dependants.	Actual workers. Total.		Actual workers. Partially agriculturist.		Dependants.
			Males.	Females.	Males.	Females.			Males.	Females.	Males.	Females.	
	1	986	987	988	989	990	991	992	993	994	995	986	997
	Hyderabad State ...	*68,750*	*26,328*	*278*	*700*	...	*42,144*	*5,554*	*2,936*	...	*69*	...	*2,618*
1	Hyderabad City ...	50,281	18,548	207	6	...	31,526	5,099	2,544	...	6	...	2,555
2	Atraf-i-balda ...	529	253	...	2	...	276	...	...	...	...	...	...
	Warangal Division ...	*2,431*	*926*	...	*54*	...	*1,505*	...	...	...	...	...	...
3	Warangal ...	1,990	701	...	35	...	1,289	...	...	...	...	...	...
4	Karimnagar ...	441	225	...	19	...	216	...	...	...	...	...	...
5	Adilabad ...	...	...	...	...	...	...	...	...	...	...	...	...
	Medak Division ...	*2,513*	*1,161*	*71*	*42*	...	*1,281*	...	...	...	...	...	...
6	Medak ...	1,249	530	71	5	...	648	...	...	...	...	...	...
7	Nizamabad ..	588	356	...	25	...	232	...	...	...	...	...	...
8	Mahbubnagar ...	443	170	...	11	...	273	...	...	...	...	...	...
9	Nalgonda ..	233	105	...	1	...	128	...	...	...	...	...	..
	Aurangabad Division.	*4,161*	*2,398*	...	*75*	...	*1,763*	*455*	*392*	...	*63*	...	*63*
10	Aurangabad ...	1,784	1,189	...	63	...	595	455	392	...	63	...	63
11	Bhir ...	712	290	...	10	...	422	...	...	...	...	...	...
12	Nander ..	624	310	...	2	...	314	...	...	...	...	...	...
13	Parbhani ...	1,041	609	...	...	...	432	...	...	...	...	...	...
	Gulbarga Division ...	*8,835*	*3,042*	...	*521*	...	*5,793*	...	...	...	...	...	...
14	Gulbarga ...	5,678	2,153	...	267	...	3,525	...	...	...	...	...	...
15	Osmanabad ...	318	116	...	...	...	202	...	...	...	...	...	...
16	Raichur ...	494	245	...	114	...	249	...	...	...	...	...	...
17	Bidar ...	2,345	528	...	140	...	1,817	...	...	...	...	...	...

TABLE XV.

OCCUPATION OR MEANS OF LIVELIHOOD.

PART A.—GENERAL TABLE.

and liberal arts.

Public force.

Army. 140.—Army (Native States). Total workers and dependants.	Actual workers. Total. Males.	Females.	Partially agriculturist. Males.	Females.	Dependants.	Order 43.—Navy. 141.—Navy. Total workers and dependants.	Actual workers. Total. Males.	Females.	Partially agriculturist. Males.	Females.	Dependants.	Total Order 44. Total workers and dependants.	Actual workers. Total. Males.	Females.	Partially agriculturist. Males.	Females.	Dependants.	Serial Number.
998	999	1000	1001	1002	1003	1004	1005	1006	1007	1008	1009	1010	1011	1012	1013	1014	1015	
63,196	***23,392***	***278***	***631***	...	***39,526***	...	...	...	...	...	***95,648***	***41,943***	...	***4,395***	...	***53,705***	
45,182	16,004	207	...	...	28,971	...	...	...	...	...	...	12,697	3,761	...	...	...	8,936	1
529	253	...	9	...	276	...	...	...	...	...	...	4,623	2,013	...	77	...	2,620	2
2,431	***926***	...	***54***	...	***1,5[illegible]***	...	...	...	...	...	...	***13,945***	***5,342***	...	***1,020***	...	***8,603***	
1,990	701	...	35	...	1,289	...	...	...	...	...	...	2,661	1,148	...	227	...	1,513	3
441	225	...	19	...	216	...	...	...	...	...	...	9,353	3,211	...	657	...	6,142	4
...	...	...	...	...	...	...	...	...	...	...	...	1,931	983	...	136	...	948	5
2,513	***1,161***	***71***	***42***	...	***1,281***	...	...	...	...	...	...	***25,894***	***12,663***	...	***1,465***	...	***13,231***	
1,249	530	71	5	...	648	...	...	...	...	...	...	13,404	6,557	...	756	...	6,847	6
588	356	...	25	...	232	...	...	...	...	...	...	1,960	1,126	...	236	...	834	
443	170	...	11	...	273	...	...	...	...	...	..	5,528	2,963	...	259	...	2,565	8
233	105	...	1	...	128	...	...	...	...	...	...	5,002	2,017	...	214	...	2,955	9
3,706	***2,006***	...	***12***	...	***1,700***	...	...	...	...	...	...	***32,808***	***15,437***	...	***1,306***	...	***17,371***	
1,329	797	...	...	...	532	...	...	...	...	...	...	2,612	1,049	...	57	...	1,563	10
713	290	...	10	...	422	...	...	...	...	...	...	12,542	5,126	...	537	...	7,416	11
624	310	...	2	...	314	...	...	...	...	...	...	1,327	680	...	...	...	647	12
1,041	609	...	...	...	432	...	...	...	...	...	...	16,327	8,582	...	712	...	7,745	13
8,835	***3,042***	...	***521***	...	***5,793***	...	...	...	...	...	...	***8,671***	***2,727***	...	***827***	...	***2,944***	
5,678	2,153	...	267	...	3,525	...	...	...	...	...	...	1,911	895	...	57	...	1,016	14
318	116	...	...	...	202	...	...	...	...	...	...	1,218	572	...	9	...	646	15
494	245	...	114	...	249	...	...	...	...	...	...	1,663	792	...	401	...	87	16
2,345	528	...	140	...	1,817	...	...	...	...	...	...	879	466	...	60	...	411	17

TABLE XV.

OCCUPATION OR MEANS OF LIVELIHOOD.

PART A.—GENERAL TABLE.

Serial Number.	District.	Class C.—Public administration. Sub-Class VI.—Public force.—(concld.) Order 44.—Police. 142.—Police. Total workers and dependants.	142.—Police. Actual workers. Total. Males.	Total. Females.	Partially agriculturist. Males.	Partially agriculturist. Females.	Dependants.	143.—Village watchmen. Total workers and Dependants.	Actual workers. Total. Males.	Total. Females.	Partially agriculturist. Males.	Partially agriculturist. Females.	Dependants.
	1	1016	1017	1018	1019	1020	1021	1022	1023	1024	1025	1026	1027
	Hyderabad State ...	***35,135***	***12,456***	...	***1,088***	...	***22,679***	***60,513***	***29,487***	...	***3,307***	...	***31,026***
1	Hyderabad City ...	12,697	3,761	...	...	...	8,936	...	...	...	...	...	...
2	Atraf-i-balda ...	2,468	733	...	37	...	1,735	2,165	1,280	...	40	...	885
	Warangal Division ..	***4,175***	***1,284***	...	***216***	...	***2,891***	***9,770***	***4,058***	...	***804***	...	***5,712***
3	Warangal ...	1,079	472	...	61	..	607	1,582	676	...	166	...	906
4	Karimnagar ...	2,689	629	...	154	...	2,060	6,664	2,582	...	503	...	4,082
5	Adilabad ...	407	183	...	1	...	224	1,524	800	...	135	...	724
	Medak Division ...	***5,129***	***2,007***	...	***73***	...	***3,122***	***20,765***	***10,656***	...	***1,392***	...	***10,109***
6	Medak ..	1,655	638	...	30	...	1,017	11,749	5,919	...	726	...	5,830
7	Nizamabad ..	890	497	...	32	...	393	1,070	629	...	204	...	441
8	Mahbubnagar ...	436	270	...	9	...	166	5,092	2,693	...	250	...	2,399
9	Nalgonda ..	2,148	602	...	2	...	1,546	2,854	1,415	...	212	...	1,439
	Aurangabad Division.	***6,629***	***2,818***	...	***257***	...	***3,811***	***26,179***	***12,619***	...	***1,049***	...	***13,560***
10	Aurangabad ...	1,953	685	...	23	...	1,268	659	364	...	34	...	295
11	Bhir ...	1,830	929	...	8	...	901	10,712	4,197	...	529	...	6,515
12	Nander ...	930	359	...	...	...	571	397	321	...	...	...	76
13	Parbhani ..	1,916	845	...	226	...	1,071	14,411	7,737	...	486	...	6,674
	Gulbarga Division ...	***4,037***	***1,853***	...	***505***	...	***2,184***	***1,634***	***874***	...	***22***	...	***760***
14	Gulbarga ..	902	394	...	57	...	508	1,009	501	...	...	...	508
15	Osmanabad ...	775	314	...	3	...	461	443	258	...	6	...	185
16	Raichur ..	1,663	792	...	401	...	871	...	...	...	...	...	...
17	Bidar ..	697	353	...	44	...	344	182	115	...	16	...	67

TABLE XV.

OCCUPATION OR MEANS OF LIVELIHOOD.

PART A.—GENERAL TABLE.

and liberal arts.—(*contd.*)

Sub-Class VII.—Public administration.

Total Order 45.						Order 45.—Public administration. 144.—Service of the State (Imperial Government).						Serial Number.
Total workers and dependants.	Actual workers. Total. Males.	Actual workers. Total. Females.	Actual workers. Partially agriculturist. Males.	Actual workers. Partially agriculturist. Females.	Dependants.	Total workers and dependants.	Actual workers. Total. Males.	Actual workers. Total. Females.	Actual workers. Partially agriculturist. Males.	Actual workers. Partially agriculturist. Females.	Dependants.	
1028	1029	1030	1031	1032	1033	1034	1035	1036	1037	1038	1039	
346,184	***149,366***	***7,343***	***17,549***	***3,265***	***189,475***	***4,567***	***922***	***167***	...	...	***3,478***	
27,015	10,786	587	2	...	15,642	4,342	871	162	...	...	3,309	1
12,352	5,508	525	319	25	6,319	...	...	...	...	...	...	2
49,629	***22,795***	***896***	***3,102***	***360***	***25,938***	...	...	...	...	...	...	
14,160	6,312	352	828	57	7,496	...	...	...	...	...	...	3
21,122	9,736	357	1,553	303	11,029	...	...	...	...	...	...	4
14,347	6,747	187	724	...	7,413	...	...	...	...	...	...	5
66,115	***20,645***	***1,467***	***2,990***	***765***	***24,003***	...	...	...	...	...	...	
19,252	8,951	582	1,346	674	9,719	...	...	...	...	...	...	6
9,501	3,790	444	590	68	5,267	...	...	...	...	...	...	7
7,723	3,762	283	409	15	3,678	...	...	...	...	...	...	8
9,639	4,142	158	645	8	5,339	...	...	...	...	...	...	9
75,680	***32,795***	***1,547***	***4,529***	***343***	***42,308***	***225***	***51***	***5***	...	...	***169***	
25,865	10,301	309	1,807	55	15,255	225	51	5	...	...	169	10
10,638	4,482	558	535	23	5,598	...	...	...	...	...	...	11
13,813	6,326	325	1,053	69	7,162	...	...	...	...	...	...	12
25,334	11,686	355	1,134	196	13,293	...	...	...	...	...	...	13
135,423	***56,837***	***2,321***	***6,607***	***1,775***	***76,265***	...	...	...	...	...	...	
54,490	24,699	926	2,640	282	28,865	...	...	...	...	...	...	14
13,392	4,747	54	641	3	8,501	...	...	...	...	...	...	15
32,182	11,517	516	1,265	462	20,149	...	...	...	...	...	...	16
35,359	15,874	825	2,061	1,025	18,660	...	...	...	...	...	...	17

TABLE XV.

OCCUPATION OR MEANS OF LIVELIHOOD.

PART A.—GENERAL TABLE.

Class C.—Public administration

Sub-Class VII.—Public

Order 45.—Public

Serial Number.	District.	145.—Service of Native and foreign States. Total workers and dependants.	Actual workers. Total. Males.	Total. Females.	Partially agriculturist. Males.	Partially agriculturist. Females.	Dependants.	146.—Municipal and other local (not village) Muzrai service. Total workers and dependants.	Actual workers. Total. Males.	Total. Females.	Partially agriculturist. Males.	Partially agriculturist. Females.	Dependants.
	1	1040	1041	1042	1043	1044	1045	1046	1047	1048	1049	1050	1051
	Hyderabad State ...	***130,831***	***60,464***	...	***4,695***	...	***70,367***	***8,926***	***3,702***	***652***	***174***	***23***	***4,871***
1	Hyderabad City ...	18,591	8,613	...	...	...	9,978	4,082	1,302	425	2	...	2,853
2	Atraf-i-balda ...	6,280	2,902	...	14	...	3,378	120	...	88	...	...	32
	Warangal Division ...	***24,211***	***11,051***	...	***892***	...	***13,160***	***804***	***462***	***18***	...	...	***324***
3	Warangal ..	7,601	3,525	...	150	...	4,076	803	462	17	...	...	324
4	Karimnagar ...	9,004	4,062	...	356	...	4,942	1	...	1	...	...	...
5	Adilabad ...	7,606	3,464	...	386	...	4,142	...	...	...	...	...	...
	Medak Division ...	***20,538***	***9,253***	...	***814***	...	***11,285***	***1,031***	***488***	***90***	***112***	***20***	***453***
6	Medak	7,376	3,437	...	499	..	3,939	511	212	51	80	20	248
7	Nizamabad ...	5,064	2,402	...	117	...	2,662	223	121	...	23	...	102
8	Mahbubnagar ...	3,392	1,500	...	135	...	1,892	295	154	39	9	...	102
9	Nalgonda.. ...	4,706	1,914	...	63	...	2,792	2	1	...	...	...	1
	Aurangabad Division	***31,244***	***14,535***	...	***1,562***	...	***16,709***	***2,801***	***1,389***	***32***	***60***	***3***	***1,380***
10	Aurangabad ...	8,857	4,122	...	843	...	4,735	...	...	...	...	...	...
11	Bhir	4,849	2,402	...	67	...	2,447	32	21	2	7	...	9
12	Nander	5,544	2,751	...	352	...	2,793	2,297	1,238	23	53	3	1,036
13	Parbhani ...	11,994	5,260	...	300	...	6,734	472	130	7	...	...	235
	Gulbarga Division ...	***29,967***	***14,110***	...	***1,413***	...	***15,857***	***88***	***61***	...	...	...	***27***
14	Gulbarga ..	9,657	4,372	...	380	...	5,285	75	52	...	...	...	23
15	Osmanabad ...	6,710	2,891	...	84	...	3,819	13	9	...	...	...	4
16	Raichur	5,542	2,720	...	655	...	2,822	...	...	...	...	...	...
17	Bidar	8,058	4,127	...	294	...	3,931	...	...	...	...	...	...

TABLE XV.

OCCUPATION OR MEANS OF LIVELIHOOD.

PART A.—GENERAL TABLE.

and liberal arts.—(*contd.*)

administration.

administration.

147.—Village officials and servants other than watchmen.						Total Order 46.						
Total workers and dependants.	Actual workers. Total. Males.	Actual workers. Total. Females.	Actual workers. Partially agriculturist. Males.	Actual workers. Partially agriculturist. Females.	Dependants.	Total workers and dependants.	Actual workers. Total. Males.	Actual workers. Total. Females.	Actual workers. Partially agriculturist. Males.	Actual workers. Partially agriculturist. Females.	Dependants.	Serial Number.
1052	1053	1054	1055	1056	1057	1058	1059	1060	1061	1062	1063	
201,860	***84,278***	***6,523***	***12,680***	***3,242***	***111,059***	***101,187***	***30,137***	***12,953***	***4,026***	***947***	***58,097***	
...	...	...	...	...	...	8,223	2,709	269	...	...	5,245	1
5,932	2,606	437	308	25	2,909	2,165	645	642	46	35	878	2
24,614	***11,282***	***878***	***2,210***	***360***	***12,484***	***13,818***	***4,070***	***2,054***	***730***	***224***	***7,694***	
5,756	2,325	335	678	57	3,096	4,098	1,521	422	335	7	2,155	3
12,117	5,674	356	1,197	303	6,087	5,241	1,314	1,038	280	186	2,889	4
6,741	3,283	187	335	...	3,271	4,479	1,235	594	115	31	2,650	5
24,546	***10,904***	***1,377***	***2,064***	***745***	***12,265***	***15,750***	***4,051***	***2,738***	***641***	***255***	***8,961***	
11,365	5,302	531	767	654	5,532	3,350	866	580	194	116	1,904	6
4,314	1,267	444	450	68	2,503	2,370	645	320	64	26	1,405	7
4,036	2,108	244	265	15	1,684	3,670	388	449	91	39	2,833	8
4,931	2,227	158	582	8	2,546	6,360	2,152	1,389	292	74	2,819	9
41,380	***16,823***	***1,510***	***2,907***	***340***	***23,050***	***28,888***	***9,126***	***4,420***	***1,046***	***137***	***15,342***	
16,783	6,128	304	964	55	10,351	8,264	2,141	1,035	221	25	5,088	10
5,757	2,059	556	461	23	3,142	4,912	1,921	534	315	25	2,457	11
5,972	2,337	302	648	66	3,333	6,275	2,367	869	186	31	3,039	12
12,868	6,296	348	834	196	6,224	9,437	2,697	1,982	324	56	4,758	13
105,368	***42,466***	***2,321***	***5,194***	***1,772***	***60,381***	***32,343***	***9,536***	***2,830***	***1,563***	***296***	***19,977***	
44,758	20,275	926	2,260	282	23,557	10,477	2,617	1,116	347	33	6,744	14
6,669	1,847	54	557	3	4,768	8,068	3,018	509	250	17	4,541	15
26,640	8,797	516	610	462	17,327	9,623	2,505	954	766	205	6,167	16
27,301	11,747	825	1,767	1,025	14,729	4,175	1,396	254	200	41	2,525	17

TABLE XV.

OCCUPATION OR MEANS OF LIVELIHOOD.

PART A.—GENERAL TABLE.

Serial Number.	District.	Class C.—Public administration											
		Sub-Class VII.—Profession											
		Order 46.—											
		148.—Priests, ministers, etc.						149.—Religious mendicants, inmates of monasteries, etc.					
		Total workers and dependants.	Actual workers.				Dependants.	Total workers and dependants.	Actual workers.				Dependants.
			Total.		Partially agriculturist.				Total		Partially agriculturist.		
			Males.	Females.	Males.	Females.			Males.	Females.	Males.	Females.	
	1	1064	1065	1066	1067	1068	1069	1070	1071	1072	1073	1074	1075
	Hyderabad State ...	***57,809***	***14,931***	***8,075***	***2,250***	***629***	***34,803***	***33,743***	***11,507***	***4,261***	***1,391***	***271***	***17,975***
1	Hyderabad City ...	5,381	1,610	245	...	...	3,526	882	335	9	...	...	538
2	Atraf-i-balda ...	2,034	543	638	38	35	853	...	...	...	...	...	...
	Warangal Division ...	***10,403***	***2,994***	***1,586***	***650***	***193***	***5,823***	***3,056***	***943***	***393***	***61***	***30***	***1,720***
3	Warangal ...	4,032	1,498	412	335	7	2,122	...	...	...	...	...	...
4	Karimnagar ...	5,127	1,261	993	280	186	2,873	3	...	...	...	...	3
5	Adilabad ...	1,244	235	181	35	...	828	3,053	943	393	61	30	1,717
	Medak Division ...	***15,470***	***3,997***	***2,702***	***633***	***255***	***8,771***	***14***	...	...	...	...	***14***
6	Medak ...	3,221	824	556	186	116	1,841	...	...	...	...	...	...
7	Nizamabad ...	2,352	643	315	64	26	1,394	...	...	...	...	...	...
8	Mahbubnagar ...	3,665	383	449	91	39	2,833	...	...	...	...	...	...
9	Nalgonda ...	6,232	2,147	1,382	292	74	2,703	14	...	...	...	...	14
	Aurangabad Division	***11,297***	***2,554***	***1,785***	***273***	***45***	***6,958***	***15,316***	***5,589***	***2,403***	***701***	***88***	***7,324***
10	Aurangabad ...	3,940	681	203	49	5	3,056	3,918	1,339	800	164	20	1,779
11	Bhir ...	1,690	567	207	78	25	916	2,852	1,233	293	216	...	1,326
12	Nander ...	592	183	62	48	13	347	5,257	1,990	759	130	14	2,508
13	Parbhani ...	5,075	1,123	1,313	98	2	2,639	3,289	1,027	551	191	54	1,711
	Gulbarga Division ...	***13,224***	***3,233***	***1,119***	***656***	***101***	***8,872***	***14,475***	***4,640***	***1,456***	***629***	***153***	***8,319***
14	Gulbarga ...	4,209	994	418	244	30	2,797	4,706	1,158	608	61	...	2,940
15	Osmanabad ...	871	253	93	...	...	525	6,764	2,506	389	232	16	3,869
16	Raichur ...	6,280	1,452	485	354	42	4,343	1,042	303	340	201	125	399
17	Bidar ...	1,864	534	123	58	29	1,207	1,963	673	119	135	12	1,171

TABLE XV.

OCCUPATION OR MEANS OF LIVELIHOOD.

PART A—GENERAL TABLE.

and liberal arts.—(*contd*).

and liberal arts.

Religion.

150.—Catechists, readers, church and mission service.						151.—Temples, burial or burning ground service, pilgrim conductors, circumcisers.						Total Order 47.						Serial Number.
Total workers and dependants.	Actual workers.				Dependants.	Total workers and dependants.	Actual workers.				Dependants.	Total workers and dependants.	Actual workers.				Dependants.	
	Total.		Partially agriculturist.				Total.		Partially agriculturist.				Total.		Partially agriculturist.			
	Males.	Females.	Males.	Females.			Males.	Females.	Males.	Females.			Males.	Females.	Males.	Females.		
1076	1077	1078	1079	1080	1081	1082	1083	1084	1085	1086	1087	1088	1089	1090	1091	1092	1093	
2,217	***783***	***114***	***39***	...	***1,320***	***7,418***	***2,916***	***503***	***346***	***47***	***3,999***	***6,863***	***2,543***	***36***	***289***	...	***4,284***	
880	202	5	...	...	673	1,080	562	10	...	...	508	2,289	797	...	...	...	1,492	1
119	97	4	8	...	18	12	5	...	...	...	7	...	...	...	...	...	...	2
308	***117***	***59***	***13***	...	***132***	***51***	***16***	***16***	***6***	***1***	***19***	***284***	***92***	***4***	***10***	...	***188***	
66	23	10	...	...	33	...	...	...	...	...	...	67	41	...	3	...	26	3
111	53	45	...	...	13	...	...	...	...	...	...	110	18	4	...	...	88	4
131	41	4	13	...	86	51	16	16	6	1	19	107	33	...	7	...	74	5
255	***50***	***36***	***8***	...	***169***	***11***	***4***	...	...	...	***7***	***179***	***83***	...	***2***	...	***96***	
129	42	24	8	...	63	...	...	...	...	...	...	34	20	...	...	...	14	6
18	2	5	...	...	11	...	...	...	...	...	...	21	7	...	2	...	14	7
5	5	...	...	...	...	...	...	...	...	...	...	15	9	...	...	...	6	8
103	1	7	...	...	95	11	4	...	...	...	7	109	47	...	...	...	62	9
515	***271***	***1***	***8***	...	***243***	***1,760***	***712***	***231***	***64***	***4***	***817***	***2,418***	***928***	***32***	***141***	...	***1,458***	
165	58	1	1	...	106	241	63	31	7	...	147	869	284	9	76	...	576	10
...	...	...	...	...	...	370	121	34	21	...	215	712	361	13	48	...	338	11
124	78	...	7	...	46	302	116	48	1	4	138	229	78	6	15	...	145	12
226	135	...	...	...	91	847	412	118	35	...	317	608	205	4	2	...	399	13
140	***46***	***9***	***2***	..	***85***	***4,504***	***1,617***	***246***	***276***	***42***	***2,641***	***1,693***	***643***	...	***136***	...	***1,050***	
15	1	...	...	...	14	1,547	464	90	42	3	993	841	217	...	23	...	624	14
...	...	...	...	...	...	433	259	27	18	1	147	278	83	...	3	...	195	15
...	...	...	...	...	...	2,301	750	126	211	38	1,425	69	47	...	2	...	22	16
125	45	9	2	...	71	223	144	3	5	..	76	505	296	...	108	...	209	17

TABLE XV.

OCCUPATION OR MEANS OF LIVELIHOOD.

PART A.—GENERAL TABLE.

Serial Number.	District.	Class C.—Public administration / Sub-Class VIII.—Professions / Order 47.—Law. 152.—Lawyers of all kinds, including Kazis, law agents and mukhtiars. Total workers and dependants.	Actual workers. Total. Males.	Actual workers. Total. Females.	Partially agriculturist. Males.	Partially agriculturist. Females.	Dependants.	153.—Lawyers' clerks, petition writers, etc. Total workers and dependants.	Actual workers. Total. Males.	Actual workers. Total. Females.	Partially agriculturist. Males.	Partially agriculturist. Females.	Dependants.
	1	1094	1095	1096	1097	1098	1099	1100	1101	1102	1103	1104	1105
	Hyderabad State ...	***6,835***	***2,531***	***36***	***289***	...	***4,268***	***28***	***12***	...	...	...	1[illegible]
1	Hyderabad City ...	2,281	793	...	...	...	1,488	8	4	...	...	...	[illegible]
2	Atraf-i-balda ...	...	...	...	...	...	...	...	...	...	...	...	...
	Warangal Division ...	***284***	***92***	***4***	***10***	...	***188***	...	...	...	...	...	...
3	Warangal ...	67	41	...	3	...	26	...	...	...	...	...	...
4	Karimnagar ...	110	18	4	...	...	88	...	...	...	...	...	...
5	Adilabad ...	107	33	...	7	...	74	...	...	...	...	...	...
	Medak Division ...	***179***	***83***	...	***2***	...	***96***	...	...	...	...	...	...
6	Medak ...	34	20	...	...	...	14	...	...	...	...	...	...
7	Nizamabad ...	21	7	...	2	...	14	...	...	...	...	...	...
8	Mahbubnagar ...	15	9	...	...	...	6	...	...	...	...	...	...
9	Nalgonda ...	109	47	...	...	...	62	...	...	...	...	...	...
	Aurangabad Division.	***2,398***	***920***	***32***	***141***	...	***1,446***	***20***	***8***	...	...	...	1[illegible]
10	Aurangabad ...	869	284	9	76	...	576	...	...	...	...	...	...
11	Bhir ...	712	361	13	48	...	338	...	...	...	...	...	...
12	Nander ...	229	78	6	15	...	145	...	...	...	...	...	...
13	Parbhani ...	588	197	4	2	...	387	20	8	...	...	...	1[illegible]
	Gulbarga Division ...	***1,693***	***643***	...	***136***	...	***1,050***	...	...	...	...	...	...
14	Gulbarga ...	841	217	...	23	...	624	...	...	...	...	...	...
15	Osmanabad ...	278	83	...	3	...	195	...	...	...	...	...	...
16	Raichur ...	69	47	...	2	...	22	...	...	...	...	...	...
17	Bidar ..	505	296	...	108	...	209	...	...	...	...	...	...

TABLE XV·

OCCUPATION OR MEANS OF LIVELIHOOD.

PART A.—GENERAL TABLE.

and liberal arts.—(*contd*).

and liberal arts.—(*contd.*)

Total Order 48.						Order 48.—Medicine. 154.—Medical practitioners of all kinds, including dentists, oculists and veterinary surgeons.						Order 48.—Medicine. 155.—Midwives, vaccinators, compounders, nurses, masseurs, etc.						Serial Number.
Total workers and dependants.	Actual workers. Total. Males.	Actual workers. Total. Females.	Actual workers. Partially agriculturist. Males.	Actual workers. Partially agriculturist. Females.	Dependants.	Total workers and dependants.	Actual workers. Total. Males.	Actual workers. Total. Females.	Actual workers. Partially agriculturist. Males.	Actual workers. Partially agriculturist. Females.	Dependants.	Total workers and dependants.	Actual workers. Total. Males.	Actual workers. Total. Females.	Actual workers. Partially agriculturist. Males.	Actual workers. Partially agriculturist. Females.	Dependants.	
1106	1107	1108	1109	1110	1111	1112	1113	1114	1115	1116	1117	1118	1119	1120	1121	1122	1123	
30,973	***13,383***	***3,880***	***824***	***316***	***13,710***	***23,760***	***12,651***	***1,093***	***710***	***75***	***10,016***	***7,213***	***732***	***2,787***	***114***	***241***	***3,694***	
4,338	967	657	...	...	2,714	2,753	879	105	...	...	1,769	1,585	88	552	...	...	945	1
2,547	1,780	102	9	...	665	2,377	1,752	73	9	...	552	170	28	29	...	...	113	2
4,575	***1,377***	***614***	***245***	***35***	***2,584***	***3,597***	***1,244***	***307***	***245***	***14***	***2,046***	***978***	***133***	***307***	...	***21***	***538***	
2,680	812	216	78	18	1,652	2,040	696	67	78	1	1,277	640	116	149	...	17	375	3
1,787	527	393	167	17	864	1,482	524	238	167	13	720	305	3	158	...	4	144	4
108	38	2	...	...	68	75	24	2	...	...	49	33	14	...	...	...	19	5
7,376	***1,471***	***2,233***	***183***	***272***	***3,672***	***2,931***	***992***	***350***	***69***	***52***	***1,589***	***4,445***	***479***	***1,883***	***114***	***220***	***2,083***	
3,236	789	636	129	147	1,811	1,286	426	143	31	35	717	1,950	363	493	98	112	1,094	6
219	83	32	15	5	104	199	83	19	15	2	97	20	...	13	...	3	7	7
2,346	298	1,012	17	86	1,036	743	184	167	1	14	392	1,603	114	845	16	72	614	8
1,575	301	553	22	34	721	703	299	21	22	1	383	872	2	532	...	33	338	9
9,495	***6,861***	***50***	***56***	...	***2,584***	***9,464***	***6,857***	***36***	***56***	...	***2,571***	***31***	***4***	***14***	...	...	***13***	
130	49	6	...	...	75	130	49	6	...	...	75	...	...	...	...	...	...	10
250	105	25	12	...	120	237	101	21	12	...	115	13	4	4	...	...	5	11
8,981	6,670	5	44	...	2,306	8,981	6,670	5	44	...	2,306	...	...	...	...	...	...	12
134	37	14	...	...	83	116	37	4	...	...	75	18	...	10	...	...	8	13
2,642	***927***	***224***	***331***	***9***	***1,491***	***2,638***	***927***	***222***	***331***	***9***	***1,489***	***4***	...	***2***	...	...	***2***	
758	107	113	27	...	538	754	107	111	27	...	536	4	...	2	...	...	2	14
195	53	...	1	...	142	195	53	...	1	...	142	...	...	...	...	...	...	15
1,111	650	41	300	7	420	1,111	650	41	300	7	420	...	...	...	...	...	...	16
578	117	70	3	2	391	578	117	70	3	2	391	...	...	...	...	...	...	17

TABLE XV.

OCCUPATION OR MEANS OF LIVELIHOOD.

PART A.—GENERAL TABLE.

Serial Number.	District.	Class C.—Public administration / Sub-Class VIII.—Professions / 49—Instruction. / 156.—Professors and teachers of all kinds (except law, medicine, music, dancing and drawing), and clerks and servants connected with education. Total workers and dependants.	Actual workers. Total. Males.	Actual workers. Total. Females.	Partially agriculturist. Males.	Partially agriculturist. Females.	Dependants.	Total Order 50. Total workers and dependants.	Actual workers. Total. Males.	Actual workers. Total. Females.	Partially agriculturist. Males.	Partially agriculturist. Females.	Dependants.
	1	1124	1125	1126	1127	1128	1129	1130	1131	1132	1133	1134	1135
	Hyderabad State ...	***23,574***	***8,360***	***1,995***	***671***	***222***	***13,219***	***46,442***	***16,665***	***7,501***	***1,597***	***766***	***22,276***
1	Hyderabad City ...	5,228	1,484	367	...	...	3,377	4,425	1,676	116	25	...	2,6[illegible]
2	Atraf-i-balda ...	1,147	716	20	5	1	411	2,018	717	433	24	30	8[illegible]
	Warangal Division ...	***5,211***	***2,159***	***656***	***344***	***134***	***2,396***	***9,526***	***3,469***	***1,752***	***562***	***42***	***4,305***
3	Warangal ...	2,694	1,227	243	109	5	1,224	5,980	2,204	1,140	271	28	2,64[illegible]
4	Karimnagar ...	2,041	800	371	232	129	870	3,131	1,174	436	288	10	1,521
5	Adilabad ...	476	132	42	3	...	302	406	91	176	3	4	13[illegible]
	Medak Division ...	***4,469***	***1,696***	***506***	***123***	***6***	***2,267***	***14,141***	***5,389***	***2,475***	***395***	***428***	***6,27[illegible]***
6	Medak ...	1,258	375	160	31	5	723	2,772	843	624	112	155	1,30[illegible]
7	Nizamabad ...	515	225	84	34	...	206	2,415	840	433	177	11	1,14[illegible]
8	Mahbubnagar ...	1,485	747	169	36	1	569	2,595	826	846	51	138	92[illegible]
9	Nalgonda ...	1,211	349	93	22	...	769	6,359	2,880	572	55	124	2,90[illegible]
	Aurangabad Division	***3,689***	***798***	***173***	***48***	***3***	***2,718***	***7,327***	***2,686***	***519***	***223***	***3***	***4,12[illegible]***
10	Aurangabad ..	1,561	264	41	24	3	1,256	2,029	813	159	19	1	1,0[illegible]
11	Bhir ..	556	162	115	1	...	279	655	239	28	1	...	38
12	Nander ...	300	103	7	8	...	190	2,228	713	96	163	2	1,41[illegible]
13	Parbhani ...	1,272	269	10	15	...	903	2,415	921	236	40	...	1,2[illegible]
	Gulbarga Division ..	***3,830***	***1,507***	***273***	***151***	***78***	***2,050***	***9,005***	***2,728***	***2,206***	***368***	***263***	***4,0[illegible]***
14	Gulbarga ...	1,169	410	50	42	...	709	4,580	1,389	882	82	17	2,3[illegible]
15	Osmanabad ...	388	140	15	3	...	233	503	223	68	2	5	2[illegible]
16	Raichur ...	900	459	57	70	8	384	2,485	715	970	263	232	8[illegible]
17	Bidar ...	1,373	498	151	36	70	724	1,437	401	286	21	9	7[illegible]

TABLE XV.

OCCUPATION OR MEANS OF LIVELIHOOD.

PART A.—GENERAL TABLE.

and liberal arts.—(*contd*).

and liberal arts.—(*contd*).

Order 50.—Letters and arts and sciences.

157.—Public Scribes, Stenographers, etc.						158.—Architects, Surveyors, engineers and their employes.						159.—Others (authors) photographers, artists, sculptors, astronomers, meteorologists, botanists, astrologers, etc.						
Total workers and dependants.	Actual workers. Total. Males.	Actual workers. Total. Females.	Actual workers. Partially agriculturist. Males.	Actual workers. Partially agriculturist. Females.	Dependants.	Total workers and depend-	Actual workers. Total. Males.	Actual workers. Total. Females.	Actual workers. Partially agriculturist. Males.	Actual workers. Partially agriculturist. Females.	Dependants.	Total workers and dependants.	Actual workers. Total. Males.	Actual workers. Total. Females.	Actual workers. Partially agriculturist. Males.	Actual workers. Partially agriculturist. Females.	Dependants.	Serial Number.
1136	1137	1138	1139	1140	1141	1142	1143	1144	1145	1146	1147	1148	1149	1150	1151	1152	1153	
...	...	...	...	...	...	***1,166***	***419***	...	***1***	...	***747***	***11,502***	***5,031***	***1,463***	***263***	***95***	***5,008***	
...	...	...	...	...	...	969	305	...	...	...	664	924	495	...	20	...	429	1
...	...	...	...	...	...	...	...	...	...	...	...	191	71	11	3	5	109	2
...	...	...	...	...	...	***78***	***36***	...	...	...	***42***	***4,041***	***1,443***	***914***	***140***	***26***	***1,684***	
...	...	...	...	...	...	78	36	...	...	...	42	3,685	1,349	846	138	26	1,490	3
...	...	...	...	...	...	...	...	...	...	...	...	325	79	68	2	...	178	4
...	...	...	...	...	...	...	...	...	...	...	...	31	15	...	...	...	16	5
...	...	...	...	...	..	***49***	***33***	...	***1***	..	***16***	***5,683***	***2,765***	***812***	***58***	***64***	***2,406***	
...	...	...	...	...	...	...	...	..	...	..	...	703	361	103	36	28	239	6
...	...	...	...	...	...	11	4	...	1	...	7	170	59	39	...	2	72	7
...	...	...	...	...	...	2	1	...	...	...	1	748	248	314	2	18	186	8
...	...	..	...	...	...	36	28	...	...	...	8	4,062	2,097	56	20	16	1,909	9
...	...	...	...	...	...	***41***	***26***	...	...	...	***15***	***534***	***173***	***25***	***4***	...	***336***	
...	...	...	...	...	...	36	21	...	...	...	15	463	144	21	..	...	298	10
...	...	...	...	...	...	1	1	...	...	...	...	17	11	...	1	...	6	11
...	...	...	...	...	...	...	...	...	...	...	...	42	14	...	3	...	28	12
...	...	...	...	...	...	4	4	...	...	...	...	12	4	4	...	...	4	13
...	...	...	...	...	...	***29***	***19***	...	...	...	***10***	***129***	***84***	***1***	***38***	...	***44***	
...	...	...	...	...	...	15	6	...	...	...	9	105	73	...	35	...	32	14
...	...	...	...	...	...	14	13	...	...	...	1	...	...	...	...	...	...	15
...	...	...	...	...	...	...	...	...	...	...	...	...	...	...	..	...	...	16
...	...	...	...	...	...	...	...	...	...	...	...	24	11	1	3	...	12	17

TABLE XV.

OCCUPATION OR MEANS OF LIVELIHOOD.

PART A.—GENERAL TABLE.

Serial Number.	District.	Class C.—Public administration and liberal arts.—(concld). Sub-Class VIII.—Professions and liberal arts.—(concld). Order 50.—Letters and arts and sciences.—(concld). 160.—Music composers and masters, players on all kinds of musical instruments (not military), singers, actors, and dancers. Total workers and dependants.	Actual workers. Total. Males.	Actual workers. Total. Females.	Actual workers. Partially agriculturist. Males.	Actual workers. Partially agriculturist. Females.	Dependants.	Class D.— Sub-Class IX.—Persons living on their income. Order 51.—Persons living principally on their income. 161.—Proprietors (other than of agricultural land), fund and scholarship holders and pensioners. Total workers and dependants.	Actual workers. Total. Males.	Actual workers. Total. Females.	Actual workers. Partially agriculturist. Males.	Actual workers. Partially agriculturist. Females.	Dependants.
	1	1154	1155	1156	1157	1158	1159	1160	1161	1162	1163	1164	1165
	Hyderabad State ...	***33,774***	***11,215***	***6,038***	***1,333***	***671***	***16,521***	***28,377***	***8,650***	***2,289***	***204***	***14***	***17,438***
1	Hyderabad City ...	2,532	876	116	5	...	1,540	22,852	6,656	2,083	...	...	14,111
2	Atraf-i-balda ...	1,827	616	422	21	25	759	217	34	32	...	...	151
	Warangal Division ...	***5,407***	***1,990***	***838***	***422***	***16***	***2,579***	***722***	***167***	***43***	***17***	***8***	***512***
3	Warangal ...	2,226	819	294	133	2	1,113	108	18	2	1	...	83
4	Karimnagar ...	2,806	1,095	368	286	10	1,343	78	17	5	3	...	56
5	Adilabad ...	375	76	176	3	4	123	541	132	36	13	8	373
	Medak Division ...	***8,409***	***2,591***	***1,963***	***336***	***364***	***3,855***	***830***	***230***	***10***	***77***	...	***590***
6	Medak ...	2,069	482	521	76	127	1,066	593	150	7	72	...	441
7	Nizamabad ..	2,234	777	394	176	9	1,063	13	5	...	1	...	6
8	Mahbubnagar ...	1,845	577	532	49	120	736	40	24	...	3	...	16
9	Nalgonda ..	2,261	755	516	35	108	990	179	51	8	1	...	125
	Aurangabad Division	***6,752***	***2,487***	***494***	***219***	***3***	***3,771***	***1,658***	***496***	***83***	***82***	***3***	***1,079***
10	Aurangabad ...	1,530	648	138	19	1	744	750	180	47	29	1	523
11	Bhir ..	637	227	28	...	...	382	516	173	16	13	...	327
12	Nander ..	2,186	699	96	160	2	1,391	201	38	16	...	2	147
13	Parbhani ...	2,399	913	232	40	...	1,254	191	105	4	40	...	82
	Gulbarga Division ..	***8,847***	***2,625***	***2,205***	***330***	***263***	***4,017***	***2,098***	***1,065***	***38***	***28***	***3***	***995***
14	Gulbarga ...	4,460	1,310	882	47	17	2,268	662	308	28	11	3	326
15	Osmanabad ...	489	210	68	2	5	211	92	41	1	11	...	50
16	Raichur ...	2,485	715	970	263	232	800	641	251	...	...	...	390
17	Bidar ...	1,413	390	285	18	9	738	703	465	9	6	...	229

TABLE XV.

OCCUPATION OR MEANS OF LIVELIHOOD.

PART A.—GENERAL TABLE.

Miscellaneous.												
Sub-Class X.—Domestic service.												
Total Order 52.						Order 52.—Domestic service. 162.—Cooks, water carriers, door keepers, watchmen and other in door servants.						Serial Number.
Total workers and dependants.	Actual workers. Total. Males.	Actual workers. Total. Females.	Actual workers. Partially agriculturist. Males.	Actual workers. Partially agriculturist. Females.	Dependants.	Total workers and dependants.	Actual workers. Total. Males.	Actual workers. Total. Females.	Actual workers. Partially agriculturist. Males.	Actual workers. Partially agriculturist. Females.	Dependants.	
1166	1167	1168	1169	1170	1171	1172	1173	1174	1175	1176	1177	
421,147	***140,971***	***75,814***	***7,214***	***3,667***	***204,362***	***406,181***	***133,663***	***75,580***	***6,867***	***3,663***	***196,938***	
109,505	37,296	14,510	84	...	57,699	97,562	31,703	14,305	64	...	51,554	1
13,224	4,944	2,473	150	99	5,807	12,925	4,777	2,473	150	99	5,675	2
65,338	***23,265***	***10,171***	***1,516***	***307***	***31,902***	***64,809***	***22,952***	***10,158***	***1,511***	***307***	***31,699***	
18,473	5,835	3,225	74	42	9,413	18,255	5,723	3,221	74	42	9,311	3
33,436	14,337	4,069	1,297	187	15,030	33,200	14,173	4,069	1,292	187	14,958	4
13,429	3,093	2,877	145	78	7,459	13,354	3,056	2,868	145	78	7,430	5
87,328	***31,196***	***17,069***	***2,064***	***481***	***39,063***	***85,561***	***30,211***	***17,053***	***1,807***	***477***	***38,297***	
17,400	4,337	4,075	418	213	8,988	17,173	4,243	4,070	383	210	8,860	6
15,228	6,684	2,623	268	82	5,921	15,066	6,647	2,618	267	81	5,801	7
22,474	6,408	3,026	227	65	13,040	21,808	6,073	3,022	225	65	12,713	8
32,226	13,767	7,345	1,151	121	11,114	31,514	13,248	7,343	932	121	10,923	9
71,456	***24,499***	***15,849***	***1,130***	***824***	***31,108***	***71,344***	***24,435***	***15,849***	***1,130***	***824***	***31,060***	
20,138	4,069	6,381	422	693	9,688	20,138	4,069	6,381	422	693	9,638	10
12,888	4,149	3,257	114	21	5,482	12,880	4,141	3,257	114	21	5,482	11
16,214	6,260	2,544	222	91	7,410	16,208	6,256	2,544	222	91	7,408	12
22,216	10,021	3,667	372	19	8,528	22,118	9,969	3,667	372	19	8,482	13
74,296	***19,771***	***15,742***	***2,270***	***1,956***	***38,783***	***73,980***	***19,888***	***15,742***	***2,205***	***1,956***	***38,653***	
29,520	7,939	6,120	1,088	1,062	15,461	29,440	7,904	6,120	1,033	1,062	15,416	14
6,001	2,262	797	60	15	2,942	5,952	2,237	797	60	15	2,918	15
23,855	4,431	6,093	688	479	13,331	23,668	4,305	6,093	628	479	13,270	16
14,920	5,139	2,732	434	400	7,049	14,920	5,139	2,732	434	400	7,049	17

TABLE XV.

OCCUPATION OR MEANS OF LIVELIHOOD.

PART A—GENERAL TABLE.

Serial Number.	District.	Class D.— Sub-Class X.—Domestic service.—(concld). Order 52.—Domestic service.—(concld). 163—Private grooms, coachmen, dog boys, etc. Total workers and dependants.	Actual workers. Total. Males.	Actual workers. Total. Females.	Actual workers. Partially agriculturist. Males.	Actual workers. Partially agriculturist. Females.	Dependants.	Sub-Class XI—Insufficiently … Total Order 53. Total workers and dependants.	Actual workers. Total. Males.	Actual workers. Total. Females.	Actual workers. Partially agriculturist. Males.	Actual workers. Partially agriculturist. Females.	Dependants.
	1	1178	1179	1180	1181	1182	1183	1184	1185	1186	1187	1188	1189
	Hyderabad State ...	***14,966***	***7,308***	***234***	***347***	***4***	***7,424***	***380,148***	***110,010***	***111,369***	***6,278***	***6,931***	***158,769***
1	Hyderabad City ...	11,943	5,593	205	20	...	6,145	31,195	9,944	6,221	3	2	15,030
2	Atraf-i-balda ...	299	167	...	...	...	132	18,265	4,379	5,935	96	145	7,951
	Warangal Division ..	***529***	***313***	***13***	***5***	...	***203***	***54,957***	***14,788***	***16,937***	***778***	***846***	***23,232***
3	Warangal ...	218	112	4	...	...	102	15,813	4,771	3,108	308	28	7,934
4	Karimnagar ...	236	164	...	5	...	72	18,248	3,976	8,724	377	770	5,548
5	Adilabad ...	75	37	9	...	...	29	20,896	6,041	5,105	93	42	9,750
	Medak Division ...	***1,767***	***985***	***16***	***257***	***4***	***766***	***128,831***	***36,611***	***42,790***	***3,756***	***3,515***	***49,530***
6	Medak ..	227	94	5	35	3	128	34,256	8,752	8,148	1,841	1,614	17,356
7	Nizamabad ..	162	37	5	1	1	120	18,034	4,937	7,276	611	293	5,921
8	Mahbubnagar ...	666	335	4	2	...	327	26,283	10,998	7,459	239	182	7,826
9	Nalgonda ..	712	519	2	219	...	191	50,258	11,824	19,907	1,065	1,426	18,527
	Aurangabad Division.	***112***	***64***	...	...	...	***48***	***68,415***	***17,635***	***18,948***	***350***	***815***	***31,832***
10	Aurangabad ...	...	...	...	...	...	...	19,621	4,960	4,417	177	700	10,244
11	Bhir ..	8	8	...	...	...	...	13,883	3,622	4,121	52	...	6,140
12	Nander ...	6	4	...	...	...	2	18,595	3,933	7,211	17	18	7,451
13	Parbhani ...	98	52	...	...	...	46	16,316	5,120	3,199	104	97	7,997
	Gulbarga Division ..	***316***	***186***	...	***65***	..	***130***	***78,485***	***26,753***	***20,538***	***1,292***	***1,614***	***31,194***
14	Gulbarga ...	80	35	...	5	...	45	31,776	8,158	8,953	132	1,401	14,665
15	Osmanabad ...	49	25	...	...	...	24	7,354	1,537	2,884	8	3	2,933
16	Raichur ...	187	126	...	60	...	61	21,033	12,457	3,035	873	7	5,541
17	Bidar ..	...	...	...	...	...	...	18,322	4,601	5,666	279	203	8,058

TABLE XV.

OCCUPATION OR MEANS OF LIVELIHOOD.

PART A.—GENERAL TABLE.

Miscellaneous—(*contd.*)

described occupation.

Order 53.—General terms which do not indicate a definite occupation.

164.—Manufacturers, businessmen and contractors otherwise unspecified.						165.—Cashiers, accountants, book-keepers, clerks and other employes in unspecified offices, warehouses, and shops.						Serial Number.
Total workers and dependants.	Actual workers. Total. Males.	Actual workers. Total. Females.	Actual workers. Partially agriculturist. Males.	Actual workers. Partially agriculturist. Females.	Dependants.	Total workers and dependants.	Actual workers. Total. Males.	Actual workers. Total. Females.	Actual workers. Partially agriculturist. Males.	Actual workers. Partially agriculturist. Females.	Dependants.	
1190	1191	1192	1193	1194	1195	1196	1197	1198	1199	1200	1201	
6,828	***2,080***	***992***	***70***	***28***	***3,756***	***8,073***	***3,869***	***81***	***29***	***13***	***4,123***	
1,273	383	79	...	...	811	2,455	1,073	8	3	2	1,374	1
453	138	85	4	5	230	134	111	...	...	...	23	2
2,236	***434***	***686***	***12***	***6***	***1,116***	***223***	***109***	...	...	...	***114***	
958	250	87	3	6	621	55	23	...	...	...	32	3
1,083	64	599	3	...	420	43	15	...	...	...	28	4
195	120	...	6	...	75	125	71	...	...	...	54	5
7,917	***894***	***95***	***34***	***17***	***928***	***568***	***271***	***46***	***15***	***11***	***251***	
814	320	21	25	...	473	237	99	...	3	...	138	6
688	331	72	6	17	285	184	76	46	12	11	62	7
113	68	...	...	...	45	59	45	...	...	...	14	8
302	175	2	3	...	125	88	51	...	...	...	37	9
610	***156***	***35***	***15***	...	***419***	***768***	***527***	***27***	***2***	..	***214***	
534	126	35	14	...	373	57	32	...	...	...	25	10
9	4	...	...	...	5	375	287	...	2	...	88	11
53	18	...	1	...	35	125	88	...	...	...	37	12
14	8	...	...	...	6	211	120	27	...	...	64	13
339	***78***	***12***	***5***	...	***252***	***3,925***	***1,778***	...	***9***	...	***2,147***	
175	29	...	3	...	146	294	119	...	9	...	175	14
51	27	...	...	...	24	109	89	...	...	...	20	15
6	3	1	1	...	2	3,520	1,569	...	...	...	1,951	16
107	16	11	1	...	80	2	1	...	...	...	1	17

TABLE XV.

OCCUPATION OR MEANS OF LIVELIHOOD.

PART A.—GENERAL TABLE.

Serial Number.	District.	Class D.— Sub-Class XI.—Insufficiently described occupation.—(concld.) Order 53—General terms which do not indicate a definite occupation.—(concld.) 166—Mechanics otherwise unspecified. Total workers and dependants.	Actual workers. Total. Males.	Females.	Partially agriculturist. Males.	Females.	Dependants.	167—Labourers and workmen otherwise unspecified. Total workers and dependants.	Actual workers. Total. Males.	Females.	Partially agriculturist. Males.	Females.	Dependants.
	1	1202	1203	1204	1205	1206	1207	1208	1209	1210	1211	1212	1213
	Hyderabad State ...	***1,090***	***506***	...	...	...	***584***	***364,157***	***103,555***	***110,296***	***6,176***	***6,890***	***150,306***
1	Hyderabad City ...	1,047	486	...	...	...	561	26,420	8,002	6,134	...	...	12,284
2	Atraf-i-balda ...	...	...	...	...	...	...	17,678	4,130	5,850	92	140	7,69[illegible]
	Warangal Division ...	***43***	***20***	...	...	...	***23***	***52,455***	***14,225***	***16,251***	***766***	***834***	***21,979***
3	Warangal ..	43	20	...	...	...	23	14,757	4,478	3,021	305	22	7,258
4	Karimnagar ...	...	...	...	...	...	...	17,122	3,897	8,125	374	770	5,100
5	Adilabad ...	...	...	...	...	...	...	20,576	5,850	5,105	87	42	9,621
	Medak Division ..	...	...	...	...	...	...	***126,346***	***35,346***	***42,649***	***3,707***	***3,487***	***48,251***
6	Medak ...	...	...	...	...	...	...	33,205	8,333	8,127	1,813	1,614	16,74[illegible]
7	Nizamabad ...	...	...	...	...	...	...	17,162	4,530	7,158	593	265	5,474
8	Mahbubnagar ...	...	...	...	...	...	...	23,111	10,885	7,459	239	182	7,767
9	Nalgonda ...	...	...	...	...	...	...	49,863	11,598	19,905	1,062	1,426	18,36[illegible]
	Aurangabad Division	...	...	...	...	...	...	***67,037***	***16,952***	***18,886***	***333***	***815***	***31,199***
10	Aurangabad ..	...	...	...	...	...	...	19,030	4,802	4,382	163	700	9,846
11	Bhir ...	...	...	...	...	...	...	13,499	3,331	4,121	50	...	6,047
12	Nander ..	...	...	...	...	...	...	18,417	3,827	7,211	16	18	7,379
13	Parbhani ...	...	...	...	...	...	...	16,091	4,992	3,172	104	97	7,927
	Gulbarga Division ...	...	...	...	...	...	...	***74,221***	***24,900***	***20,526***	***1,278***	***1,614***	***28,795***
14	Gulbarga ...	...	...	...	...	...	...	31,307	8,010	8,953	120	1,401	14,344
15	Osmanabad ...	...	...	...	...	...	...	7,194	1,421	2,884	8	3	2,399
16	Raichur ...	...	...	...	...	...	...	17,507	10,885	3,034	872	7	3,588
17	Bidar ..	...	...	...	...	...	...	18,213	4,584	5,655	279	203	7,[illegible]

TABLE XV.

OCCUPATION OR MEANS OF LIVELIHOOD.

PART A.—GENERAL TABLE.

Miscellaneous.—(*contd*).

Sub-Class XII.—Unproductive.

Order 54.—Inmates of Jails, asylums and hospitals.						Order 55.—Beggars, vagrants, prostitutes.						
168—Inmates of Jails, asylums and hospitals.						169.—Beggars, vagrants, procurers, prostitutes, receivers of stolen goods, cattle poisoners.						
Total workers and dependants.	Actual workers. Total.		Actual workers. Partially agriculturist.		Dependants.	Total workers and dependants.	Actual workers. Total.		Actual workers. Partially agriculturist.		Dependants.	Serial Number.
	Males.	Females.	Males.	Females.			Males.	Females.	Males.	Females.		
1214	1215	1216	1217	1218	1219	1220	1221	1222	1223	1224	1225	
3,428	***3,198***	***131***	...	...	***99***	***272,711***	***82,182***	***65,728***	***5,123***	***3,172***	***124,801***	
851	746	29	...	...	76	17,260	4,599	3,949	...	...	8,712	1
...	...	...	...	...	...	13,800	4,212	3,723	118	61	5,865	2
506	***500***	***1***	...	...	***5***	***51,751***	***16,243***	***11,692***	***1,140***	***290***	***23,816***	
484	483	1	...	...	...	20,912	6,264	5,346	369	53	9,302	3
22	17	...	...	...	5	21,546	7,494	3,972	656	180	10,080	4
...	...	...	...	...	...	9,293	2,485	2,374	115	57	4,434	5
590	***544***	***28***	...	...	***18***	***63,032***	***20,961***	***16,233***	***1,213***	***1,033***	***25,863***	
39	21	...	...	...	18	15,813	4,483	4,606	461	570	6.721	6
486	472	14	...	...	...	12,306	4,937	3,066	365	134	4,303	7
52	50	2	...	...	...	13.210	4,543	3,375	291	281	5,322	8
13	1	12	...	...	...	21,673	6,995	5,156	106	43	9,522	9
751	***723***	***28***	...	...	...	***50,753***	***15,881***	***12,448***	***1,051***	***657***	***22,424***	
681	654	27	...	...	...	8,004	1,601	1,973	135	20	4,430	10
26	26	...	...	...	...	9,019	3,012	1,728	63	28	4.279	11
22	22	...	...	...	...	9,100	2,529	2,533	157	230	4,038	12
22	21	1	...	...	...	24,630	8,739	6,214	696	379	9,677	13
730	***685***	***45***	...	...	...	***76,115***	***20,286***	***17,713***	***1,601***	***1,131***	***38,116***	
693	648	45	...	...	...	21,165	4,749	4,926	155	355	11,490	14
7	7	...	...	...	...	8,178	3,115	1,473	63	31	3,590	15
26	26	...	...	...	...	27,146	6,683	6,328	936	451	14,135	16
4	4	...	...	..	...	19,626	5,739	4,986	447	294	8,901	17

TABLE XV.

OCCUPATION OR MEANS OF LIVELIHOOD.

PART B.—SUBSIDIARY OCCUPATIONS OF AGRICULTURISTS.

ACTUAL WORKERS ONLY.

TABLE XV.

OCCUPATION OR MEANS OF LIVELIHOOD.

PART B.—SUBSIDIARY OCCUPATIONS OF AGRICULTURISTS—ACTUAL WORKERS ONLY.

(1).—RENT-RECEIVERS—(LANDLORDS).

Serial Number.	District.	Total number of rent receivers (actual workers).		Number of actual workers who returned subsidiary occupations.		Details of							
						Rent payers.		Agricultural labourers.		Government employes of all kinds.		Money-lenders and grain dealers.	
		Males.	Females.	Males.	Females.	Males.	Females.	Males.	Females.	Males.	Females.	Males.	Females.
	1	2	3	4	5	6	7	8	9	10	11	12	13
	Hyderabad State ...	***234,108***	***113,407***	***22,539***	***7,864***	***6,142***	***2,522***	***6,379***	***2,773***	***1,561***	...	***1,002***	[illegible]
1	Hyderabad City ...	1,351	263	18	4	...	...	...	3	...	...	3	...
2	Atraf-i-balda ...	6,495	2,150	478	385	37	37	89	136	39	...	33	[illegible]
	Warangal Division...	***30,381***	***17,796***	***3,115***	***933***	***498***	***164***	***846***	***311***	***284***	...	***224***	[illegible]
3	Warangal ...	16,129	8,920	1,595	480	307	89	343	130	107	...	97	[illegible]
4	Karimnagar ...	8,432	3,914	704	199	47	9	211	100	122	...	76	[illegible]
5	Adilabad ...	5,820	4,962	816	254	144	66	292	81	55	...	51	[illegible]
	Medak Division ...	***65,061***	***40,684***	***9,269***	***3,695***	***3,443***	***1,562***	***2,593***	***1,195***	***557***	...	***223***	[illegible]
6	Medak	25,098	16,895	5,812	2,384	2,659	1,194	1,623	787	239	...	151	[illegible]
7	Nizamabad ..	6,756	3,302	687	281	63	40	227	78	92	...	8	[illegible]
8	Mahbubnagar ...	16,002	6,428	1,665	479	444	137	363	129	171	...	38	[illegible]
9	Nalgonda... ...	17,205	14,059	1,105	551	277	191	380	201	55	...	26	[illegible]
	Aurangabad Division	***64,975***	***19,450***	***3,333***	***1,189***	***827***	***375***	***882***	***437***	***301***	..	***132***	[illegible]
10	Aurangabad ...	26,741	11,637	1,126	448	209	108	370	181	82	...	43	[illegible]
11	Bhir	8,234	1,152	437	167	109	50	170	81	40	...	18	[illegible]
12	Nander	21,289	3,565	527	194	56	43	148	69	28	...	27	[illegible]
13	Parbhani ...	8,711	3,096	1,243	380	453	174	194	106	151	...	44	[illegible]
	Gulbarga Division ...	***65,845***	***33,064***	***6,326***	***1,658***	***1,337***	***384***	***1,969***	***691***	***380***	...	***387***	[illegible]
14	Gulbarga ..	28,649	12,233	2,431	663	421	64	745	336	150	...	95	[illegible]
15	Osmanabad ...	3,224	2,255	642	123	115	16	212	40	84	...	64	[illegible]
16	Raichur	20,103	11,483	1,760	368	312	106	633	140	61	...	103	[illegible]
17	Bidar	13,869	7,093	1,493	504	489	198	379	175	85	...	125	[illegible]

TABLE XV.

OCCUPATION OR MEANS OF LIVELIHOOD.

PART B.—SUBSIDIARY OCCUPATIONS OF AGRICULTURISTS—ACTUAL WORKERS ONLY.

(1)—RENT-RECEIVERS—(LANDLORDS).

subsidiary occupations returned.																		
Other traders of all kinds.		Priests.		Clerks of all kinds (Not Govt.)		School Masters.		Lawyers.		Estate Agent and Managers.		Medical Practitioners.		Artisans.		Others.		Serial Number.
Males.	Females.	Males.	Females.	Males.	Females.	Males.	Females.	Males.	Females.	Males.	Females.	Males.	Females.	Males.	Females.	Males.	Females.	
14	15	16	17	18	19	20	21	22	23	24	25	26	27	28	29	30	31	
1,403	**661**	**553**	**93**	**681**	...	**438**	**66**	**192**	..	**171**	**46**	**493**	**17**	**1,116**	**261**	**2,408**	**1,232**	
...	1	...	...	2	...	4	...	...	...	2	...	3	...	4	...	...	...	1
46	150	7	2	8	...	...	2	1	...	6	...	6	...	7	27	199	25	2
229	**120**	**87**	**15**	**118**	...	**27**	**12**	**14**	...	**51**	**13**	**129**	**3**	**135**	**23**	**473**	**237**	
120	58	23	3	81	...	15	8	5	...	41	8	96	2	81	15	279	144	3
57	52	7	...	29	...	7	3	...	...	5	4	27	...	21	6	95	22	4
52	10	57	12	8	...	5	1	9	...	5	1	6	1	33	2	99	71	5
418	**184**	**61**	**22**	**249**	...	**124**	**17**	**14**	...	**86**	**10**	**228**	**5**	**499**	**135**	**804**	**392**	
117	26	45	8	94	...	69	12	...	...	20	8	69	1	406	84	320	225	6
40	34	10	4	17	...	8	1	4	...	...	2	4	2	16	6	198	104	7
227	106	...	8	110	...	38	2	5	...	32	...	125	2	22	17	90	62	8
34	18	6	2	28	...	9	2	5	...	4	...	30	...	55	28	196	101	9
209	**20**	**175**	**12**	**169**	...	**75**	**27**	**38**	...	**20**	**4**	**34**	**5**	**139**	**29**	**332**	**247**	
77	7	34	2	61	...	32	21	16	.	10	1	15	...	48	5	129	113	10
27	...	18	1	9	...	21	4	6	.	...	...	2	2	13	2	4	2	11
32	5	24	6	34	...	5	2	7	..	2	...	5	1	61	7	98	56	12
73	8	99	3	65	...	17	...	9	..	8	3	12	2	17	6	101	76	13
501	**186**	**223**	**42**	**135**	...	**208**	**8**	**125**	...	**36**	**19**	**93**	**4**	**332**	**56**	**600**	**331**	
249	131	109	22	74	...	113	7	87	...	12	7	48	1	222	19	106	63	14
55	27	14	6	7	...	3	1	1	...	...	...	2	...	45	6	40	24	15
102	4	46	3	17	...	68	...	9	...	3	3	25	1	29	23	352	85	16
95	24	54	11	37	...	24	...	28	...	21	9	18	2	36	8	102	59	17

TABLE. XV.

OCCUPATION OR MEANS OF LIVELIHOOD.

PART B.—SUBSIDIARY OCCUPATIONS OF AGRICULTURISTS—ACTUAL WORKERS ONLY.

(2)—RENT PAYERS—(ACTUAL CULTIVATORS.)

Serial Number.	District.	Total number of rent payers (actual workers.)		Number of actual workers who returned subsidiary occupations.		Details of									
						Rent receivers.		Agricultural labourers.		General labourers.		Government employes of all kinds.		Money-lenders and grain dealers.	
		Males.	Females.	Males.	Females.	Males.	Females.	Males.	Females.	Males.	Females.	Males.	Females.	Males.	Females.
	1	2	3	4	5	6	7	8	9	10	11	12	13	14	15
	Hyderabad State ...	***1,367,676***	***727,383***	***81,214***	***18,637***	***8,472***	***3,285***	***14,835***	***7,045***	***2,145***	***1,498***	***2,888***	...	***2,466***	[illegible]
1	Hyderabad City ...	1,480	393	112	17	29	...	14	...	9	...	11	...	8	...
2	Atraf-i-balda ...	44,779	22,587	1,969	1,769	128	77	617	586	38	312	123	...	31	[illegible]
	Warangal Division ...	***262,299***	***137,428***	***8,791***	***2,966***	***778***	***266***	***1,842***	***1,080***	***337***	***134***	***972***	...	***544***	***109***
3	Warangal ...	93,067	47,161	3,988	1,552	593	176	626	583	175	42	311	...	211	55
4	Karimnagar ...	98,130	51,039	3,290	986	112	16	667	343	100	78	541	...	222	49
5	Adilabad ...	71,102	39,228	1,513	428	73	74	549	154	62	14	120	...	111	[illegible]
	Medak Division ...	***259,252***	***178,309***	***19,863***	***8,898***	***4,725***	***2,245***	***5,097***	***3,453***	***1,096***	***781***	***798***	...	***842***	***175***
6	Medak ...	41,623	23,932	7,661	[illegible]	3,095	1,207	2,036	1,041	188	96	145	...	244	[illegible]
7	Nizamabad ...	44,323	38,898	2,646	1,894	155	300	875	1,064	157	214	213	...	57	[illegible]
8	Mahbubnagar ...	71,595	41,803	5,886	2,176	894	463	1,323	617	537	282	311	...	167	[illegible]
9	Nalgonda ...	101,711	73,676	3,670	1,863	581	275	863	731	214	189	129	...	74	[illegible]
	Aurangabad Division	***391,310***	***216,934***	***7,235***	***2,193***	***890***	***230***	***2,433***	***982***	***324***	***168***	***500***	...	***523***	[illegible]
10	Aurangabad ...	108,673	58,009	1,774	517	220	35	540	261	106	56	84	...	150	[illegible]
11	Bhir ...	97,722	52,012	1,084	279	121	48	283	120	21	25	153	...	141	[illegible]
12	Nander ...	94,856	58,054	1,873	678	172	56	763	298	84	32	142	...	154	[illegible]
13	Parbhani ..	90,059	48,859	2 504	719	377	91	847	303	113	[illegible]	121	...	[illegible]	[illegible]
	Gulbarga Division ..	***408,556***	***171,732***	***13,244***	***2,794***	***1,922***	***467***	***4,832***	***944***	***341***	***103***	***484***	...	***818***	[illegible]
14	Gulbarga ...	104,423	51,518	4,423	[illegible]	832	240	1,139	401	156	48	95	...	244	[illegible]
15	Osmanabad ..	93,155	34,201	1,939	307	80	15	868	166	19	15	187	..	223	
16	Raichur ..	113,239	[illegible]	4,309	645	271	135	2,289	222	101	9	44	...	[illegible]	[illegible]
17	Bidar ...	97,739	42,105	2,573	549	739	77	536	155	65	31	158	...	138	

TABLE XV.

OCCUPATION OR MEANS OF LIVELIHOOD.

PART B.—SUBSIDIARY OCCUPATIONS OF AGRICULTURISTS—ACTUAL WORKERS ONLY.

(2)—RENT PAYERS—(ACTUAL CULTIVATORS.)

subsidiary occupations returned.																						
Other traders of all kinds.		Fishermen and boatmen.		Cattle breeders and milkmen.		Village watchmen.		Weavers.		Barbers.		Oil pressers.		Washermen.		Potters.		Blacksmiths and Carpenters.		Others.		Serial Number.
Males.	Females.	Males.	Females.	Males.	Females.	Males.	Females.	Males.	Females.	Males.	Females.	Males.	Females.	Males.	Females.	Males.	Females.	Males.	Females.	Males.	Females.	
16	17	18	19	20	21	22	23	24	25	26	27	28	29	30	31	32	33	34	35	36	37	
3,[illegible]25	***1,492***	***1,727***	***60***	***2,734***	***1,473***	***1,348***	...	***1,334***	***570***	***1,433***	...	***889***	***330***	***1,504***	***757***	***1,388***	***437***	***1,558***	***71***	***2,668***	***1,181***	
12	13	1	...	2	2	7	...	...	2	5	...	6	...	...	...	...	...	6	...	2	...	1
472	381	53	3	58	12	10	...	83	72	45	...	2	31	73	55	51	80	12	4	173	115	2
[illegible]227	***196***	***458***	***14***	***707***	***374***	***216***	...	***350***	***108***	***244***	...	***154***	***50***	***304***	***149***	***313***	***101***	***418***	***4***	***427***	***381***	
272	56	136	7	383	197	102	...	174	72	148	...	52	37	173	100	196	53	314	1	122	173	3
387	134	216	6	249	142	62	...	145	33	68	...	63	10	111	43	76	33	82	2	189	97	4
68	6	106	1	75	35	52	..	31	3	28	...	39	3	20	6	41	15	22	1	116	111	5
1,[illegible]462	***610***	***735***	***18***	***1,284***	***508***	***419***	...	***506***	***185***	***507***	...	***204***	***117***	***692***	***435***	***361***	***171***	***496***	***15***	***948***	***185***	
199	87	220	4	513	170	101	...	196	62	102	...	48	57	181	104	51	24	231	4	108	41	6
211	128	119	3	109	35	9	...	32	15	61	...	76	18	79	38	32	17	11	6	450	21	7
897	324	286	5	332	141	201	...	104	47	167	...	44	15	235	97	140	38	49	2	199	90	8
155	71	110	6	330	162	96	...	174	61	177	...	36	27	197	196	138	92	205	3	191	33	9
548	***147***	***148***	***16***	***243***	***288***	***350***	...	***139***	***30***	***206***	...	***217***	***62***	***167***	***46***	***149***	***32***	***183***	***27***	***221***	***99***	
89	12	31	11	69	57	40	...	27	9	47	...	86	6	34	7	47	6	64	9	138	46	10
143	32	52	...	24	20	36	...	13	1	28	...	5	2	24	2	...	2	32	3	8	4	11
174	83	32	4	87	71	85	...	16	13	53	...	20	40	32	16	18	11	31	11	10	9	12
139	20	30	1	63	140	189	...	83	7	78	...	104	14	77	21	84	15	56	4	65	40	13
607	***145***	***335***	***9***	***440***	***289***	***355***	...	***256***	***173***	***426***	..	***306***	***70***	***268***	***72***	***514***	***83***	***443***	***21***	***897***	***401***	
199	80	134	2	182	179	188	...	155	143	203	..	133	19	96	29	296	24	256	9	115	102	14
244	29	...	...	44	16	45	...	33	11	45	...	18	...	24	10	18	...	45	2	46	37	15
80	13	107	6	109	35	31	...	3	...	101	...	86	26	78	12	144	7	76	2	576	158	16
84	23	94	1	105	56	91	...	65	19	77	...	69	25	70	21	56	22	66	8	160	104	17

TABLE XV.

OCCUPATION OR MEANS OF LIVELIHOOD.

PART B.—SUBSIDIARY OCCUPATIONS OF AGRICULTURISTS—ACTUAL WORKERS ONLY.

(3)—FARM SERVANTS AND FIELD LABOURERS.

Serial Number.	District.	Total number of farm servants and field labourers (actual workers.)		Number of actual workers who returned subsidiary occupations.		Details…											
						Rent receivers.		Rent payers.		General labourers.		Village watch-men.		Cattle breeders and milkmen		[illegible]	
		Males.	Females.	Males.	Females.	Males.	Females.	Males.	Females.	Males.	Females.	Males.	Females.	Males.	Females.	Males.	Females.
	1	2	3	4	5	6	7	8	9	10	11	12	13	14	15	16	17
	Hyderabad State ...	***790,731***	***896,825***	***23,135***	***14,596***	***3,383***	***2,367***	***3,645***	***1,954***	***4,683***	***2,871***	***797***	...	***2,238***	[illegible]	[illegible]	[illegible]
1	Hyderabad City ...	515	550	84	3	...	...	...	...	8	...	...	...	...	[illegible]	[illegible]	[illegible]
2	Atraf-i-balda ...	26,404	41,650	1,306	697	53	51	185	94	230	169	5	...	42	[illegible]	—	3
	Warangal Division ...	***158,168***	***219,651***	***3,978***	***2,269***	***433***	***101***	***455***	***235***	***724***	***336***	***131***	...	***476***	[illegible]	***108***	***134***
3	Warangal ...	43,358	78,876	2,340	1,044	215	42	190	73	408	95	49	...	300	128	43	53
4	Karimnagar ...	58,713	95,351	973	742	80	11	150	71	139	148	33	...	149	57	59	21
5	Adilabad ...	56,097	45,424	665	483	138	48	115	91	177	93	49	...	27	8	6	60
	Medak Division ...	***159,403***	***239,713***	***9,961***	***7,414***	***2,031***	***1,834***	***2,175***	***1,357***	***1,459***	***1,185***	***167***	...	***1,120***	***513***	***79***	***137***
6	Medak ...	32,683	34,567	6,410	4,146	1,527	1,292	1,385	816	843	583	75	...	735	162	47	40
7	Nizamabad ...	32,261	45,150	898	834	97	53	270	90	173	197	7	...	121	70	1	77
8	Mahbubnagar ...	40,776	80,238	1,328	1,619	255	352	280	233	202	244	45	...	101	208	9	17
9	Nalgonda ...	53,683	79,738	1,325	815	152	137	240	218	241	161	40	...	163	73	22	3
	Aurangabad Division ...	***209,193***	***194,831***	***2,915***	***1,454***	***328***	***100***	***330***	***92***	***630***	***439***	***180***	...	***150***	***89***	***127***	***51***
10	Aurangabad ...	61,149	43,262	1,035	432	146	44	47	19	162	129	34	...	46	36	37	9
11	Bhir ...	54,789	51,443	281	281	38	33	38	41	55	55	21	.	34	9	9	14
12	Nander ...	48,063	51,610	641	402	43	10	115	11	179	121	24	..	37	24	52	16
13	Parbhani ...	45,192	48,516	958	339	101	13	130	21	234	134	71	...	33	20	29	12
	Gulbarga Division ...	***237,048***	***200,430***	***4,891***	***2,759***	***538***	***281***	***500***	***176***	***1,632***	***742***	***344***	...	***450***	***241***	***148***	***281***
14	Gulbarga ...	81,080	46,983	1,726	1,093	384	241	134	51	383	418	186	...	120	127	59	[illegible]
15	Osmanabad ...	62,695	62,895	364	242	3	7	59	47	26	27	52	...	...	12	12	..
16	Raichur ...	28,495	34,442	1,782	703	2	1	137	33	1,080	167	4	...	227	49	27	...
17	Bidar ...	64,778	56,110	1,019	721	149	32	170	45	143	130	102	...	103	53	50	244

TABLE XV.

OCCUPATION OR MEANS OF LIVELIHOOD.

PART B.—SUBSIDIARY OCCUPATIONS OF AGRICULTURISTS—ACTUAL WORKERS ONLY.

(3).—FARM SERVANTS AND FIELD LABOURERS.

subsidiary occupations returned.																				
ishermen and oatmen.		Rice Pounders.		Traders of all kinds.		Oil pressers.		Weavers.		Potters.		Leather workers.		Washermen.		Blacksmiths and Carpenters.		Others.		Serial Number.
ales.	Females.	Males.	Females.	Males.	Females.	Males.	Females.	Males.	Females.	Males.	Females.	Males.	Females.	Males.	Females.	Males.	Females.	Males.	Females.	
18	19	20	21	22	23	24	25	26	27	28	29	30	31	32	33	34	35	36	37	
599	**60**	**693**	**1,642**	**1,139**	**716**	**279**	**234**	**953**	**465**	**519**	**292**	**730**	**305**	**789**	**641**	**402**	**48**	**1,824**	**1,316**	
...	...	...	...	...	...	...	...	...	...	...	...	...	...	...	...	43	3	33	...	1
78	8	5	29	208	69	3	5	123	60	88	10	21	33	116	31	41	2	108	90	2
125	**20**	**230**	**313**	**145**	**194**	**50**	**73**	**336**	**131**	**94**	**60**	**328**	**128**	**102**	**88**	**74**	**13**	**167**	**250**	
48	7	200	175	58	72	22	21	304	115	51	50	260	80	62	73	50	5	80	55	3
60	6	19	128	63	96	15	36	14	15	33	6	68	29	19	13	10	7	62	98	4
17	7	11	10	24	26	13	16	18	1	10	4	...	19	21	2	14	1	25	97	5
215	**10**	**352**	**894**	**573**	**316**	**98**	**63**	**308**	**215**	**167**	**141**	**369**	**135**	**331**	**323**	**112**	**10**	**405**	**281**	
37	...	293	635	519	130	42	30	209	142	106	45	257	46	189	128	43	1	103	76	6
83	4	15	74	14	81	12	9	9	5	5	25	11	9	26	38	12	5	40	97	7
70	4	7	157	30	95	37	22	60	56	32	42	41	53	71	111	6	1	82	24	8
25	2	37	8	10	10	7	2	30	12	24	29	60	27	43	46	51	3	180	84	9
82	**17**	**27**	**128**	**117**	**66**	**65**	**30**	**53**	**13**	**81**	**35**	**8**	**4**	**56**	**23**	**48**	**8**	**663**	**359**	
20	5	6	46	33	15	23	1	2	7	24	3	1	...	17	15	6	1	412	102	10
12	1	15	11	21	...	4	9	...	2	...	9	5	...	1	4	8	2	20	91	11
11	8	4	57	36	33	16	6	7	2	8	13	2	...	27	3	22	3	58	95	12
39	3	2	14	27	18	22	14	25	2	49	10	...	4	11	1	12	2	173	71	13
99	**5**	**79**	**278**	**96**	**71**	**63**	**63**	**133**	**46**	**89**	**46**	**4**	**5**	**184**	**176**	**84**	**12**	**448**	**336**	
26	3	35	47	36	37	13	2	49	25	45	7	2	...	25	13	21	3	208	82	14
15	...	2	22	17	8	1	...	51	8	4	5	...	...	3	6	14	6	105	94	15
47	2	11	172	26	1	37	53	20	3	19	17	...	...	104	138	5	2	36	65	16
11	...	31	37	17	25	12	8	13	10	21	17	2	5	52	19	44	1	99	95	17

TABLE XV.

OCCUPATION OR MEANS OF LIVELIHOOD.

PART C.--SHOWING FOR CERTAIN MIXED OCCUPATIONS THE NUMBER OF PERSONS WHO RETURNED EACH AS THEIR (*A*) PRINCIPAL AND (*B*) SUBSIDIARY MEANS OF LIVELIHOOD.

TABLE XV.

OCCUPATION OR MEANS OF LIVELIHOOD.

PART C.—SHOWING FOR CERTAIN MIXED OCCUPATIONS THE NUMBER OF PERSONS WHO RETURNED EACH AS THEIR

(A) PRINCIPAL (B) SUBSIDIARY MEANS OF LIVELIHOOD.

Serial Number.	District.	Fisherman and palanquin bearer.							
		Total number of persons (actual workers) who returned occupation of fisherman as their principal occupation.		Number of persons in the two preceding columns who returned occupation of palanquin bearer as their subsidiary occupation.		Total number of persons (actual workers) who returned occupation of palanquin bearer as their principal occupation.		Number of persons in the two preceding columns who returned occupation of fisherman as their subsidiary occupation.	
		Males.	Females.	Males.	Females.	Males.	Females.	Males.	Females.
	1	2	3	4	5	6	7	8	9
	Hyderabad State ...	***37,954***	***5,520***	***711***	...	***987***	***47***	***201***	...
1	Hyderabad City ...	395	...	49	...	165	...	55	...
2	Atraf-i-balda ...	820	255	11	...	279	...	20	...
	Warangal Division ...	***10,788***	***1,645***	***177***	...	***135***	***31***	***47***	...
3	Warangal ...	1,952	668	101	...	50	...	19	...
4	Karimnagar ...	6,343	43	48	...	80	31	54	...
5	Adilabad ...	2,493	934	28	...	5	...	3	...
	Medak Division ...	***10,209***	***1,930***	***126***	...	***390***	***16***	***76***	...
6	Medak ...	2,033	638	67	...	173	8	18	...
7	Nizamabad ...	5,470	294	28	...	129	...	2	...
8	Mahbubnagar ...	1,226	129	22	...	88	8	27	...
9	Nalgonda ...	1,480	869	9	...	...	...	...	...
	Aurangabad Division ...	***3,041***	***818***	***224***	...	***5***	...	***1***	...
10	Aurangabad ...	1,046	446	53	...	5	...	1	...
11	Bhir ...	150	39	40	...	...	...	...	...
12	Nander ...	1,044	128	50	...	...	...	...	...
13	Parbhani ...	801	205	81	...	...	...	...	...
	Gulbarga Division ...	***12,701***	***872***	***124***	...	***13***	...	***2***	...
14	Gulbarga ...	940	311	62	...	13	...	2	...
15	Osmanabad ...	96	8	15	...	...	...	...	...
16	Raichur ...	11,110	198	23	...	...	...	...	...
17	Bidar ...	555	355	24	...	...	...	...	...

TABLE XV.

OCCUPATION OR MEANS OF LIVELIHOOD.

PART C.—SHOWING FOR CERTAIN MIXED OCCUPATIONS THE NUMBER OF PERSONS WHO RETURNED EACH AS THEIR

(A) PRINCIPAL, (B) SUBSIDIARY MEANS OF LIVELIHOOD.

Agricultural labourer and shoe maker.								Serial Number.
Total number of persons (actual workers) who returned occupation of agricultural labourer as their principal occupation.		Number of persons in the two preceding columns who returned occupation of shoe maker as their subsidiary occupation.		Total number of persons (actual worker) who returned occupation of shoe maker as their principal occupation.		Number of persons in the two preceding columns who returned occupation of agricultural labourer as their subsidiary occupation.		
Males.	Females.	Males.	Females.	Males	Females.	Males.	Females.	
10	11	12	13	14	15	16	17	
790,731	***896,825***	***1,753***	***627***	***101,423***	***41,983***	***1,976***	***700***	
515	550	4	...	1,800	506	15	5	1
26,404	41,650	118	8	10,830	4,030	154	38	2
158,168	***219,651***	***467***	***151***	***27,089***	***7,418***	***393***	***198***	
43,358	78,876	290	36	9,715	3,522	90	45	3
58,713	95,351	145	89	14,594	2,808	244	133	4
56,097	45,424	32	26	2,780	1,088	59	20	5
159,403	***239,713***	***389***	***169***	***43,558***	***21,629***	***595***	***126***	
32,683	34,587	167	66	12,254	6,496	256	25	6
32,261	45,150	45	17	6,681	4,583	59	33	7
40,776	80,238	113	55	10,514	5,878	197	51	8
53,683	79,738	64	31	14,109	4,672	83	17	9
209,193	***194,831***	***357***	***141***	***6,620***	***3,478***	***327***	***134***	
61,149	43,262	156	63	1,786	755	111	51	10
54,769	51,443	58	30	2,023	1,418	93	29	11
48,063	51,610	54	35	976	496	19	16	12
45,192	48,516	89	13	1,835	819	104	38	13
237,048	***200,430***	***418***	***158***	***11,526***	***4,922***	***492***	***204***	
81,080	46,983	161	51	2,724	1,310	153	77	14
62,695	62,895	36	32	2,054	603	114	27	15
23,495	34,442	100	34	4,654	1,778	94	25	16
64,778	56,110	121	41	2,114	1,231	131	75	17

TABLE XV.

OCCUPATION OR MEANS OF LIVELIHOOD.

PART C.—SHOWING FOR CERTAIN MIXED OCCUPATIONS THE NUMBER OF PERSONS WHO RETURNED EACH AS THEIR

(A) PRINCIPAL (B) SUBSIDIARY MEANS OF LIVELIHOOD.

Serial Number.	District.	Shepherd and blanket weaver.							
		Total number of persons (actual workers) who returned occupation of shepherd as their principal occupation.		Number of persons in the two preceding columns who returned occupation of blanket weaver as their subsidiary occupation.		Total number of persons (actual workers) who returned occupation of blanket weaver as their principal occupation.		Number of persons in the two preceding columns who returned occupation of shepherd as their subsidiary occupation	
		Males.	Females.	Males.	Females.	Males.	Females.	Males.	Females.
	1	2	3	4	5	6	7	8	9
	Hyderabad State ...	***128,428***	***58,546***	***2,437***	***394***	***19,905***	***7,647***	***1,179***	***227***
1	Hyderabad City ...	426	276	15	...	16	...	2	...
2	Atraf-i-balda ...	6,592	2,766	35	5	1,326	916	17	8
	Warangal Division ...	***27,327***	***10,897***	***270***	***33***	***5,604***	***1,431***	***246***	***50***
3	Warangal ...	9,837	6,635	57	13	1,305	182	75	5
4	Karimnagar ...	13,310	2,627	142	15	2,502	1,133	93	[illegible]
5	Adilabad ...	4,180	1,635	71	5	1,797	116	78	8
	Medak Division ...	***43,705***	***22,751***	***382***	***73***	***6,000***	***2,567***	***141***	***68***
6	Medak ...	5,647	3,610	143	25	918	631	68	[illegible]
7	Nizamabad ..	8,908	3,009	28	4	728	192	11	17
8	Mahbubnagar ...	9,772	3,647	162	32	2,952	233	31	25
9	Nalgonda ..	19,378	12,485	49	12	1,402	1,511	31	9
	Aurangabad Division.	***24,171***	***9,366***	***609***	***60***	***1,881***	***1,216***	***375***	[illegible]
10	Aurangabad ...	4,639	3,345	141	14	602	203	110	11
11	Bhir ...	5,418	908	68	4	561	541	35	29
12	Nander ..	6,769	3,985	58	19	482	369	52	7
13	Parbhani ...	7,345	1,128	342	23	236	103	178	10
	Gulbarga Division ...	***26,207***	***12,488***	***1,126***	***223***	***5,078***	***1,517***	***398***	***44***
14	Gulbarga ...	8,337	3,297	525	51	1,658	1,210	124	17
15	Osmanabad ...	5,383	3,289	85	11	2,149	142	88	[illegible]
16	Raichur ...	5,845	1,968	110	42	680	67	27	1
17	Bidar ...	6,642	3,934	406	119	591	98	159	10

TABLE XV.

OCCUPATION OR MEANS OF LIVELIHOOD.

PART C.—SHOWING FOR CERTAIN MIXED OCCUPATIONS THE NUMBER OF PERSONS WHO RETURNED EACH AS THEIR

(A) PRINCIPAL, (B) SUBSIDIARY MEANS OF LIVELIHOOD.

Cattle breeder and milk seller.								Serial Number.
Total number of persons (actual workers) who returned occupation of cattle breeder as their principal occupation.		Number of persons in the two preceding columns who returned occupation of milk seller as their subsidiary occupation.		Total number of persons (actual workers) who returned occupation of milk seller as their principal occupation.		Number of persons in the two preceding columns who returned occupation of cattle breeder as their subsidiary occupation.		
Males.	Females.	Males.	Females.	Males.	Females.	Males.	Females.	
10	11	12	13	14	15	16	17	
13,153	**10,446**	**931**	**815**	**1,848**	**4,935**	**324**	**311**	
1,141	628	36	42	132	219	47	20	1
509	641	4	19	85	126	6	15	2
3,501	**2,902**	**217**	**221**	**338**	**2,523**	**138**	**141**	
1,654	1,379	108	133	150	538	91	104	3
1,157	1,053	59	51	188	1,985	34	28	4
690	470	50	37	...	...	13	9	5
4,115	**1,794**	**161**	**159**	**1,282**	**2,053**	**63**	**59**	
615	306	85	69	985	872	30	24	6
3,282	718	23	19	294	98	12	11	7
92	79	23	22	3	985	3	6	8
126	691	30	49	...	98	18	18	9
1,444	**1,962**	**290**	**184**	**11**	**14**	**18**	**15**	
262	1,034	156	43	...	...	9	6	10
510	211	17	20	...	...	4	5	11
489	295	14	46	11	14	...	...	12
183	422	103	75	...	...	5	4	13
2,443	**2,519**	**223**	**190**	...	...	**52**	**61**	
1,411	1,033	105	108	...	...	28	24	14
55	6	5	4	...	...	7	9	15
761	1,310	12	24	...	...	8	12	16
216	170	101	54	...	...	9	16	17

TABLE XV.

OCCUPATION OR MEANS OF LIVELIHOOD.

PART C.—SHOWING FOR CERTAIN MIXED OCCUPATIONS THE NUMBER OF PERSONS WHO RETURNED EACH AS THEIR

(A) PRINCIPAL, (B) SUBSIDIARY MEANS OF LIVELIHOOD.

Serial Number.	District.	Grain dealer and money-lender.							
		Total number of persons (actual workers) who returned occupation of grain dealer as their principal occupation.		Number of persons in the two preceding columns who returned occupation of money-lender as their subsidiary occupation.		Total number of persons (actual workers) who returned occupation of money-lender as their principal occupation.		Number of persons in the two preceding columns who returned occupation of grain dealer as their subsidiary occupation.	
		Males.	Females.	Males.	Females.	Males.	Females.	Males.	Females.
	1	2	3	4	5	6	7	8	9
	Hyderabad State ...	***37,380***	***14,815***	***1,612***	***472***	***4,519***	***1,630***	***721***	***309***
1	Hyderabad City ...	2,404	825	106	53	362	34	43	24
2	Atraf-i-balda ...	2,535	719	52	30	265	42	16	[illegible]
	Warangal Division ..	***10,043***	***2,979***	***212***	***84***	***775***	***221***	***105***	***69***
3	Warangal ...	3,245	1,018	69	7	68	72	27	[illegible]
4	Karimnagar ...	5,600	1,544	56	26	48	44	16	7
5	Adilabad ...	1,198	417	87	21	659	105	62	16
	Medak Division ...	***12,088***	***6,068***	***276***	***104***	***424***	***404***	***109***	***39***
6	Medak ..	3,483	2,672	80	21	53	36	39	19
7	Nizamabad ..	2,965	957	36	33	90	116	10	11
8	Mahbubnagar ...	1,907	899	118	41	255	252	52	6
9	Nalgonda ...	3,733	1,540	42	9	26	...	8	3
	Aurangabad Division.	***4,699***	***1,681***	***523***	***123***	***1,683***	***428***	***207***	***68***
10	Aurangabad ...	987	262	193	50	293	70	17	[illegible]
11	Bhir ...	181	124	98	11	184	157	71	17
12	Nander ...	2,138	758	72	37	411	53	30	[illegible]
13	Parbhani ...	1,393	537	160	25	795	148	89	[illegible]
	Gulbarga Division ...	***5,611***	***2,543***	***443***	***108***	***1,010***	***501***	***241***	***63***
14	Gulbarga ...	1,565	1,030	189	24	466	284	83	21
15	Osmanabad ...	172	34	74	10	167	16	44	[illegible]
16	Raichur ...	1,782	1,094	39	21	89	78	53	1
17	Bidar ...	2,092	385	141	53	288	123	61	4

TABLE XV.

OCCUPATION OR MEANS OF LIVELIHOOD.

PART C.—SHOWING FOR CERTAIN MIXED OCCUPATIONS THE NUMBER OF PERSONS WHO RETURNED EACH AS THEIR

(A) PRINCIPAL, (B) SUBSIDIARY MEANS OF LIVELIHOOD.

Barber and musician.								
Total number of persons (actual workers) who returned occupation of barber as their principal occupation.		Number of persons in the two preceding columns who returned occupation of musician as their subsidiary occupation.		Total number of persons (actual workers) who returned occupation of musician as their principal occupation.		Number of persons in the two preceding columns who returned occupation of barber as their subsidiary occupation.		Serial Number.
Males.	Females.	Males.	Females.	Males.	Females.	Males.	Females.	
10	11	12	13	14	15	16	17	
36,672	***8,013***	***789***	...	***11,215***	***6,038***	***591***	...	
2,013	...	94	...	876	116	54	...	1
2,151	207	21	...	646	422	14	...	2
8,766	***1,483***	***129***	...	***1,990***	***838***	***44***	...	
3,650	154	53	...	819	294	24	...	3
3,450	819	20	...	1,095	368	7	...	4
1,666	510	56	...	76	176	13	...	5
8,793	***1,405***	***110***	...	***2,591***	***1,963***	***78***	...	
1,879	607	63	...	482	521	31	...	6
1,367	337	19	...	777	394	20	...	7
1,896	275	16	...	577	532	19	...	8
3,651	186	12	...	755	516	8	...	9
6,655	***729***	***189***	...	***2,487***	***494***	***272***	...	
1,742	257	103	...	648	138	184	...	10
1,339	104	12	...	227	28	20	...	11
1,581	136	37	...	699	96	28	...	12
1,993	232	37	...	913	232	40	...	13
8,294	***1,189***	***246***	...	***2,625***	***2,205***	***129***	...	
2,926	338	96	...	1,310	882	54	...	14
1,710	148	55	...	210	68	24	...	15
1,687	426	14	...	715	970	25	...	16
1,971	277	81	...	390	285	26	...	17

TABLE XV.

OCCUPATION OR MEANS OF LIVELIHOOD.

PART C.—SHOWING FOR CERTAIN MIXED OCCUPATIONS THE NUMBER OF PERSONS WHO RETURNED EACH AS THEIR

(A) PRINCIPAL, (B) SUBSIDIARY MEANS OF LIVELIHOOD.

Serial Number.	District.	Musician and priest.							
		Total number of persons (actual workers) who returned occupation of musician as their principal occupation.		Number of persons in the two preceding columns who returned occupation of priest as their subsidiary occupation.		Total number of persons (actual workers) who returned occupation of priest as their principal occupation.		Number of persons in the two preceding columns who returned occupation of musician as their subsidiary occupation.	
		Males.	Females.	Males.	Females.	Males.	Females.	Males.	Females.
	1	2	3	4	5	6	7	8	9
	Hyderabad State ..	***11,215***	***6,038***	***213***	***11***	***14,931***	***8,075***	***145***	***6***
1	Hyderabad City ...	876	116	13	11	1,610	245	17	6
2	Atraf-i-balda ...	646	422	...	...	543	638	...	...
	Warangal Division ...	***1,591***	***838***	***27***	...	***2,994***	***1,586***	***37***	...
3	Warangal	819	294	21	...	1,498	412	23	...
4	Karimnagar ...	1,095	368	6	...	1,261	993	1	...
5	Adilabad ...	76	176	...	...	235	181	13	...
	Medak Division ...	***2,591***	***1,963***	***38***	...	***3,997***	***2,702***	***6***	...
6	Medak ...	482	521	24	...	824	556	4	...
7	Nizamabad ...	777	394	6	...	643	315	...	...
8	Mahbubnagar ...	577	532	...	...	383	449	...	...
9	Nalgonda ...	755	516	8	...	2,147	1,382	2	...
	Aurangabad Division	***2,487***	***494***	***84***	...	***2,554***	***1,785***	***45***	...
10	Aurangabad ...	648	138	25	...	681	203	19	...
11	Bhir ...	227	28	2	...	567	207	8	...
12	Nander ...	699	96	55	...	183	62	16	...
13	Parbhani ...	913	232	2	...	1,123	1,313	2	...
	Gulbarga Division ...	***2,625***	***2,205***	***51***	...	***3,233***	***1,119***	***43***	...
14	Gulbarga	1,310	882	10	...	994	418	4	...
15	Osmanabad	210	68	25	...	253	93	17	...
16	Raichur	715	970	...	...	1,452	485	18	...
17	Bidar	390	285	16	...	534	123	4	...

TABLE XV.

OCCUPATION OR MEANS OF LIVELIHOOD.

PART D.—DISTRIBUTION BY RELIGION.

SECTION (1) DETAILS FOR THE STATE.

TABLE XV.

OCCUPATION OR MEANS OF LIVELIHOOD.

PART D.—DISTRIBUTION BY RELIGION.

SECTION (1) DETAILS FOR THE STATE.

Class.	Sub-Class.	Order and Group. Serial No.	Order and Group. Description.	Total number of workers and dependants.	Distribution by Religion. Hindu.	Jain.	Musalman.	Christian.	Parsi.	Animistic.	
1	2	3	4	5	6	7	8	9	10	11	
			Hyderabad State ...	*13,374,676*	*11,626,146*	*21,026*	*1,380,990*	*54,296*	*1,529*	*285,722*	4
A	...	...	**Production of raw materials...**	*8,408,192*	*7,455,929*	*6,960*	*667,212*	*29,345*	*216*	*247,150*	1,
	I	...	**Exploitation of the surface of the earth.**	*8,389,718*	*7,438,953*	*6,960*	*666,110*	*28,960*	*216*	*247,139*	1,
	II	...	**Extraction of minerals ...**	*18,474*	*16,976*	...	*1,102*	*385*	...	*11*	
B	...	...	**Preparation and supply of material substances.**	*3,141,052*	*2,875,372*	*10,607*	*226,130*	*9,836*	*846*	*17,820*	4
	III	...	**Industry.**	*1,872,733*	*1,761,669*	*1,796*	*102,271*	*4,097*	*94*	*2,664*	14
	IV	...	**Transport ... ...**	*133,951*	*102,818*	*80*	*21,883*	*3,946*	*122*	*4,997*	13
	V	...	**Trade ... ...**	*1,134,368*	*1,010,885*	*8,761*	*101,976*	*1,793*	*630*	*10,159*	16
C	...	...	**Public administration and liberal arts.**	*747,998*	*527,538*	*811*	*206,322*	*9,937*	*256*	*1,003*	2,13
	VI	...	**Public force ... ..**	*164,398*	*93,385*	*2*	*66,989*	*3,283*	*16*	*102*	62
	VII	...	**Public administration ..**	*346,184*	*249,272*	*225*	*92,461*	*2,230*	*138*	*826*	1,03
	VIII	...	**Professions and liberal arts ...**	*209,039*	*168,531*	*584*	*35,321*	*4,061*	*69*	*75*	39
	IX	...	**Persons living on their income**	*28,377*	*16,350*	...	*11,551*	*364*	*33*	...	7
D	...	...	**Miscellaneous ... ...**	*1,077,434*	*767,307*	*2,648*	*281,326*	*5,178*	*211*	*19,749*	1,0
	X	...	**Domestic service ... ...**	*421,147*	*222,557*	*1,391*	*190,387*	*1,943*	*56*	*4,168*	64
	XI	...	**Insufficiently described occupations ... ...**	*380,148*	*319,587*	*545*	*45,077*	*2,757*	*154*	*11,902*	12
	XII	...	**Unproductive ... ...**	*276,139*	*225,163*	*712*	*45,862*	*478*	*1*	*3,679*	24
A.—Production of raw materials.	I.—Exploitation of the surface of the earth.	(i)	**Pasture and Agriculture ...**	*8,281,829*	*7,335,910*	*6,960*	*662,976*	*28,844*	*216*	*245,543*	1,30
		(a)	**Ordinary Cultivation ...**	*7,619,505*	*6,699,604*	*6,801*	*652,361*	*28,146*	*213*	*231,014*	1,36
		1	Income from rent of agricultural land.	**731,803**	620,618	697	95,822	1,755	152	12,581	17
		2	Ordinary cultivators ...	**4,064,950**	3,573,266	4,421	336,342	11,681	54	138,504	6
		3	Agents, managers, of landed estate, (not planters), clerks, rent collectors, etc.	**34,540**	18,445	...	15,599	415	7	...	7
		4	Farm servants and field labourers.	**2,788,212**	2,487,275	1,683	204,598	14,295	...	79,929	4
		(b)	**Growers of special products and market gardening.**	*22,894*	*19,106*	*51*	*3,637*	*10*	...	...	...
		5	Tea, coffee, cinchona and indigo plantations.	...	...	...	...	...	...	...	...
		6	Fruit, flower, vegetable, betel, vine, arecanut, etc., growers.	**22,894**	19,106	51	3,637	10	..	...	...
		(c)	**Forestry... ... ...**	*41,774*	*26,301*	*15*	*2,471*	*378*	*3*	*12,604*	
		7	Forest officers, rangers, guards, etc.	**839**	384	4	443	35	3	...	...
		8	Wood cutters, fire-wood, lac, catechu, rubber, etc, collectors and charcoal burners.	**40,905**	25,917	11	2,028	343	...	12,604	

TABLE XV.

OCCUPATION OR MEANS OF LIVELIHOOD.

PART D.—DISTRIBUTION BY RELIGION.

SECTION (1) DETAILS FOR THE STATE.

Class.	Sub-class.	Order and Group. Serial No.	Order and Group. Description.	Total number of workers and dependants.	Distribution by Religion. Hindu.	Jain.	Musalman.	Christian.	Parsi.	Animistic.	Others.
1	2	3	4	5	6	7	8	9	10	11	12
A.—Production of raw materials.—(concld)	I.—Exploitation of the surface of the earth.	(d)	**Raising of farm stock** ...	***597,728***	***590,888***	***93***	***4,507***	***310***	...	***1,918***	***12***
		9	Cattle and buffalo breeders and keepers.	42,418	40,872	17	667	...	...	862	...
		10	Sheep, goat and pig breeders.	109,739	106,648	...	2,799	15	...	277	...
		11	Breeders of other animals (horses, mules, camels, asses, etc.)	413	348	...	...	2	...	63	...
		12	Herdsmen, shepherds, goat-herds, etc.	445,158	443,020	76	1,041	293	...	716	12
		(e)	**Raising of small animals** ...	***18***	***11***	...	...	...	...	***7***	...
		13	Birds, bees, silkworms, etc ...	18	11	...	...	...	...	7	...
		ii	**Fishing and hunting** ...	***107,889***	***103,043***	...	***3,134***	***116***	...	***1,596***	...
		14	Fishing	78.269	76,077	...	2.017	7	...	169	...
		15	Hunting	29,620	26,966	...	1,117	109	...	1,428	...
	II.—Extraction of minerals.	iii	**Mines**	***15,325***	***14,031***	...	***909***	***385***	...	...	...
		16	Coal mines and petroleum wells.	11.872	10,579	...	908	385	..	...	...
		17	Mines and metallic minerals (gold, iron, manganese, etc.)	3,453	3,152	...	1	...	...	..	...
		iv	**Quarries of hard rocks.** ...	***3,149***	***2,945***	...	***193***	...	...	***11***	...
		18	Other minerals (jade, diamonds, limestone, etc.)	3,149	2,945	...	193	...	...	11	...
		v	**Salt, etc....**	...	...	...	...	...	...	...	...
		19	Rock, sea and marsh salt ...	...	...	...	...	...	...	...	...
		20	Extraction of saltpetre, alum, and other substances soluble in water.	...	...	...	...	...	...	...	...
B.—Preparation and supply of material substances.	III.—Industry.	vi	**Textiles**	***517,750***	***469,166***	***890***	***55,172***	***1,211***	***54***	***253***	***4***
		21	Cotton ginning, cleaning and pressing.	69.943	43,452	34	26,388	29	37	2	1
		22	Cotton spinning, sizing and weaving.	302,745	275,909	850	24,820	926	...	240	...
		23	Jute spinning, pressing and weaving.	1,098	1,087	...	7	...	...	4	...
		24	Rope, twine and string ...	28,954	28,938	...	4	12	...	...	...
		25	Other fibres (cocoanut, aloes, palm-leaf, flax, hemp, straw, etc. ...	10	10	...	...	...	...	...	...
		26	Wool carders and spinners, weavers of woollen blankets, carpets, etc.	89,095	88,589	...	286	220	...	...	...
		27	Silk spinners and weavers ...	1,901	1,573	6	312	...	...	7	3
		28	Hair, camel and horse hair, bristles work, brush makers, etc.	77	77	...	...	...	...	...	...
		29	Persons occupied with feathers.	204	204	...	...	...	...	...	...
		30	Dyeing, bleaching, printing, preparation and sponging of textiles.	22,310	19,704	...	2,604	2	...	...	...
		31	Other (lace, crape, embroideries, fringes, etc.,) and insufficiently described textile industries.	1,413	623	...	751	22	17	...	...

TABLE XV.

OCCUPATION OR MEANS OF LIVELIHOOD.

PART D.—DISTRIBUTION BY RELIGION.

SECTION (1) DETAILS FOR THE STATE.

Class.	Sub-Class.	Order and Group. Serial No.	Order and Group. Description.	Total number of workers and dependants.	Distribution by Religion. Hindu.	Jain.	Musalman.	Christian.	Parsi.	Animistic.	Others.
1	2	3	4	5	6	7	8	9	10	11	12
B.—Preparation and supply of material substances.—(contd.)	III.—Industry.—(contd.)	vii	**Hides, skins and hard materials from the animal kingdom.**	*15,930*	*14,842*	...	*1,050*	*38*	...	...	...
		32	Tanners, curriers, leather dressers and dyers, etc.	7,061	6,464	...	597	...	...	...	...
		33	Makers of leather articles, such as trunks, water bags, etc.	7,946	7,762	...	183	1	...	...	...
		34	Furriers	462	282	...	143	37	...	...	...
		35	Bone, ivory, horn, shell, etc., workers.	461	334	...	127	...	...	...	...
		viii	**Wood**	*146,747*	*141,168*	*8*	*3,365*	*637*	*1*	*1,554*	*14*
		36	Sawyers, carpenters, turners and joiners, etc.	87,903	84,017	6	2,958	105	1	802	14
		37	Basket makers and other industries of woody material, including leaves.	58,844	57,151	2	407	532	...	752	...
		ix	**Metals**	*88,772*	*83,688*	*58*	*4,879*	*74*	*4*	...	*69*
		38	Forging and rolling of iron and other metals.	409	409	...	...	...	...	...	...
		39	Plough and agricultural implement makers.	9	...	...	9	...	...	...	...
		40	Makers of arms, guns, etc.	257	224	...	29	4	...	...	...
		41	Other workers in iron and makers of implements and tools, principally or exclusively of iron.	73,586	70,456	...	3,024	41	...	...	65
		42	Workers in brass, copper and bell metal.	12,925	11,981	58	878	...	4	...	4
		43	Workers in other metals (tin, zinc, lead, quick-silver, etc.)	1,096	519	...	577	...	...	...	...
		44	Workers in mints, die-sinkers, etc.,	490	99	...	362	29	...	...	...
		x	**Ceramics**	*103,514*	*103,427*	...	*87*	...	...	...	...
		45	Makers of glass and crystal ware.	...	...	...	...	...	...	...	...
		46	Makers of porcelain and crockery	...	...	...	...	...	...	...	...
		47	Potters and earthen pipe and bowl makers.	102,373	102,286	...	87	...	...	...	...
		48	Brick and tile makers.	1,141	1,141	...	...	...	...	...	...
		49	Others (mosaic, talc, mica, alabaster, etc., workers.)	...	...	...	...	...	...	...	...
		xi	**Chemical products properly so-called, and analogous.**	*19,211*	*17,739*	...	*1,472*	...	...	...	...
		50	Manufacture of matches and explosive materials.	39	25	...	14	...	...	...	...
		51	Manufacture of ærated and mineral waters	...	...	...	...	...	...	...	...
		52	Manufacture of dyes, paint and ink.	50	23	...	27	...	...	...	...
		53	Manufacture and refining of vegetable and mineral oils.	18,091	17,481	...	610	...	...	...	...
		54	Manufacture of paper, cardboard and *papier mache.*	535	107	...	428	...	...	...	...
		55	Others (soap, candles, lac, cutch, perfumes and miscellaneous drugs.)	496	103	...	393	...	...	...	...

TABLE XV.

OCCUPATION OR MEANS OF LIVELIHOOD.

PART D.—DISTRIBUTION BY RELIGION.

SECTION (1) DETAILS FOR THE STATE.

Class.	Sub-Class.	Order and Group. Serial No.	Order and Group. Description.	Total number of workers and dependants.	Distribution by Religion. Hindu.	Jain.	Musalman.	Christian.	Parsi.	Animistic.	Others.
1	2	3	4	5	6	7	8	9	10	11	12
B.—Preparation and supply of material substances.—(contd.)	III.—Industry.—(contd.)	xii	**Food Industries**	*119,245*	*103,493*	*118*	*15,370*	*111*	*21*	*132*	...
		56	Rice pounders and huskers and flour grinders.	7,308	6,515	4	783	...	...	6	...
		57	Bakers, and biscuit makers .	2,869	916	...	1,842	111	...	...	...
		58	Grain parchers, etc. ...	2,082	2,045	29	8	...	...	...	...
		59	Butchers	21,192	10,166	...	11,026	...	...	...	...
		60	Fish curers	13	13	...	...	...	...	...	...
		61	Butter, cheese and ghee makers.	...	...	...	...	...	...	...	...
		62	Makers of sugar, molasses and *gur*.	249	249	...	...	...	...	...	...
		63	Sweetmeat makers, preparers of jam and condiments, etc.	1,652	1,343	50	259	...	...	...	...
		64	Brewers and distillers ...	443	388	29	5	...	21	...	...
		65	Toddy drawers	79.852	79,732	...	...	...	...	120	...
		66	Manufacturers of tobacco, opium and *ganja*.	3,585	2,126	6	1,447	...	...	6	...
		xiii	**Industries of dress and the toilet.**	*642,448*	*628,419*	*654*	*12,060*	*1,141*	...	*133*	*41*
		67	Hat, cap, and turban makers.	391	60	25	306	...	...	...	...
		68	Tailors, milliners, dressmakers and darners, embroiderers on linen.	70,859	62,966	602	7,099	171	...	...	21
		69	Shoe, boot and sandal-makers.	269,048	267,693	7	322	927	...	79	20
		70	Other industries pertaining to dress, gloves, socks, gaiters, belts, buttons, umbrellas, canes, etc.	1,124	1,124	...	...	...	...	...	...
		71	Washing, cleaning and dyeing	214,921	211,260	...	3,624	37	...	...	...
		72	Barbers, hairdressers and wig-makers.	85,880	85,091	20	709	6	...	54	...
		73	Other industries connected with the toilet (tattooers, shampooers, bath houses, etc.)	225	225	...	...	...	...	...	...
		xiv	**Furniture industries** ...	*255*	*121*	...	*57*	*77*	...	...	...
		74	Cabinet makers, carriage painters, etc.	255	121	...	57	77	...	...	...
		75	Upholsterers, tent makers, etc.	...	...	...	...	...	...	...	...
		xv	**Building industries** ...	*111,194*	*103,521*	*27*	*5,125*	*63*	*3*	*451*	*4*
		76	Lime burners, cement workers	643	576	...	67	...	...	...	...
		77	Excavators, plinth builders and well-sinkers.	2,149	2,058	...	...	21	...	70	...
		78	Stone and marble workers, masons and bricklayers.	101,530	96,180	27	4,924	16	3	376	4
		79	Others (thatchers, building contractors, house painters, tilers, plumbers, locksmiths, etc.)	6,872	6,707	...	134	26	...	5	...
		xvi	**Construction of means of transport.**	*2,910*	*2,432*	...	*428*	*50*	...	...	...
		80	Cart, carriage, *palki*, etc., makers and wheelwrights.	2,518	2,052	...	420	46	...	...	...
		81	Saddlers, harness-makers, whip and lash makers.	392	380	...	8	4	...	...	...
		82	Ship and boat builders ...	...	...	...	...	...	...	...	...

TABLE XV.

OCCUPATION OR MEANS OF LIVELIHOOD.

PART D.—DISTRIBUTION BY RELIGION.

SECTION (1) DETAILS FOR THE STATE.

Class.	Sub-Class.	Order and Group. Serial No.	Order and Group. Description.	Total number of workers and dependants.	Distribution by Religion. Hindu.	Jain.	Musalman.	Christian.	Parsi.	Animistic.	Others
1	2	3	4	5	6	7	8	9	10	11	12
B.—Preparation and supply of material substances.—(contd.)	III.—Industry.—(contd.)	**xvii**	**Production and transmission of physical forces. (heat, light, electricity, motive, power, etc.)**	***78***	...	...	...	***75***	***1***	...	...
		83	Gas works, electric light and ice factories.	**78**	...	...	...	75	1	...	
		xviii	**Industries of luxury and those pertaining to literature and the arts and sciences.**	***97,951***	***95,772***	***41***	***1,692***	***289***	***9***	***141***	[illegible]
		84	Printers, lithographers, engravers, etc.	**697**	251	...	276	167	1	...	[illegible]
		85	Newspaper and magazine, managers and editors, journalists, etc.	**47**	7	...	27	13	...	...	...
		86	Bookbinders and stitchers, envelope makers, etc.	**129**	4	...	123	...	...	...	[illegible]
		87	Makers of musical instruments	**358**	319	...	4	35	..	...	...
		88	Makers of watches, and clocks, and optical, photographic and surgical instruments.	**204**	31	...	158	7	8	...	...
		89	Workers in precious stones and metals, enamellers, imitation jewellery makers, gilders, etc.	**93,489**	92,785	41	500	19	...	141	[illegible]
		90	Makers of bangles, rosaries, bead and other necklaces, spangles, lingams and sacred threads.	**2,871**	2,237	...	586	48	...	...	...
		91	Toy, kite, cage, fishing tackle etc., makers, taxidermists, etc.	**125**	115	...	10	...	...	...	...
		92	Others, including managers, persons other than performers, employed in theatres and other places of public entertainment, employes of public societies, race course service, huntsmen, etc.	**31**	23	...	8	...	...	...	...
		xix	**Industries concerned with refuse matter.**	***6,728***	***4,881***	...	***1,514***	***331***	***1***	...	[illegible]
		93	Sweepers, scavengers, dust and sweeping contractors.	**6,728**	4,881	...	1,514	331	1	...	[illegible]
	IV.—Transport.	**xx**	**Transport by water** ...	***2,667***	***2,278***	...	***389***	...	...	...	...
		94	Harbour works, dockyards and pilots.	...	...	...	...	...	...	...	...
		95	Ship owners and their employes, ship brokers, ships' officers, engineers, mariners and firemen.	...	...	...	...	...	...	...	...
		96	Persons employed on the maintenance of streams, rivers and canals (including construction.)	**2,336**	1,987	...	349	...	...	...	...
		97	Boat owners, boat men and tow men.	**331**	291	...	40	...	...	...	...

TABLE XV.

OCCUPATION OR MEANS OF LIVELIHOOD.

PART D.—DISTRIBUTION BY RELIGION.

SECTION (1) DETAILS FOR THE STATE.

Class.	Sub-Class.	Order and Group. Serial No.	Order and Group. Description.	Total number of workers and dependants.	Distribution by Religion. Hindu.	Jain.	Musalman.	Christian.	Parsi.	Animistic.	Others.
1	2	3	4	5	6	7	8	9	10	11	12
B.—Preparation and supply of material substances.—(contd.)	IV.—Transport.—(concld.)	xxi	**Transport by road .. ...**	***111,476***	***88,958***	***34***	***16,655***	***917***	***7***	***4,790***	***115***
		98	Persons employed on the construction and maintenance of roads and bridges.	51,879	47,356	3	4,055	377	...	86	2
		99	Cart owners and drivers, coachmen, stable boys tramway, mail, carriage, etc., managers and employes (excluding private servants.)	47,907	35,587	19	10,690	91	...	1,487	33
		100	*Palki*, etc., bearers and owners	1,674	1,637	...	37	...	...	...	...
		101	Pack elephant, camel, mule, ass and bullock owners and drivers.	1,335	702	...	205	428	...	...	...
		102	Porters and messengers ...	8,681	3,676	12	1,668	21	7	3,217	80
		xxii	**Transport by rail ... ...**	***18,609***	***11,265***	***16***	***4,067***	***2,924***	***110***	***207***	***20***
		103	Railway employes of all kinds other than construction coolies.	13,794	7,746	15	3,690	2,199	110	14	20
		104	Labourers employed on railway construction.	4,815	3,519	1	377	725	...	193	...
		xxiii	**Post office. Telegraph and Telephone services.**	***1,199***	***317***	...	***772***	***105***	***5***	...	...
		105	Post office Telegraph and Telephone services.	1,199	317	...	772	105	5	...	...
	V.—Trade.	xxiv	**Banks, establishments of credit, exchange and insurance.**	***22,223***	***18,035***	***990***	***3,122***	***17***	***20***	***7***	***32***
		106	Bank Managers, Money-lenders, exchange and insurance agents, money changers and brokers, and their employes.	22,223	18,035	990	3,122	17	20	7	32
		xxv	**Brokerage, commission and export.**	***3,588***	***1,769***	***12***	***1,627***	***90***	***90***	...	...
		107	Brokers, commission agents, commercial travellers, warehouse owners and employes.	3,588	1,769	12	1,627	90	90	...	...
		xxvi	**Trade in textiles ... ...**	***81,139***	***67,214***	***1,534***	***11,878***	***308***	***4***	***185***	***16***
		108	Trade in piece-goods, wool, cotton, silk, hair and other textiles.	81,139	67,214	1,534	11,878	308	4	185	16
		xxvii	**Trade in skins, leather and furs.**	***15,218***	***10,382***	...	***4,472***	***27***	...	***337***	...
		109	Trade in skins, leather, furs, feathers, horns, etc.	15,218	10,382	...	4,472	27	...	337	...

TABLE XV.

OCCUPATION OR MEANS OF LIVELIHOOD.

PART D.—DISTRIBUTION BY RELIGION.

SECTION (1) DETAILS FOR THE STATE.

Class.	Sub-Class.	Order and Group. Serial No.	Order and Group. Description.	Total number of workers and dependants.	Distribution by Religion. Hindu.	Jain.	Musalman.	Christian.	Parsi.	Animistic.	[illegible]
1	2	3	4	5	6	7	8	9	10	11	12
B.—Preparation and supply of material substances.—(contd.)	V.—Trade.—(contd.)	xxviii	**Trade in wood ... ...**	*8,511*	*8,243*	*141*	*115*	*3*	...	*9*	[illegible]
		110	Trade in wood (not firewood), cork, bark, etc.	8,511	8,243	141	115	3	...	9	[illegible]
		xxix	**Trade in metals ... ...**	*959*	*345*	...	*613*	...	*1*	...	[illegible]
		111	Trade in metals, machinery, knife, tool, etc., sellers.	959	345	...	613	...	1	...	...
		xxx	**Trade in pottery ... ...**	*11,228*	*11,020*	...	*298*	...	...	...	...
		112	Trade in pottery... ...	11,228	11,020	...	208	...	...	...	...
		xxxi	**Trade in chemical products ...**	*2,454*	*1,262*	...	*1,084*	*105*	...	...	[illegible]
		113	Trade in chemical products, (drugs, dyes, paints, petroleum, explosives, etc.)	2,454	1,262	...	1,084	105	...	...	[illegible]
		xxxii	**Hotels, cafes, restaurants, etc.**	*241,975*	*238,646*	*26*	*2,774*	*155*	*161*	*197*	[illegible]
		114	Vendors of wine, liquors, aerated waters, etc.	241,714	238,587	26	2,650	86	152	197	[illegible]
		115	Owners and managers of hotels, cookshops, *sarais*, etc., and their employes.	261	59	...	124	69	9	...	...
		xxxiii	**Other trade in food stuffs ...**	*391,941*	*354,760*	*2,277*	*31,811*	*271*	*15*	*2,771*	[illegible]
		116	Fish dealers	24,960	24,153	...	804	3	...	...	...
		117	Grocers and sellers of vegetable, oil, salt and other condiments.	112,156	101,971	1,487	8,171	20	...	495	[illegible]
		118	Sellers of milk, butter, ghee, poultry, eggs, etc.	17,040	16,810	...	215	...	15	...	...
		119	Sellers of sweetmeats, sugar, *gur* and molasses.	4,656	3,634	114	849	...	...	59	...
		120	Cardamom, betel-leaf, vegetables, fruit and areca nut sellers.	97,564	84,317	4	12,252	149	...	842	...
		121	Grain and pulse dealers ...	106.171	97,690	588	6,675	...	...	1,204	[illegible]
		122	Tobacco, opium, *ganja*, etc., sellers.	4.615	2,387	84	2,131	3	...	...	[illegible]
		123	Dealers in sheep, goats and pigs	19,400	18,915	...	378	...	...	107	...
		124	Dealers in hay, grass and fodder.	5,379	4,883	...	336	96	...	64	...
		xxxiv	**Trade in clothing and toilet articles**	*16,622*	*11,786*	*48*	*4,625*	*127*	...	*34*	[illegible]
		125	Trade in ready made clothing and other articles of dress and the toilet (hats, umbrellas, socks, ready-made shoes, perfumes, etc.)	16,622	11,786	48	4,625	127	...	34	

TABLE XV.

OCCUPATION OR MEANS OF LIVELIHOOD.

PART D.—DISTRIBUTION BY RELIGION.

SECTION (1) DETAILS FOR THE STATE.

Class.	Sub-Class.	Order and Group. Serial No.	Order and Group. Description.	Total number of workers and dependants.	Distribution by Religion. Hindu.	Jain.	Musalman.	Christian.	Parsi.	Animistic.	Others.
1	2	3	4	5	6	7	8	9	10	11	12
D.—Preparation and supply of material substances.—(concld.)	V.—Trade.—(concld.)	xxxv	**Trade in furniture ...**	***7,670***	***6,198***	***122***	***1,260***	***78***	***2***	***8***	***2***
		126	Trade in furniture, carpets, curtains and bedding.	6,117	4,969	6	1,052	78	2	8	2
		127	Hardware, cooking utensils, porcelain, crockery, glassware, bottles, articles for gardening, the cellar, etc.	1,553	1,229	116	208	...	...	...	...
		xxxvi	**Trade in building materials ...**	***1,260***	***969***	...	***291***	...	...	...	...
		128	Trade in building materials (stones, bricks, plaster, cement, sand, tiles, thatch, etc.	1,260	969	...	291	...	...	...	...
		xxxvii	**Trade in means of transport ...**	***15,597***	***13,282***	***50***	***892***	***19***	***3***	***1,351***	...
		129	Dealers and hirers of elephants, camels, horses, cattle, asses, mules, etc., sellers (not makers of carriages, saddlery, etc.)	15,597	13,282	50	892	19	3	1,351	...
		xxxviii	**Trade in fuel ... ...**	***25,880***	***20,688***	...	***4,231***	***44***	***15***	***902***	...
		130	Dealers in firewood, charcoal, coal, cowdung, etc.	25,880	20,688	...	4,231	44	15	902	...
		xxxix	**Trade in articles of luxury and those pertaining to letters and the arts and sciences.**	***46,316***	***39,036***	***678***	***6,419***	***158***	***1***	***24***	...
		131	Dealers in precious stones, jewellery (real and imitation), clocks, optical instruments, etc.	7,265	7,089	39	138	...	1	...	...
		132	Dealers of common bangles, bead necklaces, fans, small articles, toys, hunting and fishing tackle, flowers, etc.	38,144	31,613	639	5,852	16	...	24	...
		133	Publishers, booksellers, stationers, dealers, in music, pictures, musical instruments and curiosities.	907	336	...	429	142	...	...	...
		xl	**Trade in refuse matter ...**	...	...	...	...	...	...	...	...
		134	Dealers in rags, stable refuse, etc.	...	...	...	...	...	...	...	...
		xli	**Trade of other sorts ...**	***241,787***	***207,250***	***2,883***	***26,554***	***391***	***318***	***4,334***	***57***
		135	Shopkeepers otherwise unspecified.	239,765	205,454	2,878	26,336	391	318	4,331	54
		136	Itinerant traders, pedlars, hawkers, etc.	30	22	5	...	...	...	...	3
		137	Conjurors, acrobats, fortune tellers, reciters, exhibitors of curiosities and wild animals.	1,992	1,774	...	218	...	...	...	...
		138	Other trades (including farmers of pounds, tolls and markets).	...	...	...	...	...	...	...	...

TABLE XV.

OCCUPATION OR MEANS OF LIVELIHOOD.

PART D.—DISTRIBUTION BY RELIGION.

SECTION (1) DETAILS FOR THE STATE.

Class.	Sub-class.	Order and Group. Serial No.	Description.	Total number of workers and dependants.	Distribution by Religion. Hindu.	Jain.	Musalman.	Christian.	Parsi.	Animistic.	[illegible]
1	2	3	4	5	6	7	8	9	10	11	[illegible]
C.—Public administration and liberal arts.	VI.—Public force.	**xlii**	**Army ... ...**	***68,750***	***27,356***	***2***	***37,961***	***3,041***	...	...	
		139	Army (Imperial.)... ...	**5,554**	1,852	1	1,128	2,471	...	...	
		140	Army (Native States.) ...	**63,196**	25,504	1	36,833	570	...	...	
		xliii	**Navy ... ...**	...	...	...	...	...	...	...	
		141	Navy	...	...	...	...	...	...	...	
		xliv	**Police ... .**	***95,648***	***66,029***	...	***29,028***	***241***	***16***	***102***	[illegible]
		142	Police	**35,135**	9,823	...	24,912	111	16	41	[illegible]
		143	Village watchmen ...	**60,513**	56,206	...	4,116	130	...	61	...
	VII.—Public administration.	**xlv**	**Public administration ...**	***346,184***	***249,272***	***225***	***92,461***	***2,230***	***138***	***826***	[illegible]
		144	Service of the State ...	**4,567**	2,720	...	1,217	566	11	[illegible]	[illegible]
		145	Service of Native and Foreign States.	**130,831**	64,391	225	63,769	906	71	[illegible]	[illegible]
		146	Municipal and other local (not village) service.	**8,936**	5,969	...	2,521	162	56	99	[illegible]
		147	Village officials and servants other than watchmen.	**201,860**	176,178	...	24,954	596	...	[illegible]	...
	VIII.—Professions and liberal arts.	**xlvi**	**Religion ... ...**	***101,187***	***87,309***	***397***	***11,053***	***2,303***	***1***	***7***	[illegible]
		148	Priests, ministers, etc. ..	**57,809**	50,914	258	5,099	1,487	...	...	[illegible]
		149	Religious mendicants, inmates of monasteries, etc.	**33,743**	29,287	89	4,157	188	...	7	[illegible]
		150	Catechists, readers, church and mission service.	**2,217**	597	...	993	611	...	...	[illegible]
		151	Temple, burial or burning ground service, pilgrim conductors, circumcisers.	**7,418**	6,511	50	804	17	1	...	[illegible]
		xlvii	**Law ... ...**	***6,863***	***3,942***	***8***	***2,829***	***76***	***8***	...	...
		152	Lawyers of all kinds, including *kazis*, law agents and *mukhtiars*.	**6,835**	3,922	8	2,821	76	8	...	...
		153	Lawyers, clerks, petition writers, etc.	**28**	20	...	8	...	...	...	...
		xlviii	**Medicine... ... ...**	***30,973***	***25,059***	***8***	***5,635***	***244***	***14***	***13***	...
		154	Medical practitioners of all kinds, including dentists, oculists and veterinary surgeons.	**23,760**	18,666	6	4,951	122	2	13	...
		155	Midwives, vaccinators, compounders, nurses, masseurs, etc.	**7,213**	6,393	2	684	122	12	...	...
		xlix	**Instruction ... ...**	***23,574***	***14,018***	***147***	***8,314***	***1,019***	***37***	***28***	
		156	Professors and teachers of all kinds and clerks and servants connected with education.	**23,574**	14,018	147	8,314	1,019	37	28	

TABLE XV.

OCCUPATION OR MEANS OF LIVELIHOOD.

PART D.—DISTRIBUTION BY RELIGION.

SECTION (1) DETAILS FOR THE STATE.

Class.	Sub-Class	Order and Group. Serial No.	Order and Group. Description.	Total number of workers and dependants.	Distribution by Religion. Hindu.	Jain.	Musalman.	Christian.	Parsi.	Animistic.	Others.
1	2	3	4	5	6	7	8	9	10	11	12
C.—Public administration and liberal arts.—(concld.)	VIII.—Professions and liberal arts.—(concld.)	1	**Letters and arts and sciences ..**	***46,442***	***38,203***	***24***	***7,490***	***419***	***9***	***27***	***270***
		157	Public scribes, stenographers, etc.	...	...	...	...	...	...	...	...
		158	Architects, surveyors, engineers and their employes.	1,166	527	...	445	175	9	...	10
		159	Others (authors, photographers, artists, sculptors, astronomers, meteorologists, botanists, astrologers, etc.)	11,502	10,570	12	803	80	...	...	37
		160	Music composers and masters players on all kinds of musical instruments (not military), singers, actors and dancers.	33,774	27,106	12	6,242	164	...	27	223
	IX.—Persons living on their income.	li	**Persons living principally on their income.**	***28,377***	***16,350***	...	***11,551***	***364***	***33***	...	***79***
		161	Proprietors (other than of agricultural land) fund and scholarship holders and pensioners.	28.377	16,350	...	11,551	364	33	...	79
D.—Miscellaneous.	X.—Domestic service.	lii	**Domestic service ... ...**	***421,147***	***222,557***	***1,391***	***190,387***	***1,943***	***56***	***4,168***	***645***
		162	Cooks, water carriers, doorkeepers, watchmen and other in-door servants.	406,181	209,242	1,373	189,248	1,654	44	4,168	452
		163	Private grooms, coachmen, dog boys, etc.	14,966	13,315	18	1,139	289	12	...	193
	XI.—Insufficiently described occupations.	liii	**General terms which do not indicate a definite occupation.**	***380,148***	***319,587***	***545***	***45,077***	***2,757***	***154***	***11,902***	***126***
		164	Manufacturers, business men and contractors, otherwise unspecified.	6,828	2,920	6	3,611	114	28	131	18
		165	Cashiers, accountants, book-keepers, clerks, and other employes in unspecified offices ware-houses and shops.	8,073	5,771	45	2,042	128	63	...	24
		166	Mechanics otherwise unspecified.	1,090	926	45	...	32	63	...	24
		167	Labourers and workmen otherwise unspecified.	364,157	309,970	449	39,424	2,483	...	11,771	60
	XII.—Unproductive.	liv	**Inmates of Jails, asylums and hospitals.**	***3,428***	***2,401***	...	***956***	***15***	...	...	***56***
		168	Inmates of jails, asylums and hospitals.	3,428	2,401	...	956	15	...	...	56
		lv	**Beggars, vagrants, prostitutes.**	***272,711***	***222,762***	***712***	***44,906***	***463***	***1***	***3,679***	***188***
		169	Beggars, vagrants, prostitutes, receivers of stolen goods, cattle poisoners, etc.	272,711	222,762	712	44,906	463	1	3,679	188

TABLE XV.

OCCUPATION OR MEANS OF LIVELIHOOD.

PART D.—DISTRIBUTION BY RELIGION.

SECTION (2) DETAILS FOR THE CITY OF HYDERABAD.

TABLE XV.

OCCUPATION OR MEANS OF LIVELIHOOD.

PART D.—DISTRIBUTION BY RELIGION.

SECTION (2) DETAILS FOR THE CITY OF HYDERABAD.

Class.	Sub-Class.	Order and Group. Serial No.	Order and Group. Description.	Total number of workers and dependants.	Distribution by Religion. Hindu.	Jain.	Musalman.	Christian.	Parsi.	Animistic.	[illegible]
1	2	3	4	5	6	7	8	9	10	11	12
			Hyderabad City	*500,623*	*262,131*	*379*	*219,896*	*16,240*	*808*	*41*	*1,1*[illegible]
A	...	...	**Production of raw materials** ...	*49,391*	*32,509*	*33*	*16,463*	*119*	*162*	*23*	[illegible]
	I	...	**Exploitation of the surface of the earth.**	*48,879*	*32,111*	*33*	*16,384*	*84*	*162*	*23*	[illegible]
	II	...	**Extraction of minerals**	*512*	*398*	...	*79*	*35*	...	...	...
B	...	...	**Preparation and supply of material substances.**	*155,073*	*112,907*	*209*	*36,821*	*4,566*	*409*	*9*	[illegible]
	III	...	**Industry**	*65,615*	*52,297*	*61*	*12,140*	*1,047*	*43*	...	*27*
	IV	...	**Transport**	*18,462*	*9,390*	*15*	*6,884*	*2,079*	*12*	*5*	*77*
	V	...	**Trade.**	*70,996*	*51,220*	*133*	*17,797*	*1,440*	*354*	*4*	*48*
C	...	...	**Public administration and liberal arts.**	*137,348*	*35,434*	*74*	*92,733*	*8,333*	*158*	...	*61*[illegible]
	VI	...	**Public force**	*62,978*	*14,357*	*1*	*45,129*	*3,122*	*16*	...	*35*[illegible]
	VII	...	**Public administration**	*27,015*	*7,885*	...	*17,686*	*1,246*	*79*	...	*11*[illegible]
	VIII	...	**Professions and liberal arts**	*24,503*	*9,336*	*73*	*11,398*	*3,601*	*30*	...	*6*[illegible]
	IX	...	**Persons living on their income** ...	*22,852*	*3,856*	...	*18,250*	*364*	*33*	...	*7*[illegible]
D	...	...	**Miscellaneous**	*158,811*	*81,281*	*63*	*73,879*	*3,222*	*79*	*9*	*27*[illegible]
	X	...	**Domestic service**	*109,505*	*46,148*	*15*	*61,401*	*1,736*	*12*	...	*19*
	XI	...	**Insufficiently described occupations** ...	*31,195*	*24,085*	*45*	*5,490*	*1,418*	*67*	*7*	[illegible]
	XII	...	**Unproductive**	*18,111*	*11,048*	*3*	*6,988*	*68*	...	*2*	
A.—Production of raw materials.	I.—Exploitation of the surface of the earth.	i	**Pasture and Agriculture**	*47,554*	*30,886*	*33*	*16,311*	*57*	*162*	*23*	[illegible]
		(a)	**Ordinary Cultivation.**	*33,425*	*17,236*	*22*	*15,885*	*22*	*159*	*22*	[illegible]
		1	Income from rent of agricultural land...	**5,327**	1,250	22	3,891	7	152	...	
		2	Ordinary cultivators	**3,771**	2,518	...	1,253	...	...	...	...
		3	Agents, managers, of landed estate, (not planters), clerks, rent collectors, etc.	**22,200**	11,626	...	10,478	15	7	...	[illegible]
		4	Farm servants and field labourers ...	**2,127**	1,842	...	263	...	...	22	...
		(b)	**Growers of special products and market gardening.**	*3,988*	*3,866*	...	*122*	...	...	...	...
		5	Tea, coffee, cinchona and indigo plantations.	...	...	...	...	...	...	...	...
		6	Fruit, flower, vegetable, betel, vine, arecanut, etc., growers.	**3,988**	3,866	...	122	...	...	...	...
		(c)	**Forestry...**	*3,420*	*3,185*	*11*	*186*	*35*	*3*	...	...
		7	Forest officers, rangers, guards, etc. ...	**353**	155	...	160	35	3	..	..
		8	Wood cutters, fire-wood, lac, catechu, rubber, etc., collectors and charcoal burners.	**3,067**	3,030	11	26	...	...	...	..

TABLE XV.

OCCUPATION OR MEANS OF LIVELIHOOD.

PART D.—DISTRIBUTION BY RELIGION.

SECTION (2) DETAILS FOR THE CITY OF HYDERABAD.

Class.	Sub-Class.	Order and Group. Serial No.	Order and Group. Description.	Total number of workers and dependants.	Distribution by Religion. Hindu.	Jain.	Musalman.	Christian.	Parsi.	Animistic.	Others.
1	2	3	4	5	6	7	8	9	10	11	12
A.—Production of raw materials—(concld.)	I.—Exploitation of the surface of the earth.	(d)	**Raising of farm stock ... ...**	*6,721*	*6,599*	...	*118*	...	...	*1*	*3*
		9	Cattle and buffalo breeders and keepers.	4,034	3,918	...	116	...	...	...	...
		10	Sheep, goat and pig breeders ...	95	95	...	...	...	...	...	...
		11	Breeders of other animals, (horses, mules, camels, asses, etc)	214	214	...	...	...	...	...	...
		12	Herdsmen, shepherds, goat herds, etc. ...	2,378	2,372	...	2	...	...	1	3
		(e)	**Raising of small animals ... ...**	...	...	...	...	...	...	...	...
		13	Birds, bees, silkworms, etc.	...	...	...	...	...	...	...	...
		ii	**Fishing and hunting ... ...**	*1,325*	*1,225*	...	*73*	*27*	...	...	...
		14	Fishing	818	807	...	11	...	...	...	...
		15	Hunting	507	418	...	62	27	...	...	...
	II.—Extraction of minerals.	iii	**Mines ... ...**	*323*	*209*	...	*79*	*35*	...	...	...
		16	Coal mines and petroleum wells ...	322	209	...	78	35	...	...	...
		17	Mines and metallic minerals (gold, iron, manganese, etc.)	1	...	...	1	...	...	...	...
		iv	**Quarries of hard rocks ... ...**	*189*	*189*	...	...	...	...	...	...
		18	Other minerals (jade, diamonds, limestone, etc.)	189	189	...	...	...	...	...	...
		v	**Salt etc. ... ...**	...	...	...	...	...	...	...	...
		19	Rock, sea, and marsh salt	...	...	...	...	...	...	...	...
		20	Extraction of saltpetre, alum and other substances soluble in water.	...	...	...	...	...	...	...	...
B.—Preparation and supply of material substances.	III.—Industry.	vi	**Textiles ... ...**	*7,033*	*4,733*	...	*2,258*	*22*	*17*	...	*3*
		21	Cotton ginning, cleaning and pressing ...	1.455	710	...	745	...	...	...	...
		22	Cotton spinning, sizing and weaving ...	3.223	2,785	...	438	...	...	..	...
		23	Jute spinning, pressing and weaving ...	...	...	...	...	...	..	...	...
		24	Rope, twine and string	52	52	...	...	...	...	...	...
		25	Other fibres (cocoanut, aloes, palm-leaf, flax, hemp, straw, etc).	...	...	...	...	...	...	...	...
		26	Wool carders and spinners, weavers of woollen blankets, carpets, etc..	53	28	...	25	...	...	...	...
		27	Silk spinners and weavers	352	157	...	192	...	...	...	3
		28	Hair, camel and horse hair, bristles work, brush makers, etc.	2	2	...	...	...	...	...	...
		29	Persons occupied with feathers ...	38	38	...	...	...	...	...	...
		30	Dyeing, bleaching, printing, preparation and sponging of textiles.	665	551	...	114	...	...	...	...
		31	Other (lace, crape, embroideries, fringes, etc.,) and insufficiently described textile industries.	1,193	410	...	744	22	17	...	...
		vii	**Hides, skins and hard materials from the animal kingdom.**	*396*	*179*	...	*180*	*37*	...	...	...
		32	Tanners, curriers, leather dressers and dyers, etc.	161	161	...	...	...	...	...	...
		33	Makers of leather articles, such as trunks, water bags, etc.	37	...	...	37	..	...	...	...
		34	Furriers	193	18	...	143	37	...	...	...
		35	Bone, ivory, horn, shell, etc., workers ...	...	...	...	...	...	...	...	...

TABLE XV.

OCCUPATION OR MEANS OF LIVELIHOOD.

PART D.—DISTRIBUTION BY RELIGION.

SECTION (2) DETAILS FOR THE CITY OF HYDERABAD.

Class.	Sub-Class.	Order and Group. Serial No.	Order and Group. Description.	Total number of workers and dependants.	Distribution by Religion. Hindu.	Jain.	Musalman.	Christian.	Parsi.	Animistic.	Others
1	2	3	4	5	6	7	8	9	10	11	12
B.—Preparation and supply of material substances.—(contd.)	III.—Industry.—(contd.)	viii	**Wood**	*4,008*	*3,786*	...	*125*	*97*	...	...	[illegible]
		36	Sawyers, carpenters, turners and joiners, etc.	3,405	3,183	...	125	97	...	...	[illegible]
		37	Basket makers and other industries of woody material, including leaves.	663	663	...	...	...	...	...	[illegible]
		ix	**Metals**	*2,312*	*1,076*	...	*1,165*	*71*	...	...	...
		38	Forging and rolling of iron and other metals.	...	...	...	...	...	...	...	...
		39	Plough and agricultural implement makers.	9	...	...	9	...	...	...	...
		40	Makers of arms, guns, etc.	46	14	...	28	4	...	...	...
		41	Other workers in iron and makers of implements and tools principally or exclusively of iron.	1,161	726	...	397	38	...	...	...
		42	Workers in brass, copper and bell metal	194	179	...	15	...	...	...	...
		43	Workers in other metals (tin, zinc, lead, quick silver, etc.)	496	58	...	438	...	...	...	...
		44	Workers in mints, die-sinkers, etc. ...	406	99	...	278	...	...	...	...
		x	**Ceramics**	*2,238*	*2,238*	...	...	...	...	...	...
		45	Makers of glass and crystal ware. ...	...	...	...	...	...	...	...	...
		46	Makers of porcelain and crockery ...	...	...	...	...	...	...	...	...
		47	Potters and earthen pipe and bowl makers	1,973	1,973	...	...	...	...	...	...
		48	Brick and tile makers ...	265	265	...	...	...	...	...	...
		49	Others (mosaic, talc, mica, alabaster, etc., workers.)	...	...	...	...	...	...	...	...
		xi	**Chemical products properly so called, and analogous.**	*448*	*138*	...	*310*	...	...	...	...
		50	Manufacture of matches and explosive materials	39	25	...	14	...	...	...	...
		51	Manufacture of ærated and mineral waters	...	...	...	...	...	...	...	...
		52	Manufacture of dyes, paint and ink ...	50	23	...	27	...	...	...	...
		53	Manufacture and refining of vegetable and mineral oils.	345	80	...	265	...	...	...	...
		54	Manufacture of paper, card board and *papier mache.*	...	...	...	...	...	...	...	...
		55	Others (soap, candles, lac, cutch, perfumes and miscellaneous drugs.)	14	10	...	4	...	...	...	...
		xii	**Food Industries**	*12,837*	*8,709*	*50*	*3,973*	*84*	*21*	...	...
		56	Rice pounders and huskers and flour grinders.	147	147	...	...	...	...	...	...
		57	Bakers, and biscuit makers ...	2,789	1,769	...	936	84	...	...	...
		58	Grain parchers, etc.	1,132	1,132	...	...	...	...	...	...
		59	Butchers	4,349	2,341	...	2,008	...	...	...	...
		60	Fish curers	...	...	...	...	...	...	...	...
		61	Butter, cheese and ghee makers ...	...	...	...	...	...	...	...	...
		62	Makers of sugar, molasses and *gur* ...	...	...	...	...	...	...	...	...
		63	Sweetmeat makers, preparers of jam and condiments, etc.	1,048	810	50	188	...	...	...	...
		64	Brewers and distillers	403	287	...	95	...	21	...	...
		65	Toddy drawers	384	384	...	...	...	...	...	...
		66	Manufacturers of tobacco, opium and *ganja*	2,585	1,839	...	746	...	...	...	...
		xiii	**Industries of dress and the toilet** ...	*19,537*	*17,645*	*7*	*1,710*	*155*	...	...	...
		67	Hat, cap and turban makers... ..	132	6	...	126	...	...	...	...
		68	Tailors, milliners, dress makers and darners, embroiderers on linen.	5,402	4,766	7	499	110	...	...	...
		69	Shoe, boot and sandal makers ...	4,271	4,196	...	36	39	...	...	...
		70	Other industries pertaining to dress, gloves, socks, gaiters, belts, buttons, umbrellas, canes, etc.	...	...	...	...	...	...	...	...
		71	Washing, cleaning and dyeing ...	6,067	5,377	...	690	...	...	...	...
		72	Barbers, hairdressers and wig makers.	3,665	3,300	...	359	6	...	...	...
		73	Other industries connected with the toilet (tattooers, shampooers, bath houses, etc.)	...	...	...	...	...	...	...	...

TABLE XV.

OCCUPATION OR MEANS OF LIVELIHOOD.

PART D.—DISTRIBUTION BY RELIGION

SECTION (2) DETAILS FOR THE CITY OF HYDERABAD.

Class.	Sub-Class.	Order and Group. Serial No.	Order and Group. Description.	Total number of workers and dependants.	Distribution by Religion. Hindu.	Jain.	Musalman.	Christian.	Parsi.	Animistic.	Others.
1	2	3	4	5	6	7	8	9	10	11	12
B.—Preparation and supply of material substances.—(contd.)	III.—Industry.—(contd.)	**xiv**	**Furniture industries ...**	***215***	***103***	...	***35***	***77***	...	...	...
		74	Cabinet makers, carriage painters, etc....	215	103	...	35	77	...	...	...
		75	Upholsterers, tent makers, etc. ...	...	...	...	...	...	...	...	...
		xv	**Building industries ...**	***5,487***	***5,312***	...	***138***	***37***	...	...	...
		76	Lime burners, cement workers ...	265	198	...	67	...	...	...	...
		77	Excavators, plinth builders and well-sinkers.	...	...	...	...	...	...	...	...
		78	Stone and marble workers, masons and bricklayers.	5,142	5,060	...	71	11	...	...	...
		79	Others (thatchers, building contractors, house painters, tilers, plumbers, lock-smiths, etc.)	80	54	...	...	26	...	...	...
		xvi	**Construction of means of transport ...**	***2,135***	***1,785***	...	***317***	***33***	...	...	...
		80	Cart, carriage, palki, etc., makers, and wheelwrights.	2,113	1,775	...	309	29	...	...	...
		81	Saddlers and harness makers, whip and lash makers.	22	10	...	8	4	...	...	...
		82	Ship and boat builders ...	...	...	...	...	...	...	...	...
		xvii	**Production and transmission of physical forces, (heat, light, electricity, motive power etc)**	***78***	...	...	...	***75***	***1***	...	***2***
		83	Gas works, electric light and ice factories.	78	...	...	...	75	1	...	2
		xviii	**Industries of luxury and those pertaining to literature and the arts and sciences.**	***6,074***	***4,613***	***4***	***1,163***	***289***	***3***	...	***2***
		84	Painters, lithographers, engravers, etc...	485	244	...	74	167	...	...	...
		85	Newspaper and magazine managers and editors, journalists, etc.	47	7	...	27	13	...	...	...
		86	Bookbinders and stitchers, envelope makers, etc.	83	4	...	77	...	...	...	2
		87	Makers of muscial instruments ...	65	26	...	4	35	...	...	...
		88	Makers of watches and clocks and optical, photographic and surgical instruments	153	31	...	112	7	3	...	...
		89	Workers in precious stones and metals, enamellers, immitation jewellery makers, gilders, etc.	3,971	3,681	4	267	19	...	...	...
		90	Makers of bangles, rosaries, bead and other necklaces, spangles, lingams and sacred threads.	1,242	608	...	586	48	...	...	...
		91	Toy, kite, cage, fishing tackle, etc., makers, taxidermists, etc.	22	12	...	10	...	...	...	...
		92	Others, including managers, persons other than performers, employed in theatres and other places of public entertainment, employes of public societies, race course service, hunts-men, etc.	6	...	...	6	...	...	...	...
		xix	**Industries concerned with refuse matter.**	***2,817***	***1,980***	...	***766***	***70***	***1***	...	...
		93	Sweepers, scavengers, dust and sweeping contractors.)	2,817	1,980	...	766	70	1	...	...

TABLE XV.

OCCUPATION OR MEANS OF LIVELIHOOD.

PART D.—DISTRIBUTION BY RELIGION

SECTION (2) DETAILS FOR THE CITY OF HYDERABAD.

Class.	Sub-Class.	Order or Group. Serial No.	Order or Group. Description.	Total number of workers and dependants.	Distribution by Religion. Hindu.	Jain.	Musalman.	Christian.	Parsi.	Animistic.	O[illegible]
1	2	3	4	5	6	7	8	9	10	11	12
B.—Preparation and supply of material substances.—(contd.)	IV.—Transport.	**xx**	**Transport by water**	***5***	***5***	...	...	...	...	...	...
		94	Harbour works, dockyards and pilots ..	...	...	...	...	...	...	...	...
		95	Ship owners and their employes, ship-brokers, ships officers, engineers, mariners and firemen.	...	...	...	...	...	...	...	...
		96	Persons employed on the maintenance of streams, rivers and canals (including construction.)	...	...	...	...	...	...	...	...
		97	Boat owners, boatmen and towmen ...	5	5	...	...	...	...	...	...
		xxi	**Transport by road**	***12,252***	***7,172***	***8***	***4,829***	***164***	***7***	***4***	[illegible]
		98	Persons employed on the construction and maintenance of roads and bridges.	194	85	...	32	73	...	4	...
		99	Cart owners and drivers, coachmen, stable boys tramway, mail, carriage, etc., managers and employes (excluding private servants.)	9,439	5,922	...	3,423	91	...	...	[illegible]
		100	*Palki*, etc., bearers and owners ..	357	322	...	35	...	...	...	...
		101	Pack elephant, camel, mule, ass and bullock owners and drivers.	205	...	...	205	...	...	...	...
		102	Porters and messengers	2,057	843	8	1,134	...	7	...	[illegible]
		xxii	**Transport by rail**	***5,308***	***2,024***	***7***	***1,457***	***1,810***	...	***1***	[illegible]
		103	Railway employes of all kinds other than construction coolies.	4,616	1,676	7	1,389	1,539	..	1	[illegible]
		104	Labourers employed on railway construction.	692	253	...	68	271	...	...	...
		xxiii	**Post office, Telegraph and Telephone services.**	***897***	***189***	...	***598***	***105***	***5***	...	...
		105	Post office telegraph and telephone services.	897	189	...	598	105	5	...	...
	V.—Trade.	**xxiv**	**Banks, establishments of credit, exchange and insurance.**	***2,246***	***1,879***	***32***	***283***	***17***	***20***	***1***	***1***
		106	Bank managers, money-lenders, exchange and insurance agents, money-changers and brokers, and other employes.	2,246	1,879	32	283	17	20	1	1
		xxv	**Brokerage, commission and export.** ...	***2,788***	***1,286***	***12***	***1,310***	***90***	***90***	...	...
		107	Brokers, commission agents, commercial travellers, warehouse owners and employes.	2,788	1,286	12	1,310	90	90	...	...
		xxvi	**Trade in textiles.**	***3,100***	***1,479***	...	***1,311***	***310***	...	...	...
		108	Trade in piece goods, wool, cotton, silk, hair and other textiles.	3,100	1,479	...	1,311	310	...	...	...
		xxvii	**Trade in skins, leather and furs** ...	***584***	***125***	...	***459***	...	...	...	...
		109	Trade in skins, leather, furs, feathers, horns, etc.	584	125	...	459	...	...	...	...
		xxviii	**Trade in wood**	***696***	***628***	...	***68***	...	...	...	...
		110	Trade in wood (not firewood), cork, bark, etc.	693	628	...	68	...	...	...	...

TABLE XV.

OCCUPATION OR MEANS OF LIVELIHOOD.

PART D.—DISTRIBUTION BY RELIGION.

SECTION (2) DETAILS FOR THE CITY OF HYDERABAD.

Class.	Sub-Class.	Order and Group. Serial No.	Order and Group. Description.	Total number of workers and dependants.	Distribution by Religion. Hindu.	Jain.	Musalman	Christian.	Parsi.	Animistic	Others.
1	2	3	4	5	6	7	8	9	10	11	12
B.—Preparation and suply of material substances.—(contd.)	V.—Trade.—(contd.)	**xxix**	**Trade in metals ... ...**	***620***	***64***	...	***555***	...	***1***	...	...
		111	Trade in metals, machinery, knife, tool, etc., sellers.	**620**	64	...	555	...	1	...	...
		xxx	**Trade in pottery ... ...**	***695***	***674***	...	***21***	...	...	...	...
		112	Trade in pottery	**695**	674	...	21	...	...	...	...
		xxxi	**Trade in chemical products ... ...**	***1,577***	***493***	...	***976***	***105***	...	...	***3***
		113	Trade in chemical products (drugs, dyes, paints, petroleum, explosives, etc.)	**1,577**	493	...	976	105	...	...	3
		xxxii	**Hotels, cafes, restaurants, etc. ...**	***6,789***	***5,416***	...	***1,158***	***155***	***60***	...	...
		114	Vendors of wine, liquors, ærated waters, etc.	**6,610**	5,307	...	1,158	86	59	...	...
		115	Owners and managers of hotels, cook-shops, *sarais*, etc., and their employes.	**179**	109	...	...	69	1	...	...
		xxxiii	**Other trade in food stuffs ... ...**	***30,529***	***23,931***	***84***	***6,485***	...	...	***3***	***26***
		116	Fish dealers	**1.232**	1,211	...	21	...	...	...	...
		117	Grocers and sellers of vegetable oil, salt and other condiments.	**3,224**	2,494	...	718	...	...	...	12
		118	Sellers of milk, butter, ghee, poultry, eggs, etc.	**1,664**	1,456	...	208	...	...	...	...
		119	Sellers of sweetmeats, sugar, *gur* and molasses	**991**	601	36	354	...	...	...	...
		120	Cardamom, betel-leaf, vegetables, fruits and areca nut sellers.	**11.728**	8,108	...	3,614	...	...	...	4
		121	Grain and pulse dealers	**7,162**	6,753	48	348	...	...	3	10
		122	Tobacco, opium, *ganja*, etc., sellers ...	**2.703**	1,644	...	1,059	...	...	...	...
		123	Dealers in sheep, goats and pigs ...	**26**	15	...	11	...	...	...	...
		124	Dealers in hay, grass and fodder ..	**1,801**	1,649	...	152	...	...	...	...
		xxxiv	**Trade in clothing and toilet articles ...**	***1,476***	***916***	...	***431***	***127***	...	...	***2***
		125	Trade in ready-made clothing and other articles of dress and the toilet (hats, umbrellas, socks, ready-made shoes, perfumes, etc.)	**1,476**	916	...	431	127	...	...	2
		xxxv	**Trade in furniture ... ...**	***665***	***555***	...	***32***	***78***	...	...	...
		126	Trade in furniture, carpets, curtains and bedding.	**571**	493	...	...	7[illegible]	...	...	...
		127	Hardware, cooking utensils, porcelain, crockery, glassware, bottles, articles for gardening, the cellar, etc.	**94**	62	...	[illegible]	...	...	...	...
		xxxvi	**Trade in building materials ... ...**	***319***	***238***	...	***81***	...	...	...	...
		128	Trade in building materials (stones, bricks, plaster, cement, sand, thatch, etc.)	**319**	238	...	81	...	...	...	...
		xxxvii	**Trade in means of transport ... ...**	***417***	***204***	...	***191***	***15***	***3***	...	...
		129	Dealers and hirers of elephants, camels, horses, cattle, asses, mules, etc., sellers (not makers) of carriages, saddlery, etc.	**417**	204	...	191	1[illegible]	[illegible]	...	...
		xxxviii	**Trade in fuel ... .**	***2,535***	***1,769***	...	***759***	***6***	***1***	...	...
		130	Dealers in firewood, charcoal and coal, cowdung, etc.	**2,535**	1,769	...	759	6	1	...	...

TABLE XV.

OCCUPATION OR MEANS OF LIVELIHOOD.

PART D.—DISTRIBUTION BY RELIGION.

SECTION (2) DETAILS FOR THE CITY OF HYDERABAD.

Class.	Sub-class.	Order of Group. Serial No.	Description.	Total number of workers and dependants.	Distribution by Religion. Hindu.	Jain.	Musalman	Christian.	Persi.	Animistic.	Other
1	2	3	4	5	6	7	8	9	10	11	12
B.—Preparation and supply of material substances.—(concld.)	V.—Trade.—(concld.)	xxxix	**Trade in articles of luxury and those pertaining to letters and the arts and sciences.**	*3,595*	*1,650*	...	*1,803*	*142*	...	...	...
		131	Dealers in precious stones, jewellery (real and imitation), clocks, optical instruments, etc.	1,012	884	...	128	...	...	...	...
		132	Dealers of common bangles, bead, necklaces, fans, small articles, toys, hunting and fishing tackle, flowers, etc.	2,215	681	...	1,534	...	...	...	...
		133	Publishers, booksellers, stationers, dealers, in music, pictures, musical instruments and curiosities.	368	85	...	141	142	...	...	...
		xl	**Trade in refuse matter**	...	...	...	...	...	...	...	...
		134	Dealers in rags, stable refuse, etc. ...	...	...	...	...	...	...	...	...
		xli	**Trade of other sorts**	*12,365*	*9,913*	*5*	*1,874*	*391*	*179*	...	[illegible]
		135	Shopkeepers otherwise unspecified ...	12,304	9,869	5	1,857	391	179	...	[illegible]
		136	Itinerant traders, pedlars, hawkers, etc.	...	...	...	...	...	...	...	...
		137	Conjurors, acrobats, fortune tellers, reciters, exhibitors of curiosities and wild animals.	61	44	...	17	...	...	...	...
		138	Other trades (including farmers of pounds, tolls and markets).	...	...	...	...	...	...	...	...
C.—Public administration and liberal arts.	VI.—Public force.	xlii	**Army**	*50,281*	*11,990*	*1*	*35,083*	*3,041*	...	...	*16*
		139	Army (Imperial.)	5,099	938	1	1,587	2,471	...	...	10
		140	Army (Native States.)	45,182	11,052	...	33,496	570	...	...	6
		xliii	**Navy**	...	...	...	...	...	...	...	...
		141	Navy	...	...	...	...	...	...	...	...
		xliv	**Police**	*12,697*	*2,367*	...	*10,046*	*81*	*16*	...	*18*
		142	Police...	12,697	2,367	...	10,046	81	16	...	18
		143	Village Watchmen	...	...	...	...	...	...	...	...
	VII.—Public administration.	xlv	**Public administration**	*27,015*	*7,885*	...	*17,686*	*1,246*	*79*	...	*11*
		144	Service of the State	4,342	432	...	3,335	566	9	...	[illegible]
		145	Service of native and foreign States ...	18,591	5,703	...	12,194	519	56	...	[illegible]
		146	Municipal and other local (not village) service.	4,082	1,750	...	2,157	161	14	...	[illegible]
		147	Village officials and servants other than watchmen.	...	...	...	...	...	...	...	[illegible]
	VIII.—Professions and liberal arts.	xlvi	**Religion**	*8,223*	*3,599*	*53*	*2,462*	*2,093*	*1*	...	[illegible]
		148	Priests ministers, etc.	5,381	2,878	53	1,028	1,407	...	...	[illegible]
		149	Religious mendicants, inmates of monasteries, etc.	882	...	...	704	178	...	...	[illegible]
		150	Catechists, readers, church and mission service.	880	145	...	244	491	...	...	[illegible]
		151	Temple, burial or burning ground service, pilgrim conductors, circumcisers.	1,080	576	...	486	17	1	...	[illegible]
		xlvii	**Law**	*2,289*	*582*	...	*1,623*	*76*	*8*	...	...
		152	Lawyers of all kinds, including *kazis*, law agents and *mukhtiars*.	2,281	574	...	1,623	76	8	...	...
		153	Lawyers clerks, petition writers, etc. ...	8	8	...	...	...	...	...	[illegible]

TABLE XV.

OCCUPATION OR MEANS OF LIVELIHOOD.

PART D.—DISTRIBUTION BY RELIGION.

SECTION (2) DETAILS FOR CITY OF HYDERABAD.

Class.	Sub-Class.	Order and Group. Serial No.	Order and Group. Description.	Total number of workers and dependants.	Distribution by Religion. Hindu.	Jain.	Musalman	Christian.	Parsi.	Animistic.	Others.
1	2	3	4	5	6	7	8	9	10	11	12
C.—Public administration and liberal arts.—(concld.)	VIII.—Professions and liberal arts.—(concld.)	xlviii	**Medicine ... .**	***4,338***	***2,261***	***2***	***1,876***	***187***	***12***	...	...
		154	Medical practitioners of all kinds, including dentists, oculists and veterinary surgeons.	2,753	914	2	1,712	113	12	...	...
		155	Midwives, vaccinators, compounders, nurses, masseurs, etc.	2,585	1,347	...	164	74	...	...	...
		xlix	**Instruction ... .**	***5,228***	***1,194***	***6***	***3,128***	***897***	...	...	***3***
		156	Professors and teachers of all kinds and clerks and servants connected with education.	5,288	1,194	6	3,128	897	...	...	3
		l	**Letters and arts and sciences ..**	***4,425***	***1,700***	***12***	***2,309***	***348***	***9***	...	***47***
		157	Public scribes, stenographers, etc.	...	...	...	...	...	...	...	...
		158	Architects, surveyors, engineers, and their employes.	969	275	...	562	113	9	...	10
		159	Others (authors, photographers artists, sculptors, astronomers, meteorologists, botanists, astrologers, etc.)	924	322	12	480	73	...	...	37
		160	Music composers and masters, players on all kinds of musical instruments (not military), singers, actors and dancers.	2,532	1,103	...	1,267	162	...	...	...
	IX.—Persons living on their income.	li	**Persons living principally on their income.**	***22,852***	***3,856***	...	***18,520***	***364***	***33***	...	***79***
		161	Proprietors (other than of agricultural land) fund and scholarship holders and pensioners.	22,852	3,856	...	18,520	364	33	...	79
D.—Miscellaneous.	X.—Domestic service.	lii	**Domestic service ... .**	***109,505***	***46,148***	***15***	***61,401***	***1,736***	***12***	...	***193***
		162	Cooks, water carriers, door-keepers, watchmen and other in door servants.	97,582	35,387	15	60,507	1,448	12	...	193
		163	Private grooms, coachmen, dog boys, etc.	11,943	10,761	...	694	288	...	...	...
	XI.—Insufficiently described occupations.	liii	**General terms which do not indicate a definite occupation.**	***31,195***	***24,085***	***45***	***5,490***	***1,418***	***67***	***7***	***83***
		164	Manufacturers, business men and contractors, otherwise unspecified.	1,273	767	...	448	48	4	...	6
		165	Cashiers, accountants, book-keepers, clerks, and other employes in unspecified offices, warehouses and shops.	2,455	944	45	1,279	100	63	...	24
		166	Mechanics otherwise unspecified ..	1,047	1,018	...	...	29	...	...	...
		167	Labourers and workmen otherwise unspecified.	26,420	21,356	...	3,763	1,241	...	7	53
	XII.—Unproductive.	liv	**Inmates of Jails, asylums and hospitals.**	***851***	***424***	...	***412***	***15***	...	...	...
		168	Inmates of jails, asylums and hospitals...	851	424	...	412	15	...	...	...
		lv	**Beggars, vagrants, prostitutes ...**	***17,260***	***10,624***	***3***	***6,576***	***53***	...	***2***	***2***
		169	Beggars, vagrants, procurers, prostitutes, receivers of stolen goods, cattle poisoners.	17,260	10,624	3	6,576	53	...	2	2

TABLE XV—E.

Occupation or means of Livelihood.

STATISTICS OF INDUSTRIES.

This table exhibits statistics of factories, mills, etc., in which at least twenty persons were employed on the 10th March 1911; and is divided into four parts: Part I gives information regarding each kind of factory, etc. distinguishing between those factories in which mechanical power is employed and those in which it is not; and classifies them according to the number of persons employed. Part II contains district figures without these details. Parts III and IV are designed to show the caste and nationality of owners and managers respectively.

TABLE XV-E

Part I.
Provincial Summary.

STATISTICS OF INDUSTRIES.

Description of Factory, Mine, etc.	Classification of Factory, etc., according to number of persons employed (including management.)	Number of Factories.	Total number of persons employed.		Classification of: Direction, Supervision and Clerical work. Europeans and Anglo-Indians.		Indians.	
			Males.	Females.	Males.	Females.	Males.	Females.
1	2	3	4	5	6	7	8	9
Total Hyderabad State ...	...	*121*	*19,461*	*4,856*	*103*	*10*	*1,345*	*5*
Mines	Total ...	*3*	*7,976*	*2,347*	*57*	...	*343*	...
Collieries	Total ...	1	6,302	1,996	25	...	334	...
Collieries using mechanical power.	Total ...	1	6,302	1,996	25	...	334	...
	From 400 & over...	1	6,302	1,996	25	...	334	...
Gold mines	Total ...	2	1,674	351	32	...	9	...
Mines using mechanical power ...	Total ...	2	1,674	351	32	...	9	...
	From 100 to 200...	1	155	19	6	...	1	...
	„ 400 & over...	1	1,519	332	26	...	8	...
Quarries of Hard Rocks ...	Total ...	*3*	*997*	*64*	*6*	...	*17*	...
Shahabad stone quarries ...	Total ...	2	95	24	...	...	1	...
Quarries in which mechanical power is not used.	Total ...	2	95	24	...	...	1	...
	From 50 to 100...	2	95	24	...	...	1	...
Granite dressing works ...	Total ...	1	902	40	6	...	16	...
Works in which mechanical power is used.	Total ...	1	902	40	6	...	16	...
	From 400 & over...	1	902	40	6	...	16	...
Textile Industries ...	Total ...	*63*	*4,530*	*2,179*	*3*	...	*557*	*5*
Cotton ginning and pressing factories.	Total ...	18	896	639	...	...	118	2
Factories in which mechanical power is used.	Total ...	18	896	639	...	...	118	2
	From 20 to 50...	6	137	31	...	...	37	...
	„ 50 to 100...	7	322	220	...	...	61	2
	„ 100 to 200...	4	295	253	...	...	17	...
	„ 200 to 400...	1	142	135	...	...	3	...
Cotton ginning factories ...	Total ...	15	683	489	...	...	253	...
Factories in which mechanical power is used.	Total ...	15	683	489	...	...	253	...
	From 20 to 50...	3	70	21	...	...	27	...
	„ 50 to 100...	8	293	292	...	...	102	...
	„ 100 to 200...	4	320	176	...	...	124	...

TABLE XV-E.

STATISTICS OF INDUSTRIES.

Part I.
Provincial Summary.

Persons employed.								Remarks.
Skilled workmen.				Unskilled labourers.				*N. B.*—The state of business is indicated thus in figures— (1)—Much brisker than usual. (2)—Brisker than usual. (3)—Somewhat brisker than usual. (4)—Normal. (5)—Somewhat slacker than usual. (6)—Slacker than usual. (7)—Much slacker than usual.
Europeans and Anglo-Indians.		Indians.		Age 14 and over.		Under 14.		
Males.	Females.	Males.	Females.	Males.	Females.	Males.	Females.	
10	11	12	13	14	15	16	17	18
230	...	***7,378***	***248***	***9,595***	***3,750***	***810***	***843***	
18	...	***2,600***	...	***4,919***	***1,742***	***39***	***605***	
7	...	2,511	...	3,425	1,423	...	573	Steam and Electricity 1 (4) 1
7	...	2,511	...	3,425	1,423	...	573	
7	...	2,511	...	3,425	1,423	...	573	
11	...	89	...	1,494	319	39	32	Steam ... 1 (2) 1
11	...	89	...	1,494	319	39	32	
3 8	... ...	45 44	... ...	95 1,399	19 300	5 34	... 32	Steam oil and air ... 1 / 3 (4) 1 / 3
...	...	***624***	...	***305***	***58***	***45***	***6***	
...	...	59	...	35	24	...	...	(4) 2
...	...	59	...	35	24	...	...	
...	...	59	...	35	24	...	...	
...	...	565	...	270	34	45	6	Steam 1 (4) 1
...	...	565	...	270	34	45	6	
...	...	565	...	270	34	45	6	
1	...	***1,739***	***234***	***1,736***	***1,748***	***494***	***192***	
...	...	187	...	494	573	97	64	Steam 18 (3) 1
...	...	187	...	494	573	97	64	
... ...	.. ..	39 45 61 42	... ...	42 167 203 82	31 187 230 125	19 49 14 15	... 31 23 10	... ... (4) 5 ... ... (5) 3 ... ... (6) 4 ... ... (7) 4 (Closed) 1 18
...	...	63	40	284	411	83	38	Steam ... 14 (3) 3
...	...	63	40	284	411	83	38	Oil Engine ... 1 / 15 (4) 3
... ...	... ...	2 22 39	... 40 ...	41 159 84	21 249 141	... 10 73	... 3 35	... ... (5) 3 ... .. (6) 1 ... ... (7) 1 (Closed) 4 15

TABLE XV-E.

Part I.
Provincial Summary.

STATISTICS OF INDUSTRIES.

Description of Factory, Mine, etc.	Classification of Factory, etc., according to number of persons employed (including management.)	Number of Factories.	Total number of persons employed.		Classification of — Direction, Supervision and Clerical work. — Europeans and Anglo-Indians.		Indians.	
			Males.	Females.	Males.	Females.	Males.	Females.
1	2	3	4	5	6	7	8	9
Cotton presses	Total ...	9	289	201	1	...	41	...
Factories in which mechanical power is used.	Total ..	9	289	201	1	...	41	...
	From 20 to 50...	5	143	49	...	..	19	...
	„ 50 to 100...	4	146	152	1	...	22	...
Cotton ginning (and rice) mills ...	Total ...	6	131	115	...	...	37	...
Mills in which mechanical power is used.	Total ...	6	131	115	...	...	37	...
	From 20 to 50...	4	74	52	...	...	22	...
	„ 50 to 100...	2	57	63	...	...	15	...
Cotton spinning and weaving mills	Total ...	3	2,221	661	2	...	96	
Mills in which mechanical power is used.	Total ...	3	2,221	661	2	...	96	
	From 400 & over...	3	2,221	661	2	...	96	
Cotton sari factories ...	Total ..	2	33	7	...	...	...	...
Factories in which mechanical power is not used.	Total ..	2	33	7	...	...	...	...
	From 20 to 50...	2	33	7	...	...	...	...
Carpet factories	Total ...	2	114	4	...	...	1	...
Factories in which mechanical power is not used.	Total ...	2	114	4	...	...	1	...
	From 20 to 50...	1	40	4	...	...	...	...
	„ 50 to 100...	1	74	...		...	1	...
Cotton and silk sari factories ...	Total ...	7	131	35	...	...	5	...
Factories in which mechanical power is not used.	Total ...	7	131	35	...	...	5	...
	From 20 to 50...	7	131	35	...	...	5	...
Silk mills...	Total ...	1	32	28	...	...	6	...
Mills using mechanical power ...	Total ...	1	32	28	...	...	6	...
	From 50 to 100...	1	32	28	...	...	6	...
Leather and other Industries	Total ...	*13*	*607*	*75*	...	...	*54*	...
Tanneries...	Total ...	13	607	75	...	...	54	...
Tanneries in which mechanical power is not used.	Total ...	13	607	75	...	...	54	...
	From 20 to 50...	8	221	16	...	...	22	...
	50 to 100...	4	225	51	...	...	23	...
	100 to 200...	1	161	8	8	...	9	...

TABLE XV-E.

STATISTICS OF INDUSTRIES.

Part I.
Provincial Summary.

Persons employed.								Remarks.
Skilled workmen.				Unskilled labourers.				*N. B.*—The state of business is indicated thus in figures :— (1)—Much brisker than usual. (2)—Brisker than usual. (3)—Somewhat brisker than usual. (4)—Normal. (5)—Somewhat slacker than usual. (6)—Slacker than usual. (7)—Much slacker than usual.
Europeans and Anglo-Indians.		Indians.		Age 14 and over.		Under 14.		
Males.	Females.	Males.	Females.	Males.	Females.	Males.	Females.	
10	11	12	13	14	15	16	17	18
...	...	22	...	216	201	9	...	Steam ... 9 (2) 2
...	...	22	...	216	201	9	...	
...	...	17	...	105	49	2	...	... ... (3) 3
...	...	5	...	111	152	7	...	... ... (5) 4 9
...	...	...	...	94	115	...	...	Steam ... 6 (2) 3
...	...	...	...	94	115	...	...	
...	...	...	...	52	52	...	...	... ... (5) 3
...	...	...	...	42	63	...	...	6
1	...	1,433	170	402	400	287	88	Steam ... 3 (4) 1
1	...	1,433	170	402	400	287	88	... ... (7) 2 3
1	...	1,433	170	402	400	287	88	
...	...	...	...	33	7	...	...	... ... (4) 1
...	...	...	...	33	7	...	...	... ... (5) 1 2
...	...	...	...	33	7	...	...	
...	...	3	...	96	2	14	2	... ... (3) 1
...	...	3	...	96	2	14	2	
...	...	...	...	30	2	10	2	... ... (5) 1
...	...	3	...	66	...	4	...	2
...	...	19	18	103	17	4	...	... ... (3) 1
...	...	19	18	103	17	4	...	... ... (4) 3
...	...	19	18	103	17	4	...	... ... (5) 3 7
...	...	12	6	14	22	...	...	Steam ... 1 (6) 1
...	...	12	6	14	22	...	...	
...	...	12	6	14	22	...	...	
...	...	***157***	***6***	***363***	***56***	***33***	***13***	
...	...	157	6	363	56	33	13	... ... (3) 1
...	...	157	6	363	56	33	13	... ... (4) 7
...	...	126	3	67	13	6	...	... ... (5) 4
...	...	31	3	144	35	27	13	... ...
...	...	...	...	152	8	...	...	... ... (6) 1 13

TABLE XV-E.

STATISTICS OF INDUSTRIES.

Part I.
Provincial Summary.

Description of Factory, Mine, etc.	Classification of Factory, etc., according to number of persons employed (including management.)	Number of Factories.	Total number of persons employed.		Classification of — Direction, Supervision and Clerical work. — Europeans and Anglo-Indian.		Indians.	
			Males.	Females.	Males.	Females.	Males.	Females.
1	2	3	4	5	6	7	8	9
Wood, etc. Industries ..	Total ...	*2*	*91*	*5*	...	...	*5*	...
Carpentry and blacksmithy works	Total ..	1	45	...	...	...	3	...
Works in which mechanical power is not used.	Total ...	1	45	...	...	...	3	...
	From 20 to 50...	1	45	...	...	...	3	...
Timber yards ...	Total ..	1	46	5	...	...	5	...
Yards in which mechanical power is not used.	Total ..	1	46	5	...	...	5	...
	From 50 to 100 ..	1	46	5	...	...	5	...
Metal Industries ...	Total ...	*3*	*772*	*5*	*4*	...	*86*	...
Cast iron foundry ...	Total ..	1	61	5	...	...	3	...
Foundry using mechanical power.	Total ..	1	61	5	...	...	3	...
	From 50 to 100...	1	61	5	...	...	3	...
Weights and measures making factories.	Total ...	1	34	...	...	...	9	...
Factories in which mechanical power is not used.	Total ...	1	34	...	...	...	9	...
	From 20 to 50...	1	34	...	...	...	9	...
Mints	Total ...	1	677	...	4	...	74	...
Mints using mechanical power ...	Total ...	1	677	...	4	...	74	...
	From 400 & over .	1	677	...	4	...	74	...
Earthenware Industries ...	Total ..	*1*	*14*	*11*	...	...	...	...
Tile factory	Total ...	1	14	11	...	...	...	...
Factories in which mechanical power is not used.	Total ...	1	14	11	...	...	...	...
	From 20 to 50..	1	14	11	...	...	...	...
Industries connected with Chemical Products ...	Total ...	*3*	*105*	...	*2*	...	*34*	...
Aerated water factories (Ice factory).	Total ...	3	105	...	2	...	34	...
Factories in which mechanical power is used.	Total ...	2	85	...	2	...	32	...
	From 20 to 50...	1	26	...	1	...	2	...
	„ 50 to 100...	1	59	...	1	...	30	...
Factories in which mechanical power is not used.	Total ...	1	20	...	...	...	2	...
	From 20 to 50...	1	20	...	...	...	2	...

TABLE XV-E.

STATISTICS OF INDUSTRIES.

Part I.
Provincial Summary.

Persons employed.								Remarks.
Skilled workmen.				Unskilled labourers.				*N.B.*—The state of business is indicated thus in figures :— (1)—Much brisker than usual. (2)—Brisker than usual. (3)—Somewhat brisker than usual. (4)—Normal. (5)—Somewhat slacker than usual. (6)—Slacker than usual. (7)—Much slacker than usual.
Europeans and Anglo-Indians.		Indians.		Age 14 and over.		Under 14.		
Males.	Females.	Males.	Females.	Males.	Females.	Males.	Females.	
10	11	12	13	14	15	16	17	18
...	...	***53***	...	***24***	***5***	***6***	...	
...	...	23	...	13	...	6	...	Steam ... ... (7) 1
...	...	23	...	13	...	6	...	
...	...	23	...	13	...	6	...	
...	...	30	...	11	5	...	...	... ... (2) 1
...	...	30	...	11	5	...	...	
...	...	30	...	11	5	...	...	
13	...	***176***	...	***463***	***5***	***30***	...	
...	...	12	...	46	5	...	...	Oil Engine ... 1 (4) 1
...	...	12	...	46	5	...	...	
...	...	12	...	46	...	...	...	
...	...	...	...	25	...	...	...	... ... (4) 1
...	...	...	...	25	...	...	...	
...	...	...	...	25	...	...	...	
13	...	164	...	392	...	30	...	Steam ... 1 (2) 1
13	...	164	...	392	...	30	...	
13	...	164	...	392	...	30	...	
...	...	***3***	***1***	***1***	***4***	***10***	***6***	
...	...	3	1	1	4	10	6	... ... (5) 1
...	...	3	1	1	4	10	6	
...	...	3	1	1	4	10	6	
...	...	***25***	...	***19***	...	***25***	...	
...	...	25	...	19	...	25	...	Steam ... 2 (2) 1
...	...	7	...	19	...	25	...	
...	...	4	...	19	...	...	...	... ... (3) 1
...	...	3	...	...	...	25	...	2
...	...	18	...	...	...	...	...	
...	...	18	...	...	...	...	...	

TABLE XV-E.

STATISTICS OF INDUSTRIES.

Part I.
Provincial Summary.

Description of Factory, Mine, etc.	Classification of Factory, etc., according to number of persons employed (including management.)	Number of Factories.	Total number of persons employed.		Classification of — Direction, Supervision and Clerical work. — Europeans and Anglo-Indians.		Indians.	
			Males.	Females.	Males.	Females.	Males.	Females.
1	2	3	4	5	6	7	8	9
Food Industries ...	Total ...	*15*	*692*	*99*	*2*	...	*83*	...
Flour mills	Total ...	1	34	4	...	...	8	...
Mills in which mechanical power is used.	Total ...	1	34	4	...	...	8	...
	From 20 to 50...	1	34	4	...	...	8	...
Rice mills	Total ...	6	138	25	1	...	23	...
Mills using mechanical power ...	Total ...	6	138	25	1	...	23	...
	From 20 to 50...	6	138	25	1	...	23	...
Rice (and oil) mills	Total ...	1	34	6	...	...	3	...
Mills using mechanical power ...	Total ..	1	34	6	...	...	3	...
	From 20 to 50...	1	34	6	...	...	3	...
Distilleries.	Total ...	4	138	17	1	...	23	...
Distilleries using mechanical power.	Total ...	2	80	2	1	...	20	...
	From 20 to 50...	1	30	...	...	...	9	...
	" 50 to 100...	1	50	2	1	...	11	...
Distilleries in which mechanical power is not used.	Total ...	2	58	15	...	...	3	...
	From 20 to 50...	2	58	15	...	...	3	...
Water works	Total ...	1	207	...	...	...	23	...
Water works using mechanical power.	Total ...	1	207	...	...	...	23	...
	From 200 to 400...	1	207	...	...	...	23	...
Bidi factories	Total ..	1	127	25	...	...	2	...
Factories in which mechanical power is not used.	Total ...	1	127	25	...	...	2	...
	From 100 to 200...	1	127	25	...	...	2	...
Forage presses	Total ...	1	14	22	...	...	1	...
Presses in which mechanical power is not used.	Total ...	1	14	22	..	...	1	...
	From 20 to 50...	1	14	22	...	...	1	...
Industries of Dress ...	Total ...	*3*	*87*	*3*	...	...	*1*	...
Aurangabad dress (Mashrus and Himrus) factories.	Total ...	3	87	3	...	...	1	...
Factories in which mechanical power is not used.	Total ...	3	87	3	...	...	1	...
	From 20 to 50...	3	87	3	...	...	1	—

TABLE XV-E.

STATISTICS OF INDUSTRIES.

Part I.
Provincial Summary.

Persons employed.								Remarks.
Skilled workmen.				Unskilled labourers.				*N.B.*—The state of business is indicated thus in figures:— (1)—Much brisker than usual. (2)—Brisker than usual. (3)—Somewhat brisker than usual. (4)—Normal. (5)—Somewhat slacker than usual. (6)—Slacker than usual. (7)—Much slacker than usual.
Europeans and Anglo-Indians.		Indians.		Age 14 and over.		Under 14.		
Males.	Females.	Males.	Females.	Males.	Females.	Males.	Females.	
10	11	12	13	14	15	16	17	18
...	...	***212***	***7***	***297***	***71***	***98***	***21***	
...	...	...	...	25	4	1	...	Steam ... 1 (4) 1
...	...	...	...	25	4	1	...	
...	...	...	...	25	4	1	...	
...	...	18	7	79	17	17	1	Steam ... 6 (2) 2
...	...	18	7	79	17	17	1	... ... (3) 3
...	...	18	7	79	17	17	1	... ... (5) 1/6
...	...	14	...	14	6	3	...	Steam ... 1 (4) 1
...	...	14	...	14	6	3	...	
...	...	14	...	14	6	3	...	
...	...	2	...	110	17	2	...	
...	...	...	...	57	2	2	...	Steam ... 2 (2) 1
...	...	...	...	21	...	...	...	
...	...	..	...	30	2	2	...	
...	...	2	...	53	15	...	...	... ... (5) 1/2
...	...	2	...	53	15	...	...	Steam ... 1 (4) 2
...	...	173	...	11	...	...	...	
...	...	173	...	11	...	...	...	
...	...	173	...	11	...	...	...	
...	...	...	...	50	5	75	20	... ... (1) 1
...	...	...	...	50	5	75	20	
...	...	...	...	50	5	75	20	
...	...	5	...	8	22	...	...	... ... (7) 1
...	...	5	...	8	22	...	...	
...	...	5	...	8	22	...	...	
...	...	***44***	...	***30***	***3***	***12***	...	
...	...	44	...	30	3	12	...	... ... (6) 3
...	...	44	...	30	3	12	...	
...	...	44	...	30	3	12	...	

TABLE XV-E.

Part I.
Provincial Summary.

STATISTICS OF INDUSTRIES.

Description of Factory, Mine, etc.	Classification of Factory, etc., according to number of persons employed (including management.)	Number of Factory.	Total number of persons employed.		Classification of — Direction, Supervision and Clerical work. — Europeans and Anglo-Indians.		Indians.	
			Males.	Females.	Males.	Females.	Males.	Females.
1	2	3	4	5	6	7	8	9
Furniture Industries ...	Total ...	*1*	*36*	...	...	...	*10*	...
Furniture factory (Government Industrial School).	Total ...	1	36	...	...	...	10	...
Furniture factories in which mechanical power is not used Government Industrial School	Total ...	1	36	...	...	...	10	...
	From 20 to 50 ...	1	36	...	...	...	10	...
Construction of Means of Transport ...	Total ...	*8*	*3,460*	*61*	*25*	*10*	*145*	...
Railway workshops ...	Total ...	3	3,259	61	24	10	138	...
Factories in which mechanical power is used.	Total ...	2	3,231	61	23	10	137	...
	From 100 to 200	1	192	1	...	...	7	...
	„ 400 & over ..	1	3,039	60	23	10	130	...
Factories in which mechanical power is not used.	Total ..	1	28	...	1	...	1	...
	From 20 to 50 ...	1	28	...	1	...	1	...
Coach building factories ..	Total ...	3	130	...	...	...	1	...
Factories in which mechanical power is not used.	Total ...	3	130	...	...	...	1	...
	From 20 to 50 ...	2	71	...	...	...	1	...
	„ 50 to 100 ...	1	59	...	...	...	...	...
Motor car works ...	Total ...	1	41	...	1	...	8	...
Works in which mechanical power is not used.	Total ...	1	41	...	1	...	8	...
	From 20 to 50 ...	1	41	...	1	...	8	...
Bicycle works ...	Total ...	1	30	...	...	...	3	...
Works in which mechanical power is not used.	Total ...	1	30	...	...	...	3	...
	From 20 to 50 ...	1	30	...	...	...	3	...
Production and transmission of Physical Forces ..	Total ...	*1*	*34*	*6*	...	...	*3*	...
Electric works ...	Total ...	1	34	6	...	...	3	...
Works in which mechanical power is used.	Total ...	1	34	6	...	...	3	...
	From 20 to 50 ...	1	34	6	...	...	3	...
Industries of Luxury ..	Total ..	*2*	*60*	*1*	*4*	...	*4*	...
Printing presses	Total ...	2	60	1	4	...	4	...
Presses in which mechanical power is not used.	Total ...	2	60	1	4	...	4	...
	From 20 to 50...	2	60	1	4	...	4	...

TABLE XV-E.

STATISTICS OF INDUSTRIES.

Part I.
Provincial Summary.

Persons employed.								Remarks.
Skilled workmen.				Unskilled labourers.				*N. B.*—The state of business is indicated thus in figures:— (1)—Much brisker than usual. (2)—Brisker than usual. (3)—Somewhat brisker than usual. (4)—Normal. (5)—Somewhat slacker than usual. (6)—Slacker than usual. (7)—Much slacker than usual.
Europeans and Anglo-Indians.		Indians.		Age 14 and over.		Under 14.		
Males.	Females.	Males.	Females.	Males.	Females.	Males.	Females.	
10	11	12	13	14	15	16	17	18
...	...	*19*	...	*7*	...	...	...	
...	...	19	...	7	...	...	...	... ... (1) 1
...	...	19	...	7	...	....	...	
...	...	19	...	7	...	...	...	
198	...	*1,687*	...	*1,393*	*51*	*12*	...	
196	...	1,516	...	1,377	51	8	...	
196	...	1,510	...	1,357	51	8	...	Steam ... 2 (2) 1
3	...	111	...	63	1	8	...	... ... (4) 1
193	...	1,399	...	1,294	50	...	...	2
...	...	6	...	20	...	...	...	... ... (1) 1
...	...	6	...	20	...	...	...	
...	...	117	...	8	...	4	...	... ... (4) 2
...	...	117	...	8	...	4	...	
...	...	58	...	8	...	4	...	... ... (5) 1
...	...	59	...	...	...	...	...	3
2	...	29	...	6	...	...	...	... ... (5) 1
2	...	29	...	6	...	...	...	
2	...	29	...	6	...	...	...	
...	...	25	...	2	...	...	...	... ... (1) 1
...	...	25	...	2	...	...	...	
...	...	25	...	2	...	...	...	
...	...	*15*	...	*16*	*6*	...	...	
...	...	15	...	16	6	...	...	Electricity ... 1 (4) 1
...	...	15	...	16	6	...	...	
...	...	15	...	16	6	...	...	
...	...	*24*	...	*22*	*1*	*6*	...	
...	...	24	...	22	1	6	...	... ... (2) 1
...	...	24	...	22	1	6	...	
...	...	24	...	22	1	6	...	... ... (4) 1/2

TABLE XV-E.

Part II.
Distribution by Districts.

STATISTICS OF INDUSTRIES.

Description of Factory, Mine, etc.	District.	No. of Factories.	Total number of persons employed.		Classification of Direction, Super. Clerical — Europeans and Anglo-Indians.	
			Males.	Females.	Males.	Females.
1	2	3	4	5	6	7
Total Hyderabad State	...	*121*	*19,461*	*4,856*	*103*	*10*
Total Hyderabad City .	...	*24*	*5,677*	*284*	*36*	*10*
Textile Industries.						
Cotton spinning and weaving mills. ..	Hyderabad City.	1	835	185	1	...
Leather and other Industries.						
Tanneries	Do.	2	77	4	...	...
Wood, etc., Industries.						
Carpentry and blacksmithy works ..	Do.	1	45	...	...	...
Timber yards	Do.	1	46	5	...	...
Metal Industries.						
Cast iron foundry	Do.	1	61	[illegible]	...	...
Mints	Do.	1	677	...	4	...
Earthenware Industries.						
Tile factory	Do.	1	14	11	...	...
Industries connected with Chemical Products.						
Aerated water factories (Ice factory) ..	Do.	3	105	...	2	...
Food Industries.						
Flour mills	Do.	1	34	4	...	...
Distilleries	Do.	1	50	2	1	...
Water works	Do.	1	207	...	...	...
Construction of Means of Transport.						
Railway workshops	Do.	2	3,231	61	23	10
Coach building factories	Do.	3	130	...	...	...
Motor-car works	Do.	1	41	...	1	...
Bicycle works	Do.	1	36	...	...	...
Production and transmission of Physical Forces.						
Electric works	Do.	1	34	6	...	...
Industries of Luxury.						
Printing presses	Do.	2	60	1	4	...
Total Atraf-i-Balda ...	...	*5*	*114*	*31*	...	...
Leather and other Industries.						
Tanneries	Atraf-i-balda.	4	100	9	...	...
Food Industries.						
Forage presses	Do.	1	14	22	...	...

TABLE XV-E.

STATISTICS OF INDUSTRIES.

Part II.
Distribution by Districts.

persons employed.										Remarks.
vision and work.		Skilled workmen.				Unskilled labourers.				
Indians.		Europeans and Anglo-Indians.		Indians.		Age 14 and over.		Under 14.		
Males.	Females.	Males.	Females.	Males.	Females.	Males.	Females.	Males.	Females.	
8	9	10	11	12	13	14	15	16	17	
1,345	5	230	...	7,378	248	9,595	3,750	810	843	
341	...	212	...	2,934	171	2,049	97	105	6	
18	...	1	...	750	170	65	15	...	...	
11	...	...	...	34	...	19	4	13	...	
3	...	...	...	23	...	13	...	6	...	
5	...	...	...	30	...	11	5	...	...	
3	...	...	...	12	...	46	5	...	...	
74	...	13	...	164	...	392	...	30	...	
...	...	...	...	3	1	1	4	10	6	
34	...	...	...	2[illegible]	...	19	...	25	...	
8	...	...	...	...	...	25	4	1	...	
11	...	...	...	...	...	36	2	2	...	
23	...	...	...	173	...	11	...	...	...	
157	...	186	...	1,510	...	1,357	51	8	...	
1	...	...	...	117	...	8	...	4	...	
3	...	2	...	29	...	6	...	...	...	
3	...	...	...	25	...	2	...	...	...	
3	...	...	...	15	...	16	6	...	...	
4	...	...	...	24	...	22	1	6	...	
10	...	...	...	86	3	16	28	2	...	
9	...	...	...	81	3	8	6	2	...	
1	...	...	...	5	...	8	22	...	...	

TABLE XV-E.

Part II.
Distribution by Districts.

STATISTICS OF INDUSTRIES.

Description of Factory, Mine, etc.	District.	No. of Factories.	Total number of persons employed.		Classification of Direction, Super. Clerical Europeans and Anglo-Indians.	
			Males.	Females.	Males.	Females.
1	2	3	4	5	6	7
Total Warangal Division ..	...	*17*	*6,903*	*2,219*	*25*	...
Total Warangal District ..	...	*16*	*6,870*	*2,192*	*25*	...
Mines.						
Collieries	Warangal.	1	6,302	1,996	25	...
Textile Industries.						
Cotton presses	Do.	3	73	63	...	...
Cotton ginning (and rice) mills	Do.	6	131	115	...	..
Leather and other Industries.						
Tanneries	Do.	4	309	18	...	...
Food Industries.						
Distilleries	Do.	2	55	...	...	...
Total Adilabad District ..	...	*1*	*33*	*27*	...	...
Textile Industries.						
Cotton presses	Adilabad.	1	33	27	...	...
Total Medak Division ..	...	*10*	*1,140*	*100*	*7*	...
Total Medak District ..	...	*2*	*921*	*43*	*6*	...
Quarries of Hard Rocks						
Granite dressing works	Medak.	1	902	4	6	...
Food Industries.						
Rice mills	Do.	1	19	3	...	..
Total Nizamabad District ..	...	*7*	*185*	*56*	*1*	...
Textile Industries.						
Silk mills	Nizamabad.	1	32	28	...	...
Food Industries.						
Rice mills	Do.	5	119	22	1	...
Rice (and oil) mills	Do.	1	34	6	...	...
Total Nalgonda District ..	...	*1*	*34*	*1*	...	...
Leather and other Industries						
Tanneries	Nalgonda.	1	34	1	...	...

TABLE XV-E.

STATISTICS OF INDUSTRIES.

Part II.
Distribution by Districts.

persons employed.										
vision and work.		Skilled workmen.				Unskilled labourers.				Remarks.
Indians.		Europeans and Anglo-Indians.		Indians.		Age 14 and over.		Under 14.		
Males.	Females.	Males.	Females.	Males.	Females.	Males.	Females.	Males.	Females.	
8	9	10	11	12	13	14	15	16	17	
437	...	7	...	2,513	...	3,931	1,646	...	573	
417	...	7	...	2,513	...	3,908	1,619	...	573	
334	...	7	...	2,511	...	3,425	1,423	...	573	
15	...	...	...	...	...	58	63	...	...	
37	...	...	...	...	...	94	115	...	...	
21	...	...	...	...	...	238	18	...	...	
10	...	...	...	2	...	43	...	...	...	
10	...	...	...	...	...	23	27	...	...	
16	...	...	...	...	...	23	27	...	...	
57	...	...	...	640	13	377	80	66	7	
21	...	...	...	565	...	280	37	49	6	
16	...	...	...	563	...	276	34	45	6	
5	...	...	...	...	...	10	3	4	...	
27	...	...	...	41	13	97	42	16	1	
6	...	...	...	12	6	14	22	...	...	
18	...	...	...	18	7	69	14	13	1	
3	...	...	...	14	...	14	6	3	...	
2	...	...	...	31	...	...	1	1	...	
2	...	...	...	31	...	...	1	1	...	

TABLE XV-E.

Part II.
Distribution by Districts.

STATISTICS OF INDUSTRIES.

Description of Factory, Mine, etc.	District.	No. of Factories.	Total number of persons employed.		Classification of Direction, Super… Clerical… Europeans and Anglo-Indians.	
			Males.	Females.	Males.	Females.
1	2	3	4	5	6	7
Total Aurangabad Division ...	...	*32*	*1,929*	*1,087*	...	...
Total Aurangabad District ...	Aurangabad.	*12*	*936*	*326*	...	...
Textile Industries.						
Cotton ginning and pressing factories ...	Do	2	60	57	...	...
Cotton ginning factories	Do	2	40	42	...	...
Cotton presses	Do	3	105	52	...	...
Cotton spinning and weaving mills ...	Do	1	608	172	...	...
Industries of Dress.						
Aurangabad dress (Himrus and Mushrus) factory.	Do	3	87	3	...	...
Furniture Industries.						
Furniture factory (Government Industrial School.)	Do	1	36	...	...	...
Total Nander District ...	Nander.	*9*	*602*	*504*	...	...
Textile Industries.						
Cotton ginning and pressing factories ...	Do	7	541	444	...	...
Cotton ginning factories	Do	1	28	45	...	...
Food Industries.						
Distilleries	Do	1	33	15	...	...
Total Parbhani District ...	...	*11*	*391*	*257*	...	...
Textile Industries.						
Cotton ginning and pressing factories ...	Parbhani.	4	98	7	...	...
Cotton ginning factories	Do	6	258	236	...	...
Cotton presses	Do	1	35	14	...	...
Total Gulbarga Division ...	...	*33*	*3,698*	*1,135*	*38*	...
Total Gulbarga District ...	...	*19*	*1,605*	*617*	*8*	...
Mines.						
Gold mines	Gulburga.	1	155	19	6	...
Quarries of Hard Rocks.						
Shahabad stone quarries	Do	2	95	24	...	...

TABLE XV-E.

STATISTICS OF INDUSTRIES.

Part II. Distribution by Districts.

persons employed.										
vision and work.		Skilled workmen.				Unskilled labourers.				Remarks.
Indians.		Europeans and Anglo-Indians.		Indians.		Age 14 and over		Under 14.		
Males.	Females.	Males.	Females.	Males.	Females.	Males.	Females.	Males.	Females	
8	9	10	11	12	13	14	15	16	17	
198	***3***	...	...	***590***	***28***	***1,030***	***1,026***	***114***	***33***	
83	***3***	...	...	***385***	...	***413***	***323***	***58***	...	
6	...	...	...	10	...	44	57	...	...	
5	...	...	...	2	...	33	42	...	...	
6	...	...	...	15	...	82	52	2	...	
52	3	...	...	295	...	217	169	44	...	
1	...	...	...	44	...	30	3	12	...	
10	...	...	...	19	...	7	...	...	...	
46	...	...	...	***112***	...	***416***	***471***	***29***	***33***	
33	...	...	...	112	...	367	411	29	33	
11	...	...	...	...	...	17	45	...	...	
2	...	...	...	...	...	31	15	...	...	
69	...	...	...	***93***	***28***	***202***	***232***	***27***	...	
30	...	...	...	34	...	15	7	19	...	
36	...	...	...	55	25	159	211	8	...	
3	...	...	...	4	...	28	14	...	...	
222	***2***	***11***	...	***618***	***36***	***2,192***	***873***	***523***	***224***	
128	...	***3***	...	***533***	***21***	***507***	***431***	***429***	***168***	
1	...	3	...	45	...	93	19	5	...	
1	...	...	...	59	...	35	24	...	...	

TABLE XV-E.

Part II.
Distribution by Districts.

STATISTICS OF INDUSTRIES.

Description of Factory, Mine, etc.	District.	No. of Factories.	Total number of persons employed.		Classification of Direction, Super[vision] Clerical[...] Europeans and Anglo-Indians.	
			Males.	Females.	Males.	Females.
1	2	3	4	5	6	7
Textile Industries.						
Cotton ginning and pressing factories ..	Gulbarga.	2	80	95	...	..
Cotton ginning factories	Do.	1	110	50	...	...
Cotton presses	Do.	1	43	45	1	...
Cotton spinning and weaving mills ...	Do.	1	778	304	1	...
Cotton sari weaving factories	Do.	1	15	5	...	...
Cotton and silk sari weaving factories ...	Do.	7	131	35	...	...
Leather and other Industries.						
Tanneries	Do.	1	37	15	...	...
Metal Industries.						
Weight and measures making factories ...	Do.	1	34	...	...	...
Food Industries.						
Bidi factory	Do.	1	127	25	...	...
Total Osmanabad District ...	...	*5*	*265*	*94*	...	...
Textile Industries.						
Cotton ginning and pressing factories ...	Osmanabad.	1	42	8	...	...
Cotton ginning factories	Do.	4	223	86	...	...
Total Raichur District ...	...	*9*	*1,826*	*424*	*27*	...
Mines.						
Gold mines	Raichur. ...	1	1,519	332	26	...
Textile Industries.						
Cotton ginning and pressing factories ..	Do.	2	75	28	...	...
Cotton ginning factories	Do.	1	24	30	...	...
Cotton sari and weaving factories ...	Do.	1	18	2	...	...
Carpet factories	Do.	2	114	4	...	...
Leather and other Industries.						
Tanneries	Do.	1	50	28	...	...
Construction of Means of Transport.						
Locomotive Shed, Railway and carriage works.	Do.	1	28	...	1	...

TABLE XV-E.

STATISTICS OF INDUSTRIES.

Part II.
Distribution by Districts.

persons employed.										
vision and work.		Skilled workmen.				Unskilled labourers.				Remarks.
Indians.		Europeans and Anglo-Indians.		Indians.		Age 14 and over.		Under 14.		
Males.	Females.	Males.	Females.	Males.	Females.	Males.	Females.	Males.	Females.	
8	9	10	11	12	13	14	15	16	17	
13	...	...	...	2	...	19	65	46	30	
55	...	...	...	6	...	...	25	49	25	
7	...	...	...	3	...	25	45	7	...	
26	...	...	...	388	...	120	216	243	88	
...	...	...	...	...	...	15	5	...	...	
5	...	...	...	19	18	103	17	4	...	
6	...	...	...	11	3	20	10	...	2	
9	...	...	...	...	...	25	...	...	...	
2	...	...	...	...	...	50	5	75	20	
172	***2***	...	...	...	***15***	***66***	***64***	***27***	***13***	
31	2	...	...	...	...	10	6	1	...	
141	...	...	...	...	15	56	58	26	13	
25	...	***8***	...	***82***	...	***1,619***	***378***	***67***	***46***	
8	...	8	...	44	...	1,399	300	34	32	
5	...	...	...	29	...	39	27	2	1	
5	...	...	...	...	...	19	30	...	...	
...	...	...	...	...	...	18	2	...	...	
1	...	...	...	3	...	96	2	14	2	
5	...	...	...	...	...	28	17	17	11	
1	...	...	...	6	...	20	...	...	...	

Part III.
Particulars as to Ownership of Factories, etc.

TABLE XV-E.

STATISTICS OF INDUSTRIES.

Description of Factory, Mine, etc.	Number of Factories.	Number owned by companies of which the directors are.			Number			
		Europeans and Anglo-Indians.	Indians.	Of both races.	Europeans and Anglo-Indians.		In	
						Total.	Ayyawar satani.	Chatri.
1	2	3	4	5	6	7	8	9
Total Hyderabad State.								
Total ...	*121*	*9*	*22*	*2*	*2*	*86*	*1*	*1*
Mines.								
Collieries ...	1	1	...	...	...	...	...	...
Gold mines ...	2	2	...	...	...	...	...	...
Quarries of Hard Rocks.								
Shahabad stone quarries ...	2	...	...	...	...	2	...	...
Granite dressing works ...	1	...	...	1	...	...	...	...
Textile Industries.								
Cotton ginning and pressing factories ...	18	...	2	1	...	15	...	...
Cotton ginning factories ...	15	...	3	...	...	12	...	...
Cotton presses ...	9	...	4	...	...	5	...	...
Cotton ginning (and rice) mills ...	6	...	3	...	...	3	1	...
Cotton spinning and weaving mills ..	3	...	3	...	...	...	...	...
Cotton sari factories ...	2	...	...	...	...	2	...	...
Carpet factories ...	2	...	...	...	...	2	...	...
Cotton and silk sari factories ...	7	...	...	...	...	7	...	...
Silk mills ...	1	...	...	...	...	1	...	...
Leather and other Industries.								
Tanneries ...	13	...	...	...	...	13	...	...
Wood, etc., Industries.								
Carpentry and blacksmithy works ...	1	...	...	...	...	1	...	...
Timber yards. ...	1	...	...	...	...	1	...	...
Metal Industries.								
Cast iron foundry ...	1	...	...	...	...	1	...	...
Weights and measures making factories.	1	...	...	...	...	1	...	...
Mints ...	1	...	1	...	...	...	...	...
Earthenware Industries.								
Tile factory ...	1	...	...	...	...	1	...	...

TABLE XV-E.

STATISTICS OF INDUSTRIES.

Part III.
Particulars as to Ownership of Factories, etc.

privately owned by															
dians.															
Gosain.	Gounda-la.	Gujrati Bania Nagar.	Kapu	Kayasth	Khatri.	Komati	Lingayet Bania.	Marwari Bania Muhesri.	Musalman.	Padma Sale.	Parsi.	Rajput.	Wanjari	Vellal mudliar	Teli.
10	11	12	13	14	15	16	17	18	19	20	21	22	23	24	25
1	*1*	*5*	*1*	*1*	*4*	*9*	*1*	*14*	*30*	*3*	*10*	*1*	*1*	*1*	*1*
...	...	...	...	...	...	...	...	...	...	...	...	...	...	...	...
...	...	...	...	..	...	...	...	...	...	...	...	...	...	...	...
...	...	...	...	...	...	...	...	...	2	...	...	...	...	...	...
...	...	...	...	...	...	...	...	...	...	...	...	...	...	...	...
1	...	1	...	1	...	...	1	6	2	...	3	...	...	...	...
...	...	2	...	...	...	2	...	5	...	...	3	...	...	...	...
...	...	1	...	...	...	3	...	1	...	...	...	...	...	...	...
...	...	...	..	...	...	2	...	...	...	...	...	...	...	...	...
...	...	...	...	...	...	...	...	...	...	...	...	...	...	...	...
...	...	...	...	...	...	...	...	...	2	...	...	...	...	...	...
...	...	...	...	...	...	...	...	...	2	...	...	...	...	...	...
...	...	...	...	..	2	...	...	...	1	3	...	...	...	...	1
...	...	...	...	...	1	...	...	...	...	...	...	...	...	...	...
...	...	...	...	...	...	...	...	...	13	...	...	...	...	...	...
...	...	...	...	...	...	...	...	...	...	...	...	...	...	1	...
...	...	...	...	...	...	...	...	...	1	...	...	...	...	...	...
...	...	...	...	...	...	...	...	...	1	...	...	...	...	...	...
...	...	...	...	...	1	...	...	...	...	...	...	...	...	...	...
...	...	...	...	...	...	...	...	...	...	...	..	...	...	...	...
...	...	...	...	...	...	...	...	...	...	...	1	...	...	...	...

Part III.
Particulars as to Ownership Factories, etc.

TABLE XV-E.

STATISTICS OF INDUSTRIES.

Description of Factory, Mine, etc.	Number of Factories.	Number owned by companies of which the directors are.			Number			
						In		
		Europeans and Anglo-Indians.	Indians.	Of both races.	Europeans and Anglo-Indians.	Total.	Ayyawar. satani.	Chatri.
1	2	3	4	5	6	7	8	9
Industries connected with Chemical Products.								
Aerated water factories (Ice factory) ...	3	2	1	...	...	...	...	...
Food Industries.								
Flour mills ...	1	...	...	...	...	1	...	..
Rice mills ..	6	...	...	...	...	6	...	...
Rice (and oil) mills ..	1	...	...	...	...	1	...	...
Distilleries ...	4	...	1	...	...	3	...	...
Water works ..	1	...	1	...	...	...	...	...
Bidi factory ...	1	...	...	...	...	1	...	...
Forage presses ...	1	...	...	...	1	...	...	...
Industries of Dress.								
Aurangabad dress (Himrus and Mushrus) factories.	3	...	...	...	...	3	...	..
Furniture Industries.								
Furniture factory (Government Industrial School)	1	...	1	...	...	...	...	...
Construction of Means of Transport.								
Railway workshops ...	3	3	...	...	...	...	...	...
Coach building factories ...	3	...	...	...	...	3	...	1
Motor-car works ...	1	1	...	...	...	...	...	...
Bicycle works ...	1	...	...	...	...	1	...	...
Production and transmission of Physical Forces.								
Electric works ...	1	...	1	...	...	...	...	...
Industries of Luxury.								
Printing presses ...	2	...	1	...	1	...	...	...

TABLE XV-E.

STATISTICS OF INDUSTRIES.

Part III.
Particulars as to Ownership of Factories, etc.

privately owned by															
dians.															
Gosain.	Gound-la.	Gujrati Bania Nagar.	Kapu	Kayasth.	Khatri.	Komati.	Linga-yet Bania.	Mar-wari Bania Mahes-ri.	Musal-man.	Padma Sale.	Parsi.	Rajput.	Wanjari	Vellal mudliar	Teli.
10	11	12	13	14	15	16	17	18	19	20	21	22	23	24	25
...	...	...	...	...	...	...	...	...	...	...	...	...	...	...	...
...	...	...	...	...	...	...	...	...	1	...	...	...	...	...	...
...	1	1	...	...	...	1	...	2	...	...	...	...	1	...	...
...	...	...	1	...	...	...	...	...	...	...	...	...	...	...	...
...	...	...	...	...	...	1	...	...	...	...	1	1	...	...	...
...	...	...	...	...	...	...	...	...	...	...	...	...	...	...	...
...	...	...	...	...	...	...	...	...	1	...	...	...	...	...	...
...	...	...	...	...	...	...	...	...	...	...	...	...	...	...	...
...	...	...	...	...	...	...	...	...	3	...	...	...	...	...	...
...	...	...	...	...	...	...	...	...	...	...	...	...	...	...	...
...	...	...	...	...	...	...	...	...	...	...	...	...	...	...	...
...	...	...	...	...	...	...	...	...	1	...	1	...	...	...	...
...	...	...	...	...	...	...	...	...	...	...	...	...	...	...	...
...	...	...	...	...	...	...	...	...	...	...	1	...	...	...	...
...	...	...	...	...	...	...	...	...	...	...	...	...	...	...	...
...	...	...	...	...	...	...	...	...	...	...	...	...	...	...	...

Part IV.
Particulars as to Caste or Race of the Managers of Factories, etc.

TABLE XV-E.

STATISTICS OF INDUSTRIES.

Description of Factory, Mine, etc.	Number of Factories.	Number						
		Europeans and Anglo-Indians.	In					
			Total.	Brahman.	Gosain.	Goundla.	Gujrati Bania. (Modh.)	Kapu.
1	2	3	4	5	6	7	8	9
Total Hyderabad State ...	*121*	*12*	*109*	*9*	*2*	*1*	*7*	*1*
Mines.								
Collieries	1	1	...	...	...	...	...	...
Gold mines	2	2	...	...	...	...	...	...
Quarries of Hard Rocks.								
Shahabad stone quarries	2	...	2	...	...	...	...	...
Granite dressing works	1	1	...	...	...	...	...	...
Textile Industries.								
Cotton ginning and pressing factories.	18	...	18	4	...	...	1	...
Cotton ginning factories ...	15	...	15	3	...	...	3	...
Cotton presses	9	...	9	1	...	...	2	...
Cotton ginning (and rice) mills ...	6	...	6	...	...	...	...	...
Cotton spinning and weaving mills ...	3	...	3	...	...	...	...	...
Cotton and sari factories ..	2	...	2	...	...	...	...	...
Carpet factories	2	...	2	...	...	...	...	...
Cotton and silk sari factories ...	7	...	7	...	...	...	...	...
Silk mills	1	...	1	...	...	...	...	...
Leather and other Industries.								
Tanneries	13	...	13	...	...	...	...	...
Wood etc., Industries.								
Carpentry and blacksmithy works ...	1	...	1	...	...	...	...	...
Timber Yards	1	...	1	...	...	...	...	...
Metal Industries.								
Cast iron foundry	1	...	1	...	...	...	...	...
Weights and measures making factories.	1	...	1	...	...	...	...	...
Mints	1	1	...	...	...	...	...	...

TABLE XV-E.

STATISTICS OF INDUSTRIES.

Part IV.
Particulars as to Castes or Race of the Managers of Factories, etc.

managed by

dians.

Kasar.	Khatri.	Komati.	Lingayet wani.	Marwari Bania. Mahesri	Padma-sale.	Rajput.	Telaga.	Teli.	Vellal (mudliar.)	Wanjari.	Musalman.	Parsi.
10	11	12	13	14	15	16	17	18	19	20	21	22
1	*3*	*11*	*2*	*10*	*4*	*1*	*1*	*2*	*3*	*1*	*33*	*17*
...	...	...	...	...	...	...	...	...	...	...	...	...
...	...	...	...	...	...	...	...	...	..	...	...	...
...	...	...	...	...	...	...	...	...	...	...	2	...
...	...	...	...	...	..	...	...	...	...	...	...	...
...	1	...	2	4	...	...	...	...	...	...	1	5
1	...	1	...	3	...	...	...	...	...	...	...	4
...	...	3	...	1	...	...	...	...	...	...	1	1
...	...	4	...	...	...	...	...	1	1	...	...	...
...	...	1	...	...	...	...	...	...	...	...	...	2
...	...	...	...	...	...	...	...	...	...	...	2	...
...	...	...	...	...	...	...	...	...	...	...	2	...
...	2	...	...	...	3	...	...	1	...	...	1	...
...	...	...	...	...	1	...	...	...	...	...	...	...
...	...	...	...	...	...	...	1	...	...	...	12	...
...	...	...	...	...	...	...	...	...	1	...	...	...
...	...	...	...	...	...	...	...	...	...	...	1	...
...	...	...	...	...	...	1	...	...	...	...	...	...
...	...	...	...	...	...	...	...	...	...	...	1	...
...	...	...	...	...	...	...	...	...	...	...	...	...

Part IV.
Particulars as to Caste or Race of the Managers of Factories, etc.

TABLE XV-E.

STATISTICS OF INDUSTRIES.

Description of Factory, Mine, etc.	Number of Factories.	Number						
		Europeans and Anglo-Indians	In					
			Total.	Brahman.	Gosain.	Goundla.	Gujrati Bania (Modh.)	Kapu.
1	2	3	4	5	6	7	8	9
Earthenware Industries.								
Tile factory	1	...	1	...	...	...	...	...
Industries connected with Chemical Products.								
Aerated water factories (Ice factory)...	3	2	1	...	1	...	...	...
Food Industries.								
Flour mills	1	...	1	...	...	...	...	...
Rice mills	6	...	6	...	...	1	1	...
Rice (and oil) mills	1	...	1	1	...	...	...	...
Distilleries	4	...	4	...	...	...	...	...
Water works	1	...	1	...	...	...	...	...
Bidi factory	1	...	1	...	...	...	...	...
Forage presses	1	...	1	...	...	...	...	...
Industries of Dress.								
Aurangabad dress (Himrus and Mashrus) factories.	3	...	3	...	...	...	...	...
Furniture Industries.								
Furniture Factory (Govt. Industrial school.)	1	...	1	...	...	...	...	...
Construction of Means of Transport.								
Railway workshops	3	3	...	...	...	...	...	...
Coach building factories	3	...	3	...	...	...	...	...
Motor-car works	1	1	...	...	...	...	...	...
Bicycle works	1	...	1	...	...	...	...	...
Production and transmission of Physical Forces.								
Electric works	1	...	1	...	1	...	...	...
Industries of Luxury.								
Printing presses	2	1	1	...	...	...	...	

TABLE XV-E.

STATISTICS OF INDUSTRIES.

Part IV.
Particulars as to Caste or Race of the Managers of Factories, etc.

managed by

dians.

Kasar.	Khatri.	Komati.	Lingayet wani.	Marwari Bania Mahesri.	Padma-sale.	Rajput.	Telaga.	Teli.	Vellal (mudliar.)	Wanjari.	Musalman.	Parsi.
10	11	12	13	14	15	16	17	18	19	20	21	22
...	...	...	...	...	...	...	...	...	...	...	...	1
...	...	...	...	...	...	...	...	...	...	...	...	...
...	...	...	...	...	...	...	...	...	...	...	1	...
...	...	1	...	2	...	...	...	...	...	1	...	...
...	...	...	...	...	...	...	...	...	...	...	...	...
...	...	...	...	...	...	...	...	...	1	...	1	2
...	...	...	..	...	...	...	...	...	...	...	1	...
...	...	...	...	...	...	...	...	...	...	...	1	...
...	...	...	...	...	...	...	...	...	...	...	1	...
...	...	...	...	...	...	...	...	...	...	...	3	...
...	...	...	...	...	...	...	...	...	...	...	1	...
...	...	...	...	...	...	...	...	...	...	...	...	...
...	...	1	...	...	...	...	...	...	...	...	1	1
...	...	...	...	...	...	...	...	...	...	...	...	...
...	...	...	...	...	..	...	...	...	...	...	...	1
...	...	...	...	...	...	...	...	...	...	...	...	...
...	...	...	...	...	...	...	...	...	...	...	..	...

TABLE XVI.

OCCUPATION BY SELECTED CASTES, TRIBES OR RACES.

The figures in columns 13 onwards of this table are exclusive of the numbers shown in columns 7 and 8 as following the traditional occupation, if any, of the caste. Asterisks have been placed in these columns which are affected by this arrangement.

TABLE XVI.

OCCUPATION BY SELECTED CASTES, TRIBES OR RACES.

Serial No.	Caste, tribe or race.	Traditional Occupation.	Population dealt with. Actual workers. Males.	Population dealt with. Actual workers. Females.	Population dealt with. Dependants. Males.	Population dealt with. Dependants. Females.	Number of actual workers whose traditional caste occupation was returned as their Principal means of livelihood. Males.	Principal means of livelihood. Females.	Subsidiary means of livelihood. Males.	Subsidiary means of livelihood. Females.	Number of actual workers returning their traditional occupation as their principal means of livelihood who had some subsidiary occupation. Males.	Females.
	1	2	3	4	5	6	7	8	9	10	11	12
	HINDU											
1	Bhoi ...	Fishermen ...	54,668	43,786	34,701	43,849	23,793	15,756	3,958	3,178	589	[illegible]
2	Brahman ..	Priests ...	83,159	14,210	50,033	113,839	29,564	...	5,272	...	284	...
3	Chakala ...	Washermen ...	60,227	49,136	29,564	56,699	47,212	40,293	9,652	5,069	696	[illegible]
4	Chambhar ...	Shoe makers ...	23,957	14,893	12,036	19,732	13,488	5,158	1,325	476	79	[illegible]
5	Dewang or Koshti..	Weavers ...	22,062	12,682	14,195	22,461	14,711	6,224	1,241	446	86	[illegible]
6	Dhangar ...	Shepherds ...	159,069	93,653	86,318	143,569	84,041	31,679	10,481	3,620	180	[illegible]
7	Dhobi ..	Washermen ...	20,129	17,288	13,471	15,710	12,355	10,043	1,649	753	20	[illegible]
8	Golla ...	Cowherds ...	156,889	131,544	77,740	94,587	92,411	45,733	12,915	5,308	862	[illegible]
9	Goundla ...	Toddy sellers ...	102,288	63,760	54,093	80,930	76,934	46,679	12,453	7,076	773	[illegible]
10	Hatkar ...	Cultivators. ...	20,923	12,974	13,804	20,233	12,947	6,879	1,213	352	3	[illegible]
11	Kalal ...	Liquor sellers ..	25,189	14,473	13,177	22,500	16,501	8,447	2,268	918	147	[illegible]
12	Kapu ...	Cultivators ...	214,989	161,036	115,913	156,316	164,713	103,267	11,852	10,402	1,927	914
13	Koli ...	Cultivators ...	64,084	49,798	50,348	62,610	54,766	20,247	9,902	2,163	20	[illegible]
14	Komati ...	Traders ...	73,528	34,829	40,593	74,430	62,490	27,145	8,748	2,825	488	[illegible]
15	Kummara, Kumbhar	Potters ...	47,375	34,620	30,605	39,377	33,719	20,694	4,926	2,332	263	[illegible]
16	Kurma ...	Shepherds ...	49,053	39,371	26,091	30,173	34,307	21,167	5,020	3,156	376	[illegible]
17	Lingayet ...	Traders and shopkeepers.	226,135	115,707	155,066	260,703	181,802	91,195	60,406	29,814	602	[illegible]
18	Lohar ...	Blacksmiths ...	15,059	7,251	9,769	15,765	10,558	2,703	1,846	307	40	[illegible]
19	Madiga, Mang ...	Menial service ...	363,911	307,673	217,608	256,160	192,380	89,314	24,109	12,114	3,118	[illegible]
20	Mahar, Mala ...	Menial service ...	367,869	286,668	206,525	276,536	167,377	94,473	18,039	8,931	987	460
21	Mali ...	Gardeners ..	33,443	23,261	20,787	29,606	19,143	11,060	1,681	614	14	1
22	Mangala ...	Barbers ...	24,418	16,747	15,336	20,013	17,727	5,102	3,464	933	353	[illegible]
23	Maratha ...	Cultivators ...	506,638	320,451	266,240	445,545	308,002	163,190	25,564	11,335	385	[illegible]
24	Munnur ...	Cultivators ...	73,033	55,565	42,087	57,669	46,109	29,292	3,861	1,965	276	[illegible]
25	Mutrasi ...	Hunters ...	81,925	65,813	52,548	60,484	30,171	15,014	6,176	3,427	877	[illegible]
26	Nahvi (Warik) ...	Barbers ...	18,693	10,170	11,326	18,785	12,693	2,544	1,556	284	11	1
27	Panchal ...	Smiths ...	35,734	14,105	24,256	43,615	29,950	8,648	5,134	1,332	341	[illegible]
28	Rajput ...	Soldiers ...	17,935	8,011	13,361	22,330	8,860	3,506	846	407	15	[illegible]
29	Sale ...	Weavers ...	112,781	87,289	63,187	79,873	90,671	56,702	7,411	5,425	392	[illegible]
30	Satani ...	Religious beggars ...	8,716	5,433	5,873	7,861	4,809	3,361	625	374	53	[illegible]
31	Sunar ..	Goldsmiths ...	28,484	10,763	16,794	31,996	23,324	5,047	2,634	447	66	[illegible]
32	Sutar ...	Carpenters ...	19,803	10,922	15,315	23,165	16,228	7,237	2,141	836	101	[illegible]
33	Telaga ..	Cultivators ...	150,730	119,552	82,476	105,864	84,915	51,363	9,334	6,268	1,358	[illegible]
34	Teli ...	Oil pressers ...	18,176	10,834	10,444	17,490	11,088	5,980	1,234	531	46	[illegible]
35	Uppara ...	Masons ...	16,840	14,262	12,258	13,640	9,035	6,883	1,377	802	84	[illegible]
36	Velama ...	Cultivators ...	24,826	15,445	17,879	25,637	19,162	9,899	1,332	804	82	[illegible]
37	Waddar ...	Stone breakers ...	40,812	31,693	26,884	32,410	28,093	17,299	3,148	1,659	132	[illegible]
38	Wanjari ...	Cultivators ...	54,901	41,217	32,942	44,979	35,800	21,095	4,340	6,168	21	[illegible]
	MUSALMAN.											
39	Mughal ...	...	11,104	4,342	6,581	11,384	...	...	...	...	...	...
40	Pathan ...	...	43,694	15,524	27,473	48,457	...	...	...	...	...	...
41	Sayyed ...	...	61,042	18,824	58,100	71,608	...	...	...	...	...	...
42	Shaik ...	...	328,904	109,383	170,591	376,141	...	...	...	...	...	...
	CHRISTIAN.											
43	Anglo-Indian ...	...	1,004	231	544	1,225	...	...	...	...	...	...
44	Armenian ...	...	1	...	...	1	...	...	...	...	...	...
45	European ...	...	2,756	90	1,555	981	...	...	...	...	...	...
46	Indian Christian ...	...	14,602	10,536	9,033	11,737	11,737	...	...	...	...	...
	ANIMISTIC.											
47	Bhil ...	Hunters ...	3,225	2,357	1,932	2,674	1,176	333	190	17	...	...
48	Erkala ...	Basket makers ...	600	330	369	714	111	60	29	9	...	...
49	Gond ...	Cultivators ..	38,780	32,022	23,803	29,736	25,923	14,765	40	18	...	...
50	Lambada ...	Carriers ...	48,625	34,422	28,078	30,919	7,007	4,370	567	401	142	[illegible]

TABLE XVI.

OCCUPATION BY SELECTED CASTES, TRIBES OR RACES.

RECORDED PRINCIPAL OCCUPATION OF ACTUAL WORKERS.																
I.—EXPLOITATION OF THE SURFACE OF THE SOIL.												II. EXTRACTION OF MINERALS.				Serial No.
Income from rent of land.		Cultivators of all kinds.		Agents and managers of landed estates, planters, forest officers, and their clerks, rent collectors, etc.		Field labourers, wood-cutters, etc.		Raisers of live-stock, milkmen and herdsmen.		Fishing and hunting.		Owners, managers, clerks, etc.		Labourers.		
Males.	Females.	Males.	Females.	Males.	Females.	Males.	Females.	Males.	Females.	Males.	Females.	Males.	Females.	Males.	Females.	
13	14	15	16	17	18	19	20	21	22	23	24	25	26	27	28	
609	387	9,161	3,796	...	...	7,681	17,060	2,105	594	*	*	...	...	995	1,220	1
6,358	1,897	11,775	3,894	1,353	191	...	...	200	36	...	...	505	...	...	...	2
284	115	6,081	2,678	...	...	2,874	4,028	1,243	179	94	19	...	...	342	542	3
338	206	1,568	1,074	...	...	3,520	5,534	1,081	223	50	60	...	...	181	201	4
705	186	2,343	1,316	40	...	1,678	2,873	76	54	...	...	...	...	...	...	5
6,982	3,443	28,751	15,523	15	...	24,995	35,536	*	*	...	...	..	...	1,185	...	6
527	171	2,156	1,202	...	...	3,769	4,460	66	27	3	...	...	...	56	142	7
713	891	34,347	26,174	78	1	19,102	54,824	*	*	...	...	...	...	771	27	8
183	99	15,053	6,976	...	...	6,983	12,243	289	41	16	5	...	...	397	827	9
1,121	414	*	*	107	24	4,383	3,914	60	...	...	...	...	...	224	163	10
652	211	3,101	1,694	95	54	2,190	2,424	558	145	31	18	...	...	90	105	11
2,903	850	*	*	270	57	18,111	45,545	10,160	1,642	332	7	38	...	1,878	1,562	12
2,933	1,093	*	*	116	14	12,856	20,757	3,322	1,033	361	93	53	...	404	670	13
591	252	6,319	4,632	137	30	...	...	...	...	...	...	29	...	...	...	14
679	317	5,672	3,503	...	...	3,191	7,578	...	...	...	...	...	...	202	412	15
323	124	6,122	4,070	...	...	3,893	10,378	*	*	19	...		...	415	380	16
4,674	2,457	19,821	9,541	933	...	2,477	3,118	...	...	...	...	234	...	111	119	17
434	154	1,431	1,017	...	...	992	2,554	...	...	...	...	...	...	75	70	18
5,351	3,940	45,570	30,561	...	...	87,238	157,829	...	...	1,011	220	...	...	5,120	7,469	19
7,834	3,639	54,179	30,366	...	...	92,916	124,783	...	...	505	932	...	...	8,495	5,431	20
1,933	932	*	*	141	153	6,605	8,099	1,590	115	17	6	...	...	185	224	21
310	156	2,855	2,123	...	...	1,477	7,435	...	...	...	...	...	...	303	397	22
32,827	8,906	*	*	1,931	232	84,545	103,706	24,791	2,946	126	55	90	...	2,244	3,351	23
2,235	635	*	*	168	...	9,215	18,183	3,088	451	176	...	...	...	970	785	24
535	347	22,521	12,758	262	10	15,192	27,965	252	85	*	*	...	...	623	939	25
656	362	2,161	1,521	...	...	1,650	4,107	95	104	18	5	...	...	45	70	26
521	258	3,067	2,926	46	...	...	...	...	...	...	...	...	...	201	844	27
476	446	2,800	1,423	137	...	...	...	...	...	18	...	131	...	214	177	28
653	263	8,171	5,949	...	...	7,517	18,619	...	...	...	...	...	...	1,232	1,119	29
255	56	1,147	451	17	...	325	419	...	...	...	...	...	...	55	38	30
763	242	2,029	1,401	36	...	886	2,841	...	...	...	...	...	...	105	130	31
795	495	1,748	2,210	...	...	...	...	...	...	...	...	...	...	72	69	32
1,528	204	*	*	428	...	25,253	48,315	7,393	1,819	2,727	433	24	...	1,493	2,396	33
633	234	2,068	1,054	...	...	1,424	1,545	78	...	...	...	...	...	592	252	34
416	92	2,677	1,479	...	...	2,179	3,604	...	...	...	...	...	...	807	812	35
1,373	236	*	*	...	...	2,619	3,920	61	6	...	...	...	...	37	169	36
...	...	1,071	1,187	...	...	3,733	6,285	...	...	23	17	...	...	1,678	1,278	37
3,504	773	*	*	93	...	9,654	9,587	66	73	...	...	...	...	285	1,934	38
739	191	1,668	696	222	...	712	670	226	44	55	...	45	...	43	19	39
2,693	912	5,397	2,589	867	...	3,434	3,261	777	266	291	...	128	...	474	77	40
3,745	1,466	9,103	2,941	962	...	5,036	4,777	1,589	222	359	...	108	...	371	180	41
13,515	8,308	54,014	17,970	3,727	...	30,233	28,279	7,410	1,194	968	...	707	...	8,947	1,345	42
...	...	...	...	9	...	...	...	...	...	...	...	8	...	48	...	43
...	...	...	...	...	...	...	...	...	...	...	...	...	...	...	...	44
...	...	...	...	13	...	...	...	...	...	...	...	12	...	...	...	45
409	47	1,799	1,937	89	...	3,446	4,498	1,232	68	117	11	19	...	307	95	46
...	...	325	99	1	...	234	570	56	37	*	*	...	...	...	10	47
...	...	107	48	...	...	69	60	2	2	32	12	...	...	8	..	48
210	197	*	*	...	...	8,344	14,682	2,262	686	...	...	...	...	332	349	49
32	82	24,993	11,981	62	...	6,886	13,194	5,144	1,023	149	10	...	...	470	359	50

TABLE XVI.

OCCUPATION BY SELECTED CASTES, TRIBES OR RACES.

Serial No.	Caste, Tribe or Race.	Traditional Occupation.	RECORDED PRINCIPAL													
			III.—Industries.				IV.—Transport.				V.—Trade.		VI—Public force			
			Owners, managers, clerks, etc.		Artisans and other workmen.		Owners, managers, ship's officers, etc.		Labourers, boatmen, carters, palki-bearers, etc.				Comissioned and gazetted officers.		Others	
			Males.	Females.	Males.	Females.	Males.	Females.	Males.	Females.	Males.	Females.	Males.	Females.	Males.	Females.
	1	2	29	30	31	32	33	34	35	36	37	38	39	40	41	42
	HINDU.															
1	Bhoi ..	Fishermen ...	..	...	432	78	...	...	1,191	253	848	1,760	...	..	307	...
2	Brahman ...	Priests ...	953	...	...	...	170	...	...	...	4,724	656	87	...	1,458	...
3	Chakala ...	Washermen ...	...	...	*	*	...	...	391	177	41	16	...	...	47	...
4	Chambhar ...	Shoe makers ...	...	...	*	*	...	...	289	70	700	377	...	...	36	...
5	Dewang or Koshti...	Weavers ...	...	...	*	*	...	..	...	...	1,143	232	...	...	45	...
6	Dhangar ...	Shepherds ...	27	...	2,158	1,182	...	...	680	744	...	...	...	.	228	...
7	Dhobi ...	Washermen ...	...	...	*	*	...	...	53	5	42	68	...	.	8	...
8	Golla ...	Cowherds ...	...	...	248	204	...	.	1,032	...	...	...	...	...	182	...
9	Goundla ...	Toddy sellers ...	...	...	205	86	...	...	...	...	*	*	...	...	...	...
10	Hatkar ...	Cultivators ...	...	...	212	69	...	...	45	...	248	226	2	...	72	...
11	Kalal ...	Liquor sellers ...	4	...	283	73	1	...	76	120	*	*	...	...	12	..
12	Kapu ..	Cultivators ...	97	...	973	247	106	...	1,461	457	3,102	1,525	12	...	293	..
13	Koli ...	Cultivators ...	...	...	602	264	32	...	421	207	1,425	692	...	...	181	2
14	Komati ...	Traders ...	53	...	187	308	128	...	466	...	*	*	...	...	35	...
15	Kummara, Kumbhar	Potters ..	...	1	*	*	...	...	153	107	712	578	...	...	30	...
16	Kurma ...	Shepherds ...	...	...	1,205	1,422	...	...	225	238	873	554	...	...	...	...
17	Lingayet ...	Traders and shopkeepers.	88	...	1,038	129	...	...	720	110	*	*	6	..	88	...
18	Lohar ...	Blacksmiths ...	...	...	*	*	...	...	56	44	550	136	...	...	8	...
19	Madiga, Mang ...	Menial service ...	...	...	5,961	2,525	...	...	2,877	2,530	...	...	...	...	504	24
20	Mahar, Mala ...	Menial service ...	...	...	4,912	1,921	...	...	6,471	1,433	...	...	...	...	...	...
21	Mali ...	Gardeners ...	...	...	109	38	1	...	110	4	618	791	...	..	...	...
22	Mangala ...	Barbers ...	...	...	*	*	...	...	95	67	94	58	...	...	91	...
23	Maratha ...	Cultivators ...	320	...	1,914	904	123	...	3,492	793	7,830	2,530	...	...	1,428	...
24	Munnur ...	Cultivators ...	...	...	1,162	133	...	...	497	165	1,932	1,609	...	...	251	...
25	Mutrasi ...	Hunters ...	...	...	1,149	474	...	...	1,602	700	2,716	3,346	5	...	182	
26	Nabvi (Warik) ...	Barbers ...	...	...	*	*	...	...	19	27	172	47	...	...	...	...
27	Panchal ...	Smiths ...	26	...	*	*	...	...	48	69	500	264	...	...	...	...
28	Rajput ...	Soldiers ..	39	...	600	298	160	...	205	15	1,158	587	*	..	...	...
29	Sale ...	Weavers ..	...	...	*	*	...	...	...	...	1,598	929	...	...	...	...
30	Satani ...	Religious beggars ..	...	...	46	59	...	...	47	...	...	...	...	...	...	..
31	Sunar ...	Goldsmiths ...	...	...	*	*	...	...	53	17	679	278	...	...	...	..
32	Sutar ...	Carpenters ...	47	11	*	*	...	...	31	23	195	140	...	...	...	..
33	Telaga ...	Cultivators ...	298	...	2,012	968	115	...	1,683	1,081	7,849	6,747	34	...	380	
34	Teli ...	Oil pressers ...	...	...	*	*	...	...	...	...	1,281	993	9	...	4	
35	Uppara ...	Masons ...	...	...	*	*	...	...	71	...	137	182	...	...	...	
36	Velama ...	Cultivators ...	...	...	70	289	...	...	...	...	245	216	4	...	20	
37	Waddar ...	Stone breakers ...	...	...	*1,474	*712	...	...	...	...	279	317	...	...	...	
38	Wanjari ...	Cultivators ...	...	...	83	320	...	...	595	150	1,248	1,773	...	...	...	
	MUSALMAN.															
39	Mughal ...	...	64	...	318	56	39	...	226	6	771	294	25	...	1,327	
40	Pathan ...	...	255	...	1,440	341	258	...	914	101	4,990	1,128	181	...	6,613	
41	Sayyed ...	...	251	...	1,366	687	186	...	935	130	4,986	1,115	362	...	5,455	
42	Shaik ...	...	1,738	...	25,722	4,640	365	...	10,641	1,204	26,313	6,518	1,020	...	28,670	
	CHRISTIAN.															
43	Anglo-Indian ...	...	77	...	46	...	22	...	94	...	30	...	20	...	51	
44	Armenian ...	...	...	...	...	...	...	...	...	...	...	...	—	...	...	
45	European ...	...	7	...	193	4	199	...	...	...	116	...	177	...	1,339	
46	Indian Christian ...	...	363	6	663	164	69	1	477	33	1,357	389	...	...	366	
	ANIMISTIC.															
47	Bhil ...	Hunters ...	...	...	17	...	...	...	20	1	21	26	...	...	...	
48	Erkala ...	Basket makers ...	...	...	*14	*1	...	...	...	...	18	12	...	...	...	
49	Gond ...	Cultivators ...	...	...	22	53	...	...	134	34	133	200	...	...	7	
50	Lambada ...	Carriers ..	25	...	70	88	7	...	*85	*162	749	489	...	...	40	

TABLE XVI.

OCCUPATION BY SELECTED CASTES, TRIBES OR RACES.

OCCUPATION OF ACTUAL WORKERS.

VII—Public Administration.				VIII—Arts and Professions.						IX—Persons living on their income.		X—Domestic service.		XI—Contractors, clerks, cashiers, etc., otherwise unspecified.		XII—Labourers unspecified.		XIII—Beggars, prostitutes, criminals and inmates of jails and asylums.		Serial No.
Gazetted officers.		Others.		Religious.		Lawyers, doctors and teachers.		Others.												
Males.	Females.	Males.	Females.	Males.	Females.	Males.	Females.	Males.	Females.	Males.	Females.	Males.	Females.	Males.	Females.	Males.	Females.	Males.	Females.	
43	44	45	46	47	48	49	50	51	52	53	54	55	56	57	58	59	60	61	62	
...	...	1,256	...	...	...	5	3	35	34		...	4,337	1,211	..	...	1,393	1,139	521	495	1
192	..	10,713	...	*	*	2,399	45	327	22	1,504	2,698	6,334	2,526	648	...	...	...	3,885	2,245	2
...	...	10	...	...	...	...	...	..	...	213	61	663	282	...	...	462	496	270	250	3
...	...	70	..	..	...	...	...	33	.	229	124	599	253	..	...	1,284	1,302	321	311	4
...	...	...	...	14	..	1	...	3	...	166	692	533	283	38	...	410	655	156	167	5
..	...	220	...	2	...	5	1	4	...	862	578	3,671	3,626	...	...	3,208	6,108	2,035	1,233	6
...	...	51	...	..	...		...	13	...	196	182	234	400	..	...	438	480	162	108	7
...	...	571	...	8	...	99	...	18	...	969	423	3,802	1,381	226	..	799	834	1,513	1,052	8
...	...	..	...	4	...	..	..	...	...	685	359	820	717	29	...	165	395	525	328	9
1	...	234	...	12	...	25	1	29	6	37	93	379	295	3	..	490	707	286	183	10
...	...	120	...	7	...	5	..	44	...	135	220	830	367	82	...	280	496	92	105	11
47	...	3,261	...	48	...	172	5	268	138	1,435	1,306	3,540	2,153	151	...	511	1,450	1,104	825	12
..	...	292	...	28	...	46	...	146	91	230	167	2,968	1,342	141	...	2,049	2,491	718	610	13
...	...	336	...	71	...	135	...	40	...	421	1,021	1,372	1,168	207	...	56	21	455	252	14
...	...	88	...	...	...	...	..	...	...	1,611	214	634	297	12	...	441	577	241	346	15
...	...	...	..	...	...	..	..	...	...	521	369	734	309	10	...	55	173	351	187	16
...	...	547	...	86	...	370	9	165	49	5,405	4,012	1,259	1,851	273	...	1,105	570	4,933	2,547	17
...	...	14	...	...	...	...	...	26	...	90	85	341	146	4	...	251	258	229	84	18
...	...	2,963	473	...	...	...	...	..	...	3,149	1,309	*	*	401	...	6,728	6,835	4,658	5,549	19
...	...	...	...	...	...	...	...	...	...	3,360	1,105	*	*	...	..	14,183	17,032	7,627	5,553	20
...	...	...	...	...	...	...	...	...	...	274	55	1,099	387	70	...	1,359	1,168	189	229	21
...	...	...	...	...	...	...	...	124	254	143	263	957	521	6	...	96	163	140	203	22
21	...	3,878	...	468	348	839	330	235	189	1,549	934	10,067	8,226	297	...	15,935	21,280	3,686	2,552	23
...	...	973	...	...	...	51	...	116	215	623	426	2,943	1,167	153	..	1,319	1,821	992	673	24
...	...	1,306	69	...	...	...	...	58	145	902	525	2,646	1,728	353	..	720	997	710	690	25
...	...	...	...	...	...	...	...	16	32	178	61	641	333	...	...	257	816	89	141	26
...	...	...	...	...	...	18	...	216	16	154	365	474	358	38	...	174	188	301	189	27
19	...	741	...	...	...	57	...	124	30	259	197	1,414	752	95	...	178	435	220	145	28
..	...	...	...	...	...	...	...	...	...	358	553	1,543	1,180	23		499	1,354	516	576	29
...	...	...	...	*	*	...	...	76	3	103	42	329	196	..	...	45	125	1,459	672	30
...	...	...	...	36	1	1	...	37	30	154	230	20	90	55	...	131	301	170	155	31
...	...	...	...	13	...	...	..	1	...	122	181	96	44	12	...	305	416	138	186	32
49	...	2,851	...	254	...	227	97	256	111	2,340	1,223	5,553	3,394	276	...	1,457	2,000	1,335	1,901	33
...	...	2	...	...	...	...	...	2	40	147	93	428	202	38	...	212	354	173	87	34
...	...	...	...	...	...	...	...	...	31	74	116	307	159	78	...	729	656	330	249	35
6	...	401	...	...	...	...	...	25	1	138	82	255	271	10	..	324	258	76	98	36
...	...	...	...	...	...	...	...	...	...	369	419	330	479	109	51	710	1,635	2,943	2,014	37
...	...	...	...	...	...	...	...	13	...	280	585	1,005	457	84	...	1,582	3,762	599	703	38
67	...	1,494	...	84	...	194	11	53	26	604	90	1,459	1,660	91	...	126	162	452	417	39
274	...	4,133	...	155	...	358	79	225	1,037	971	849	6,221	3,075	365	...	873	1,174	1,302	635	40
353	...	6,091	...	551	...	729	88	270	288	2,119	1,100	11,424	3,940	560	...	1,409	626	2,722	1,234	41
505	...	29,989	...	1,249	...	3,102	248	2,278	3,563	6,305	4,011	41,010	18,973	3,121	...	16,901	8,050	10,454	5,080	42
66	3	285	2	38	23	72	103	20	43	20	9	95	48	3	...	...	...	...	...	43
...	...	...	...	...	...	...	...		...	...	...	...	...	1	...	...	...	...	...	44
116	5	175	1	78	6	118	64	199	5	12	4	...	1	2	..	...	...	...	...	45
1	...	418	46	112	81	97	95	273	192	247	531	2,208	1,957	46	10	261	123	226	230	46
...	...	19	...	...	...	...	...	...	6	23	21	36	21	1	...	77	119	1,169	1,114	47
...	...	...	...	...	...	...	...	...	..	1	...	1	7	...	...	12	22	225	106	48
...	...	17	...	...	...	...	...	...	14	261	46	429	370	...	..	334	359	372	267	49
...	..	98	..	...	...	...	...	2	8	272	281	355	255	8	..	427	605	1,741	1,515	50

TABLE XVII.

TERRITORIAL DISTRIBUTION OF THE CHRISTIAN POPULATION BY SECT AND RACE.

Armenians are classed under the head "European and allied Races." They are shown separately in Table XVIII.

TABLE XVII.

TERRITORIAL DISTRIBUTION OF THE CHRISTIAN POPULATION BY SECT AND RACE.

Serial Number.	District.	ALL DENOMINATIONS.						
		Total.			Distribution by			
					European and Allied Races.		Anglo-Indian.	
		Persons.	Males.	Females.	Males.	Females.	Males.	Females.
	1	2	3	4	5	6	7	8
	STATE ...	***54,296***	***29,495***	***24,801***	***4,312***	***1,072***	***1,548***	***1,456***
1	Hyderabad City ...	16,240	9,623	6,617	4,051	866	1,030	1,07[illegible]
2	Atraf-i-balda ...	1,291	686	605	67	51	129	9[illegible]
	Warangal Division ...	***12,593***	***6,507***	***6,086***	***57***	***53***	***109***	***85***
3	Warangal ...	11,979	6,202	5,777	51	47	94	8[illegible]
4	Karimnagar ...	586	286	300	5	6	7	1[illegible]
5	Adilabad ...	28	19	9	1	...	8	1[illegible]
	Medak Division ...	***13,940***	***7,285***	***6,655***	***23***	***27***	***35***	***20***
6	Medak ...	2,203	1,124	1,079	7	14	14	8
7	Nizamabad ...	720	375	345	1	7	14	3
8	Mahbubnagar ...	451	221	230	8	5	...	3
9	Nalgonda ...	10,566	5,565	5,001	7	1	7	6
	Aurangabad Division ...	***6,849***	***3,513***	***3,336***	***65***	***37***	***94***	***81***
10	Aurangabad ...	6,369	3,222	3,147	44	31	29	3[illegible]
11	Bhir ..	2	1	1	...	...	1	1
12	Nander ...	69	40	29	...	...	15	[illegible]
13	Parbhani ...	409	250	159	21	6	49	4[illegible]
	Gulbarga Division ...	***3,383***	***1,881***	***1,502***	***49***	***38***	***151***	***10[illegible]***
14	Gulbarga ...	1,044	633	411	22	19	43	[illegible]
15	Osmanabad ...	252	130	122	...	...	11	4
16	Raichur ...	1,711	920	791	26	18	96	[illegible]
17	Bidar ..	376	193	178	1	1	1	[illegible]

TABLE XVII.

TERRITORIAL DISTRIBUTION OF THE CHRISTIAN POPULATION BY SECT AND RACE.

Race.		ANGLICAN COMMUNION.										
Indian.		Total.			Distribution by Race.							Serial Number.
					European and Allied Races.		Anglo-Indian.		Indian.			
Males.	Females.	Persons.	Males.	Females.	Males.	Females.	Males.	Females.	Males.	Females.		
9	10	11	12	13	14	15	16	17	18	19		
23,635	***22,273***	***14,261***	***8,681***	***5,580***	***3,586***	***718***	***550***	***550***	***4,545***	***4,312***		
4,542	4,678	5,534	4,171	1,363	3,415	622	364	410	392	331	1	
490	459	205	115	90	50	34	40	25	25	31	2	
6,341	***5,948***	***6,253***	***3,191***	***3,062***	***41***	***29***	***59***	***50***	***3,091***	***2,983***		
6,057	5,647	6,231	3,175	3,056	37	24	49	49	3,089	2,983	3	
274	293	17	11	6	3	5	6	1	2	...	4	
10	8	5	5	...	1	...	4	...	...	...	5	
7,227	***6,608***	***979***	***518***	***461***	***5***	***3***	***10***	***5***	***503***	***453***		
1,103	1,057	...	...	...	...	...	...	...	...	...	6	
360	335	18	11	7	...	3	8	3	3	1	7	
21[illegible]	222	5	5	...	4	...	...	...	1	...	8	
5,551	4,994	956	502	454	1	...	2	2	499	452	9	
3,354	***3,218***	***1,153***	***594***	***559***	***52***	***21***	***36***	***33***	***506***	***505***		
3,149	3,086	1,078	543	535	39	18	15	19	489	498	10	
...	...	...	...	...	...	...	...	...	...	...	11	
25	22	13	10	3	...	...	8	3	2	...	12	
180	110	62	41	21	13	3	13	11	15	7	13	
1,681	***1,362***	***137***	***92***	***45***	***23***	***9***	***41***	***27***	***28***	***9***		
508	364	64	44	20	9	5	13	8	22	7	14	
119	118	1	1	...	...	...	1	...	...	...	15	
793	705	72	47	25	14	4	27	10	6	2	16	
196	175	...	...	...	...	...	...	...	...	...	17	

TABLE XVII.

TERRITORIAL DISTRIBUTION OF THE CHRISTIAN POPULATION BY SECT AND RACE.

Serial Number.	District.	BAPTIST.						
		Total.			Distribution by Race.			
					European and Allied Races.		Anglo-Indian.	
		Persons.	Males.	Females.	Males.	Females.	Males.	Females.
	1	20	21	22	23	24	25	26
	STATE ...	***9,630***	***5,075***	***4,555***	***23***	***16***	***14***	***20***
1	Hyderabad City ...	211	125	86	16	8	9	14
2	Atraf-i-balda ...	59	27	32	1	...	...	...
	Warangal Division ...	***3,660***	***1,910***	***1,750***	***1***	***6***	...	...
3	Warangal ...	3,519	1,841	1,678	1	6	...	...
4	Karimnagar ...	141	69	72	...	...	...	...
5	Adilabad ...	...	...	...	...	...	...	...
	Medak Division ...	***5,682***	***3,005***	***2,677***	***5***	***2***	***1***	...
6	Medak ...	14	6	8	...	...	...	...
7	Nizamabad ...	25	15	10	...	...	...	...
8	Mahbubnagar ...	407	197	210	3	2	...	...
9	Nalgonda ...	5,236	2,787	2,449	2	...	1	...
	Aurangabad Division ...	***7***	***3***	***4***	...	...	...	...
10	Aurangabad ...	7	3	4	...	...	...	...
11	Bhir ...	...	...	...	...	...	...	...
12	Nander ...	...	...	...	...	...	...	...
13	Parbhani ...	...	...	...	...	...	...	...
	Gulbarga Division ...	***11***	***5***	***6***	...	...	***4***	[illegible]
14	Gulbarga ...	3	2	1	...	...	1	[illegible]
15	Osmanabad ...	...	...	...	...	...	...	...
16	Raichur ...	8	3	5	...	...	3	[illegible]
17	Bidar ...	...	...	...	...	...	...	...

TABLE XVII.

TERRITORIAL DISTRIBUTION OF THE CHRISTIAN POPULATION BY SECT AND RACE.

		CONGREGATIONALIST.									
		Total.			Distribution by Race.						
Indian.					European and Allied Races.		Anglo-Indians.		Indian.		Serial Number.
Males.	Females.	Persons.	Males.	Females.	Males.	Females.	Males.	Females.	Males	Females.	
27	28	29	30	31	32	33	34	35	36	37	
5,038	***4,519***	***353***	***186***	***169***	***3***	***2***	***2***	...	***181***	***167***	
100	64	6	3	3	3	2	...	...	...	1	1
26	32	...	...	...	...	...	...	...	...	...	2
1,909	***1,744***	...	...	...	...	...	...	...	...	...	
1,840	1,672	...	...	...	...	...	...	...	...	...	3
69	72	...	...	...	...	...	...	...	...	...	4
...	...	...	...	...	...	...	...	...	...	...	5
2,999	***2,675***	...	...	...	...	...	...	...	...	...	
6	8	...	...	...	...	...	...	...	...	...	6
15	10	...	...	...	...	...	...	...	...	...	7
194	208	...	...	...	...	...	...	...	...	...	8
2,784	2,449	...	...	...	...	...	...	...	...	...	9
3	***4***	***194***	***103***	***91***	...	...	...	...	***103***	***91***	
3	4	194	103	91	...	...	...	...	103	91	10
...	...	...	...	...	...	...	...	...	...	...	11
...	...	...	...	...	...	...	...	...	...	...	12
...	...	...	...	...	...	...	...	...	...	...	13
1	...	***155***	***80***	***75***	...	...	***2***	...	***78***	***73***	
1	...	...	...	...	...	...	...	...	...	...	14
...	...	137	70	67	...	...	2	...	68	67	15
...	...	3	2	1	...	...	...	...	2	1	16
...	...	15	8	7	...	...	...	...	8	7	17

TABLE XVII.

TERRITORIAL DISTRIBUTION OF THE CHRISTIAN POPULATION BY SECT AND RACE.

Serial Number.	District.	GREEK.											
		Total.			Distribution by Race.						Total.		
					European and Allied Races.		Anglo-Indians.		Native.				
		Persons.	Males.	Females.	Males.	Females.	Males.	Females.	Males.	Females.	Persons.	Males.	Females.
	1	38	39	40	41	42	43	44	45	46	47	48	49
	STATE ...	*2*	...	...	*1*	...	*1*	...	...	...	*24*	*15*	*9*
1	Hyderabad City ..	1	...	...	1	...	...	...	...	...	3	2	1
2	Atraf-i-balda ..	...	...	...	...	...	...	...	...	...	2	1	1
	Warangal Division ..	...	...	...	...	...	...	...	...	...	*4*	*2*	*1*
3	Warangal ..	...	...	...	...	...	...	...	...	...	4	2	
4	Karimnagar ..	...	...	...	...	...	...	...	...	...	...	...	...
5	Adilabad ..	...	...	...	...	...	...	...	...	...	...	...	...
	Medak Division ..	...	...	...	...	...	...	...	...	...	*14*	*9*	
6	Medak ..	..	...	...	...	...	...	...	...	...	...	...	...
7	Nizamabad ..	...	...	...	...	...	...	...	...	...	...	...	...
8	Mahbubnagar ..	...	...	...	...	...	...	...	...	...	...	...	...
9	Nalgonda ..	...	...	...	...	...	...	...	...	...	14	9	
	Aurangabad Division ..	*1*	...	...	...	...	*1*	...	...	...	...	...	..
10	Aurangabad ...	1	...	...	...	...	1	...	...	...	...	...	..
11	Bhir ...	...	...	...	...	...	...	...	...	...	...	...	..
12	Nander ..	...	...	...	...	...	...	...	...	...	...	...	..
13	Parbhani ...	...	...	...	...	...	...	...	...	...	...	...	.
	Gulbarga Division ...	...	...	...	...	...	...	...	...	...	*1*	*1*	.
14	Gulbarga ...	...	...	...	...	...	...	...	...	...	1	1	.
15	Osmanabad	...	...	...	...	...	...	...	...	...	...	...	
16	Raichur ...	...	...	...	...	...	...	...	...	...	...	...	
17	Bidar ..	...	...	...	...	...	...	...	...	...	...	...	

TABLE XVII.

TERRITORIAL DISTRIBUTION OF THE CHRISTIAN POPULATION BY SECT AND RACE.

LUTHERAN.						METHODIST.									
Distribution by Race.						Total.			Distribution by Race.						Serial Number.
European and Allied Races.		Anglo-Indians.		Natives.					Europeans and Allied Races.		Anglo-Indians.		Indian.		
Males.	Females.	Males.	Females.	Males.	Females.	Persons	Males.	Females.	Males.	Females.	Males.	Females.	Males.	Females.	
50	51	52	53	54	55	56	57	58	59	60	61	62	63	64	
...	...	*1*	...	*14*	*9*	*8,614*	*4,484*	*4,130*	*234*	*77*	*78*	*104*	*4,172*	*3,949*	
...	...	...	...	2	1	1,320	654	666	211	34	43	86	400	546	1
...	...	...	...	1	1	643	340	303	1	...	2	2	337	301	2
...	...	...	...	*2*	*2*	*774*	*377*	*397*	*4*	*7*	*1*	...	*372*	*390*	
...	...	...	...	2	2	336	168	168	2	6	1	...	165	162	3
...	...	...	...	...	...	426	204	222	2	1	...	...	202	221	4
...	...	...	...	...	...	12	5	7	...	...	...	...	5	7	5
...	...	...	...	*9*	*5*	*4,014*	*2,050*	*1,964*	*8*	*17*	*9*	*5*	*2,033*	*1,942*	
..	...	...	...	...	...	2,176	1,110	1,066	7	14	9	5	1,094	1,047	6
...	...	...	...	...	...	644	328	316	...	2	...	...	328	314	7
...	...	...	...	...	...	6	3	3	...	...	...	...	3	3	8
...	...	...	...	9	5	1,188	609	579	1	1	..	...	608	578	9
...	...	...	...	...	...	*35*	*19*	*16*	...	...	*3*	*1*	*16*	*15*	
...	...	...	...	...	...	13	8	5	...	...	1	...	7	5	10
...	...	...	...	...	...	...	...	...	...	...	...	...	...	...	11
...	...	...	...	...	...	15	6	9	...	...	2	1	4	8	12
...	...	...	...	...	...	7	5	2	...	...	...	..	5	2	13
...	...	*1*	...	...	...	*1,828*	*1,044*	*784*	*10*	*19*	*20*	*10*	*1,014*	*755*	
...	...	1	...	...	...	653	410	243	5	9	...	...	405	234	14
...	...	...	...	...	...	95	50	45	...	...	1	...	49	45	15
...	...	...	...	...	...	779	424	355	4	9	18	8	402	338	16
...	...	...	...	...	...	301	160	141	1	1	1	2	158	138	17

TABLE XVII.

TERRITORIAL DISTRIBUTION OF THE CHRISTIAN POPULATION BY SECT AND RACE.

Serial Number.	District.	MINOR PROTESTANT DENOMINATIONS.									PRESBY[TERIAN]		
		Total			Distribution by Race.						Total.		
					European and Allied Races.		Anglo-Indians.		Indian.				
		Persons.	Males.	Females.	Males.	Females.	Males.	Females.	Males.	Females.	Persons.	Males.	Females.
	1	65	66	67	68	69	70	71	72	73	74	75	76
	STATE ...	***427***	***229***	***198***	***3***	***5***	...	***3***	***226***	***190***	***1,148***	***573***	***575***
1	Hyderabad ..	4	...	4	...	1	...	...	...	3	128	86	42
2	Atraf-i-balda ...	6	3	3	...	...	...	...	3	3	5	3	2
	Warangal Division ...	***364***	***207***	***157***	...	...	..	...	***207***	***157***	***2***	***2***	...
3	Warangal ..	364	207	157	...	...	...	...	207	157	2	2	...
4	Karimnagar ..	...	...	...	...	...	...	...	...	...	...	...	...
5	Adilabad ..	...	...	...	...	...	...	...	...	...	...	...	...
	Medak Division ..	***19***	***6***	***13***	***1***	***3***	...	***3***	***5***	***7***	...	...	...
6	Medak ..	2	1	1	...	...	...	...	1	1	...	...	...
7	Nizamabad ...	..	...	...	...	...	...	...	...	...	...	...	...
8	Mahbubnagar ..	17	5	12	1	3	...	3	4	6	...	...	...
9	Nalgonda ..	...	...	...	...	...	...	...	...	...	...	...	...
	Aurangabad Division ...	***31***	***11***	***20***	...	...	...	...	***11***	***20***	***1,011***	***480***	***531***
10	Aurangabad ..	31	11	20	...	...	...	...	11	20	943	443	50[illegible]
11	Bhir ...	...	...	...	...	...	...	...	...	...	...	...	...
12	Nander ...	..	...	...	...	...	...	...	...	...	...	...	...
13	Parbhani ..	...	...	...	...	...	...	...	...	...	68	37	31
	Gulbarga Division ...	***3***	***2***	***1***	***2***	***1***	...	...	...	...	***2***	***2***	...
14	Gulbarga ..	...	...	...	...	...	...	...	...	...	2	2	...
15	Osmanabad ...	...	...	...	...	...	...	...	...	...	...	...	...
16	Raichur ...	3	2	1	2	1	...	...	...	...	...	...	...
17	Bidar ...	...	...	...	...	...	...	...	...	...	...	...	...

TABLE XVII.

TERRITORIAL DISTRIBUTION OF THE CHRISTIAN POPULATION BY SECT AND RACE.

TERIAN.						PROTESTANTS (UNSECTARIAN OR SECT NOT SPECIFIED).									Serial Number.
Distribution by Race.						Total			Distribution by Race.						
European and Allied Races.		Anglo-Indian.		Indian.					Europeans and Allied Races.		Anglo-Indian.		Indian.		
Males.	Females.	Males.	Females.	Males.	Females.	Persons.	Males.	Females.	Males.	Females.	Males.	Females.	Males.	Females.	
77	78	79	80	81	82	83	84	85	86	87	88	89	90	91	
89	*43*	*9*	*8*	*475*	*524*	*1,346*	*688*	*658*	*9*	*9*	*42*	*28*	*637*	*624*	
78	35	7	6	1	1	125	47	78	4	8	27	20	16	50	1
3	2	...	...	...	...	...	...	...	...	...	...	...	...	...	2
2	...	...	...	...	...	*21*	*14*	*7*	*1*	...	*5*	*3*	*8*	*4*	
2	...	...	...	...	...	19	13	6	1	...	5	3	7	3	3
...	...	...	...	...	...	...	...	...	...	...	...	...	...	...	4
...	...	...	...	...	...	2	1	1	...	...	...	...	1	1	5
...	...	...	...	...	...	*53*	*25*	*28*	...	...	...	...	*25*	*28*	
...	...	...	...	...	...	...	...	...	...	...	...	...	...	...	6
...	...	...	...	...	...	2	2	...	...	...	...	...	2	...	7
...	...	...	...	...	...	15	10	5	...	...	...	...	10	5	8
...	...	...	...	...	...	36	13	23	...	...	...	...	13	23	9
5	*6*	*2*	*2*	*473*	*523*	*1,089*	*561*	*528*	...	*1*	*2*	...	*559*	*527*	
1	5	2	2	440	493	1,072	551	521	...	1	1	...	550	520	10
...	...	...	...	...	...	...	...	...	...	...	...	...	...	...	11
...	...	...	...	...	...	...	...	...	...	...	...	...	...	...	12
4	1	...	...	33	30	17	10	7	...	...	1	...	9	7	13
1	...	...	...	*1*	...	*58*	*41*	*17*	*4*	...	*8*	*2*	*29*	*15*	
1	...	...	...	1	...	2	2	...	2	...	...	...	...	...	14
...	...	...	...	...	...	2	2	...	...	...	1	...	1	...	15
...	...	...	...	...	...	32	28	4	2	...	7	2	19	2	16
...	...	...	...	...	...	22	9	13	...	...	...	...	9	13	17

TABLE XVII.

TERRITORIAL DISTRIBUTION OF THE CHRISTIAN POPULATION BY SECT AND RACE.

Serial Number.	District.	ROMAN CATHOLIC.											
		Total.			Distribution by Race.						Total.		
					European and Allied Races.		Anglo-Indian.		Indian.				
		Persons.	Males.	Females.	Males	Females.	Males.	Females.	Males.	Females.	Persons.	Males.	Females.
	1	92	93	94	95	96	97	98	99	100	101	102	103
	STATE ...	***18,473***	***9,553***	***8,920***	***358***	***201***	***848***	***744***	***8,347***	***7,975***	***5***	***2***	[illegible]
1	Hyderabad City ...	8,892	4,525	4,367	317	155	577	535	3,631	3,677	5	2	[illegible]
2	Atraf-i-balda ...	371	197	174	12	15	87	68	98	91	...	...	...
	Warangal Division ...	***1,515***	***804***	***711***	***8***	***11***	***44***	***32***	***752***	***668***	..	...	...
3	Warangal ...	1,504	794	710	8	11	39	31	747	668	...	...	...
4	Karimnagar ...	2	2	...	...	...	1	...	1	...	...	...	...
5	Adilabad ...	9	8	1	...	...	4	1	4	...	...	...	...
	Medak Division ..	***3,179***	***1,672***	***1,507***	***4***	***2***	***15***	***7***	***1,653***	***1,498***	...	...	...
6	Medak ...	11	7	4	...	...	5	3	2	1	...	...	...
7	Nizamabad ...	31	19	12	1	2	6	...	12	10	...	...	...
8	Mahbubnagar ..	1	1	...	...	...	...	...	1	...	...	...	...
9	Nalgonda ...	3,136	1,645	1,491	3	...	4	4	1,638	1,487	...	...	...
	Aurangabad Division ...	***3,328***	***1,741***	***1,587***	***8***	***9***	***50***	***45***	***1,683***	***1,533***	...	...	...
10	Aurangabad ...	3,030	1,559	1,471	4	7	9	9	1,546	1,455	...	...	...
11	Bhir ...	2	1	1	...	...	1	1	...	...	...	...	...
12	Nander ...	41	24	17	...	...	5	3	19	14	...	...	...
13	Parbhani ..	255	157	98	4	2	3[illegible]	32	118	64	...	...	...
	Gulbarga Division ...	***1,188***	***614***	***574***	***9***	***9***	***75***	***57***	***530***	***508***	...	...	...
14	Gulbarga ...	319	172	147	5	5	28	19	139	123	...	...	...
15	Osmanabad ...	17	7	10	...	...	6	4	1	6	...	...	...
16	Raichur ...	814	414	400	4	4	41	34	369	362	..	...	...
17	Bidar ...	38	21	17	...	...	...	...	21	17	...	...	...

TABLE XVII.

TERRITORIAL DISTRIBUTION OF THE CHRISTIAN POPULATION BY SECT AND RACE.

SYRIAN (ROMO-SYRIAN.)						INDEFINITE BELIEFS.									Serial Number.
Distribution by Race.						Total.			Distribution by Race.						
European and Allied races.		Anglo-Indian.		Indian.					European and Allied Races.		Anglo-Indian		Indian.		
Males.	Females.	Males.	Females.	Males.	Females.	Persons.	Males.	Females.	Males.	Females.	Males.	Females.	Males.	Females.	
104	105	106	107	108	109	110	111	112	113	114	115	116	117	118	
...	...	*2*	*2*	...	*1*	*11*	*7*	*4*	*5*	*1*	*1*	...	*1*	*3*	
...	...	2	2	...	1	11	7	4	5	1	1	...	1	3	1
...	...	...	...	...	...	...	...	...	...	...	...	...	...	...	2
...	...	...	...	...	...	...	...	...	...	...	...	...	...	...	
...	...	...	...	...	...	...	...	...	...	...	...	...	...	...	3
...	...	...	...	...	...	...	...	...	...	...	...	...	...	...	4
...	...	...	...	...	...	...	...	...	...	...	...	...	...	...	5
...	...	...	...	...	...	...	...	...	...	...	...	...	...	...	
...	...	...	...	...	...	...	...	...	...	...	...	...	...	...	6
...	...	...	...	...	...	...	...	...	...	...	...	...	...	...	7
...	...	...	...	...	...	...	...	...	...	...	...	...	...	...	8
...	...	...	...	...	...	...	...	...	...	...	...	...	...	...	9
...	...	...	...	...	...	...	...	...	...	...	...	...	...	...	
...	...	...	...	...	...	...	...	...	...	...	...	...	...	...	10
...	...	...	...	...	...	...	...	...	...	...	...	...	...	...	11
...	...	...	...	...	...	...	...	...	...	...	...	...	...	...	12
...	...	...	...	...	...	...	...	...	...	...	...	...	...	...	13
...	...	...	...	...	...	...	...	...	...	...	...	...	...	...	
...	...	...	...	...	...	...	...	...	...	...	...	...	...	...	14
...	...	...	...	...	...	...	...	...	...	...	...	...	...	...	15
...	...	...	...	...	...	...	...	...	...	...	...	...	...	...	16
...	...	...	...	...	...	...	...	...	...	...	...	...	...	...	17

TABLE XVIII.

EUROPEANS, ARMENIANS AND ANGLO-INDIANS BY RACE AND AGE.

TABLE XVIII.

EUROPEANS, ARMENIANS AND ANGLO-INDIANS BY RACE AND AGE.

Serial No.	District.	Total.			EUROPEAN AND ALLIED												
					British Subjects.												
					All ages.			0–12		12–15		15–30		30–50		50 and over	
		Total.	Males.	Females.	Total.	Males.	Females.	Males.	Females.	Males.	Females.	Males.	Females.	Males.	Females.	Males.	Females.
	1	2	3	4	5	6	7	8	9	10	11	12	13	14	15	16	17
	STATE ...	***8,388***	***5,860***	***2,528***	***5,230***	***4,251***	***979***	***238***	***305***	***20***	***22***	***3,239***	***270***	***682***	***323***	***102***	***59***
1	Hyderabad City ...	7,020	5,081	1,939	4,803	4,012	791	207	250	17	18	3,177	214	525	264	86	4[illegible]
2	Atraf-i-balda ...	342	196	146	118	67	51	17	17	2	1	13	13	31	17	4	3
	Warangal Division ...	***304***	***166***	***138***	***97***	***49***	***48***	***6***	***17***	..	***3***	***11***	***13***	***31***	***9***	***1***	***6***
3	Warangal	275	145	130	85	43	42	6	16	...	2	10	12	26	7	1	5
4	Karimnagar... ...	19	12	7	11	5	6	...	1	...	1	1	1	4	2	...	1
5	Adilabad	10	9	1	1	1	...	...	...	...	...	...	...	1	...	...	...
	Medak Division ...	***105***	***58***	***47***	***40***	***17***	***23***	...	***4***	...	..	***5***	***9***	***12***	***10***	...	..
6	Medak	43	21	22	21	7	14	...	3	...	..	4	5	3	6	...	...
7	Nizamabad	25	15	10	8	1	7	...	1	..	..	...	3	1	3	...	...
8	Mahbubnagar ...	16	8	8	7	6	1	...	...	..	...	...	...	6	1	...	...
9	Nalgonda	21	14	7	4	3	1	...	...	...	...	1	1	2	...	..	...
	Aurangabad Division	***277***	***159***	***118***	***97***	***62***	***35***	***3***	***9***	...	...	***25***	***13***	***29***	***11***	***5***	***2***
10	Aurangabad ...	134	73	61	73	43	30	3	9	...	...	15	10	22	10	3	1
11	Bhir	2	1	1	...	...	...	...	...	...	..	...	...	...	...	...	...
12	Nander	22	15	7	...	..	...	...	...	...	...	...	...	...	...	...	...
13	Parbhani	119	70	49	24	19	5	...	...	...	...	10	3	7	1	2	1
	Gulbarga Division ...	***340***	***200***	***140***	***75***	***44***	***31***	***5***	***8***	***1***	...	***8***	***8***	***24***	***12***	***6***	***3***
14	Gulbarga	112	65	47	41	22	19	2	6	1	...	3	5	11	6	5	2
15	Osmanabad	15	11	4	...	...	...	...	...	...	...	...	...	...	...	...	...
16	Raichur	208	122	86	34	22	12	3	2	...	...	5	3	13	6	1	[illegible]
17	Bidar	5	2	3	...	...	...	...	...	...	...	...	...	...	...	...	...

TABLE XVIII.

EUROPEANS, ARMENIANS AND ANGLO-INDIANS BY RACE AND AGE.

RACES.													Serial No.
Others.													
All ages.			0—12		12—15		15—30		30—50		50 and over.		
Total.	Males.	Females.	Males.	Females.	Males.	Females.	Males.	Females.	Males.	Females.	Males.	Females.	
18	19	20	21	22	23	24	25	26	27	28	29	30	
152	***60***	***92***	***7***	***5***	***2***	***3***	***17***	***25***	***27***	***42***	***7***	***17***	
112	38	74	7	5	2	3	8	20	15	31	6	15	1
...	...	...	...	...	...	...	...	...	...	...	...	...	2
13	***8***	***5***	...	...	...	...	***3***	***2***	***5***	***3***	...	...	
13	8	5	...	...	...	...	3	2	5	3	...	...	3
...	...	...	...	...	...	...	...	...	...	...	...	...	4
...	...	...	...	...	...	...	...	...	...	...	...	...	5
10	***6***	***4***	...	...	...	...	***1***	***1***	***5***	***3***	...	...	
...	...	...	...	...	...	...	...	...	...	...	...	...	6
...	...	...	...	...	...	...	...	...	...	...	...	...	7
6	2	4	...	...	...	...	...	1	2	3	...	...	8
4	4	...	...	...	...	...	1	...	3	...	...	...	9
5	***3***	***2***	...	...	...	...	***2***	...	...	***2***	***1***	...	
2	1	1	...	...	...	..	1	...	...	1	...	...	10
...	...	...	...	...	...	...	...	...	...	...	...	...	11
...	...	...	...	...	...	...	...	...	...	...	...	...	12
3	2	1	...	...	...	...	1	...	...	1	1	...	13
12	***5***	***7***	...	...	...	...	***3***	***2***	***2***	***3***	...	***2***	
...	...	...	...	...	...	...	...	...	...	...	...	...	14
...	...	...	...	...	...	...	...	...	...	...	...	...	15
10	4	6	...	...	...	...	3	2	1	2	...	2	16
2	1	1	...	...	...	...	...	...	1	1	...	...	17

TABLE XVIII.

EUROPEANS, ARMENIANS AND ANGLO-INDIANS BY RACE AND AGE.

Serial No.	District.	ARMENIANS.												
		All ages.			0–12		12–15		15–30		30–50		50 and over.	
		Total.	Males.	Females.	Males	Females.	Males.	Females.	Males.	Females.	Males.	Females.	Males.	Females.
	1	31	32	33	34	35	36	37	38	39	40	41	42	43
	STATE ...	*2*	*1*	*1*	...	*1*	...	...	...	...	*1*	...	...	...
1	Hyderabad City ...	2	1	1	...	1	...	...	...	...	1	...	...	...
2	Atraf-i-balda ..	...	...	...	...	...	...	...	...	...	...	...	...	...
	Warangal Division .	...	...	...	...	...	...	...	...	...	...	...	...	...
3	Warangal	...	...	...	...	...	...	...	...	...	...	...	...	...
4	Karimnagar... ...	...	...	...	...	...	...	...	...	...	...	...	...	...
5	Adilabad	...	...	...	...	...	...	...	...	...	...	...	...	...
	Medak Division ...	...	...	...	...	...	...	...	...	...	...	...	...	...
6	Medak	...	...	...	...	...	...	...	...	...	...	...	...	...
7	Nizamabad	...	...	...	...	...	...	...	...	...	...	...	...	...
8	Mahbubnagar ...	...	...	...	...	...	...	...	...	...	...	...	...	...
9	Nalgonda	...	...	...	...	...	...	...	...	...	...	...	...	...
	Aurangabad Division	...	...	...	...	...	...	...	...	...	...	...	...	...
10	Aurangabad... ..	..	...	...	...	...	...	...	...	...	...	...	...	...
11	Bhir	...	...	...	...	...	...	...	...	...	...	...	...	...
12	Nander	...	...	...	...	...	...	...	...	...	...	...	...	...
13	Parbhani	...	...	...	...	...	...	...	...	...	...	...	...	...
	Gulbarga Division ...	...	...	...	...	...	...	...	...	...	40	41	...	...
14	Gulbarga	...	...	...	...	...	...	...	...	...	...	...	...	...
15	Osmanabad	...	...	...	...	...	...	...	...	...	...	...	...	...
16	Raichur	...	...	...	...	...	...	...	...	...	...	...	...	...
17	Bidar	...	...	...	...	...	...	...	...	...	...	...	...	...

TABLE XVIII

EUROPEANS, ARMENIANS AND ANGLO-INDIANS BY RACE AND AGE.

ANGLO-INDIANS.													Serial No.
All ages.			0—12		12—15		15—30		30—50		50 and over.		
Total.	Males.	Females.	Males.	Females.	Males.	Females.	Males.	Females.	Males.	Females.	Males.	Females.	
44	45	46	47	48	49	50	51	52	53	54	55	56	
3,004	***1,548***	***1,456***	***489***	***435***	***108***	***101***	***396***	***467***	***382***	***315***	***173***	***138***	
2,103	1,030	1,073	326	304	84	83	263	334	219	234	138	118	1
224	129	95	43	35	8	4	29	30	33	21	6	5	2
194	***109***	***85***	***31***	***30***	***5***	***4***	***30***	***26***	***38***	***20***	***5***	***5***	
177	94	83	31	30	5	4	26	25	28	19	4	5	3
8	7	1	...	...	...	...	1	...	5	1	1	...	4
9	8	1	...	...	...	...	3	1	5	...	...	...	5
55	***35***	***20***	***13***	***9***	...	***1***	***4***	***6***	***15***	***3***	***3***	***1***	
22	14	8	8	2	...	...	1	3	4	2	1	1	6
17	14	3	3	...	...	1	2	1	8	1	1	...	7
3	...	3	...	3	...	...	...	...	...	...	...	...	8
13	7	6	2	4	...	...	1	2	3	...	1	...	9
175	***94***	***81***	***25***	***27***	***4***	***3***	***24***	***29***	***34***	***17***	***7***	***5***	
59	29	30	5	11	...	...	6	10	15	8	3	1	10
2	1	1	...	...	...	...	...	...	...	1	1	...	11
22	15	7	4	1	1	...	7	5	3	1	...	...	12
92	49	43	16	15	3	3	11	14	16	7	3	4	13
253	***151***	***102***	***51***	***30***	***7***	***6***	***36***	***42***	***43***	***20***	***14***	***4***	
71	43	28	15	8	...	2	6	11	18	4	4	3	14
15	11	4	3	1	1	...	6	2	1	1	...	...	15
164	96	68	33	21	6	4	24	29	23	14	10	...	16
3	1	2	...	...	...	...	...	...	1	1	...	1	17

PROVINCIAL TABLE I.

AREA AND POPULATION OF TALUKAS.

1. The figures for the census of 1891 for the city by wards and for districts by Talukas are not available.

2. Owing to the general readjustment of districts between 1901 and 1911 the Talukas have undergone changes to such an extent as to render the figures for 1901 valueless for purposes of comparison. The process of adjustment of population to correspond with the present Taluka areas would entail labour quite out of proportion to the results. Hence the omission of figures for 1901.

3. The population of troops has now been correctly included in that of Chadarghat instead of in that of the city as was done in the last census.

PROVINCIAL TABLE I.

AREA AND POPULATION OF TALUKAS.

Serial No.	Taluka.	Area in square miles.	Number of. Towns.	Number of. Villages.	Number of occupied houses.	Population. 1911. Persons.	Population. 1911. Males.	Population. 1911. Females.	Population. 1901 (both sexes.)	Percentage of variation. 1901 to 1911	Percentage of variation. 1891 to 1901.	Number of persons per square mile in 1911.
	1	2	3	4	5	6	7	8	9	10	11	12
	STATE ...	***82,698***	***85***	***20,151***	***2,713,845***	***13,374,676***	***6,797,118***	***6,577,558***	***11,141,142***	***+20·0***	***—3·4***	***162***
	Hyderabad City ...	***50***	***1***	...	***111,509***	***500,623***	***258,454***	***242,169***	***448,466***	***+11·6***	***+8·0***	***10,012***
1	**City Proper** ...	***11·46***	...	...	***45,537***	***207,562***	***105,342***	***102,220***	***192,861***	***+7·6***	...	***18,112***
	City Andarun ...	***2·0***	...	...	***27,058***	***131,335***	***66,755***	***64,580***	***128,043***	***+2·5***	...	***65,668***
	Ward I ...	0·56	...	...	6,272	34,369	17,578	16,791	31,007	+10·8	...	[illegible]
	Ward II ...	0·50	...	...	7,520	34,880	17,602	17,278	31,849	+9·5	...	[illegible]
	Ward III ...	0·65	...	...	7,415	34,667	17,582	17,085	29,717	+16·6	...	[illegible]
	Ward IV ...	0·29	...	...	5,851	27,419	13,993	13,426	35,470	—22·6	...	[illegible]
	City Berun ...	***9·46***	...	...	***18,479***	***76,227***	***38,587***	***37,640***	***64,818***	***+17·6***	...	***8,058***
	Ward V (Berun. I)...	2·17	...	...	8,739	36,806	18,694	18,112	32,952	+11·6	...	[illegible]
	Ward VI (Berun. II)...	4·81	...	...	5,808	25,151	12,689	12,462	22,728	+10·6	...	[illegible]
	Ward VII (Berun. III)...	2·48	...	...	3,932	14,270	7,204	7,066	9,138	+56·1	...	[illegible]
2	**Chadarghat** ...	***20·84***	...	...	***37,297***	***161,600***	***82,853***	***78,747***	***142,263***	***+13·5***	...	***7,754***
	Ward VIII (Chad. A)...	4·19	...	...	5,743	24,906	12,619	12,287	20,787	+19·8	...	[illegible]
	Ward IX (Chad. B)...	6·15	...	...	7,723	38,628	20,233	18,395	27,546	+40·2	...	[illegible]
	Ward X (Chad. C)...	0·44	...	...	7,539	31,193	16,073	15,120	36,571	—14·7	...	[illegible]
	Ward XI (Chad. D)...	0·59	...	...	5,485	24,672	12,558	12,114	24,446	+0·9	...	[illegible]
	Ward XII (Chad. E)...	4·00	...	...	4,576	20,153	10,002	10,151	15,969	+26·2	...	[illegible]
	Troops ...	5·47	...	...	6,231	22,048	11,368	10,680	16,944	+30·1	...	[illegible]
3	**Residency Bazars** ...	***0·53***	...	...	***4,089***	***17,971***	***9,504***	***8,467***	***16,904***	***+6·3***	...	***33,907***
4	**Secunderabad including Bolarum** ...	***17·17***	...	...	***24,586***	***113,490***	***60,755***	***52,735***	***96,438***	***+17·6***	...	***6,610***
	Atraf-i-balda District	***2,561***	***2***	***868***	***104,527***	***520,159***	***265,184***	***254,975***	...	...	...	***203***
5	Sharqi ...	600	...	175	27,619	140,800	72,058	68,742	...	...	..	[illegible]
6	Gharbi ...	320	1	113	13,676	66,926	33,880	33,046	...	...	...	[illegible]
7	Shumali ...	508	...	149	16,808	84,514	43,267	41,247	...	...	...	166
8	Junubi ...	492	...	193	19,704	98,960	50,929	48,031	...	...	...	[illegible]
9	Pattlur ...	486	...	143	13,482	67,681	34,029	33,652	...	...	...	[illegible]
10	Homnabad ...	23	1	5	2,861	12,706	6,356	6,350	...	...	...	[illegible]
11	Kharka ...	132	...	90	10,377	48,572	24,665	23,907	...	...	...	[illegible]
	Warangal Division ...	***20,970***	***18***	***4,002***	***502,670***	***2,657,477***	***1,368,101***	***1,289,376***	...	...	...	***127***
	Warangal District ...	***7,943***	***5***	***1,244***	***172,285***	***905,414***	***467,413***	***438,001***	...	...	...	***114***
12	Warangal ...	916	3	190	46,529	245,190	126,150	119,040	...	...	...	[illegible]
13	Khamammett ...	700	1	161	25,700	135,975	69,210	66,765	...	...	...	[illegible]
14	Mahbubabad ...	990	...	210	30,909	166,481	85,896	80,585	...	...	...	[illegible]
15	Madhra ...	966	...	186	24,257	126,901	65,346	61,555	...	...	...	[illegible]
16	Pakhal ...	720	...	154	11,353	58,662	30,436	28,226	...	...	...	[illegible]
17	Paloncha ..	1,763	...	152	15,766	85,132	43,409	41,723	...	...	...	[illegible]
18	Mulag ...	1,096	...	129	5,322	27,313	14,441	12,872	...	...	...	[illegible]
19	Yellandlapad ...	792	1	62	12,449	59,760	52,525	27,235	...	...	...	[illegible]

PROVINCIAL TABLE I.

AREA AND POPULATION OF TALUKAS.

Serial No.	Taluka.	Area in square miles.	Number of. Towns.	Number of. Villages.	Number of occupied houses.	Population. 1911. Persons.	Population. 1911. Males.	Population. 1911. Females.	Population. 1901 (both sexes.)	Percentage of variation. 1901 to 1911.	Percentage of variation. 1891 to 1901.	Number of persons per square mile. in 1911.
	1	2	3	4	5	6	7	8	9	10	11	12
	Karimnagar District.	***5,733***	***7***	***1,135***	***209,963***	***1,131,637***	***586,260***	***545,377***	...	...	...	***197***
20	Karimnagar ...	949	2	175	34,317	201,429	104,636	96,793	...	...	...	212
21	Jagtial ..	860	3	235	46,823	235,083	120,665	114,418	...	...	...	273
22	Jamikunta ...	552	...	130	25,716	151,599	79,548	72,051	...	...	...	275
23	Mahadeopur ...	1,106	1	142	14,942	77,241	39,509	37,732	...	...	...	70
24	Parkal ...	509	...	110	20,764	107,695	55,737	51,958	...	...	...	212
25	Sirsilla ...	697	1	170	33,928	170,994	88,901	82,093	..	...	...	245
26	Sultanabad ...	1,060	...	173	33,468	187,596	97,264	90,332	...	...	...	177
	Adilabad District ...	***7,294***	***3***	***1,623***	***120,422***	***620,426***	***314,428***	***305,998***	...	...	...	***85***
27	Adilabad ..	1,300	1	263	17,602	90,510	45,225	45,285	...	...	...	70
28	Chinnur ...	978	1	171	15,652	83,339	42,466	40,873	...	...	...	85
29	Asafabad ...	612	...	185	6,600	37,727	19,422	18,305	...	...	...	62
30	Lakshatipet ...	558	...	125	12,695	64,773	33,159	31,614	...	...	...	116
31	Kinwat ...	1,218	...	249	18,065	94,369	48,607	45,762	...	...	...	77
32	Nirmal ...	480	1	188	20,943	95,998	47,572	48,426	...	...	...	200
33	Rajura ..	823	...	175	7,619	39,374	20,204	19,170	...	...	...	48
34	Sirpur ...	1,062	...	213	17,212	94,141	47,359	46,782	...	...	...	89
35	Yelgadap (Jagir) ...	263	...	54	4,034	20,195	10,414	9,781	...	..	...	77
	Medak Division ...	***17,739***	***13***	***3,955***	***594,654***	***3,046,705***	***1,548,882***	***1,497,823***	...	...	...	***172***
	Medak District ...	***3,215***	***4***	***957***	***133,930***	***687,137***	***348,410***	***338,727***	...	...	...	***214***
36	Medak ...	563	1	163	25,624	127,192	64,485	62,707	...	...	...	226
37	Andol ...	450	...	172	21,898	113,320	56,803	56,517	...	...	...	252
38	Bagbat ...	451	...	142	17,032	84,575	42,962	41,613	...	...	...	188
39	Kalabgur ..	390	2	172	25,139	126,917	63,883	63,034	...	...	...	325
40	Siddipet ...	1,174	1	247	38,707	208,218	106,910	101,308	...	...	...	177
41	Narsapur (Jagir) ...	102	...	34	3,313	16,113	8,083	8,030	...	...	...	158
42	Hatnura (Jagir) ...	71	...	23	1,611	7,951	3,951	4,000	...	...	..	112
43	Doulatabad (Jagir) ...	14	...	4	606	2,851	1,333	1,518	...	...	...	204
	Nizamabad District...	***3,273***	***5***	***761***	***122,612***	***568,009***	***283,621***	***284,388***	...	...	...	***174***
44	Nizamabad ...	789	1	150	24,311	111,842	55,737	56,105	...	...	...	142
45	Armur ...	989	2	184	35,487	154,935	76,663	78,272	...	...	...	157
46	Bodhan ...	587	1	162	23,095	113,879	56,366	57,513	...	...	...	194
47	Kamareddipet ...	555	...	130	22,997	111,502	56,745	54,757	...	...	...	201
48	Yellareddipet ...	353	1	135	16,722	75,851	38,110	37,741	...	...	..	215
	Mahbubnagar District	***5,147***	***2***	***1,183***	***149,029***	***747,178***	***379,712***	***367,466***	...	...	...	***145***
49	Mahabubnagar ...	676	1	211	31,317	154,783	79,103	75,680	...	...	...	229
50	Nagarkarnul ..	420	...	135	17,195	88,586	44,534	44,052	...	...	...	211
51	Amrabad ...	1,030	...	71	7,747	39,208	19,718	19,490	...	...	...	36
52	Kalvakurti ...	877	...	143	18,612	97,181	49,501	47,680	...	...	...	111
53	Makhtal ...	612	1	149	23,056	120,664	61,143	59,521	...	...	...	197
54	Pargi ...	377	...	259	24,266	116,006	59,263	56,743	...	...	...	308
55	Jatpol (Jagir) ..	356	...	79	7,828	38,310	19,454	18,856	...	...	...	108
56	Gopalpet (Jagir) ...	144	...	22	3,691	17,314	8,774	8,540	...	...	...	120
57	Wanparti (Jagir) ...	605	...	114	15,317	75,126	38,222	36,904	...	...	...	124

PROVINCIAL TABLE I.

AREA AND POPULATION OF TALUKAS.

Serial No.	Taluka.	Area in square miles.	Number of. Towns.	Number of. Villages.	Number of occupied houses.	Population. 1911. Persons.	Population. 1911. Males.	Population. 1911. Females.	Population. 1901 (both sexes.)	Percentage of variation. 1901 to 1911.	Percentage of variation. 1891 to 1901.	Number of persons per square mile in 1911.
	1	2	3	4	5	6	7	8	9	10	11	12
	Nalgonda District ...	*6,104*	*2*	*1,197*	*189,083*	*1,044,381*	*537,139*	*507,242*	...	...	...	[illegible]
58	Nalgonda ..	1,003	1	193	32,211	186,205	95,400	90,805	...	...	...	[illegible]
59	Bhongir ..	1,285	1	242	38,405	205,159	105,383	99,776	...	...	...	[illegible]
60	Cherial ..	739	...	191	34,639	187,265	96,750	90,515	...	...	...	[illegible]
61	Devarkonda ...	989	...	185	21,870	119,107	61,721	57,386	...	...	...	[illegible]
62	Huzurnagar ...	578	...	87	15,004	80,799	41,300	39,499	...	...	...	[illegible]
63	Mirialguda ..	795	...	147	19,398	109,393	56,208	53,185	...	...	...	[illegible]
64	Suriapet ...	720	...	152	27,556	156,453	80,377	76,076	...	...	...	217
	Aurangabad Division	*19,268*	*22*	*5,662*	*633,502*	*2,976,541*	*1,496,102*	*1,480,439*	...	...	...	[illegible]
	Aurangabad District	*6,212*	*5*	*1,828*	*182,748*	*869,787*	*437,495*	*432,292*	...	...	...	[illegible]
65	Aurangabad ..	786	1	234	25,685	122,295	62,194	60,101	...	...	...	[illegible]
66	Ambarh ...	900	...	214	26,677	120,475	59,917	60,558	...	...	...	[illegible]
67	Bhokardan ...	991	...	336	29,041	130,213	65,408	64,805	...	...	...	[illegible]
68	Gangapur ...	546	...	200	13,274	64,672	32,595	32,077	...	...	...	[illegible]
69	Jalna ..	744	2	250	29,773	137,681	69,216	68,465	...	...	...	[illegible]
70	Kannad ..	687	...	194	16,549	81,731	40,941	40,790	...	...	...	[illegible]
71	Paithan ...	608	1	167	16,518	77,730	38,708	39,022	...	...	...	[illegible]
72	Vaijapur ...	572	1	139	14,004	74,525	37,382	37,143	...	...	...	[illegible]
73	Khuldabad ...	129	...	41	3,515	25,033	13,643	11,390	...	...	...	[illegible]
74	Sillod ...	249	...	53	7,712	35,432	17,491	17,941	...	...	...	[illegible]
	Bhir District ...	*4,132*	*4*	*1,019*	*124,038*	*622,531*	*314,738*	*307,793*	...	...	...	[illegible]
75	Bhir ...	640	1	199	27,165	126,607	64,130	62,477	...	...	...	[illegible]
76	Mominabad ...	983	2	245	35,158	164,658	83,442	81,216	...	...	...	[illegible]
77	Asbti ..	740	...	127	14,481	68,600	34,673	33,927	...	...	...	[illegible]
78	Gevrai ...	564	...	154	19,157	86,311	43,452	42,859	...	...	...	[illegible]
79	Manjlegaon ...	702	1	220	29,127	135,452	68,426	67,026	...	...	...	[illegible]
80	Patoda ...	503	...	74	8,950	40,903	20,615	20,288	...	...	...	[illegible]
	Nander District ...	*3,797*	*6*	*1,302*	*146,065*	*704,549*	*352,638*	*351,911*	...	...	...	*186*
81	Nander ...	562	1	211	20,106	103,009	52,283	50,726	...	...	...	183
82	Biloli ...	508	1	175	19,615	95,645	47,657	47,988	...	...	...	[illegible]
83	Deglur ...	733	1	243	27,799	137,398	68,777	68,621	...	...	...	[illegible]
84	Hadgaon ...	704	...	203	17,403	90,976	45,531	45,445	...	...	...	129
85	Kandahar ...	630	1	235	30,956	137,780	69,594	68,186	...	...	...	219
86	Mudhol ...	660	2	235	30,186	139,741	68,796	70,945	...	...	...	[illegible]
	Parbhani District ...	*5,127*	*7*	*1,513*	*170,651*	*779,674*	*391,231*	*388,443*	...	...	...	[illegible]
87	Parbhani ...	546	1	250	28,979	131,952	65,772	66,180				[illegible]
88	Basmat ...	665	1	206	22,512	100,704	51,230	49,474	...	...	...	[illegible]
89	Hingoli ...	723	1	214	22,841	105,627	53,666	51,961	...	...	...	[illegible]
90	Jintur ...	1,456	...	320	27,759	129,544	64,977	64,567	...	...	...	[illegible]
91	Kalamnuri ...	594	...	201	16,662	81,240	40,571	40,669	...	...	...	[illegible]
92	Pathri ...	600	2	167	28,391	126,081	63,123	62,958	...	...	...	[illegible]
93	Palam ...	543	2	155	23,507	104,526	51,892	52,634	...	...	...	[illegible]

PROVINCIAL TABLE I.

AREA AND POPULATION OF TALUKAS.

Serial No.	Taluka.	Area in square miles.	Number of. Towns.	Number of. Villages.	Number of occupied houses.	Population. 1911. Persons.	Population. 1911. Males.	Population. 1911. Females.	Population. 1901 (both sexes.)	Percentage of variation. 1901 to 1911.	Percentage of variation. 1891 to 1901.	Number of persons per square mile in 1911.
	1	2	3	4	5	6	7	8	9	10	11	12
	Gulbarga Division ...	***22,110***	***32***	***5,521***	***766,983***	***3,673,171***	***1,860,395***	***1,812,776***	...	...	...	***166***
	Gulbarga District ..	***6,719***	***10***	***1,585***	***238,247***	***1,150,983***	***582,447***	***568,536***	...	...	...	***171***
94	Gulbarga ...	773	1	249	45,813	212,034	108,402	103,632	...	...	...	274
95	Chincholi ...	825	...	138	17,498	77,561	38,888	38,673	...	...	...	94
96	Kodangal ...	622	2	163	24,235	119,944	61,369	58,575	...	...	...	193
97	Seram ...	448	1	103	18,417	70,921	35,535	35,386	...	...	...	158
98	Yadgir ...	507	1	130	21,827	111,922	56,301	55,621	...	...	...	221
99	Andola ...	709	...	149	17,764	88,535	44,510	44,025	...	...	...	125
100	Shahpur ..	546	...	151	21,685	109,239	54,674	54,565	...	...	...	200
101	Shorapur ...	527	1	175	22,738	108,115	54,405	53,710	...	...	...	205
102	Kalgi (Jagir) ...	121	...	43	7,150	32,032	16,069	15,963	...	...	...	265
103	Afzalpur (Jagir) ...	414	...	47	6,012	40,537	20,829	19,708	...	...	...	98
104	Chitapur (Jagir) ...	360	1	67	9,724	59,993	30,182	29,811	...	...	...	167
105	Aland (Jagir) ...	402	1	76	12,585	60,386	31,041	29,345	...	...	...	150
106	Firozabad (Jagir) ...	256	1	25	6,284	28,870	14,562	14,308	...	...	...	113
107	Tandur (Jagir) ...	211	1	69	6,605	30,894	15,680	15,214	...	...	...	146
	Osmanabad District..	***3,517***	***6***	***869***	***137,654***	***635,977***	***324,969***	***311,008***	...	...	...	***181***
108	Osmanabad ...	468	2	95	19,845	94,198	48,317	45,881	...	...	...	201
109	Kalam ...	605	...	143	22,273	105,347	53,757	51,590	...	...	...	174
110	Parenda ...	734	...	171	21,169	97,533	49,289	48,244	...	...	...	133
111	Owsa ...	336	2	129	19,793	87,416	44,425	42,991	...	...	...	260
112	Tuljapur ...	606	2	134	25,938	123,939	63,551	60,388	...	...	...	207
113	Lohara (Jagir) ...	450	...	122	15,490	70,797	36,554	34,243	...	...	...	157
114	Ganjoti (Jagir) ...	324	...	75	12,141	56,747	29,076	27,671	...	...	...	175
	Raichur District ...	***6,791***	***9***	***1,658***	***208,765***	***996,684***	***503,541***	***493,143***	...	...	...	***147***
115	Raichur ...	700	2	190	28,593	139,908	71,110	68,798	...	...	...	200
116	Alampur ...	232	...	43	6,436	30,880	15,486	15,394	...	...	...	133
117	Deodrug ...	547	1	170	17,635	88,970	44,588	44,382	...	...	...	163
118	Gangawati ...	459	1	140	13,698	63,740	31,890	31,850	...	...	...	139
119	Kushtagi ...	714	...	218	18,118	92,567	47,008	45,559	...	...	...	130
120	Lingsugur ...	774	1	187	20,136	97,529	49,037	48,492	...	...	...	126
121	Manvi ...	676	1	153	20,721	95,258	47,978	47,280	...	...	...	141
122	Sindhnur ...	672	1	140	16,113	78,021	39,021	39,000	...	...	...	116
123	Koppal (Jagir) ...	551	1	148	16,160	80,234	40,235	39,999	...	...	...	146
124	Yelbarga (Jagir) ...	493	...	101	16,093	72,399	36,591	35,808	...	...	...	147
125	Gadwal (Jagir) ...	813	1	118	26,653	113,818	58,428	55,390	...	...	...	140
126	Amarchinta (Jagir) ...	161	...	50	8,378	43,360	22,169	21,191	...	...	...	269
	Bidar District ...	***5,983***	***7***	***1,409***	***182,317***	***889,527***	***449,438***	***440,089***	...	...	...	***[illegible]75***
127	Bidar ...	620	2	171	24,835	120,461	60,085	60,376	...	...	...	194
128	Nilanga ...	651	...	141	18,131	84,679	42,889	41,790	...	...	...	130
129	Ahmadpur ...	680	...	221	25,363	113,032	57,452	55,580	...	...	...	166
130	Udgir ...	676	1	164	15,473	100,242	51,137	49,105	...	...	...	148
131	Janwada ...	440	...	125	13,083	63,175	32,171	31,004	...	...	...	144
132	Hasanabad (Jagir) ...	103	...	41	4,566	20,892	10,337	10,555	...	...	...	192
133	Bhalki (Jagir) ...	101	1	22	5,274	23,945	12,101	11,844	...	...	...	237
134	Partabpur (Jagir) ...	222	...	58	10,195	48,007	24,630	23,377	...	...	...	216
135	Chincholi (Jagir) ...	184	1	47	8,038	37,097	18,870	18,227	...	...	...	202
136	Narayankher (Jagir) ...	221	...	100	10,395	51,217	25,977	25,240	...	...	...	232
137	Chitgopa (Jagir) ...	290	...	94	18,638	86,617	43,000	43,617	...	...	...	299
138	Ghorwadi (Jagir) ...	250	...	57	8,848	41,268	20,664	20,604	...	...	...	165
139	Ekeli (Jagir) ...	207	1	52	5,918	27,546	13,798	13,748	...	...	...	133
140	Kalyani (Jagir) ...	272	1	70	9,338	43,758	22,241	21,517	...	...	...	161
141	Murag (Jagir) ...	160	...	46	4,099	27,541	14,086	13,455	...	...	...	172

PROVINCIAL TABLE II.

POPULATION OF TALUKAS BY RELIGION AND EDUCATION.

PROVINCIAL TABLE II.

POPULATION OF TALUKAS BY RELIGION AND EDUCATION.

Serial No.	Taluka.		DISTRIBUTION BY					
			Hindu.		Jain.		Musalman.	
			Males.	Females.	Males.	Females.	Males.	Females.
	1		2	3	4	5	6	7
	Hyderabad State	...	***5,897,158***	***5,728,988***	***11,032***	***9,994***	***706,821***	***674,169***
	Hyderabad City	...	***135,638***	***126,493***	***223***	***156***	***111,770***	***108,126***
1	City Municipality	...	25,810	22,812	14	7	40,865	41,678
2	Chadarghat Municipality	...	63,635	61,097	42	26	55,776	53,424
3	Residency Bazars	...	6,297	5,556	15	12	2,674	2,418
4	Secunderabad including Bolarum	...	39,896	37,028	152	111	12,455	10,606
	Atraf-i-Balda District	...	***231,505***	***223,698***	***58***	***52***	***30,602***	***28,746***
5	Sharqi	...	64,835	62,172	1	...	5,880	5,504
6	Gharbi	...	28,900	28,351	9	10	4,868	4,571
7	Shumali	...	38,211	36,492	...	...	4,520	4,303
8	Junubi	...	43,814	41,596	...	...	6,488	5,961
9	Patlur	...	28,796	28,732	2	2	4,829	4,542
10	Homnabad	...	4,931	4,826	36	30	1,380	1,491
11	Kharka	...	22,018	21,529	10	10	2,637	2,368
	Warangal Division	...	***1,194,071***	***1,128,967***	***115***	***111***	***66,897***	***59,373***
	Warangal District	...	***372,793***	***351,091***	***21***	***14***	***26,709***	***23,370***
12	Warangal	...	113,593	107,512	9	5	9,142	8,701
13	Khammamett	...	59,058	57,411	1	...	4,965	4,587
14	Mahbubabad	...	65,250	62,374	6	7	3,566	2,901
15	Madhra	...	55,894	52,827	...	...	3,977	3,281
16	Pakhal	...	23,756	22,091	...	...	1,002	742
17	Paloncha	...	25,495	24,331	...	...	1,539	1,312
18	Mulug	...	9,597	8,489	...	...	592	424
19	Yellandlapad	...	20,147	16,056	5	2	1,926	1,322
	Karimnagar District	..	***556,441***	***518,213***	***35***	***29***	***24,345***	***22,178***
20	Karimnagar	...	98,816	91,069	31	27	5,221	5,193
21	Jagtial	...	114,247	108,525	3	1	5,346	4,941
22	Jamikunta	...	75,828	68,759	...	...	3,199	2,796
23	Mahadeopur	...	36,048	34,773	...	...	1,437	1,102
24	Parkal	...	53,251	49,712	1	1	1,912	1,677
25	Sirsilla	...	85,212	78,844	...	...	3,383	3,019
26	Sultanabad	...	93,039	86,531	...	...	3,847	3,448
	Adilabad District	...	***264,837***	***259,663***	***59***	***68***	***15,843***	***13,825***
27	Adilabad	...	37,776	38,158	2	1	3,239	2,973
28	Chinnur	...	39,873	38,573	...	...	1,502	1,288
29	Asafabad	...	11,809	11,268	7	4	882	612
30	Lakhsetipet	...	28,486	27,317	...	...	1,023	780
31	Kinwat	..	44,712	42,429	6	5	2,794	2,395
32	Nirmal	...	43,333	44,511	...	...	3,572	3,328
33	Rajura	...	13,828	13,206	44	58	591	482
34	Sirpur	...	36,350	35,924	...	...	1,596	1,404
35	Yelgadap (Jagir)	...	8,670	8,277	...	...	644	563
	Medak Division	...	***1,397,884***	***1,355,271***	***72***	***70***	***111,379***	***109,049***
	Medak District	..	***312,690***	***302,862***	***57***	***63***	***32,269***	***32,815***
36	Medak	...	58,499	56,666	...	...	4,947	5,100
37	Andol	...	50,135	49,915	45	47	5,750	5,796
38	Baghat	...	37,354	35,904	1	...	5,194	5,382
39	Kalabgur	...	54,246	53,468	8	10	9,318	9,264
40	Siddipet	...	100,596	95,025	...	...	5,834	5,825
41	Narsapur (Jagir)	...	7,198	7,126	...	...	652	[illegible]
42	Hatnura (Jagir)	...	3,526	3,511	...	...	380	445
43	Doulatabad (Jagir)	...	1,135	1,247	3	6	194	265
	Nizamabad District	...	***261,053***	***262,106***	***13***	***5***	***21,036***	***20,915***
44	Nizamabad	..	50,228	51,129	10	3	5,230	4,727
45	Armur	..	72,415	73,641	...	...	4,217	4,603
46	Bodhan	...	49,998	51,247	3	2	6,207	6,100
47	Kamareddipet	...	53,640	51,661	...	...	2,735	2,763
48	Yellareddipet	..	34,772	34,428	...	...	2,647	2,702

PROVINCIAL TABLE II.

POPULATION OF TALUKAS BY RELIGION AND EDUCATION.

RELIGION.						NUMBER OF LITERATE PERSONS.						
Christian.		Animist.		Others.		0—15		15—20		20 and over.		Serial No.
Males.	Females.	Males.	Females.	Males.	Females.	Males.	Females.	Males.	Females.	Males.	Females.	
8	9	10	11	12	13	14	15	16	17	18	19	
29,498	24,801	149,023	136,699	3,889	2,907	38,291	5,392	34,574	3,678	271,224	15,010	
9,623	6,617	38	3	1,162	774	6,478	2,274	6,606	1,698	48,746	6,583	
32	56	...	...	34	27	1,511	379	1,699	337	12,762	1,269	1
1,559	1,523	36	2	392	315	1,942	580	2,387	548	17,341	2,216	2
445	421	...	...	73	60	609	284	489	194	2,836	679	3
7,587	4,617	2	1	663	372	2,416	1,031	2,031	614	15,807	2,399	4
686	608	2,258	1,812	78	68	1,526	200	1,193	147	10,887	561	
17	18	1,312	1,037	13	11	299	51	229	31	2,449	131	5
20	24	68	73	15	17	233	42	162	20	1,956	56	6
303	258	183	154	50	40	311	66	202	46	2,022	160	7
158	123	469	351	...	...	271	16	297	24	2,115	110	8
179	179	223	197	...	...	277	18	178	22	1,238	61	9
9	3	...	...	...	...	21	4	29	1	341	17	10
...	...	...	...	...	...	124	3	96	3	766	26	11
6,507	6,086	100,115	94,468	396	371	5,898	498	5,096	322	39,201	1,557	
6,202	5,777	61,473	57,548	215	201	2,578	260	2,264	160	16,208	778	
360	304	2,916	2,376	130	142	1,110	124	959	69	6,129	330	12
2,343	2,196	2,822	2,555	21	16	449	71	388	37	2,802	176	13
442	358	16,612	14,932	20	13	344	17	326	14	2,545	61	14
2,568	2,489	2,901	2,848	6	10	295	14	287	9	2,011	68	15
13	16	5,662	5,376	3	1	47	...	41	1	526	6	16
36	30	16,324	16,040	12	10	109	5	95	5	704	41	17
5	2	4,244	3,957	3	...	35	6	29	1	216	7	18
435	382	9,992	9,464	20	9	189	23	139	24	1,270	89	19
286	300	5,041	4,557	112	100	2,493	167	2,188	121	16,867	590	
172	188	328	254	68	62	589	56	596	38	3,864	115	20
13	20	1,046	915	10	16	395	18	348	16	2,818	77	21
65	71	453	418	3	5	384	28	279	27	2,147	113	22
1	...	2,012	1,848	11	9	126	6	133	3	1,125	32	23
10	5	559	561	4	2	233	11	184	8	1,490	32	24
18	11	274	217	14	2	537	33	398	31	3,361	151	25
7	5	369	344	2	4	229	15	250	8	2,062	70	26
19	9	33,601	32,363	69	70	824	68	644	31	6,131	189	
4	...	4,192	4,146	12	7	154	25	103	10	1,078	28	27
4	2	1,087	1,010	...	...	121	2	129	3	958	18	28
4	1	6,719	6,429	1	...	52	6	47	7	330	48	29
1	...	3,646	3,515	3	2	62	1	46	...	622	17	30
...	...	1,063	897	32	36	71	16	67	6	648	25	31
2	1	660	581	5	5	144	10	86	3	975	23	32
1	...	5,739	5,423	1	1	49	4	42	...	390	13	33
3	5	9,410	9,449	...	...	136	3	100	1	855	12	34
...	...	1,085	922	15	19	34	1	24	1	275	5	35
7,285	6,655	31,902	26,463	360	318	8,009	883	7,233	512	54,860	2,217	
1,124	1,079	2,179	1,837	91	71	2,595	288	2,194	163	15,643	685	
387	402	594	493	58	46	563	107	629	47	2,822	157	36
167	158	700	594	6	7	267	28	190	30	2,195	64	37
39	33	363	229	10	5	329	45	281	44	1,970	166	38
73	46	226	237	12	10	644	41	449	18	3,601	124	39
458	441	17	14	5	8	726	61	573	24	4,505	142	40
...	...	233	164	...	...	17	4	26	...	232	5	41
...	...	45	46	...	...	17	2	27	...	195	4	42
...	...	1	...	...	...	12	...	19	...	123	3	43
375	345	972	848	172	169	987	69	1,002	53	8,882	272	
61	47	127	113	81	86	150	22	202	19	1,753	69	44
3	5	9	5	19	18	253	6	202	4	1,872	51	45
1	...	142	149	15	15	138	16	161	12	1,476	54	46
73	81	289	226	8	6	320	23	313	12	2,507	73	47
237	212	405	355	49	44	126	2	124	6	1,274	25	48

PROVINCIAL TABLE II.

POPULATION OF TALUKAS BY RELIGION AND EDUCATION.

Serial No.	Taluka.	DISTRIBUTION BY					
		Hindu.		Jain.		Musalman.	
		Males.	Females.	Males.	Females.	Males.	Females.
	1	2	3	4	5	6	7
	Mahbubnagar District	***341,109***	***331,641***	...	...	***30,353***	***29,16***
49	Mahbubnagar	70,446	67,377	...	...	7,372	7,2[illegible]
50	Nagarkarnul	41,138	40,728	...	...	2,933	2,880
51	Amrabad	16,568	16,857	...	...	1,202	1,098
52	Kalvakurti	44,753	43,449	...	...	3,086	2,923
53	Makhtal	54,664	53,478	...	...	6,088	5,709
54	Pargi	51,831	49,591	...	...	6,214	6,203
55	Jatpol (Jagir)	17,618	17,351	...	...	1,022	825
56	Gopalpet (Jagir)	8,300	8,113	...	...	452	384
57	Wanparti (Jagir)	35,791	34,637	...	...	1,954	1,899
	Nalgonda District	***483,032***	***458,662***	***2***	***2***	***27,721***	***26,151***
58	Nalgonda	88,341	84,056	...	...	5,695	5,551
59	Bhongir	98,746	93,366	2	2	5,957	5,858
60	Cherial	88,569	82,976	...	...	4,713	4,602
61	Devarkonda	52,858	50,223	...	...	2,457	2,096
62	Huzurnagar	33,784	32,811	...	...	2,811	2,442
63	Mirialguda	49,926	47,822	...	...	2,578	2,347
64	Suriapet	70,808	67,408	...	...	3,510	3,257
	Aurangabad Division	***1,317,224***	***1,310,409***	***7,019***	***6,471***	***157,875***	***180,137***
	Aurangabad District	***367,581***	***366,671***	***2,880***	***2,616***	***57,629***	***53,820***
65	Aurangabad	48,229	47,173	284	263	12,829	11,828
66	Ambarh	53,874	54,678	547	497	4,886	4,785
67	Bhokardan	56,802	56,398	224	204	7,312	7,165
68	Gangapur	27,919	27,579	276	249	3,376	3,238
69	Jalna	58,931	58,595	385	318	8,441	8,082
70	Kannad	34,628	34,832	323	309	4,432	4,179
71	Paithan	33,167	33,197	259	234	4,837	4,875
72	Vaijapur	31,480	31,421	471	427	3,105	2,988
73	Khuldabad	7,134	6,717	50	52	6,407	4,574
74	Sillod	15,417	15,778	61	63	2,004	2,096
	Bhir District	***285,573***	***280,481***	***1,820***	***1,569***	***26,749***	***25,151***
75	Bhir	57,480	56,227	350	263	6,186	5,877
76	Mominabad	74,998	73,128	336	340	7,994	7,658
77	Ashti	32,229	31,635	462	385	1,973	1,887
78	Gevrai	39,496	39,242	293	231	3,607	3,330
79	Manjlegaon	62,089	61,188	235	213	5,842	5,358
80	Patoda	19,281	19,061	144	137	1,147	1,046
	Nander District	***313,495***	***314,157***	***477***	***463***	***36,708***	***35,461***
81	Nander	43,470	42,541	69	52	8,160	7,629
82	Biloli	43,020	43,465	33	27	4,575	4,487
83	Deglur	61,816	61,687	86	75	6,738	6,758
84	Hadgaon	41,788	41,984	73	83	3,525	3,200
85	Kandahar	62,608	61,234	180	196	5,836	5,819
86	Mudhol	60,793	63,246	36	30	7,874	7,594
	Parbhani District	***350,575***	***349,100***	***1,842***	***1,823***	***36,789***	***35,688***
87	Parbhani	58,516	59,115	164	186	6,975	6,763
88	Basmat	46,110	45,036	166	176	4,734	4,122
89	Hingoli	48,255	46,633	357	336	4,818	4,751
90	Jintur	58,637	58,507	351	337	5,476	5,968
91	Kalamnuri	36,380	36,528	345	336	3,550	3,637
92	Pathri	56,386	56,392	319	337	6,326	4,140
93	Palam	46,291	46,889	140	115	4,910	5,084

PROVINCIAL TABLE II.

POPULATION OF TALLUKAS BY RELIGION AND EDUCATION.

RELIGION.						NUMBER OF LITERATE PERSONS.						
Christian.		Animist.		Others.		0—15		15—20		20 and over.		Serial No.
Males.	Females.	Males.	Females.	Males.	Females.	Males.	Females.	Males.	Females.	Males.	Females.	
8	9	10	11	12	13	14	15	16	17	18	19	
221	***230***	***7,991***	***6,401***	***38***	***26***	***1,847***	***203***	***1,645***	***122***	***14,174***	***584***	
123	143	1,140	899	22	14	446	82	317	50	3,235	194	49
35	48	428	366	...	...	240	18	249	12	1,492	75	50
8	5	1,938	1,528	2	2	65	4	61	6	731	17	51
22	9	1,640	1,289	...	...	244	23	283	11	1,961	75	52
6	1	385	833	...	...	285	35	265	16	2,215	85	53
12	15	1,172	934	4	...	271	9	214	12	2,213	56	54
...	...	812	679	2	1	44	6	46	3	295	12	55
...	...	22	13	...	...	85	11	79	4	510	20	56
15	9	454	350	8	9	167	15	131	8	1,522	50	57
5,565	***5,001***	***20,760***	***17,377***	***59***	***49***	***2,580***	***323***	***2,392***	***174***	***16,161***	***676***	
957	854	391	832	16	12	544	69	468	45	3,205	145	58
163	142	498	387	17	23	594	49	543	36	3,576	195	59
283	235	3,177	2,760	8	2	460	63	454	13	3,183	99	60
283	226	6,113	4,838	10	3	221	42	229	22	1,506	57	61
2,091	1,955	2,611	2,287	3	4	167	5	142	4	1,262	19	62
830	682	2,874	2,334	...	...	232	38	221	29	1,356	80	63
958	907	5,096	4,499	5	5	342	57	335	26	2,073	81	64
3,513	***3,336***	***9,184***	***8,924***	***1,287***	***1,162***	***7,507***	***818***	***6,332***	***488***	***54,171***	***1,956***	
3,222	***3,147***	***5,956***	***5,836***	***227***	***200***	***2,254***	***564***	***2,021***	***217***	***15,534***	***887***	
450	435	278	268	144	104	611	174	531	87	4,187	38[illegible]	65
246	259	[illegible]58	33[illegible]	6	3	163	22	211	19	1,071	4[illegible]	66
68	47	894	987	8	4	200	98	150	50	1,305	11[illegible]	67
558	517	465	494	1	...	206	25	156	[illegible]	1,031	1[illegible]	68
920	538	486	470	53	46	[illegible]07	59	276	6[illegible]	1,644	12[illegible]	69
...	...	1,545	1,457	13	13	201	12	174	[illegible]	1,318	39[illegible]	70
60	47	384	369	1	...	207	165	169	81	1,587	13[illegible]	71
907	873	1,418	1,431	...	...	262	6	230	[illegible]	1,453	14	72
33	31	19	10	...	...	6[illegible]	...	80	1	643		73
...	...	6	4	1	...	[illegible]	7	44	[illegible]	392	1[illegible]	74
1	***1***	***407***	***428***	***188***	***163***	***1,820***	***50***	***1,453***	***36***	***12,183***	***287***	
...	...	47	54	67	56	253	15	240	6	2,450	5[illegible]	75
1	1	73	62	40	32	[illegible]8[illegible]	7	520	9	3,904	8[illegible]	76
...	...	9	26	...	...	258	1	139	4	1,240	1[illegible]	77
...	...	15	52	1	4	208	11	162	1	1,380	7[illegible]	78
...	...	185	196	75	71	842	15	32[illegible]	14	2,781	47	79
...	...	38	44	5	...	7[illegible]	3	63	2	628	10	80
40	***29***	***1,194***	***1,142***	***724***	***639***	***1,507***	***88***	***1,297***	***71***	***11,548***	***272***	
20	15	32	28	532	461	378	24	272	16	2,327	80	81
...	...	16	7	13	2	220	5	153	8	1,522	10	82
4	...	119	96	14	11	242	10	230	8	2,204	72	83
...	...	109	149	36	29	150	1	155	3	1,202	13	84
3	2	827	849	76	86	263	8	208	27	1,720	30	85
13	12	21	13	59	50	274	10	279	14	2,573	61	86
250	***159***	***1,627***	***1,516***	***146***	***160***	***1,926***	***146***	***1,561***	***64***	***14,906***	***510***	
31	28	41	46	45	42	271	8	250	10	2,508	43	87
186	108	17	13	17	19	272	42	256	19	2,353	101	88
19	12	187	187	30	42	352	41	257	16	2,135	83	89
6	4	505	429	2	2	380	12	244	5	2,243	49	90
...	...	276	248	20	20	129	17	91	3	1,150	9[illegible]	91
8	7	60	64	24	21	239	22	253	10	2,594	85	92
...	...	541	532	10	14	183	5	207	1	1,933	41	93

PROVINCIAL TABLE II.

POPULATION OF TALUKAS BY RELIGION AND EDUCATION.

Serial No.	Taluka.	DISTRIBUTION BY					
		Hindu.		Jain.		Musalman.	
		Males.	Females.	Males.	Females.	Males.	Females.
	1	2	3	4	5	6	7
	Gulbarga Division ...	*1,620,836*	*1,584,150*	*3,545*	*3,134*	*228,298*	*218,144*
	Gulbarga District ...	*490,220*	*480,185*	*880*	*733*	*86,152*	*83,174*
94	Gulbarga ...	86,382	83,161	219	157	21,315	19,884
95	Chincholi ...	31,459	31,731	12	7	5,868	5,594
96	Kodangal ...	55,768	53,416	...	...	5,231	4,850
97	Seram ...	41,906	41,682	25	36	7,010	6,597
98	Yadgir ...	48,891	48,183	39	34	7,354	7,393
99	Andola ...	37,516	37,175	61	51	6,911	6,787
100	Shahpur ...	46,038	45,994	33	23	7,968	8,066
101	Shorapur ...	47,751	47,055	25	13	6,348	6,402
102	Kalgi (Jagir) ...	13,549	13,620	21	19	2,472	2,303
103	Afzalpur (Jagir) ...	17,083	16,267	35	29	3,404	3,157
104	Chitapur (Jagir) ...	14,689	14,610	56	45	1,854	1,771
105	Aland (Jagir) ...	24,804	23,297	327	303	5,806	5,650
106	Firozabad (Jagir) ...	10,903	10,787	23	15	2,627	2,594
107	Tandur (Jagir) ...	13,481	13,207	4	1	1,989	1,832
	Osmanabad District ...	*292,192*	*280,241*	*1,817*	*1,612*	*30,602*	*28,846*
108	Osmanabad ...	43,090	40,948	268	255	4,923	4,657
109	Kalam ...	49,696	47,971	353	307	3,541	3,169
110	Paronda ...	45,166	44,148	494	456	3,618	3,629
111	Owsa ...	38,922	37,579	196	157	5,255	5,207
112	Tuljapur ...	56,456	53,722	287	277	6,721	6,315
113	Lohara (Jagir) ...	32,579	30,694	115	82	3,858	3,466
114	Ganjoti (Jagir) ...	26,283	25,179	104	78	2,684	2,403
	Raichur District ...	*453,629*	*446,788*	*393*	*314*	*48,402*	*45,076*
115	Raichur ...	62,802	61,210	21	17	7,967	7,283
116	Alampur ...	12,785	12,857	...	...	2,619	2,451
117	Deodrug ...	40,128	40,023	1	1	4,387	4,337
118	Gangawati ...	28,293	28,515	3	2	3,551	3,298
119	Kushtagi ...	43,594	42,421	23	16	3,330	3,052
120	Lingsugur ...	43,140	43,051	22	13	5,453	5,048
121	Manvi ...	43,157	42,743	2	...	4,809	4,524
122	Sindhnur ...	35,111	35,090	64	50	3,839	3,558
123	Koppal (Jagir) ...	36,250	36,505	155	126	3,794	3,282
124	Yelbarga (Jagir) ...	33,636	33,109	98	87	2,853	2,610
125	Gadwal (Jagir) ...	54,035	51,382	4	2	4,340	3,975
126	Amarchinta (Jagir) ...	20,668	19,882	...	...	1,460	1,278
	Bidar District ...	*384,795*	*376,936*	*455*	*475*	*63,142*	*61,648*
127	Bidar ...	47,038	47,111	12	16	12,858	13,075
128	Nilanga ...	37,757	37,025	191	208	4,899	4,527
129	Ahmadpur ...	51,640	50,157	142	117	5,641	5,335
130	Udgir ...	44,952	43,164	41	48	5,982	5,735
131	Janwada ...	28,680	27,672	6	...	3,427	3,297
132	Hasnabad (Jagir) ...	8,623	8,867	4	7	1,708	1,659
133	Bhalki (Jagir) ...	10,754	10,511	14	19	1,333	1,314
134	Partabpur (Jagir) ...	21,869	20,810	2	2	2,632	2,457
135	Chincholi (Jagir) ...	15,787	15,396	4	8	3,074	2,817
136	Narayenkher (Jagir) ...	23,493	22,827	...	...	2,414	2,346
137	Chitgopa (Jagir) ...	34,415	34,942	11	14	8,507	8,601
138	Ghorwadi (Jagir) ...	18,038	18,049	6	4	2,577	2,398
139	Ekeli (Jagir) ...	11,997	11,077	8	12	2,446	2,521
140	Kalyani (Jagir) ...	18,179	17,508	12	18	4,049	3,991
141	Murag (Jagir) ...	12,391	11,820	2	2	1,595	1,554

PROVINCIAL TABLE II.

POPULATION OF TALUKAS BY RELIGION AND EDUCATION.

RELIGION.						NUMBER OF LITERATE PERSONS.						
Christian.		Animist.		Others.		0—15		15—20		20 and over.		Serial No.
Males.	Females.	Males.	Females.	Males.	Females.	Males.	Females.	Males.	Females.	Males.	Females.	
8	9	10	11	12	13	14	15	16	17	18	19	
1,881	*1,532*	*5,529*	*5,029*	*306*	*217*	*8,866*	*722*	*8,114*	*513*	*63,355*	*2,136*	
633	*411*	*4,469*	*3,973*	*93*	*60*	*3,383*	*166*	*2,795*	*143*	*21,194*	*549*	
55	45	402	368	29	17	913	43	636	37	4,272	174	94
6	1	1,532	1,335	11	5	172	5	178	9	1,477	27	95
13	14	348	291	9	4	496	10	340	10	2,502	66	96
15	13	44	51	18	15	160	10	193	22	1,830	30	97
41	19	24	23	2	2	245	25	193	17	1,343	25	98
1	...	16	11	5	1	71	7	114	3	1,053	30	99
323	214	312	274	...	...	219	25	222	9	1,599	23	100
82	29	202	211	2	...	341	21	329	23	2,264	82	101
26	21	...	...	1	...	103	3	89	4	792	20	102
1	—	306	255	...	...	105	3	93	3	682	7	103
12	6	87	87	1	1	68	...	52	...	442		104
...	...	104	95	...	...	317	7	169	2	1,131	2	105
52	40	942	857	15	15	84	7	92	4	497	50	106
6	9	200	165	...	...	89	...	95	...	910	18	107
130	*122*	*163*	*143*	*68*	*44*	*1,799*	*114*	*1,531*	*75*	*12,771*	*402*	
9	6	2	1	23	14	339	12	250	9	2,046	61	108
99	93	68	86	...	...	279	11	223	1	2,157	45	109
...	...	9	11	2	...	288	28	238	16	1,921	66	110
20	22	27	22	5	4	386	19	319	26	2,403	65	111
1	...	53	45	33	26	359	29	324	12	2,499	66	112
1	1	...	...	1	...	68	3	91	...	872	4	113
...	...	4	11	1	...	71	12	86	11	873	95	114
920	*791*	*138*	*130*	*59*	*44*	*1,898*	*313*	*2,002*	*214*	*15,048*	*753*	
300	283	3	1	8	4	324	104	298	73	2,594	236	115
82	86	...	...	...	...	65	6	85	3	675	6	116
72	21	...	...	...	...	143	36	116	16	1,074	32	117
...	...	38	32	5	3	79	14	418	18	1,356	22	118
1	...	56	69	2	1	261	29	166	26	1,262	40	119
403	370	...	...	19	10	257	32	227	26	1,953	102	120
...	...	...	...	10	13	191	13	157	7	1,515	112	121
1	...	...	...	6	2	175	16	154	6	1,525	56	122
6	6	...	...	...	...	188	19	185	14	1,420	27	123
4	2	...	...	...	...	50	8	33	3	334	48	124
40	20	...	...	9	11	152	26	125	17	941	64	125
2	2	39	28	...	...	10	10	40	5	205	8	126
198	*178*	*789*	*783*	*89*	*69*	*1,798*	*129*	*1,786*	*81*	*14,346*	*432*	
133	133	2	1	42	40	401	31	311	24	2,489	169	127
...	...	30	26	12	4	180	4	197	5	1,565	10	128
...	...	29	18	...	...	172	10	183	8	1,917	57	129
2	1	143	151	17	8	138	37	165	17	1,217	69	130
18	11	29	16	11	8	118	1	115	3	1,022	16	131
2	1	...	...	...	...	31	3	20	...	273	6	132
...	...	...	...	...	...	55	...	62	1	319	9	133
1	...	126	108	...	...	75	2	52	2	591	12	134
...	...	5	6	...	...	66	...	88	1	850	8	135
5	2	58	57	7	8	89	...	124	...	864	9	136
...	...	67	60	...	...	159	9	252	2	1,171	9	137
...	...	43	153	...	...	100	8	88	2	685	20	138
...	...	165	138	...	...	82	14	31	8	485	13	139
1	...	...	...	...	...	50	...	51	...	610	13	140
36	30	62	49	...	...	62	15	54	8	488	12	141